TREES AND TIMBER
IN THE ANCIENT
MEDITERRANEAN
WORLD

TREES AND TIMBER
IN THE ANCIENT
MEDITERRANEAN
WORLD

RUSSELL MEIGGS

OXFORD
AT THE CLARENDON PRESS

Oxford University Press, Great Clarendon Street, Oxford OX2 6DP
Oxford New York
Athens Auckland Bangkok Bogota Buenos Aires Calcutta
Cape Town Chennai Dar es Salaam Delhi Florence Hong Kong Istanbul
Karachi Kuala Lumpur Madrid Melbourne Mexico City Mumbai
Nairobi Paris São Paolo Singapore Taipei Tokyo Toronto Warsaw
and associated companies in
Berlin Ibadan

Oxford is a registered trade mark of Oxford University Press

Published in the United States by
Oxford University Press Inc., New York

© Oxford University Press 1982

Special edition for Sandpiper Books Ltd., 1998

British Library Cataloguing in Publication Data
Data available

ISBN 0-19-814840-2

1 3 5 7 9 10 8 6 4 2

Printed in Great Britain
on acid-free paper by
Bookcraft (Bath) Ltd.,
Midsomer Norton

PREFACE

SERIOUS work on this book was begun in 1972 and I expected to complete it in 1976. Progress at first was brisk. There was much more evidence to find than was generally assumed and, after an uncertain start, the overall structure of the book emerged without difficulty. But at the close of 1975 the end was not yet in sight. The problems had been defined more clearly, but not the solutions, and there was much more essential reading than I had anticipated. Long notes in barely legible writing with technical terms left in their original German or French are painful reminders of the middle years. The last stages of digestion were more rewarding and I was sorry when, for practical reasons, I was persuaded to give myself a deadline without further indulgence in appendices.

Within the limits of a preface it is impossible to name all those many friends, including foreign scholars trapped in the library, who have enabled me to write more than a superficial summary. But I hope that the unnamed will realize how much I appreciate their contribution. Some names must, however, be mentioned. Without the patient encouragement of Elwyn Jones and Philip Stuart of the Oxford University Forestry Faculty my innocence in botany would be much more sharply exposed. Professor David Oates and Stephanie Dally helped me to get the Assyrian inscriptions on which I mainly relied in better perspective. Joseph Shaw helped me to understand and enjoy Minoan architecture. In general matters I have gained most from long sessions with Charles Venables, whose knowledge of English trees and woods is unrivalled, Donald Davidson, formerly Forestry Adviser in the Near East for the Overseas Development Administration, Peter Kuniholm of Cornell University, a pioneer of dendrochronology, Don Hughes, who moved from the American forestry service to teaching ancient history at Denver University, and John Bintliff, who has worked intensively on Greek soils.

In Italy I found the company and advice of Professor Pietro Piussi particularly stimulating, and the generous hospitality and help of the officers of the Italian Forestry Service made a short visit to the Sila forest area much more rewarding than I could have hoped. In Lebanon David and Doris Dodge, with their intimate knowledge of the country and affection for the mountains, enabled me to see more of the great forest areas than I had thought possible in a mere fortnight. I also had the good fortune to be introduced to the forests of the Troodos mountains by Dr Andrew Polycarpou, who was then Director of the Department of Forests in Cyprus. In Turkey, David French and Özdemir Demirtaş helped me to make the most of a too short visit. Among many correspondents who very kindly answered my sometimes unreasonable enquiries I would mention Nigel Hepper, of the Kew Herbarium, whose drawings of the distinctive features of cedar, fir, and juniper add life to a difficult appendix, Professor Pairman Brown, Professor Toumis, and Oliver Rackham. In the early stages Professor Sterling Dow kindly passed to me a collection of references from a Harvard seminar, several of which were new to me.

Alan Hall read a very early draft of the text, and his basic criticisms encouraged me to be more ambitious and more specific. Peter Brunt read the penultimate draft with the most generous thoroughness and saved me from many careless mistakes and unconscious errors. Thomas Braun read the proofs of several chapters with a keen eye for improvements in style and substance. Anna Crabbe added deft touches to some of the chapters. In the final stages I was fortunate to find Nicholas Purcell, who shared my interests and whose sharp critical judgement has proved invaluable; I also owe to him the map of the Campus Martius. And once again I must thank those in the Clarendon Press who have steered the manuscript into a book.

My debts to Institutions are very considerable. Without a generous grant from the Leverhulme Trustees I would have had to modify the whole scale of my study. An invitation from the Rockefeller Foundation to become a scholar in residence in their Villa Serbelloni at Bellagio provided the ideal setting for thinking out the main problems of composition in congenial company. Nor can I forget the tolerance and practical help of the librarians of the Ashmolean and Forestry libraries in Oxford with their staffs.

I am very grateful to the museums and individuals who

allowed me to use their photographs, to Marion Cox for her drawings, and to N. A. Griffiths for making my description of the Parthenon roof more intelligible. Translations from J. B. Pritchard's *Ancient Near-Eastern Texts Relating to the Old Testament* are quoted by permission of the Princeton University Press and J. N. Postgate has kindly allowed me to use his translation of an important Assyrian letter.

Only those who have suffered from my correspondence can appreciate how much I owe to Rosamund Broadley, who from draft to draft has converted a script which I can barely read myself into copy acceptable to the printer. Finally, I cannot but resist the reluctance of my wife to be thanked publicly.

R. M.

Garsington
July 1982

CONTENTS

PLATES

(at end)

FIGURES

ABBREVIATIONS

AA	*Archäologischer Anzeiger: Beiblatt zum Jahrbuch des deutschen archäologischen Instituts*
AJA	*American Journal of Archaeology*
AM	*Mitteilungen des deutschen archäologischen Instituts: Athenische Abteilung*
ANET	J. B. Pritchard (ed.) *Ancient Near-Eastern texts relating to the Old Testament*[3] (Princeton, 1969)
Ant. Class.	*L'Antiquité classique*
AR	*Records of ancient Egypt* (5 vols., Chicago, 1906–7)
ARAB	D. D. Luckenbill, *Ancient records of Assyria and Babylonia* (2 vols., Chicago, 1926–7)
BAR	*British Archaeological Records*
BC	Caesar, *Bellum Civile*
BCH	*Bulletin de correspondance hellénique*
BG	Caesar, *Bellum Gallicum*
BSA	*Annual of the British School at Athens*
CAD	*Chicago Assyrian Dictionary*
cu.	cubit
ESAR	T. Frank, *An economic survey of ancient Rome* (Baltimore, 1933–40)
FAO	The Food and Agriculture Organisation of the United Nations
FD	*Fouilles de Delphes* 5 (3)
FGH	F. Jacoby, *Die Fragmente der griechischen Historiker* (Berlin and Leyden, 1923–)
GHI	*Greek historical inscriptions*
Hesp.	*Hesperia*
Hist.	*Historia, Zeitschrift für alte Geschichte*
HP	Theophrastus, *Enquiry into plants* (*Historia plantarum*)
ID	*Inscriptions de Délos*: comptes des hiéropes, nos. 290–510 (2 vols., F. Durrbach, Paris, 1916–17)
IG	*Inscriptiones Graecae* (Berlin, 1873–)
IGLS	*Inscriptions grecques et latines de la Syrie*, L. Jalabert, R. Mouterde (Beirut, 1929–)
ILS	*Inscriptiones Latinae Selectae*, H. Dessau (Berlin, 1955–6)
JEA	*Journal of Egyptian Archaeology*
JHS	*Journal of Hellenic Studies*
JNES	*Journal of Near Eastern Studies*
Journ. Arch.	*Journal of the British Archaeological Society*

Journ. Arch. Sci.	*Journal of Archaeological Science*
JRS	*Journal of Roman Studies*
Lucan	*Pharsalia*
Mon. Ant.	*Monumenti antichi (Accademia nazionale dei Lincei)*
NH	Pliny's *Natural history*
OGIS	*Orientis Graecae Inscriptiones Selectae*
PBSR	*Papers of the British School at Rome*
PGM	*Petermanns geographische Mitteilungen*
PM	Sir Arthur Evans, *The palace of Minos* (4 vols., London, 1921–36)
RE	Pauly-Wissowa-Kroll, *Real-Encyclopädie der classischen Altertumswissenschaft* (Stuttgart, 1894–)
REG	*Revue des études grecques*
RR	Varro, *Res Rusticae*
SEG	*Supplementum Epigraphicum Graecum*
SHA	*Scriptores Historiae Augustae*
SIG	Dittenberger, *Sylloge Inscriptionum Graecarum* (Leipzig, 1915–24)
Sylva	J. Evelyn, *Sylva*[3]: *A discourse on forest trees and the propagation of timber* (London, 1679)
TAPA	*Transactions of the American Philological Association*
ZA	*Zeitschrift für ägyptische Sprache und Altertumskunde*

INTRODUCTION

WHEN peace collapsed in September 1939 I was teaching Greek and Roman history and preparing a book on Roman Ostia. The shock that war had actually come was blunted in the early months by the apparent stalemate on the western front, and when officials came down from the War Office to select volunteers for military intelligence there was almost a holiday atmosphere about the business. I thought that my knowledge of Italian and French might be useful in the Mediterranean, but very few were chosen and I was not among them. By February 1940 the false lull was not quite over, but we were no longer in a holiday mood. I received a telegram from a former colleague who had been absorbed by the Civil Service asking me if I could leave Oxford and join his Department, as they were desperately short of staff. If I was willing, how soon could I come for interview? I replied that one day's notice was sufficient, and waited for more than a month.

After an insignificant interview, I was assigned to the timber section of the Raw Materials Department of the Ministry of Supply and for my apprenticeship I was attached to a senior civil servant who had spent the six months before war broke out in helping to plan the blueprint for the organisation of the country's civilian resources. As a result of the intensive pressure of this work he was only too eager to cut short my passive apprenticeship. One of the pressing problems that he had not had time to tackle was the widespread infringement of wartime regulations to control the felling of trees and the distribution of timber; as a result his desk was piled high with appeals from the regions for action to be taken in the courts before the authority of the Department's control was completely undermined. I was allowed to open negotiations with the Department of the public prosecutor and soon sufficient prosecutions were being brought to restore confidence.

This was my first and last constructive contribution from Ministry Headquarters; there followed what seemed a long period of routine conferences, memoranda to be drafted, other people's memoranda to be redrafted, and material to be prepared which would enable the Minister not to answer the questions he had to face in Parliament. For such exercises my temperament was poorly suited and, as my superior realised this no less clearly, I was able to negotiate a transfer to the Department responsible for timber production from home woodlands. My responsibility as Chief Labour Officer in the Department was the building up of the labour force and the negotiation of wages and conditions of service. The work was divided between office and field and it brought me into close relations with a wide range of foresters and timber merchants, whose company I much enjoyed. Visiting forests and sawmills with them I came to be keenly interested in their work, and developed something approaching an affection for trees.

It was probably because of this new-found enthusiasm that I was asked to review the translation in the Loeb series of the elder Pliny's books on trees in his *Natural history* (books 12–16), when it was published in 1945. I had not read these books before and was so delighted to find echoes of topics that had become almost familiar that I decided that when pressures eased I would try to fuse my two lives as ancient historian and· as timber administrator by writing a book on timber in the ancient world. It was a very long time before this could be anything but a vague ambition, because there was a long-standing commitment to Ostia from before the war, and both teaching and academic administration became much more demanding after the war than in the comparatively carefree days of the inter-war period. It was not until after retirement in 1970 and the completion in 1972 of commitments still outstanding that I was able to divorce myself temporarily from the mainstream of Greek and Roman history and luxuriate in a comparatively untrodden field.

My original decision had been emotional rather than rational, but I was still satisfied that the subject was sufficiently important to be worth attempting. Wood had from Palaeolithic times been one of man's basic raw materials, as Pliny recognised when in passing from the animal kingdom to the products of the soil he began with trees. The early Greek rationalists too were right in regarding the discovery of fire as a great step forward in the development of civilisation. Indeed, wood remained man's only reliable means of making fire until the exploitation of coal in the sixteenth century; without fire the use of metals would have been virtually confined to copper.

Man's needs in wood were still very modest in the Neolithic Age, but became more demanding with the emergence of palace states and the growth of trade in the Bronze Age. From the classical period onwards, war no less than peace depended on timber as navies increased and siege equipment became more sophisticated. The extravagances of war were sharply reduced when Augustus reorganised the Roman empire for peace and there was no serious opposition to Roman power. The main timber problem now became the maintenance of adequate supplies of building-timber and fuel for the great urban concentrations. Nowhere was the problem more acute than in the city of Rome. Its solution is a major achievement of which our sources tell us very little.

While I have never felt any doubt about the social and economic importance of timber, my confidence in my own competence has often wavered. It would have been easy to write in two years a short and readable book which left most of the questions unasked and very few answered, but the more serious book I had in mind required an understanding of botany, geology, and carpentry which had to be built on negligible foundations. I have exploited friends, acquaintances, and strangers shamelessly, but I am still nervous in the company of botanists and geologists. These handicaps I have tried to minimise by concentrating primarily on the problems of demand and supply, which in a historical study is perhaps justified.

The title of the book is vague enough to need further definition. *Trees and Timber in the Ancient Mediterranean World* suggests much more than is offered. With the arrogance of a classic I have made my ancient world the world of the Greeks, Romans, and Phoenicians from the Bronze Age to the fall of the Roman Empire. Spain and Gaul, however, are virtually ignored. Both were well forested but, so far as our evidence goes, they did not play an important part in supplying others. In retrospect I realise that I may have been too ambitious in casting my net so wide in time and space; a better book could perhaps have been written by concentrating on the woodlands of Italy with special emphasis on the supply of timber to the city of Rome. But there were too many relevant problems in Greek history that interested me and I had always been fascinated by the splendid descriptions of the cedars of Lebanon in the Old Testament. Had I followed reason rather than enthusiasm I should never have seen the Lebanon mountains and so should have missed one of my most memorable experiences.

After some hesitation I decided that the most satisfactory way of using the fragmentary evidence was to examine separate aspects of the subject in chapters that could be self-contained, but in a sense interdependent. The intention of most of the chapters is explicit in their titles, but four require a brief explanation. Since the main focus of the study is on the worlds of Greece and Rome, a chapter on the cedars of Lebanon may seem an anomaly, but the Phoenician states which exploited the Lebanon forests played an important part in Mediterranean history. Down to the middle of the sixth century BC the historical importance of the cedars lay in the rivalry of civilisations based on Mesopotamia and the Nile. When Persia became the undisputed master of Asia and Egypt, the forests of Cilicia, Syria, Cyprus, and Phoenicia provided the fleets with which she successfully resisted Greek control of the eastern Mediterranean, and these forests were no less important after the death of Alexander in the struggle for power between the rulers of Syria and Egypt.

The long chapter on the timber trade arose from the need to reduce repetition in the various chapters. The problems of extraction and transport are an integral part of the study of the timber supplies of Athens and Rome, as of the cedars of Lebanon; but the problems in each area have much in common. The paramount importance of transporting timber whenever possible by water rather than by land is common to them all. Timber-felling and conversion underwent very little radical change between the Bronze Age and the nineteenth century and though there were regional diversities of which we know very little, even the development of tools, which has not been studied here in detail, seems to have followed a roughly common pattern. I have included in this chapter a short discussion of prices and wages which will disappoint economic historians. The fault lies partly in the sources. From the Romans we have no evidence for wages, and for prices only a few record figures.

From the Greeks we have more than 200 prices, but the Greeks were strangely unprofessional in their accounts, and there is a frustrating lack of precision in their descriptions. In the prices recorded only seven give all the details required to make comparisons significant, and all come from a single consignment. Such terms as oak timbers, twelve-foot timbers (with width and thickness unspecified), are the rule. As a result the general statements in the text remain very anaemic; but since so little work has been published on the temple commissioners' accounts which provide our main evidence, I have discussed the most important of them in an appendix.

The chapter on Mediterranean forests is an attempt to set out the main general factors governing the distribution and growth of trees in the Mediterranean region, again in order to reduce the repetition of general principles in individual chapters. It is not intended to break new ground but to help those who are even less familiar with trees and forests than I was when I started. The final chapter on deforestation arose from a consideration of the contribution made by the ancient world to the almost desperate state of Mediterranean forests today. But to assess the part played by the ancient world in the squandering of natural resources one needs to know something of the history of the forests between the end of the Roman Empire and today. Even a summary sketch based on inadequate reading will, I hope, be sufficient to show that the ancient world and the goat have been required to take too large a share of the blame.

The nature of the subject imposes many problems of presentation, and not least the vocabulary of trees and timber. The ambiguities here, however, are not confined to the ancient languages. In English the line between wood and timber remains very blurred and other words tend to be used whose literal meaning is different from what they are intended to convey. The terms hardwood and softwood are often used in the British timber trade as virtually synonymous with deciduous and evergreen; but the hardwoods include lime which is a very soft wood, and the softwoods include box and yew which are very hard woods. In German *Nadelholz*, which literally means needle-wood, is widely used for most conifers, though strictly speaking it should apply only to pines and perhaps cedars. We should not be surprised, therefore, if the legal distinction in

Latin between *materia*, meaning wood to be used for building or in making articles, and *lignum*, meaning wood for burning, is not always observed, or that *xylon* in Greek should cover wood of every description.

More serious is the difficulty of identifying species, and here again modern languages offer a parallel. The 'red cedar' which is one of the commonest native trees in the eastern seaboard of the United States of America is botanically a juniper, *Juniperus virginiana*, and the English plane becomes an American sycamore. In Britain the pine botanically known as *Pinus silvestris* is still often called a Scots fir; in Germany it is usually known as *Kiefer*, but also as *Föhre*, *Waldföhre*, or *Rotföhre*. Similarly Theophrastus knew that the names given to the various species of oak in Macedon were different from those given on Mt. Ida, and that the Arcadian names for the main species of pines distinguished by the Greeks were the reverse of those accepted in the rest of Greece. The botanist can only be completely satisfied with the official botanical name, but the general reader would find such language as *Quercus pubescens Willd* for a species of oak that is common in Italy and Greece very indigestible; nor is it easy to feel sympathy towards names that seem to be singularly ill-chosen. Why should the commonest coastal pine in the Mediterranean, which does not grow in a desert climate, be named *Pinus halepensis*, from Aleppo, a desert town? And why should the commonest mountain pine in Italy be named *Pinus laricio*, when it has no association with the larch? But even if the claims of precision were considered paramount it would not often be possible to give the botanical name, because our sources rarely distinguish between the various species of oak and pine and when they do their judgement is not always sound. I have therefore confined the discussion of oak and pine species to the general chapter on Mediterranean forests and normally used the wider terms in the main text.

The confusion between cedar and juniper is more difficult to unravel. One soon discovers that the Greek word *kedros* and the Latin word *cedrus* do not always mean cedar. The statement in a recent history of Macedon that cedar was one of the country's useful timbers was based on a Greek archaeological report of 1939 which stated that the piles of a prehistoric lake village which had been excavated near Kastoria were made of *kedros*, which still grew in the district. This would be very surprising, for no native cedars have ever been recorded in Europe. The simple explanation is that the trees, as Professor Tsoumis assures me, are junipers. In some cases identification is clear from the context, more often the ambiguity remains. The difficulties of identifying Greek and Latin tree names should not, however, be exaggerated. The various oaks have much in common and the only widespread species that is of inferior value as timber, the Turkey oak, is in Latin usually given a separate name, *cerrus*. The great majority of trees are named consistently and can be identified by the descriptions of Greek and Latin writers, especially Theophrastus and Pliny.

It is a very different matter when we are faced with tree names in Akkadian, Hebrew, and Egyptian, as I learnt to my cost too late. When, in 1972, I had decided on the structure of the book I thought that the easiest chapter to shape in a first draft was chronologically the earliest. I had recently become increasingly interested in the Bronze Age and since very early days had been fascinated by the awe felt by the Hebrews of the Old Testament for the cedars of Lebanon. Naïvely I thought that with a combination of the writings of the prophets and the inscriptions of Mesopotamian and Egyptian kings the chapter would virtually write itself. I assembled the evidence avidly, read all the botanical studies of the area that I could find in Oxford, and finished the chapter in two months. But in my reading I had been considerably puzzled by some translations of Assyrian texts, not on philological grounds, but because it seemed to me that some of the woods were being used for purposes for which they were poorly suited. It was not long before I had discovered from a generous professor of Assyriology that very few indeed of the Akkadian tree names were non-controversial, but that the word for cedar, *erinu*, could be regarded as secure. At this point I realised that the chapter must be completely rewritten after I had recovered a degree of confidence from chapters that came more nearly within my competence.

When I returned to the discarded chapter, fortified by a visit to the Lebanon forests in 1975, I received a more severe check. From the start I had assumed that it was the cedars of Lebanon that Egypt most prized for the uses which her limited range of native trees could not satisfy, and I thought that this was the

generally accepted view. I now found that this consensus
had been violently broken and that an increasing number of
Egyptologists accepted the thesis first published by Loret in
1916. He argued strongly that the word most commonly used by
the Egyptians for imported wood (*ash*-wood) was fir, or possibly
fir and pine, rather than cedar. I prefer to retain the earlier
orthodoxy, but to justify this conservatism in the main text
would unbalance a long chapter and so I have set my arguments
in an appendix. In accepting the identification of the Akkadian
words for box and cypress I am following the main authorities,
but the identification of pine, juniper, and other trees is more
controversial and I have therefore enclosed them in brackets.

More practical matters have also caused embarrassment.
Since yards, feet, and inches could now seem a sentimental
anachronism, measurements should be expected in metres; but
in the case of timber there is a serious objection. Both Greeks and
Romans expressed timber measurements in terms of cubits
(normally one and a half feet), feet, palms, fingers. They
therefore speak, for example, of ten-foot beams and twelve-cubit
boards. To describe them as 3.05 metre beams and 5.49 metre
boards would imply a production of random length, which
would be misleading. And to say that in Diocletian's edict on
maximum prices the highest-priced timber was fir of 22.86
metres rather than fifty cubits would be distracting. Since the
Roman foot and one of the Greek feet correspond very nearly
with the British and American foot, all timber measurements
and spans to be covered are expressed in feet, with palms and
fingers converted to inches, as in the appendix on weights and
measures.

The metric system is used for distances, including the height of
mountains, but not for the height of trees which is more closely
linked with timber measurements. A somewhat similar compromise has been made for place names. To avoid confusion
between the republic of Lebanon and the mountain range I
have used the name Phoenicia for the combined territories of the
Phoenician states, even when they were part of the Roman
province of Syria, and I have retained the name of Macedon for
what is now northern Greece. For Africa, on the other hand, to
follow the Romans in using Africa as the name of a Roman
province limited to Tunisia and eastern Algeria could be mis-

leading and the modern names of Tunisia, Algeria, and Morocco have been used.

The main work on this book has been done in libraries in Oxford, Rome, Beirut, and Florence. I should have liked to balance this reading by more walking in Mediterranean forests, but time and finance have imposed limits. I have, however, been considerably helped by my travels. Whereas a better reader of maps would have had little difficulty in visualising the physical geography of the region, I had a very vague appreciation of the problems of extracting large cedar logs from the Lebanon mountains and transporting them to Assyria or Babylon until I saw the structure of the mountain range and could follow from various viewpoints the natural routes to the Euphrates; and many Akkadian texts came to life when, on being driven from Beirut to Damascus, I could see Mt. Hermon floating into view at the southern end of the rich Bekaa valley and the arid slopes of Antilebanon facing me. Citrus-wood, which was the mahogany of the Roman furniture world in the early Empire and in high demand, became much less remote when I was able to see it growing and also being worked in Morocco. A day spent in the Maenalon forest in Arcadia with the helpful guidance of the district forest officer was a good introduction to Greek fir (*Abies cephalonica*), and a walk on Mt. Parnes in Attica encouraged a more realistic approach to Athenian timber problems. The chapter on Rome's timber supplies would have been weaker had I not been able to see something of the once well-forested mountains of the Tiber basin in Tuscany and Umbria.

One of the main attractions of the subject when I started was the comparative neglect of it by historians. After spending many years with the Athenian Empire, where most of the problems have been discussed for a hundred years until they are nearly threadbare and to write a single paragraph might require the reading of at least twenty specialised articles, the prospect of not having to wade through a thick undergrowth of controversy seemed very refreshing. There have been many occasions in the last few years when I would have warmly welcomed more fore-runners, not excluding doctoral theses, on the more frustrating parts of the subject. There is no lack of articles and books on Mediterranean trees and forests, but, apart from discussions of the importance of ship-timber to naval power, very little has been written directly on the problems of demand and supply in relation to changing historical patterns. Adolfo di Bérenger's *Studi di archeologia forestale*, first published in 1859–65 and republished in a limited edition by the Italian Academy of Forest Sciences in 1965, is still the best comprehensive review of the ancient sources, though he wrote before the present range of Greek and Latin inscriptions could be used; for Bérenger, besides being a distinguished professional forester, had a remarkably wide knowledge of the classics. H. Blümner's *Technologie und Terminologie der Gewerbe und Künste bei Griechen und Römern*, published in 1875–87, has still the best analysis of the use of wood by the Greeks and Romans. A. Seidensticker's *Waldgeschichte des Altertums*, in two volumes (1886), was intended as a source-book for the study of the history of ancient forests, and his massive collection of references remains useful; but it was designed for foresters and not related to historical developments. More recently E. C. Semple's chapter on timber in *The geography of the Mediterranean region: its relation to ancient history* (1932) is an excellent study in miniature, and *Ancient forestry* by O. Makkonen, professor of forestry at Helsinki University, published in *Acta Forestalia Fennica* 82 (1967) and 95 (1969), is particularly valuable for a forester's reflections on Theophrastus, and his list of Greek and Latin species with their identification. I have also been helped considerably in my study of the Greek timber trade by two excellent reviews of the evidence for the Greeks' use of timber, both compressed but comprehensive: *Ta xylika domes ton arkhaion Hellenon* (vol. 1, Athens, 1955) by A. K. Orlandos (trans. V. Hadjimichalis, *Les Matériaux de construction et la technique architecturale des anciens Grecs*, Paris, 1966), and *Manuel d'architecture grecque* (vol. 1, Paris, 1965) by R. Martin.

The most that I can hope is that this wider exploration of the subject will tempt historians into a field which is too important to be ignored, and in which much new ground can be won.

Most of the footnotes are confined to references, especially to Greek and Latin texts. I have also appealed for illustration to John Evelyn's *Sylva*, for Evelyn combined a familiarity with Pliny and Theophrastus with a keen practical interest in forestry and timber production. References are to the third edition published in 1679, the last edition to be personally revised.

Discussions that are essential to the argument are marked with an asterisk.

The organisation of the bibliography, which is confined to books and articles that I have used, is based on the convenience of readers rather than strict logic. Since most of the sources for the chapter on the cedars of Lebanon have little or no relevance to the rest of the Mediterranean world I have confined them to a separate section, marking with an asterisk those whose interest is primarily botanical.

I

THE NATURE OF THE EVIDENCE

THE evidence on which this study of the supply and distribution of timber in the ancient world is based is abundant but widely dispersed and much of it very frustrating. Timber suffers in comparison with pottery and metals because, except in the dryest climates, it disintegrates unless it is sealed from the atmosphere. Even then it needs special conservation treatment very soon after discovery; many excellent examples of ancient woodworking have been lost in recent years because they have not been treated soon enough. There is, however, much more antique wood in museums than is generally imagined.

Excavations in Egypt naturally have been the most productive because of the dryness of the climate, and there are sufficient wooden coffins, statues, models, chests, and other objects, including tools, to enable us to appreciate the techniques of Egyptian woodworking. The microscopic analysis of a large number of samples provides a fair indication of the varied use of native and imported timbers over a period of more than three thousand years. In the Russian Crimea wooden coffins and sarcophagi, some almost complete, displaying exquisite joinery and very attractive carving, have been recovered in sealed tombs of the fourth century BC and the Hellenistic period. In Phrygia a royal tomb of the late eighth century BC was found to have a well-preserved funeral chamber of closely jointed pine boards and outer protecting walls of juniper logs. Waterlogged ground is also a good preserver. The famous temple of Hera on the island of Samos was built in a marshy area which preserved a considerable number of dedications in wood—statuettes, bowls, plates, and fragments of furniture. In two ancient spring sanctuaries in France hundreds of wooden statues were found, some crude, others finely carved—dedications to the goddess of the spring—preserved in a bed of mud. At Valkenburg in Holland, near the Rhine, the plan of complete buildings in a

Roman fort can be recovered from the surviving timbers. Among the discoveries in the recent excavation of Vindolanda, a Roman fort near Hadrian's Wall in Britain, there were a large number of writing-tablets, many of them well preserved in marshy ground. But the most spectacular addition to the corpus of ancient timbers has come from the development of under-water archaeology.

We now know in great detail how the average Greek and Roman merchantman was built, and most of the woods that were used. The timbers of one ship in particular, a fourth-century BC merchantman sunk off the north coast of Cyprus, were so well preserved that it has been possible to reconstruct almost the entire ship with the original timbers. The wood used was almost exclusively pine. Valuable evidence can also be found by the archaeologist in buildings even when the timbers themselves have disappeared. It was common practice in walls built with mud-brick to add timbers to give strength and cohesion. They can often be traced by grooves left in the walls where the vertical or horizontal timbers have themselves dis-integrated; and sometimes there is a residue of carbonised wood which can be identified. In rare cases ancient woods and even carbonised wood can be recognised at once by the timber expert, but many such immediate identifications have had to be reversed when the wood has been examined microscopically. It is a great disappointment that at Herculaneum, where more carbonised wood has been preserved than at any other classical site, none has yet been scientifically identified.

Next in importance to the timber itself are the contemporary records that have survived, of which there are many of many kinds; but much of their evidence is very opaque. The most colourful form the backbone of the chapter on the cedars of Lebanon. They are the proud boasts of Egyptian and Meso-potamian monarchs, who include their cutting of timbers on the mountains of Phoenicia and Syria side by side with the flattering record of their military triumphs, to be a permanent memorial in the palaces they have built, on the site of their operations, or on the cliff-face at the mouth of the Nahr-el-Kelb where the coast road has to make a detour inland between Byblos and Beirut.

In the Greek world public accounts are the most valu-able records. It was an essential feature of the fully developed democracy of Athens that the people as a whole should control the executive and one expression of this control was the publication of their accounts by the boards of commissioners who were appointed by the people to supervise the implementation of building programmes. Important fragments survive of the building accounts of the Parthenon on the Athenian acropolis. They set out money received, the main expenditure on materials and wages, and the balance handed over at the close of the year. They are in very summary form and the surviving references to timber are tantalisingly fragmentary, but the accounts of the final phase of the building of the Erechtheum are much more complete and more detailed, throwing useful light on the use of wood in the building. For timber usage the most interesting document is an Athenian decree of the late fourth century BC setting out in detail the specification for a large arsenal for the storage of naval equipment. The complete text has survived (p. 213).

The same principle of public accounting was followed by the authorities who were responsible for managing the finances of the great religious centres. Substantial records survive from Eleusis, Delphi, Delos, and Epidaurus. These all include records of timber purchases, sometimes with transport costs, and in one of the series from Epidaurus we have the complete accounts of the building of a temple, which specify the timbers that were used. In most of these accounts we are less fortunate. A few entries name the timbers and give their measurements and prices; more often neither the name nor the measurements are recorded. This vagueness may be the main reason why these documents have remained so long neglected and have not even become a mine for the extraction of doctoral theses. The only comprehensive attempt to extract their full value known to me is a study by A. Burford of the accounts from Epidaurus which includes a discussion of the structure of the timber trade implied by the texts.[1] The criticism of details by some reviewers obscured the boldness of the attempt. The author at least showed the kind of work that needs to be done.

These are the most important documents for our investigation into the Greek timber trade. Among other inscriptions the most important are a long series of Athenian naval inventories and substantial fragments of decrees which throw light on the dependence of Athens on Macedonian ship-timbers. No such records were published by the Romans but we are lucky to have the text of a contract for building a decorative doorway at Puteoli (Pozzuoli) in 105 BC which not only specifies the form of the doorway, but, unlike the Athenian specification for the naval arsenal, names the woods that are to be used and where they are to be used (p. 242).

Unlike the Athenians and other Greek democracies, the Romans did not require their magistrates and commissioners to set up in public an inscribed account of their handling of public monies, and so our evidence for the Roman timber trade is considerably poorer than for the Greek; but Roman funerary inscriptions are more informative than the Greek. Though there are no colourful records of the careers of timber merchants to match those of builders, bakers, and fullers, a number of short inscriptions from the tombs of timber-workers throw a little light on the structure of the timber trade and on the status of timber-workers. The Greeks are much more reticent in their cemeteries, but one Greek timber-worker left a refreshingly personal epitaph: 'The best Phrygian in wide-wayed Athens he was, Mannes of Oryma (in Caria), whose fair tomb this is. And by heaven I never saw a better timber-feller than myself.'[2]

A relief from a tombstone in Ravenna shows a shipwright, *faber navalis*, at work,[3] and another from near Florence displays the main tools of the timber-worker.[4] A relief from Gaul illustrates the manhandling of a large tree-trunk.[5] In a relief of the second millennium BC from the great temple at Karnak, Phoenician princes are depicted felling very stylised trees for the benefit of the Egyptian conqueror (pl. 2), and an Assyrian palace relief provides good evidence for the transport of big timbers by sea (pl. 3A). But by far the most impressive illustrations of timber-working in Antiquity are the magnificent reliefs that wind around the column erected by Trajan in his Forum to commemorate his victories over the Dacians: timber operations, including felling, carrying, bridge building, and camp construction, figure largely in the record (pls. 15 and 16).

Though archaeology and epigraphy provide useful support, the framework of our study must be built up from the literary evidence. Two authors in particular, one Greek and the other

Latin, will play a dominant part and deserve a less restricted introduction. Theophrastus was born in 370 BC at Eresus on the island of Lesbos and died at Athens in 285 BC. He had come to Athens to study under Plato and became Aristotle's pupil and succeeded him as head of the Lyceum. Like Aristotle he was immensely industrious and covered a very wide range of knowledge. Like Aristotle too he wrote on politics, and on various aspects of nature, including fire-stones and weather-signs; both were masters of classification. By coincidence the only two of his works to survive in full are both concerned with botany. His *Aetiology of plants* is a discussion of their physiology; the *Enquiry into plants*, to which we shall frequently refer, is concerned with their classification and description, and the first five of nine books are devoted to trees.[6] One of the factors which led him to this field may have been the new interest in the variety of nature which was stimulated by Alexander's spectacular campaigns in the east. Alexander had taken with him into Asia geographers and botanists whose descriptions of the new flora and fauna, particularly of India, were widely read. But Theophrastus' interest in trees, shrubs, and other plants was not purely theoretical. In his will he asked to be buried in the garden of the Lyceum, which Aristotle had bequeathed to him, and made provision for the grant of freedom to the slave-gardeners after four further years in the garden.[7]

Theophrastus, so far as we know, was the first to attempt to classify trees as well as plants and shrubs, by examining their differences in appearance, habit, and properties. He was not merely concerned with the form and function of the bark, leaf, and flower, but included a detailed study of root systems and a discussion of the various forms of propagation. He is rightly recognised as a founder of botany and the Greek and Latin writers who concerned themselves with farming and nature accepted his authority. In the Renaissance he was highly respected and many of his formulations remain permanently valid: botanists without prejudices in favour of the classics who can be coaxed to read him are surprised how far he progressed. He was, however, a pioneer. He may have had no literary predecessors on whose foundations he could build, and his own personal experience was limited, for, apart from accompanying Aristotle to Assos in the Troad, he seems to have spent all his life in Lesbos and Athens: most of the information he had to analyse was based on the observation of others.

The work as we have it probably evolved from a series of lectures and seminars at the Lyceum. Most of the examples he cites are from Mt. Ida, Mt. Olympus in Mysia, Macedonia, and Arcadia, regions noted for their forests, and the evidence from these regions he introduces by such phrases as 'The Arcadians say that', 'In Macedon it is said that'. It has been widely inferred that the lectures were based on reports from these areas collected by friends or pupils. This will also help to explain some inconsistencies in the text. It is, for instance, impossible to reconcile all the various distinctions he describes between *peuke* and *pitys*, the names given by the Greeks to pines. In this case his problem was complicated by a different usage of the two words in different districts.

Theophrastus bases his conclusions primarily on deduction from observation, but he inherits some assumptions which interfere with his scientific approach. He assumed that by analogy with the animal kingdom all trees would be either masculine or feminine, and within this framework the facts of observation had to be fitted.[8] His basic assumption, not unnaturally, is that the fruit-bearing trees are female, while those that produce no fruit are male. But in some species observation seemed to show that trees which would otherwise seem male were also fruit-bearing; and so a compromise had to be accepted. When both male and female were fruit-bearing the female had better and more abundant fruit. But Theophrastus had to admit that some people reversed the roles. The nature of the difference is not like that between different species of oak or of pine, but more like the difference between cultivated and wild, and the standard of reference is clearly the difference between man and woman.

His description of lime is typical: 'the wood of the male tree is hard, yellow, more fragrant, and denser; the wood of the female is whiter. The bark of the male is thicker and when it is stripped off it is hard and so does not bend, whereas the bark of the female is thinner and flexible.'[9] In the fir Theophrastus sees a difference in the leaves: 'those of the male are sharper, more needle-like, and more bent'; but human sex differentials are also applied: 'the wood of the female is whiter, softer, and easier to work'.[10]

The woodcutter put it very simply: 'Whenever a male tree is cut with an axe it gives shorter lengths, it is more twisted, harder to work, and darker in colour, while the female gives longer lengths.'[11] Throughout Antiquity the conviction persisted that in trees as well as among humans the male must be tougher and stronger than the female. It was presumably for this reason that Pliny, following a source unknown to us, maintained that of the two varieties of cypress the pyramidal (*Cupressus pyramidalis*) was the female and the wide-branching (*Cupressus horizontalis*) the male.[12] Neither Theophrastus nor his Greek and Roman successors seem fully to have understood the importance of pollination in the production of seed. Nor did they realise that most species of trees have male and female flowers on the same tree.

The headings of the books which deal with trees give a fair indication of the scope of the work. Book 1, *Of the parts of plants and their composition, and of their classification*; book 2, *Of propagation*; book 3, *Of wild trees*; book 4, *Of the trees and plants special to particular districts and positions*; book 5, *Of the timber of various trees and their uses*. The arrangement is logical, the style undistinguished but clear, the approach scientific and impersonal. There are no diverting anecdotes and no moral disquisitions. We cannot therefore feel that we know Theophrastus personally. A random collection of anecdotes by Diogenes Laertius writing more than four hundred years after Theophrastus' death is no substitute for contemporary evidence and the rest of his works.

Pliny, whose *Natural history* is our second most important source, we can know much better.[13] His personality informs his writing and his nephew has left an account of his career and of his method of working. Theophrastus was an academic in the best sense of that much abused word; Pliny had an active career in the Roman imperial service, but combined with it an insatiable appetite for acquiring and communicating knowledge. But while Theophrastus had no predecessors to lean on, Pliny could draw on a considerable number of Greek and Roman authorities. He was born in AD 23 at Comum in north Italy, but spent most of his life in Rome or on imperial service in the provinces. His family had sufficient capital and connections to launch him on a public career, and after making his mark by pleading at the bar in Rome, he was sent to take command of a cavalry squadron on the Rhine. Here he had the good fortune to form a friendship with Titus, son of the future emperor Vespasian, which was to stand him in good stead later. There followed a series of administrative posts as an imperial agent, *procurator*, in the provinces, in Spain and probably Africa. When, after the civil war of 69, in which rival armies fought to establish their candidates as emperor, Vespasian emerged as the final victor, Pliny was called to the palace and assigned to special duties which culminated in the command of the main Roman naval base at Misenum. It was there, while attempting to rescue refugees from the violent eruption of Vesuvius in AD 79, that he met his end, partly because his absorbing interest in the physical phenomena preoccupied his attention.

In spite of his active career Pliny managed to complete a formidable series of publications. From his experience as a cavalry commander he wrote a short technical treatise *On the use of the javelin by cavalry*, and a long *History of the Romans' wars against the Germans*. His early experience of the courts led to a manual on the training of orators, and when Nero's savagery made it dangerous to write anything that could be interpreted as political, he took refuge in a book *On careless language*. Two major works crowned his achievement—a *History of Rome* over the last two generations, beginning where Aufidius Bassus had ended, and a *Natural history* in thirty-seven books.

His nephew explains how he was able to crowd so much into such a busy public life.[14] He got up before dawn, had the useful gift of snatching sleep whenever he needed it, and disciplined himself to use every moment to the full. With the help of his slaves he covered a vast amount of reading. In the summer, after a light midday meal, he would lie in the sun reading a book, invariably taking notes and copying out selected passages: 'There is no book, however bad, that hasn't something useful in it.' He even used the journeys in his carriage to collect material and would take a secretary with him to read and mark passages. No time should be wasted, and when one of his friends asked his reader to repeat a sentence which he had pronounced badly Pliny's reaction was sharp: 'But you understood, didn't you? Why then ask for it again? Your interruption has cost us at least ten verses.' His nephew records that when his uncle was serving as a procurator in Spain he was offered 400,000 sesterces (as much as the property qualification for the second administrative grade in the empire) for his notes, and there were then considerably less of them than when he died. By the time he came to write his *Natural history* in his fifties he had collected a massive accumulation of notes and quotations from a very wide reading of Greek and Latin authors.

The *Natural history* was completed in AD 77 and dedicated to the emperor's son Titus. After a long passage of laborious flattery, he explained the intention of the work. It is an attempt, he says, to describe the entire world of nature, and the chief merit he claims is that such a comprehensive study has never been attempted before by any Greek or Roman writer. He has not chosen a fancy title and his readers may find the going hard, but it is a supremely difficult task. Even if he has not succeeded there is honour and glory in having made the attempt. He has consulted some 2,000 volumes, very few of which are studied even by scholars because they are so specialised. From a hundred selected authors he has assembled 20,000 topics that deserve attention. He has included many other matters that previous authors have ignored or which were only discovered after they had written. 'We do not doubt that there are many things which we too have overlooked, for we are only human, and we are fully employed with official duties. It is in our spare time, at night, that we do our writing.'

Most ancient authors borrow from their predecessors and rarely acknowledge their obligations: Pliny claims credit for prefacing each book with a table of contents and a list of the authors he has used. These lists are so long that some modern scholars have refused to believe that they are a genuine record of what Pliny has read; but there is no need for such scepticism. From his practice of reading voraciously and making notes and excerpts we should expect a wide distribution of sources. No doubt it gave Pliny great pleasure to display the extent of his 'researches', but having myself worked on a system not very different from his, I find it very easy to believe that he had personally collected or remembered passages from each of the 123 authors he lists in one or more of the books reserved for trees. The lists are misleading if it is inferred that Pliny read carefully through these authors to develop an argument. He did not deliberately collect evidence from Homer; similarly, he had not read completely through Virgil to find passages that would be useful to him. On the other hand, he realised that Theophrastus remained the recognised authority on trees and there are clear references to specific passages. Similarly, he accepted Cato as the traditional authority on farming principles and is familiar with his text, which he quotes accurately.

Pliny devotes six books (12–17) to trees. His earlier books are concerned with the physical nature of the universe, and he proceeds to trees before agricultural crops or minerals because they were the first to sustain man. They gave him their fruit to eat, their foliage relieved the discomfort of the cave, and their bark provided his clothes. Later they brought great benefit to man: 'We use a tree to plough the seas and bring the lands closer together; we use trees for building houses; even the images of the deities were once made from trees.' But at this point the moralist intervenes; images were made of wood 'before man had thought of paying for the corpses of giant animals' (a clumsy denuncia-tion of ivory).

After these disconnected preliminaries comes a description of exotic trees which somewhat illogically begins with the plane tree, the main feature of which to Pliny is that it was introduced to Italy not because it was useful, but simply for the pleasure of its shade: it also appealed to Pliny because there were more famous plane trees than trees of any other species. He then surveys the trees of Asia and Africa, which most of his readers will not have seen. In the long catalogue he shows most interest in the trees from which the Romans got their spices and the citrus trees of north Africa which provided the wood for their most fashionable tables. The common feature in these special choices is that they provide extravagant luxuries that have helped to degrade Roman society. But he includes also an invaluable history of parchment. Books 14 and 15 are mainly devoted to vines and wines, and olives and other fruit-trees; book 16 is reserved for forest trees and 17 for cultivated trees.

There are interesting points which concern us in the other books, but the long book on forest trees is by far the most relevant to our study. Whereas he can list more than fifty Latin or Greek authorities in his other books on trees, he claims only twenty-one for forest trees. Eleven of these he names in his text, but this gives no indication of their relative importance. He mentions Homer four times, Theophrastus once only, and

Vitruvius not at all. But that Homer called Achilles' spear an ash is something that every schoolboy would know, and the other references are more probably taken from a Homeric scholar than from Homer.[15] He makes no attempt to use Homer's epics to illustrate the properties or use of trees. His only reference to Theophrastus is to correct a statement about ivy which he has not understood;[16] on the other hand, Theophrastus is one of his main authorities in his description of trees. For the uses of various woods he has often followed Vitruvius.

The transition from fruit-trees to forest trees is made by beginning with the oaks whose acorns provided valuable food for animals, and at some time and in some places for men also. Before embarking on the oaks, he pauses to ask what it is like for a land to have no trees. This enables him to describe the strange country of the Chauci, that miserable people whose land was treeless and regularly flooded by the sea, as he knew from his military service on the Rhine. He may even have served under the Roman general Corbulo who planned to incorporate the tribe within the empire, but was required to abandon his aggressive campaign by the emperor Claudius. In describing oaks Pliny is more concerned with antiquarian questions about wreaths than with the differentiation of species and of their different uses. When he passes to conifers his main interest is in their production of resin. His transition from conifers to hardwoods is strangely artificial: 'It is because of their timber that nature has produced the rest of the trees'—as though firs and pines, which were the most used building-timbers, were only valued for their by-products.

After descriptions of the commonest hardwoods Pliny turns to general factors by which the various species are differentiated: the influence of climate and soil, the form of leaf, root, and bark, the processes of budding and fruiting, and the right time for felling. Towards the end of the book interesting facts which have not found a place earlier are strung together without a serious attempt to form a logical sequence. We should be grateful for Pliny's eagerness to record strange events and notable records— the largest tree ever seen in Rome, the time taken to build emergency fleets in the first and second Punic wars, the tallest cedar, the longest beam—for such information we can rarely find in other sources; but for the differentiation of species and the properties of their woods we soon realise that he is almost always dependent on his sources, and often misunderstands them. Unlike Theophrastus he was no botanist and it is doubtful how many species he would have recognised himself in the forest.

These weaknesses become clear when we compare Pliny's text with the passages in Theophrastus which he is following. Theophrastus says that the plane is rare in Italy; Pliny misunderstands the Greek word for rare, *spania*, and assumes that it refers to Spain.[17] According to Theophrastus the wood of yew on Mt. Ida had a yellow colour like cedar and when the bark was removed the wood was sometimes sold as cedar. In Pliny the yew has become ash, but ash-wood is white and not in the least like cedar: Pliny confused two Greek words, *milos* (yew) and *melia* (ash).[18] In another passage Theophrastus says that there are two kinds of pine (*peuke*) on Mt. Ida, one of which is called the pine of Ida, the other the coastal pine. In Pliny this becomes the difference between the mountain and the coastal larch.[19] There are other passages in which Pliny translates *peuke*, Theophrastus' pine, by *larix*, larch. When he says that larch does not grow again from its root if it has been cut down or burnt, he is clearly drawing on Theophrastus who says that *peuke* does not grow again when its root is burnt, though some maintain that the coastal pine (*pitys*) does, as happened at Pyrrha on the island of Lesbos when the *pitys*-wood on its mountain was burnt down.[20]

But the most interesting example of Pliny's confusion of pine and larch is in a strange passage where he makes Homer, in the *Odyssey*, say that Circe was burning larch together with cedar and thyon-wood on her fire.[21] The confusion of Circe with Calypso is a very venial error. They were both women, both had special powers, and they both lived on islands: Pliny was probably following Virgil.[22] But how did larch come into the story? It was not in Homer's vocabulary and the Greeks had no word for the tree until they borrowed the Latin word. It was essentially a European mountain tree and even in Italy it did not grow south of the Alps. Homer's line cannot be emended to introduce larch but Detlefsen long ago suggested that *peuke* could be fitted in. We can infer that Pliny, as in our other examples, has translated *peuke* by *larix*.[23] He has also mistranslated Theophrastus' chestnut ('the Euboic nut') by walnut, in one case certainly, in another probably.[24]

Pliny had probably followed others in believing that the Latin word *fagus* means the same as the Greek word *phegos*. They certainly must descend from a common ancestor, but there is no doubt that *phegos* in Greek means an oak, and specifically the Valonia oak, and that *fagus* in Latin means a beech. Theophrastus includes *phegos* in his classification of oaks and says that its acorns are the sweetest; Pliny says that the acorns of *fagus* are the sweetest.[25] We can follow the generally accepted explanation of the confusion, that people moving southwards into Greece from areas where beech was the dominant tree transferred their beech name to the oak when they came to a country where the beech did not grow and the oak was the most impressive tree. In historical times the beech is not recorded south of Thessaly.

Pliny does not always follow his source mechanically. Theophrastus, after distinguishing deciduous trees and evergreens, adds that some trees which are normally deciduous can in some situations keep their leaves. As illustrations he cites vines and figs at Elephantine and Memphis in Egypt, to which he has already referred. He now adds a famous plane tree at Gortyn in Crete and another in Cyprus which keep their leaves while all the other plants in the neighbourhood shed theirs. He also cites an oak within sight of Sybaris in south Italy 'which does not shed its leaves and is said not to come into bud until after the rising of the Dog Star'. Pliny uses the same story in the same context and is proud to point out that, although it was reported by Greek authors, he was the first Latin author to draw attention to it. He makes two small changes from Theophrastus. For Sybaris he substitutes Thurii, because, even when Theophrastus wrote, Sybaris had been destroyed and replaced by a new settlement at nearby Thurii. Theophrastus' specific 'rising of the Dog Star' becomes the more general 'midsummer'.[26] Pliny would have been disappointed to be told that he had been anticipated by Varro in his treatise on agriculture, including the change to Thurii—embarrassing, because he refers elsewhere several times to Varro's treatise. Pliny refers to Elephantine and Memphis, but says nothing here about the two plane trees at Gortyn in Crete and in Cyprus, because he has used them already in his list of famous plane trees.[27]

Sometimes, however, in establishing his independence he slightly distorts Theophrastus' meaning. In a discussion of the effects of climate on timber Theophrastus gives the accepted grading of quality in the building-timbers used in Greece. The best quality comes from Macedon, the second best from Pontus, the third from the (river) Rhyndacus, the fourth from the territory of the Aenianians (south of Thessaly), and the worst from Parnassus and Euboea; the quality of Arcadian wood is left open. Pliny adds the mountain forests of the west and adapts the list of Theophrastus.[28] He substitutes for the Rhyndacus Bithynia through which the river flows. He also simplifies by upgrading Pontic timber to an equality with Macedonian, and by downgrading Aenianian timber from the fourth to the lowest category; and he prefers to slip Arcadia into the same category rather than leaving the question open. He also arbitrarily changes the description of the poor firs of Euboea and Parnassus from Theophrastus' 'knotty and rough' to 'knotty and twisted'.

In some passages one can see that Pliny has drawn on more than one source without realising their incompatibilities. In expanding on the theme that some woods last longer in some situations than others, he says that beech and walnut have a good reputation for use in water, but a little later in the same section he says that beech and Turkey oak quickly decay and that aesculus-oak also will not withstand damp.[29] The first statement probably derives from Theophrastus, who says that beech and chestnut (mistranslated by Pliny) do not decay in water; the second statement comes from Vitruvius.[30] The explanation of the apparent contradiction is that Vitruvius is speaking of the use of these woods in building. They should not be exposed to the weather, but beech lasts well if completely submerged in water: Theophrastus knew that beeches grown in central Italy were used for ships' keels.[31]

Pliny's main description of cypress and other scattered references to the tree are a conflation from different sources that form an incongruous composite;[32] and it is very difficult from his descriptions to distinguish the various pines. While in one place he gives a fair general description of the larch, in others, as we have seen, he confuses it with Theophrastus' pine, and he includes it among the evergreens though alone among conifers it sheds its leaves in the autumn.[33] This is a surprising mistake, because larch grew freely in the Alps and anyone coming from Comum should have been familiar with this eccentricity.

We can see Pliny making good use of Theophrastus in his detailed description of citrus-wood (*Callitris quadrivalvis*), which particularly interested him because it was the source of the most expensive tables in the late Republic and early Empire. Most of the supply came from Mauretania. Theophrastus had referred to this tree, which the Greeks called *thyon*, and briefly described it: 'It grows at its best near the temple of Zeus Ammon and in the district of Cyrene. . . . Men can still recall that some of the roofs in ancient times were made of it. For the wood is absolutely proof against decay.'[34] Pliny is surprised that Theophrastus makes no mention of citrus-wood tables, 'and indeed there is no record of one before the time of Cicero, which proves how recently they have come to Rome'.[35] Where Pliny draws on Theophrastus we can make the necessary corrections, but in his descriptions of conifers he goes mainly to other sources which have not survived and he is a very frustrating guide.

Though Pliny was not by nature a botanist, his interests were wide and he drew on a very wide range of sources. We could expect him to turn to the recognised authorities on trees, including the specialised studies of olives and vines; it is endearing to find him also quoting from the memoirs of generals. It helps us to form a more balanced picture of Mucianus, the governor of Syria who master-minded Vespasian's successful bid for the imperial purple, when we learn from Pliny that, while governing Lycia, he held a dinner-party for eighteen members of his staff within the hollow of a plane tree.[36] It is records such as this that particularly appeal to Pliny. Another curiosity he owed to Suetonius Paullinus who, in a campaign against troublesome nomads in Mauretania (*c*.AD 42), was the first Roman general to cross the Atlas range. In his account of the campaign he emphasised the spectacular height of the snow-capped mountains and described some remarkable trees, of a species unknown to the Romans, growing in dense forests. They were exceptionally tall, with smooth trunks free from knots, their leaves like those of the cypress. They had a strong scent and were covered with a light, wool-like down from which clothes could be made.[37] We are still left to wonder what they were.

His concern with imperial finances in his administrative posts gives him a natural interest in prices, such as we very rarely find in other sources. He also flavours his narrative with observations from his own personal experience. In his description of the ash he observes that, according to Greek writers, ash leaves are poisonous to animals. This he can support: 'We can state from personal experience that if a ring of ash leaves is placed round a snake and a fire the snake will rather escape into the fire than into the ash leaves.'[38] His vivid description of the gigantic oaks in Germany derives from his military service on the Rhine: 'These oaks grow with a very great appetite, and when they are undermined by the waves or driven on by the winds they carry away with them enormous islands of earth, fast bound by their roots; and so balanced they sail upright. Our fleets have often been terrified by the formidable array of their enormous branches when they seemed to be driven on deliberately against their bows as the ships lay at anchor by night. They could find no way of evading the danger and were forced to mount a naval battle against trees.'[39]

In a discussion of fruit-trees that fruit more than once a year he quotes two examples cited by Varro of trees that produce three crops in the year and adds that this occurs regularly at Tacape in Africa. The soil and crops of this district he describes in very great detail in a later book and includes the market price of land.[40] A plot of four square cubits costs four denarii, and he even adds that the local cubit was the measure not from the elbow to the fingertips, but to the closed fist. One senses the practical interest of the government official. Pliny had probably been a procurator in the province of Africa.

Whereas Theophrastus' approach is impersonal, and free from his own prejudices, Pliny is obsessed with the erosion of the traditional Roman values. It was fashionable as the standard of living rose, especially among the rich, to look back nostalgically to the sturdy and thrifty Sabine farmer, and the courage and discipline which enabled the Romans to extend their rule over the whole of Italy and beyond. Most of the writers of the imperial period who indulged in such themes were repeating clichés; they attacked the extravagance of the day and enjoyed it; they liked to hark back to the time when the Forum was not built over and the Capitoline hill was covered with brambles, but they would have been miserable without their marble temples, baths, and lavish spectacles. Pliny, however, was genuine in his disgust at current social trends, and though his style of writing is sometimes obscure and never distinguished, and though he is uncritical and superstitious, he offers a wealth of information that cannot be found in any other Greek or Roman writer whose works have survived. How else should we know that the great Cicero was criticised because his son when slightly drunk had thrown a goblet at Agrippa,[41] or that the emperor Tiberius would only have his hair cut between two moons?[42]

Our two next most important sources are Vitruvius and Strabo. Vitruvius, who probably came from north Italy, had studied the theory and practice of architecture as a young man. In the Civil War he supported Caesar, and when Caesar was murdered he transferred his allegiance to Octavius, who appointed him with three colleagues to a commission to organise the construction and maintenance of his artillery. After the decisive battle of Actium, when Octavian had become the undisputed master of the Roman world, Vitruvius dedicated to him a treatise on architecture, expressing the hope that it would be useful to him in the great building projects that he had in mind. In his treatise he discusses the qualifications of the architect, the basic elements of town planning, building materials, and the construction of public and private buildings. He includes a detailed description of a basilica which he himself designed at Fanum, where the great north road from Rome reaches the Adriatic, and in his last book he takes advantage of his experience with artillery to describe a series of machines that have been used in peace or war. There is no explicit evidence for the date of the treatise, but it should be before 27 BC when Octavian became Augustus; to Vitruvius he is still *imperator* or *imperator Caesar*. He shows no knowledge of any of the great buildings of the Augustan principate and does not even mention Agrippa, who had already transformed Rome's water-supply and sewage system and was later to play a leading part in replanning an imperial Rome.

Vitruvius is concerned with fine architecture, with temples, basilicas, theatres, and elegant houses rather than warehouses and multiple dwellings. In taste he is conservative, firmly rooted in Greek theory and practice, still thinking almost exclusively in

terms of post-and-beam construction. He is familiar with concrete but does not realise its revolutionary potential, which did
not emerge clearly until the Flavian period. He sees the contemporary changes in the housing of the common people, when
apartment blocks had to be built high to meet the needs of a
massive increase in population, but he does not seem to grasp
their full social significance. He reserves his detailed description
for the houses of the rich, based on the atrium and expanding
horizontally; but such houses were already becoming restricted
to a very narrow class. He would have been regarded as old-
fashioned by progressive architects, and there is no evidence
that he played any part in the Augustan rebuilding of Rome as
architect or adviser.[43] Vitruvius in fact probably had more
influence during the Renaissance than in his own day, but the
wide-scale use of his treatise by Pliny shows that it was still read
a hundred years after his death. For our purposes his main
usefulness is that he included wood in the building materials
which he discusses in detail and is a useful guide to the usage of
the various woods by Roman builders.[44]

The contribution of Strabo (c.63 BC–AD 20) is very different.
He was born at Amaseia on the south coast of the Black Sea, a
Greek city with a strong admixture of native blood. His mother's
family had exercised considerable influence in the great days
when Mithridates Eupator built up the kingdom of Pontus until
he became a serious threat to Roman domination in Asia Minor.
But when the crisis came the family chose the side of Rome.
They retained much of their wealth and Strabo was able to
study under some of the best teachers of the day at home and
abroad. He prided himself on being a philosopher who had
studied all branches of knowledge and his writings included
philosophical treatises and a historical study beginning where
Polybius had ended; but the only work to survive is his geographical description of the known world in seventeen books.
Behind this work lies a long series of geographies which go back
to the Milesian Hecataeus (c.500 BC). The primary objective of
these treatises had been virtually to translate a map into words,
to establish the relation of places to one another and to state the
distances between them, though the catalogue was relieved by
brief historical, geographical, and sociological notes on places of
major importance or interest.

Strabo agreed with Polybius that a historian or geographer must travel and he claims to have gone as far east as Armenia and as far west as the west coast of Italy; in the south he has seen Ethiopia. His travels, however, seem not to have been designed primarily to collect material for his geography but to see interesting places or to meet interesting people. His work is mainly based on wide reading in libraries, and its quality depends largely on the quality of his sources. The work indeed is very uneven and if none but his two books on Greece had survived we should think very poorly of it, for he is obsessed with Homer and his description of Greece takes on the flavour of a Homeric scholar's commentary on place names in the *Iliad* and *Odyssey*. Eratosthenes had tried to put an end to this form of scholarship more than two hundred years earlier: 'You will find the scenes of the wanderings of Odysseus when you find the cobbler who sewed up the bag of the wind.' To Strabo this was sacrilegious heresy and he was at great pains not only to locate the place names in the *Iliad*, but also to identify the places visited by Odysseus. But he had a shrewd appreciation of Roman politics and a great respect for Roman administration. He pays tribute to Augustus' achievement and his flattery is neither fulsome nor hypocritical.

The centres which interested Strabo most were Alexandria and Rome. He spent several years in Alexandria and had the great advantage of a personal friendship with Aelius Gallus, who governed Egypt from 26 to 22 BC. This enabled him to describe in great detail Gallus' frustrated expedition into Arabia, and to travel up the Nile to Ethiopia. Strabo also knew Rome well: he claims to have seen Servilius Isauricus, who campaigned successfully against the pirates in Pamphylia and Isauria in 78 BC and died at Rome in 44 BC. He witnessed the execution in 36 BC of a pirate chief in the arena at Rome and he was there again in 7 BC.[45] He could see the architectural transformation of Rome under Augustus and he was intelligent enough to appreciate the problem of supplying such a large urban concentration with timber and other building materials. He also draws attention to the timber resources of other parts of Italy and mentions a visit to Populonia, where the iron-ore from Elba was smelted because the timber supply on the island had been exhausted. Apart from his personal experience in Rome and his voyage up the west coast of Italy, he seems to have had a personal interest in Campania. There is a refreshing liveliness in his description of Italy that is completely lacking in his description of Greece. For Italy, as also for Spain, he provides a fair basis for a rough distribution map of forests: in his description of Greece he does not even mention any forest. There is, however, compensation in Pausanias, who in the Antonine period wrote a description of Greece. His main interests were in religious cults and antiquities, and for us he is most valuable for his description of archaic sculptures in wood, but he also makes occasional reference to forests that he passes in his travels.

Further evidence for the distribution of forests can be found in the historians. Livy's narrative of the war against Hannibal, and the history of early Rome by Dionysius of Halicarnassus, throw considerable light on the nature and distribution of Italian forests; and Polybius adds a description of Cisalpine Gaul.[46] Macedonian forests form an integral part of Livy's narrative of the Roman war against Perseus King of Macedon in 191–186 BC. From Caesar's account of his Gallic campaigns we can see how thickly forested Gaul was, and in the late Empire Ammianus Marcellinus happens to give us one of the very few pieces of evidence for the manhandling of massive timbers. We also rely largely on historians for our accounts of timber consumption by navies and armies. For timber on the farm we turn naturally to Cato and the writers on agriculture who succeeded him, particularly Varro and Columella.

All the literary sources so far mentioned could be expected to contribute to our enquiry. What is surprising is the amount of useful information that can be gleaned in the most unlikely places. One would not expect the most comprehensive analysis of deforestation to come from Plato (p. 188) and it is odd that the only prose account of cutting oars should be in a description of an imaginary picture.[47] There are indeed very few Greek or Latin prose authors who will not yield useful information if diligently searched. Poets are different and have to be approached cautiously.

There is no need, however, for caution in using the earliest of the poets, Homer and Hesiod. It is clear, as we shall see later, that Homer, though his heroes are more than life-size, is thoroughly familiar with the work of the feller in the forest and with the usage of the various woods. Hesiod is reliable in his *Works and Days* because he is giving serious advice to those who work the land and he knows the life of a farmer from his own experience. There is also a genuine feeling for nature in the lyric poets of the archaic period. The themes of most of their surviving poems do not invite the kind of information we need, but in crossing from the mainland to Thasos one recalls Archilochus' description of the island, 'standing out like the back of an ass, garlanded with untamed forest'.[48] By the classical period the intensive political life of the city-state and the philosopher's growing interest in man obscure the feeling for nature. Socrates thought that he had nothing to learn from trees and the open country; it was people in the city who could teach him.[49] When Euripides introduces a ladder made of *kedros*-wood we should not take this as evidence that the Greeks of his day or any other day made ladders of cedar or juniper. In the Hellenistic period there may have been something of a return to nature; the background of the idylls of Theocritus genuinely reflects the Sicilian landscape.

We might hope for more help from the Latin poets of the Augustan age, for Virgil and Horace were both born in well-wooded country, and Horace clearly enjoyed his Sabine farm with its woodlands which he owed to his patron Maecenas. From Virgil especially, whose father is said to have built up a small fortune by buying woods[50] and who, on the firm prompting of Maecenas, was able to write four books of *Georgics* on the farmer's life, we might expect a mine of information, but confidence is soon shaken. Within a single book of the *Aeneid* he ascribes three different woods, maple, fir, and pine, to the Trojan horse and not for structural reasons.[51] Similarly, the Trojan ships, usually called firs, become pines when it suits the narrative or metre.[52] When Aeneas sends his men to collect wood for the funeral pyre of Misenus, drowned in the bay of Naples, they enter an age-old wood and proceed to fell spruce, ilex, ash, oak, and mountain ash.[53] This is not evidence that such a strange assortment of trees could grow in the same wood in Campania; the passage derives from Virgil's appreciation of a similar passage in Ennius. Catalogues of trees which are only metrically compatible began with Homer and had a long history after Virgil.[54]

In his *Eclogues* and *Georgics* we can see another tendency in Virgil, which derives from his absorption in Greek literature. It is generally accepted that when in his first eclogue he makes his shepherd take rest in the shade of a beech, *fagus*, he is echoing Theocritus whose shepherd rests under an oak, *phegos*.[55] Virgil is more interested in the sound than the substance; he certainly did not believe that *fagus* was an oak. Similar Greek echoes can be found even in the *Georgics*. When Virgil writes of an axle of beech, *faginus axis*, he is thinking of Homer's *pheginos axon*, axle of oak;[56] beech is a very poor wood for an axle, which needs the strength of an oak or some other very hard wood. In his description of making a plough he prescribes a light lime-wood for the yoke where again one would have expected a particularly strong wood.[57] Such things did not disturb Seneca; 'Virgil sought not what was nearest to the truth, but what was most appropriate.'[58] His aim was not to teach the farmer but to please his readers. So we should not be misled by his description of 'the windswept Caucasus providing useful timber, pine for ships, cedar and cypress for houses'.[59] There is no reason to believe that there were ever cedars in the Caucasus range. It is formally possible that Virgil's *cedros* meant junipers rather than cedars, for *cedrus*, the word for cedar, was sometimes used for juniper; but no such justification is needed. It is the attraction of alliteration that explains the choice, *cedros cupressosque*, preceded two lines earlier by *franguntque feruntque*.

In Horace also there is the same combination of a love of nature and the strong influence of Greek literature. Some have inferred from the description of his ship of State as a Pontic pine, *Pontica pinus*, that Rome imported pine from the Black Sea forests.[60] It is extremely improbable that the Romans imported pine from such a distant area when Italy was so well stocked with fir and pine. But the fine quality of the Pontic pine was well known to the Greeks and *Pontica pinus* has a satisfying sound. On the other hand, when Horace speaks of the oak and ilex on his Sabine farm it is what one should expect in that neighbourhood. But if we discount the poetry and think only of our own narrow requirements, it must be admitted that the Flavian poets are more useful to us than the Augustans. We shall have many occasions to call on Martial's neat epigrams and Juvenal's biting satires.

In investigating the distribution of species two further approaches can be used. Place names, when their antiquity is securely attested, can be significant. The proliferation of names derived from *pitys* is fair evidence of the wide spread of the coastal pine (*pitys*). Pityeia on the south coast of the Propontis between Parium and Priapus was included in Homer's Trojan catalogue and Strabo confirms that there were pines on the mountain above the town.[61] Pityussa was the name of a small island off the coast of Troezen[62] and it is no coincidence that the prize at the Isthmian games nearby was a wreath of pine (*pitys*): Aleppo pine still grows freely in the area. The same name, Pityussa, was given to two islands off the south coast of Spain, Ebusa and Ophiousa.[63] According to Pliny Samos was once also called Pityussa[64] as, according to Strabo, were Lampsacus on the south shore of the Hellespont and the island of Chios.[65]

As might be expected the oak (*drys*) has left its mark widely. Dryopis was the name of a district with shifting boundaries in central Greece:[66] It was an oak forest that concealed the Persian force sent by Xerxes to trap the Greeks at Thermopylae. According to Herodotus the Phocaean defenders who were guarding the mountain path were taken by surprise.[67] Oak-men, Dryopes, are recorded in the Argolid and Laconia, and in the islands.[68] There was Drymaea in Boeotia near the border with Phocis,[69] and a district called Drymos at the north end of Euboea under Mt. Telethrios, near Oreus.[70] Dryoscephalae, oak-heads, was the name of a pass linking Attica with Boeotia.[71] On the other side of the Aegean, Dryusa, so Pliny tells us, was an earlier name for the island of Samos;[72] Dryussa was an island off the coast near Clazomenae.[73]

The wide range of the elm (*ptelea*) in Greece is reflected in the name Pteleum, which is found on the south coast of Thessaly near the river Peneus, on the west coast of the Peloponnese, and behind the Gulf of Ambracia.[74] Thucydides records a fort named Pteleum in the territory of Erythrae in Ionia.[75] From Pausanias' description of his travels in Greece we can infer that cypress was one of the commonest trees in the Peloponnese. It gave its name to Cyparissia on the south-west coast, which is included by Homer in his Achaean catalogue,[76] and cypress-wood is referred to in tablets which were baked when Nestor's palace in Messenia was destroyed by fire at the end of the Bronze

Age.[77] Homer also includes a Cyparissos near Delphi in his
Achaean catalogue. It is not recorded later, but Pausanias
reports that the name was changed to Anticyra.[78] Castanea
attests the importance of the chestnut in Thessaly, confirmed by
Theophrastus,[79] and Xylopolis (Timbertown), sited by Pliny
and Ptolemy in Macedonian Mygdonia,[80] was aptly named, for
the Mygdonian mountains were well wooded.

Latin adds three names. Buxentum, a Roman colony on the
south-west coast of Italy, is presumably named from the
boxwood of the district. Laricinum is in Noricum in a district
where the larch (*larix*) grows well, and Pliny has preserved the
name of the *Querculani*, the oak(*quercus*)-men, one of the Early
Latin peoples who cannot yet be located.[81] More important are
surviving tree names inside Rome which reflect the trees that
the Romans found when they first settled on the Palatine hill
(p. 219).

Further evidence of local landscape may be obtained by
pollen analysis. Pollen grains have the great advantage for the
archaeologist that they are virtually indestructible provided
that they are sealed from the atmosphere. If suitable sites can be
found in lake-beds, peat, or marsh, a long tube can be sunk and a
core taken from the deposit: the stratified grains should reveal
the changing pattern of the vegetation. Pollen analysis is,
however, a complex operation. It is not merely a comparison of
the quantity of grains of different species. The distance that the
various species will carry has to be considered: some grains are
heavier than others and will not travel so far; wind-blown grains
will travel much further than those that are carried by insects;
account also has to be taken of the prevailing wind. These
factors are not given due weight in all reports, but the positive
achievements of this comparatively new discipline are already
striking. It is mainly by pollen analysis that it has been possible
to build up in outline the history of European vegetation and
climate since *c.*40,000 BC. The main concentration has hitherto
been on prehistoric periods, but reconstructions based on pollen
analysis in two areas, one in Greece and the other in Italy,
should encourage more pioneers in the period that concerns us.
Scholars working with the University of Minnesota's Messenian
expedition have produced a credible outline of the woodland
pattern in Messenia during the Bronze Age (p. 104), and cores

taken from lake Monterosi in Latium have shown the changes in vegetation when the Romans opened up the country which the Ciminian forest had once dominated, by driving the Via Cassia through Sutrium into central Etruria (p. 246). On the other hand, it is disconcerting that two pollen analysts should conclude that the plain of Drama in Macedon was covered with oak forest throughout the classical period, when Theophrastus has recorded that the plain or a large part of it had recently been drained and was in his day (c.300 BC) all cultivated.[82]

There is another discipline, still younger, that may make a significant contribution in our field of study. Dendrochronology is based on the study of the annual growth rings of trees. Since it has been shown that ring patterns are consistent within the same climatic zone, undated samples can be cross-dated by the ring pattern on growing trees or beams from buildings whose date is known. The ring patterns of the bristle-cone pine have provided a chronological framework for the history of south-west America and the collation of dated samples of European oaks has provided firm dates for buildings that were hitherto undated, and even for the oak boards of paintings whose date or authorship was disputed.

No such spectacular results can be expected from the ancient Mediterranean world. There are no remaining trees from our period still growing. Although round timbers are not uncommonly found in excavations, their date is rarely certain and dated beams are still rarer. Sufficient results have already been achieved to make it possible to date by ring patterns many medieval churches and other buildings in the Middle Ages, but it will be more difficult to build an adequate framework of dated samples for the classical period and earlier. There is, however, one site in which the value of dendrochronology has been considerable. When the Americans cut into the most impressive of the tumuli of the Phrygian capital of Gordium they found the tomb chamber undisturbed. The chamber itself was built with carefully sawn boards, neatly mortised together, and to protect the chamber from the pressure of the immense mound an outer protection of round logs was added. The ring pattern was clear on both boards and logs, and other samples were collected from carbonised wood in the city itself and other burials. As a result P. Kuniholm has been able to provide a master tree-ring chronology covering 806 years which can be approximately dated by the pottery and bronze vessels that were found in the tomb chamber. The inferences arising will be discussed in an appendix (p. 460). A very different type of example was provided by a recent discovery. In a drain leading from the Colosseum, which was blocked in the late Empire, a substantial remnant was found of an oak beam showing a clear ring pattern. This pattern exactly matched the pattern established in the Trier region of Germany for the years AD 70–86, which fits the building of the Colosseum.[83]

2

MEDITERRANEAN FORESTS

In the course of these studies we shall be specially concerned with the forests of Italy, Greece, Macedon, and the Near East, but it may be useful first to discuss certain basic factors by which all Mediterranean woodlands are influenced to a greater or lesser degree.[1] For in terms of climate and soil these forests belong to a roughly homogeneous region which takes its name from the sea which is its dominant feature.

The Mediterranean region lies between the great land mass of Europe and the wide desert belt of Africa and the most characteristic feature of its climate is the combination of mild wet winters and long dry summers. From May to September rain is extremely rare. The winters are very different from those of central Europe and the British Isles; the sun is rarely absent for long and heavy rain can be quickly followed by bright sun even in January and February. Though in most areas the total rainfall in the winter is adequate, it tends to come in the form of concentrated downpours rather than steady rain. This increases the danger of erosion, especially when trees have been clear-felled on steep hillsides; torrents of rain may sweep away the soil before the new growth has had time to establish itself. The long dry months of summer also make natural regeneration more difficult than in lands where rain is more evenly spread over the year. If spring comes early and the dry weather begins in April there may not be enough moisture in the soil to sustain the growing seedlings until the rains come again.

The typical Mediterranean climate applies primarily to the coastal areas. The great central plateau of Spain has a different geological foundation and a different climate, and winters are significantly colder and summers tend to be hotter. Trees such as the olive and fig, which cannot withstand sharp frosts, have no place here and the same conditions apply broadly to the central Anatolian plateau. Not even all coastal areas have the same pattern. In north Africa, the western half including Morocco, Algeria, Tunisia corresponds closely in climate to the south coasts of Spain and France; but between Tunisia and Egypt the influence of the desert is paramount—only Cyrene and a few other limited areas can support any trees but the acacia and the palm, which have adapted themselves to desert conditions. The fertility of Egypt depends entirely on irrigation by the Nile. The Delta was called by Hecataeus and Herodotus the 'gift of the river'; it was land recovered from the sea by the silting of the river and unsuited to tree-growing. In Upper Egypt the valley of the Nile was less than twenty kilometres wide and on each side it was hemmed in by desert. The rich soil deposited by the river and the irrigation system made possible by the flood waters could sustain the densest population in the Mediterranean, but only a limited range of trees could grow in such a dry climate. For big timbers Egypt had to look outside her own borders.

It has often been thought that the climate of Mediterranean lands has changed significantly since the period with which we are concerned. The frequency of floods in the records of Roman historians and references to the freezing of the Rhine and Danube have led some to infer that the climate was wetter and colder in the classical period than now. The study of vegetation by pollen analysis has indeed shown major changes in climate in the 10,000 years that followed the last Ice Age, but the modern vegetation patterns in Mediterranean countries today correspond very closely with the ancient records. Although there have been periods of drought and periods of excessive rain, no major change of climate can be assumed. Floods in Rome loom large in the record because they were regarded as portents. If it were not for the more effective modern means of control we should hear much more of Tiber floods today.

The Greeks and Romans associated trees primarily with hills and mountains. A disgruntled oligarch cynically analysing the Athenian democracy and explaining the importance of sea power says: 'No one city has both timber and flax, but where flax is common the land is level and treeless.'[2] This is not because trees will not grow on plains, but because the plains have to be cleared for agriculture; food crops are more important than timber. Most of the timber with which we shall be concerned came from the mountain ranges that are a special feature of the

Mediterranean region. Some run parallel to the sea, rising behind the coastal plain: in Spain, the Sierra Nevada in the south and the Cantabrian and Galician mountains in the north; in the south of Asia Minor, the Taurus range towering above the Cilician plain, and, when the coast turns southwards, Mt. Amanus in Syria and the long Lebanon range to the south. Italy is divided by the Apennines down to Lucania, with a further forested area to the south in Calabria. The Pindus range runs from north to south through Macedon and northern Greece, but in the Peloponnese the mountain pattern is more complex, with a range of mountains along the southern coast of the Corinthian Gulf, the parallel ranges of Taygetus and Parnon flanking Laconia, and the quadrilateral of mountains which surrounds Arcadia.

The distribution of species in the Mediterranean depends partly on rainfall. It is natural that the west coasts of Portugal and Morocco, facing the Atlantic Ocean, should have cooler summers and more rain; similarly the western Mediterranean, being nearer the ocean, will receive more rain than the east. That is why the cork-oak, which needs a moist location, is widely spread in north-west Africa, Spain, and Portugal, but is much less common in Italy, rare in Greece, and not found east of Greece. By contrast the carob tree, which likes a dry climate, is common in the east and not found west of Italy. The character of the soil is also important. Geologically most of the mountains of the Mediterranean region were formed in the Tertiary Age. Limestone is the main foundation, some of it very hard and less favourable to tree growth, but most softer, disintegrating under the pressures of wind and rain, and forming soils that can sustain good forests. In such areas there tend to be cavities and cracks in the rock by which rain finds its way into subterranean streams or reservoirs which store water to furnish gushing springs. There are also outcrops from an earlier geological period as in south Italy where, in contrast to the limestone of the Apennines, the Sila and Aspromonte forests have a granite foundation.

Altitude also plays a very important part in the distribution of species. Trees that grow well at the level of the coast may not withstand the colder temperatures of the higher zones, and trees that flourish in the higher zones may find the sun too hot and the rain too little at the coastal level. For convenience altitude may be divided into three zones, although the divisions are arbitrary and not fixed. Some species that are typical of the lower zone may extend to the middle zone and even to the higher zone and few species will be rigidly confined to the zone which most favours them. The dividing lines may be placed at *c*.500 metres and *c*.1,200 metres, though in the more southerly areas they will be a little higher.

The lowest zone feels the full force of the long summer heat and the evergreen oaks and coastal pines support these conditions best. In drier areas, as in parts of southern California, which has a very similar climate, the natural vegetation may always have been a maquis of drought-resisting evergreen shrubs, with occasional pines or ilex. The middle zone is generally characterised by deciduous trees, sometimes growing in pure stands but more often mixed. In most countries the oak is by far the commonest tree in this zone, but the range is wide including maple, elm, sycamore, cypress, pine, and some of the junipers. By streams that bring down the rain-water, and particularly the melting snows, alders, poplars, and willows find a natural home, and the same pattern is found in the mountain valleys of the Apennines, Lebanon, and the Atlas mountains of Algeria and Morocco.

It is from the middle zone that most of the furniture woods come, and this zone also is most suited to a form of silviculture which in England is known as coppicing. Long before the Bronze Age men must have observed that some trees die completely when they are cut down, while others throw up new shoots from their roots. Broadly it is one of the main differences between conifers few of which coppice, and broadleaf trees which mostly coppice well. From this basic observation developed the custom of cutting down trees before they are mature and cutting the regrowth at regular intervals. This was the most economic way of producing stakes, posts, and fencing for farms and also firewood, which was in constant demand. Chestnut and oak proved to be the best adapted to coppicing, but good returns could be obtained from many other deciduous trees, including maple and hornbeam.

While deciduous trees tended to dominate the middle zone, the upper zone was normally dominated by conifers. Some of the oaks penetrated into the lower levels of this zone, as did maples, but the commonest components, varying from area to area, were pine, beech, fir, cedar, and juniper. It was the juniper that could stand the highest altitudes. No cedars and few firs are found higher than 2,000 metres; junipers have been recorded on Antilebanon up to 2,700 metres.

In Greece and Italy the fir was the dominant species in the upper zone and in both countries it was regarded as the most useful timber for boat-building and general construction. In the Apennines and in the Macedonian mountains it was the common European fir, *Abies alba*, often called silver fir; in central and southern Greece fir grew on most of the mountains that were more than 1,000 metres high, but it was a different variety, named from the island where it was first differentiated, *Abies cephalonica*. In the eastern Mediterranean, from the Taurus range to Lebanon, there is a third variety, *Abies cilicica*. The differences in appearance are slight, but the two more southern varieties are generally regarded as inferior in quality. Theophrastus ranked the timber of Parnassus and the mountains of Euboea considerably below the Macedonian, and though he does not specify firs in the comparison of these areas, they were recognised as the most important timbers.[3] In the mountains which rise along the south coast of the Black Sea at its eastern end, there is a fourth variety of fir, *Abies nordmanniana*, which is closer in quality to the fir of Macedon. In the coastal mountain ranges of the eastern Mediterranean behind the plains of Cilicia, Syria, and Phoenicia cedar becomes one of the dominant species in the upper zone. In all three areas it is accompanied by fir, but the relative importance of fir is uncertain, especially on Lebanon. Today fir grows fairly well at the north end of the range, but is not found further south than the forest of Ehden.

Of the large number of pines distributed throughout the world only five have a significant place among Mediterranean trees.[4] The commonest pine of all, *Pinus silvestris*, which is widespread throughout Europe and conspicuous in such fragments of natural pine forest as still survive in Scotland, is unsuited to the much warmer and drier climate of the Mediterranean; but it penetrates into Macedon and is common in the Black Sea forests, in both of which temperatures are lower and rainfall higher than in Greece or Italy. The most widespread of the Mediterranean pines is the Aleppo pine, *Pinus halepensis*, which is normally found by the coast, but can penetrate inland as in Greece in the district of Olympia, and in Italy as far as Spoleto; though more common on the coastal plain, it can be found up to *c*.800 metres and occasionally higher. It tends to be twisted by the wind, rarely grows higher than fifty feet, and its wood is not strong; today in many areas it is valued most for the resin it supplies. It is found in the south of Spain and France, north-west Africa, and especially in Greece. In the islands of the Aegean and further east it is very rare, and more often replaced by *Pinus halepensis* var. *brutia*, a variety only recently distinguished from *halepensis*, but tending to grow straighter and stronger. It can be seen at its best in Thasos, Cyprus, and Turkey. Another pine that grows well by the sea in Italy and the western Mediterranean is *Pinus pinaster* (sometimes called *Pinus maritima*). It produces stronger wood, grows taller and straighter than the other coastal pines, and can be found up to *c*.1,000 metres.

More useful to the builder are the mountain pines which can be found up to 1,200 metres and sometimes higher. Of these there are several species, of which the commonest in the Mediterranean is divided into two varieties, *laricio* and *nigra*. The natural area of *Pinus laricio*, often called the Corsican pine because the finest examples were found in Corsica, is Italy with the western Mediterranean. *Pinus nigra* belongs rather to Greece and the eastern Mediterranean. These mountain pines are the pines most used in ships and in building. The last of the five pines, *Pinus pinea*, called from its shape the umbrella pine and less appropriately the stone-pine, is the easiest to distinguish, by its broad and rounded crown. Today it dominates many coastal landscapes, especially in Italy and Lebanon, but its expansion is due more to its attractiveness in the landscape than its usefulness as timber. The wood is of poor quality and in the classical world it was appreciated most for the nuts from its cones. When Virgil wrote that the fir was the first of the trees of the mountain, ash in the wood, and pine in the garden, he presumably had *Pinus pinea* in mind. With the aid of a botanist it is not difficult to distinguish these five species of pine by the different formation of their leaves, cones, branches, and bark, but the ancient classification was less sophisticated and it is rarely possible to determine from literary references which particular pine is meant.

The evergreen oaks, like the pines, are distributed according to conditions of soil and climate. In the western Mediterranean the ilex (holm-oak) has an important place in the coastal and middle zones. It can grow up to fifty feet and if it has room its branches spread widely. It is valued for its shade, appreciated especially by shepherds, and for the strength of its wood, and the fine charcoal it produces. The kermes oak, *Quercus coccifera*, which takes its name from the scarlet-producing insect which it hosts, is also widespread in the western Mediterranean. It is a small tree, with prickly leaves, rarely growing higher than twenty feet, but its wood too is very strong. In the eastern Mediterranean these two evergreens are superseded by *Quercus calliprinos*, very similar to *Quercus coccifera* but larger in girth and growing taller, when it survives the grazing of goats.

Deciduous oaks are more intractable.[5] In England only two varieties and their hybrids are native, *Quercus pedunculata* and *Quercus sessiliflora*. They can be distinguished by leaf, acorn, and branching habits, but in the quality of their wood they are similar and to most of us they are simply oaks. In no Mediterranean country is the oak pattern so simple. In Greece, according to Theophrastus, the classification of oaks and their names differed from district to district. On Mt. Ida they divided the oaks into five varieties, in Macedon into four, and the names did not correspond, nor is it easy to identify them botanically.[6] In Italy the situation is less opaque. Pliny names four varieties, *quercus*, *robur*, *aesculus*, and *cerrus*.[7] Of these *cerrus*, corresponding to the Greek *aspris*, can be identified by the descriptions. It is *Quercus cerris*, the Turkey oak, which was not uncommon in Italy, Greece, and the Near East. It is the fastest-growing and tallest of the oaks, but the wood had a poor reputation in both Italy and Greece. In England it is not a native, but it has been introduced into parks and gardens. *Robur* and *aesculus* were regarded as the most valuable of the oaks, corresponding roughly to our English oaks, *robur* to *pedunculata*, *aesculus* to *sessiliflora*. *Quercus*, like *drys* in Greek, was often used for the whole oak family, but clearly it was also regarded as a separate species. Different varieties of oaks are found today in other areas of the Mediterranean, but we have no ancient sources from which we could even guess the importance or identification of oaks in these areas, and have to make inferences from the modern distribution.

It would be interesting to know to what extent building contracts in Greece and Rome specified the species of oak that was to be used. It may be significant that the temple commissioners of Epidaurus and Delos, both of whom bought considerable quantities of oak, made no distinctions. None of the various words given by Theophrastus for the varieties of Greek oaks appear in the temple accounts, only *drys*, which corresponds to *quercus* in Latin and oak in English. On the other hand, it must be admitted that the full text of a contract for building a doorway with a porch in a wall enclosing a sacred area in Puteoli in 105 BC goes into considerable detail.[8] For two doorposts *aesculus*-oak is to be used; for the lintel over the doorway, and for two beams that support the roof of the porch, *robur*-oak; fir (*abies*) is to be used for the roofing to support the tiles. The implication is that *robur* is a significantly stronger wood than *aesculus* and that the timber merchant and architect were given no freedom of choice. On the other hand, the Athenian decree that provides for the building of a naval arsenal in the Piraeus gives the measurements of the various timbers in great detail, but does not specify what woods are to be used; this seems to be left to the architect.[9]

Two other trees, cypress and juniper, have had an important place in Mediterranean forests. The original home of the cypress is still in dispute, but it was already firmly established in Asia Minor and Greece at the beginning of our period, and by the end it was common also in Italy. It was well suited to the climate, because it likes the heat and needs less rainfall than most of the conifers. There are two distinctive varieties, one with branches rising close to the stem, *Cupressus sempervirens pyramidalis*, the other with branches extending outwards, *horizontalis*. Both varieties were well known to Pliny, but most botanists believe that the spreading cypress was the original and, in our period, the more common form. According to Theophrastus the cypress was particularly abundant in Crete, Lycia, and Rhodes,[10] but it also grew well on the Taurus, Amanus, and Lebanon coastal ranges. It could also tolerate the drier, inland climate of the anti-Taurus range and, possibly, Antilebanon. The cypress is normally less tall than the cedar but can grow up to 100 feet, and while seen more often in the middle zone, it can extend into the upper zone.

The juniper has some of the properties of the cypress. It is even more drought-resistant but, unlike the cypress, it can also withstand fairly sharp cold. The junipers are a large family and, after the pines and the oaks, are probably the most widely distributed trees in the Mediterranean. Of the many species the most important to us are the tall junipers in the Near East, *Juniperus excelsa* and *foetidissima*, growing up to eighty feet, and *Juniperus drupacea*, much less common and rarely found over sixty feet. As both Greeks and Romans use the same word for juniper and cedar, there is serious danger of confusion. An appendix is more suitable for the discussion of this issue.[11]

In addition to trees that have a natural home in Mediterranean lands, there are some which are more European than Mediterranean but penetrate into the area. The presence of *Pinus silvestris* in Macedon and in the Black Sea mountains has already been mentioned. Similarly beech, which is one of the commonest trees in central Europe, accompanies European fir (*Abies alba*) down the Apennines but in Greece is not found south of Thessaly. It is also one of the most widespread trees in the mountains of the south coast of the Black Sea. Here too the spruce has an important place with fir, pine, and beech. How widely the spruce was spread in Italy during our period is made uncertain by mistranslation from Greek into Latin and will be briefly discussed later. Larch, however, seems never to have been acclimatised in Italy. Vitruvius says that it was discovered by Caesar in the Alps and was subsequently marketed in north Italy.[12]

Forests are not unchanging. Disturbance by violent windstorm, fire, or overcutting can change the balance in a forest, and trees which reproduce easily, like the pine, will expand at the expense of those that seed less regularly and grow slowly. In Cyprus the cedar has been restricted to a single forest above Paphos, largely under pressure from the pine. More drastic changes have been brought about by man's intervention. It is one of the more engaging attributes of the Romans that their governing class, just as the Assyrian kings, liked to introduce trees that they had admired in other countries. Lucullus included a cherry tree in the triumph following his successful campaign in Asia Minor against Mithridates and within 120 years it had even reached Britain.[13] From the east the Romans introduced and distributed the walnut and citrus trees. The plane, which originated in the east, came through Greece to Italy where it soon became very popular, especially in parks.[14] The cypress similarly came to Italy long after it had been firmly established in Greece and north Africa.[15]

Further changes have taken place since the Roman period. It is not easy from the present poor status of the fir in Italian forests to realise that in our period it was the dominant species in the Apennines and the Romans' most valued and used timber for shipbuilding and major constructions. This is the result of heavy cutting by the Romans and the popes, but it is surprising that the attempts to re-establish it have not been more successful. The chestnut, on the other hand, is probably much more widespread now than in our period. It is not included by Dionysius of Halicarnassus in his list of trees in the Sila forest; now it is the commonest tree on the middle slopes below pine, fir, and beech. There are now fine cedar forests in south-west France, but they are not native; they were developed from seed collected in north Africa. A Roman landowner returning to Italy today would be even more surprised to see eucalyptus, which comes from Australia, being planted on a large scale in the south, and Douglas fir, whose natural home is western America, growing well in the Vallombrosa national forest near Florence. Caution is needed when making inferences from the present to the past.

3

THE CEDARS OF LEBANON

They stood still and gazed at the forest,
They looked at the height of the cedars,
They looked at the entrance to the forest,
Where Humbaba was wont to walk was a path;
Straight were the tracks and good was the going.
They beheld the cedar mountain, abode of the god,
Throne-seat of Irnini.
From the face of the mountain
The cedars raise aloft their luxuriance.
Good is their shade, full of delight.[1]

THE epic of Gilgamesh was the most widespread and popular
of all the ancient stories from the Near East and fragments of
texts have been recovered in Sumerian, Akkadian, Hittite,
and Hurrian. The episode of the visit of Gilgamesh with his
companion Enkidu to a forest to destroy the guardian monster
and cut the trees can be traced back to the third millennium BC.
In the original form of the epic the episode may have been sited
in the mountains to the east of Mesopotamia,[2] but most of
the Akkadian fragments, including the fragment quoted, were
recovered from the library of the Assyrian king Assurbanipal
(668–633 BC) and by his time Mesopotamian rulers had for long
looked to forests in the west for their finest timber, and particularly their cedar-wood. It is a great tribute to these cedars
that they should catch the imagination of peoples more than 500
kilometres distant. The same feeling for the magnificence of the
cedar permeates the Old Testament and nowhere better than in
the verses of Ezekiel:

Look at Assyria: it was a cedar in Lebanon,
    whose fair branches overshadowed the forest,
towering high with its crown finding a way through the foliage.
Springs nourished it, underground waters gave it height,
their streams washed the soil all around it

and sent forth their rills to every tree in the country.
So it grew taller than every other tree.
Its boughs were many, its branches spread far;
    for water was abundant in the channels.
In its boughs all the birds of the air had their nests,
under its branches all wild creatures bore their young,
and in its shadow all great nations made their home.
    A splendid great tree it was, with its long spreading boughs,
for its roots were beside abundant waters.[3]

But the writers of the Old Testament knew that the cedar forest
was not merely admired for its beauty; it provided the most
sought-after wood in the Near East. It supplied the main
timbers for their own temple, which Solomon had secured from
Hiram King of Tyre.

The pre-eminence of the cedars of Lebanon in the Bible tends
to obscure the nature of the timber resources of the eastern
Mediterranean lands. Lebanon is but one of three mountain
systems that run parallel to the line of the coast. To the west is
the great Taurus range dominating the Cilician plain and rising
to heights of 3,885 and 3,734 metres. When the coastline turns to
the south the Amanus range of Syria rises up north of the river
Orontes. To the south of the river comes Mt. Cassius (1,759 m.),
and after it Jebel Ansarieh, a range of high hills. Between these
hills and Lebanon there is a break where the Nahr-el-Kabir (the
classical river Eleutherus) reaches the sea. South of the gap the
Lebanon range runs parallel to the coastline for a little more
than 100 kilometres, separated from the sea by a narrow plain
never more than eight kilometres wide. At the mouth of the
Nahr-el-Kelb, ten kilometres north of Beirut, the rocky hills
drop down to the sea and force the coastal road to make a short
inland detour. In the north the plain is not very productive but
southward it becomes more fertile and today citrus fruit and
bananas grow well. The Lebanese range reaches its highest
point near the northern end at Qurnat-as-Sawoa (3,083 m.).
Slightly north of Beirut Mt. Sannim is a little more than
500 metres lower (2,548 m.), and south of Beirut the crest falls
gradually until Lebanon ends behind Sidon. The mountains rise
up sharply from the plain and are cut by deep valleys, which
makes lateral communication difficult. South of Sidon the hills
behind Tyre are considerably lower.

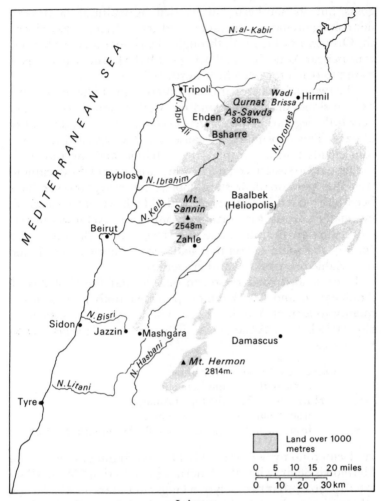

1 Lebanon

To the east and roughly parallel to the Lebanon runs another mountain range of approximately the same height, Antilebanon, at the south end of which, but separated from it, is the spreading mass of Mt. Hermon, rising to a height of 2,814 metres and keeping its snow into summer. Between Lebanon and Antilebanon lies the upland Bekaa valley, some fifteen kilometres wide. Today at the northern end it offers a meagre pasture for goats but its southern half is rich agricultural land with flourishing orchards, vegetables, and grain. In it rise two rivers, the Orontes flowing north through lake Homs into the Mediterranean near Antioch, and flowing south the Litani which curves round to reach the sea a little north of Tyre.

The two main ranges are very different in character. On the eastern slopes of Lebanon and on Antilebanon there is today very little vegetation, no conifers except junipers, and a scatter of oaks. This is primarily because they are screened from the rain clouds that are trapped by Lebanon and the rainfall is inadequate to sustain cedars, fir, pine, and most of the deciduous trees that grow on the western slopes. They may, however, have been less barren in the period with which we are concerned, especially towards the north and south ends. Nebuchadnezzar cut cedars on the east slope of Lebanon near the north end (p. 82) and some cedars that had become buried were found near Zahle towards the southern end.[4]

There is also good reason to believe that the west face of Antilebanon and Mt. Hermon provided timber of sufficient quality to attract Assyrian kings. The Song of Songs seems to regard Lebanon, Amanus, Antilebanon, and Hermon all as forest areas:

> Come from Lebanon, my bride;
>   come with me from Lebanon.
> Hurry down from the top of Amana,
>   from Senir's top and Hermon's,
>   from the lions' lairs and the hills the leopards haunt.[5]

In Deuteronomy we are told that the Sidonians' name for Hermon is Senir, while the Amorites call it Syrion.[6] We shall see later (p. 76 f.) that two Assyrian kings cut cedars on Mt. Sirara, which is generally thought to be a modified form of Syrion, both meaning Hermon. Their choice should not surprise us. Mt. Hermon, though now almost bare of trees, should have had a good cover of conifers and, on lower levels, oaks and other deciduous trees, for there is no high barrier between the mountain and the sea and it has as much rain as the western slopes of Lebanon. Antilebanon is considerably less favoured, but in the passage quoted from the Song of Songs Senir is distinct from Hermon. That Antilebanon as well as Hermon could be called Senir is shown in the record of an Assyrian campaign against Damascus in which it is said that the prince of Damascus had made Senir, a mountain facing the Lebanon, his fortress.[7] It was, however, on the western slopes of Lebanon that the best and largest reserves of timber were to be found.

The forest areas that we are now considering have been sadly denuded over the centuries, but ancient records combined with scattered relics of natural forest give some indication of the vegetation patterns during our period. The most colourful records are the royal inscriptions of Mesopotamian and Egyptian kings, who thought it natural to include records of their tree-felling in the accounts of their military campaigns and to hand down to posterity a description of the palaces they built. Unfortunately we cannot make full use of their records until all the tree words in Egyptian, Akkadian, and Hebrew are convincingly identified. Even then we should not have a completely satisfactory picture because the royal records are concerned only with the timbers that were taken. From these records alone we should not realise that oak, very rarely mentioned, was one of the commonest trees on these mountains. Greek and Roman historians and geographers add a little supporting evidence, but Theophrastus' *Enquiry into plants* provides what may be crucial evidence on some important issues.

Fortunately we have an invaluable control for the distribution of species. Since it is now generally agreed that there has been no major change in climate in the region since *c*.5000 BC, fragmented survivals of natural forest and an examination of plant communities should be the basis of any reconstructions. The combined studies of foresters, geographers, and botanists since the Second World War have produced a broadly convincing picture of the Lebanon forests.[8] And what is valid for Lebanon will be valid, with minor modifications, for the Taurus and Amanus mountains, which enjoy a very similar climate. We owe in particular to these studies a more realistic appreciation of the place of the cedar in the forests of the Lebanon range. Even as late as 1862 J. D. Hooker, a Fellow of the Royal Society and one of the most distinguished botanists of the day, who made a detailed study of the famous Bsharre cedar-grove, could argue that this grove was probably always the only true cedar forest in the whole Lebanon range.[9] Irresponsible guides continued to

assure tourists that no other cedars had survived. Recent surveys
have discovered fourteen remnant groups dispersed over the
whole range from Tripolis to Sidon.

The coastal cities of Phoenicia were so thickly populated that
the narrow coastal plain must have been taken over very early
for agriculture. The lower slopes up to *c*.500 metres would be
occupied by trees that could stand the long rainless summer;
especially evergreen oaks, either the Kermes oak (*Quercus
coccifera*), a small tree but providing very strong wood, or *Quercus
calliprinos*, a bigger tree but rarely more than twenty feet high.
Of the conifers cypress and the coastal pines could withstand the
summer heat and lack of rain. Of the pines *Pinus halepensis* and
Pinus brutia were certainly present; doubts have been raised
about *Pinus pinea*, the umbrella pine which was mainly valued
for its nuts. Its wide prominence in the landscape today is the
result of modern planting in the mid-nineteenth century, but
the pine-nuts found in Egyptian coffins probably came from
Lebanon pines. None of these three pines would normally grow
to more than sixty feet.

Between *c*.500 and *c*.1,200 metres these species are joined by
deciduous oaks, the commonest of which is *Quercus infectoria*, a
useful building wood but rarely growing higher than forty feet,
a wide range of other hardwoods including elm, ash, maple,
and two of the smaller junipers, the prickly *Juniperus oxycedrus*,
often a bush, rarely more than twenty feet high, and *Juniperus
phoenicea*, a little higher but rarely more than thirty feet. Above
c.1,000 metres cypress and pines become rarer and different oaks
are found, *Quercus brantii* and *Quercus libani*, both providing
useful timber but smaller than *Quercus infectoria*, and in the north
end of the range, *Quercus cerris*, the Turkey oak, which had a
poor reputation throughout Antiquity. But the zone above
1,200 metres is primarily the zone of the tallest conifers, cedars,
and firs, and of the junipers *Juniperus foetidissima* and *Juniperus
excelsa* growing exceptionally up to eighty feet, and *Juniperus
dupracea*, less tall and much less common. The highest altitude of
surviving cedars is in the famous Bsharre grove at 1,960 metres
and no cedar has ever been recorded above 2,000 metres on
Lebanon. Junipers are better able to withstand extremes of
drought and cold: *Juniperus excelsa* has been seen on Antilebanon
at 2,700 metres.

While it is clear that cedar, fir, and juniper were best suited in the uppermost of the three zones, it is far from clear what was the relative strength of the three. In the popular view, deriving largely from the Bible, the cedar was dominant throughout the Lebanon range, and all other species were by comparison negligible. Cedar was thought to be the prize which all the states of the Near East coveted, and for which the empires of Egypt and Mesopotamia were prepared to fight. What was approaching a consensus was rudely broken when V. Loret, whose basic work on Egyptian flora added authority to his judgement, gave reasons in 1916 for inferring that Egyptian *ash*-wood, which is the name of by far the commonest of Egypt's imported woods, was not cedar, but fir, or possibly fir and pine.[10] His conclusion, which has been accepted by the majority of Egyptologists in Germany, France, and Britain, needs to be reconsidered. To set out the reasons for preferring the traditional translation as cedar would involve too long a diversion. The arguments are given in an appendix.

The kings of Mesopotamia and Egypt chose cedar before fir for several reasons. As a tree it was a patrician, the fir plebeian. The wood of the cedar, unlike the fir, resisted rot and insects and was very durable, as was demonstrated in the temple of Artemis at Ephesus, the roof-beams of which were of cedar and still in good condition four hundred years later.[11] It also had an attractive aromatic scent, took a good polish, and was appreciated by carpenters and cabinet-makers because it had a close, straight grain and was easy to work. The wood of cypress and juniper had very similar qualities. Like the cedars their wood was of a reddish-brown colour; they too had an aromatic scent, and the juniper was stronger than the cedar. But both cypress and juniper were less handsome and neither could compare with the cedar in height. This emphasis on height will surprise those who judge from the cedars we see in European parks and gardens. The main characteristics of these cedars when mature are the wide spread, in layer formation, of the branches and the massiveness of the trunk. Such is the character of the cedars in the Bsharre grove, but in the Taurus and Atlas mountains cedars can still be found growing to a height of more than 100 feet, and Pliny says that the largest cedar on record, grown in Cyprus, was 130 feet high.[12] Such heights could be produced when the trees grew close together in high forest conditions, forcing their way up to the light in competition with their neighbours and leaving their lower branches no room to develop. If, however, the cedar has ample space, its branches will be longer and strong and it will only rarely exceed eighty feet.

The fir also had a good reputation in the Mediterranean world. Both the Greeks and Romans regarded it as the best timber for building both houses and warships which depended upon speed. It grew more rapidly than the cedar and was normally taller, but its trunk was slimmer and in close forest it shed its lower branches more easily than the cedar. Like the cedar it had a good, straight grain, and, being lighter, it was even easier to work. But the fir was vulnerable to rot and insect attack and its life was considerably shorter. Cedars and junipers can produce excellent timber even after 600 years; it would be exceptional to find sound timber in a fir more than 300 years old. The relative importance of firs in the forests we are considering is very difficult to assess. In modern times they have clearly formed a major component in the Taurus and Amanus forests; in the Lebanon forests they are considerably less conspicuous. There are still good fir forests and forests of fir mixed with cedar in the north-west of the range, but no firs have been recorded south of the Ehden forest, leaving three-quarters of the range without them, while cedar remnants continue at intervals down to Niha, less than ten kilometres from the southern end. The explanation could be that the fir has been more heavily overcut than the cedar or that it has been more vulnerable to the omnivorous goat. The more probable reason is that the summer temperatures were too high and the rainfall too low in the southern half of the range.

The evidence of Theophrastus should not be ignored and two passages are relevant. In a discussion of mountain trees he says that some major mountains, such as Parnassus and Cyllene in Greece, the Macedonian and the Mysian Olympus, have all kinds of trees because of the variety of situations—marshy, dry, deep-soiled, rocky—but there are other mountains which have a single species either pure or dominant, and he cites as examples the cypress in Crete, the cedar on the mountains of Cilicia and Syria, and the terebinth in some parts of Syria.[13] In another passage where he is discussing ship-timbers he says that fir, pine, and cedar provide the most useful ship-timbers. Triremes are made of fir because it is a light wood, and merchantmen of pine because it does not decay, while some use pine because they have an inadequate supply of fir, and the peoples of Syria and Phoenicia use cedar because they have not even much pine.[14] The natural indication of these two passages is that cedar was by far the commonest tree in Lebanon and that pine was a minor constituent and fir negligible. Theophrastus is writing at a time when the Greeks became interested in the forests of the east as a result of Alexander's conquests. His other references to Syria have an authentic ring.

Another Greek writer, the historian Diodorus (c.50 BC), also provides important evidence for the relative strength of species on Lebanon. In describing the building of a large fleet in 315 BC by Antigonus in Phoenicia he says that the Lebanon forest is full of cedar and cypress timbers of extraordinary beauty and size.[15] Today there is very little cypress on the Lebanon range and it tends to be overlooked, but Diodorus at this point of his universal history was using a good source; and in an Akkadian list of toponyms Lebanon is called a cypress mountain, as well as a cedar mountain.[16] It is not surprising to find ample evidence of its use in Egypt.

Throughout the Bronze Age and the archaic period the history of Lebanon is bound up with the powers that controlled Mesopotamia and the valley of the Nile, for both looked to the Lebanon and to Mt. Amanus in Syria for timbers of special quality. There is no reason to believe that during this period there was a serious shortage of wood in Egypt for general purposes; the very liberal use of wood for models and toys would otherwise be very difficult to explain.[17] Later, in the Hellenistic and Roman periods, papyri show clearly that wood was very scarce, but by then the area of cultivated land had been considerably expanded to meet the needs of an increasing population. The extreme dryness of the climate, however, had always limited the range of trees that could survive.

The evidence for native species and their use is good. Egypt, like Syria, became much more familiar to the Greeks after Alexander's conquests, and more particularly his establishment of a Greek colony at Alexandria. The list of Egyptian trees in Theophrastus provides a firm foundation; Pliny follows him

2 The Near East

closely, with some characteristic misunderstandings, and adds a little information from another source.[18] A great variety of Egyptian documents illustrate the usage of timbers native and imported and surviving timbers provide an invaluable control. Egypt, thanks to the dryness of its climate, is unique in the preservation of ancient wood. Lucas in his basic study of Egyptian materials gives lists of native and imported woods that have been scientifically identified,[19] and it can be hoped that this list will soon be substantially extended, since without microscopic examination identifications have often been found to be mistaken.

Of the native woods the acacia was the most widespread and the most useful. There is an embarrassing number of species in the acacia family, but the sources make no subtle distinctions; even Theophrastus only distinguishes between the black acacia which is weak and soon decays and the white which is strong and more durable. The tree branches low and the branches tend to be curving; that is why, as Herodotus tells us, one of the commonest types of cargo boat on the Nile, called a *baris*, was made of pieces of acacia two feet long, fitted together like bricks.[20] But it would be misleading to infer that the acacia produces only short lengths. Theophrastus says that roof-timbers of twelve cubits could be cut from it, and that owing to its strength the wood was used for the ribs of ships.[21] It could also be used for the main timbers of the hull. In the sixth century BC Amasis could boast that he had found the sacred barge of Osiris at Thebes made of acacia and rebuilt it with cedar.[22] Theophrastus does, however, admit that the tree is not very straight in its growth. The acacia, with its spiky leaves, could flourish in extreme drought and was the appropriate wood for the Jews in the Sinai desert to make their ark, tabernacle, table, and altar;[23] but it was also used for furniture, coffins, chests, boxes, and bows.

The most widely used wood after the acacia was the sycomore fig, which was common also in Palestine, a large tree of many branches and a very wide crown. Its leaves and wood closely resemble the mulberry and like the mulberry it was popular for its fig-like fruit as well as the usefulness of its wood. What seems to have impressed Theophrastus most was its peculiar manner of fruiting on the stem and the custom of seasoning the wood by sinking it in water until the internal moisture dried out. Theophrastus says that it was useful for many purposes, but without specifying them. There is evidence for its common use for coffins and statues and further identification will surely extend its known range.[24]

A third wood appreciated by Theophrastus was that of the persea (*Minusops schimperi*). 'It strongly resembles the pear tree in leaves, branches, and general form. . . . Its wood is strong and attractive, dark like the nettle-tree. With it they make images (*agalmata*), beds, and other such things.'[25] Theophrastus is much less flattering about the *balanos* (*Balanites aegyptiaca*), so called from its acorn-like fruit. It has a considerable girth and grows tall but is very twisted. In spite of this, it is used for shipbuilding and other purposes because of its strength.[26]

The palms of Egypt were more widely used.[27] The date-palm was soft and fibrous and could not carry weight, but the poorer classes found split palms very useful for the roofing of their houses. The doum-palm was compact and hard, and much stronger. According to Theophrastus the Persians valued it highly and made the feet of their couches out of it. Theophrastus also includes a description of the carob in his list of Egyptian trees, but claims that it grew in Syria, Ionia, Cnidus, and Rhodes but not in Egypt. This may be doubted, since Strabo reports that it was common in Ethiopia; but it was certainly appreciated as a furniture wood: Egyptian kings included chairs and tables of the wood in their lists of booty won by their victories.[28] Theophrastus omits the willow and tamarisk presumably because they are not peculiarly Egyptian, nor would we expect him to include papyrus, which, according to Pliny, was used to make small objects, as well as for firewood, and could be plaited to make boats.[29] But it is surprising that he does not include sidder, a strong wood of which several samples have survived suggesting its general usefulness. The earliest comes from a third-dynasty coffin. Other examples include a bow, dowels (requiring great strength), and a mummy label.[30]

Few of these Egyptian trees grew higher than forty feet and much of their wood was curved, often requiring elaborate packing with small pieces. What Egypt most needed were the long lengths that could be supplied by tall conifers. This helps to explain some features of Egyptian architecture which were

strange to the Greeks. Herodotus was very struck by the roof of
the Egyptian labyrinth, which, from above, looked like a sea of
stone.[31] If his travels in Egypt were as extensive as he implies, he
should not have been surprised, because Egyptian architects
normally roofed their temples with slabs of stone, supported by
serried rows of stone columns; they also tended to use stone for
doorposts where the Greeks would use wooden posts or a facing
of wooden boards. The Greeks would also have been surprised
by the lack of timber in Egyptian mud-brick walls. From the
Bronze Age onwards in Greece, Asia Minor, and Syria it was
common practice to strengthen mud-brick walls with horizontal
timbers or a framework of horizontals and verticals.

The Egyptians did, however, build long timbers into specially
thick walls from face to face and this need was not easy to satisfy
from native trees.[32] They probably also imported timber for the
roofs of their finer early tombs, for some of the burial chambers
were over twenty feet wide and there are no traces of internal
supports.[33] This particular need passed when rock tombs were
developed, but kings and nobles would have welcomed cedar
and cypress or other conifers for their roofs; the common people
were satisfied with split palm-trunks or other native woods.
More important was the demand for the best-quality woods for
the Nile boats of kings and gods.

The Egyptians also appreciated the woods of better quality
for cabinet-making. From Ethiopia they could get 'ebony' as
an admirable foil for ivory or white woods, especially box.
True ebony was not known in the Mediterranean world until
it was discovered in India, but the name seems to have been
given to several different species whose heartwood was very
dark. Egypt could also look to her nearest neighbours in the
north. Palestine and Jordan were not then the virtually treeless lands of recent times. The oaks of Bashan, between Gilead
and Mt. Hermon, were famous and pine (*Pinus halepensis*) grew
well.[34] But though there could have been a significant trade in
timber from Palestine, it was not sufficiently important to be
reflected in royal pronouncements. Palestine was eclipsed by the
forests of Phoenicia and Syria whose fame rested largely on their
tall conifers and especially cedars, and on the boxwood which
was indispensable for the palace-furniture makers (p. 280). In
addition to cedar, fir, juniper, and box, samples of cypress, pine,

maple, yew, lime, and elm have been identified. All these woods could have been found in the Lebanon range, except yew and lime which need a colder temperature and do not come south of Amanus. Since Lebanon was nearer than Amanus, the great bulk of Egypt's timber imports will have come from Phoenician ports, and particularly Byblos (p. 358). When the Phoenician cities were hostile or closed by an enemy, Amanus would not be accessible. Egypt could then turn to Cyprus, which was well forested with cedar, pine, and cypress.

The Mesopotamian kingdoms had somewhat similar difficulties. Whatever the early vegetational history of Mesopotamia may have been, and whether the shore-line has advanced or receded, it seems clear that by the classical period the land was very poorly supplied with serviceable trees. There was an abundant supply of reeds near the coast, but the only serviceable tree was the palm.[35] These resources were adequate, with the help of dung, to provide fuel and roofing for modest buildings of mud-brick, but temples and palaces needed more substantial timbers. There were, however, much nearer supplies than Lebanon. To the east of the Tigris the long range of the Zagros mountains could probably have supplied oaks and other hardwoods, cypress, and juniper, but in the south-east Elam was a strong neighbour which, in spite of frequent wars, was never securely controlled from Mesopotamia. When power in Mesopotamia passed to the north with the rise of Assyria the situation was rather different. The Assyrians occupied the land on the right bank of the Tigris between the Upper and the Lower Zab and, though their own territory was poorly wooded, the Zagros mountain range was very near.

It is clear from the record of a campaign of Sargon II (725–705 BC) against the kingdom of Urartu that these mountains were well forested:[36]

High mountains covered with all kinds of trees, whose surface was a jungle, over whose area shadows stretched as in a cedar forest ... Great cypress beams from the roof of his substantial palace I tore out and carried to Assyria ... The trunks of all those trees which I had cut down I gathered them together and burnt them with fire.[36]

The Assyrians exploited their victory, but their hold on this difficult country was never secure:

As for the timbers which they (Urartians) held back in the city of Eziat, I sent the Ituai together with a city ruler. I sent them out to reconnoitre. The second officer of their city rulers together with nine men were wounded with the bow.[37]

The kingdom of Urartu included the mountains of the northern Zagros and the eastern Taurus. In both areas they could find oak and cypress, and at the higher levels pine and juniper.[38] But even if the Assyrians had been able to control this mountainous area effectively, and rely on securing adequate supplies from it of these woods, the attraction of the cedars to the west would still have remained very strong.

It was inevitable that sooner or later the interests of Egypt and Mesopotamia should clash. There was little to encourage Egypt to expand in the south and west, where there was mainly desert; the only profitable direction for expansion was to the north through Palestine to the richer lands of Phoenicia and Syria. Similarly, Mesopotamian Assyria found it much more attractive to expand westwards rather than into the mountainous country to the north and east. For a long time Assyria presented no serious challenge to Egypt. Syria was nearer than Lebanon and it was from Amanus that the Mesopotamians first procured their cedars, and not before the middle of the third millennium. But fragments of cedar-wood from the pre-dynastic period in the fourth millennium have been found in Egypt and on the Palermo stone there is the first surviving record of timber imports: when Snefru of the fourth dynasty was king (*c.*2600 BC): 'Bringing forty ships filled with cedar logs. Shipbuilding (of) cedar-wood, one "Praise of the Two Lands" ship 100 cubits (long) and of *meru*-wood two ships, 100 cubits long. Making the doors of the royal palace (of) cedar-wood.'[39]

This first inscribed record of timber from Lebanon illustrates two of the most important uses for which Egypt had to look outside her own territory, and the names of the two woods concerned, *ash*-wood and *meru*-wood, recur more often than any other imported woods in the record.

A document in the British Museum from approximately a thousand years later provides an interesting complement. The papyrus, which is very fragmentary, records operations in a royal dockyard near Memphis which is supervised by the Crown prince, probably in the reign of Tuthmosis III (*c.*1450 BC).[40]

The main business covered by the report is the issue of timbers in small numbers to individual workers, perhaps foremen. The two series that interest us most are the issue of long lengths of *ash*-wood and *meru*-wood, presumably for the main construction.[41] Each entry gives the part of the ship for which the wood is required and the length of the timber. The two woods are issued for different parts of the ship, but the terms cannot yet be translated.

The commonest number of timbers issued is seven and they vary in lengths from thirteen to twenty-eight cubits. The *ash*-wood timbers tend to be slightly shorter, but in the same general range with very few indeed under fifteen cubits; and the number of *ash*-wood timbers is more than four times as large as the *meru*-wood total. The only other wood mentioned in the record is the native sycomore, but less than a dozen sycomore boards are issued. It is interesting to note that there is no standardisation of lengths and that the precise length of each individual timber is recorded. The longest timber issued was thirty cubits (45 ft.) long and it was *ash*-wood for a mast. Two other masts of *ash*-wood, of forty and forty-two cubits, are recorded in other Egyptian documents.[42] It has been assumed throughout this chapter that *ash*-wood is cedar. Flagstaves and masts which required long, straight timbers were among the most important uses of the wood. *Meru*-wood may be cypress, but the evidence is less firm.

The cedar which was brought to King Snefru was also used for the doors of his palace, and cedar-wood continued to be one of the favourite woods for monumental doors both in the Near East and in the world of Greece and Rome. Long timbers of up to thirty feet were required for the boards of doors, and in Egypt, as in Assyria, temple and palace doors were normally bound with decorative metal bands. In the mortuary temple of Seti I at Thebes the doors were of cedar, 'wrought with Asiatic copper and made high and large'.[43] In the temple of Osiris at Abydos the doorposts were of stone, but the doors of cedar.[44]

The inscription which records the arrival of forty shiploads of cedars does not specify the forest in which the timber was cut, nor the port from which the ships sailed. It was almost certainly Byblos, which, from early in the third millennium BC, seems to have had a special relationship with Egypt.[45] When Tuthmosis III needed ships to carry his army across the Euphrates, he had them built 'on the mountains of God's Land near the Lady of

Byblos', and Montet has shown that the region of Negau which is frequently referred to as a source of timber for Egypt is to be found in the mountains behind Byblos.[46] An Egyptian sage, painting at an uncertain date a picture of general misery, includes a lament: 'Men do not sail northwards to [Byblos] today. What shall we do for cedar for our mummies, with the produce of which priests are buried and with the oil of which [chiefs] are embalmed?'[47] The name of the port is not preserved, but the restoration of Byblos is almost inevitable. It is to Byblos also that, as we shall see (p. 68), in a much later period of weakness (c. 1100 BC), Egypt turns for timber for the ship of Amon-Re. Excavation at Byblos gives substance and colour to the close association. The exhibits in one of the rooms of the Beirut Museum consist almost exclusively of Egyptian objects from life-size statues to small vases: most of them were Egyptian dedications in the temple of our Lady of Byblos (Baalat Gebal) dating from the early third millennium to near the end of the second.

The flow of timber from Lebanon depended on Egypt being strong and rich enough to impress the Phoenician cities, and this involved periodic campaigns to reassert Egyptian authority. It must have been very low when Egypt was overrun by tough invaders from the north, the so-called Hyksos people, who controlled Egypt for over a hundred years. But the expulsion of the Hyksos by Ahmose I (c. 1580 BC) was followed by a period of strong imperial expansion and Tuthmosis III was long remembered as the greatest of Egypt's warrior kings. Campaigns in the south made Egypt's southern frontier secure and to the north a series of successful expeditions brought all the land up to the Euphrates under firm Egyptian control. Having won his way through Palestine by a victory at Megiddo, Tuthmosis was free to plunder as he advanced and in his record of booty he includes chairs of ivory, ebony, and carob-wood and an ebony-and-gold statue of one of his enemies. (The ebony must have come from Egypt.) The Phoenician cities offered no serious resistance after the battle of Megiddo and were prepared to accept orders. They were required to build ships for the crossing of the Euphrates:

When my majesty crossed over to the marshes of Asia, I had many ships of cedar built on the mountains of God's Land near the Lady of Byblos. They were placed on chariots with cattle drawing (them).

They journeyed in [front of] my majesty, in order to cross the great
river (Euphrates) which lies between this foreign country and
Naharin.[48]

The Phoenician harbours were filled with ships ready to sail to
Egypt with the 'impost of Lebanon'. The Egyptian king can
proudly say: 'They have brought to me the choicest products of
[———] consisting of cedar, (juniper), and (cypress)—all the
good sweet woods of God's land.'[49] In his eighth campaign one
of his officials cut timber 'above the clouds' sixty cubits long.[50]

In little more than a hundred years the Egyptian empire of
the north was in the process of disintegration and the archive of
tablets from Tel-el-Amarna, which became the new capital of
Egypt for two generations (early second millennium), presents
an increasingly gloomy picture. The correspondence with the
cities of Syria and Phoenicia clearly reflects the decline of
Egyptian power. The penetration of the Hittites from the
Anatolian plateau into Syria created a general restlessness, but
at a time when a strong demonstration of power was needed, her
kings did not leave Egypt. The prince of Byblos appeals
repeatedly for help, for the king himself to come north or at the
least to send his archers. While he protests his loyalty he paints a
picture of treachery on every side.[51] Enemies ravage his land, he
has no water, no wood, and no place to bury his dead. The
prince of Tyre also remains loyal and begs for help, but there is
no response:[52] Sidon has deserted and finally there is an anti-
Egyptian uprising in Tyre itself. Since enemies now controlled
the open country and he could no longer get timber from
Lebanon, the Egyptian king turns instead to Cyprus, where
there were ample supplies of cedar, cypress, and pine. There is a
plaintive letter from Cyprus: 'My people speak to me about my
wood which the king of Egypt took from me. So, my brother,
give me the worth (of it).'[53] But Cyprus realised that she might
need Egypt's help and undertook to build ships for the
Egyptians.

While the foreign interests of Egypt were being neglected a
religious revolution was attempted to submerge all cults in the
worship of the sun, but the priestly establishment was too strong.
Amnhotep IV, who had taken the name Akhenaton, was
assassinated and Tel-el-Amarna was abandoned. Under Seti I
(1318–1301) there was a national revival. An Egyptian army

marched north and re-established Egyptian influence in Phoenicia, and the king had a relief cut for the great temple of Amon at Karnak showing Lebanon subjects felling cedars for the king, though the sculptor's trees are highly stylised (pl. 2).[54]

Seti's successor Rameses II continued an imperialist policy and set out to break Hittite power in Syria. In a great pitched battle at Kadesh in 1293 neither side could achieve a victory, and in 1273 both found it convenient to make a formal peace settlement. The balance of power was precarious, for in many cities allegiance was divided and the restlessness that had followed the southward penetration of the Hittites continued. But it was not long before decisive changes came over the region. In the second half of the thirteenth century new forces were on the move, raiding and ravaging and finally moving down through Syria and Lebanon by land and sea against Egypt. They left a long trail of destruction behind them. Ugarit (Ras Shamra), which had been one of the most flourishing trading cities in Syria, was razed to the ground and never recovered; Byblos and Sidon were sacked; Tyre being on an island survived. The forces of the raiders were finally defeated in the Delta, but they left Egypt considerably weaker.

The destruction caused by the raiders as they moved on Egypt now seems in retrospect to be part of a much larger pattern. Within two generations the main centres of Mycenaean Greece had been destroyed and the Hittite capital of Boğazköy in Anatolia was in ruins. New peoples came into Asia Minor and into Greece and gradually a very different Mediterranean world emerged. Egypt, exhausted by a century of war, withdrew within her own frontiers, and there was no longer a Hittite empire in Anatolia to overshadow Syria. The great change that had come over the Near East is dramatically illustrated by the story of Wen Amon, an official of the temple of Amon at Thebes who was sent to Byblos to secure timber for the great ceremonial barge of Amon.

The setting is in the eleventh or, possibly, the twelfth century, and even if the story is a romance and not an actual report the circumstantial detail seems authentic.[55] When he starts on his journey there is no centralised control in Egypt and Wen Amon depends on the goodwill of the high priest of Amon at Tanis in

the Delta to help him on his way. After a long delay a passage on
a Syrian ship is secured for him and he receives gifts to take to
Byblos. When his ship puts in at Dor, a town of the Tjeker, one of
the ship's crew deserts and takes with him most of the gold and
silver vessels intended for the prince of Byblos. The prince of Dor
shows little sympathy, but Wen Amon manages somehow (the
text is fragmentary at this point) to seize some silver from a
Tjeker ship and proceeds to Byblos where he sets up his tent on
the shore of the harbour, nursing a statue of Amon-of-the-road
which he has brought with him. For twenty-nine days he fails to
obtain an audience with Zakar-Baal the prince of Byblos and
instead receives repeated instructions to leave the harbour. But
suddenly there is a dramatic change. While the prince was
making offerings to his god one of the youths of his court became
possessed and cried out: 'Bring up the god! Bring the messenger
who is carrying him. Amon is the one who sent him. He is the
one who made him come!' Wen Amon is summoned to the
presence but the interview does little to cheer him.

The scene is charming: the prince of Byblos was 'sitting in his
upper room with his back to a window, so that the waves of the
great Syrian sea broke against the back of his head'. But negotiations were difficult:

'I have come after the woodwork for the great and august barque of
Amon-Re, King of the Gods. Your father did (it), your grandfather
did (it), and you will do it too!' So I spoke to him. But he said to me:
'To be sure they did it! And if you give me (something) for doing it,
I will do it!'

Wen Amon has to send back to Egypt for more gifts with no
hope of getting any timber till they come. When at last they
arrived the prince sent 300 men and 300 cattle with supervisors
into the forest to cut down the trees, where they were left to dry
out for a season and then brought down to the sea-shore. This
was by no means the end of Wen Amon's troubles. When all was
nearly ready eleven ships of the Tjeker arrived and appealed to
the prince to arrest Wen Amon who, they said, had stolen their
silver. The prince had religious scruples about arresting a
messenger of Amon in his own land: 'Let me send him away, and
you go after him to arrest him.' Wen Amon was not caught by
the Tjeker but blown off course to Cyprus, where he was only

saved from the natives by the appearance of the queen. From this point the text is lost.

The decline of Egyptian authority, so clearly reflected in the story of Wen Amon, provided the opportunity for the Hebrews to enjoy a short period of power and apparent prosperity in the tenth century. Under two strong kings, David and Solomon, the two kingdoms of Judah and Israel were united and the royal revenues substantially increased. It had been David's ambition to build a great temple and palace at Jerusalem, but it was left to his son Solomon to carry out his designs. Although the main construction was to be in stone, timber was needed for the roof, the panelling of the walls, the columns, the floors, and the doors. Palestine had cypress and pine, but if Solomon was to compete with other kings he would need to secure Lebanon cedars. This he was able to do as a result of the good relations already established by his father with Hiram King of Tyre. Although negotiations were conducted with the king of Tyre, the cedars may not have come from the territory of Tyre, for the hills behind the city seem too low to carry cedars. The Lebanon range ended behind Sidon and the cedars probably came from the south end of the range. But Tyre, which had escaped destruction at the end of the Bronze Age, emerged as the strongest of the Phoenician cities and presumably controlled Sidon in the tenth century. It may be significant that Solomon refers to the Sidonian fellers.

After the usual exchange of courtesies Solomon explains his needs:

I propose to build a house in honour of the name of the Lord my God, following the promise given by the Lord to my father David . . . If therefore you will now give orders that cedars be felled and brought from Lebanon, my men will work with yours, and I will pay you for your men whatever sum you fix; for, as you know, we have none so skilled at felling timber as your Sidonians.

Hiram welcomes the contract: 'Blessed be the Lord today who has given David a wise son to rule over this great people'; but he is also business-like:

In this matter of timber, both cedar and (cypress), I will do all you wish. My men shall bring down the logs from Lebanon to the sea and I will make them up into rafts to be floated to the place you appoint;

I will have them broken up there and you can remove them. You, on your part, will meet my wishes if you provide the food for my household.

So far the only difficulty is in identifying the second wood which Hiram is said to have agreed to supply. A note of extravagance, however, seems to intrude in the description of the auxiliary labour sent by Solomon to help in the less skilled work of stripping the branches from the trunks and hauling the trunks from the forest. The version in the first book of Kings says that Solomon raised a forced levy of 30,000 men whom he sent to Lebanon in monthly relays of 10,000. Such numbers seem to be pure fantasy: they would have very seriously embarrassed their hosts.[56]

Some details are provided about the use of the timber. The temple was 90 × 30 × 45 feet, with a vestibule of 15 × 30 feet. Cedar was used for the roof-beams and the walls were completely covered with cedar panelling. At the inner end of the temple the first thirty feet were reserved as an inner shrine to receive the Ark of the Covenant; the cross-wall was also panelled with cedar and an altar of cedar stood in the shrine. The floor was made of boards of a different wood, which was also used for the two leaves of the main entrance door. Translations old and new have varied widely, but the choice lies between juniper and cypress and to me the evidence seems slightly to favour cypress which, with cedar, was most favoured for monumental doors.[57] The only other woods mentioned in the account in the book of Kings is wild olive, which was used for two cherubim, each fifteen feet high, in the inner sanctuary. Olive-wood is strong and long-lasting, and is still much used for carving in the Near East, but normally only for small pieces: as the cherubim were overlaid with gold, the joins would not have shown. Olive-wood was also used for the double door in the inner shrine; at the main entrance to the temple the door-frame was of olive-wood, but not the two leaves.

Cedars were also lavishly used in the palace and adjoining buildings. The so-called House of the Forest of Lebanon was larger than the temple, 150 × 75 × 45 feet. The wide span of seventy-five feet, more than twice the width of the temple, needed internal supports for the roof. There were four rows of cedar columns with beams of cedar over them and further lengths of cedar on top of the walls, which were made of carefully cut blocks of stone. These two series of cedar beams formed the basis of the roof, with smaller cedar timbers over them and a sealing of mud. Cedar was also used for the panelling of the Hall of Judgement.

The record in the first book of Kings, our main source for Solomon's buildings, was written some three hundred years after the temple was completed, but the measurements of the temple and the other buildings could be easily checked and are likely to be correct, as are the statements about the use of the main timbers. One may, however, expect the story to be embroidered for the greater glory of the people. The fact that Solomon had to hand over to Hiram twenty cities in addition to annual deliveries of corn and oil is tactfully omitted until later in the narrative, and the scale of operations is magnified by swelling the numbers employed.

Nor should the statement that the king made cedar as plentiful as sycamore fig in the Shephelah be pressed; but it is possible that the use of cedar by Solomon was not confined to the temple, palace, and associated buildings. The accounts of his reign list a wide range of buildings including store-cities, and towns where he kept his chariots and horses. In excavation at Beer-Sheba it was found that the earliest settlement dated from the tenth century BC and traces of buildings suggested large-scale storage. The identification of wood samples showed, as might be expected, that the main woods used were acacia and tamarisk, which are both well suited to the very dry climate; but seven samples were identified as cedar. It is at least possible that Beer-Sheba was one of Solomon's store-cities.[58]

Solomon's contract for timber for his temple and palace led to further co-operation with the king of Tyre:

King Solomon built a fleet of ships at Ezion-geber, near Elath on the shore of the Red Sea, in Edom. Hiram sent men of his own to serve with the fleet, experienced seamen, to work with Solomon's men; and they went to Ophir and brought back four hundred and twenty talents of gold, which they delivered to King Solomon.

This seems to have been a joint enterprise. A little later we are told that Hiram's fleet, which had brought gold from Ophir, also brought cargoes of *almug*-wood and precious stones. This

wood was used to provide (?stools) for the temple and the
palace, and harps and lutes for the singers. 'No such *almug*-wood
has been imported or even seen since that time.' The wood
cannot be identified, but the association with Ophir suggests
that it should have come from Africa south of Egypt or from
Arabia. There are, however, differences in the account in
Chronicles which by some have been regarded as important.
The word there is called *algum* rather than *almug*, and it is included with cedar and (cypress) in the woods requested by
Solomon; but the association with Ophir is repeated. It is very
doubtful whether the differences derived from valid evidence.[59]*

The achievement of David and Solomon in creating a united
kingdom and displaying such affluence was but a brief interlude. The glory of Jerusalem was at the expense of the rest of the
country, whose economy was not capable of sustaining such
grandeur, and it was possible only because there was no great
power yet dominating or threatening the land between Egypt
and Mesopotamia. David and Solomon were in danger of
making Jerusalem more Phoenician than Jewish, anticipating
the Herods who tried to bring Palestine into the cultural
cosmopolitanism of the Graeco-Roman world: but the religious
forces of Judaism were too strong for both.

The Phoenician cities, and particularly Tyre, reached the
height of their prosperity between the eleventh and eighth
centuries BC, because Egypt made no attempt to revive her
imperial ambitions and the small Hittite principalities in Syria
lacked the protection and encouragement of a Hittite empire in
Anatolia. But the consolidation of Assyrian power led to a new
chapter in the history of Lebanon.

The earliest evidence of Mesopotamian concern for the
western forests comes from the second half of the third millennium BC when Sargon of Akkad (*c*.2300–2200 BC) could claim
that his god Enlil had given him the upper country as far as the
cedar forest and silver mountain. In the next century one of his
successors from northern Mesopotamia Naram-Sin (2291–
2258) was given by his god Nergal Amanus the cedar mountain,
and the upper sea.[60] A similar claim was later made by Gudea,
prince of Lagash (*c*.2000), in southern Mesopotamia.[61]

When he was building the temple of Ningirsu, Ningirsu, his beloved
king, opened up for him (all) the (trade) routes from the Upper to the

Lower Sea, and he cut cedar logs 60 cubits long together with other timbers on Amanus the mountain of cedar.[61]

No mention of Lebanon is made in any of these three inscriptions in the third millennium and we can safely infer that the Mesopotamians were concerned only with the forests to the north of Lebanon, and particularly Amanus. For most of the second millennium we have no evidence of Mesopotamian expeditions to the west, and though the argument from silence is dangerous, it may be that the strong power of Mitanni proved a barrier to western ambitions.

It was in this period of comparative weakness in Assyria that the state of Mari on the middle Euphrates enjoyed a brief period of power and prosperity and one of her kings could boast proudly of his expedition to the sea:

Since the distant days when the God built Mari, no king living in Mari had reached the sea, had conquered the mountains of cedar and box, and had not cut their trees. Jahdan-lim, son of Jaggid-lim, the brave king, the wild ox among kings, with force and power went to the shore of the sea.[62]

He also claims to have cut other woods, one (*surmenu*) very probably cypress, the other (*elammaku*) beyond the range of rational guessing. The emphasis on cedar and box is a striking tribute to their pre-eminence. That cedar should be placed first was to be expected; box owes its place here because it was one of the cabinetmaker's favourite woods and the best-quality box was to be found on the Amanus range which was the king of Mari's objective rather than Lebanon. It is significant that the boxwood which the prince of Byblos supplied to Egypt came from the port of Ugarit (Ras Shamra) near the mouth of the Orontes. Mari's period of prosperity was comparatively short-lived, but it was not until the general destruction at the close of the Bronze Age and the collapse of the Hittite empire that the Assyrians could hope to build up a western empire.

It was at roughly the same time as Wen Amon's journey to Byblos that a king from Ashur, Tiglath-Pileser I (1114-1078), led an expedition against the Phoenicians: 'I went to the Lebanon. I cut (there) timber of cedars for the temple of Anu and Adad, the great gods, my lords, and carried (them to Ashur). . . . I received tribute from Byblos, Sidon, and Arvad.'[63] But it was not until the ninth century that Tiglath-Pileser's conquest was repeated and consolidated. Assur-Nasir-Pal (883–859 BC) was the first of a long series of Assyrian conquerers using a highly efficient and ruthless army to dominate Syria and Phoenicia and eventually to confront Egypt. He has left a record of his expedition on the large pavement slabs of the temple of Ninurta in Calah where he had built a new royal residence: 'At that time I seized the entire extent of the Lebanon mountain and reached the Great Sea of the Amurru country (north of Phoenicia).'[64] He received tribute from the coastal cities and this time Tyre, which was not included in the cities that had submitted to Tiglath-Pileser I, had to submit. At the end of his campaign he cut logs of cedar and other timbers on Mt. Amanus.

Shalmeneser III (858–821) consolidated his father's conquests in the west. In his eighteenth year he crossed the Euphrates for the sixteenth time[65] and in his twenty-sixth year he crossed Amanus for the seventh time.[66] His primary concern was to crush all opposition from the cities of Syria, most of which were ruled by Hittite princes; but he also crossed the Amanus mountain range into Cilicia. In his operations beyond Amanus he makes no mention of timber, but, like his predecessors, he appreciated the forests of Amanus and on four campaigns he cut cedars there. He also demanded cedar from some of the Syrian princes who submitted to him, ranking timber with metals and cattle.[67] From one prince he demanded three talents of gold, 100 talents of silver, 300 talents of copper, 300 talents of iron, 1,000 copper vessels, 1,000 brightly coloured garments of (wool) and linen, a daughter of the prince with a large dowry, twenty talents of purple wool, 500 cattle, 500 sheep. His annual tribute was to be one talent of silver, two talents of purple wool, 200 cedar logs. A second prince who ruled at the foot of Amanus was required to give him a considerably smaller supply of metal and cattle, 200 cedar logs, and two measures of cedar resin, and to send annually 100 cedar logs and one measure of cedar resin. A third prince was required to include 300 cedar logs in his annual tribute.

Of the next two kings we know much less, but Tiglath-Pileser III (744–727) emerges as a powerful ruler. He brought all the coastal cities from the mouth of the Orontes to Tyre under his firm control and reached Judaea, but he was also a

great builder and delighted to describe the great palace which
he built at Nimrud (Calah).[68] His successor Sargon II (721–
705) was also a strong ruler. He has left a grim detailed record of
a great campaign in his eighth year against the kingdom of
Urartu to the north-east of Assyria.[69] His intention was clearly
to break the power of the kingdom and by the wholesale
destruction of life and property to ensure that Assyria could
continue the westward expansion of her empire without any fear
of incursions from the north or east. But there may be signs of
serious restiveness in Phoenicia, for it was probably in Sargon's
reign that a letter was sent from Tyre with alarming news:

> With regard to the ruler of Tyre, of whom the king said that I was to
> speak kindly to him—all the quays are open to him (and) his subjects
> enter and leave the quay-houses as they wish (and sell and buy).
> Mount Lebanon is at his disposal, and they go up and down as they
> wish, and bring down the wood.
> I levy taxes on anyone who brings down wood, and I have
> appointed tax-collectors over the quays of all Mount Lebanon, and
> they keep watch . . .
> I appointed a tax-collector over those who come down to the quays
> which are in Sidon, but the Sidonians chased him off.
> Then I sent the Ituaeans into Mount Lebanon, and they made the
> people grovel.
> Afterwards they sent to me, and they brought the tax-collector
> (back) into Sidon.
> I made a statement to them, that they might bring down the wood
> and do their work with it, (but) that they were not to sell it to the
> Egyptians or to the Palestinians or I would not allow them to go up to
> the mountain.[70]

It is interesting to note the importance attached by the Assyrians
to Lebanon timber not only for tax purposes, but also as a
practical means of damaging Egypt.

Sargon's successor Sennacherib (704–681) was, like his
father, a vigorous campaigner and an enthusiastic palace
builder. Early in his reign he had to deal with Babylon, which
had long been ruled by Assyria but was now in open revolt.
Sennacherib decided to take his force by river, but to build
ships he needed timber and craftsmen from the west. 'Hittite
people (from Syria), plunder of my bow, I settled in Nineveh.
Mighty ships (after) the workmanship of their land they built

dexterously. Tyrians, Sidonians, and Cyprians, sailors, captives
I ordered (to descend) the Tigris with them to Opis.'[71] With
their help the revolt was savagely crushed. But Sennacherib's
main ambition was to carry Assyrian conquest further in the
west and challenge Egypt directly. There were probably at least
two campaigns, but the only one for which we have evidence is
the final one. Sennacherib had to fight his way through Palestine and a vivid record of his siege of Lachish has been recovered
from the ruins of the palace at Nineveh and is now in the British
Museum. Hezekiah, king of the Jews, was shut up 'like a bird in
a cage' and hoped to buy his safety by a lavish 'gift' of treasure.
The Assyrians departed, but not as they intended. In the Jewish
tradition 'the angel of the Lord went out and struck down a
hundred and eighty-five thousand men in the Assyrian camp'.[72]
In the tradition which Herodotus heard in Egypt the Egyptians
were encamped at the entry from Palestine to Egypt, prepared
to face battle with the invader. But there was no battle. During
the night mice from the fields ate all the quivers, bows, and
shield-straps and in the morning the Assyrians fled. The miracle
of the plague was commemorated by a statue of the Egyptian
priest-king holding a mouse in his hand, with an inscription:
'Look on me and honour the gods.'[73]

Isaiah draws a vigorous picture of the pride and arrogance of
Sennacherib:

> You have sent your servants to taunt the Lord,
>   and said:
> With my countless chariots I have gone up
> high in the mountains, into the recesses of Lebanon.
> I have cut down the tallest cedars,
>   the best of its (junipers),
> I have reached its highest limit of forest and meadow.[74]

This surely is an echo of an inscription in the palace of
Sennacherib:

That I might accomplish the construction of my palace, and bring
to an end the work of my hands, at that time. Ashur and Ishtar, who
love my priesthood, and have called me by name, showed me how to
bring out the mighty cedar logs which had grown large in the days
gone by and had become enormously tall as they stood concealed in
the mountains of Sirara (?Hermon).[75]

Sennacherib died soon after his return, the succession was disputed, and it was more than a year before Esarhaddon (680–669) was firmly established. Before resuming the offensive against Egypt he struck quickly against Tyre and Sidon, where old links with Egypt increased their resentment of Assyrian control, and he thought it wise to improve relations with Babylon, still smarting from Sennacherib's harsh treatment. As a gesture of reconciliation Esarhaddon built a great temple of all the Babylonian gods: 'With mighty beams [of cedar], products of Mt. Amanus . . . I spanned its roof. Door-leaves of (cypress), whose odour is pleasant, I bound with a band of gold and silver and hung them in their doors.'[76] For the building of his own palace at Nineveh, his new capital, he turned to the west and summoned twenty-two princes from north Syria, the sea-coast cities, and Cyprus to send levies for the operation:

> Great beams and tall trunks, logs (or planks) of cedar and (cypress), from Mt. Sirara (?Hermon) and Mt. Lebanon . . . from out of the mountains I had them dragged to Nineveh with toil and pain. . . . Long cedar beams I stretched over it (for its roof), door-leaves of cypress, whose scent is sweet, I covered with a sheathing of silver and copper, and hung (them) in its doors.[77]

It was not until near the end of his reign that Esarhaddon was free to realise the dream of Sennacherib. The weakness of Egypt had been exposed by her failure to bring any support to the coastal cities, which were naturally sympathetic, and when the Assyrian army at full strength reached the border of Egypt there was little serious fighting. For a short time Egypt became a province of the Assyrian empire.

The time was short because the Assyrians had overstrained their resources by maintaining the largest and most expensively equipped army that the Near East had yet seen. Their lines of communication had been drawn too long and their manpower could not sustain a garrison large enough to hold Egypt down. By the middle of the seventh century Egypt, supported by help from Lydia, who had good reason to fear Assyrian power, was once again ruled by an independent Pharaoh. Her example was followed by Babylon, an unwilling subject of Assyria, whose revolt had been savagely crushed by Sennacherib. Babylon found an ally in the Medes who threatened Assyria from the

north and in 612 the combined forces of Media and Babylon
destroyed Nineveh. Nahurn expressed the mood of Assyria's
victims:

> Your wounds cannot be assuaged, your injury is mortal;
> all who have heard of your fate clap their hands in joy.
> Are there any whom your ceaseless cruelty has not borne down?[78]

The fall of Nineveh was not quite the end, but after the fall of
Harran in 610 resistance petered out.

In this brief survey of the timber taken from the forests of
western Asia by the Assyrians the evidence has been taken
mainly from campaign records. These are usefully supplemented by what may be called palace inscriptions. The commonest
uses for the timber brought from the west was for roofs and
monumental doors of temples and palaces. Throughout the
Near East there was a common simple roof-form. Timbers, sawn
or round, were placed over the area to be spanned and they were
supported by the walls, which were made of mud-brick. Over
these beams were set smaller timbers and over them brushwood
or reeds covered by a thick layer of mud. The commonest roof-
timbers recorded were cedar, followed by cypress. Kings prided
themselves on the length of the beams but also appreciated their
fragrance, as Tiglath-Pileser III show in his description of his
palace at Nimrud: 'With long cedar beams, whose fragrance is
as good as that of the cypress tree, products of Amanus,
Lebanon, and Ammannama (?Hermon) I roofed them (the
palaces) and brought them to faultless completion.'[79] Assurbanipal (668–627 BC) records:

> Great cedars, which had grown exceedingly tall on Mt. Lebanon,
> (cypress) logs whose odour is pleasant, which Adad had made beauti-
> ful on Mt. Sirara (?Hermon), which the kings of the sea-coast, my
> vassals, had felled . . . with these I roofed Ehulhul the abode of gladness
> (the temple of Sin at Harran).[80]

Cedar and cypress are, I think, the only trees specifically
associated with roofs in the inscriptions, but it would be an
unnatural simplification to believe that no other woods were
used for the purpose by Assyrian kings. Layard, in his excavation in the middle of the nineteenth century of an area of the
north-west palace and temple at Nimrud, identified a beam that

he found his Arab workers cheerfully burning as cedar from its fragrance.[81] In Mallowan's excavation in the nineteen-fifties of another area of the palace one beam was thought to be mulberry, and several fragments from different beams were microscopically examined at the Princes Risborough laboratory and all found to be pine.[82] There is another surprising feature that has been revealed by excavation at several palace sites. Layard emphasised the narrowness of the rooms in the Nimrud palace; even the throne room which was 17.5 metres long was only five metres wide, very odd proportions, especially for kings who wished to display a visual record of their military and hunting triumphs.[83]

Layard and Mallowan inferred that the width of the rooms was restricted by the size of the timbers that were available. This, however, is not what we should expect from the emphasis in the records on the height of the cedars. The difficulty is slightly reduced when it is realised that the walls are much thicker than seems to be necessary, as much as from 4.4 metres to 4.8 metres in the royal apartments, and in the throne room 5.6 metres.[84] If the beams were carried over the whole width of both walls, lengths of more than fifty feet would have been needed. Why didn't the Assyrians, like the Minoans later and the Greeks, introduce internal supports in the form of columns or pillars to spread the weight of the cross-beams over a wider span? We don't know. Why didn't they introduce timber verticals to the mud-brick walls to help carry the weight? Perhaps because of a general shortage of timber.

Do these surprises invalidate the evidence of the records we have been quoting? Should we be sceptical of the dependence of Assyria on the western forests, particularly Lebanon and Amanus? Is the emphasis on cedar and cypress misplaced? Should we be thinking of smaller trees and shorter lengths? We have no good ground for reducing the lengths of timber to the length that palace rooms required. As we have seen, cedars will grow up to and even beyond eighty feet and in the Old Testament and in Theophrastus the height of the cedars is one of their main features. Gudea claimed that he brought back from his expedition to Amanus cedar logs of sixty and fifty cubits (p. 72) and an Egyptian official in the reign of Tuthmosis III also boasted of sixty-cubit cedars. It might have been more practical to cut down the longest logs to the size actually required, but Assyrian kings with their appetite for grandeur would have preferred to have the full length.

The dominance of cedar alone, or, more rarely, with cypress, in the campaign records may be misleading. Gudea claimed that he brought back logs of three other woods as well as cedar. Shalmeneser III includes the cutting of cedars on Amanus in four years of his reign: in one year cypress is also included, in the three other years cedar is alone. But the annual records are very compressed and it is sufficient to mention only the most important. It is unlikely that if junipers or firs or pines were growing in the same part of the forest only cedars would be taken. It is, however, safe to infer that cedar and cypress were the most prized trees on Lebanon and Amanus.

One might imagine from the campaign records that all the timber for palaces and temples came from the western forests. There is a corrective in letters sent to Sargon II by officials when he was building a new palace at Khorsabad. The governor of Assur reports that he is sending, as required by His Majesty, 372 heavy timbers, 808 of second size, 2,313 of third size, 11,807 of fourth size—a total of 15,200 whole (timbers) and 13,157 (inferior). The woods are not specified; presumably they came from stock. Other timbers are sent by Assyrian officials operating in the country of Urartu. One of them sends 500 great timbers which were felled by an Urartian; another is going to send 470 timbers by river.[85] From Urartu territory in the Zagros mountains and the eastern Taurus the Assyrians might expect cypress, juniper, and pine. There is no surviving inscription recording the cutting of cedars by Sargon, but in his palace at Khorsabad there is a splendid relief, now in the Louvre, showing Phoenician boats, loaded with large beams destined for his palace (pl. 3A).

Cedar and cypress were not the only timbers used for palace and temple roofs, but they were thought to be the best. The same applies to monumental doors, which were clearly an important feature of palace architecture. Here surely cedar and cypress were the favourite woods because of their fragrance and durability, and they retained their pre-eminence in the Greek and Roman worlds. Normally the door-leaves were bound with bands of metal, rarely gold or silver, more often bronze or copper. A convincing reconstruction of such a door can be seen in the British Museum, based on the bronze bands that were found at Balawat, a small settlement fourteen kilometres from Nimrud. The bronze bands, ten in number, illustrate the various campaigns of Shalmeneser III.

One record, literally translated, means 'a palace of cedar, a palace of (cypress), a palace of (juniper), a palace of boxwood, a palace of (mulberry), a palace of (pistachio), a palace of (tamarisk)'.[86] This cannot mean a series of palaces. What is implied is that for different wings, areas, or rooms of the palace different woods were chosen, a nice reflection of the Assyrians' respect for wood. The main opportunity for displaying wood was in the panelling. The Persian palace at Persepolis, for instance, and Solomon's temple and palace at Jerusalem were both panelled with cedar. Or the main emphasis could be in the furniture. It is clear that a wide variety of woods was used for interior work, but few of the names can be securely identified. It is significant that in the recent excavations at Nimrud the wooden writing-tablets were found to be of walnut, which still grows in the district, but none of the many tree names in the records had been assigned to walnut.[87]

With the collapse of Assyria the stage was soon set for a new alignment of forces. Media and Babylon had become allies to crush Assyria, but they now went their different ways. Media's main objective was to advance westwards, which involved conflict with Lydia; Babylon's natural line of expansion was to follow in Assyria's tracks against Syria and Phoenicia; Egypt, under a new and vigorous dynasty, was anxious to reassert her old claims. Necho, king of Egypt, attempted to strike early before Babylonian power was consolidated, but he was held up by Jewish resistance at the vital pass of Megiddo and at the decisive battle of Carchemish on the Euphrates he was defeated; in the ensuing period it became increasingly clear that Egypt was 'a broken reed'. For at this point Babylon produced a young ruler, Nebuchadnezzar (605–562 BC), of dynamic energy and wide ambitions. In a series of campaigns he reduced the Phoenicians of the seaboard, broke down the walls of Jerusalem, and carried its population into captivity. He has left a memorial on the north-east slopes of the Lebanon.

The record of his campaign is included in a long inscription carved on limestone rocks in the Wadi Brisa. Two copies were made, one in old Babylonian, the other in neo-Babylonian. The former is accompanied by a relief, now very badly worn, of the king killing a lion. Beside the neo-Babylonian text there is a second relief showing the king cutting down a tree: 'What no former king had done (I achieved): I cut through steep mountains, I split rocks, opened passages, and (thus) I constructed a straight road for the (transport of the) cedars.'[88]

When Nebuchadnezzar died in 562 the prophet Isaiah remembered his exploitation of Lebanon:

> The whole world has rest and is at peace;
>   it breaks into cries of joy.
> The pines themselves and the cedars of Lebanon exult over you.
>   Since you have been laid low, they say,
>   no man comes up to fell us.[89]

With the death of Nebuchadnezzar Babylon's brief revival as a major power was over. There followed a series of weak kings, religious quarrels, and a general disintegration, until the priests transferred their allegiance to a foreign conqueror who respected their old-established cults and opened the gates to Cyrus King of Persia.

The rise of Persia was swift and dramatic. Within a generation she absorbed Media, crushed Lydia, and, after the surrender of Babylon, was able to win Egypt with very little fighting: the balance of power had been irretrievably broken. All the great cedar forests were now under Persian control, and it was by the decrees of Persian kings that the Jews, having been restored to their country by Cyrus, were able to secure cedars from the Phoenicians for the rebuilding of their temple;[90] and when in the fifth century Nehemiah secured the authority of Artaxerxes to fortify Jerusalem, he was careful to ask for a letter to the keeper of the royal forest 'instructing him to supply me with timber to make beams for the gates of the citadel, which adjoins the palace, and for the city wall, and for the palace which I shall occupy.'[91] The Persian kings themselves accepted the verdict of the kings of Egypt and Mesopotamia that the cedar was the royal timber, and the longer distance did not deter them from following their example. In the proud inscription in which Darius commemorates the building of his palace in Susa he first describes the digging of the foundations and the preparation of the mud-brick, and then continues: 'The cedar timber, this a mountain by name Lebanon, from there it was brought. The Assyrian people, they brought it to Babylon; from Babylon the Carians and Ionians brought it to Susa.'[92] The historian Curtius Rufus, recording the burning by Alexander of the slightly later palace at Persepolis, emphasises the use of cedar in the building.[93] According to Polybius cedar was also used, with cypress, for the royal palace in the Median capital at Ecbatana.[94]

In the following period the nature of our evidence changes. We no longer have the royal records of Mesopotamia and Egypt but have to rely almost exclusively on passing references in historians. It is certain that the pattern of exploitation of the western forests changed considerably. When Mesopotamia and Egypt lost their independence and became provinces in a Persian empire their building policies became considerably less ambitious and they no doubt had to be content mainly with timber from nearer home, but the demand for ship-timber increased sharply. The Phoenicians provided the backbone of the Persian fleet, which was built from the forests of Cilicia, Syria, and Phoenicia. Large fleets were equipped to crush the Ionian revolt (499-494 BC) and to accompany Xerxes' invasion of Greece (480-479 BC), and when the Persians were driven out of Greece and their fleet was destroyed at the battle of Mycale (479 BC) a new fleet had to be built to defend the eastern Mediterranean against a Greek league under Athenian leadership. In major battles at the river Eurymedon and off Cyprus there were heavy losses and when Egypt revolted and was supported by a Greek expeditionary force a new fleet of 300 ships had to be built. Egypt was recovered and a Greek attempt to resume the offensive was abandoned. This marked the temporary end of hostilities between Greece and Persia (c.450 BC), and the strain on the forests was eased for more than a century. But Lebanon was exploited again when Alexander committed himself to the siege of Tyre.

When Alexander died and his marshals fought for the succession, control of the forests of the eastern Mediterranean became an important factor, as we shall see later, in the struggle between the Ptolemies of Egypt and Antigonus followed by the Seleucids

in Syria. Diodorus describes the building of a large fleet by
Antigonus from the forests of Lebanon and Taurus (p. 134).
When the Ptolemies were not strong enough to control Phoenicia
they relied on Cyprus for their naval timber, and when Rome
had crippled the power of Syria and Egypt the pirates of Lycia
and Cilicia, who had no organised fleet to challenge them,
depended on the timbers of the Taurus range. But when Rome
had eliminated the pirates the demand for ship-timber in the
eastern Mediterranean was insignificant until the period of
Rome's civil wars. The last we hear of the exploitation of the
forests for shipbuilding was when Antony and Cleopatra
challenged Octavian, and Lebanon and the Taurus were again
required to provide the timber for a large fleet;[95] but the battle of
Actium (31 BC), which confirmed Octavian as the undisputed
master of the Roman world, was the last naval battle in the
Mediterranean before the disintegration of the Roman empire.

We catch occasional glimpses of the supply of timbers for
building during the Hellenistic period. Josephus preserves
the terms of a decree which Antiochus III of Syria issued to
reward the city of Ptolemais for help given to him by them in
his war with Egypt: 'It is my will that the work on the temple
be completed, namely the stoas and whatever other parts
remain unbuilt. Let the timber be brought free of duty from
Judaea proper, from the other nations, and in particular from
Lebanon.'[96] Some 250 years later Agrippa II (AD 50–68) turned
to Lebanon for timber for the temple at Jerusalem and 'brought
down the timber required (presumably of cedar-wood) with
great expense and difficulty; the beams were marvellous both for
their straightness and length.'[97] After the Jewish revolt broke
out, John of Gischala appreciated these qualities and used them
to strengthen the fortifications.

The cedars of Lebanon may also have been used for another
famous building. Of all the buildings inspired by Rome in the
early Empire the great temple of Jupiter Heliopolitanus at
Baalbek is the most spectacular. In photographs the building
may seem almost vulgarly extravagant, but doubts vanish when
it is seen in its setting. Attention has often been drawn to the
immense size and weight of some of the blocks of stone, and the
huge monolithic columns that were brought all the way from
Assouan in Egypt, but little notice has been taken of the great

timbers required for the roof. The central span needed beams of sixty feet or a little more. Such a size would not have been unfamiliar in contemporary Rome, but it is doubtful whether such long beams had ever been used in Syria or Phoenicia. In the ruins of Byblos, Tyre, and Sidon I could find no evidence of any span longer than thirty feet. It is difficult not to think of Agrippa, who had played the leading part in the Augustan transformation of Rome, and was clearly attracted by engineering challenges. In Athens he had built a new Odeum in the city centre with a span of eighty feet, and there were no internal supports (p. 216). Agrippa's aim was to convince the Athenians, who had not forgotten the sack of the city by Sulla and whose sympathies had been more with Pompey than with Caesar, that the Augustan settlement was the dawn of a new era. Was the Baalbek temple a reflection of the same policy? The fusion of native and Roman cults would seem to have a political flavour.

The status of Heliopolis in the early Empire is controversial. Coins were issued under Septimius Severus with the proud title of *Colonia Julia Augusta Felix*, but there is no firm evidence of colonial status earlier. The title implies a connection with Berytus (Beirut), *Colonia Julia Felix*, and the colony of Berytus was established with two legions shortly after the battle of Actium.[98] Strabo, however, reports that Agrippa established the colony with two legions, presumably in 14 BC during his eastern tour, and he adds that the territory of Berytus was extended to include a large part of the Bekaa valley up to the source of the river Orontes.[99] This would include Heliopolis. Of an earlier colony Strabo seems to know nothing, but it is evident that the two legions V Macedonica and VIII Augusta[100] were settled at Berytus much earlier than Agrippa's visit.

The most plausible solution of the apparent conflict in the evidence is that Roman colonists were sent by Agrippa from Berytus to Heliopolis to guard an important line of communication. Whether Heliopolis was formally a colony from that time is less certain but for our purpose less important.[101] If the commencement of the building of the great temple is rightly dated to the early Empire[102] it is a bold but not irresponsible guess to associate the ambitious design with Agrippa.

Very different questions are raised by more than a hundred inscriptions commissioned by Roman imperial agents that have

been found in Lebanon. They are inscribed in very large letters
on limestone rocks, some of the texts extending over two rocks.
They cover a large area from the north of the Lebanon range
to the hinterland of Beirut and in altitude they vary from
500 metres to 1,800 metres. The commonest text is *Imp(eratoris)*
Had(riani) Aug(usti) d(e)f(initio) s(ilvarum) a(rborum) g(enera) IV
c(etera) p(rivata): 'the demarcation of the forests of the emperor
Hadrian Augustus; four species of trees; the rest are private' (i.e.
not claimed by the emperor).[103] The date is AD 138, when the
twentieth year of Hadrian's rule was commemorated, and the
action taken by his agents probably followed instructions given
by the emperor when, on one of his long and conscientious tours
of inspection of the provinces, he visited the Phoenician cities.
The emperor was asserting publicly that in the large area
covered by the markers (which includes the forests most accessible from Byblos, from which Egypt had once received substantial supplies of timber) four species of trees could only be
taken with the authority of the emperor or his agents. The
remaining species could be cut without such authority. No other
inscriptions of this nature have been found elsewhere in the
Roman empire and it would be naïve to expect general
agreement on the answer to the two most obvious questions that
arise: 'Which were the four species?' and 'Why did Hadrian take
this action at this time?'

Without further evidence we cannot hope to do more than
make a short list of trees among those that are thought to have
grown on Lebanon at the time which would be particularly
worth preserving. The choice should lie within six species: cedar,
cypress, juniper, fir, pine, oak. Juniper could possibly be
eliminated if the purpose was to conserve ship-timber. This has
been suggested on the basis of a passage in Vegetius who, in a
treatise on military and naval affairs in the fourth century AD,
says that four species were particularly suitable for ship-timber:
fir, pine, cypress, larch.[104] But Vegetius includes larch which
was a European tree not found in western Asia, and he omits
cedar which, according to Theophrastus, was the principal
timber for triremes in Syria and Phoenicia. It is more likely that
the criterion of selection was the general value for all purposes. It
would be particularly interesting to know if fir was included; for
if, as Theophrastus seems to imply,[105] there was very little fir

when he wrote (*c*.300 BC), it might have become negligible by Hadrian's time, four hundred years later.

Hadrian's action has usually been accepted as evidence for deforestation, a sign that timber reserves were seriously threatened, but this is not a necessary inference. The immediate cause presumably was that valuable trees were being taken without authority from forests that belonged to the emperor. The loss to the imperial exchequer was a sufficient motive for making imperial ownership more explicit. It can also be argued that notices would not have been inscribed on bare mountain slopes. Their wide distribution is inconsistent with wide-scale deforestation. We have no means of estimating the extent to which the forests of Cilicia and Syria had been depleted by the end of the Roman Empire. The Taurus had been least affected, and Amanus less heavily than Lebanon; but in the early fourth century, when an impressive new Christian basilica was built at Tyre, it was still possible to find cedar of good quality. Eusebius extolled the size and grandeur of the building, including 'the costly cedars of Lebanon overhead, of which Holy Scripture is not silent: "The trees of the Lord shall be glad, even the cedars which he planted".'[106]

4

BRONZE AGE PALACES AND HOMER

WHEN we pass from the Middle East to the Aegean world in the Bronze Age there is a sharp change in the nature of our enquiry. Our main evidence for timber usage in the Middle East comes from literary sources, notably the Bible, and the long series of royal inscriptions. The only contemporary writings that survive from the Minoan and Mycenaean civilisations are the administrative records of a palace bureaucracy, consisting almost exclusively of inventories. We therefore have to rely primarily on the archaeological evidence and our main sources become the reports of excavations in Minoan Crete and Mycenaean Greece.

The mainspring of Minoan and Mycenaean societies was the palace, which was the political, religious, and administrative centre of the district it controlled; and since it had to provide for public as well as private quarters, workshops for the production of palace requirements and a surplus for trade, and ample storage, the buildings were large and complex. The pattern of building and administrative system derived from further east and is well illustrated in the palace of Mari on the Upper Euphrates. There the earliest walls are composed of mud-brick.[1] This was the natural form of construction in areas that were poorly supplied with stone, but it was also often used when stone was freely available, for it was an easier material to handle and considerably more economical in labour. Even a rubble wall where the stones are not specially selected and not worked takes considerably longer to build. Nor should mud-brick walls be lightly dismissed as short-lived. If they are penetrated by damp they disintegrate, but they can be protected. It became standard practice to defend them from damp rising from the ground by building on a stone socle, to cover the top of the wall with timber, and to plaster the face. When such precautions are taken a well-built mud-brick wall can last more than a hundred years.

It is less capable of carrying weight than timber and if more than two storeys are to be built the thickness of the wall has to be proportionately increased. But it is considerably less vulnerable to fire than timber; in fact, as the ruins of palaces destroyed by fire demonstrate, fire hardens mud-brick. Even Vitruvius, who was a practising architect in the time of Augustus, more than a thousand years later than the Minoan palaces, had a great respect for such walling.[2] In the excavations of the palace of Mari traces were found of rows of half-round timbers running through some of the thicker walls. Timber was associated more widely with mud-brick in Minoan and Mycenaean palaces.[3]

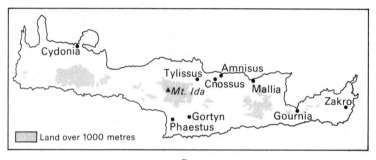

3 Crete

Unlike Mari, Cnossus, Phaestus, and the other palace centres of Minoan Crete had ample supplies of building-stone within easy reach. Many of the walls in the earliest palaces and other settlements were of rubble and in the latest phase before the destruction of most of the palaces (c.1450 BC) ashlar walls of carefully cut and evenly coursed stones were being built. But walls of mud-brick continued in use to the end for less important walls and particularly for upper storeys. In these walls grooves often show where timbers have disintegrated but left their shape, and sometimes carbonised remains have survived. From the very little firm evidence that is available it seems that in the early Minoan period (c.2800–2000 BC) the use of wood was very tentative, confined to short lengths of small dimension, whose only usefulness could have been to prevent vertical cracks. Later, long horizontals were used which served a double purpose: they helped to consolidate the walls and made it easier to absorb the shock of earthquakes, which were frequent and sometimes violent; they could also serve as sills and lintels for window-frames.

Vertical timbers had a useful part to play when second storeys were built. Mud-brick walls cannot sustain heavy weights; vertical timbers in the wall helped to support the cross-beams on which the upper floor was laid; and some of the thicker walls had struts tying their two faces together. In the later phases this use of horizontal and vertical timbers developed into a genuine half-timber construction in which strong timbers provided a framework for panels of masonry. Those who look for standard measurements or standard treatment of timbers in the walls of Minoan palaces will be disappointed. Sometimes the timber is used in the round, sometimes the trunk is cut longitudinally down the middle leaving one side round; in other walls the timbers are squared. Usually the timber-faces are level with the wall, but sometimes they project a little. More often they are covered by the same plaster as the walls, but frescos confirm that they were also sometimes exposed. The intervals between verticals and between horizontals tend to be irregular.

Of the construction timbers the main weight-carriers were beams which supported the upper floor, providing at the same time the ceiling of the ground-floor rooms, and the beams that supported the roof. There is very little evidence for the floors of upper storeys, but in one case at least, in the Zakro palace on the south-east coast of Crete, there was a wooden floor of boards resting on the bearer beams. No tiles have been found on palace sites and it is assumed that all roofs were flat, as most still are in Crete. On top of the beams that provided the ceiling was a layer of brushwood or reeds which in turn was covered by a thick coat of mud. Such roofs would not stand up to a central or north European climate, but the rainy season in Crete covers little more than three months. From December to March the roof will have been very heavy, but the high heat of summer dried out the effect of the rains.

The weight-carrying beams had not only to be strong, but some of them also had to be long, covering spans of up to eighteen feet (5.49 m.). In the Pillar Crypt of the Royal Villa at Cnossus, which has a span of thirteen feet nine inches (4.20 m.), the sockets of the ceiling beams can still be seen.[4] The main timber, between the north and south walls, was formed by cutting the trunk of a tree longitudinally down the middle. It is surprising to find that it tapers from about twenty-eight inches (71 cm.) to twenty-two inches (56 cm.) in a length of less than fourteen feet. Cuts were made in the top of this beam into which the smaller cross-timbers could fit; their sockets in the east and west walls show that they were left in the round. The main beam is supported by a substantial pillar of gypsum in the centre of the room, but such a large and comparatively short beam needed no such support. The channels round the base of the pillar seem to be designed to draw off and collect libations; the pillar clearly had some religious significance.[5] In the Temple Tomb at Cnossus there were two main beams, both squared, on the east–west axis, measuring twenty feet (8.10 m.) and eighteen and one-half feet (5.60 m.) and both one foot nine inches (53 cm.) square in cross-section.[6] These also, like the main beam in the Crypt of the Royal Villa, had cuts on their tops to take the eight smaller transverse north–south beams. In a few rooms for which there is not the explicit evidence of sockets there were larger spans to be covered. In the Royal Villa at Hagia Triada there is a room which is twenty feet wide and some of the great staterooms on the upper floors may have been up to twenty-three feet wide; but it is unlikely that any of the beams used were over twenty-seven feet long.

When spans were wide the main beams could be supported by rectangular piers or columns. The columns were always of wood, the piers were built of masonry, sometimes with the corners protected by wood. Their commonest use was in the so-called polythyron in large rooms of major importance in the palaces. This was a form of screen in which alternating piers and doors divided the room into two halves which could be united by opening the doors, a system used in all the palaces, though not always with the same number of doors. The purpose is clearly not merely for communication; one door or at most two would have been sufficient for that. The main reason was probably to be able to adapt to change of temperature, wind, and rain; it also provided greater flexibility. When the doors were all open the whole space became one room; when they were all closed one half remained open to the fresh air and light from the light-well, the other half became an independent room, protected from bad weather but lighted only indirectly, from windows which were probably inserted in the walls over the doors. The pier could also be used decoratively, alternating with columns to support the roofs of long porticoes, especially in the great ceremonial courts of the palaces, though it would have been more economical in labour to use wooden columns throughout. The explanation is the same instinct that led to the alternation of rounded and rectangular niches in Roman imperial architecture.

Piers were the more effective weight-carriers, columns were more often used to add grace, lightness, and variety to the architecture. Wood was invariably used for the columns, because the rounded surface of stone presented much more difficulty for the chisel than wood; a wooden column was little more than a tree-trunk cross-cut to the required length and stripped of its bark. The finished surface was the work of the adze and, if a finer surface was needed, the chisel. The diameter of columns varied considerably from roughly one foot to two feet according to the weight that they had to support, and trees would be selected according to the size required. The commonest use of the column was to emphasise entrances, to mark the transition from light-well to the room it lights, or to support the roofs of porticoes. The largest and most impressive column was set at the top of the magnificently wide stairway that leads to the main entrance of the palace at Phaestus. It stood in the centre of the propylon and had to support the weight of two large timbers spanning thirty-two feet (9.75 m.).[7] At Cnossus there are columns fulfilling the same function for the entrance to the wide staircase leading up from the west side of the great ceremonial court in the palace and for the entrance to the pavilion of the Caravanserai; but in both these cases the column stood on one of the lower steps.

In lands where summer heat is strong the shade of porticoes is as welcome as the play of a fountain. It is therefore not surprising that in almost all the residential quarters of the palaces there was a portico looking out on to garden or open country. There were longer porticoes in the great central courts where they served a double purpose: they gave shade and invited a pleasant promenade, but they also provided support for verandas on the upper floor from which spectators could watch the ceremonial spectacles in the court below. Unlike the smaller porticoes, whose roofs were supported entirely by columns, the long porticoes of the great courts had rectangular piers alternating with columns. But of the various uses of the column the most attractive is in the Great Staircase of the residential quarter of the palace at Cnossus, where they stand, sunk in a shallow bed, on the sills, supporting the landings and adding a monumental dignity to the staircase.[8]

A few carbonised fragments of columns have survived, but the main evidence for their use and size comes from the stone bases on which most of them were set to protect them from damp. Almost all these bases are round, but there is a small group in the palace at Phaestus which seem deliberately oval, and this should imply oval columns.[9] No capitals have been found but the general pattern can be seen in some of the frescos. They seem to have been composed of two separate pieces, a bulging neck and a square block on which the architrave rested, anticipating the echinus and abacus of the Doric capital. The extent to which columns were fluted is uncertain, but in three cases imprints on plaster suggest sixteen, twenty-four, and twenty-eight flutings.[10] From one substantial fragment Evans estimated that the height was five times the diameter at the base, but paintings suggest much slenderer columns and of three bases in front of a light-well in the storage area at Phaestus two showed the same measurements but the third was different; they all, however, supported the same architrave and must therefore have been of the same height. Minor variation in the diameters of columns is to be expected when the column is in fact part of a tree-trunk: the irregularity of some of the beams suggests that the Minoans would not have pared down a column to provide a precisely matching diameter if the difference was very small.

In one column at Cnossus, from which eight feet of carbonised wood had survived from a probable length of ten feet, Evans measured a significant downward taper of at least three-eighths of an inch.[11] In some frescos there is no such taper, but two provide good parallels[12] and though Evans excluded the column in the grand relief over the Lion Gate at Mycenae, it too has in fact a slight downward taper. Various explanations have been offered of this apparent anomaly. The least acceptable is that it was to prevent the wooden column trying to continue life as a tree by sending out new shoots. The suggestion that the purpose was to protect the foot of the columns from water falling from the capital is hardly more persuasive, for the column on which Evans's inference was based came from the interior of the palace and was not exposed to the weather. The only functional explanation which cannot be dismissed at once is that the wider diameter at the top would provide a larger surface on which to rest the entablature and would leave more free space at floor level. But the gain at both ends is too small to make a significant difference. The downward taper cannot be dismissed, but unless and until more examples are found in paintings or in the buildings it is better to regard it as a temporary fashion.

The other most important use of timber in construction was for doors and windows. All doors were of wood and so far as we know none of them had bands of copper, bronze, or silver. The threshold was normally in stone, but sometimes in wood, and the door-frame, jambs, and lintel were regularly of wood, though sometimes the jambs were in masonry faced with timber boards. Pivots were used to hang the doors, fitting into lintel and threshold. Windows also were framed in timber, sometimes using the horizontals bedded in the wall, and wood was also needed for the shutters. The main staircases were in stone, but the less important were in wood, sometimes with the first few steps in stone.

The best-preserved illustration of Minoan timber usage is in the domestic wing of the palace at Cnossus and especially in the largest of the rooms. This hall, which dates from the last phase of the Middle Minoan period (c.1500 BC), was called by Evans the Hall of the Double Axes from the many figures of the double axe on the walls of the area from which it drew its light.[13] This name, though perhaps misleading, is too well established to discard, especially since suggested alternatives tend to beg questions; whatever the name, it is clear from the size of the room, 40 × 26 feet (12.19 × 7.92 m.), and its decoration that this was the king's main reception-room. The lighting comes from a light-well at the west end and two columns carrying an architrave mark the entry to the hall. The floor was paved with gypsum flags, and gypsum veneers covered the dado. The walls above were plastered and painted, but beneath the plaster it can be seen that they were framed with vertical and horizontal timbers (pl. 6). The verticals rest on masonry a little above floor level.

On top of them a series of horizontal beams was laid all round the room at lintel level; on them was set a second series of verticals continuing the lines of the first, and on them was laid a second series of horizontal beams on which rested the beams of the ceiling.

The hall was divided by a polythyron, a partition of five piers framing four doors. The bases of the piers are well preserved and provide a secure foundation for reconstruction. In each doorway there were two pivot-holes to hold the pivots of the two door-leaves, and on each side of each pier there was a recessed panel into which the doors neatly fitted, so preserving the full width of the doorway when the doors were open. Above the doors were square openings which may have held some translucent material that could spread a diffused light without letting in the cold air in winter; but since a ladder would be needed to open and close the windows, it is more probable that they were simply open sources of light. A similar partition with the same number of piers and doors was built at the end of the room, and a shorter partition on the south-east side. The only trace of furnishings that remained came from a throne in wood in the western half of the room which seems to have had a wooden canopy supported by four columns.[14] Impressions of the columns on the plaster showed that they were fluted, with roughly twenty-eight flutes. On the plaster covering the horizontal beams at lintel level there was a painted frieze of spiralling waves, and since in other examples of this design it was accompanied by large painted figure-of-eight shields, Evans suggested that real shields with wooden frames covered by layers of bull-hide were hung on the walls over the frieze.

The evidence on which we have so far drawn comes almost entirely from the palaces, for these are the buildings that have been most systematically and intensively explored, but excavations at Gournia, Mallia, Tylissus, Palaikastro, and other settlements show that the same building principles applied in private housing. When we leave buildings to review the wider usages of timber we can do little but ask questions. We can be certain that shipbuilding made extensive demands, for the Cretan Minos was traditionally associated with the control of the seas. The wide distribution of Minoan products in the west, in mainland Greece, and more extensively in the eastern

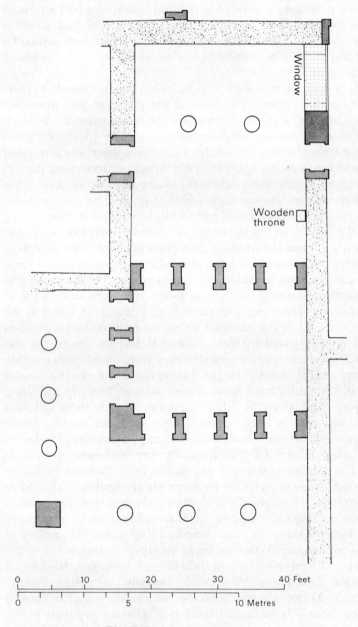

Window

Wooden throne

| 0 | 10 | 20 | 30 | 40 Feet |

| 0 | 5 | 10 Metres |

4 The Hall of the Double Axes

Mediterranean implies a large boat-building trade producing merchantmen and warships. Fine illustrations of ships of the period can be seen in a magnificent fresco found at Akrotiri on the island of Santorini in 1973 and now in the National Museum in Athens.[15] We shall later give reasons for thinking that Cretan forests could supply all the timber that was needed for her shipping. In sheer quantity the amount of wood required for fuel probably surpassed the combined requirements of the builders of ships and houses. Wood or charcoal were needed for domestic cooking, for public sacrifices, and for metallurgy, in particular for fusing copper with tin to make bronze for arms and tools.

The other main requirements may be briefly listed. By our standards the Minoans used little furniture, but their tables, chairs, couches, beds were all made of wood and, perhaps most important of all, their chests, shelves, and boxes. It would be more interesting to know the dividing line between wood and pottery in household utensils such as bowls, dishes, trays, but the indestructability of pottery has obscured the important part played by wood in the kitchen. The excavations in the area of the temple of Hera at Samos, which was built on marshy ground, are a reminder that in the archaic period craftsmen took pride in making their wooden bowls, plates, and other vessels beautiful as well as useful.[16] It would be even more interesting to know to what extent, if any, wood was used to carve human figures, small or large. We are familiar with the little ivory figures of the snake goddess or priestess from Cnossus and the ivory figure usually thought to be of a young god. There are also stylised figures in pottery which probably have religious associations, but no figures, large or small, in stone have yet been found and it is reasonable to assume that none or very few indeed were made. The argument from silence does not, however, apply equally to wood. Wooden objects cannot be expected to survive from Antiquity unless they have been sealed from the atmosphere, either by a very dry climate as in Egypt, or by preservation in mud or marsh as at Samos. No such sites have yet been excavated in Crete. The question is surely not whether there is any reason to believe that the Minoans did carve in wood, but whether there is any reason to explain why they didn't.

In this context it is reasonable to consider again a suggestion tentatively made by Evans. In the East Hall of the domestic quarters of the palace at Cnossus he found, amidst remains of carbonised wood, four massive bronze objects elegantly modelled which could only be curling locks of hair, one of these no less than six inches (15 cm.) long.[17] Elsewhere he had found the locks of a sphinx's head in steatite. Nothing had survived of the figures to which bronze and steatite were attached, and the most natural explanation was that the material was wood. Evans inferred that the bronze curls had been originally attached to a statue in wood rather larger than life-size, and probably a goddess. This remains a good suggestion and should at least persuade us to keep an open mind. Closed minds found it difficult to accommodate the series of large terracotta figures of priestesses or a goddess found in 1968 on the island of Keos, for which there seemed to be no precedent.[18] In the wide ambience of Minoan and Mycenaean religion, where so little is understood, there is ample scope for new surprises. If it were not for the literary evidence we should considerably underestimate the quality and quantity of sculpture in wood during the archaic period (c.750–500 BC).

Were the Minoans able to satisfy all their timber requirements from the forests of Crete? Evans had doubts. Noticing two changes in building practice at Cnossus he was led to believe that in the late Minoan period (after c.1550 BC) there was a growing shortage of timber. The two new features were the wide-scale use of gypsum in places where timber had been previously used, especially in door-frames, and a decrease in the use of vertical timbers in the walls accompanied by a decline in the size of horizontals. He regarded these two changes as ominous signs of timber demand exceeding supply; 'a main cause of the downfall of Minoan dominion is to be sought in the gradual deforestation of the island'.[19] Evans was careful not to overstate his case, but it was not long before his tentative suggestion had become for the general reader an established historical fact; an acute shortage of timber was widely accepted as the explanation of the collapse of the Minoan thalassocracy. But Evans wrote before the violent eruption of the volcano on the island of Santorini had been found to be an integral part of the Minoan story, when it was not known that Mycenaean Greeks had gained control of Cnossus before the destruction of the palaces, and before the palace at Zakro had been found. The effects of the volcano and the rise of Mycenaean power are sufficient alone to account for the Minoan decline, and comparison with the palaces of Phaestus and Zakro suggests that there was no shortage of timber. Phaestus had always used less mud-brick walling than Cnossus but there is no reduction in the use of wood for doors, windows, and columns, and in the later palace it became common practice to protect door-jambs and wall-ends with timber boards;[20] there is no sign of a timber shortage in Zakro where no fewerthan ten saws were found. The main change noted by Evans at Cnossus was a change of fashion, encouraged by the ample deposits of gypsum nearby.

Nor does what little we know of the later history of Cretan forests accord with an acute shortage in the Bronze Age. Strabo, writing in the first quarter of the first century AD, describes the island as 'mountainous and well-wooded (daseia)';[21] and an Athenian comedy produced during the early stages of the Peloponnesian War (431–421 BC) included cypress from Crete in a list of Athenian imports.[22] Theophrastus links Crete with Rhodes and Lycia as 'warm places that have cypress in great abundance'.[23] He also cites the cypress of Crete as his example of native plants that grow spontaneously even if the ground is only lightly disturbed:[24] Pliny accepts Crete as the original home of the cypress tree.[25] The cypress continued to dominate in Crete into the Middle Ages and was much appreciated by the Venetians as a major source of supply for their fleets.[26]

It was natural therefore to believe that cypress would have been the most widely used wood in the construction of the palaces, and Evans was encouraged in this belief by the 'expert examination' of carbonised samples as cypress-wood,[27] and the largest fragment (p. 93) was also accepted as cypress.[28] It seems very probable, however, that it was the same fragment which, when microscopically examined, was found to be fir (*Abies cephalonica*).[29] The availability of fir was also revealed by the analysis of seven miniature axe-handles from the cave at Arkolantiri: it was found that five were made of fir and two, almost certainly, of Lebanon cedar.[30]

The discovery of tool-handles of cedar was a surprise, because no cedars had been recorded on Crete in modern times and it is generally believed that it was not a Cretan tree. But one would not expect tool-handles to be made from imported cedar when suitable cypress was available in Crete and there is other possible evidence. Mt. Kedros in Crete might have been given its name from cedar. More positively, Vitruvius says that *cedrus* grew particularly well in Crete, Syria, and Africa.[31] Cedar was also recorded by a seventeenth-century traveller who visited Crete. Fynes Morrison, a Fellow of Peterhouse, Cambridge, in the story of his travels published in 1617, listed the resources of the island: 'corne, all manner of Pulse, of Oyle, all kinds of flesh, of Canes of Sugar, of Honey, of Cedar trees, of all coloured dyings, of Cypress trees (whereof many sweet-smelling chests are made, and carried into forraine parts), and of all the necessities of life'.[32]

This evidence, however, is not conclusive. In Greek and Latin the words *kedros* and *cedrus* are used for juniper as well as cedar, and Cretans still call the juniper *kedros*. Did a Cambridge scholar of the early seventeenth century know the difference between the two trees? Perhaps the strongest argument for believing that there were cedars on Crete in the Bronze Age is the passage in Pliny. In linking Crete with Africa as well as Syria his source surely had in mind the famous cedars of the Atlas range of mountains. But if the cedars were heavily overcut during the Bronze Age, they could have lost ground in the archaic period to trees that reproduce more easily, as in Cyprus where the pines almost succeeded in driving out the cedars. Three other woods have also been identified microscopically—holm-oak (*Quercus ilex*) from Amnisus, Cnossus, and Myrtos;[33] and olive and pine from Myrtos.[34] The only evidence for pine comes from carbonised wood found in the early Minoan settlement at Myrtos and of eighteen samples collected it was present in only one, but pine grows freely in Crete today and pines of fine quality which can be seen in comparatively inaccessible places such as the Samaria gorge may be natural descendants from natives. Chariot-wheels of elm-wood and of willow are included in a palace inventory from Cnossus, and Cretan willow is referred to by Pliny.[35] By inference from the modern distribution of species and the analogy of the Lebanese forest range we can probably add oak, ash, maple, black mulberry, and tamarisk. The climate was not cold enough for beech, spruce, or larch.

Fir and cypress will have been the main timbers for general

construction and shipbuilding, supplemented by pine and perhaps cedar. Cypress, because of its attractive scent and immunity from decay and insect attack, was preferred for chests and boxes; oak and maple with fir and pine could have been used for furniture. It is doubtful whether the island had any timber worries until after the heavy inroads of the Venetians. The question is rather whether Crete, which supplied Athens with cypress in the Periclean period, exported any timber in the Bronze Age. Minoan pottery is found in Egypt, which, as we have seen, depended on overseas sources for her best-quality wood. The Lebanon forests were her nearest and best suppliers, and when hostile powers controlled Syria and Lebanon Egypt could turn to Cyprus, as she did both in the Bronze Age and in the Hellenistic period. But when Cyprus also was controlled by enemies Egypt would have been very glad to have cypress, cedar, or fir from Crete. We need positive evidence, however, before we assume a timber trade between Crete and Egypt.

While Minoan power and wealth were at their height (c.1700–1450 BC) the people of the Greek mainland, whom for convenience we call Mycenaeans from the pre-eminence of Mycenae, were considerably less advanced in technology, trade, and general culture. The finest objects in their grandest tombs were Minoan or strongly influenced by Minoan models, and they had no buildings to compare with the Cretan palaces. But by 1450 BC or soon afterwards Mycenaean Greeks had won control of Cnossus and the other main centres of Minoan power had been broken. Minoan settlements in Ionia and the eastern Mediterranean were abandoned or destroyed and the Mycenaeans became the main traders with the Near East. From the Minoans the Mycenaeans inherited the palace system of government and administration. As in the Cretan palaces there were public and private rooms, and substantial accommodation for production and storage, but there were significant differences in plan, notably the dominance of the great hall, the megaron, which was entered from a courtyard through porch and vestibule.

The palaces of the mainland are not as well preserved as those of Crete. At Mycenae a large part of the palace has fallen down the hillside; the Theban palace is buried under buildings in a busy part of the modern city and only a very limited exploration has been possible; all traces of the palace on the acropolis of Athens have been lost. The best preserved are the palaces of Tiryns and Pylos, and as techniques were more sophisticated when the Pylos palace was excavated (1952–64), the palace of Pylos will be our main point of reference.

The palace of Pylos was discovered by Blegen in 1939, and its location and building periods correspond so closely with Homer's account of Nestor's kingdom that even those who are generally sceptical of the value of epic tradition have accepted the title of Nestor's palace. It was Nestor's father Neleus who had come down from Thessaly and established his principality at Pylos in the Peloponnese. Nestor was past fighting age when Agamemnon led the Achaeans against Troy, but he joined the expedition and was continuously prominent in counsel, somewhat garrulous but highly respected. In Homer his kingdom is the only important centre of power beside Sparta in the western Peloponnese, and in the tablets baked by the fire that destroyed the palace the name Pylos recurs frequently.[36]

The palace was built on a low ridge some nine kilometres inland from the bay of Navarino in the south-west of the Peloponnese. The original building has been dated to the early thirteenth century, but it was considerably modified and enlarged later in the century; it was burnt to the ground c.1200 BC, in or very near the period when the other main centres of Mycenaean power were destroyed. In its final form there were two residential blocks, the more important of which included the megaron, the main reception-room. There was a separate group of rooms concerned mainly with workshops and also, detached from the residential blocks, a large building which seems to have been used for the storage of wine. The site had not been reoccupied, and though it had been often raided for building material, some of the walls were still preserved to a height of more than a metre and the plans of the ground floors could be clearly traced.[37]

The main building material of the two residential blocks was stone, laid in regular courses of squared blocks on external walls and on most internal walls as rubble coated with plaster. Repairs to walls were sometimes made with mud-brick and from the large quantities of disintegrated brick found throughout these two blocks it can be assumed that mud-brick was also used, though not perhaps exclusively, for upper rooms. The walls of the workshops and wine magazine were entirely of mud-brick on a low stone socle. In both stone and brick walls that were carrying weight horizontal and vertical timbers were bedded in the wall and in many walls the grooves can still be seen. The walls are best preserved in the central block which includes the megaron, and a brief description of this great hall offers perhaps the best illustration of the use of timber by the Mycenaeans.[38]

The megaron is approached from the main entrance to the palace, which is emphasised by a propylon consisting of an inner and outer portico with a fluted column in the centre of each façade. From the propylon one passes into a large open court, which leads into another portico, which prefaces the vestibule of the megaron. This is the largest room in the palace, $c.44 \times 37$ feet (12.46×11.28 m.) and the best-appointed. Its doorway, twelve feet (3.66 m.) wide, was also the widest and, unlike the other doors of the central block, had two leaves. In the centre of the room was an impressively large hearth, slightly raised above floor level, and round it were four fluted columns framing a rectangular area of $c.20 \times 16$ feet (6.16×4.88 m.). The diameter of these columns is very similar to that of the two columns in the entrance propylon ($c.1\frac{1}{2}$ ft.), but the flutings are much wider, thirty-two compared with sixty-four; they carried a wooden epistyle on which they supported a wooden balcony round the four sides of the room. They also supported a second series of columns above them which provided a frame for a lantern over the hearth, through which light came into the hall, and the smoke from the fire was carried up by two large terracotta pipes. The lower walls of the megaron were in stone, the upper parts above the balcony and the lantern were probably in mud-brick.

For the support of the balcony the spans that had to be covered from the central columns to the walls varied between ten and thirteen feet (3.31 and 3.89 m.); the length provided no problem but the timber had to be strong. The length of epistyle required between column and column varied from fourteen to sixteen feet (4.26 to 5.36 m.). Timbers were also used to frame the walls. In both sides of the walls there were verticals, with irregular intervals varying from fifty-five to eighty centimetres. The evidence for horizontals is less good. There seem normally to have been one row at floor level, another about seventy centimetres higher, but not at the same level in all walls. As no tiles were found in the excavation it is assumed that the roof was flat. It would have been supported by beams resting on the mud-brick walls of the upper floor and the four columns over the columns of the ground floor.

There is enough evidence from other palaces, and particularly from Tiryns, to show that, with minor variants, timber usage at Pylos was typical, and very similar to Minoan practice in its fully developed form. The evidence is barely full enough to make a fair comparison of the use of timber within the walls, but the basic principles seem to have been the same. There is a striking similarity also in the use of timber casing for the jambs of doors. There are, however, two timber-intensive features in the Minoan palace plan that the Mycenaeans do not adopt. The light-well with its wooden columns, and the very common pier and door partitions have not yet been found on the mainland. This, however, is not due to a shortage of timber, for at Pylos at least there is good reason to believe that there were ample supplies of timber in the neighbourhood, and there are certainly no signs of restrictions in its use in the palace. From two sources we can learn a little of what was available locally and what was used.

A detailed study of the flora and fauna of Messenia by American scholars, undertaken as part of a comprehensive survey, archaeological, historical, and geographical, has provided a fair outline of the distribution of species in the area during the Bronze Age.[39] By far the most widespread was the oak on the plains and the lower slopes; there were fir forests at the higher altitudes and pine forests along the coast. Alder and poplar were growing in the more marshy areas and there was some cypress, reflected in the place-name Kyparissia already established. Pollen analysis seems to show that in the late Bronze Age a pine forest near the modern Kalamata was destroyed, but the attribution of this to the growth of population needs further support.

Clay tablets that were baked hard when the palace was burnt down add a little more specific evidence. These tablets, very similar in character to those found at Cnossus, are mainly concerned with palace inventories, giving lists of various categories of objects with ideograms of the objects listed. As at

Cnossus chariots were made in a palace workshop and chariot inventories are well represented. One tablet shows that cypress was used.[40] This could probably have been found locally, but some of the wood used in furniture had come a long distance. Among the tables are three combining ebony with ivory inlays, and there was also an ebony chair with an ebony footstool, both with ivory inlays.[41] The combination of ivory and ebony was fashionable in Egypt and the Near East during the Bronze Age and the chair with footstool, in particular, can be closely parallelled in Egypt (pl. 4). The luxurious furniture was probably imported, though it might possibly have been made in a palace workshop. The Mycenaeans certainly imported a substantial quantity of ivory, probably from Syria or Phoenicia. Ebony, the only source for which, until trade developed with India, was Ethiopia and neighbouring lands, could be acquired in Phoenician trading cities. The combination of yew and box in two other tables[42] was also familiar in the Near East and at Phrygian Gordium (p. 461), but though they were probably not available in Messenia, both could have been found in Arcadia.

There is no firm evidence for wood-carving by the Mycenaeans. Pausanias had no hesitation in accepting dates before the Trojan War for some of the oldest figures in wood that he saw or heard of, but he had no critical judgement himself and relied on local tradition, which in such cases is notoriously unreliable. However, if we are right in believing that the Minoans used wood as well as stone and ivory for their figures, it would be natural to expect the Mycenaeans to do the same. They made figures of terracotta, ivory, and at least one head in limestone; it would be extraordinary if they did not also carve in wood.

The Mycenaean world was also the background of the two great epics attributed to Homer. In the *Iliad* and *Odyssey* we seem to come nearer to the forests than we shall ever come in later classical literature or archaeology. The poet is clearly familiar with the work of the woodsman and carpenter and he knows the main uses of the different woods. But we are at once faced with an embarrassing complication. The *Iliad* and the *Odyssey* were both written at least four hundred years after the events which they purport to narrate and scholars, pedants, and dilettantes have never tired of investigating their relevance to the Bronze

Age. It is clear that behind them lies a long tradition of oral poetry which in words and phrases may have kept alive genuinely Mycenaean echoes. It is also clear that there are features of the poems which fit the eighth and seventh centuries BC better than the thirteenth or twelfth. Material objects of both periods are embedded in the texts and the battle-pieces fit neither period satisfactorily. There is also continuing controversy over the authorship of the two poems and their respective dates. There is a wide measure of agreement that the *Iliad* was the earlier poem and written in the late eighth or early seventh century, but many scholars would place the *Odyssey* considerably later and assign it to a different author. Before becoming engulfed in such controversies it will be more wholesome to turn first to the poems themselves. Meanwhile, for convenience, we shall give Homer's name to both poems.

Though Homer's heroes, including Odysseus, are primarily warriors, they are also hunters and the hunting-scenes in both narrative and simile are vivid and drawn directly or indirectly from nature. The story of Odysseus' famous wound from a wild boar which waited in a hidden lair in a wooded glen is compelling in its detail,[43] and the picture of a lion snatching away a goat from sharp-toothed dogs and carrying it through the thick undergrowth high above the ground is surely not drawn from an ivory relief or the scene on a surviving Mycenaean pot.[44] Homer draws freely on trees and forests in his similes, which often take on a life of their own. The commonest example is the comparison of a warrior's fall in battle to the felling or falling of a tree. In its simplest form there is no elaboration. The twin sons of Diokles, killed by Aeneas, 'fell like tall fir trees'.[45] When Ajax son of Telamon strikes down Imbrios son of Mentor, 'he fell like an ash which is cut with the bronze axe on the peak of a mountain seen from afar and brings down its tender leaves to the ground'.[46] The distant visibility of the mountain is not relevant to the comparison but the decorative expansion is slight. It is more substantial when Asios is killed by Diomedes: 'he fell as an oak falls, or a poplar, or a tall pine, which craftsmen cut down in the mountains with their newly whetted axes to make ship-timbers'.[47] There is even more distracting detail when Hector is killed by a giant stone hurled by Ajax: 'He span like a top round and round and fell to the ground, as when an oak is struck by the bolt of father Zeus and uprooted, and there rises a grim smell of brimstone.'[48]

Ajax is also associated with the most incongruous development of the theme. Simoeisios, speared by Ajax, 'fell to the ground in the dust like a poplar that has grown up smooth on the edge of a great marsh, and its branches grow at the top. A chariot-maker cuts it down with his gleaming iron axe to bend a felloe for a specially fine chariot, and so it lies drying out by the river banks.'[49] This is a fascinating illustration of the craftsman's practice but it takes us far away from Simoeisios and the battle. Trees can also stand firm: when the Trojans had driven the Achaeans from the plain and were on the point of storming their camp, two Achaean warriors stood their ground in front of the high gate 'as when high-leafing oak trees which day after day resist the wind and the rain are held firm by their roots thick and long'.[50] The oak was not chosen to satisfy the metre; it was the most deep-rooted of trees.

Homer also turns to the forest to sharpen attention on the noise of battle. The clash of arms is compared to a forest buffeted by the wind: 'As when the east and south winds vie with one another to strike the deep forest in the mountain glens, the oak and the ash and the smooth-barked cornel tree. Their tapering branches clash together with a fearsome noise and there is the crashing of breaking branches.'[51] The sound of oxhide and bronze being smitten was like 'the ringing sound of men felling trees in the mountain glen, and the sound travels far'.[52]

More striking are Homer's forest-fire similes: 'The noise of battle was like that of a fire blazing in mountain glens when it rises to burn up the forest, nor is the sound of wind so great among the high-leafing oaks when it roars and rages loudest.'[53] Few acts of nature strike terror like forest fires even today when we are so much better equipped to deal with them, and it is entirely appropriate that the image should be used for Achilles, the greatest warrior of them all: 'As rages a devouring fire through the deep hollows of a parched mountain and the deep forest burns, and the wind drives it and wheels it around, so stormed he over the whole field of battle with his spear, like a god.'[54] Floods have something of the ruthlessness of the forest fire. When Ajax charges into battle he carries all before him 'as when a flooding river swollen in the mountains by the rain of

Zeus comes down over the plain and carries with it many leafless oaks and many pines, and pours a mass of flotsam into the sea'.[55]

In one of his battle similes Homer introduces a peaceful scene which is strangely inappropriate. The battle has raged all day: 'As long as it was morning and the day divine was rising, so long did the weapons of both sides strike and the people fell, but at the time when a woodcutter has prepared his food in the mountain glen, his hands wearied with the cutting down of tall trees, when weariness comes over his soul and he is seized with a longing for sweet food . . . then did the Danaans by their valour break through the serried ranks.'[56] This comes as a shock for we have been led to expect that the fighting men, like the woodcutter, would be weary and hungry by the evening and break off the battle, but the realism of this glimpse of the woodsman's life obscures the weakness of the simile.

The detailed description of the gathering of wood for the funeral pyre of Patroclus is also very close to nature.[57] Agamemnon calls for men from all the camp huts to collect wood and puts Meriones in charge. They go out with mules and well-woven ropes to bundle the logs. They climb Mt. Ida, 'going up, down, and along' as on a zigzag path, until they come to the shoulder of the mountain and there they cut oaks. We cannot be certain that Homer chose his language carefully here, but oaks were among the several species that grew well on Mt. Ida and oak, the strongest burner among woods, was particularly appropriate for cremation. It may also be significant that they go no further than the shoulder of the mountain; had they proceeded further towards the summit conifers would have been dominant. The men load the mules, presumably with a roped bundle of logs on each side, and carry some themselves. The mules make their way down to the plain 'cutting up the earth with their feet as they make their way through the thick undergrowth'. The mules stamp firmly to maintain their balance over rough ground, and they are eager to get back.

When assessing Homer's familiarity with trees and their usage we should allow him a poet's licence when he approaches catalogues of three or more trees. In describing Calypso's home he surrounded it with 'alders and poplars and sweet-scented cypress',[58] but when she takes him to the end of the island 'where the trees grow tall' there are 'alders and poplars and heaven-high firs'.[59] Poplars and alders both like damp places and are commonly found accompanying mountain streams down their valley, but neither cypress nor fir is a natural companion. It has been suggested that Homer envisages alder and poplar in a valley and fir on the hillside above: there were no such subtleties in his mind. Fir was introduced because Homer knew that firs provided the best ship-timber and that is what Odysseus would want. Nor should any weight be attached to the conjunction of oak, aspen (*acherois*), and pine as trees whose fall is likened to that of heroes in battle.[60] Later poets, Greek and Latin, were only too glad to follow Homer's precedent and lists tended to get longer and more incongruous.

The listing together of trees which would not normally be associated in nature should not be taken as evidence that Homer didn't understand the habits and usage of the different trees he mentions. He knew that plane trees tend to be found near springs and that alder and poplar are fond of water.[61] He knew that fir trees grow at high altitudes and are the tallest of trees; other trees grow high but only the fir grows heaven-high.[62] The comparison of the quick-moving hands of a serving maiden spinning to the quivering leaves of a poplar is imaginative and not likely to be drawn from a common store.[63] And in Homer's world, unlike Hesiod's, trees are not only useful raw material. When wounded Sarpedon was carried from the battlefield by his friends they set him beneath 'an oak tree of rare beauty',[64] and it was a beautiful plane tree under which the Achaeans were about to sacrifice Agamemnon's daughter Iphigenia before they sailed to Troy.[65]

The range of trees in the two epics is fairly wide and the commonest is the oak. A scholiast commenting on the use of the word *drytomos*, literally a cutter of oaks, when no specific reference to oaks was intended, says that there was once a time when all trees were called oaks.[66] This is probably no more than a guess, but it is botanically probable that in most parts of central, southern, and western Greece the oak was in our period the most widely distributed of trees up to a height of *c*.800 metres. There is at least enough positive evidence to show that oak was the dominant species in Messenia during the Bronze Age, and the usages attributed by Homer are appropriate. As a strong wood it is used for a threshold in the palace of Odysseus.[67]

Eumaeus the swine-herd of Odysseus used cleft oak for fencing round the palace piggeries, a form of fencing that is still common.[68] Oak leaves are fed to the cattle of the sun, though, according to later judges, they might have preferred elm or poplar.[69] But most of the references to the oak are in similes and in landscape. It is the tree from which Zeus speaks at Dodona.[70] On Achilles' shield it was under an oak that heralds were preparing the feast while the king was watching the harvest on his demesne;[71] it was under an oak that the wounded Sarpedon was rested; high-leafing oaks and tall pines and quarried stone enclosed the courtyard of the Cyclops.[72]

The spear of Achilles in Homer was made of ash from Mt. Pelion.[73] The stock epithet applied to both Homer's words for spear, *dory* and *enchos*, is ashen, *meilinos*, and the spear is often simply 'the ash'. The wood (with cornel-wood) is especially suitable for the spear because it is strong, but flexible and withstands the shock of impact: that is why it is still often used for oars, hockey sticks, and cricket bats. But the use of ash (as well as oak) for a threshold in Odysseus' palace is also appropriate because of its strength.[74] Homer's references to elms are not very revealing. When Achilles has to struggle against the river Scamander and is in danger of being swept away 'he seized with his hands an elm tree, tall and well-grown, and the tree up-rooted tore away all the bank and checked the fair waters with its thick branches and stretched across the river himself, falling all within him'.[75] In another passage the use of elm is even less distinctive. When Andromache's father was slain by Achilles his body was spared and a mound was raised over it as a memorial, 'and round it the mountain nymphs planted elms'.[76]

We should have expected cypress here, but we do not know how early the cypress was associated with death and mourning. Homer mentions it only twice. It grows on Calypso's isle where its sweet scent makes it appropriate, but it is also used for the doorposts in Odysseus's palace,[77] where it is justified by its strength.[78] The poplar is nearly always associated with water. In the island of the Phaeacians there is a grove of poplars with a spring in it, near the city, where the king has an orchard:[79] in Ithaca there is a spring outside the city where the people come to draw water and 'round it was a grove of water-nourished poplars'.[80] But in two similes already noticed we come closer to the poplar. In one Homer notes the quivering leaf, in the other he points to the usefulness of the wood for bending and so for making the felloes of a chariot wheel.[81]

Olive-wood is used in Homer where we should expect it. The form of the tree rarely provides long lengths, but it is a hard wood and wears well. Its commonest use was in tool-handles and so the great double-headed axe given by Calypso to Odysseus had 'a handle of olive-wood of great beauty, fitting well in the socket'.[82] Peisander's axe-head also had an olive-wood handle, described as long and well-finished.[83] Olive was also an appropriate wood for the giant club of the Cyclops, though to provide the size implied would have required a whole tree, for in length it was 'like the mast of a twenty-oared ship, and such also was its thickness'.[84] Odysseus cut off a length of a fathom (c.6 ft.). The cornel tree, which was regarded by Xenophon and many others as superior to ash for spears, is mentioned only once in the *Iliad*, in company with oak and ash, and it is described as 'smooth-barked',[85] a reasonable description of a tree that has a tall, thin trunk. The single reference in the *Odyssey* couples its fruit with the acorn as good for pigs.[86]

Among evergreens fir (*elate*) is the most prominent in both *Iliad* and *Odyssey*. Theophrastus at the end of the fourth century BC gives pride of place to the fir among ship-timbers and for general construction.[87] It is also, he claims, the best wood for making oars.[88] In Homer firs were among the trees shown by Calypso to Odysseus for his boat-building. Fir is presumably used for the mast of his boat, as it is for the mast in the ship prepared for the voyage home of Telemachus after his visit to Menelaus in Sparta.[89] And just as a spear in Homer is often called an ash, so fir, without qualification, is used for oars.[90] The fir is also used in general construction. The palace of Odysseus has beams of fir and high columns, like the megaron in the palace of Nestor at Pylos.[91] The Myrmidons had cut beams of fir to make a temporary home for Achilles before Troy and had roofed it with a soft thatch cut in the meadow (presumably the beams were for the ceiling and not for the wall) and they made a great court with stakes closely set; 'and the door was barred by a single bolt of fir; it took three men of the Achaeans to drive home that great bar, and draw it back; but Achilles could drive it home alone'.[92]

The pine is strangely inconspicuous in Homer. In a simile in the *Iliad* which is repeated *pitys* is cut down in the mountains to provide ship-timbers,[93] and in the *Odyssey* the tall *pitys* is used with oak and stone to form a court for the Cyclops by his cave.[94] *Peuke* occurs twice, but only in the *Iliad*. It is carried down in large numbers with oak by the mountain torrent in flood and a stump on the plain is the relic either of an oak or a pine.[95] It is unclear in Homer, as it is in later writers, whether the two words *pitys* and *peuke* represented two different species of pine or the same tree. Box (*pyxos, pyxinos*) is mentioned only once, for a yoke used by mules.[96] There is no reference in Homer to a growing cedar, but in Priam's palace in Troy there was a chamber of cedar-wood where fine dresses were kept,[97] and Calypso burns logs of cedar on her fire.[98] In both cases it is the scent of the wood that is significant. With cedar Calypso also burns thyine-wood and if this wood, as seems likely, is to be identified with Theophrastus' *thyon* and Roman *citrus* (*Callitris quadrivalvis*), its home is in north Africa and it too is an aromatic wood.[99] The absence of beech from the two epics, whether as tree or wood, is not surprising, for beech is not found in Greece south of Thessaly; it is only rarely mentioned in the mainstream of Greek literature.

Odysseus' boat-building introduces us to the shipwright's tools. Calypso first gives him 'a great axe of bronze, sharp-edged on both sides, well-fitted to his hand' and 'an adze that would give a good finish'. He cut down twenty trees, 'axed them with his bronze axe, and finished them cunningly making them straight by the line'.[100] The intermediate stage between felling the tree and smoothing the surface of the boards with the adze is done with the axe. The tree-trunk would first be squared and then split with the help of wedges. No mention is made of a saw and it is doubtful whether saws were used in the Bronze Age or early archaic period for boat-building. It was a more important tool for the furniture maker. When the timbers were cut they had to be joined together. Calypso then gave Odysseus a drill, *teretra*, with which holes could be bored for the dowels, *gomphoi*.[101]

In the *Iliad* and *Odyssey* the woodworker occupies an important place in society. The craftsman who works with timbers, *tektona douron*, is ranked with the seer, the doctor, and the singer of songs,[102] and the woodcutter is no witless labourer. Nestor, in briefing his son for the chariot race in the funeral games of Patroclus, tells him that he must use his head and not simply rely on his horses: 'It is by cunning rather than strength that the woodcutter is successful, and by cunning that the helmsman on the wine-dark sea steers his swift ship, when it is buffeted by the wind.'[103]

It remains to consider briefly whether any significant contribution is made to any of the main Homeric problems by a study of the references to trees and timber in the *Iliad* and *Odyssey*. Jaroslav Levy, in an article published in 1961, argued that the evidence of tree names suggested different environments and that the *Odyssey* was substantially later than the *Iliad*.[104] The trees concerned are *pitys* and *peuke*, and *phegos*. It is generally thought that in Theophrastus *peuke* refers to the mountain pine, and *pitys* to the coastal pine. Levy's case is that in the *Iliad pitys* is a mountain pine, cut for ship-timber, whereas *peuke* is a lowland pine. In the Homeric hymns and Hesiod *pitys* does not occur, and *peuke* is the only word used for pine. Levy infers that the *Odyssey* was roughly contemporary with the Homeric hymns. But this does not follow from the evidence, for in the *Iliad peuke* is a tree which, with oaks, is carried down by the flooding mountain torrents, and therefore grows high up, though a stump on the plain may be either a *peuke* or an oak.[105] In the *Odyssey*, however, *peuke* does not occur at all: *pitys* is mentioned only once, as one of the materials used to form a court round the cave of the Cyclops.[106] Levy regards this as sufficient reason for dismissing the line as a later interpolation, but this is positively reckless. The references to *pitys* and *peuke* in both poems are much too few and imprecise to support any conclusion about the dates of the two poems or their authorship.

The argument from the use of *phegos* is stronger. Levy translates the word as chestnut, and since it is used in the *Iliad* and not in the *Odyssey* he infers that the *Iliad* was composed in chestnut country, whereas chestnuts did not grow where the *Odyssey* was composed. The identification, however, of the *phegos* with the chestnut must be rejected. It is based on a passage in Theophrastus in which he says that the fruit of the *phegos* was particularly sweet, but in this passage Theophrastus is discussing the different kinds of oak.[107] It is extremely unlikely that Theophrastus would have included *phegos* among the oaks if the

name was not given to an oak in his day. Nor do the references
to *phegos* in the *Iliad* suit the chestnut as well as the oak. The
phegos under which the wounded Sarpedon is rested is 'very
beautiful', a description which suits the oak much better than
the chestnut.[108] The adjective *pheginos* is applied to an axle for
which again oak would be more suitable.[109]

There remains the question whether the differences between
the two poems are statistically significant. In the *Iliad phegos* is
mentioned six times, *pheginos* once; *drys*, the more general word
for oak, occurs nine times, *dryinos* once. In the *Odyssey drys* is
mentioned four times, *dryinos* once; neither *phegos* nor *pheginos* is
mentioned at all. The figures are sufficient to raise doubts about
a single authorship, but they are too few to be decisive. They
may add a little ammunition to those who do not believe in a
common authorship, but they do not help us to distinguish
Mycenaean from archaic in the poem.

Similarly the reference to citrus-wood (Homer's *thyon*) in
the *Odyssey* is a little surprising.[110] Some scholars may doubt
whether the Greeks either in the Mycenaean period or in the
eighth century, when it is widely thought that the *Iliad* was
composed, could have been familiar with a wood which, so far as
we know, was confined to north Africa. There is, however,
nothing in Homer's references to trees and timber in the two
epics that would be demonstrably out of place in either the
Mycenaean period or the eighth and seventh centuries. There
may be an exception in the poplar simile in the *Iliad* already
mentioned (p. 107). Poplar, a wood that is easily bent, might be
chosen for the felloe of a wheel at either date, but does the Bronze
Age chariot-maker go out to choose his own tree? The linear
tablets show that an inventory of chariots was kept by the palace
officials and the inference is that they were also made on palace
premises. If the relevant tablet is correctly translated, woodcutters are required to bring saplings to the workshop of the
Pylos palace.[111] The style seems barely compatible with individual craftsmen going out into the country to choose their own
tree. In the archaic period when Greek states no longer had
chariot forces and the demand for chariots was limited to the
racing chariot, such individual craftsmanship is more appropriate. It is perhaps significant that the axe in this passage is
made of iron, whereas swords and spearheads are normally of

bronze in Homer. There is a similar anachronism in the *Odyssey*, also in a simile. In the gruesome description of the gouging out of the eye of the Cyclops the hissing of the eye as the stake is thrust in is compared to the sound made 'when a smith dips a great axe or adze in water to temper it, for that is how iron gains its strength'.[112] This is almost certainly a practice unknown in the Bronze Age palaces.

But there was probably little change in the woodsman's craft in the Dark Ages that followed the collapse of Mycenaean culture. With the breakdown of palace organisation there will have been considerably less demand for sophisticated furniture and high-class joinery, but the properties of the various woods had been learnt long before the palaces were destroyed and would not be forgotten. With the decline in the use of stone for building, timber gained in importance, and in the temples of the eighth, seventh, and early sixth centuries BC the need of timber for doors, columns, and roofs maintained the status of the carpenter.

5

FORESTS AND FLEETS

In 1926 a Harvard historian, R. G. Albion, published a volume
on the British navy. Under the title *Forests and sea power* he
examined not the strategy, tactics, and leadership that lay
behind the development of British naval supremacy, but the
spreading oaks of southern England, the white pine of Maine
and New Hampshire, and the prosaic record of timber stocks in
the royal dockyards. He did not strain his evidence to extract
sensational conclusions: Nelson and not the timber merchants
remained primarily responsible for the victory of Trafalgar. But
his study illuminated certain phases of British naval history. He
showed, for instance, that one of the main reasons for the failure
of the British fleets in the War of American Independence was
the weakness of the masts, which resulted from a failure to
anticipate the cutting-off of the supplies of white pine from New
England on which the navy had come to rely. The difficulties
caused by the French Continental blockade in the Napoleonic
War were accentuated by a short-sighted timber-purchasing
policy which had failed to build up adequate stocks of the right
timber for essential repairs. British foreign policy in the Baltic
was largely dictated by the urgent need to control or at least
have access to the large conifer forests of Sweden, Finland, and
Russia and the oak that came down the rivers from central
Europe to the Polish ports. The decisive part played by the
British navy in world history abundantly justified the study: it is
only surprising that such an approach had not been seriously
attempted before.

To translate the theme to the ancient world needs perhaps
more justification.[1] In reviewing the decisive phases of ancient
history we think more of the land than of the sea. The rivalries
between Egypt and the kingdoms of Mesopotamia were fought
out by the armies; the Persian empire was won by land and
remained land-centred; the Roman empire was built up and

maintained by the legions. But in the Mediterranean world the influence of sea power was rarely dormant and sometimes decisive. When the historian Thucydides was growing up, the focal point of the Greek-speaking world was the Athenian empire, which had changed a small city-state with only moderate natural resources into the richest and most powerful community in the Mediterranean. That empire was the fruit of naval power and when Thucydides prefaced his account of the great war between Athens and the Peloponnesian League (431-405 BC) with a compressed review of early Greek history, his main accent was on the growth of navies. He realised that the wealth and magnificence of Periclean Athens had been won by the Athenian triremes and he was practical enough to know that naval power depended on access to good shipbuilding timber. When the great armada which had sailed out of the Piraeus with such high hopes was destroyed at Syracuse in 413, Thucydides understood that it was not only a question of finding new crews but also of getting new supplies of ship-timber when Athens no longer had the power to impress potential suppliers.[2] Fleets depended on forests, and when much later Antony gave Cleopatra queen of Egypt a well-forested area of Cilicia it was not intended as a hunting-park or a status symbol; it was to provide timber for an Egyptian fleet.[3]

The Roman fleet was overshadowed by the legions, but in the first war against Carthage (264-241 BC) the Romans soon realised that the Carthaginians could not be driven from Sicily so long as they could be reinforced with men and materials from Africa. History might have run a very different course if Italy had not been well forested. During the imperial period even less is heard of Roman fleets; but the effective organisation of permanent fleets round the Mediterranean by Augustus made a significant contribution to the peace and prosperity of the early Empire. The firm suppression of piracy was the essential foundation for a free flow of trade between east and west.

Britain's wooden walls were largely, but by no means exclusively, built of oak and the quality of her warships was in some measure due to the strength of the oaks that matured slowly on the heavy soils of Kent, Sussex, and Hampshire. When the crisis of the Napoleonic Wars revealed acutely the increasing dependence of the navy on foreign supplies there was a brisk planting of acorns in the New Forest and in the Forest of Dean. In the ancient story oak has a much less massive role. It was used for their ships by the Veneti, a Gallic tribe living in Britanny, but strength in the Atlantic was more important than speed.[4] In naval warfare in the Mediterranean speed was the first essential. Speed requires lightness and oak is heavy.

There is ample evidence in Greek and Roman writers about shipbuilding timbers and there are no serious inconsistencies in the sources. The fullest and best statement comes from Theophrastus:

Fir (*elate*), mountain pine (*peuke*), and cedar (*kedros*) are the standard ship-timbers. Triremes and long ships (warships) are made of fir because it is light, while round ships (merchantmen) are made of pine because it does not decay. Some people, however, make their triremes of pine also, because they have no adequate supply of fir, while in Syria and Phoenicia they use cedar, because they are short of pine as well as fir. In Cyprus they use coastal pine (*pitys*) which grows in the island and seems to be of better quality than mountain pine (*peuke*). These woods are used for the main timbers, but for the trireme's keel oak is used because it has to stand up to the hauling . . . They make the cutwater and catheads, which require special strength, of ash, mulberry, or elm.[5]

That fir was normally the shipwright's first choice is confirmed from widely varying sources. Plato, in outlining the character of his ideal city, is anxious that there should be 'no good fir nor mountain pine, not much cypress, and little coastal pine which shipwrights have to use for the interior parts of merchant vessels, because this would encourage trade, the great corrupter'.[6] Alexander, on the Hydaspes, needing a fleet to carry his army down to the Indus, is glad to find a plentiful supply of fir, pine, and cedar.[7] In Virgil fir (*abies*) is accepted as a poetic name for a trireme.[8] Theophrastus is also right in drawing a distinction between warships, the commonest type of which in his day was the trireme, and merchantmen. Merchantmen had to stay at sea for long periods and strength was more important than speed. The effectiveness of triremes depended on speed and so they were lightly built, tended to hug the coast, and, whenever they could, the crews landed for the night. The primacy of fir is most decisively illustrated in the text of an alliance between Amyntas King of Macedon and the Chalcidians in the early fourth century BC: 'The Chalcidians may export pitch, all building-timbers, and all ship-timbers except firs unless their government requires them. The Chalcidian government may take out firs, provided that they report first to Amyntas and pay the prescribed dues.'[9]

The fir is a mountain tree, normally growing at or near the highest timber level, and rarely found below 800 metres. Quality depends largely on climate, temperature, and soil, and of the four varieties in the Mediterranean area *Abies alba*, the silver fir, which was limited to Italy and Sicily, and Macedon, had the highest reputation.[10] The pine grows at lower altitudes, is more widespread and diversified, but can be roughly divided into coastal and mountain pines. It was the mountain pine *Pinus laricio* in Italy and the west, and *Pinus nigra* in Greece and the eastern Mediterranean, that produced the stronger and bigger timbers and was most appreciated by shipbuilders. The main advantage of fir over pine was that it was lighter and, when grown in high forest conditions where the trees are closer together and compete for the light, produced longer lengths of straight timber. In such conditions the fir also sheds its lower branches earlier than the pine and is therefore more free from knots. This virtue in the fir made it particularly valuable for oars, whose strength was vital to the trireme.

This special importance of the oar is reflected in literary sources and inscriptions where oars are mentioned separately from general ship-timber.[11] When Perdiccas King of Macedon made an alliance with Athens he undertook not to export Macedonian oars to anyone but the Athenians.[12] The best wood for oars came from young trees for they were more flexible, and special care had to be taken in the shaping of the oar, as Theophrastus explains: 'The fir has many layers, like the onion (a picturesque way of describing annual growth-rings), for there is always a layer below the one that is visible; and that is why when they shave the wood to make oars they try to remove the layers one by one evenly. If they do this, the oar is strong; if they do not strip off the layers evenly the oar is weak.'[13] The regular listing of *kōpai adokimoi*, oars unfit for use, often because they were worm-eaten, in Athenian naval inventories of the fourth century BC shows how important it was to ensure that the trireme was not handicapped by weak oars which might snap at a critical moment.[14] But for the main timbers good pine was better than poor fir and if Aristophanes introduces two triremes of pine in his *Knights* Athens is unlikely to have had an all-fir fleet in the fifth century.[15]

Theophrastus does not include cypress among his ship-timbers, but where there were ample supplies it was more than adequate. When Alexander shortly before his death was contemplating an expedition against Arabia, he relied mainly on the shipbuilders of Cilicia, Cyprus, and Phoenicia, but he also used cypresses that had become acclimatised in Babylon.[16] Vegetius, writing in the late Roman Empire about military and naval organisation, included cypress with pine and fir as the best ship-timbers,[17] and it was used in the sixth century for the fleet of Theodoric (p. 152).

In Herodotus' day, when the importance of sea power was emphasised by the growth of the Athenian empire, people tended to look back to the almost mythical days of King Minos of Cretan Cnossus. Of Minoan history and culture they knew considerably less than we know today, but there remained a strong tradition, kept alive by place names and cult practices, that Minos King of Crete had once ruled the seas.[18] Excavation has disclosed the attractive culture of Bronze Age Crete—the magnificence of the palaces, the exquisite taste and craftsmanship of the pottery, and the wide ramifications of trade and overseas settlement. It would be reasonable, even without the support of tradition, to assume a considerable fleet, or fleets. There was certainly no lack of suitable timber (p. 99). Meanwhile, as the Mycenaean Greek states developed on the mainland, they too needed ships. It is now clear that at some time before *c.*1450 BC Greeks from the mainland had gained control of Cnossus, the most important palace centre, and from that base had probably destroyed Minoan power at least in the centre and east of the island. Greeks in the Peloponnese would have had no difficulty in finding sufficient fir and pine to build effective fleets.

The destruction of the Mycenaean centres of power on the mainland was followed by a recession in trade and a general impoverishment. Horizons were restricted and it was some three hundred years before the old sea routes were opened up again. The clearest sign of the revival was the great colonisation move-

ment which began in the middle of the eighth century BC and
took Greeks from the mainland to south Italy and Sicily in the
west, to the Black Sea and its approaches in the east, and in the
north to the peninsulas of Chalcidice and the coast of Thrace.
One of the most important results of colonisation was a great
increase in trade, which in turn called for warships to defend
merchantmen. According to Thucydides the first real sea battle
was fought between Corinth and her colony Corcyra in the
middle of the seventh century.

   Thucydides, however, makes it clear that there were no considerable Greek fleets before the Persian invasion. When Xerxes
assembled the forces of the Persian empire to crush Greece only
one state was able to contribute more than fifty ships to the
combined fleet. Of the 350 Greek ships which defeated the
Persian fleet at the decisive battle of Salamis in August 480 BC
Athens, according to Herodotus, provided 200.[19] It was this that
made Herodotus insist that the main credit for crushing Xerxes
should go to Athens. For if Athens had accepted Persian over-
tures and abandoned the struggle the Persians would have
controlled the sea and could have landed troops wherever they
wished. However bravely the Spartans fought, their allies would
inevitably have dispersed to defend their own cities. Before the
invasion the Athenian fleet had been of little consequence. The
small island of Aegina in the Saronic Gulf had been able to fight
with her on equal terms and Thucydides says that both the
Athenian and Aeginetan fleets were small and that most of their
ships were pentekonters.[20] Such indirect evidence as can be
gathered from Herodotus suggests that the total number of
Athenian warships did not exceed seventy.

   The explanation of the dramatic increase in numbers lies in
the decision of a popular Assembly meeting on the Pnyx at
Athens early in the year 482. According to the story accepted by
Herodotus and Aristotle, the main question at issue was the use
of a sudden access of unexpected silver from a particularly rich
strike in the silver-mining area of the Laurium peninsula.[21]
There were precedents in Greek states for the distribution of
such windfalls to the people and this may have been expected,
but Themistocles, who saw further into the future than his
contemporaries, managed to persuade the people to use the
money for a massive and urgent shipbuilding programme. The

vote may have been influenced by a recurrence of friction with
Aegina, but Themistocles had the much greater danger from the
east in mind. The eastern Greeks had revolted from Persia in 500
BC, and Athens and Eretria had sent ships to help them. After
initial successes the revolt disintegrated, Persian rule was
securely restored, and preparations were made to punish the
two mainland cities that had interfered. In 490 a comparatively
small Persian force sailed across the Aegean, sacked Eretria,
landed at Marathon, and expected Athens to surrender. The
Persians were decisively defeated on the plain of Marathon, but
it was certain that they would return with considerably larger
forces. The vote of the Athenian Assembly in 482 should be
regarded as one of the most important events in the history of
western civilisation.

Athenian orators of the fifth and fourth centuries never
allowed the Assembly to forget the glorious part that Athens
and particularly the Athenian fleet played in the liberation of
Greece, but not even an anecdote survives to throw light on the
practical steps taken to implement the decree of 482. The
building of at least 100 and possibly 200 triremes in two years
presented formidable problems to a state that had probably
never built more than ten triremes in a year before. How was the
labour, skilled and unskilled, recruited? Where were the ships
built? Where did the timber come from? The first two questions
are more easily answered than the third. There will have been a
considerable number of fishermen and others in the small ports
round the Attic coast who would have been familiar with the
general principles of boat-building, and slaves could have been
recruited as auxiliary labour. The main difficulty would be in
increasing the number of skilled men who could supervise the
building of a trireme. For this the Athenians must have cast their
net wider and called on experienced shipwrights from other
states, as Dionysius of Syracuse did in the early fourth century
when he decided to build a large fleet urgently.[22] Perhaps the
majority of the triremes were built on the long faintly sloping
sand-shore of Phaleron bay, which was the Athenian naval
headquarters before it was transferred to the Piraeus. There can
be little doubt that others were built in some of the small ports of
the Attic coast.

It is much more difficult to determine how the timber was

assembled. Theophrastus, emphasising that the number of areas which could supply good ship-timber was strictly limited, gives a list: 'in Europe Macedon, parts of Thrace, and south Italy; in Asia the territories of Sinope and Amisus (both on the south shore of the Black Sea), Mt. Olympus in Mysia, and Mt. Ida (in the Troad), where the supply was not extensive'.[23] He adds that Syria had cedar which was there used for triremes, implying that it would not be regarded elsewhere as ship-timber. From the late fifth century at least, and throughout the fourth century, there is ample evidence that Athens relied primarily on Macedon for her ship-timber; the association probably began much earlier. The first Pisistratus in his second exile from Athens (556–546 BC) had lived in Macedon and had learnt to appreciate the silver of Mt. Pangaeus. When his son Hippias was driven out of Athens and failed to secure the support of Sparta he was invited to settle in Macedon,[24] which implies a family friendship with the Macedonian king, who controlled the export of timber. According to Herodotus, Alexander, son of the king of Macedon, had already been formally recognised as *proxenos* and benefactor of Athens,[25] a title based on benefits received or hoped for, before the Persian invasion; and though he accompanied Xerxes, Herodotus emphasises that Alexander did everything in his power to help Athens. It is tempting to accept the suggestion by M. B. Wallace that the service for which Alexander was publicly honoured was the supply of timber for the Athenian fleet which fought at the battle of Salamis.[26] This would be a conveniently simple solution, but there are difficulties.

When Darius returned from his expedition against the Scythians he left a Persian force under a senior commander to extend Persian control along the north coast of the Aegean, and before the end of the sixth century the king of Macedon had submitted without a fight. Shortly afterwards a Greek tyrant, Histiaeus, who had led a Milesian contingent to join Darius on his Scythian expedition, had been allowed as a reward to establish a settlement at Myrcinus on the river Strymon. It was not long before the Persian army commander urged Darius to recall his friend because 'there was abundant ship-timber and a wealth of oars as well as silver-mines in the area'.[27]

The sensational Athenian victory at Marathon might have

encouraged the Macedonians to reconsider their relations with Persia, but when it was widely known that the Persians were raising a massive imperial levy to crush Greece it is very doubtful whether the Macedonian king or his son would have risked provoking Persia. It is even more unlikely that the Persian commander who had insisted on the expulsion of a Greek adventurer would have tolerated the sending of ship-timber to Athens. The urgent cutting of timber for some 200 triremes would have been a very conspicuous operation and in 482–480 BC Persians were busy building up supplies along the invasion route and digging a canal through the Athos promontory. The shipping of so much timber to Athens could not have been unnoticed. Macedon should be ruled out. For the same reason Athens could not have imported timber from Thrace nor from Asia Minor, which were also under Persian control: of the areas listed by Theophrastus only south Italy remains.

It must have been well known in Greece from their contacts with colonies in Italy that the forests of Calabria in south Italy were rich in timber. Thucydides makes Alcibiades, when he deserted the Athenian fleet at Syracuse and went to Sparta, claim that it was the intention of Athens, when she had defeated Syracuse, to build more ships intensively in the west, 'because Italy had an abundance of timber'. With a vastly enlarged fleet the Athenians would return to Greece and so bring the war against Sparta and the Peloponnesians to a decisive end.[28] In 408/7 the commissioners of Eleusis included in their inventory of stock thirty large timbers from Thurii, a port from which timber from the Sila forest was exported.[29] There is no earlier evidence of an Athenian timber trade with Italy, but from the fragmentary nature of our sources one could not expect it. There are, however, signs that Themistocles, who was responsible for the creation of the new fleet, was interested in the west.

Before the battle of Salamis, when there was a serious danger that the commanders of the Peloponnesian contingents would withdraw their ships to be nearer their army, Themistocles threatened to take the Athenians to Siris in the south of Italy if the Peloponnesians sailed away.[30] There are other hints that he was interested in the west. His two eldest daughters were called Sybaris and Italia, and the island of Corcyra, which is strategically placed on the route to Italy and Sicily, was under some obligation to him.[31] Themistocles, whose foresight and powers of analysis Thucydides so much admired, could well have thought through the implications of his policy and made plans for getting the timber for his new fleet from the west. The difficulties of this solution lie rather in the practical problem of felling the trees, carrying them down by river to the coast, bringing them to Phalerum and other Attic shipbuilding centres, and converting the timber into triremes within the short space of two years.

The only other alternative was to rely on the mountain forests on the borders of Attica, supplemented perhaps from the mountains of Euboea. It will be argued later that sufficient fir, pine, and oak could have been found from these sources (p. 189), but the quality of the wood was considerably poorer, and a large wagon-building programme would have been an essential preliminary if large quantities of heavy timber had to be brought from Mt. Parnes or Mt. Cithaeron to the coast. The fact that we have no allusion in Greek literature to the source of the timber lends a little support against the use of home timber. Had Mt. Parnes made a major contribution to the victory of Salamis we should probably have found an echo somewhere. On balance it is easier to believe that Italian timber was used, possibly supplemented from Euboea. The shortage of time available is not a decisive objection. Pliny records that the Romans in their first war against Carthage built a fleet of 120 ships in sixty days and, in a later year, 220 ships in forty-five days.[32]

Wherever the timber was cut during these two years very little of it can have been properly seasoned, though the Greeks and Romans were fully aware of the importance of not using unseasoned wood for shipbuilding. When in the Roman civil war which broke out in 49 BC Caesar needed a fleet to match the defenders of Massilia, he had twelve ships built at Arles and had to use them at once. In battle his men 'were handicapped because their ships were slow and heavy; for they had been made quickly from timber that was still humid and so lacked the normal speed of war ships'.[33] When Scipio built a new fleet in 205 BC to carry the war against Carthage and Hannibal over to Africa, he drew his new ships out of the water to dry over the winter.[34] Vegetius adds a warning: 'When ships which have been built with green timber sweat out their moisture they contract and develop cracks; there is nothing more dangerous to sailors.'[35] But if the greenness of the timber made the Greek ships heavier and slower this was not a serious handicap: in the narrow waters of Salamis there was little room for manœuvre and strength was more important than speed.

The achievements of the new fleet in 480 and 479 in the battles of Salamis and Mycale heightened Athenian ambitions and when the Ionians invited Athens to lead an alliance of Greek states to protect the Greek world from the threat of Persia, the Athenians, led by Aristides, accepted. In her new role Athens had to maintain a strong fleet and access to good timber remained essential. Even if little or no timber had been taken from Attica in the crisis of 482–480, local supplies could not stand a continuous drain, and the quality of the timber was poor. In the late fifth and throughout the fourth century Athens depended heavily on Macedon,[36] but it is uncertain how soon the relationship was established. The first explicit evidence comes from the fragmentary record of the treaty referred to above between the Macedonian king Perdiccas and the Athenians, which may be dated between 440 and 413.[37] A little later, in 411, we find Andocides, an exiled Athenian aristocrat, trying to pave the way for his return to grace by using the friendship of his family with the Macedonian royal family to secure oars which he sold at cost price to the Athenian fleet based at Samos.[38]

The vital factor governing Macedonian supplies was the personal attitude of the king, for Macedonian timber was a royal monopoly. It has been suggested above that it was the friendship of the Pisistratids with the Macedonian royal family that led to the Athenian import of Macedonian timber, and that the timber relationship was a factor in the public honouring at Athens of the king's son Alexander before the Persian invasion (p. 123). But since the Macedonian royal family was almost as notorious as the Persian for palace intrigues and attempted coups, it was natural that Athens should think of alternative sources of supply. To the east of Macedon were the well-forested mountains of Thrace, a country which in the first half of the fifth century was divided between a number of independent warlike tribes. In the west of Thrace the rich island of Thasos had extended her influence to the mainland and was exploiting the economic resources of the Strymon valley. After the withdrawal of the Persians, the Athenians also developed an interest in this area and competition in Thrace led to friction and eventually war with Thasos.[39] While the Athenian fleet was still besieging the city of Thasos, an attempt was made by Athens to establish a colony at a strategic centre where several trade routes met some three kilometres up river from the coast. The colony was established but the settlers, moving inland, were caught by an army of Thracian tribesmen and virtually annihilated.[40] A second attempt, in 437/6, was more successful and the site, formerly called Nine Ways, was renamed Amphipolis. But thirteen years later, during the great Peloponnesian War, a Spartan general, who had brought a small force to support a revolt from Athens by the cities of Chalcidice, marched swiftly on Amphipolis and seized the town before its defence was effectively organised (424).[41]

The seriousness of the loss of Amphipolis is emphasised by Thucydides: 'the city was useful to Athens for the ship-timber that it sent and the silver revenue',[42] but in spite of repeated attempts, Athens was never able to regain control of the area. The timber from Amphipolis in its last years had been particularly valuable to Athens because relations with the Macedonian king had broken down. At some time before 432, possibly when Amphipolis was established, the Athenians had made a formal alliance with King Perdiccas, but in circumstances that are not recorded they had later supported the king's brother in his bid for the throne.[43] The natural reaction of Perdiccas was to stir up trouble for Athens among the Greek cities of Chalcidice: from 432 he regarded the Athenians as enemies. It was very fortunate for Athens that shortly after the fall of Amphipolis it suited the interests of Perdiccas to renew his alliance with Athens.[44] He had hoped to use the Spartan force in Chalcidice against western tribes pressing on his border, but the partnership had proved thoroughly unsatisfactory.

Macedonian supplies were temporarily reassured, but a much more serious crisis faced Athens when the great expeditionary force that had been sent out to crush Syracuse and bring Sicily under Athenian control was destroyed in 413. Thucydides gives a vivid pen picture of the desperate situation at Athens— the lack of men, money, ships, and timber; 'but they must not surrender, they must build a fleet, and get the timber wherever they could'.[45] The situation, however, was now more critical than in 482. Such timber as remained on Parnes, Cithaeron, and Pentelicus was no longer accessible, for the Spartans had occupied Decelea and forced the Athenians of the countryside to take refuge in the city. The mountains of Euboea, though their fir was of poorer quality, would have been very useful in the emergency, but in 411 the island revolted from Athens. During the blockade of Syracuse the Athenians had made arrangements to collect timber stockpiled near Caulonia, in Calabria, but Syracusan raiders had burnt it;[46] they could now have bought ship-timber from the same source in south Italy, but merchant-men loaded with timber would have been very vulnerable to interception by Spartan or Corinthian triremes. Thessaly may have afforded some relief, for through most of the fifth century the Thessalians had been formally allies of Athens; Pelion and Ossa were well-wooded mountains whose timber could have been shipped from Pagasae.

The acute difficulty of timber supply is reflected in Xeno-phon's account of the last phase of the Peloponnesian War. The destruction of the Athenian fleet at Syracuse encouraged Sparta to send a fleet to the east side of the Aegean to support Athenian allies who could be persuaded to revolt. To check the disintegra-tion of her empire the Athenians needed to build as many ships as possible as soon as possible; she was only, however, able to send very small detachments until 406. It is surprising, therefore, that in 406, when the main Athenian fleet in eastern waters was blockaded in Mytilene, a new fleet of no less than 110 triremes set out from the Piraeus, only thirty days after the news reached Athens. The explanation of this sensational effort may be found in an Athenian decree honouring Archelaus, who had succeeded Perdiccas on the Macedonian throne. Nearly half of each line of the inscription is missing, but key words and phrases provide an adequate base for a reasonable reconstruction of the general sense.[47] The particular service for which Archelaus is being honoured seems to have been that he allowed Athenian ship-wrights to proceed to Macedon to build ships with timber that would normally have been shipped to Athens. Merchantmen under sail with heavy timber cargoes would have been more vul-nerable to interception by an enemy than oar-powered triremes.

When the new Athenian fleet accepted battle with the Spartan fleet by the Arginusae islands off the coast of Lesbos, the Athenians, who normally adopted offensive tactics, drew up their ships in a defensive formation. It is tempting to think that this was partly because the timber had not been properly seasoned; the use of green timber would have made the ships heavier and slower. Xenophon, however, merely says that the Athenians were the poorer sailors, and this was probably the main reason.[48] The crews were largely recruited from slaves who were promised freedom: the majority must have been very inexperienced. The Athenians, however, won the battle; the Spartan crews had, in fact, little more experience than the Athenians, and the Spartan commander was too careless of his own life: he fell overboard when his ship rammed an enemy.

The great victory of the Athenian fleet was almost immediately nullified by an act of emotional madness fed by political feuds. It was alleged that survivors from some Athenian triremes that had sunk could have been rescued: the generals were tried together by an angry Assembly and those who had returned to Athens were put to death. As a result the Athenian fleet lost confidence, weak generals were elected, and within two years the Athenian fleet had been destroyed at Aegospotami, by the carelessness, and possibly in one case the corruption, of the commanders. Athens was starved into surrender and was left by the peace terms with only twelve triremes to protect her shores.

While there is good evidence to show that during the Peloponnesian War Athens depended mainly on Macedon for her ship-timber, the sources of the timber for the Peloponnesian fleets are not recorded. Their ineffectiveness, however, was not due to difficulties of getting timber. The strength of the Peloponnesian League lay in the army and there was no deliberate attempt to meet the Athenians at sea until the major part of the Athenian fleet had been destroyed at Syracuse. But ships were needed by the League to protect expeditionary forces crossing the Corinthian Gulf and were once used to bring help to an Athenian ally in revolt. Thucydides, in his review of the resources of both sides at the beginning of the war, gives a list of the Spartan allies who provided ships for the League fleet: Corinth, Megara, Sicyon, Pellene, Elis in the Peloponnese, and from the north-west two Corinthian colonies, Ambracia and Leucas.[49] Of these the only

state which had maintained a strong fleet was Corinth, where
there was a long shipbuilding tradition. In peace time Corinth,
who by the fifth century can have had little good timber in her
own restricted territory, could have drawn supplies either from
the Peloponnese or from her colonies on the north-west coast.[50]*
When war broke out the latter source became much less accessible, because an Athenian squadron stationed at Naupactus
controlled the entry to the Corinthian Gulf. But there were
probably ample supplies of fir and pine on the mountains that
rise up from the narrow coastal Achaean plain and on Mt.
Cyllene in the north of Arcadia. The same mountains could also
meet the needs of Sicyon and Pellene; Elis could draw on the
forests of Arcadia.

There was, however, a serious timber crisis when, after the
Athenian disaster at Syracuse, the war was transferred to the
east side of the Aegean, where Sparta anticipated widespread
support from discontented Athenian allies. For the first year she
made a little progress, but in 410 her fleet was surprised off
Cyzicus and almost completely destroyed, as the report to
Sparta admitted: 'Our ships are lost; Mindarus is gone; the men
are starving; we don't know what to do.'[51] The Spartans were
saved by Pharnabazus, the Persian satrap of the Hellespontine
region, who was relying on Sparta to help him recover the Greek
cities in his satrapy that had become part of the Athenian
empire. He provided immediate relief for the survivors and told
the ship captains and the commanders of city contingents to
replace the ships that they had lost by building new ones at
Antandros with timber from Mt. Ida.[52] For the remaining years
of the war Sparta relied mainly on ships from Rhodes and other
states which had revolted from Athens, or on new ships built
at Ephesus.

For a generation after the end of the Peloponnesian War there
was no major new power in the Aegean. There were, however,
important developments in the west where, after a period of
unrest, Dionysius seized power at Syracuse. The Carthaginians,
who had been decisively defeated when they invaded Sicily at
the time of Xerxes' invasion of Greece, had launched another
attempt to establish Phoenician supremacy in 410. They had
quickly won control of the west and had, after a long siege,
captured Acragas, the second strongest city of the island.

Dionysius made it his first objective to build up the armed forces of Syracuse in order to turn the tide of Carthaginian aggression. He brought in shipwrights from Greece and organised the cutting of timber in two areas. Half his men were sent to nearby Mt. Etna, 'which in those days was still full of excellent fir and pine', and half to south Italy.[53] When he had accumulated a sufficient stock of timber he built, according to Diodorus, more than 200 ships. With these added to the 110 ships he already possessed Dionysius had the largest fleet in the Mediterranean: without it Sicily might have been completely lost to the Greeks.

In the Aegean no single navy was dominant, but when Sparta had proved incapable of taking over the role of Athens, and had lost the support of Corinth and Thebes, her strongest allies in the Peloponnesian War, Athens was able gradually to build up her fleet again and to appeal once more to fifth-century allegiances. Though she had lost the financial resources of a tributary empire, her Piraeus was still the largest and best-organised port in the Aegean and attracted more trade than any other; there is no evidence that she lacked the money to buy enough timber for her naval programmes. The detailed inventories of her naval stock that survive show that she was not short of ships. Although there is no record from the fourth century of any Athenian fleet with more than 100 ships in action, there were 283 triremes listed in the inventory of 357/6.[54] This number needs to be qualified, because there was not sufficient equipment to put so many ships to sea at once. The full complement of a ship included 200 oars, 170 for the three banks of rowers and thirty spares; two large steering oars; a mast with yard-arm and two stays to support it; three poles and three ladders. In 357/6 there were oars for 233 triremes, steering oars for 234, ladders for 232, and 185 main masts. But in none of the surviving inventories is the number of ships that could be fully equipped less than 150 and the number increased after the middle of the century. Athens was not troubled by a shortage of ship-timber; it was more difficult to find the money to finance the crews. When, however, relations with Macedon were strained or broken, as they were during the reigns of Philip and his son Alexander, different suppliers had to be found. A speaker in the Athenian Assembly during the early stages of Alexander's eastern campaign said that it was difficult to get timber for the fleet and it had to come from a long distance (possibly south Italy).[55]

It may seem strange that Macedon, whose ship-timber was unrivalled in the Aegean world, should have no strong fleet herself. But within her own territories she was self-sufficient and she concentrated her resources on the army, which was continuously needed to protect her vulnerable frontiers. When Alexander led his expedition from Europe into Asia he had no Macedonian ships, and had to rely on a fleet composed of small contingents from various Greek states. This fleet was useful to him in his siege of Miletus, but when Ionia and Lydia had been won and he was ready to move away from the coast, he took the bold risk of disbanding his fleet. He was not fully confident of the Greeks' loyalty, and his fleet was too small if the Persian fleet, provided mainly by the Phoenicians, brought it to battle. The Persian fleet did in fact attempt a counter-offensive and at first had some important successes, but at the critical point they lost the very able Greek mercenary who shared the command and the news from the east was very discouraging. Alexander's gamble succeeded brilliantly, for he was able to eliminate the Persian fleet by taking their naval bases with his army. After his victory at Issus most of the Phoenician cities submitted, and during the siege of Tyre Cypriote kings also brought their ships to help him.[56]

Alexander was not blind to the usefulness of a fleet. After the defeat of the Indian prince Porus by the Hydaspes he had a fleet built from the fir, pine, and cedar of neighbouring mountains.[57] This fleet he used later to transport most of his army down to the Indus and the sea and Nearchus took it back to Babylon on a voyage of coastal exploration. Alexander made plans for building a fleet from the forests of Hyrcania to explore the Caspian Sea, and at the end of his life he was planning the annexation of Arabia and organising the building of a larger fleet. Ships were to be built by the skilled shipwrights of Cyprus, Phoenicia, and Cilicia and in Babylon, which had always been very timber-poor, he used the cypresses from parks and groves.[58] In this large shipbuilding programme Alexander may already have been thinking of an expedition to the west, but at the age of thirty-two he died, without having made any provision for the succession (323 BC).

When the news of Alexander's death spread through his empire it was soon evident that there would be a struggle for power between the marshals. There followed a long period of alliances made and broken, of wars and peaces, and it was more than fifty years before a comparatively stable pattern emerged. By then Macedon, Syria, and Egypt had become the main bases of power, to be joined later by the Attalid kingdom of north-west Asia Minor with its capital at Pergamum: to advance their claims these Hellenistic kingdoms needed strong fleets. Of Greek communities only Rhodes remained a naval power. She had built up a strong trading position in the fourth century, but her territorial ambitions were very limited and her suppression of piracy performed a useful service for all. Macedon, Syria, and Pergamum had no timber problems. The reputation of Macedonian forests had been long established: a strong ruler of Syria could command the rich forest resources of Cilicia, Syria, and Phoenicia; Pergamum could rely on the firs, pine, and oak of Mt. Ida. Rhodes had to supplement her native supplies of cypress and pine by imports, but most trading ports were open to her and normally she needed to go no further than Lycia, which had ample resources of cedar and cypress.

Ptolemy in Egypt had no such advantages, for Egypt's woodlands could not supply the long timbers that were needed to build warships. Ptolemy, who had been close to Alexander in the last stage of his conquests, had been sent to govern Egypt, but when he saw that there was no agreed solution to the succession he decided to build up an independent power in Egypt. This power was to be based on the development of Egypt's wealth with the aid of Greek technology and commercial skills, supported if necessary by Greek mercenaries. Unlike the Pharaohs, Ptolemy and his successors were anxious to maintain close links with the Greek world and especially with Greece itself. To follow this policy and to defend Egypt from any threat by sea a strong fleet was necessary, and most of the timber for the ships had to be imported. The nearest sources of supply were Phoenicia, Syria, and Cyprus and in the period immediately following the death of Alexander Ptolemy had no serious rival in the eastern Mediterranean, for Antigonus, another of Alexander's generals, who was making his bid for power from Syria, was at first preoccupied with rivals in Asia Minor and in

Macedon itself. This enabled Ptolemy to extend his influence into Phoenicia and Cyprus where there was an old legacy of goodwill to Egypt, and along the coasts of Cilicia, Lycia, and Caria.

To meet this challenge Antigonus needed a fleet as well as an army. Diodorus describes in detail the measures taken:

> He collected fellers and sawyers from all parts, and also shipwrights, and he brought the timber down to the sea from the Lebanon. 8,000 men were employed to fell and saw the timber and 1,000 yokes of oxen were used to bring the timber down. The Lebanon mountain range runs along the territories of Tripolis, Byblos, and Sidon, and is full of cedar and cypress of specially fine quality and size. He established shipbuilding centres in Phoenicia at Tripolis, Byblos, and Sidon, and a fourth in Cilicia for timber brought down from the Taurus mountains. There was another centre in Rhodes, where the Rhodians had agreed to make ships from timber supplied to them.[59]

This fleet was needed when Antigonus had extended his control by land through Phoenicia and down to Sinai and decided to drive Ptolemaic influence out of Cyprus. There had been considerable support for Ptolemy in Cyprus, particularly in cities where Greek influence was strong, and when Antigonus' son Demetrius landed on the island, the city of Salamis was in no mood to surrender. When Demetrius settled down to besiege the city Ptolemy fitted out a large naval and military force to defend his influence; but in a major battle off Salamis his fleet was decisively defeated (306) and he had to abandon the island.[60]

Pressure on Ptolemy was relieved by the preoccupation of Antigonus and his son with rivals in the west, which culminated in the battle of Ipsus (301) in which Antigonus was killed. Egypt had taken no part in the battle and was ignored in the settlement which followed. Syria and Phoenicia were awarded to Seleucus, another of Alexander's generals, but Ptolemy had taken advantage of the concentration of forces at Ipsus to occupy Phoenicia and in 296, while Seleucus was busy annexing Cilicia, he recovered Cyprus. Phoenicia, however, and south Syria remained a constant source of friction, flaring up into no less than five wars of fluctuating fortune. But by the end of the century it had become clear that Egypt was not strong enough to control Phoenicia with its important cedar forests. Following a decisive victory by Antiochus III, the Seleucid monarch, at

Panium near the source of the Jordan in 200, Ptolemy Epiphanes (209–181) agreed to surrender all claims to territory outside Egypt with the exception of Cyprus, which was strongly held. The island had an Egyptian military governor with Egyptian garrisons in all the main cities, and it remained under Egyptian control until it was made a Roman province in 58 BC. Throughout this period the island's timber was of crucial importance to the Ptolemies.

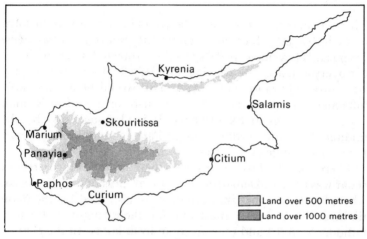

5 Cyprus

Today the most widespread trees in Cyprus are the pines (both *P. nigra* and *P. brutia*) and cypress, but there were also cedars in the western mountains. The only specific reference to them in Antiquity is by Pliny who notes that the tallest recorded cedar grew in Cyprus and was used by Demetrius for his famous eleven-oar warship. Pliny, however, often makes mistakes in such matters and his evidence was discounted by all the early botanists who studied the flora of the island. It was not until 1879 that Pliny was vindicated by Sir Samuel Baker, who described the circumstances in a letter to his publisher:

A few days ago I was conversing with the old monk upon the question of 'Chittim wood', and I suggested my own theory, that Solomon required the highly scented cypress of this island (for the temple). My venerable informant declared that a wood exists to this day in Cyprus which is supposed to be the original species referred to in the Scriptures: this is a pine which is only found upon the mountain between Kyko and Khrysokhus. The grain and surface when planed are exceedingly close and smooth, and the timber is strong and durable, far exceeding in quality all other varieties. The native name for the tree is kandro. I have sent a monk to gather the cones of the tree which I shall send to England for seed, together with a sample of the foliage. [A postscript was added:] My messenger has returned with a branch and cones of the tree. There is no longer a doubt, it is a beautiful species of cedar.

These cedars differ from the cedars of Lebanon only in the form of their leaves, which are significantly shorter, *Cedrus libani brevifolia*. They have been specially protected since their rediscovery and are now growing impressively. In our period they were probably more widespread. This would be a reasonable inference from the report of cedar pit-props found in Roman copper workings at Skouriotissa. It is also suggested by the finding of a buried cedar trunk at Panaya considerably below the present range of the cedars.

There may be further traces of these cedars. Pliny's record cedar was used for Demetrius' eleven-oar, presumably as a mast. Theophrastus implies that cedars were also used for the main timbers. They were remarkable for their length of thirteen fathoms (*c*.78 ft.) and their freedom from knots. In the context Theophrastus is referring to the fine quality of the cedars on the mountains of Syria, especially in the parks. Trees, he says, grow especially well when left alone and he cites as an example the trees of Cyprus, which were preserved by the kings, because they took great care of them and also because it was difficult to transport them.[61] High up on the mountains (at *c*.1500 m.) they were much less accessible than the pines. The example of Demetrius may have been followed by Ptolemy Philadelphus (285–246). In the temple of Aphrodite at Paphos he set up a statue of Pyrgoteles, son of Zoes to commemorate his building of two massive ships of the new model, a 'thirty' and a 'twenty'.[62] The wood is not specified but the surviving cedars are in a forest above Paphos.

The use of cedar by Hellenistic kings for shipbuilding may seem difficult to reconcile with Theophrastus' statement that, while the peoples of Syria and Phoenicia use cedar to build ships, the people of Cyprus use *pitys-pine* (p. 118), but pine was probably commoner than cedar and growing at a lower altitude was much more accessible. Kings of Syria and Egypt would think on more ambitious lines than the Cypriots.

The ships which Pyrgoteles built illustrate the obsession with size of the Hellenistic kings in their military and naval innovations. During the fifth century the trireme with its three banks of oarsmen had been the standard form of warship, but at the beginning of the fourth century Dionysius, tyrant of Syracuse developed, according to Diodorus, new types of ships, including *tetrereis* and *pentereis*, in a big shipbuilding programme. Diodorus also says that there were more than 100 triremes and *pentereis* in the fleet of Sidon in 351. But the Greeks of the mainland were slow to follow. The new types are not mentioned in the accounts of naval battles in the Aegean before the time of Alexander, and in the Athenian naval inventories *tetrereis* appear first in 330/329, when there were eighteen newly built; in the inventory of 325/4 the number of *tetrereis* had been increased to forty-three and seven *pentereis* had been added.[63] By analogy with *tetrereis* one would expect *pentereis* to have five banks of oars, but it is generally recognised that any such construction would be technically impracticable, and since there is soon a further development to 'fifteens' and 'sixteens' some different explanation is needed. The simplest solution is to believe that the first stage was to put two men to an oar, with two banks for a quadrireme and three banks for a quinquereme (2: 2: 1). Beyond six, however, a new system is required and this is probably an extension of the two-man oar to a multiple-rower sweep as in the Venetian galley of the seventeenth and eighteenth centuries.[64]

The main reason for these developments was a change in battle tactics. The fourth century had witnessed the development of artillery. Catapults appear for the first time in the Athenian naval inventory of 326/5 and they played an important part in naval battles.[65] Instead of relying on speed and manœuvre to ram the enemy, Hellenistic navies relied largely on crippling the enemy with artillery and then boarding. The marines therefore had a much more important role to play and their number was accordingly increased. To meet these needs ships had to be considerably larger and stronger. Demetrius, son of Antigonus, whom we have met as the victor of the battle of

Salamis (306), played an important part in these developments. He was primarily remembered for the sieges he undertook, but he seems also to have led the way in naval innovations. At the battle of Cyprian Salamis, while Ptolemy's ships were all quadriremes or quinqueremes, Demetrius had ten 'sixes' and seven 'sevens'.[66] Later Demetrius was to build still larger ships, an 'eleven' and finally a 'fifteen' and a 'sixteen'.[67] Of his 'eleven' we have a little further information. Theophrastus, a contemporary, records that the timbers cut for the ship were thirteen fathoms long, about seventy-eight feet (c.24 m.),[68] and Pliny implies that the mast was from the tallest cedar ever recorded, of 130 feet (39.6 m.).[69] Such measurements suggest a ship considerably larger than a quinquereme. But this was not the end of the race.

As we have seen, Ptolemy Philadelphus built a 'twenty' and a 'thirty' and finally the climax came with the 'forty' of Ptolemy Philopator (221–203). The dimensions of this extravaganza have been recorded, but the record is barely credible: length 280 cubits (103.63 m.); beam thirty-eight cubits (17.37 m.); height from water-level to top of stern fifty-three cubits (24.08 m.); height from water-line to top of prow forty-eight cubits (21.94 m.). It had four steering oars thirty cubits (14 m.) long, and its *thranite* oars, which were the longest, were thirty-eight cubits (17.37 m.) long. During a trial run it had more than 4,000 oarsmen and on the deck 2,850 marines.[70] The mention of thranite oars, used for the highest of the three banks of the trireme, implies that the 'forty' also had three banks. If there were roughly 180 oars in each bank, each worked by eight men, there would have been more than 4,000 rowers. But such figures seem to belong to dream-land. They would be more credible if we could accept Casson's ingenious solution that before the 'forty' a different type of ship had been developed with two hulls, anticipating the modern catamaran.[71] But such a revolutionary change of design should have left clearer traces in our sources. We have no record of the fighting qualities of these monsters in action, but they soon passed out of fashion. At the battle of Actium (31 BC) Antony and Cleopatra had nothing larger than a 'ten' and Octavian's largest ship was a 'six'.[72] When the Roman fleet was reorganised by Augustus the flagship was a 'six' but the ships of the line were either triremes or quinqueremes.

The giant armed merchantman of Hiero II king of Syracuse (269–215) was a companion in spirit of Philopator's 'forty'. In the detailed description of this grand folly the measurements are not given and the figure for the total complement is lost, but 300 craftsmen with assistants are said to have worked for a whole year to complete the vessel and it carried a cargo of 60,000 measures of grain, 10,000 jars of salted Sicilian fish, 20,000 talents of wool, and 20,000 talents of miscellaneous cargo. Like Dionysius before him he took his timbers from Mt. Etna and south Italy: from Etna he took his main timbers (presumably fir and pine), and they were 'enough to build sixty quadriremes'.[73] The size of the main mast, which was cut in south Italy, is not given, but it was very difficult to find and needed an expert engineer to supervise its transport to the shore. The ship was intended primarily to carry a cargo but it had many of the symptoms of a luxury cruiser, including gymnasium, reading-room, and baths; but, presumably because it would be a tempting prize for pirates, it also carried defensive towers and a catapult specially designed by Archimedes. The ship may have given great pleasure to Hiero and perhaps even more to Archimedes, but it failed miserably as a commercial asset or as a prestige-builder. It was too large for most of the harbours on its intended run; so it was presented as a gift to the king of Egypt, but it remained dock-bound in the harbour at Alexandria (not unlike the *Queen Mary* ending her days as an 'attraction' off the Californian coast). It may have preceded Ptolemy Philopator's 'forty' there.

In the century that followed the death of Alexander more ships were brought to battle in the Aegean and in the eastern Mediterranean than in any other century of ancient history and the increase in the size of the warship increased the scale of the demand for timber, which at first fell mainly on the forest belt that stretches along the mountain chains behind the coast from Lycia to Lebanon and on the mountains of Macedon. From 264 to 200 the forests of Italy and of Tunisia were called on to supply ship-timber on an even larger scale.

While the Hellenistic kingdoms were manœuvring for power a new state was growing up in the west. No one at the time could have dreamt that the kingdom of Macedon, from which Alexander had launched his conquest of the east, would in less than two hundred years become a province in a Roman empire. When Alexander died Rome had recovered from the sack of the city by the Gauls (390 BC) and, once again firmly in control of central Italy, she could resume her advance in the south. The Romans were still a land power depending entirely on the legions, but in 311 they had taken steps to organise a small fleet of twenty ships, with their headquarters at Rome. Very little is heard of this fleet until it was humiliated by the ships of Tarentum in 272, but since Tarentum was soon afterwards captured by land forces the naval defeat had no serious consequences except to discourage interest in the fleet. The conquest of Tarentum by the legions and Rome's increasing association with the Greek cities of south Italy did, however, lead inevitably to involvement in Sicily, where the Greek cities had for two centuries been threatened by Carthaginian support for the Phoenicians of the west of the island.

The incidents that led to the first war between Rome and Carthage are not in themselves important, for war between the two powers was bound to come sooner or later. It came when Messina in Sicily appealed for help to both Carthage and Rome and when it came Rome had made no attempt to keep her small fleet in proper condition for war. At first this did not seem to be a serious handicap. Roman legions were transported in ships borrowed from Tarentum and the other Greek cities of south Italy across the narrow straits and it was soon found that the Carthaginian forces could not match their fighting strength. After three years, however, it was realised that there could be no final settlement of the struggle for Sicily so long as Carthage controlled the seas and could bring over men and material without fear of interception. With typical determination the Romans decided to build and maintain a fleet of 100 quinqueremes and twenty triremes and to carry on war by sea as well as by land. It was stated later that this first fleet, which fought in 260, had been launched only sixty days after the timber had been felled.[74]

Although the crews had been trained on land, they could not expect to be a match for the Carthaginians in a traditional naval battle; but the fighting qualities of the marines would be decisive if the enemy ships could be boarded. This was achieved by fitting a new device to their ships, a boarding bridge thirty-six feet (*c.*11 m.) long and four feet (1.2 m.) wide with a strong spike at the end, which was manœuvred by a pulley on top of a twenty-four-foot (7.3 m.) pole. When two ships collided the bridge was raised by the pulley, and swivelled round so that when it was let down the spike stuck fast in the enemy's deck.[75] The 'crow', as the new device was called, was sensationally successful at the battle of Mylae and for four years the Romans controlled the seas round Sicily; but their attempt to carry the war to Africa was premature and on the return voyage their fleet was overwhelmed by a destructive storm and lost some 270 ships. The Romans showed their resilience by building another fleet of 220 ships in three months, but two more fleets were lost before the war was ended. Finally, one more fleet was built by private subscription and the decisive battle off the Aegates islands was won in 242.

Polybius says that during the twenty-four years of the first Punic War the Romans lost 700 quinqueremes.[76] If account is taken of the much smaller number of triremes that were lost, the number of Roman ships built in those years must have approached one thousand. We are told that the Romans relied for their first fleet on copying a Carthaginian quinquereme that had run aground in the straits of Messina and that later they copied the construction of a Rhodian ship. There is no other evidence in surviving accounts of the measures taken to produce so many ships. It might be expected that Rome would have taken advantage of the shipbuilding experience of her naval allies and commissioned them to build the quinqueremes and triremes that she needed, but there is no hint of this in the sources and the tradition that the first big fleet was launched no more than sixty days after the trees had been felled would be difficult to explain if the shipbuilding was spread over several ports. If the work was in fact concentrated, the ships were probably built at Rome. When the first fleet was built in 311 Rome was the navy's headquarters and so it remained: Roman fleets in the first Punic War sailed from Rome and ultimately returned to Rome. To build the number of ships now required the skilled labour in Rome could have been increased by attracting shipwrights from the southern ports. The timber, mainly fir and pine, will have come by the Tiber and its tributaries from Etruria and Umbria.

During the first Punic War the Carthaginian losses must have been almost as heavy as those of the Romans. They had suffered less from storms but more in battle and at the critical time when Rome was almost exhausted they failed to build sufficient ships to fight on equal terms. There is no reason to believe that this failure was due to the difficulty of finding adequate supplies of ship-timber. Conditions of soil and climate on the north coast of Africa from western Tunisia to the straits of Gibraltar were very similar to conditions on the south coast of Gaul. The coastal belt had sufficient rainfall to sustain good forests and both Hero-dotus and Strabo emphasise the tree-wealth of the region. The commonest trees in the woodlands within easy reach of Car-thage today are the cork-oak and Aleppo pine. In the valleys there is a thin scatter of ash, elm, poplar, willow, and alder.[77] The cover in the classical period was probably very similar.

In the Phoenician homeland from which Carthage was colonised fleets were built with the cedars of Lebanon and there were cedars in north-west Africa. The main cedar areas were in the Atlas mountains in what are now Morocco and western Algeria, but cedars also grew and still grow in the Aures mountains more than 200 kilometres south-west of Carthage. This would have seemed a very long haul if there were other suitable woods much nearer, and we can be satisfied that there were. In Appian's account of the third Punic War, which led to the final destruction of Carthage in 146 BC, the two Roman consuls expected the city to surrender without fighting. When they met stubborn resistance and saw that there was no hope of taking the city by assault, they had to find timber to build their siege equipment. One of the consuls led a force across Lake Tunis, but in a surprise attack by a Carthaginian cavalry force he is said to have lost 500 woodcutters, which suggests that he expected to find ample supplies.[78] In spite of his losses he was able to take back sufficient timber to make ladders, and two enormous ram-tortoises. Of the trees most accessible from Carthage the cork-oak was completely unsuitable; its wood is soft and spongy and the tree's habit of growth rules out long lengths. Pine, however, was often used for warships as well as merchantmen. In a ship sunk off the north-western shore of Sicily, whose form suggests that it was a Punic warship, most of the planking was pine, but where strength was more important as for the ribs, dowels, and tenons, oak was used, supplemented by maple in some of the ribs and the after end of the keel. Shavings found in the ship showed that a wider variety of woods were used in the superstructure: beech, fir, and pistachio, and probably cedar (one sample only); and a fragment of walnut had survived.[79] It is probable that the ship was built in Sicily or north Africa, but the range of woods would not be surprising on other coasts in the central and eastern Mediterranean.

The pattern of the second Punic War was very different from the first. There were no major sea battles, but the war was spread over a much wider area and the Roman fleet played an important role in protecting the Italian coast, preventing supplies reaching Hannibal by sea, supporting the Roman armies in Spain and Sicily, and ensuring that Philip of Macedon, who had made an alliance with Hannibal, sent him no help. The fleet had therefore to be maintained at considerable strength through the long war and it is probable that, as in the first war, the ships were built in Rome. The only evidence that survives, however, is in Livy's account of the ships built by Scipio in 205 in his preparations for taking the war to Africa. Firs, he tells us, were promised by three Etruscan towns, Rusellae, Perusia, and Clusium, while Scipio also used firs from state forests.[80] The ships were built at Rome and the timber came by river. This, however, was not a major programme; in spite of Livy's enthusiasm, only twenty quinqueremes and ten triremes were built and when he did take his army to Africa Scipio used only forty warships to convoy the transports. According to Pliny the ships were built in no more than forty days, which suggests that Scipio may not have waited for the firs promised by the Etruscan cities. Scipio's purpose in part at least was to impress the city of Rome where many senators were less than lukewarm about what they regarded as the African gamble. The shipbuilding in Rome would also help to attract volunteers from central Italy. Scipio's bold plans were completely successful. His army was landed in Africa and Hannibal was urgently recalled. He was still strong enough in south Italy to build a fleet from the Sila forest[81] and he made the passage to Africa safely; but in the decisive battle of Zama he was defeated and Carthage had to surrender. With the crushing of Carthage Rome took possession of Spain, which had been Hannibal's main source of manpower and materials. There was now no potential rival to Rome in the western Mediterranean, but the Macedonian king's agreement with Hannibal led to Rome's increasing involvement in the world of the Hellenistic kingdoms.

Rome's victories in the east, which eventually reduced the Hellenistic kingdoms to Roman provinces, were won by the legions, but the Romans understood the potential danger of a strong hostile fleet. When Carthage had been crushed in the second Punic War Rome restricted her fleet to ten ships and these were to be triremes and not quinqueremes, which had become the standard warship. When Philip of Macedon, who had made an alliance with Hannibal, had been defeated at Cynoscephalae (197) the Macedonians were allowed to keep only five warships and a sixteen, which was too cumbersome to be effective.[82] Rome's victory over Antiochus of Syria at Magnesia (189) was followed by a peace settlement in which Rome's main objective was to ensure that Syrian kings did not interfere in the affairs of the Greek world. It was insufficient to make Antiochus undertake not to cross the Taurus range. In his attempt to extend his power in Greece and the Aegean he had used a hundred warships and a large number of auxiliary vessels. Antiochus was now forbidden to sail beyond the Calycadnus river and Cape Sarpedonium, and his fleet was reduced to ten undecked ships, which were only to be used for defence.[83] When Rhodes, which had the strongest fleet in the Greek world, showed signs of anti-Roman sympathies her wings too were sharply clipped.

In the fourth century Rhodes, with the partial eclipse of Athens, had become an increasingly prosperous trading centre and had built up a powerful fleet to safeguard her interests. To Hellenistic kings who lacked the energy or resources to maintain a strong fleet the protection offered to commerce by the Rhodian fleet was very welcome, and Rhodes, following a carefully calculated policy of preserving the balance of power, profited from their goodwill. After the great earthquake in 227 which reduced a large part of the city to ruins, the Hellenistic kingdoms vied with one another in their gifts.

Timber figured prominently in these gifts. The Macedonian king Antigonus Doson promised 10,000 timbers ranging from sixteen cubits (7.31 m.) to eight cubits (3.66 m.) to serve as *sphekiskoi* and 5,000 *stroteres* of seven cubits, with 1,000 talents of solid pitch and 1,000 measures of liquid pitch. Ptolemy's gifts from Egypt included ship-timbers for ten quinqueremes and ten triremes, 40,000 cubits, with good measure, of squared pine-wood. From Syria Seleucus sent 10,000 cubits of timber and 1,000 talents of resin.

These gifts are not all easy to interpret. From Macedon we should expect ship-timbers in view of their generally accepted superiority, and this is how Walbank in his commentary on Polybius understands the words; but the normal meaning of *sphekiskoi* is rafters, and *stroteres*, when associated with them, are timbers laid over the rafters. Unless other examples can be found of *sphekiskoi* being ship-timbers we should, with Holleaux, assume that the Macedonian gift consisted of roof-timbers for which there would have been a massive demand after the earthquake, and roof-timbers, like ships, were normally coated with pitch.[84]

Ptolemy sent pine and this is at first surprising, for Egypt could not have supplied good ship-timber from her own woods and in the Bronze Age cedar-wood had been Egypt's main timber import. According to Theophrastus the peoples of Syria and Phoenicia used cedar for their ships because they did not even have much pine,[85] and Pliny confirms that the Egyptian kings also used cedar.[86] The clue to the apparent anomaly may lie in what follows in Theophrastus: 'The people of Cyprus use *pitys*-pine because this pine grows there and seems to be better than *peuke*-pine.' Ptolemy no longer had free access to the cedars of Lebanon, but he controlled Cyprus; the timber sent to Rhodes was probably Cyprian pine, of which there may be other evidence.

In 306 Demetrius son of Antigonus of Syria had promised to send timber to the Athenians for 100 triremes and a record of its arrival in Athens has been preserved. The decree authorising payment for the transport was passed by the Assembly in midsummer 305, and in the currently accepted restoration of the text the timbers are described as pines.[87] This is not what we should expect from Theophrastus, who implies a shortage of pine in Syria, but in the previous year Demetrius had invaded Cyprus and Ptolemy, defeated in a sea battle, had to abandon the island and its forests. The timbers sent to Athens may have been pines from Cyprus. Demetrius was later to use Cyprian cedar.[88]

It is far from clear what is meant by Ptolemy's 40,000 cubits of squared timber, or the 10,000 cubits from Seleucus. We should expect to be told the length of the timbers and the number of each length, a combination such as 1,200 timbers of twenty cubits, and 400 timbers of fifteen cubits. Probably the timbers from Syria were also squared, and could be converted by the Rhodians to required sizes, whereas the Macedonian timber had been cut to size before dispatch.

In less than a hundred years the prospects of Rhodes were to be transformed. When Rome had crushed Philip of Macedon at the battle of Cynoscephalae (197) and Antiochus of Syria had been forced to renounce his amibition to extend his empire into Asia Minor (188), the position of Rhodes, which depended on a balance of power, was more precarious. Should she still struggle to pursue a policy of neutrality, or should she accept Roman policies and concentrate on maintaining at all costs friendly relations with Rome? Opinions were sharply divided and largely on a class basis, the propertied classes more concerned with the safer course, the common people hostile to Rome.

Matters came to a head as a result of the attitude of Rhodes to Philip's son Perseus, who had come to the Macedonian throne in 178. Early in his reign the Rhodians had escorted his bride Laodice from Syria and had accepted a considerable supply of ship-timbers from Perseus; and at a grand Rhodian naval review Perseus had decorated with golden tiaras the upper bench of rowers in the ship that brought his bride.[89] Feeling against Rhodes was also stirred up at Rome by appeals from Lycia, which the Rhodians claimed the right to control. Meanwhile Rome became increasingly suspicious of the intentions of Perseus and in 171 decided on war. Rhodes, which remained inactive through three years of the war, finally decided to send an embassy to Rome to offer to mediate, but when the embassy arrived Perseus had already been decisively defeated at the battle of Pydna (168). The Romans saw in this late Rhodian gesture confirmation of their suspicions and decided to treat Rhodes as a friend of Perseus. They required her to surrender her possessions on the mainland and crippled her trade by making the island of Delos a free port. In the settlement imposed on Perseus Rome 'forbade the Macedonians to cut their ship-timber or to allow others to cut it'.[90] There could be no greater tribute to the importance of Macedonian ship-timber. Rome was determined that no other state should indulge in naval power, but she was not prepared to build up a strong navy herself; she was content to rely on the provinces and allied kingdoms to police their own local waters.

It was against this background of Roman indifference that piracy became a serious menace. In the Mediterranean there were certain areas which positively encouraged piracy. What the pirates needed were good harbours or sheltered coves, good ship-timber easily accessible, and safe refuges to which they could withdraw in the event of attack. These conditions were particularly well satisfied in three areas. The Rif Atlas mountains, close behind the north-west African coast, had ample reserves of cedar and other conifers, and good harbours within easy reach; Dalmatia, on the east side of the Adriatic, also had a well-forested mountain chain behind a coast that was heavily indented; and there were similar conditions on the coasts of Lycia and Cilicia, where the Taurus mountains tower over the coastal plain.[91] Rome had met with considerable trouble from the pirates of the Dalmatian coast during the second half of the third century and until she controlled the mountains behind the coast the trade of the Adriatic was continuously at risk. When Greece and Macedon had been made Roman provinces there were sufficient forces available to intimidate the coastal peoples from the interior.

Of African pirates we hear little in our sources because the main course of history was being decided in the eastern Mediterranean; there was, however, a pirate problem in the west. But the strongest pirate bases were in Lycia and Cilicia. Even during the period of the Athenian Empire in the fifth century, when Athens had the will and the resources to maintain a strong navy, traders knew that they ran serious risks as they sailed along the south coast of Asia Minor on the way to Cyprus, Syria, Phoenicia, or Egypt.[92] Periodic attempts by the Romans to crush the pirates of this area in the late second and early first century had proved singularly ineffective.

As a result of Roman neglect piracy, by the first century, was becoming a serious danger to trade throughout the

Mediterranean, and this neglect was perhaps encouraged by a useful service that the pirates provided for the Roman nobility. For it was the pirates who by their raids provided the majority of the slaves that were sold in the market at Delos, and the rising prosperity of the Roman governing class created a growing demand for slaves, particularly for the great landowners. The freedom of movement enjoyed by the pirates is well illustrated in Cicero's savage attack on the corruption and incompetence of Verres when he governed Sicily. But the pirates went too far. They raided the west coast of Italy, plundered the port of Gaieta, kidnapped two Roman praetors, sailed into the Tiber mouth, destroyed the fleet which had come down river from Rome under the command of a consul, and sacked Rome's harbour town.[93]

Such bold action implied good organisation; the pirates had become the most formidable naval power in the Mediterranean. Their strongest bases were in Cilicia where they could live on the mountain slopes behind the coastal plain, grow their own food, and withdraw into inaccessible country if attacked. They had excellent ship-timber in these mountains, and there were adequate harbours and anchorages. When the Romans were at last rudely woken to the danger, they created a special command for Pompey, who had the greatest military reputation of the day, and gave him ample resources to sustain a major campaign. This campaign was won more by good organisation than by active fighting. The Mediterranean was divided into zones which Pompey assigned to his officers. He himself sailed first to the west and quickly crushed such opposition as was offered; meanwhile his officers were dealing with the Dalmatian pirates and preventing them from sailing out of the Adriatic to join other pirate forces. Stragglers were swept eastwards and a naval victory was won off Coracesium on the Cilician coast. Within three months resistance was ended and by his generous terms Pompey succeeded in converting the pirates into peaceful farmers; it is an interesting postscript that he burned their stocks of timber.[94] Only the broad outline of the war against the pirates has survived in our sources and we hear nothing of any special shipbuilding programme. But there is an interesting echo in the record of the later Roman Civil War. When fighting broke out in Africa between Pompeians and Caesarians there were ten triremes that had been laid up at Utica since the pirate war. It is probable that in 67 new ships were built at several points in the Mediterranean.

In the civil war which broke out in 49 BC Pompey had good reason to remember his operations against the pirates. Caesar, confident in the strength of the legions with which he had conquered Gaul, had marched on Rome to assert his rights; Pompey had been called on by the senate to defend the constitution. With few troops at his immediate disposal Pompey soon found that it was impossible to hold Italy and he decided to move to the east, where he had won his most recent victories, and build up his forces to return. Caesar followed him to Brundisium but was unable to prevent him from sailing, for the shipping of the district had been confiscated by Pompey. Caesar had to build up his own fleet. He had to wait for ships to come from Cisalpine Gaul, Picenum, and from south Italy, but that would take time and meanwhile Spain, where Pompey (who had governed the province) had strong influence, might create trouble.[95] Instead of waiting at Brundisium Caesar carried through a swift but effective campaign in Spain.

When he returned to Brundisium preparations for his fleet had gone slowly, but he risked a crossing in bad weather and managed to elude the large fleet which Pompey had assembled on the east coast of the Adriatic. The creation of this large fleet, which included separate Rhodian, Asiatic, and Egyptian squadrons, illustrates once again Pompey's supreme ability in organisation.[96] His strategy failed because Caesar was always prepared to take risks and, as in the past, his boldness was accompanied by good fortune. Pompey's hope depended on his fleet, which was overwhelmingly superior, being able to prevent large Caesarian forces landing. He perhaps overlooked how ineffective his warships would be in rough weather.

In the second period of civil war which followed the assassination of Caesar fleets played a more important part. The unity of the triumvirate which had been formed to avenge Caesar and to make impossible a return to the old style of republican misgovernment was soon seen to be hollow. The interests and ambitions of Caesar's adopted son Octavian and Caesar's friend and general Antony were irreconcilable and the drift to open conflict was almost inevitable. Antony had chosen to base his

power on the east, where he looked forward to a triumph over
the Parthians which would make his personal position un-
assailable.

Octavian had the more invidious and difficult responsibilities
of settling veterans in Italy. This was bound to arouse strong
resentment in those who were dispossessed, and the resentment
led to some savage fighting which left a bitter taste. A more
serious crisis followed when Pompey's younger son Sextus tried
to revive the appeal of his father's name. Basing himself first on
Africa he gave a welcome to political refugees, enlisted pirates
and slaves, who were given their freedom, and built a considerable fleet. With his ships he hoped to cut off Rome's supplies of
grain from overseas and so starve the city into surrender.

Octavian had no naval experience and his fleet was totally
inadequate. When the early clashes merely emphasised his
weakness he realised that his own future depended on building a
large new fleet in the shortest time possible. He could now rely
on the active help of Agrippa who had been campaigning
successfully in Gaul, and was the ablest of his supporters.
Instructions were sent to all cities on the west coast which had a
boat-building tradition, and, since there was an acute shortage
of harbours, lake Avernus was made into a vast inland harbour
connected to the sea by canal.[97] The thickly wooded banks of the
lake were stripped of their trees, shipwrights got busy with the
timber, and, as in the early days of the first Punic War, crews
were trained in the basic essentials of rowing before they went to
sea.[98] As a result of these emergency measures Octavian within a
year could considerably outnumber Sextus' fleet. The decisive
battle was soon won thanks largely to the skill of Agrippa.

Antony meanwhile had dissipated his strength. The Parthian
expedition on which his main hopes were based ended in
a humiliating retreat, and his political judgement became
clouded by the ambitions and attractions of Cleopatra. When he
realised from his political friends in Rome that popular favour
was moving increasingly towards Octavian, he decided to strike
first. No details are recorded of the steps taken by Antony to
assemble the very considerable fleet that was with him in 31 BC
in Epirus, but a story which survived because of its moral value
suggests that there was some urgent tree-felling in unlikely
places. When Octavian after his victory at Actium followed

Antony to Egypt, he demanded the surrender of P. Turullius, a
senator who was a friend of Antony but had taken part in the
murder of Caesar. He was executed, and his death was taken as
vengeance also for the gods, because 'he had cut timber for his
fleet from the sacred grove of Asklepios on the island of Cos'.[99]

The victory of Actium marked the end of the Civil War.
Octavian was to become Augustus and to lay the foundations of
an imperial structure which lasted for more than four hundred
years. By a revolutionary reform in naval organisation he
provided for the free flow of trade in the Mediterranean world.
Permanent fleets were stationed at key points round the
Mediterranean to protect the coasts and patrol the sea lanes,
and two main naval bases were established at Ravenna and
Misenum. The pines that now dominate the coast at Ravenna
do not derive from Roman forests, but there was a place called
Pineta, The Pines, near Ravenna. The city itself was famous for
its buildings of wood, and it had a very large guild of builders.[100]
There is no such evidence from Misenum, but there were
adequate supplies of timber within easy distance. There was
indeed a large forest on the coast nearby, *Gallinaria*, which
Strabo describes as waterless and sandy and *thamnodes*, literally
meaning bushy; it was probably more like scrub than forest,
perhaps a pine forest that had been overcut during the
Republic.[101] The Apennine background of Campania, however, was well wooded and Vitruvius implies that the firs were of
good quality.[102]

It was not until the empire began to disintegrate that
merchantmen no longer felt secure. By the fifth century the
Vandals who had settled in Africa were strong enough to raid
Italy and new ships had to be built. Sidonius, writing in 458
a panegyric for Majorianus who had been made emperor by
the senate and people in Rome, praises his energy in building
a fleet: 'While you build your fleet on both Italian shores, all the
trees of the forest fall and are taken down to the sea; and you,
O Apennine, cut down on both your slopes too heavily over long
ages, rich in naval timber, send down to the sea as much wood as
water.'[103] This laboured passage is fair evidence that ship-
timber could still be found on both sides of the Apennine range,
but the poet implies equally clearly that supplies had become
less plentiful. This was the result not so much of the demands

of the fleets as of the need for long timbers for Rome's basilicas
and other public buildings.

We have a more detailed description of the steps taken to
build a fleet from the early sixth century. Theodoric, leader of
the Ostrogoths, had successfully invaded Italy, seized power
from Odoacer, and established his capital at Ravenna. In spite
of his violent start he was content to style himself king of Italy
without claiming the imperial title, and proved to be a
conscientious and effective ruler. Towards the end of his reign
(526) he decided to meet the continuing threat from sea raiders
by building a fleet of 1,000 *dromones* (a new type of ship designed
to carry troops and cargo as well as oarsmen). These were
intended to carry public corn and deal with any attacks by
hostile ships.

Four dispatches cover the enterprise. In the first he sends
instructions to Abundantius, his praetorian prefect, to send out
surveyors to search for suitable ship-timber, and to buy
cypresses and pines throughout Italy near the shore: they were
to fix a fair price, safeguarding the interests of the owners. 'These
are the only trees to be considered (among coastal trees); there
is no need to put a value on the rest which are worthless (for
our purpose).' In a second dispatch he commends Abundantius
for the progress he has made and adds that any trees needed
for the building of the ships that can be found on either bank
of the Po must be cut, and here he has the fir in mind: 'Let our
Po send down its own ships and let the fir whose growth has been
fed by the water of the river learn to move over the waves of
the sea.'

In two further dispatches he calls on another member of his
staff to do what he can to ensure that the praetorian prefect's
instructions are carried out. Sufficient skilled craftsmen must be
sent to Ravenna by the Ides of June to build the ships, and the
supply of timber must be speeded up. 'If any timbers suitable for
building *dromones* can be found in the royal estates on the banks
of the Po, allow the surveyors of my praetorian prefect to cut
them down. For we wish to set this example from our own estates
so that no one can complain of an order which applies to the
emperor as well.' Landowners must be reassured that this is not
confiscation but a necessary response to an urgent public need.
They are not being asked to sacrifice trees from their parks, but

only forest trees which will not be missed. There are also transport problems. Fishermen are building dams across rivers to improve their private fishing prospects, obstructing the flow of goods. Theodoric demands that this abuse be sternly suppressed.[104]

But with Theodoric we are already moving towards the Middle Ages.

6

TIMBER FOR ARMIES

THE association of forests with fleets is a common theme in Greek and Latin literature. The army's use of timber receives considerably less emphasis, but armies consumed more timber than fleets. On campaign armies needed fuel to cook their food and provide warmth when it was cold; they often had to cut their way through forests, or clear-fell whole areas to deny cover to an enemy; rivers had to be bridged and roads made; timber played a major part in defence works and above all in sieges. Fortunately sieges are very fully illustrated in our sources. They provided tension and colour and appealed particularly to the dramatic school of historians, who found the fluctuating emotions that are inseparable from a long-drawn-out siege an attractive opportunity to display their talents.

The importance of timber operations to an army is well documented by Caesar's own account of his campaigns in Gaul (58–50 BC). The legions could carry emergency rations with them, but they relied on getting their water and fuel where they encamped. We frequently read of parties being sent out to bring in water and wood, *aquari et lignari*.[1] Sometimes they needed timber for construction, *materia* rather than logs for burning, *ligna*. The distinction comes out clearly in Caesar's account of the attack by rebel Gauls in the early autumn of 54 on the camp commanded by Cicero's brother Quintus in the territory of the Nervii. The Gauls had successfully overrun one legionary camp, killing the commander and decimating the legion; they then moved swiftly on Cicero's camp. A small, fast-moving Gallic cavalry unit cut off some of the Roman troops, who had gone out of the camp into the woods *lignationis et munitionis causa*, to collect fuel and to strengthen the defences:[2] 'from the timber which they had brought back for the defences towers of 120 feet had been raised with incredible speed'.[3] Although there were no specialised units in the legion, a large proportion of the men had been recruited from rural districts and were familiar with a countryman's work in the woods.

When Caesar wanted to teach the Germans a sharp lesson he decided to build a bridge over the Rhine rather than rely on boats to take his men across. To build a bridge over such a wide and fast-flowing river required considerable engineering skills; the work was completed in ten days. Caesar's description of the construction reminds us that the Roman ruling class, whose careers lay in the provinces and in the army as well as in the debating chamber, were capable of supervising construction work intelligently.[4] The felling and the conversion of the timber to the sizes required was the work of legionaries.

Caesar's men showed their versatility no less strikingly in solving a very different problem. In 52 it seemed that with the capture of Alesia after a long-drawn-out siege Gaul had been finally crushed, but in the winter of 51–50 Caesar learnt that widespread risings were being planned by the Gauls. At Rome the political situation was approaching a crisis and Caesar realised that a successful revolt in Gaul would be politically as well as militarily disastrous. He returned while it was still winter, divided his army to make as wide a show of strength as possible, and himself led three legions against the Bellovaci of the north-west, the strongest of the Gallic tribes. The Bellovaci had concentrated all their forces in a fortified camp on high ground in well-wooded country near Clermont protected by marsh, which made it impossible to besiege the camp or to make a major assault.

Caesar first built a strongly fortified camp for his legions and felt out the enemy's strength in minor skirmishes. This made little impression and some of his own parties were badly mauled. To force the enemy to fight or abandon their position it was necessary to move his men and his artillery across the marsh. The narrative is very condensed: 'the marsh was covered with bridges. Caesar led his men across and quickly reached the high ground' (on the other side of the valley).[5] Sufficient of the 'bridges' have survived to show what lies behind this brief statement. A thick layer of brushwood was laid on the floor of the marsh and pinned down by long pyramidal spikes with large heads; on the brushwood surface small timbers were laid at odd intervals, and over them round timbers mostly of a standard

length of thirteen feet were laid lengthwise, a foot apart, with the
heads of the spikes projecting between them. Over the round
timbers boards were laid transversely, providing a level surface
that could take carts as well as men. No attempt was made to
nail or mortice the timbers together, for this was not intended as
a permanent road.[6] It was a temporary improvisation that was
not subsequently maintained, to be discovered about seventy
centimetres below the peat that had grown over it.

The legions could also provide sufficient craftsmen to repair
ships. In Caesar's second invasion of Britain in 54 he faced a
major crisis. He was advancing through Kent when news came
that a violent storm had wrought havoc in his fleet: no less than
forty ships had been destroyed, the remainder could be
repaired, but they had been severely damaged. Caesar was able
to collect craftsmen from his legions and summon others from
the legions left in Gaul. After ten days in which the men had
worked night and day he felt sufficiently secure to resume his
advance towards the Thames.[7] No less impressive was the speed
and efficiency with which the legions could construct and bring
into action their siege equipment.

Caesar's first campaign in 58 had been nominally to protect
Gallic tribes from the increasing encroachment of Germans
from across the Rhine. But when Caesar, after defeating and
expelling the Germans, left his legions in Gaul while he attended
to civilian business on the Italian side of the Alps, it was clear to
the Gauls that Caesar had come to stay. The northern tribes,
realising the danger, determined to strike first and when in the
spring Caesar returned to his legions he found the Gauls already
on a war footing. He decided to act vigorously and was able to
crush the most dangerous of the tribes, the Nervii, before all the
forces of the rebels could unite. Having broken the Nervii Caesar
moved against the other tribes. The superiority of the Romans
in a pitched battle had been amply demonstrated by his
victories over the Germans and the Nervii. The Gauls therefore
preferred to rely on the strong defences of their fortified hills,
which had provided security in inter-tribal wars; but they had
no experience of Roman siege techniques. When the Roman
covered approaches had been brought up, and the mound had
been raised against the wall, they saw a tower being built in
the distance. At first they jeered and mocked the Romans for

assembling such an enormous construction so far away: 'What were such puny men (for most Gauls, being big themselves, look down on our short stature) relying on to place such a heavy tower against the wall?' But when they saw the tower being moved up and getting near to the wall they were so amazed by such a strange and unfamiliar sight that they sued at once for peace.[8]

Caesar was fortunate in his Gallic campaigns to be fighting in well-forested country with ample supplies of oak, fir, and pine to match all his needs. There was no difficulty in finding timber to build a fleet on the Loire to fight the Veneti, or in the territory of the coastal tribes to invade Britain; the speed with which his bridge over the Rhine was built would have been impossible unless there were plenty of tall forest-grown trees in the neighbourhood. The only difficulty in getting timber for fuel or siege works lay in ambushes or raids by the Gauls. But the forests could also be a handicap. When he was fighting against the Menapii and Morini of Normandy, who had to be reduced before legions could be withdrawn to invade Britain, the tribesmen avoided a pitched battle and withdrew into the cover of their woods. Caesar proceeded to cut down the trees, but had to abandon the attempt to destroy the Gauls' cover owing to a succession of severe storms.[9]

In Caesar's campaigns in Gaul the two sides were very unevenly matched in technology, and the Gauls realised too late that their only hope of defeating the Romans lay in abandoning their towns and cutting the Romans off from supplies by a scorched earth strategy. In the more advanced areas of the Mediterranean world there were no such disparities and innovations in attack led to innovations in defence. Even when siege techniques had reached their most sophisticated development the issue was often decided by starvation rather than assault. That was the case in the first siege for which we have a detailed account.

Soon after the outbreak of the Peloponnesian War, in which Athens fought Sparta for the leadership of the Greek world (431 BC), Sparta determined to crush the little city of Plataea, which was situated within the borders of Boeotia but allied to Athens. The Athenians, however, whose main strength was in their fleet, could not risk a major battle against the Spartans

and their allies, and the Plataeans had to rely on their own
resources. When an attempt to win over the city by political
intrigue and a half-hearted direct assault had failed, the
Spartans settled down to a siege.[10] They first cut down the trees
in the immediate neighbourhood, most of them probably fruit-
trees, and with stakes cut from them made a palisade round the
town. Next they began to build up a mound against the wall and
cut timber to bind the earth of the mound and prevent its
disintegration. These timbers came from Mt. Cithaeron which
rose up behind the town, and were probably pine and fir, which
in ancient and modern times have been the dominant trees of
the mountain. As the mound grew the Plataeans raised the
height of their wall at that point with mud-bricks framed with
timber to increase its strength, and as a second line of defence
they added an inner crescent wall. When battering-rams were
brought up they dropped strong beams from the top of the wall
and broke off their heads. The Spartans succeeded in setting fire
to the wall but a rain-storm providentially put the fire out.

The Spartan hoplites had the most formidable fighting
reputation in Greece, but they were trained to fight pitched
battles and had no experience of siege warfare. It was two years
before Plataea surrendered and then it was through complete
exhaustion; meanwhile a great deal of useful timber had been
wasted. But the Athenians were little more successful. It took
two years to reduce the comparatively small town of Potidaea in
Chalcidice and the siege of Thasos (464-462 BC) lasted more
than two years. When the island of Samos revolted from Athens
in 440, its fleet, after some initial success, was driven off the sea,
and her land forces were defeated, but nearly nine months
passed before the city surrendered, and the island of Lesbos held
out for nearly a year. In none of these four cases was the city
taken by assault. They were starved into surrender, and, at the
end of the Peloponnesian War, when the Athenian fleet had
been destroyed and supplies in the city were desperately short,
the Spartans had to rely on blockade leading through starvation
to unconditional surrender.

One can admire the collective courage shown by the defenders of these towns, but it remains curious that the Greeks of the
classical period made such little progress in the technique of
siege operations. Had the Assyrian kings who led their victorious

armies through Syria and Palestine down to Egypt in the eighth and seventh centuries been spectators of the siege of Plataea they would have thought very poorly of the performance of the besiegers. The great pictorial records of their triumphs show that most of the main elements of siege warfare had already been developed. In the fine relief in the British Museum of the siege of Lachish by Sennacherib the high mound rises against the wall, and a spear-headed ram, protected from above by a defensive covering, strikes at the battlements of a high tower, while archers fire their arrows to drive the defenders off. It is a vivid picture of ruthless determination efficiently organised.[11] The Persians in their rise to power seem to have inherited some of these skills. When the Lydian capital of Sardis had fallen they had little difficulty in storming the Greek cities of the Ionian coast, and when the island of Cyprus revolted they had taken all the main cities within a year, though the great mound at Paphos preserves evidence of a much more stubborn resistance than the account of Herodotus implies.[12]

The first Greek commander to make a significant advance beyond the Assyrians was the elder Dionysius, tyrant of Syracuse in the late fifth and early fourth century. His main contribution was the development of artillery, harnessing mechanical power to the projection of missiles in the form of arrows, bolts, and stones. His co-ordination of siege devices can be appreciated in Diodorus' account of the siege of Motya off the west coast of Sicily in 396 BC. 'He brought up all manner of devices, battered the walls with his rams, and with his catapults dislodged the defenders on the battlements. And he brought up to the walls towers on wheels, with protective roofs, built to match the height of the houses.' The inhabitants of Motya had no comparable weapons, but 'they raised men in corselets on yard-arms attached to the highest masts they could find and these men from their high position threw lighted torches and burning tow on their enemies' machines'. The wood caught fire, but Dionysius' men managed to extinguish the flames and their rams broke through part of the wall.

They could now enter the town, but the streets were very narrow and were easily blocked. Wooden towers were then brought up with drawbridges that could be let down, over which the troops could force their way into the houses.[13] It is not very easy to fit this picture into what we think we know of the geography of Motya, but it illustrates the main elements of the new-style siege. The attacker's main weapons are the rams to make a break in the walls, the catapults to force the enemy off his battlements, and the movable towers to provide high platforms which enabled the attackers to fire from above into the town. The tower, the rams, and the frames of the catapults were all made of wood and fire was one of the defender's most useful weapons against them. Dionysius would not have been able to master a siege armoury on this scale if he had not had ample supplies of timber available. He was in fact well placed in that respect, because he could draw on the fir and pine of Mt. Etna and of the forests of south Italy.

There is no evidence that the cities of the Greek mainland took advantage of the new techniques in siege warfare, but Philip and Alexander of Macedon appreciated their importance. Although he preferred to open city gates by political intrigue and a tactful distribution of Macedonian gold, Philip showed in his siege of Perinthus in 341 that he had mastered the new tactics. He built towers of eighty cubits (36.58 m.), rising high above the wall, to fire on the enemy from above, he battered the wall with rams, undermined it with tunnels, and so forced an entry. He also had a wide range of catapults which were directed against the garrison on the battlements. But Perinthus was better equipped than Motya. The city had the same advantage of narrow streets and high houses and it also had its own catapults, and support from Byzantium and Persia. Philip switched his attack to Byzantium, but when threatened by substantial forces from other Greek states he decided to withdraw.[14]

Alexander inherited from his father a fully developed siege armoury and the skilled technicians who could make and maintain a siege train. Diades and Chares on whom he mainly relied had worked under the Thessalian Polyides (Philip's chief engineer), and Diades, in a treatise on the construction and use of siege machines, claimed credit for inventing the prefabricated siege tower of which the sections could be carried separately and reassembled when required.[15] Though Alexander crossed into Asia with only a small force and was intending to depend primarily on speed of movement, he took with him an essential

nucleus of siege equipment which, after his initial victory at the
river Granicus, helped him to intimidate Miletus and to
neutralise Halicarnassus. This enabled him to move swiftly
eastwards, but it was not until after his victory at Issus in 333
that his engineers played a decisive part in his campaign.

His march southwards was at first uneventful, for the
weakness of Persia had been decisively exposed and the cities of
Syria and Phoenicia submitted without a struggle until he came
to Tyre. This was the strongest of the coastal cities, because it
still had a considerable fleet and the main part of the city was on
an island with two harbours, separated from the shore by half a
kilometre of sea. Tyre also had an abundant supply of artillery
and inventive designers. The siege of Tyre, which lasted seven
months, was the most dramatic of any siege in the ancient world
that has been recorded, and it was fortunate for Alexander that
he could draw on the forests of the Lebanon range for the timber
he needed.[16] Since he had dismissed his own fleet after the fall of
Miletus, his only hope of forcing Tyre to surrender was by
building a causeway across the narrow stretch of water from
which he could use his artillery against the city walls and force
his way into the town.

There were abundant supplies of stone in the neighbourhood
and it was easy to conscript local labour for the work of piling up
the stones in the sea, but timber also was needed in the form of
stakes to serve as a framework for the stones, and also to provide
a level track for troops and machines. At first, while the
causeway was being built in shallow water, the work proceeded
smoothly, but difficulties increased as the causeway extended
into deeper water, for the workers were then vulnerable to
attacks by sea and needed special protection. Two wooden
towers were built towards the end of the mole, providing
platforms for stone-throwers and catapults to attack the city and
make it difficult for boats to approach. To protect the towers
from fire attack skins and hides were attached to the exposed
timbers. The advantage, however, did not long rest with the
besiegers. The Tyrians converted a merchantman into an
elaborate fire-ship loaded with a mass of inflammable material
and, when the wind was in the right direction, triremes towed
it towards the causeway and set fire to the pitch, sulphur,
and other material. The small crew of the fire-ship jumped

overboard and swam to safety. While the towers went up in flames, the triremes stood by and shot their missiles so that nobody could approach and quench the flames. At the same time a large number of small boats came out and burnt all the engines that had not been destroyed by the main fire, and tore up the stakes that had been sunk in front of the mole as a framework for its continuation.

This was a crucial point in the siege, the advantage having now swung strongly in favour of Tyre. Alexander, however, had learnt his lesson. He needed more fire-power, and so long as Tyre controlled the sea the issue would remain uncertain. He therefore gave orders for a widening of the causeway and a massive construction of new siege engines, supplementing his own engineers with experts from other Phoenician cities and Cyprus. He himself went to Sidon to begin to build up a new fleet. The kings of Arados and Byblos added their contingents, making a total of eighty Phoenician ships, and they were reinforced by squadrons from Cyprus, Rhodes, Cilicia, and Lycia. When these programmes had been completed Alexander was able to develop new tactics. He now had an overwhelming supply of artillery and could use his fire-power from ships as well as from the mole. The whole circuit of the wall came under fire and though the Tyrians devised ingenious machines to weaken the force of the stones and arrows, they were gradually worn down. Finally it was possible from a wooden tower on the end of the causeway to drop a drawbridge down on the wall and to force a way into the city.

It is impossible to estimate even approximately the amount of timber that was used by both sides in this long siege, but it must have had a significant effect on the timber resources of the neighbourhood of Tyre: it would be interesting to know which woods were used for their various needs, but only one piece of explicit information survives in the sources. Diodorus records that when the mole was badly damaged by a storm the Macedonians cut down specially large trees in the mountains and sank them in the sea together with their branches to break the force of the waves.[17] But for most purposes in the siege, and particularly for the frames of the catapults and stone-throwers, strength was more important than length.

In the period that followed the death of Alexander, when his marshals were carving out their independent kingdoms, sieges have a larger share in the historical record and one of the princes took his name from them—Demetrius *Poliorketes*, besieger of cities. He remained famous for the scale of his siege works and particularly for the enormous wooden towers that he built, to which the name *helepolis*, city-stormer, was given. Diodorus is our main authority for his operations and in this period he seems to be drawing on a good source. There is some useful control in technical writings, for the practical details of the construction were interesting to those who were concerned with engineering problems, and we can also compare Diodorus' account with Plutarch's *Life of Demetrius*, which is not entirely dependent on the source used by Diodorus.

Demetrius was the son of Antigonus, who had been one of Alexander's commanders and had established a powerful base in Syria. His main rival was Ptolemy, who had been sent after Alexander's death to govern Egypt and had established his independence, ruling Egypt from the Greek colony of Alexandria, whose site Alexander himself had chosen. As in the Bronze Age the most attractive line of expansion from Egypt was northwards through the economically lean Palestine to the richer lands of Phoenicia and Syria. Moreover, as we have seen, if Ptolemy was not satisfied with being confined to Egypt, he needed a fleet, and the timber for warships had to come either from the forest belt that runs from Lycia to Lebanon or from the island of Cyprus. Both Antigonus and Ptolemy were anxious to enjoy patronage and respect in Greece, for Greece was still regarded as the cultural leader in the Mediterranean and the best reservoir of mercenaries and technical experts. The rivalry of these two powers was widespread, but the open clashes came in the eastern Mediterranean, and, as Ptolemy was at a considerable disadvantage when fighting in Phoenicia or Syria, it is natural that Cyprus should assume major importance. Ptolemy had gained control of the island in the very unsettled period that followed the death of Alexander, and Antigonus sent his son to drive him out.

Demetrius landed on the Karpas peninsula at the north-eastern end of the island and made his base there.[18] Advancing towards Salamis, the island's capital, he was met by Ptolemy's general Menelaus. After a sharp engagement Menelaus took his force back to Salamis, which was well fortified with strong walls and artillery. Demetrius, realising that Salamis could not be taken by assault, withdrew to prepare for the siege. He had no siege equipment with him and sent to the mainland for skilled men, and for iron and timber and other supplies. It was presumably easier to get his timber from the forests of Cilicia or Syria, which were firmly controlled by Antigonus, than from the forests in the north and more particularly in the west of the island which might be loyal to Ptolemy. His aim was to impress the Salaminian garrison by the size of his siege machines and the one he most prided himself on was his city-stormer. Here for the first time we have a detailed description from Diodorus. Each side measured forty-five cubits and it was ninety cubits high. It was divided into nine storeys and was moved by four solid wheels, eight cubits high. On the lowest floors he placed a varied range of stone-throwing machines, the largest of which hurled stones of three talents weight; on the middle floors he put his largest catapults, and on the top floors his smallest catapults with a large number of stone-throwers and more than 200 men to operate them. He also made two enormous rams and two *tortoises* protecting rams. He brought his machines up to Salamis.

With intense fire from his stone-throwers he was able to sweep the defenders from the battlements and shake the walls with his rams. Finally a section of the wall collapsed, but it was now night and to fight a way into the town in the dark would be dangerous: the troops were held back. Realising that the situation was desperate, the garrison collected great quantities of dry wood which they piled on the siege machines and then threw firebrands down from the wall. The machines caught fire, all attempts to put the fire out failed, and they were destroyed with considerable loss of life. Demetrius continued the siege, but the issue was decided by sea. Ptolemy had sent a relief force with a large fleet to save Cyprus, but his fleet was defeated outside Salamis harbour, and Cyprus had to be temporarily abandoned.

While he was encamped on Cyprus, Demetrius had asked the island of Rhodes to join him against Ptolemy. Rhodes would have been a valuable ally because she had a strong navy, a very widespread trade, and considerable influence in the Greek world. The Rhodians, after a short phase of opposition, had remained loyal to Alexander and had given him valuable help during the siege of Tyre. Any of Alexander's successors might hope for an alliance with Rhodes, but the prosperity of the island depended largely on peace and stability and she did her best to remain neutral, though her natural sympathies, based on the pattern of her trade, were with Egypt. It was to be expected therefore that Demetrius, having driven Ptolemy from Cyprus, would bring pressure on Rhodes. When it became clear that an alliance with Demetrius on any terms acceptable to him would mean the loss of independence, Rhodes decided that war was the lesser of the two evils. The siege of Rhodes remained famous throughout Antiquity, and particularly because of the extravagant size of the siege engines brought against the city by Demetrius. The account in Diodorus, though raising difficulties on points of detail, is credible in outline and is broadly consistent with other surviving sources.[19]

Demetrius assembled what seemed an overwhelming force of 200 ships, and nearly 40,000 troops with cavalry; he was also joined by the pirates of Lycia and Cilicia, whose activities had been drastically curbed by the Rhodian fleet. The Rhodians had only some 6,000 fighting men and a fleet that was heavily outnumbered. Demetrius took with him a supply of stone-throwers and catapults, and hoped by a combined attack by sea and land to get quick possession of the harbours and so cut Rhodes off from further supplies of material or men; but, after a preliminary success, his landing-party was driven off the mole and Demetrius had to fall back on a siege by land. For this he needed much more powerful machines and more of them. He sent out for massive supplies of material and also called for experts in siege machines from all parts of the Greek world. It is doubtful whether very significant supplies of timber could be got from the neighbourhood of the city, because when he landed his army he had cut down trees on a large scale for the construction of his camp; there were, however, ample supplies in Lycia and Cilicia. The most spectacular machine that was now built was an enormous city-stormer designed by an Athenian architect Epimachus:

Having assembled a great quantity of wood of all kinds, he built a siege tower which was considerably higher than any that had yet been built. The base was square, each side was nearly fifty cubits long, and it was made of squared timbers protected by iron plates. The space within he divided by beams roughly a cubit apart, to give room for those who were to push the machine forward. The whole weight of the structure was mounted on eight large solid wheels, the discs being two cubits thick and covered with strong iron plates. Pivots had been added so that the whole machine could easily be moved in any direction, and at the four corners there were uprights, each of the same length, a little less than 100 cubits (45.72 m.), leaning in towards one another in such a way that of the nine storeys the first had an area of 4,300 square feet, and the topmost an area of 900 square feet. The three exposed sides of the machine were covered with iron plates fastened by nails to the timber to protect it from fire-missiles. The storeys had embrasures in their walls designed to match in size and form the missiles which were to be discharged through them; and these embrasures had shutters which could be put up mechanically, giving protection to those who were engaged in discharging the missiles; for they were made of hides sewn together and full of wool so that they could give way to and so absorb the hits from the stone-throwers. Each storey had two stairways to avoid confusion, one for the carrying up of what was needed, and the other for going down.

Those who had to move the machine, 3,400 men, were selected for their strength from the whole force. Some of them were inside the machine, others pushed from behind, and the skill with which the machine was designed made its movement easier. He also built two types of *tortoises*, one to pile up the mound, the other equipped with rams, and two covered ways, so that those who were going to operate the machines could come and go in safety. Meanwhile he used the ships' crews to clear the ground for a depth of half a mile over which he was intending to bring up the machines he had prepared, and the frontage covered seven towers and six stretches of wall between towers.

Diodorus emphasises the scale of these preparations by adding that the number of technicians and others that were assembled was little short of 30,000.[20] A little further information about the machines is added when they are assembled for the attack:

He set the city-stormer in the middle and divided the mound-piling *tortoises*, which were eight in number. He placed four on each side of the city-stormer and to each he attached a covered way . . . and two ram-carrying *tortoises*, which were many times larger; for the rams were 120 cubits long, strengthened with iron, with a head like the head of a ship's ram. It could easily be moved forward as it was on wheels and the motive force came from not less than 1,000 men. Before taking the machine up to the walls, he put stone-throwers and catapults on each of the storeys of the city-stormer, according to their various functions.[21]

The most difficult elements in Diodorus' account to explain or explain away are his manpower figures. Did the city-stormer really require 3,400 men to move it? Within the machine if five square feet were allowed for a man, there would be room for few more than 1,000. Could more than 2,000 be effectively employed pushing from behind? The figure could only be saved by assuming that the total provides for reliefs and casualties. Can we believe that 1,000 men could be needed to work the tortoise-rams, including the operating of the ram and moving the whole machine to a different section of the wall? And even allowing for a very large supply of catapults and stone-throwers, for which no numbers are given, is a work-force of 30,000 credible? It is difficult not to be extremely suspicious. But if these figures are no better than Herodotus' grossly inflated army lists, can we have any confidence in the size of the machines which Diodorus records or implies? In terms of timber this is of more importance to us.

Fortunately there is sufficient evidence to confirm that Diodorus' measurements for the city-stormer are not all grossly exaggerated. The technological advances in siege operations produced a steady stream of writers describing and analysing the various machines that were used. Some of their writings are preserved and Vitruvius in his treatise on architecture included a section on machines the second half of which is devoted to machines of war, for which he drew on the work of the specialists.

Three other sets of dimensions can be compared with those of Diodorus:

Source	Sides of base	Height
Diodorus (20. 91. 2)	*c.*50 cu.	*c.*100 cu.
Athenaeus Mechanicus	48 cu.	90 cu.
Vitruvius (10. 16. 4)	60 ft.	125 ft.
Plutarch (*Demetrius* 21)	48 cu.	66 cu.

The height is impressive but should not surprise, for the main function of the tower was to provide a platform from which to fire on the enemy from above. In speaking of the four corner-posts (*kiones*) Diodorus says that they were all of the same height, a little less than 100 cubits (150 ft.), and he does not suggest that the posts were composed of two or more timbers joined together. Cedars and firs would have been the tallest trees available to Demetrius. Both could have provided posts of 100 feet, but lengths of 150 feet are unacceptable.

One of the specialists, Biton, who wrote in the third quarter of the third century BC, describing the construction of a giant siege tower which Posidonius, a Macedonian, designed for Alexander, gave a brief indication of the timber used: 'All kinds of wood have to be used. Long lengths and planking should be mountain pine (*peuke*), fir, or coastal pine (*pitys*); for axles and wheels oak or ash should be used.'[22] As both Greek and Roman writers confirm, fir and pine were regarded as the best woods for general construction, but at points of special stress the stronger hardwoods were to be preferred. The work on beams, boards, and planks was rough: as Biton says of the *helepolis* which he describes: 'such works as these do not require a carefully planed or finely finished surface'. Posidonius was presumably thinking in terms of the timber with which he was familiar in Macedon. Demetrius may have found it easier to get cedar, juniper, cypress, or pine from Lycia than fir.[23]

Of the other siege engines used at Rhodes by Demetrius the ram-tortoise required most timber. Vitruvius describes the design developed by Diades. The main purpose was to give more force to the ram and at the same time to protect it. Without such protection the ram's head could too easily be broken by heavy timbers or stones from the battlements. The basic improvement was to put the ram on a roller and apply the principle of torsion, so that when pulled back by ropes and released it struck the wall with greater force. The machine had a protective covering and a tower was built over the centre, which served a double purpose. It provided a platform from which artillery could fire at the battlements, and it also enabled the use of the ram to be effectively directed. Textual difficulties throw some doubt on the measurements given by Vitruvius, but the length seems to have been thirty-two cubits (14.63 m.) and the height sixteen cubits (7.31 m.) up to the beginning of the roof.[24]

Vitruvius also gives a more detailed description of the construction of a ram-tortoise designed by Hagetor of Byzantium. Its base was sixty feet long and thirteen feet wide and, like

Diades' machine, it had a turret from which the use of the ram could be directed. The requirements included eight timbers thirty-six feet long, eighteen inches wide, and fifteen inches thick; four timbers forty-five feet long, eighteen inches wide, and nine inches thick; a large number of posts eighteen feet high, nine inches wide, and eight inches thick, and one foot nine inches apart. In Hagetor's design the ram had an iron beak, like the beak on the head of a warship's ram, from which iron plates fifteen feet long were fixed to the timber. The length of the ram was 104 feet, it was fifteen inches wide at the butt-end and one foot thick, tapering to one foot wide and nine inches thick at the top.[25] These measurements for the ram are not impossible, but they discredit the figure in Diodorus of 180 feet for the ram-tortoises used by Demetrius. A timber of that length would not stand the force of a violent impact, and no trees approaching such size are recorded by Pliny who was an avid collector of records. Diodorus has made a mistake and perhaps the most charitable explanation is that he has confused cubits and feet; but even 120 feet would be barely credible.

The other form of *tortoise* mentioned by Diodorus is a much simpler machine, because it has a simpler function. The name given to it, *chostris*, means that it was used for moving earth; Caesar speaks of it as a '*tortoise* for levelling the ground, made from the strongest timbers'. In Vitruvius' description it is a square with sides of only twenty-one feet (6.40 m.) and the frame-posts are only nine feet (2.74 m.) high.[26] Timber was also needed for the stone-throwers and catapults which were used in great numbers throughout the siege, from shipboard, siege tower, ram-tortoise, and from the ground. Nor should one forget the wastage by fire. In earlier days much damage could be done by fire-arrows from the battlements, but when the attackers had developed first the covering of leather and other soft materials and then of iron plates for their siege equipment, there could be little hope of success except by a surprise sally on a dark night from one of the gates.

The fire hazard was sharply illustrated in the siege of Massilia in 49 BC. Caesar had crossed the Rubicon and challenged the senatorial establishment led by Pompey. He had behind him an experienced army, battle-hardened and confident from the conquest of Gaul. Pompey could not muster an effective challenge

in time and evacuated Italy to build up his strength from
the resources of the east. Without a fleet Caesar could not
pursue Pompey across the Adriatic and it would have been
dangerous to cross to the east without a show of strength in
Spain; for Pompey had been governor of Spain since 55 BC and
the Spaniards remembered his successful campaign against
Sertorius in the seventies.

Caesar's route to Spain passed by Massilia and the city had to
be won over or neutralised. He summoned their leading men to
negotiate, but they pleaded to remain neutral since they had
good reason to be grateful to both Caesar and Pompey. Before
Caesar's army reached Massilia, however, one of Pompey's most
influential supporters, Cn. Domitius Ahenobarbus, entered the
town, tipped the balance in Pompey's favour, and took command of the defence. Caesar, in a hurry to reach Spain, left
C. Trebonius in charge of the siege but established the strategy
before he left. The boat-builders of Arelate, some twenty
kilometres up the Rhône, were instructed to build twelve
warships and siege engines were to be prepared as quickly as
possible and brought up against the walls.[27] Trebonius com-
mandeered a large labour force of men and mules from the
province and cut down 'all the trees far and wide in the territory
of Massilia'.[28] When the attack on the walls began the garrison
achieved some minor successes by fire-raising sorties, but they
were soon penned back within the walls. Meanwhile the twelve
warships ordered from Arelate had been built in thirty days and
the Massilian fleet had been defeated in two engagements.

With no prospect of further supplies the garrison surrendered
and agreed to wait for instructions from Caesar who was now
campaigning in Spain. But, according to Caesar's account, the
cease-fire was not respected. When the Romans were off their
guard the Massaliots launched a massive attack on the Roman
siege engines, set them on fire, and a high wind spread the
flames. Towers, mound, artillery were completely destroyed
before the Romans could realise how it had happened. But when
the Massaliots made another sortie the following day the
Romans were prepared and threw them back with little
difficulty. They now had to improvise, for they had no timber
left and no hope of quickly getting any more. They used mud-
brick to bind their mound together and had soon made it again

such a threat to the walls that the Massaliots gave up hope and surrendered.

Lucan welcomed the drama of the siege of Massilia and heightened the story. He had clearly read an account of the actual operations and he saw the dramatic value of the large-scale felling of trees to make the siege engines:

> Then all the woods far and wide were levelled to the ground and the forests were stripped of their oaks. There remained only a sacred grove which had been there since time immemorial. No Gaul dared enter and no axe had ever cut its trees. The Roman soldiers were overawed and stayed their axes until Caesar arrived, called for an axe, set it to a tree and took upon himself the guilt.[29]

It is extremely doubtful whether Lucan found this part of the story in a historian's account and it is highly probable that Caesar was in Spain at the time implied. But it was a good story and helped to build up the character he wished to give to Caesar. There is, however, no reason to doubt the stripping of local woods.

Athens had suffered no less badly from Sulla's siege in 86 BC. When Mithridates King of Pontus in 88 BC roused the Greeks of Asia Minor to massacre Roman residents and sent one of his generals to win over and occupy Greece, the Athenians were foolish enough to think that Mithridates might succeed in driving the Romans out of the Greek world. Under the influence of a popular anti-Roman leader, Aristion, they threw in their lot with Mithridates. Sulla who, as consul in 88, had been given command of the war against Mithridates, needed to win Greece back before he led his army into Asia Minor. Most of the Greek cities saw that the future lay with Rome, but Athens stubbornly resisted. Sulla was in a hurry and hoped to take the Piraeus by a surprise attack, but the assault failed, and having no siege train with him he had to get the timber for his siege engines locally. According to Plutarch he sent out 10,000 pairs of mules daily to collect timber, and when he ran out of timber and could not replace or repair his losses he cut down the sacred groves together with the Academy, which had more trees in it than any other place in the suburbs, and the Lyceum.[30] There is probably exaggeration in Plutarch's account, but we can accept a ruthless cutting of trees for the siege. Attica had never had much good timber: it had very much less when Sulla left and the constant reminder, especially in the Academy and the Lyceum, must have been a significant factor in keeping alive anti-Roman feelings in Athens.

In most campaigns it could be assumed that the army would find adequate supplies of timber in enemy country, though it may have become increasingly common to take a stock of artillery, for the machines had to be carefully made. If a shortage of suitable timber was anticipated in the campaign area, the more bulky siege equipment could be prepared in advance. Alexander's engineer Diades had shown that a siege tower could be carried in sections, and when Alexander, in his last year, needed a new fleet for an expedition against Arabia he gave instructions that ships should be built by the Phoenicians, cut into sections for transport, and reassembled in Babylon. Such prefabrication seems to be implied in Plutarch's account of Antony's bitter experience against the Parthians. In the struggle for power that followed the assassination of Caesar Antony chose to base his fortunes on the resources of the east. He saw himself returning to Rome as the triumphant conqueror of Parthia and the avenger of the humiliating defeat of a large Roman army led by Crassus at the battle of Carrhae in 53 BC.

Antony decided to avoid the shorter route across the steppe land east of the Euphrates where he would, like Crassus, be vulnerable to the Parthian archers, and invade through the rougher country of Armenia and Atropatene. Feeling that speed was essential, he left his siege train to follow him with a small escort while he advanced rapidly on the important city of Phraaspa. It soon became apparent that the city could not be taken by assault and he waited for his siege train; but the siege train never came. Antony's dispositions had been betrayed to the Parthian king, who sent out a strong cavalry force. The small escort, taken by surprise, was overwhelmed and the siege train, which, according to Plutarch, included 300 wagons and with them a ram eighty feet (24.38 m.) long, was captured.[31] The siege equipment could not be replaced because the only timber on the route was miserable in length and had poor bearing-strength. Antony had to face a long and dangerous retreat. It is fascinating to guess how the course of history would have run if he had not lost his siege train.

When Augustus had firmly consolidated his power there was a major change in the pattern of war. The army was judiciously taken out of politics and the legions were withdrawn from pacified provinces and stationed at key points on the frontiers or in unsettled areas. Their function was to protect the provinces by ensuring that there were no dangerous concentrations of hostile tribes threatening invasion and to help directly and indirectly the process of Romanisation, which was the best safeguard against revolt from within. The Roman legion was well adapted to carry out this policy. With a paper strength of 6,000 men divided into sixty centuries it was self-supporting. There was no separate corps of engineers and no forestry corps. The legionaries had to build their own camps, make their own weapons, and cut their own timber. Vegetius describes the duties of the camp commandant, a man of long military experience serving under the legion's commander, who will probably be at his post not more than five years, before moving up in his senatorial career. He is responsible for supervising the construction of the camp, whether tented or with barracks, including hospital and workshops. He has to ensure that adequate supplies of all essential materials are maintained. These include iron and charcoal for the making of tools, wood for making catapults and all the varied forms of siege equipment, including scaling-ladders with their sides in one piece without joins, specially strong wood for javelins (cornel or ash), and for bows probably yew.[32] For work on wood there had to be axes and saws, and the versatile *dolabra*, the Roman pickaxe.[33]

The evidence for the use of timber by the army during the Empire is almost exclusively archaeological and it is only recently that serious attempts have been made to correlate and interpret the evidence. A great number of military buildings have been excavated over the past century in Roman provinces, but since much of the evidence for timber usage comes only from post-holes or soil discoloration it is not surprising that the subject was long neglected. Even when post-holes were identified it was often difficult to distinguish between original construction and later rebuilding. A new stimulus, however, was given to the subject by the excavation of a fort at Valkenburg in Holland near the Rhine where substantial

elements of the timber construction were well preserved, and by
the excavation of forts in Scotland which had been built under
Domitian but abandoned after a brief occupation. Britain perhaps offers the best evidence for the impact of a Roman army
on the forest resources of a province.

When the Romans decided to make Britain a Roman province the country was well forested. In the record of his campaigns as governor of Gaul Caesar wrote that there was
timber in Britain of every kind, as in Gaul, with the exception of
beech and fir.[34] There is no evidence for firs in Britain after the
Ice Age before specimens were imported in the seventeenth
century, but Britain had soils and climate ideally suited to
beech, particularly on the chalk downs of south England and the
Chiltern hills, and there is evidence from pollen analysis of beech
in burials long before the Iron Age.[35] Oak was by far the most
widespread species, but in most districts there were adequate
supplies of elm, ash, lime, birch, and, particularly in marshy
areas, alder. Woods are involved in almost all the brief accounts
of military operations;[36] there should have been no difficulty
in finding adequate supplies of timber for military and civil
purposes.

Britain had been invaded by Caesar during the conquest of
Gaul, but his summer campaigns in 55 and 54 BC were too short
to win more than a nominal submission from the tribes of the
south-east and in the following period the Romans were too
preoccupied with civil war and imperial reorganisation to
resume Caesar's policy. It was left to the emperor Claudius to
carry forward Caesar's plans and to invade the island in AD 43
with three legions. There were few problems in overrunning the
lowlands of the south and south-east, but it was much more
difficult to impose Roman control over the highlands of Wales
and the north. To win battles in these areas was not enough; the
victories had to be consolidated by the judicious distribution of
legions and auxiliary cohorts in well-sited forts and fortresses.
More than 200 of these sites have been at least partially excavated, covering 400 years of occupation, but it was only in the first
century that timber was the main building material. Although
there are minor variations from fort to fort, there are standard
plans for legionary fortresses and for the smaller forts for
auxiliary cohorts and standard forms for the various buildings.

We can therefore cautiously generalise from individual cases and concentrate on the cohort fort at Fendoch and the legionary fortress at Inchtuthil, for which the evidence is fullest.

The historical context is provided by Tacitus in his biography of his father-in-law Agricola who was governor of Britain from AD 78 to 84. Agricola's two predecessors had advanced the northern frontier, moving the northernmost legionary camp from Lincoln to York, and had almost completed the conquest of Wales. Agricola first campaigned in north Wales, which was still restless, and then continued to advance in the north, beyond the border into southern Scotland. After a temporary halt on the Forth–Clyde line he decided to extend his advance into the north of Scotland, hoping that by bringing the northern tribes to battle he could complete the conquest of Britain. After failing in an attack on one of the legions, the enemy withdrew and concentrated their forces on Mons Graupius, probably not far from Aberdeen. There the battle was fought and decisively won by Agricola; according to Tacitus the enemy lost 10,000 men, the Romans 360.[37] This was late in the season and the Caledonian tribesmen were completely crushed; Agricola could take his army back to winter quarters. At this point, much to Tacitus' disgust, Agricola was recalled by Domitian. Later, in the preface to his *Histories*, Tacitus wrote: 'Britain had been completely subdued, but was immediately abandoned.'[38]

Tacitus' rhetorical text throws little light on the topography or the strategy of Agricola's campaigns north of the Forth–Clyde line, but a study of the forts in the area suggests a convincing reconstruction. The legionary fortress at Inchtuthil is one of the keys to the solution.[39] It was built seventeen kilometres from Perth on the north bank of the river Tay on a plateau commanding the Dunkeld Gorge, through which the Tay issues from the Highlands, the easiest route for road and railway. At the same time much smaller forts for auxiliary cohorts were built at the mouth of other glens issuing from the Highlands, the best preserved being Fendoch at the mouth of the Sma' Glen where the river Almond emerges. The natural inference is that Agricola intended to seal off the Highlands by blocking the natural gateways and to station a legion where it could reinforce any fort that was threatened or meet any highland army that broke out. Inchtuthil cannot have been built before Agricola advanced north of the Forth-Clyde line in 83: it clearly implied the intention to incorporate the north of Scotland (with the exception of the Highlands) in the Roman province.

The fortress, however, was not abandoned when Agricola was recalled, as is demonstrated by coins of 86 and 87. In or soon after 87 the Romans departed, though the fortress had not been completed. The heating system of a set of baths outside the wall had not yet been used, and the legion commander's headquarters had not been built, though the site for it had been prepared. The withdrawal was not under immediate pressure from the natives, for it was preceded by systematic demolition. The stone wall was dismantled, the pottery and glass from the stores were deliberately smashed, some eleven tons of nails of all sizes were buried to ensure that they were not used by the tribesmen to make weapons, and the main timbers were wrenched from the ground and taken away, leaving a trail of bent nails. There was a similar withdrawal at apparently the same time from the auxiliary fort at Fendoch. It seems that Agricola's forward policy was not immediately reversed, and that the main reason for the withdrawal was the increasing danger on the Danube. By 92 at the latest one of the British legions had been transferred to that front: the garrison of Britain was no longer strong enough to control the large area north of the Forth-Clyde line without endangering its hold on the south.

Since Inchtuthil and Fendoch were occupied for such a short time there is no confusion in the evidence arising from rebuilding and nowhere is the scale of timber consumption in the early phases of the Roman occupation more clearly demonstrated. The fortress is a rough square with sides of some 1,500 feet (470 m.), covering an area of a little more than fifty acres. The main defence is a turf rampart, perhaps twelve feet high, faced with a stone wall, and an external ditch twenty feet wide. The rampart was built over a layer of round timbers set transversely to the rampart and round timbers were used on top of the rampart for the military walk, which was protected by breastwork and battlements, probably in wattle. Inside the rampart an area about ten metres deep, the *intervallum*, was reserved to allow free circulation near the rampart, with the additional advantage of keeping the men's barracks out of the range of enemy missiles.

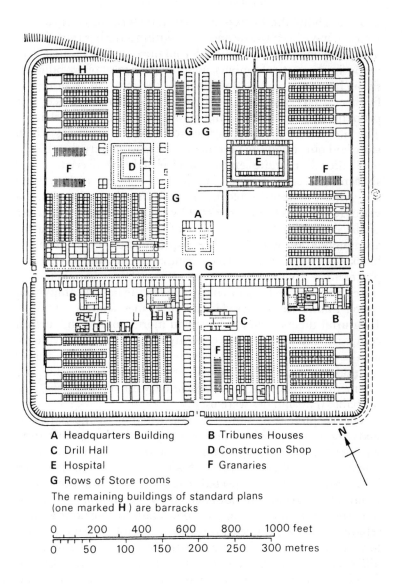

A Headquarters Building   **B** Tribunes Houses
C Drill Hall   **D** Construction Shop
E Hospital   **F** Granaries
G Rows of Store rooms

The remaining buildings of standard plans
(one marked **H**) are barracks

0	200	400	600	800	1000 feet
0	50	100	150	200	250	300 metres

6 Legionary fortress at Inchtuthil

Throughout the fortress the standard form of construction seems to have been wattle and daub within a timber framework. The plans have been deciphered from the post-holes which were made for the vertical timbers, averaging for most of the building six inches (15.2 cm.) by four inches (10.1 cm.) in section, and five feet apart, and though there is no specific evidence, it is probable that horizontal timbers were linked with the verticals. The simplest of the buildings were the men's barracks which were laid out round the periphery. There were sixty-four blocks in all, fifty-four for the centuries of nine of the cohorts which had six centuries each, and ten for the first cohort which had ten centuries. The century blocks are built in pairs and each has a veranda along its front supported by timber posts. The quarters of the centurion are at one end of the block, combining his accommodation with his office requirements. The rest of the block is divided into fourteen compartments and each compartment is divided into a small room where equipment was stored and a much larger living-room. In the tented camps from which timber camps are derived eight men shared a tent; at Inchtuthil the men should have had more room, with fourteen compartments for a century of eighty men. There is no evidence for the roofing, but one can assume a series of tie-beam trusses with rafters, and a sheathing of boards over the rafters. Since no fragments of roof-tiles were associated with the barracks, it is probable that shingles were used.

The hospital is as simple in construction as the barracks. Sixty rooms are provided in a rectangular building measuring 298 × 193 feet (90.83 × 58.83 m.). The rooms are built on each side of a circulating corridor with a rectangular space left open in the middle. An unexpected feature of the structure is that rooms and corridor are not covered by a common roof. Driplines show that the two lines of rooms and the corridor all had separate roofs, a strange feature which Richmond, the excavator, explained by a wish to avoid the need for long lengths. A different problem was raised by the granaries. It was essential for a legionary fortress to carry a substantial reserve of grain and by the time of the invasion of Britain a standard type of granary had been developed; six of them have been identified at Inchtuthil, measuring 136 × 42 feet (41.45 × 12.80 m.). All that was actually found was a series of foundation trenches for beams in which short squared posts would have been set to carry the floor of the granary. This was a refinement from the practice of the Claudian period. In the fort at Hod Hill the posts to carry the granary floor were sunk into the gravel independently without a trench.[40] A little later, when Richborough was made a supply base, the posts were set in a trench,[41] a slight advance, but in both these systems the posts, sunk directly in the ground, would be liable to rot: the provision of a timber sill into which the posts could be fitted was a considerable improvement.[42] The floor was raised so that air could circulate freely below the floor, as a protection against damp and a discouragement to insects and small rodents which would be attracted by the grain.

In the second century stone was substituted for wood in granaries and their most notable features are the thickness of the walls, averaging over three feet (91.4 cm.), and the strengthening of the side walls with buttresses. This reminder of the thrust of the grain against the walls suggests that strong timbers specially reinforced must have been used in the first century. Special selection was also needed for the timber posts up to thirty feet (9.14 m.) tall and one foot (30.5 cm.) square that provided the skeleton round which towers on each side of the gates were built, nine for each tower. These timbers had to be both strong and straight and would have been much more difficult to find than the framing timbers of the barracks and other buildings.[43]

Fendoch, covering four and a half acres, is less than a tenth of the size of Inchtuthil, but the main features are repeated, though on a much smaller scale, with the same types of construction.[44] The barracks have the same plan, but there are ten blocks only in place of sixty-four, for the fort was intended for a cohort of 1,000 men, and the men have less room; there are only two granaries and they are considerably smaller, 50 × 30 feet; but the same system was used of setting posts on timbers sunk in a trench to raise the granary floor; gates and towers were similar to those of Inchtuthil, requiring the same tall timbers for the towers. As at Inchtuthil there are clear signs that the main timbers were taken away when the fort was abandoned.

The volume of timber required for Fendoch and Inchtuthil was very considerable, and it would be interesting to know how the supply was organised. Richmond, impressed particularly by the big timbers required for the gateway towers at Fendoch, concluded that they must have been drawn from seasoned stock at a supply base, perhaps York, for the pollen analysis of a soil sample from the rampart suggested that there were no suitable trees in the vicinity.[45] He found confirmation for his view from his excavation at Inchtuthil; the building of such a large fortress would, he thought, need seasoned timbers on a massive scale, which could not have been produced by the legionaries cutting their own timber in the neighbourhood.[46] It also seemed significant that the main timbers were taken away when the fortress was abandoned.

Richmond's views, which were widely accepted, have now been strongly challenged and need to be reconsidered. In a detailed discussion of the issues W. S. Hanson has argued that the importance attached by the Romans to using dried timber has been exaggerated and that in building camps seasoning would have been an unnecessary extravagance if timber was available locally; and Britain, he thinks, was so thickly forested that there should have been no need to build up centralised stocks of standard sizes. Richmond attached considerable importance to the pollen analysis of a turf from the rampart at Fendoch which showed an abundance of grass spores and pollen from alder and birch, but none from oaks. As Hanson points out, recent work on the history of Scotland's vegetation suggests a substantial presence of oaks in the north-east, on low ground and in fertile valleys, with a scatter of elm, alder, and birch, while on the higher ground pine and birch dominated.[47]

Although there is more evidence of Roman concern for seasoning than Hanson suggests,[48] it is reasonable to draw a distinction between civil and military building. Caesar in Gaul had to use green timber throughout his campaigns and in the scenes from the Dacian wars on Trajan's Column the Romans seem to cut the timber for bridges, walls, and buildings as they need it. But beyond the Danube the Romans were campaigning in areas which have always been rich in good oak forests. The quantity and quality of woodland in the north-east of Scotland is less securely established. If we had to rely on pollen analysis alone we should be very doubtful whether adequate supplies of timber could have been found within easy distance from Inchtuthil. Published samples from the north-east indicate very low levels of oak, but in their publication it was recognised that the pollen results were barely compatible with the considerable remains of oaks found in the Buchan moss in Aberdeenshire.[49] Similarly, M. L. Anderson, in his history of Scottish forestry, emphasises the large number of oaks, including one of up to three feet in diameter, which had been used as foundations for roads both north and south of the Forth.[50]

More direct, though admittedly vague, evidence comes from the literary sources. Tacitus, in his brief account of Agricola's campaign beyond the Forth–Clyde line, says that while the fleet had the seas and its storms to fear, the army was faced by 'the recesses of the woods and hills'.[51] The accounts of a later expedition are a little more specific. In 208 the emperor Septimius Severus, having received a report from the governor of Britain that it was impossible to control the northern frontier without strong reinforcements, decided to mount a major campaign beyond the Antonine wall, and the identification of some of his marching camps shows that he followed the same route as Agricola. We have two accounts, in Dio and Herodian, and both make woods an important factor in the campaign. Dio says that he was very considerably handicapped by the need to cut down woods and fill up marshes. According to Herodian, although the emperor won several engagements, his enemy found it easy to escape and hide in the woods and marshes.[52] It is reasonable to infer that there would have been adequate quantities locally of timber to build the camps, but it is much more difficult to assess its quality. Would local oaks have produced the thirty-foot lengths of straight timber, one foot square, that were needed for the gates? This we cannot know from the evidence available to us, but Agricola, when he decided to extend Roman occupation beyond the Forth–Clyde line, should have had reports on the general character of the woodlands on the route. If he had reason to believe that tall oaks with straight trunks would be difficult to find, he could have organised the cutting of the larger timbers in the south of Scotland to be carried by sea to the river Tay.

Inchtuthil and Fendoch illustrate the standard layout of camps for legions and auxiliary cohorts, but there are many camps which do not fit neatly into either category. A camp site at Longthorpe near Peterborough, recently investigated, covers

27.3 acres, whereas a legion normally requires fifty acres and a cohort from three to five acres.[53] The camp seems to have been designed for a mixed force of legionaries and auxiliaries and the siting suggests that the function of the garrison was to watch the sensitive area between the Iceni and the warlike tribes to their north. Longthorpe was one of a small series of such camps dating from the early years of occupation, when legions had to be divided to provide a wider network of strong points to ensure security in the newly conquered area. The plan of these camps strongly resembled the legionary camp on a smaller scale and, as with Inchtuthil and Fendoch, the most difficult timbers to provide will have been the tall posts that formed the framework of the towers flanking the four gates. In the two gates that were examined at Longthorpe there was the same disposition, a wide carriageway flanked by a tower on either side framed by six posts, 10 × 10 inches in section (slightly smaller than at Inchtuthil). It is interesting to note that here too the posts were removed when the camp was abandoned, but they were sawn off at ground level rather than torn out.

Provision also had to be made at all periods for much smaller detachments. The Roman fortlet at Bamburgh Mill in Dumfriesshire, surrounded by two ditches, occupied only 0.21 acres and was probably designed for a century of eighty men.[54] The only buildings that could be traced were two small blocks of barracks with walls of wattle coated with clay and apparently a surface of plaster. But even this small camp had a substantial gate whose six post-holes could still be traced.

The construction of forts and fortresses, particularly in Wales, the north of England, and Scotland, in the years from 43 to c.100 involved a significant inroad into the forests of Britain: from the reign of Trajan onwards the scale was progressively reduced, by the increasingly widespread use of stone. When a legionary fortress was established at Chester in the Flavian period a wooden amphitheatre was built; after a short interval it was replaced by a larger amphitheatre in stone.[55] The earliest stone granaries date from Trajan's reign, after which no trace has yet been found of a wooden granary. In the second century ramparts were gradually abandoned in favour of stone walls. Hadrian's great wall across the isthmus from Tyne to Solway and the forts associated with it were built with stone, as were the headquarters and most of the buildings in forts and fortresses in the rest of the province. It is unlikely that timber framing was completely abandoned, but we need more evidence to assess its role.

The Roman army was also responsible for building up communications within the province. This involved tree-felling where natural routes led through forest, and special measures had to be taken in marshy areas. On campaigns when speed was essential the ·system used by Caesar in his Gallic campaigns (p. 155) could be adopted, and some such system may be implied by Tacitus when he calls part of the military route of penetration beyond the Rhine 'the long bridges'.[56] Permanent highways needed something more solid. In Scotland trunks of trees have been found which served as the foundation of roads.[57] Rivers had to be crossed on campaigns and roads needed bridges. Vegetius describes in some detail the various methods used by Roman troops when there was no bridge to use.[58] The bridge of boats was a natural improvisation, adopted by Xerxes when he crossed from Asia to Europe in his invasion of Greece and used by Trajan's legions in his Dacian campaigns (pl. 15A). When boats were not available, but the neighbourhood was wooded, tree-trunks could be hollowed out and provide a platform for planking. Alternatively the platform could be provided by barrels. Where there were neither boats nor timber, goatskins could be collected and stuffed to support men swimming across the river. But the method which was the most efficient if circumstances allowed was to sink large numbers of piles in close formation in the river-bed and lay planking over them.

This last was the method most commonly used for permanent bridges in the early stage of the invasion, and when the river was apt to flood the abutments had to be built up, enclosing a concrete or earth-and-rubble core in a frame of substantial timbers.[59] The planking was more solid than in temporary bridges and there were parapets supported by criss-cross tracery. In and after the second century there was a tendency with bridges, as with walls, forts, and granaries, to replace timber with stone.[60] In a bridge at Wallasey in Cheshire the width of the river to be spanned was 100 feet and there were two stone piers in the crossing.[61] There is, however, very little evidence for stone arches and it seems to have been normal even over wide rivers to retain wood for the superstructure. Trajan's bridge over the Danube is an outstanding example (pl. 15B).

The Roman impact on British woodlands was also reflected in buildings for civilians. Tacitus, in his biography of Agricola, recorded that in the winter following his first successful campaign he concentrated on the peaceful development of the province:

> In order that men who lived rough lives in scattered villages which made them easily roused to war should grow accustomed to peace and leisure by enjoying the pleasures of life, he encouraged them personally and helped them publicly to build temples, civic centres (*fora*), and proper houses (rather than huts). He praised those who actively responded and had harsh words for those who were slow. As a result competition for honour took the place of compulsion.[62]

In this he was giving new impetus to a policy that had been tested in Spain and Gaul and was adopted in Britain in the early stage of consolidation. It was in the Roman interest to encourage the Britons to leave their fortified hilltops for new settlements associated with roads which would encourage economic growth. The formless grouping of huts should be replaced by a civilised town plan with a central forum and a rectangular street grid.

The evidence for the use of timber in civil building is considerably more elusive than for its use in the military sector. Most of the towns have been continuously inhabited since Roman times and later rebuilding has obliterated or at least obscured work of the early period. Excavation, however, at Verulamium (St. Albans), which was established near a native settlement, probably illustrates common practice. Two blocks that date back to the middle of the first century reveal plans that would not have been out of place in a contemporary town in Italy, a combination of shops and living accommodation conceived as a single complex rather than a series of independent units.[63] The walls, like those in Fendoch and Inchtuthil, were based on a framework of vertical and horizontal timbers, with a filling of wattle and daub. This may have continued into and beyond the second century for private housing,[64] but, as in the military sector, stone increasingly replaced timber in public buildings. Roofing, however, still depended on timber.

One other aspect of the Roman impact on British woodlands needs emphasis. From a very early stage of the occupation the Romans exploited the mineral resources of the island. As early as AD 49 silver was being extracted from the lead-mines of the Mendips in Somerset and further lead-mines were opened later in Shropshire and Flintshire. Copper was mined for the first time in north Wales and Angelsey, and a gold-mine at Dolaucothi in Carmarthenshire was elaborately equipped with an aqueduct (c.11 km. long) and a large wooden wheel to extract water from the mine-workings. The Britons were already producing their own iron; the Romans exploited the iron-ore of the great oak forests, particularly the Kent–Sussex weald and the forest of Dean, more intensively.[65] Much later, in the seventeenth century, the consumption of wood for smelting-furnaces caused a critical shortage of timber in some areas; even in the Roman period the use of wood as fuel accounted for a significant proportion of total consumption.

The Romans also cut extensively into the forests on the Rhine and Danube frontiers. In Caesar's day they had a vague impression of an endless forest beyond the Danube, called the Hercynian forest, which was a nine-days'-journey wide and stretched eastwards from the territory of the Helvetii for at least a sixty-days' journey and no one knew how much further.[66] Beyond the Rhine, also, Germany was well forested. Pliny describes the giant oaks of the coastal area, and forests recur in all accounts of campaigns beyond the river.[67]

Later the line was advanced beyond the upper half of the Rhine and the large re-entrant angle between Rhine and Danube was incorporated in the empire.[68] In lower Germany the legionary and auxiliary forts guarded the river; in upper Germany the frontier-line was at first guarded by watch-towers, while the auxiliary cohorts were stationed in reserve and the legionary fortresses remained on the Rhine. The system was modified when Hadrian adopted the principle of a continuous barrier as in Britain. The auxiliaries were brought up to the frontier-line and in upper Germany a palisade of stout wooden stakes was sunk in deep trench, while a stone wall was built for the stretch of frontier along the Rhaetian section of the Danube. In the early third century the defences were strengthened in upper Germany by building an earth rampart with ditch behind the palisade. In the legionary and auxiliary fortifications there are minor variations from their counterparts in Britain, but they were broadly similar and there was the same sequence from earth and timber buildings, in the first century to stone buildings in and after the second century.

There is an interesting feature on the Rhine frontier that has no known parallel in Britain. Two inscriptions have been found recording dedications by a detachment of one of the Rhine legions serving under a very junior officer *in lignariis*,[69] which could mean 'in a timber store-base'. These inscriptions have been ingeniously associated with sawing operations to supply camps and forts on the Main section of the Rhine frontier with big timbers that could not easily be procured in their immediate neighbourhood. The thesis is based on two very uncharacteristic forts. The first, at Ohrenbach, is small, 60 × 68 metres, and though it is fortified with wall and ditch there is no trace of buildings.[70] Across almost the whole width of the camp there was a deep trench with scattered stones that may have come from retaining-walls. It is suggested that the trench was designed for a series of sawyers operating two-man saws in a way that was familiar in many countries into the twentieth century: one of the sawyers stands above and a lower sawyer stands in a pit or trench below. One of the two inscriptions was found at Trennfurt, eight kilometres distant, and here too there is a camp very unlike the standard military pattern. From the wide spread of blackened earth it has been inferred that this was where the timber cut at the neighbouring camp was stored.

From Britain we have a description of the Roman forces in action in Tacitus' biography of Agricola. For a northern frontier we have the much more vivid narrative on stone of Trajan's two wars that led to making Dacia a province. The story was told in a series of realistic reliefs that wound round the column which Trajan set up in his new imperial Forum completed in 112.[71] In these reliefs we can see all aspects of the campaign from the crossing of the Danube on bridges built over boats to the suicide of Decebalus and the surrender of the Dacians (pls. 15, 16). We can see troops felling trees and carrying logs, building camps with turf walls and gates with wooden towers, setting up platforms and protective screens for artillery with round timbers built up like funerary pyres. Most of the trees represented are

oaks and this was not because they were more decorative; oak
was the dominant species in these central European forests.
There are no signs of the use of saws by the troops; for shaping
the timbers as well as felling the trees they use the axe combined
with a pick as their standard tool, the *dolabra*. Perhaps the most
impressive evidence for the army's work in timber is the relief
showing the great bridge over the Danube which Trajan's
architect Apollodorus designed, with its highly sophisticated
timber superstructure resting on stone piers. There is evidence
for another engineering triumph. To speed communications it
was necessary to build a road along the Danube's bank, but for
part of its length the cliffs approached so near the bank that it
was only possible to secure the width required for a military road
by extending the surface over the river. The cuttings where the
massive beams were fitted to support the widening of the road
can still be seen.

The scale on which timber was used by the Romans in Britain
and on the northern frontiers has been emphasised but should
not be exaggerated. Both areas remained well wooded to the end
of the medieval period.

7

ATHENIAN TIMBER SUPPLIES

IT is strange that the most comprehensive statement about the timber resources of Attica comes from a philosopher. The passage has been quoted by agriculturists, foresters, geographers, historians, economists, and ecologists, but it is doubtful whether it has ever been examined in detail. In his *Critias*, Plato, as so often, is combining myth and actuality. He is building up a picture of a glorious Athens in the mythical past when everything was so very much better. That was 9,000 years ago: In the long interval the land of Attica, once so fertile, has been ruined by deforestation.

There have been many floods in those 9,000 years, and the earth carried down from the high ground has not built up a deposit of silt, as elsewhere, but has disappeared. The result is that Athens is now like one of the small islands, the skeleton of a sick body with barely any flesh on it. In those early days the land was unspoilt; there was soil high upon the mountains, and what we now call scrub had fields full of rich earth. There was abundant timber on the mountains and of this you can still see the evidence. Some of our mountains can now only support bees; it is not so long ago that trees from these mountains provided roof-timbers for the largest of our buildings, and the timbers are still sound. And there were many other tall trees cultivated which provided food in plenty for livestock. The year's rain did not, as now, run off the bare earth into the sea, but the water coming down from the hills was preserved underground and fed springs and rivers. One can still see sacred memorials where springs once existed.[1]

From this passage it has often been inferred that all the mountains of Attica had been stripped of timber by the fifth century and that Athens was almost completely dependent on imports to supply even her basic timber needs. Before accepting such extreme views we must look more closely at the passage. Which mountains has Plato in mind and when, according to him, did they lose their timber cover? The most vulnerable were the two ranges nearest to the city, Aegaleos and Hymettus, and the mention of bees calls up at once the famous honey of Hymettus. When the city population expanded these two ranges will have been the nearest large-scale reserves of timber for construction and fuel. Plato says that it was not so long ago that they carried timber which was adequate for the roofing of even the largest buildings. The mark of time is very vague, but since he can refer to roof-timbers from these mountains as still sound in his own day in the first half of the fourth century they are not likely to have been cut much more than 200 years earlier and probably less. It was probably the expansion of the city in the seventh and sixth centuries that led to overcutting on the nearest mountains. There is no reason, however, to believe that these mountains could ever have supplied in quality or quantity the more exacting demands of the fifth century.

What applies to Hymettus and Aegaleos, however, does not necessarily apply to the more distant mountains, Parnes and Cithaeron marking the border with Boeotia, and Pentelicus which dominates the east coast of Attica. There are good grounds for believing that both Parnes and Cithaeron could have supplied substantial quantities of timber. Aristophanes would not have chosen the charcoal-burners of Acharnae as a chorus for his *Acharnians* unless there was a substantial trade in charcoal from neighbouring Mt. Parnes. In the early nineteenth century Leake found an 'inexhaustible supply of timber', mainly pine and fir on the mountain[2] and today Parnes is by no means bare. On the south side Aleppo pine of poorish quality grows up to *c*.800 metres, and above the pine there is still a substantial forest of fir which is now being managed by the forestry service but is a direct descendant of the natural forest. There may be no giants, but there is plenty of timber that would be useful for shipbuilding or general construction.

For Cithaeron the evidence is rather fuller. The name of one of the passes, Dryoscephalae (Oak-heads),[3] is evidence that there were once oaks high up on the mountain, and Thucydides' description of the siege of Plataea at the beginning of the Peloponnesian war shows that the Boeotian side of the mountain was well wooded. The besieged Plataeans had ample stocks of timber for their defence works and the Spartan besiegers were able to cut all the timber they needed to consolidate their siege mound and to make their battering-rams from Cithaeron.[4] Leake, visiting the area in 1835, found a fair quantity of pine on the lower slopes and above them firs giving the name Elatia, 'The Firs', to the top of the mountain.[5] Euripides in his *Bacchae*, though perhaps by coincidence, gives the same sequence. Pentheus, King of Thebes, is determined to stamp out the wild orgies of the women on Cithaeron. Dionysus in disguise leads him up the mountain where in a grim climax he is to be torn in pieces by his mother and her frenzied companions. They first see the women in a glen surrounded by pines. Pentheus asks to go higher to see better. He then climbs a 'heaven-high' fir and meets his grisly end when the women uproot his fir with oak stakes.[6]

The main contribution of Mt. Pentelicus to the Athenian economy was its marble, which could be profitably quarried on the upper levels across the southern face of the mountain. The soil over the marble on this hotter and dryer side must always have been thin and better suited to maquis with a sprinkle of pines than to pine forest, but on the north side there are more and better soil, cooler temperatures, and more rain. This face is well stocked with Aleppo pine, which spreads eastwards towards Marathon. The pines of Pentelicus were near enough to supply Athens, but it is unlikely that serious inroads were made in the archaic period on the timber of Parnes or Cithaeron: the difficulties of transport would have been a strong deterrent if timber was available nearer the city. The main impact of the growth of the city must have fallen on Aegaleos and Hymettus.

On the plains and lowlands of Attica woodlands had to face the competition of agriculture and through the archaic period there was probably an increasing clearance of trees to provide more land for grain crops. In the passage from which we started Plato implies that in the archaic period it was not unusual to plant trees primarily for the purpose of providing fodder for sheep and cattle. These would probably be elm and poplar and perhaps oak. The assumption of the passage is that big trees are an uneconomical use of land. It would also be reasonable to infer that in Plato's day Athenian livestock was winter-fed on grain. It must soon have been realised that olives and vines brought a better return than timber trees and the planting of both probably increased sharply during the archaic period. When Solon, in order to conserve essential food supplies, imposed a ban on the export of all products of the land except olives, it is clear that Attica had more olive trees than she needed for home consumption. Olives and olive oil remained one of her most important exports throughout her history. But Athenian farmers were not so senseless as to cut down all their trees. It was useful to have timber on the farm for building and tool-making, and there was always a wide demand for wood or charcoal for cooking and, at rare intervals, for heating. We should imagine a wide scatter of small copses and smaller groups of trees over the countryside with oak, pine, and elm as the commonest and most useful species.

In comparison with what was to come later the needs of the archaic period were modest. The Athenian fleet was very small during the archaic period, nor should it have been difficult to find within Attica the timber needed for public and private buildings. It is true that the archaic temple was more dependent on wood than the temples of the fifth century: both columns and entablatures were normally of wood down to the sixth century, and walls were commonly built of mud-brick with a timber framing. But archaic temples were very small before the sixth century. The scanty remains of public buildings of the archaic period that have been found by excavation in the Agora, Athens's civic centre, also seem very unpretentious in scale. One change in building practice, however, should be noted.

In the Bronze Age, so far as we know, all roofs were flat; early in the archaic period the gable roof was introduced from the north, offering a great opportunity for architects and sculptors in the design of temple pediments, but complicating the construction of the roof. For the flat roof all that was needed was a series of beams or round timbers laid horizontally with a layer of brushwood or boards or both on top, sealed by a thick cover of mud. The gable roof depended on a ridge-beam which had to be joined to the side walls by a rafter on each side, and both rafters and ridge-beam had to be supported from a cross-beam below.[7] The rafters were covered by boards and the boards normally by battens over which were laid, often on a bed of mud, tiles to protect the wood and carry off the rain. Private houses were probably slower in adopting the new system, but as there is so little evidence for this period, discussion will be postponed until we come to the fifth and fourth centuries.

In sheer quantity the demand for fuel probably exceeded all other demands combined in the archaic period. Wood was needed for cooking, in the form of logs or charcoal, and also for metallurgy. Copper and tin had to be fused into bronze, silver had to be refined in the furnace, and iron-ore had to be converted into iron at a very high temperature. The need for smelting, which was very small at the beginning of the Iron Age, was increasing significantly in the sixth century; but the silver-mines of Laurium were not exploited intensively until the fifth century. It is by no means certain that Athens was compelled to import ordinary building-timber during the archaic period, but there may have been a small import trade in woods not available in Attica, especially for fashionable furniture and for sculpture. Athena's cult image was a very primitive figure in olive-wood and olive remained a popular wood for sculpture because it was hard and long-lasting, but it was easier to find small pieces than large. Cedar and cypress had the advantage of taking a good polish, and having a fragrant scent, as well as being virtually immune to decay and disease.[8]

There is one project of the archaic period in Athens which does not fit into this pattern. All earlier buildings would have been completely dwarfed by the great temple of Olympian Zeus which one of the Pisistratid tyrants intended to build a little south of the Acropolis. It was attributed to Pisistratus, commonly identified with the first of the tyrants, who came to power in 560 and, after being forced twice into exile, consolidated his power in a long period of stable rule. Archaeologists, however, consider that what remains from the original building must be later than the death of Pisistratus in 527 and prefer to assign the building to his grandson, the younger Pisistratus, who was archon in 522, a much less suitable context. The building was not completed, but sufficient remains to indicate the plan. In 174 BC Antiochus Epiphanes, a generous friend of Athens, undertook to complete the unfinished building, but he died too soon. It was left for Hadrian, most philhellenic of the Roman emperors, to end what had been begun more than 600 years earlier.[9] There seems to be no doubt that the original design was respected and the dimensions emphasise what an anachronism it must have seemed to later generations. It would have required timbers much stronger and larger than any that had been used previously and one wonders where the timber would have been found. It has been suggested above (p. 123) that Athenian access to Macedonian timber may go back to the first Pisistratus.

There is no good reason to believe that timber supply was a crucial issue at Athens in the archaic period; in the fifth century there was a dramatic change in circumstances. If complete statistics could be available we should probably find that timber consumption was increased more than fourfold, and for this there are four main reasons—the development of the Athenian navy, the transformation of public building standards, the growth of industry, and the increase of population in the city of Athens and the Piraeus.

At the beginning of the fifth century the Athenian navy had less than 100 ships and, as Thucydides emphasises, the majority of them were pentekonters, at a time when the trireme was firmly established as the most efficient warship.[10] But when the Persians invaded Greece in 480 the Athenians contributed more ships than all the other Greek states combined. The 200 Athenian triremes which fought at the battle of Salamis in 480 played a major part in repulsing the Persians and preserving the liberty of Greece. The sudden emergence of Athens during the invasion of Xerxes as the strongest naval power in Greece determined the direction of Athenian policy when the Persians had been driven out of Greece.

The problem that immediately faced the Greeks was the future of the Ionians and other eastern Greeks. It was natural that they should now feel the time ripe to recover the freedom which they had failed to recover in the Ionian revolt (499-494), but this they could only hope to achieve if they were strongly supported from the Greek mainland. The Athenians were not slow to accept the challenge and to become the acknowledged leader of a confederation of states to protect the Greek world from the Persians. For thirty years hostilities continued between Greeks and Persians and the Athenian fleet was the decisive factor in the successes that were gained, but it was almost inevitable that the original enthusiasm of the allies should be eroded when the danger of absorption by Persia seemed no longer real. Coercion was needed to prevent defections and Athenian control became firmer and less disinterested. When hostilities with Persia were broken off in the middle of the century, whether by formal peace or mutual understanding, the Athenians were not prepared to dissolve the league and what had originally been a union of independent allies inevitably developed into the form and language of an Athenian empire, which rested largely on the overwhelming superiority of the Athenian fleet.

The evidence for Athenian supplies of ship-timber has already been discussed (p. 123). There is no firm evidence before the last third of the fifth century, but from that point it is clear from inscriptions and literary sources that Athens relied mainly on Macedon, the fine quality of whose ship-timber was emphasised by Theophrastus. But since supplies depended on friendly relations with the Macedonian kings and Macedonian kings were rarely secure on their thrones, Athens must from time to time have been forced to turn elsewhere. Here, however, we are more concerned with the volume of timber required than with its sources. When war broke out with the Peloponnesian League in 431 Athens had a fleet of 300 triremes.

The second factor that raised new problems in the fifth century was the effect of the growth of Athenian power and wealth on the scale of public buildings, and especially temples. The immediate aftermath of the repulse of Xerxes was a very lean period. During the Persian occupation in 480 there had been considerable destruction. Thucydides says that 'the majority of the houses were in ruin and few were still standing, which Persian officers had occupied'.[11] The destruction can be traced by the layers of ash in the Agora and, as could be expected, it was particularly thorough on the Acropolis. How far beyond these two most important areas the destruction was systematic is debatable. But it is abundantly clear that the immediate need was to provide living quarters for the people and accommodation, however improvised, for the carrying on of essential public business. The ten years following 479 were no time for fine building. So far as timber was concerned, apart from ship-timbers to maintain a strong fleet, the need was for quantity rather than quality and a quick delivery. The main supplies should have come from Attica and Euboea.

By the sixties the main task of restoration was completed, and a succession of victories over the Persians, culminating in the destruction of the Persian fleet at the mouth of the river

Eurymedon in Pamphylia, had swollen the wealth as well as the pride of Athens. It was time now to think of improvement rather than restorations and replacements. The first concentration, associated with Cimon, who had been the outstanding commander in the fighting against the Persians, was in the Agora. Plane trees were planted to provide shade in the height of summer[12] and at the north end a new stoa was built, the so-called Stoa Poikile, which remained famous through a long history for its monumental paintings by Polygnotus of Thasos, who had been attracted to Athens by the patronage of Cimon.[13] We shall not know the dimensions of this building until the excavation of the north side of the Agora has reached the lower levels and revealed the ground-plan, but the tiled and gabled roof will have required strong timbers of good quality. It may have been rather more difficult to find the wooden panels for the very large paintings. Since they are said to have been removed by a Roman proconsul in the late Empire,[14] the choice should be restricted to woods that were particularly long-lasting, perhaps cypress or oak.[15]

Close to the Stoa Poikile in point of time was the Tholos, the large round building in the Agora, east of the Council House, which was designed to be the headquarters of the standing committee of the Council, each of the tribal divisions of the Council taking this duty for a tenth part of the year. The diameter was 18.2 metres (60 ft.) and the roof was the architect's main problem. He provided six columns from whose epistyles rafters could support a conical roof somewhat like a sunshade.[16] More demanding in timber was the temple of Hephaestus and Athena on Colonus hill overlooking the Agora, which was begun near the middle of the century.[17] The width of the cella was only 7.50 metres (25 ft.) and there was an inner colonnade to ease the strain, but it may not have been easy to find timbers of more than twenty feet in Attica. Work on the temple of Hephaestus was at some point interrupted, and the cult images of Hephaestus and Athena were not set up on their platform in the cella until the period of the Peace of Nicias (418).[18]

The main reason for the delay may have been a decision to concentrate on an ambitious programme to transform the Acropolis. Athenian tradition held that an oath had been taken before the battle of Plataea (479) that temples destroyed by the

Persians should not be rebuilt, but left as a permanent memorial of Persian sacrilege. This would explain why no attempt was made before 450 even to build a new temple for the city's patron goddess. And the easiest explanation of the coherent building programme which developed from the early forties is that the end of hostilities with Persia absolved the Athenians from their vow.[19] It is at least certain that the first and most important of the new buildings, the Parthenon, was begun in 447/6, and with it or soon afterwards the great chryselephantine statue of Athena Parthenos. When the great temple was nearing completion and the cult statue had been installed and dedicated (438/7), work was begun on the Propylaea, the new monumental entrance to the Acropolis. The war with Sparta's Peloponnesian League broke out in 431 before the Propylaea was completed, and it was to remain an uncompleted building, but when the first phase of the war was ended by the Peace of Nicias work was begun on a temple for Erechtheus, the traditional hero-founder of the Athenian people, in association with Athena.

The Parthenon and the Propylaea were not only considerably larger in scale than any earlier buildings in Athens, but were also much grander in the quality of their materials. In the new buildings in the Agora limestone, poros, and mud-brick were still the standard building materials and very little marble was used; the Parthenon and Propylaea were marble buildings, but they could not dispense with timber, though its importance would not have been at once apparent to a visitor. He could admire the monumental door of the Parthenon, and the coffered ceiling; he would not see the massive timbers that supported the roof. But the roof of the Parthenon was one of the architect's main triumphs. The size of the span that had to be covered was his first difficulty.

The cella was 19.20 metres (63 ft.) wide, considerably wider than any of the archaic temples in Attica, and even when an inner colonnade was added, the central span required cross-beams of roughly thirty-five feet (c.11 m.). And since the principle of the tie-beam truss had not yet been discovered, the cross-beams had, by means of props, to carry the weight of the roof and also of the marble-coffered ceiling.[20] A professor of mechanical engineering in Athens has calculated that the weight to be carried would require a beam of 0.65 × 0.65

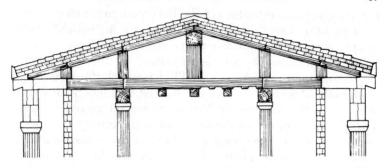

7 Cross-section of the Parthenon roof

metres,[21] but it is doubtful whether the Greeks or Romans would have calculated weights with mathematical precision. The architect of the Parthenon would more probably have chosen the largest size of his chosen timber that could be supplied. The most important timber after the cross-beams was the ridge-beam, which would have had to be about seventy feet long if in one piece, but more than one timber could have been used.

From the ridge-beam the principal rafters stretched to the outer colonnade, but the length of timbers required was reduced by the purlins that accompanied the ridge-beam on either side. At the west end of the Parthenon the purlin sockets can still be seen and measured. There were three on either side of the ridge-beam and the sockets measured 0.94 × 0.95 metres (c.3 ft.).[22] The plan of the west end provided adequate internal supports for this number, but the cella of the Parthenon at the east end of the temple had a different plan. The main prop from the cross-beam went to the ridge-beam, subsidiary props were needed for the purlins, and there were only two points on either side of the ridge-beam where the weight brought by the props to the cross-beam could be relieved by support from below. This was only possible on the cella walls and at the two ends of the inner colonnade.

There is no evidence for the size of sockets for the purlins or the ridge-beam over the cella but the sockets in the west end suggest very big timbers indeed. They could probably have been found in Macedonian fir, and possibly in cypress, but it was not unusual in Greek and Roman buildings for two timbers of the same length to be joined together. Apart from the roof-timbers the most important timbers in the Parthenon were those of the monumental door (c.10 m. high and 4.92 m. wide).[23] Here quality was as important as size and strength.

The Parthenon was a majestic setting for the great chryselephantine statue of Athena by Phidias which dominated the main cella. Athena was here the warrior goddess, with spear, shield, and helmet, holding Victory in her outstretched hand. The gleam of gold from the dress, the white ivory of the flesh, and the blue-grey eyes must have been very impressive as one passed from the bright light of the sun into the dim cella, lit only from the great doorway. One could not have seen the strong timber that was the chief supporting member of the armature of the statue. A cutting in the pedestal shows that it was 0.75 metres wide and 0.45 metres (29 × 18 in.) thick and was sunk to a depth of 1.83 metres (6 ft.) implying a total height of roughly twelve metres (c.40 ft.);[24] a timber of these dimensions must have required very special selection. The core of the statue was also in wood, but since the surface was not exposed, the size of the component parts to be fitted together was not important.

The Propylaea should have posed no major timber problem. It was an essentially marble building and the socket-holes that survive imply beams considerably smaller than those of the Parthenon. The Periclean Odeum on the south slope of the Acropolis near the theatre of Dionysus was more demanding. From the literary sources it is difficult to form a clear picture. Plutarch includes the building in the Periclean programme: the interior, he tells us, was a forest of columns and seats, and the roof was built to a single point, taking the form of the Persian king's tent.[25] The account of Vitruvius is very different. He attributes the building to Themistocles and says that stone columns were used and that the roof was composed of masts and yard-arms from the Persian spoils.[26] The excavations of 1914–31 and the more recent clearing of the site have now revealed the basic ground-plan.[27] The Odeum measured 62.40 × 68.60 metres (195 × 225 ft.) with nine rows of seven columns east and west and ten rows north and south. The date is Periclean, but Vitruvius may have been right in his description of the roofing. It is certain, at any rate, that substantial timbers were involved in the building, because when the Athenians during the siege by Sulla in 86 BC were preparing to make their last stand on the

Acropolis, they burnt down the Odeum so that the timbers could not be available for Sulla to use for siege engines.[28] Perhaps the seating of the Odeum was also in wood.

Though marble was the dominant material in this monumental rebuilding on the Acropolis, the demand implied for timber was unprecedented in quantity and quality. Our sources throw a glimmer of light on the problems involved. Pericles' building programme had raised very controversial issues, for it depended on using the reserve of tribute contributed by the allies to the Delian confederacy. This reserve had originally been kept in Apollo's sanctuary on Delos, but when the great expedition to support the revolt of Egypt from Persia had failed disastrously, it could be claimed that Delos might be vulnerable to an attack by the Phoenician fleet and the reserve was transferred from Apollo on Delos to Athena on the Acropolis (454). When Athens decided to suspend the war against Persia, Pericles persuaded the Assembly that they were morally justified in using the tribute reserve to restore what had been destroyed by the Persians.

This policy was strongly resisted by conservative elements in Athens led by Thucydides son of Melesias, and Plutarch, in his *Pericles*, has included a vivid summary of the debate.[29] Pericles is made to justify his policy, partly on the ground that the tribute was intended to provide for the protection of the allies, and, provided that Athens protected them, she was entitled to use the money as she thought fit, and partly on account of the advantages that the policy brought in the form of employment. These advantages are listed in some detail. There was a wide variety of materials which required men to work them. Materials that came from overseas would bring trade to sailors, helmsmen, and merchants; land transport would call for wagon-builders, and those who could supply oxen or mules.

It is by no means certain that there is any reliable source behind the detailed arguments of Pericles in Plutarch; it could derive from a colourful Hellenistic expansion of the bare bones of the issue.[30] But even such a source would try to keep within the bounds of the probable. The reference to wagon-builders and heavy-transport animals is a good realistic touch. A vastly increased supply of wagons would have been needed to carry the enormous quantity of heavy marble blocks from Mt. Pentelicus,

and timber coming from overseas would have had to be carried
from the Piraeus by wagon. Of the various woods that might
have been used only cypress and ebony are mentioned by
Plutarch. We could not expect him to be exhaustive, but one
can ask if there is any rational explanation of the selection of
these two.

The emphasis on cypress need not surprise us, for it was
highly valued by the Greeks and was widely used in temples. It
resisted decay, was virtually immune from insect attack, and
was one of the longest-lasting woods; in addition it had an
attractive scent. Throughout ancient history it was one of the
first choices for monumental doors, and a fragment of an
Athenian inscription which recorded elm-wood and cypress in
an uncertain context has now been shown by D. M. Lewis to be
from the accounts of the commissioners of the Parthenon.[31] The
conjunction of these two particular woods points decisively to
the grand door of the eastern entrance to the Parthenon: elm,
noted particularly for its strength, was commonly used for door-
frame and pivots; cypress would be used for the door itself. But
the more important question is whether cypress was used also for
the roof-timbers of the temples. Theophrastus names fir and
pine first among general-construction timbers[32] and the detailed
accounts of the fourth-century temple of Asklepios at Epidaurus
show that the roof-timbers were of fir, and that cypress was
reserved for the door and other special features.[33] But the sixth-
century temple of Apollo at Delphi seems to have been roofed
with cypress,[34] and new restorations of a critical inscription
make it highly probable that cypress was also used for the main
timbers of the new temple built in the fourth century (p. 436).
Both fir and pine were much more liable to decay, and length of
life was more important for temples than for secular buildings. It
is also a reasonable inference from a list of Athenian imports in a
comedy of the last third of the fifth century that cypress was
more widely used in the Parthenon: 'Crete sends us cypress for
the gods.'[35] This should refer to temples, because by the fifth
century wood was no longer used for statues by established
sculptors. It is a fair inference from the passage that cypress was
used for the main weight-bearing timbers of the Parthenon.

There may be more explicit evidence in an Athenian decree a
copy of which was found on the island of Carpathos. In this

decree the Athenian people honours an Eteocarpathian together with his sons and his community as public benefactors of
the Athenians, 'for they presented the cypress for the temple of
Athena mistress of Athens'.[36] Various privileges are conferred
on the community and provision is made for the setting-up of a
copy of the decree 'in the sanctuary of Apollo, where the cypress
was cut'. The decree ends: 'And Agatharchus the Lindian may
. . . the cypress, as he requested.' This decree has until recently
been dated to the very early fourth century, but a re-
examination of a squeeze of the original demands an earlier
date, in the third or the fourth quarter of the fifth century. The
cypress of the decree is clearly an exceptional tree, which has
developed freely in a sacred grove. A clue to the use made of the
tree may be found in the word not translated above. This word,
which is partly restored, [kathista]nai, literally means to set
down, establish, but it can be used in a wider sense. Wilhelm
suggested that it here means 'to deliver',[37] referring to the
transport of the tree from Carpathos to Athens, but the position
of this clause makes it more likely that the privilege conferred
on Agatharchus came after the delivery. In the Erechtheum
accounts the word kathistanai is used for setting a ceiling in
place[38] and this very normal usage is applicable to the cypress
from Carpathos. An exceptionally (c.80 ft.) tall cypress could
have provided a splendid ridge-beam for the main cella of the
Parthenon.

If cypress was used on a large scale in the Parthenon it will
help to explain why some at least of the *empolia* used in the
columns were made of cypress.[39] The *empolia* are small blocks of
wood inserted in the centre of the top and of the bottom of each
column-drum, with a hole into which a wooden peg was sunk
binding the two drums together and maintaining them in
position. Two of these blocks, very well-preserved, were featured
in an article published in 1962 on 'Fluctuation in rainfall during
the building of the Parthenon'.[40] Both *empolia* can be seen by the
pattern of their annual rings to come from the same tree, a
cypress aged roughly 200 years when it was felled, but the title of
the article is perhaps too precise. I have found no evidence of
cypresses growing in Attica and Crete remained famous for its
cypress trees to the end of the Roman period.[41]

The inclusion of ebony by Plutarch raises a very different

problem. Ebony was a very rare wood which, before the development of trade with India, could only be obtained from Africa. The darkness and strength of the wood made it particularly fashionable in royal furniture during the Bronze Age in the Near East, and Pausanias refers to the occasional use of ebony for dedications in Greek temples during the archaic period (p. 310). After the end of hostilities against the Persians, it could have been bought by Athenian traders in Egypt or carried by Phoenician merchants to the Piraeus. It is difficult to find a place for ebony in the building programme, but it does not seem a plausible invention for a forger, and there could perhaps be a place for ebony in the coffers of the Erechtheum. The Erechtheum accounts tell us that the frames of the coffers of the ceiling over the main cella of the temple were made of boxwood.[42] Strips or geometric patterns of dark ebony could make an excellent contrast to the whiteness of the box. Such a contrast would suit the architect of the Erechtheum, who set figures of white marble against a black background in his frieze and deliberately introduced courses of dark Eleusinian marble for decorative effect against white Pentelic.[43] There could have been no such contrast in the marble coffers of the Parthenon, but it is, at least, interesting to know that Phidias used ebony in the highly decorative throne of his great chryselephantine statue of Zeus at Olympia.[44]

One other wood is known to have been used in the Parthenon from the firmer evidence of a fragment from the record of income and expenditure published by the commissioners. In 442/1 they purchased pine-wood (*peukina*), but the quantity and price have not survived.[45] If we are right in suggesting that cypress was used for the main roof-timbers, cross-beams, rafters, ridge-beam, and purlins, the pine should be assigned to secondary timbers. The Parthenon had been begun in 447/6 and Phidias' chryselephantine statue of Athena was dedicated in 438/7. By 442/1 the builders should have been ready or nearly ready to work on the roof. Pine would have been suitable wood for the boards and battens over the rafters.

In providing for the fleet and for the public building programmes the main problem for the Athenians was to find timber of first-class quality and particularly timber in long lengths. For other demands quantity presented more problems than quality. We may consider separately the timber required for fuel, housing, and furnishings. In all those areas the demand must have grown considerably in the fifth century. The population of the rural demes is not likely to have increased significantly and may even have declined, but the prosperity that accompanied the growth of Athenian power acted as a powerful magnet to attract other Greeks, particularly from the islands, to settle in Athens or the Piraeus. During the second half of the century, when the Athenians had reorganised their harbour facilities for the benefit of traders, the number of metics (foreigners registered as residents in Attica) increased dramatically. There was ample opportunity for profitable employment in trade or industry, and well-paid service in the fleet was open to non-Athenians. With the increase of private and public prosperity more slaves were needed and could be afforded. Unfortunately, though these tendencies are non-controversial, the scale of increase in the population, free, metic, and slaves, cannot be quantified and little is gained by the detailed defence of what would be uncontrollable guesses.[46]

In many developing countries today fuel accounts for more than ninety per cent of total timber consumption, and even in Turkey nearly eighty per cent of the timber taken from the forests in 1968 was for fuel.[47] In view of the large scale of building operations in fifth-century Athens similar proportions will not apply, but the increase in population will have brought with it a larger demand for fuel. More serious was the intensive exploitation of the silver-mines of the Laurium area. Pit-props were required to support galleries, and charcoal and logs for the furnaces which separated the silver from its associates. Pines have grown freely on the peninsula of Sunium when the mines have not been in operation and the comparative treelessness of the hills today is in large part due to the reopening of the mines in the nineteenth century, but the silver owls that were poured out from the mint in the fifth century must have been very expensive in timber. Sophocles mentions a grove of trees near the temple of Poseidon on Cape Sunium,[48] but this may have been a sacred grove associated with the temple and provides no evidence for fuel supplies in the Laurium area.

There is a hint in Demosthenes' speech against Meidias that
local supplies were short. The speech, which was not in fact
delivered, is a scathing attack on a rich man who had humiliated Demosthenes by striking him at a public festival. Demosthenes' best hope of convincing the jury to support him was
to show that Meidias cared nothing for the interests of the state.
As a prime example of his unsocial extravagance and lack
of public spirit Demosthenes describes Meidias' service as
captain of a trireme in a campaign in Euboea.[49] When it was
decided to withdraw he did not join the other ship captains in
escorting the expeditionary force back to the Piraeus, but used
his ship for his own profit, bringing back from Styros on the
south-east coast of Euboea door-frames and doors, fencing-
posts, and wood (*xyla*) for his mine-workings, either pit-props or
logs for furnaces. It is not difficult to understand why he chose
doors and door-frames. Fine doors, as we shall note later, were
one of the distinctive features in the houses of the rich and fine
wood was rare in Attica, but it would not have been worth
taking fencing with pit-props or logs for burning if local supplies
in the mining area were still plentiful. It would be cheaper to
bring wood to Laurium from southern Euboea than from the
mountains on the Attic borders.[50]

Considerable quantities of fuel were also needed for smelting in or near the city. There is a stock entry in the accounts of
the colossal statue of Athena Promachos (*c*.460–450) on the
Acropolis and of the statues of Hephaestus and Athena that
were made for the temple of Hephaestus overlooking the west
side of the Agora (418): 'charcoal and logs for burning'
(*anthrakes kai xyla kausima*).[51] This refers to the fusing of copper
with tin to produce bronze. If it was standard practice to convert
iron-ore into iron in Attica rather than importing finished
articles, it will have added significantly to the fuel demand, for
the smelting of iron requires a higher temperature than either
silver or bronze. In all smelting processes charcoal was normally
preferred, because it gave a steadier and stronger heat, and
hardwoods were preferred to softwoods, because they were
denser and so produced a greater heat.[52]

One final aspect of the fuel problem needs to be mentioned.
In his funeral speech commemorating the Athenians who died
in the first year of the Peloponnesian War, Pericles emphasised

the number of opportunities for enjoyable relaxation that the Athenian people had provided for themselves in the form of games and sacrifices.[53] The more cynical author of a pamphlet analysing the realities of Athenian democracy echoes the same point. One of the reasons, he says, why it is difficult to complete business with the Council and people is that the Athenians have more public festivals than any other city. 'The multiplicity of public sacrifices', he says in another passage, 'is a natural expression of democratic policy. Poor people cannot afford sacrifices and that is why the state sacrifices so many victims: it is the people who enjoy the feast and share the victims.'[54] There were probably not a few who associated the Panathenaea primarily with a good slice of beef. The importance of sacrifices in the total timber picture is best illustrated by the accounts of the commissioners who were responsible for managing the finances of the Delian gods. Most of the timber entries in these accounts refer to building-timbers; one series, however, simply refers to wood (*xyla*) by weight in talents (a talent being roughly 56 lb.), and in one year in the fourth century the total weight of logs for sacrifices amounted to some 150 talents or twelve tons. In the same Delian accounts there are recurrent entries for the purchase of charcoal for the altars.[55] Charcoal may have been more commonly used for the smaller victims, but oxen and pigs would more naturally be roasted over logs.

There is very little evidence indeed to show how the extremely large demand for fuel which we have envisaged was met, but there is perhaps a glimpse of the firewood trade in a speech attributed to Demosthenes. Phaenippus whom the prosecutor is attacking had been appointed to a liturgy and took advantage of the law to attempt to transfer the burden to a richer man on the ground that his own resources were inadequate. The main concern of the speech was to show that Phaenippus had scandalously undervalued his own resources; we have therefore to allow for exaggeration and distortion. By stating that the circumference of the estate was forty stades (*c.*8 km.) he implies that it was very large and some scholars have inferred a farm of some 1,000 acres, a size which is otherwise unknown and most unlikely in Attica; but the size of the estate depends on its shape and as it was a so-called marginal estate, *eschatia*, either on the sea-shore or at the foot of a mountain, it could have been as little

as 200 acres.[56] The main crop on the estate was barley, but some
of the income came from wood. Demosthenes claims that
Phaenippus had six asses carrying wood which brought in
twelve drachmae a day, but he does not tell us what kind of
wood was carried, nor where it was carried.[57] The word used,
xyla, is as all-embracing as our word 'wood', but the price
quoted gives a clue. As it would have been in Demosthenes'
interest to put the price as high as possible, we may regard
twelve drachmae as a maximum and from this has to be
deducted the cost of feeding the asses and the slave in charge.
In the accounts of the Epidaurian commissioners in the late
fourth century, which is not far from the date of Demosthenes'
speech, we find that a ten-foot timber costs from three to five
drachmae;[58] the simplest explanation of such a low figure in
Demosthenes is that Phaenippus was selling firewood. The most
likely situation of the estate is near Mt. Pentelicus: the asses were
probably taking logs to Athens. Farmers within twenty kilometres of Athens could have found it profitable to sell firewood
in the city.

The stelae which record the sale of properties confiscated
from men found guilty of profaning the mysteries of Eleusis
(413 BC) include in one of the estates an oak copse and a pine
copse.[59] These oaks and pines could yield firewood from dead
branches and prunings, but their main function was probably to
provide timber for the maintenance of farm buildings. When we
find in the lease of a property by a phratry (kinship group) that
the tenant is required to provide a certain weight of wood at
certain seasons of the year, we can imagine that the wood was for
sacrifices by the phratry and was produced by coppicing.[60]
Wood could be supplemented by vine prunings which are still
widely used to fire ovens in Greece. For cooking and smelting
charcoal was a strong competitor, and charcoal was comparatively light to carry. Charcoal-burners worked where the
reserves of timber were largest, and especially on Mt. Parnes.
How far was Attica self-supporting in fuel? It is surely significant
that we hear nothing of a fuel famine in the sources, though we
are told that Thebes in neighbouring Boeotia was a poor place
to live in during the winter because there was a great shortage of
wood.[61] The easiest solution is to believe that Athens could also
rely on supplies from Euboea.

In turning to the timber needed for the building of houses a natural starting-point is an often-quoted passage in Xenophon's reminiscences of Socrates:

When stones and bricks and wood and tiles are thrown together indiscriminately they have no value, but when the materials which are not subject to decay or disintegration, namely the stones and tiles, are placed in due order on top and at the bottom, and the bricks and woodwork in the middle, as in building, then a possession of value is created, a house.[62]

In the standard Greek house of the classical period the walls were of mud-brick resting on a low foundation of stone to protect them from rising damp. Tiles imply a gabled roof with wide eaves to protect the top of the wall from the weather. In this general pattern there were variations: some roofs, particularly in poorer houses, were flat, as was the general practice in the Bronze Age, with horizontal roof-timbers, squared or round, covered by brushwood or reeds with a thick layer above of mud. Walls often had a timber framework, as was common in Minoan and Mycenaean buildings; for this, though not structurally necessary, gave the walls greater strength and elasticity.[63]

The archaeological evidence for houses of this period in the city and in the rural districts of Attica is very limited, but a substantial area of housing and shops has been excavated in Olynthus, the capital city of the Chalcidic League, which was destroyed by Philip II of Macedon in 348 BC.[64] Most of the buildings date from the fourth century, but some go back to the fifth and such traces as have been recovered in the city of Athens seem to conform to the Olynthic pattern.[65] The main focus of the house is an open court round which the rooms are built and in the commonest type a loggia or portico supported by posts is added on one side of the court with the main range of rooms behind it. In most houses there are two storeys, but some have only one, and there are windows looking onto the court. Wood is used for doors, window-frames, and shutters, for staircases, and for the roof. Doors were framed by posts and lintel of wood; some thresholds were of wood, others of stone. Not all rooms had doors; hangings were sometimes used instead.

Thucydides, in describing the evacuation of Attica in the first year of the Peloponnesian War, says that those who lived outside the city 'brought with them their children and wives and their household utensils; and they took down the woodwork (*xylosin*) of the houses'.[66] Of the woodwork the door was the most valuable part and the most vulnerable. Herodotus, in describing the Lydian strategy in their sixth-century war against Miletus of destroying the crops but leaving the farm buildings untouched, adds that *they didn't even pull out the doors*.[67] Doors are separately listed in the properties of those who were condemned for sacrilege against the Eleusinian mysteries,[68] and, as we have seen, Meidias chose doors and door-frames to bring back from Euboea. It was because so much attention was attached to them that the stealing of doors was not uncommon. The same contrast between plain walls and highly decorative doors can be seen in old Arab houses and even in African villages.

What else Thucydides had in mind for his woodwork is uncertain: window-shutters certainly, because they were easily movable. The timber framing of walls could not have been removed without the complete destruction of the house, but the most useful timbers were the rafters and boards of the roof. These, however, could not be removed without taking off the tiles and it is very doubtful whether such elaborate dismantling would have been contemplated; had they gone so far Thucydides would probably have mentioned the tiles. Presumably during the first years of war the owners expected to return to their homes; it was different in the last phase when a Spartan force occupied Decelea and the Athenians were permanently penned in their city. The destruction in Attica was now more thorough and the Boeotians in particular took advantage of it. An unidentified historian who wrote a detailed, dull, but accurate history from the point where Thucydides' text ended records that the Boeotians bought up roof-timbers and tiles at bargain prices from the Spartans.[69]

It is impossible to say how far Attica was able to supply the timber needed for housing. The rich, who were more concerned with quality, would have preferred the greater variety and finer quality available from Macedon, Italy, or Asia Minor and some of them seem to have made their own special arrangements. Timotheus, one of the most successful generals of the first half of the fourth century, was able to secure a substantial shipload of Macedonian timber as a result of his personal relations with the

Macedonian king.[70] Theophrastus' boastful man claims that he has been invited to take timber from Macedon without paying any duty.[71] The Eleusinian accounts for 408/7 include timbers from the confiscated property of Alcibiades;[72] they may have been acquired in the same way. But the great majority of Athenians would have been less demanding, and the lengths required for roofing were comparatively short.

What Attica was unable to supply could probably have been bought in Euboea. Thucydides emphasises the effects of the occupation of Decelea by the Spartans: 'The transport of supplies from Euboea which hitherto had come from Oropus by land through Decelea now had to go by sea round Sunium which was costly.'[73] This is at first puzzling because transport by water was normally much more economical than transport by land, but the sea journey to the Piraeus from Chalcis, which was the port nearest to the forests of central Euboea, was some seventy miles and conditions off Cape Sunium were often dangerous; and when the timber had been unloaded at the Piraeus it still had to be carried by wagon nine kilometres to the city. The land route, on the other hand, involved only a short sea passage to Oropus followed by a twenty-three-kilometre carriage to the city. Thucydides does not say what supplies Athens drew from Euboea, but he stresses their importance again when Euboea revolted in 411 and the Athenian fleet was defeated by the Spartans off Eretria: Euboea, he says was more important to Athens than Attica.[74] Thucydides is not thinking of grain, because Athens's main supplies came from the Crimea. But when Athens was cut off from Attica the vegetables and fruit of the Lelantine plain near Chalcis were invaluable and Euboea supplied most of the animals needed for public sacrifices, and meat; for at the beginning of the war the Athenians had removed their livestock to Euboea and other islands. It would be surprising if essential supplies did not also include wood.

When Demosthenes was trying to urge the Athenians of his own day not to appease Philip of Macedon he naturally appealed to the glories of the past and the unselfish patriotism of the leaders of the state when Athens was great. He pointed in particular to the contrast between the lavish expenditure on public buildings and the modesty of private houses: 'Our leaders were so moderate and public-spirited that anyone who knows the houses then occupied by Aristides and Miltiades and the other great men of those days can see that they are no grander than their neighbours.'[75] This is probably an exaggeration, for the house of the wealthy Callias, for instance, which is the scene of Plato's *Protagoras*, seems to be of considerable size, but the general impression from the sources is that the city was over-crowded and it is unlikely that when it had to be hurriedly rebuilt after its sacking by the Persians in 480, the general spirit of the times would have allowed individuals to acquire extravagant lots. Those houses whose ground-plan has been recovered are small, but they are far too few to support any general conclusions.

It would be even more dangerous to generalise about houses in the rural areas. In the deme centres themselves we should not expect signs of luxury in the general housing, but were the rich men of the Periclean period satisfied with the modest standards of the men of Marathon? The comparatively recent excavation of two independent houses provides a starting-point for the enquiry. One was at the foot of the northerly slope of Aegaleos and was probably built during the period of the Peace of Nicias (421–415), the other was within a fold of the southern foothills of Mt. Hymettus.[76] The plans of the two buildings are very similar and neither was pretentious in size or furnishings. The so-called Dema house, on Mt. Aegaleos, occupied an area of 22.05 × 16.10 metres; the Hymettus house was smaller, 17.7 × 13.7 metres. In both of these the central feature was a courtyard with a portico along one side supported by columns of wood with wooden epistyles. The walls were built with mud-bricks on a low footing of stone rubble. The rooms were small, no less than five being fitted into the 22.05 metres of the northern side of the larger house. The pottery found in these two houses shows that the families were comfortably placed, but there is no hint of luxury or extravagance. It would be dangerous, however, to generalise from them, especially in the light of various passages from respectable authorities which imply a different picture.

Thucydides, in describing the reactions to the evacuation of Attica at the opening of the Peloponnesian War, draws a sharp distinction between rich and poor:

Publicly they accepted the Periclean policy (of abandoning Attica) . . . but privately they felt acutely their own sufferings. The common people, starting with less, had been deprived of even that little; men of substance had lost fine possessions in the country in the form of buildings and valuable furnishings.[77]

The impression given by the unknown continuator of Thucydides is very similar. Describing the rewards of booty to the Boeotians when the Spartans had occupied Decelea, he says that the land of Attica at the time was more richly furnished than any other in Greece because the earlier Spartan invasions had done little permanent damage.[78] There must have been many Athenians who would not be satisfied with local supplies of timber for their country houses.

The demand for imported timber (excluding supplies from Euboea) was probably at its peak in the twenty years before the outbreak of the Peloponnesian War in 431. This was a period of unparalleled public building, the maintenance of the empire demanded a substantial shipbuilding programme, and the rich had enough wealth to pay the higher prices that timber from Macedon and other favoured regions must have fetched.

We have very little firm evidence for the sources from which Athens imported timber in this period, but the trade in the late fourth century is comparatively well documented. The accounts of the commissioners at Eleusis for 329/8 show that timber was being imported from Samos (probably pine or oak), from Cnidus cypress, and from Corinth elm and ash.[79] Theophrastus gives a general review of the timber trade with Greece, and he is speaking not of naval timber but of timber for building and general carpentry.[80] The best, he says, comes from Macedon, the next best from the Black Sea, and then from Bithynia. After these he lists the territory of the Aenianes on the southern border of Thessaly; the woods from Euboea and Mt. Parnassus are the worst. The comparative merits of Arcadian wood he leaves open, but transport problems would have ruled it out for Athens. It is reasonable to believe that the trade was similarly diversified in the fifth century.

When war broke out work on the public building programme stopped and timber imports were probably confined to the needs of the navy and essential maintenance work in the city and its fortifications. In the short period of the Peace of Nicias the Erechtheum was begun on the Acropolis, and the temple of Hephaestus overlooking the Agora was completed. Before the end of the century a monumental stoa of Zeus Eleutherios had been built at the north-west corner of the Agora, and the southern side had been framed by a long two-storeyed stoa of 80.47 × 14.96 metres. This building, however, reflects the effect of the war on Athenian finances. As an economy the upper part of the walls was in mud-brick, instead of marble or limestone.[81] The roof of the long portico and the joists and boards supporting the upper floor would have required a considerable quantity of timber, but there was probably less insistence on quality.

Fourth-century Athens was a very different city. The great building activity of the fifth century was one of the fruits of empire, and with the loss of the empire it was impossible for the Athenians to maintain both a strong navy and an ambitious public building programme. The Athenians wisely put their navy first and there is no suggestion in the literary sources or in the inventories of naval equipment that policy was affected by a shortage of ship-timber (p. 131). It was more difficult to find and finance the crews than the triremes. Although tentative efforts were periodically made to revive dreams of expansion and a restoration of the empire, there were neither the will nor the resources to sustain them; but in the second half of the century,

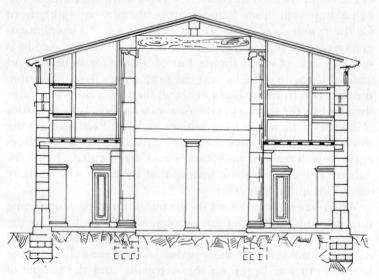

8 Cross-section of the Piraeus arsenal

by a wise management of public finances and by improving judicial and other facilities for the benefit of traders, Athenian and foreign, there was a sufficient accumulation of wealth to improve the public amenities. It was in this period that a great stadium was built south-east of the Acropolis, and the theatre of Dionysus rebuilt in marble.

Neither of these buildings involved substantial use of timber, but a large arsenal for the storage of naval equipment was also built in this period, and the decree of the Assembly which specified the plan and dimensions has fortunately been preserved. The building was to be 400 feet long from wall to wall and fifty feet wide. It had a central nave fifty feet long, flanked each side by a row of thirty-five columns thirty feet high. On each side of the central nave was a narrower aisle fifteen feet wide in which were stored the sails, ropes, and other 'hanging' naval stores in chests and cupboards on two floors. The walls were of stone with thirty-six windows in each side, and three at each end, and at each end there were two doors, fifteen and a half feet high and nine feet wide, separated by a marble pier. The roof was planned with ingenious economy:

The architect will set capitals of Pentelic marble on the columns and over the columns wooden epistyles two feet six inches wide, two feet three inches thick, fastening them on to the columns, eighteen epistyles in number on each row of columns. And he will set cross-beams of the same width and thickness as the epistyles on the columns over the central nave. He will set ridge-beams one foot nine inches wide and one foot four and a half inches thick without the cutting back on both sides (to take the rafters), setting a supporting block three feet long and one foot six inches thick on the cross-beam, and will fix the ridge-beams to the supporting block with iron pins. He will set rafters seven and a half inches thick, eleven and a quarter inches wide, and one foot three inches apart, resting on the cross-beams, and on the rafters he will set battens six inches wide, one and a half inches thick, and three inches apart; and on the battens close boarding of timbers three-quarters of an inch thick, four and a half inches wide, nailed to the battens with iron nails, and laying the tiles in a bed of mud.[82]

In most large Greek buildings of the classical period one expects to find the rafters and ridge-beams supported by props from the cross-beams, and usually with purlins parallel to the ridge-beam. The arsenal dispenses with both. Instead the side

walls serve as purlins and the ridge-beams are supported by a
solid block of timber on the centre of the cross-beam. It is a useful
simplification to use the same measurements for epistyles and
cross-beams and it is assumed that they have the same lengths,
the epistyles covering two inter-column lengths. No attempt is
made to use a single ridge-beam of fifty feet, though it might
have been possible to get such a length from Macedon. It is
interesting that though the different stones to be used are
specified—Piraeus limestone for the walls and columns, Pentelic
marble for the column capitals and the lintels over the great
doors, Pentelic or Hymettian marble for the doorposts, and
Hymettian for the thresholds—all the timbers were simply
described as 'wood'. The choice would presumably be made by
the architect. He might have used fir or oak for the main beams
and pine for the secondary timbers over the rafters.

Philon's huge arsenal was an ambitious gesture that assumed
an important future for the Athenian navy. It was not long,
however, before Athens had been crushed at the battle of
Chaeronea and had to accept humiliating conditions from
Philip of Macedon. When Alexander died there was a brief
period when it seemed that Greek forces might be able to re-
establish Greek independence from Macedon, but Greek unity
was always brittle and a campaign that had begun promisingly
ended in the decisive defeat of the land forces and the virtual
elimination of the Athenian fleet. Athens now faced a bleak, un-
promising future. Militarily she was powerless against Macedon
and Alexander's victories and the subsequent opening-up of
Asia and Egypt to Greek penetration had changed the patterns
of trade. No longer was the Piraeus the busiest harbour in the
Mediterranean.

Athens, however, remained important for her cultural heri-
tage and her schools of philosophy; and the successors, who
fought to take over as much as possible of Alexander's empire,
needed Greek mercenaries and Greek technology. And so
Athens was wooed by the kings of Egypt, Syria, Macedon, and
Pergamum. From her own resources she could no longer afford
large supplies of ship-timber; Demetrius, son of Antigonus,
visiting Athens in 307 to win her over against Macedon,
declared Athens free and promised her timber for a hundred
triremes from the forests controlled by his father (p. 364).

Architecturally Athens had to be content with her legacy from the fifth century unless friends paid the bills.

In the early second century two monumental two-storeyed stoas were built. One ran westward for 161.80 metres from the theatre of Dionysus along the southern foot of the Acropolis and provided a pleasant promenade for the audience and a useful refuge in bad weather.[83] The second provided a monumental frame for the Agora on its eastern side. It was 116.50 metres long and 19.52 metres wide, with two lines of columns and a row of shops along the back wall, and the ground-floor pattern was repeated on an upper storey, approached by a stone staircase at either end.[84] Strong beams of about fifteen feet were needed to support the upper storey and the roof. For these two stoas a very large quantity of timber was required. The theatre stoa was the gift of Eumenes II (197-159) King of Pergamum, and Attalus his brother, who succeeded him (159-138), gave his name to the new stoa in the Agora. The timber for these two stoas is not likely to have come from Macedon, which at the time was hostile both to Pergamum and Athens. Perhaps the kings' officials organised the cutting of the timber from the forests of Mt. Ida. It was a Hellenistic king also, Antiochus Epiphanes of Syria (176-165), who hoped to win recognition in Athens by undertaking to complete the great temple of Olympian Zeus which a Pisistratid had begun, another building which would depend on imported timber.

The days of the Hellenistic kingdoms were, however, comparatively short. Rome had entered their world after defeating Carthage in the second Punic War and by the middle of the second century they were all powerless. At first the Romans were content after their victories to dictate terms and maintain control by diplomacy, but there were less patient elements in Rome and sufficient hostility among the defeated to keep suspicions alive. When Macedon, defeated in three wars, showed signs of uniting under a pretender to the throne the Romans decided to adopt new policies. Macedon was made a Roman province in 148 and two years later, when there was a strong anti-Roman reaction in Corinth, the city was destroyed and the Greeks lost their precarious freedom. Athens's relations with Rome were considerably more strained than they had been with the Hellenistic kingdoms. It was for a long

time difficult not to resent the superior power of a culturally
inferior ruler, and relations with Rome were further soured
by the savage behaviour of Sulla in 86 BC, when he destroyed
the Piraeus and stripped Attica of most of its remaining timber
(p. 171).

During the Civil War Athenian sympathies were more with
Caesar's murderers than with Octavian. When therefore
Octavian, now Augustus, set out to stabilise and revive the
empire he paid particular attention to Athens. His policy is
reflected in the great Odeum that Agrippa built in the Athenian
Agora.[85] This may have been a deliberate comment on the
Periclean Odeum which was burnt by the Athenians themselves
at the time of Sulla's siege, but had been rebuilt by a king of
Cappadocia. The main feature of the Periclean building was the
forest of internal columns supporting the roof; Agrippa was
proud to show the Greeks that Romans could roof a span of
about eighty feet (24.38 m.) without any internal supports.
Perhaps the Athenians were not too displeased when the roof
collapsed a hundred years later; in restoring the building they
were careful to change the ground-plan by reducing the size of
the auditorium. Hadrian also, as might be expected from such
an eager Hellenist, left his mark on the city. He built a new
library, planned a secondary Agora, and at last completed the
Pisistratid temple of Olympian Zeus.

But though there were few opportunities for making fortunes
in Greece when she had become a Roman province with a weak
economy and a declining population, individual Greeks could
become rich in the wider opportunities offered by the economic
prosperity of the Mediterranean world. There are few major
centres in Greece which did not benefit from the public
generosity of Herodes Atticus, a leading sophist and a large
landowner. To him Athens owed the Odeum at the foot of the
south-west slope of the Acropolis, in which dramas and concerts
can still be seen and heard.[86] Philostratus, who wrote lives of the
sophists, is careful to point out that the roof-timbers of the
Odeum were of cedar-wood, 'though cedar is expensive even for
sculpture'.[87] This use of cedar was a spectacular gesture. So far
as we know, cedar had never before been used on a large scale in
any public building in Athens, nor is that surprising when
cypress, fir, and pine were available from nearer sources.

Meanwhile there was less pressure on local timber supplies. By the middle Empire there had been a sharp decline of population both in the city and in the rural districts. Less wood was required for fuel and for building. Attica may even have approached self-sufficiency in wood.

8

THE CITY OF ROME'S
TIMBER SUPPLIES

WHEN Rome had become the city with the largest population
in the Mediterranean world poets and moralists liked to recall
the days of rural innocence. Ovid was typical: 'Here where now
is Rome, the world's capital, were once trees and grassland; only
a few cattle grazed; men lived in huts and there were few to be
seen.'[1] Propertius almost repeats Ovid: 'Here, where now is
mighty Rome, all that you can see was hill and grass before the
Phrygian Aeneas came.'[2] Virgil catered for the same antiquarian taste by sending Aeneas from the Tiber mouth up river
to seek help against the Latins from the aged king Evander. His
boat passes between wooded banks and he finds the king's son
Pallas making sacrifice in a grassy grove outside the walls. In
a conducted tour from Evander's palace Aeneas sees a thick
grove where later was the Argiletum, and another grove
between the Capitol and Quirinal which Romulus was to
declare an Asylum, offering free refuge to all. The Capitol,
gleaming with marble and gold in Virgil's day, was covered
with wild brambles.[3] Such romanticism was encouraged by
place names that had become discordant with their setting.

Those who enjoy trees in their travels will recall from Rome
particularly the pine, the cypress, and the ilex, which, for their
numbers and quality, leave the most vivid impression. The
treescape of the eighth century BC was very different. The ilex is
the commonest tree in the coastal zone of Italy and was probably well established already in the Roman landscape. Pliny
knows of an ilex on the Vatican hill which he assumes to be older
than the foundation of Rome on the strength of a bronze plate
on the trunk with Etruscan lettering:[4] it must at least have been
a very ancient tree. But there were then no conifers in the
immediate neighbourhood of Rome, and though pine was
native in Italy, Pliny is probably right in recording that the

cypress was introduced from Greece;[5] it took its name *cupressus* from the Greek *kyparissos*. The early Romans grew up in a landscape dominated by broad-leaved deciduous trees. The Porta Querquetulana reminded passers-by that there were once *quercus*, oak trees, there. The nearby Caelian hill, Tacitus tells us, was also originally named from its oaks *Querquetulanus*.[6] The Viminal was the hill of the osiers, *vimina*, and in the Campus Martius there was a place called Aesculetum where, in 287 BC, when the plebs had seceded to the Janiculum, the dictator Hortensius had a law passed that resolutions of the plebs should be binding on all citizens. It took its name from the *aesculus*-oak. Fagutal was the name given to a spur of the Esquitine hill where there was a fine beech tree and a shrine of Jupiter Fagutalis. Corneta was a place north of the Forum, between the Via Sacra and the Macellum, where there had once been cornel trees.

When the small shepherd community moved down from the Alban hills to settle on the Palatine they had no shortage of wood to fear; in fact they were more concerned with clearing than preserving woodland. For their needs were modest. Virgil's generation could still see the 'house of Romulus', which had been maintained from time immemorial and restored to its original form when burnt by fire or otherwise needing repair.[7] It stood at the top of the southward-facing slope of the Palatine overlooking the Circus Maximus and was made of wattle and daub with a thatched roof. In this area archaeology has indeed revealed the ground-plans of an eighth-century settlement in which the best-preserved hut measures 4.90 × 3.60 metres (16 × 12 ft.) and is roughly rectangular, but with rounded corners.[8] There are six large post-holes on each of the long sides and between the timbers there would have been a filling of reeds or brushwood coated with clay, while a central post-hole held a support for the ridge-pole. Four smaller holes show that the entrance was preceded by a small porch. It can be assumed that the roof was thatched.

There was no difficulty in finding the small timbers needed for such modest buildings, and tool-handles and simple furniture could be easily supplied from local hardwoods, especially oak and beech. Towards the end of the fourth century BC Theophrastus knew that there were magnificent beeches in the lowlands of Latium;[9] the oak continued to play a large part in

Roman religious and secular life. But the demands for timber became less modest when Rome came into the cultural orbit of the Etruscans during and after the sixth century and passed from the hut to the house and from the altar in an open sacred area or a cave to the temple. Both public and private buildings became more ambitious, requiring bigger timbers and better quality.

From the point of view of timber the most ambitious of Rome's early buildings was the Pons Sublicius. This bridge, said to have been built when Ancus Marcius was king in the sixth century, was intended to link Rome across the Tiber with the Janiculum hill which, if occupied by an enemy, would constitute a serious threat. Roughly 100 metres in length it left Rome by the Forum Boarium a little below the island, where the current flows less strongly.[10] In its original form the bridge was probably composed of stout planks resting on a series of oak piers close together, as in the third-century bridge over the Volturnus, presumably with railings on either side. Its antiquity gave it a special sanctity and whenever it was damaged it was duly restored, and always in wood. It was not until 176 BC, when the Pons Aemilius was built, that stone piers were used for a Tiber bridge, and even then the superstructure was in wood until it was replaced by stone arches in 147.[11] But even when stone bridges became the rule, oak piles were sometimes sunk to act as a breakwater reducing the force of the current against the stone piers and oak was used to line the river bank where ships unloaded.[12]

The earliest temple for which there is firm archaeological evidence is the sixth-century temple of Fortuna and Mater Matuta in the Forum Boarium.[13] The podium was square, 36 feet (c.11 m.) × 36 feet, and five feet (1.52 m.) high. As in Etruscan temples there was a triple division, the central cella being fourteen feet wide and the two side cellas seven feet wide. The columns were of wood, twelve feet high, and their bases and capitals were protected by terracotta; the walls were of mud-brick with timber framing. Of the more important temples of Castor and Pollux and of Saturn in the Forum we know nothing, not even the dimensions, but there is no reason to believe that there would have been any difficulty in meeting the timber demand for public buildings from local hardwoods. The

Capitolium, the great temple of Jupiter, Juno, and Minerva, which was begun by an Etruscan monarch in the late sixth century and dedicated in 509, the first year of the Republic, may have been an exception. This was certainly the largest and grandest temple yet built in Rome and the formidable size of the podium, which in large part survives, suggests dimensions for the temple that seem barely credible. In the most widely accepted reconstruction the temple was 168 feet (49.73 m.) wide and 192 feet (56.63 m.) long. It had three rows of six columns in front of the cellae with three further columns on the two long sides, and the height of the columns was fifty-seven feet (18.64 m.). The interval between columns was twenty-four feet (7.85 m.) in the width and thirty-two feet (10.46 m.) in the length. To bridge such wide spans stone would have been too heavy and, as in Etruscan temples, the architraves would have been in wood, requiring fifteen beams of twenty-four feet (7.85 m.) and ten of thirty-two feet (10.46 m.), all probably in oak. The roof, whatever the design, would have required a very considerable volume of good timber.[14]

The archaeological and literary evidence for housing in this early period is even weaker than for public buildings, but Vitruvius, in the introduction to his discussion of the use of materials, briefly summarises what he assumed to have been the main developments: how, when they had gained experience and become more ambitious, men advanced from huts to houses with proper foundations, mud-brick walls, and roofs of timber and tiles.[15] Excavation has revealed traces of sixth-century houses on the Via Sacra with stone footings and mud-brick walls strengthened with timbers.[16] Mud-brick remained in common use until the end of the Republic, but Rome and the country round the city were rich in volcanic stone and even in the first century of the Republic many of the houses of the rich and influential were probably built of stone. A little light on housing conditions comes from Livy's account of the sacking of the city by the Gauls in 390 BC and the rebuilding that followed.

Livy draws a distinction between the behaviour of leaders and the common people when the Gauls swept through the city. The people blocked the entrances of their houses, the nobles left their halls, *atria*, open and awaited death with dignity.[17] The language implies that the poorer people normally had no central hall and that the *atrium* house was a mark of status. We have no archaeological evidence from Rome for the houses of the nobility in this early period, but Etruscan rock-cut tombs, which seem to reproduce the houses of the living, probably give a fair indication of houses in Rome. We can see fine wooden ceilings reproduced in stone, long ridge-beams, and even coffers, but before *c.*300 there is no suggestion of a house-plan based on an *atrium*.[18] In such dramatic scenes we should not be surprised by anachronisms in Livy.

When the Gauls were bought off, the destruction of Rome, with the exception of the Capitoline citadel, had been complete, and there was a serious proposal that the site should be abandoned and a new Rome built at Veii. According to Livy, Camillus, who had crushed Veii, persuaded the people to stand firm. It was decided to rebuild Rome as quickly as possible and emergency measures were adopted to speed the work. All citizens were allowed to cut stone and timber where they pleased on condition that they gave sureties to complete their homes within a year, and the state was prepared to provide tiles.[19] From this it would be reasonable to infer that roof-tiles were already in common use in Rome. Pliny, however, states that according to the biographer Cornelius Nepos, Cicero's contemporary, Rome was roofed with shingles down to the time of Pyrrhus (*c.*280 BC).[20]

Cornelius Nepos was too intelligent to believe that no terra-cotta roof-tiles were used before the time of Pyrrhus: he probably implied that by this time shingles had passed out of date. Fragments of terracotta tiles were found from the sixth-century houses on the Via Sacra, but there was probably a wide variety of roofing, including shingles (which were best made from oak) and, in poor quarters, thatch. The free issue of roof-tiles may have been a deliberate attempt to cut down the fire risk. But the simplest form of roof and the most economical in timber was the flat roof of squared beams or round timbers, covered with boards, brushwood, or reeds, and sealed by a thick coat of mud. This was a normal form of roofing in Greece and the Near East. It was less suited to the wetter climate of Italy, but the economy in materials and labour was no small compensation.

Very little is known about architectural development in Rome between the Gallic sack and the Punic Wars, but the times did not encourage public initiatives. This period may, however, have seen the emergence of the *atrium* house, which was to become the standard house-plan of those who could afford it. The central focus of the house was a large central hall lighted by an aperture in the centre of the roof, the *impluvium*, through which smoke escaped and rain fell into a shallow basin below, the *compluvium*. The rooms were built round the hall and drew their light from it. The house looked inward rather than outward and windows were inconspicuous; it could not expand vertically without blocking the light of the *atrium* and so upper rooms were virtually attics. Later a peristyle enclosing a garden was added, round which a second series of rooms could be built. The builders' main problem in this house was the support of the roof of the *atrium*. In the earliest examples of the new house-type, which Vitruvius called the Tuscan *atrium*, the main weight of the roof was carried by two massive beams across the width of the hall, with two shorter beams between the two main beams framing the *impluvium*. The main rafters joined this frame from the four corners. The Tuscan *atrium* can be seen in some of the earliest houses at Pompeii and Herculaneum and in the largest houses the main beams are not less than thirty feet long. The lintel in the main room, the *tablinum* facing the entrance, also had to be a very substantial timber because the entrance to the room was wide and it had to sustain the weight of the wall above. The timber requirements for these houses were considerably more exacting than for the small-roomed houses of the common people, but they could probably have been met from local sources of oak, elm, or ash.

Publicly Rome was at first occupied in recovering her control over central Italy; later she answered the appeal from Campania for protection from the Samnites of the mountains, and this soon involved her in diplomatic relations with the Greek cities of south Italy. These extended commitments led inevitably to the demand for a fleet, and in 311 two duovirs were appointed to organise a small fleet, probably consisting of two squadrons of ten triremes each, commanded by the two duovirs. These ships were stationed at Rome in the river docks, *navalia*, by the Campus Martius and we can assume that they were built in Rome, perhaps by shipwrights from south Italian cities.

Rome remained the headquarters of the fleet throughout the

two Punic Wars and it was at Rome that Scipio in 205 built his fleet to carry the war over to Africa (p. 143). The shipbuilding from the establishment of the fleet to the end of the second Punic War probably marked Rome's first major incursions into the firs of the central Apennines, but there is no evidence to indicate what proportion of the massive number of Roman ships that were sunk in storm or battle during the two Punic Wars were built in Rome. With the crushing of Carthage the need for a large Roman fleet was no longer acute, but a squadron was still maintained in Rome and the *navalia* were restored c.100 BC.[21] In 67 an organised fleet of pirates entered the Tiber mouth and defeated the Roman fleet commanded by a consul (p. 148). This humiliation is the last we hear of the Roman squadron; in the reorganisation of Augustus, Misenum and Ravenna became the home bases of the Roman fleet. No more warships were built in Rome.

The defeat of Carthage in the second Punic War marked a major turning-point in the history of Rome. She had seized Sardinia and Corsica shortly after the first war and one of the prizes of the second war was Spain, which had been Hannibal's main source of men and material. With the elimination of Carthage Rome had no rival in the west and the attempt of Philip of Macedon to join forces with Carthage led to Rome's search for friends in Greece as a counterweight. This led almost inevitably to war with Macedon when Carthage had been crushed, and increasing involvement in the Greek-speaking world. Within a hundred years Rome had broken the power of the kingdoms which had been carved out of Alexander's empire. Macedon and Greece had lost their freedom and become provinces, followed by Pergamum whose last king left his kingdom to Rome in his will. Syria had been excluded from Asia Minor and was soon to become a province; Egypt had lost all real independence and was waiting to be absorbed.

Rome was the unchallenged mistress of the Mediterranean, and this dramatic expansion was bound to have a profound effect on Roman society. The influence of Greece had been felt through the Greek colonies of south Italy even before the first Punic War, but from 200 to 140 Rome was continuously concerned with the politics of the states and leagues of Greece, which became familiar ground for her diplomats and generals.

The increasing familiarity with the culture of Greece exercised an increasing influence on Roman thinking, writing, and building, and it was naturally the Roman nobility, who provided the generals and diplomats, that were most affected. Their horizons were widened and they were no longer satisfied with the comparative crudities of a warrior state. The material rewards of successful wars provided the means for the satisfaction of new tastes public and private.

This infusion of wealth and Hellenism encouraged higher standards for the town and country houses of the rich, and new forms of public buildings. The architects' main inspiration came from the peristyle squares that had spread widely in the cities of Greece and Asia Minor during the Hellenistic period. Livy's annalistic record of the second century BC provides a long list of public porticoes bearing the family names of the magistrates who supervised their construction or presented them to the state from the spoils of war. The Porticus Aemilia was the first, built in 193 in the dock quarter outside the Porta Trigemina.[22] Two others, built in 168 and 147, bore the names of the Octavii and the Metelli. Others were named from their associations, 'the portico where the timber merchants do their business', *porticus inter lignarios*, also in the dock quarter (192), and *porticus Spei* (199), the portico by the temple of Hope.[23] Porticoes varied considerably in form and scale. They could be merely covered pavements with roof supported by columns or piers, but they could also be independent buildings where one could walk and talk, between lines of columns, sheltered from rain or sun. None of the second-century porticoes have been securely identified and their dimensions are unknown, nor do we know what materials were used. We should expect tufa columns, but the entablatures over the columns were probably of wood, and timber was needed for the rafters, boards, and battens of the ceiling and roof; but the spans were not large and there should have been no difficulty in finding supplies. A second form of new building raised a less simple demand.

The basilica, the 'royal building', was the Roman answer to the Greek stoa, though its form owed more to the Greek peristyle. Its function was to provide a sheltered setting for legal hearings, commercial transactions, and social meetings, and its natural place was in or near the Forum, Rome's civic centre.

Basilica plans varied considerably in detail, but the common feature which dominates all plans is a long peristyle hall. Normally this hall was surrounded by much narrower aisles on all four sides, and in some cases double aisles. These side aisles commonly had an upper floor, but the central hall was always higher and usually relied on clerestory lights.[24] The architects' main problem was the roofing of the central hall, involving spans of more than forty feet (12.19 m.). The Greeks

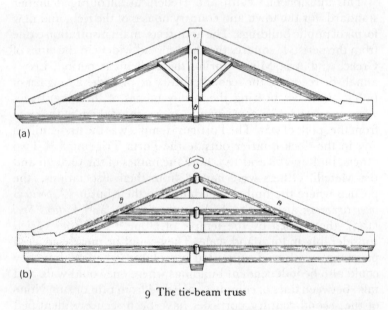

(a)

(b)

9 The tie-beam truss

of the classical period would have found it impossible to roof such wide spans without adding inner colonnades to reduce the weight on the cross-beam, but at some date after the fifth century, and probably in the Hellenistic period, it was discovered that if two rafters and a cross-beam were firmly joined together in a triangle, the cross-beam being in tension was not under pressure as in the prop system, and merely had to be protected against sagging by being joined to rafters and ridge-beam. The standard Roman system for roofing basilicas and temples was by a ridge-beam and a series of tie-beam trusses. The long timbers that were required for the basilica—more than forty feet (12.19 m.) and later up to eighty feet for the cross-

beams and more than twenty-five feet (7.62 m.) for the rafters—
could only rarely be cut from oaks or other hardwoods; but the
fir which had already been exploited for building warships was
the best building-timber in Italy; firs grew well in the Apennine
forests and at the higher altitudes the trees grew straight and tall
and their wood was strong.

Cato the censor was the pioneer of this new form when he
bought up properties in the north-west corner of the Forum. It is
a nice irony that the stubborn statesman who fought so hard to
preserve the Roman character from the corrupting influence of
Hellenism should have been the first to be responsible for a
building which was ultimately derived from Greek architecture.
The Basilica Porcia was built in 184, but it was burnt down in
52 BC and no evidence has survived of its plan or dimensions; nor
do we know anything except the names of the Basilica
Sempronia (169) or the Basilica Opimia (121). The Basilica
Aemilia, however, had a continuous history through many
restorations into the late Empire. It was built in 171 on the north
side of the Forum, and had a row of shops on its south side,
probably with living quarters above them. Most of the elements
that can still be seen in the excavated building come from
restorations, particularly those in the late Republic and early
Empire. Different materials were used, but the basic plan and
dimensions were unchanged. Cross-beams of about fifty-five feet
(16.76 m.) were needed.[25]

Another important feature of the second century was the
development of concrete construction, when it was discovered
that a mixture of volcanic sand and lime provided a material of
considerable strength which could be used effectively for walls,
with a facing of small tufa blocks. This new form of construction
increasingly replaced mud-bricks and so reduced the demand
for timber framing, but this was more than offset by the growth
in population and in public wealth and the rising scale of private
and public building.

In this context emphasis needs to be placed on the timber
merchants' interest in the city's entertainments. According
to the tradition accepted by Livy, the site of the Circus Maximus in the valley between the Palatine and Aventine hills was
used for public spectacles as early as the reign of Tarquinius
Priscus, towards the end of the seventh century BC.[26] Places

were allocated to the nobility where they could put up seating to
watch the horse-racing and boxing. Livy notes that most of the
horses and boxers came from Etruria and it is reasonable to
believe that such shows were inaugurated by Rome's first
Etruscan king. The seating was in wood, and wood was still used
for the starting-stalls for the horses, which were built in 329 BC.[27]
By this time the area was mainly used for horse- and chariot-
racing and seats were needed for an increasing population. By
the time of Augustus the Circus could accommodate 150,000
spectators and though the first tier was now in stone, timber was
still used for the two upper tiers. This seating stretched for more
than 1,200 metres round the track.[28]

Most other public entertainments depended on temporary
construction. Gladiatorial displays, for instance, were held in the
Forum in an improvised arena. Plutarch, in his *Gaius Gracchus*,
records how Gracchus, when his influence was being undermined by the senate's tactics, attempted to strengthen his hold
on the common people. Temporary seating had been erected by
the magistrates in the Forum for a gladiatorial display and the
seats were being sold. Gracchus told the magistrates to take
down the seating so that the common people could see what
should be a public show. When he was ignored he waited for the
night before the appointed day and, with the workers in his
following, tore the structure down.[29] It was not until 34 BC that a
permanent amphitheatre was built in Rome. It is even more
surprising that there was no permanent theatre until the closing
years of the Republic. The Greek colonies of south Italy and
Sicily had long since built theatres on the Greek model and in
the second century BC the plays of Plautus and Terence, which
were to have a longer life than any other plays in Latin, were
being performed in Rome. But there was a widespread feeling
that performances in the theatre, whether play, dance, or music
were effeminate and corrupting; and the feeling was so strong
that a theatre in stone which was begun in 155 was pulled down
before it was completed and temporary structures in wood had
to be put up for both plays and shows.[30] At first spectators had to
stand, but from at least the triumph of Mummius, who had
destroyed Corinth in 146, timber seating was provided.

The temporary structures were at first very simple, but by the
late Republic the competition for winning popular favour had

become a major scandal. Scaurus, stepson of the dictator Sulla, whose immense wealth was derived mainly from the Sullan proscriptions, tried to pave his way to high office by the sensational spectacle which he provided as aedile in 58 BC. The theatre built for the purpose was later said by Pliny to be the greatest building, temporary or permanent, that man had ever set up.[31] Of the three storeys in the stage-set the lowest was in marble, the second was lined with glass mosaic, and the third had panels of gilded wood. There were, according to Pliny, 3,000 columns and 2,000 statues in the decoration, and the auditorium in timber provided room for 80,000 spectators. One may reasonably suspect considerable exaggeration in the number of columns and statues, and 80,000 spectators would imply a theatre larger than the Colosseum, which is absurd; but even so, the timber required should have brought a good profit to the contractor. There is an appropriate postscript. Scaurus took back the surplus material to enjoy in his villa at Tusculum, but his slaves were so angry that they set fire to the villa and it was all burnt; it was worth 40,000,000 sesterces. 'The thought of such extravagance', moralises Pliny, 'distracts the mind and compels me to digress from my subject, and to add an even more degrading use of timber.'

The exhibition which so much shocked Pliny was the spectacular appeal to the public by C. Curio when he was tribune in 51 BC. Curio intended to play an important part in the political manœuvres that were to lead to civil war in 49, but he relied on the ingenuity of his design rather than the costliness of his materials. Two theatres were built back to back, each revolving on its own pivots. In the morning they were used as theatres, but in the afternoon they were turned round to form together a complete amphitheatre for tougher spectacles.[32] Meanwhile more important people than Scaurus and Curio were investing in public buildings to advance their political prospects. In 55 BC Pompey, whose successful campaigns against Mithridates King of Pontus had added further wealth to his considerable fortune, dedicated the first permanent theatre in Rome. The younger generation regarded this as a sensible economy, saving the expense of a succession of wooden structures as temporary as a circus tent, but some of the more conservative spirits protested against this breaking of a long tradition.[33] To make his theatre more acceptable Pompey built a temple of Venus Victrix at the top of the auditorium so that the semicircular tiers of seats seemed like a monumental stairway to the temple. However, it was not only the more conservative who regretted the passing of the wooden theatre. Vitruvius had a reply to the charge that it made no sense to build new theatres each year: wooden floors were excellent for the acoustics.[34]

Pompey's theatre was the crowning feature of a larger plan which included a luxurious quadriporticus behind the theatre, and a new senate house, but, while he was completing his building programme, Caesar's fortune from his victories in Gaul was preparing the way for a response to Pompey's challenge. L. Aemilius Paulus was carrying out a major restoration of the Basilica Aemilia and it was generally known that Caesar's money was making it possible.[35] At the same time plans were being made for a new basilica on the south side of the Forum which would match the Aemilia on the north side and so provide a frame for this western end of the Forum. In 54 Cicero tells Atticus that with Caesar's agent Oppius he is buying up land at very high cost for a new Forum which Caesar planned to relieve congestion in the centre of the city. Cicero was also excited about the prospect of a big new public enclosure, the Saepta, envisaged by Caesar in the Campus Martius to give more dignity to the voting of the tribes. In place of the present 'sheep's pen' (ovile) there would be a large area surrounded by a wall, with high porticoes round all four sides stretching a full Roman mile.[36]

In these activities Pompey and Caesar were in a sense reviving an old tradition. The great enrichment of Roman architecture in the middle Republic came from the public spirit and political ambition of Rome's leading families, and from the wealth derived directly or indirectly from the victories of the legions and the expansion of the empire. In the period of friction that was initiated by the reforms of the Gracchi (133-122 BC) political leaders were too preoccupied with the challenge to their authority to attend to the improvement of the city. The strong dictatorship of Sulla provided a short interlude of building of which the most enduring monument was the great Tabularium where public records were kept, overlooking the Forum from the Capitoline hill. But in the generation that succeeded Sulla the rich tended to be more concerned with their private estates and town houses than in investing the profits of war in public buildings. It is significant that the tribune Rullus, introducing a radical bill in 63 BC for the distribution of public land, inserted a clause that required generals 'to make a declaration to the commissioners appointed by the law of any gold or silver that they had acquired from spoils, booty, or public gift, *and had neither reported nor spent on any public monument*'.[37] It was a reminder that nobles in the second century had recognised their public responsibilities. But in reviving the old tradition Caesar and Pompey were more concerned than their predecessors with the struggle for personal pride and power. Whatever their motives, they pointed the way to the transformation of Rome into a truly imperial city.

Caesar's agents who were responsible for placing contracts and supervising the work must have felt increasing doubts as the political atmosphere became more tense. When Caesar made demands which those who had most influence in the senate could not accept, and crossed the Rubicon, civil war began and major building plans must have been temporarily abandoned. Suetonius, in discussing the causes of the war, reports that Pompey kept on saying that it was because Caesar could not complete out of his own pocket the public works that he had begun, nor satisfy the expectations that he had aroused, that he had thrown everything into confusion.[38] This may have proved a good debating point, but it would not have impressed those who remembered how well Caesar lived beyond his means at other people's expense in the sixties. Had he been allowed to take his second consulship constitutionally in 48 BC, he would have had no difficulty in raising the money to finance the plans that he had set in motion. The absolute power, however, that came with his dictatorship enabled him to give his imagination a wider range.

The changes Caesar made and contemplated in the urban landscape of Rome within five years are breath-taking, especially when it is remembered that for nearly half this short period he was commanding his legions in the field and that his schemes included major projects in Italy outside Rome. Within the city his main purpose was to bring order and dignity into the centre of the city by extending the area of monumental buildings. The building of a new Forum with an open area framed by porticoes, a handsome temple of Venus Genetrix at the end, and offices and shops along the sides would relieve the pressure on the old overcrowded Forum, and the design of a large new theatre between the Forum and the river would give distinction to a district near the Forum which was still featureless. But Caesar's most dramatic dream was to extend the area of public buildings into the Campus Martius. The exercise-ground thereby lost was to be re-created in the Campus Vaticanus, by changing the Tiber's course from the Milvian Bridge to take it round the foot of the Vatican hill.[39] He died before he could take this scheme beyond the drawing-board, but he lived to see his Forum Iulium and Basilica Iulia dedicated in 46 BC, though they were not yet completed. The Circus Maximus had been restored after a serious fire. Three new temples, probably small, had been built. Work had been begun on the Saepta, but had not proceeded far, and in 44 he had been asked by the Senate to build a new senate house.

The assassination of Caesar on 15 March 44 was followed by a political struggle between Republicans and Caesareans and it was two years before the lines were clearly drawn. By the end of 42 a triumvirate had been formed to avenge Caesar and the liberators had had to leave Italy and build up their forces in the east. At Rome the triumvirs resumed work on Caesar's uncompleted buildings and in the early thirties generals who celebrated triumphs continued the policy which Pompey and Caesar had revived. In 42 L. Munatius Plancus built a new and much larger temple of Saturn on the site of the old at the south-west corner of the Forum from spoils won in Gaul and Rhaetia, and in 36 Calvinus, who had been successful in Spain, completely rebuilt the Regia, the official residence in the Forum of the Pontifex Maximus. After 36, as the strains between Antony and Octavian were intensified, buildings became instruments of propaganda.

The period of brittle peace and high political tension came to an end with the decisive victory of Octavian at the battle of Actium in 31. In 29 he was able to return to Rome and his annexation of Egypt gave added conviction to his propaganda that the war had been against Egypt and not against the Romans. After a magnificent triumph in 29 Octavian, consul in

28 with Agrippa, set the stage for the clarification of his constitutional position. It was a shrewd bid for the support of all classes when he solemnly undertook a massive programme of temple restoration: 'I restored eighty-two temples of the gods in the city when I was consul for the sixth time, in accordance with a resolution of the senate, neglecting none which at that time needed to be restored.'[40] In the following year he graciously accepted specific powers conferred by the senate and the title of Augustus. Rome was tired of political feuds and civil war and Augustus was supremely clever in retaining power while maintaining good relations with the senate.

In his attitude to the senate and to republican loyalties Augustus learned from Caesar's mistakes, but Caesar was his model for his physical transformation of Rome. The Forum Iulium and the Basilica Julia, dedicated before completion in 46, were completed and dedicated again in 29, and when the basilica was burnt down it was completely rebuilt and enlarged, and named after Gaius and Lucius, sons of Augustus' daughter Julia. In the same year Caesar's new senate house, which had been begun in 44 and made slow progress in the triumviral period, was completed. The Saepta, for which Lepidus, the weakest of the three triumvirs, had been responsible in the thirties, was completed by Agrippa in 26 BC. The theatre which Caesar had designed to eclipse Pompey's had not been begun when Caesar died; Augustus carried out his intentions and named the new theatre after his nephew Marcellus.

Augustus also partially carried out Caesar's intentions in the Campus Martius, but wisely chose not to tackle Caesar's most ambitious schemes, when there was so much to be done without undue risks. He never contemplated changing the bed of the Tiber, but he fully agreed with Caesar on the kind of development that was needed in the Campus Martius. In this his main agent was Agrippa, who had already shown his exceptional engineering skills in overhauling Rome's water-supply and system of drains. The area to which Agrippa gave his name was in the south-east of the Campus Martius. The Pantheon still carries Agrippa's name on the architrave of the pronaos, but this was a mark of Hadrian's respect, for the great rotunda and its pronaos are the work of Hadrian; Agrippa's temple was of standard rectangular form. Behind the Pantheon

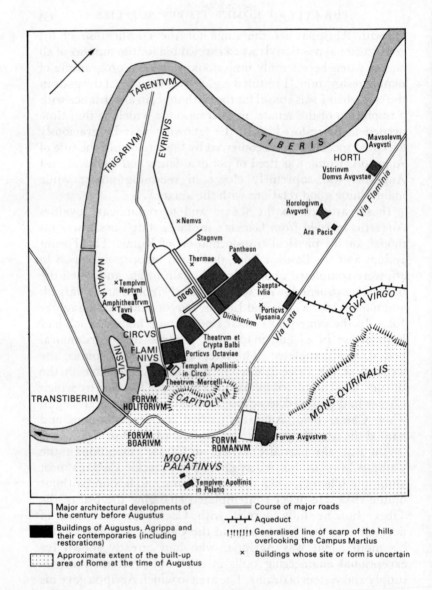

☐ Major architectural developments of the century before Augustus	══ Course of major roads
■ Buildings of Augustus, Agrippa and their contemporaries (including restorations)	┬┴┬┴ Aqueduct
⦂⦂⦂ Approximate extent of the built-up area of Rome at the time of Augustus	ꞮꞮꞮꞮꞮ Generalised line of scarp of the hills overlooking the Campus Martius
	✕ Buildings whose site or form is uncertain

10 The Campus Martius

a new basilica was built in honour of Neptune, in memory of the vital victory over Sextus Pompeius. Nearby Agrippa built the first of the imperial public baths and towards the end of his life he designed a companion building to the Saepta in which the votes were to be counted, the Diribitorium; but it was left to Augustus to complete the work after Agrippa's death in 12 BC. Several new porticoes, including one that was named Porticus Vipsania after Agrippa's sister, helped to increase the amenities of the area.

Augustus had made his own contribution to the Campus Martius when he built his family tomb there in the twenties, an enormous tumulus ringed with cypress trees. But the monument on which he prided himself most was his Forum, focused on a magnificently dominating temple of Mars the Avenger under whose protection he had exacted vengeance for the murder of Caesar. In front the temple was flanked by two colonnaded halls, one on each side.

In this rapid survey of public building between the rivalry of Pompey with Caesar in the late fifties BC and the death of Augustus in AD 14 many temples and porticoes, mentioned and dated in the sources, but little more than names to us, have been ignored. Enough, however, has been said to show that there was an unprecedented building fever in these years, and this needs emphasis.[41] Not all the buildings included in the survey made serious demands on timber. The Mausoleum of Augustus, for instance, was a concrete construction of concentric rings faced with blocks of tufa or travertine and would have used very little wood indeed; nor can the theatre of Marcellus have been very different in its materials, though even in such buildings timber was needed for scaffolding, forms for concrete, ladders, and lifting equipment. But for basilicas, temples, and porticoes the quantity of timber required was considerable and the quality had to be good. Pliny knew that the contract for the timber used in the Forum of Augustus specified that the felling must be done at the rising of the dog-star;[42] it is clear that proper attention was paid to quality. In temples and basilicas quality had to be combined with size and here the main problem was to find adequate quantities of long straight lengths for the roofs. Temples had tended to become both wider and longer since the middle Republic and widths of up to forty feet (12.19 m.) were not unusual. In basilicas the span of the central hall was rarely less; for the Augustan Basilica Julia it was forty-nine feet (14.94 m.), for the Neptune Basilica fifty-eight feet (17.68 m.).

The architect of Augustus' temple of Mars, however, did not like to take unnecessary risks and reduced the span by adding a row of interior columns on each side. Agrippa seems to have enjoyed the challenge. In his Odeum built in the Agora of Athens he covered a span of eighty feet (24.38 m.) without any internal support (p. 216), but his boldest achievement was in the Diribitorium. Dio, writing in the early third century, says that it was the largest building ever constructed with a single roof.[43] Pliny gives a clue to the span when he says that within living memory a beam 100 feet (30.48 m.) long and one and a half feet thick which was left over from the Diribitorium had been exhibited in the Saepta because of its incredible size.[44] The subsequent history of the Diribitorium is controversial, but it is certain that by the time Dio wrote it had been decided that the roof could not be replaced (p. 255).

The building programmes of Caesar and Augustus demanded timber of first quality and particularly for long lengths; but in terms of quantity the increasing demands for housing and fuel were considerably more important. Both derived from the massive increase in the population of the city. The evidence for the number of people living in Rome during the principate of Augustus is more convincing than for any other large city of the ancient world at any time, and, though a precise figure cannot be expected, few scholars who have studied the evidence would accept a figure less than 700,000.[45] It is much more difficult to trace the stages by which such a total was reached.

The first clear sign of a public awareness that an increase in the city's population was creating problems comes at the end of a long period of imperial expansion, when the final crushing of Carthage and the annexation of Macedon and Greece seemed to have paved the way for peace and stability. But the end of the wars was followed by a long period of social strains and political conflict. The building of a new aqueduct, the Aqua Marcia (144–140 BC) is a recognition that there were too many people in Rome for the existing water-supply. Although the attempt of the Gracchi (133–122) to distribute public land to the landless was designed primarily to produce effective recruits for the legions, it was also hoped that it would relieve the over-population of Rome, but the provision of cheap corn by public subsidy initiated by Gaius Gracchus in 123 suggests that there were still a significant number of people in the city who could not earn a living wage.

In 58 a law was passed guaranteeing a monthly ration of free corn to all Roman citizens living in the city, and, as political tensions increased through the decade, the prospects of political bribery from public figures eager for office encouraged migration to Rome to join political demonstrations. After the collapse of the Republic the rising standard of public amenities and the employment created by the massive building programmes of Caesar and Augustus provided powerful incentives to leave the country for the city; and when so many big contracts were being placed master builders and other contractors must have felt that the purchase of more slaves was a sound investment.

The dramatic increase in population intensified the demand for timber in two main areas. It is easy to appreciate, though impossible to quantify, the rise in the amount of wood required for fuel. More wood or charcoal was needed for cooking, for heating, for industry, and for cremation. During this period burial had been almost entirely abandoned in favour of cremation and funeral pyres consumed great quantities of logs, preferably of oak or other hardwoods. The demands of industry were also affected. Tiles had long been the standard form of roofing and more housing for more people meant more tiles, but the production of fired bricks was only slowly developing. Other industries that were dependent on fuel such as baking, tanning, bronze-casting, pottery, and tool-making will have expanded and consumed more. Although for most of the year houses in Rome needed no heating, there could be spells of sharp cold, particularly in January and February, when braziers with charcoal would be indispensable to those who could afford them; but the furnaces that heated the public baths had to be fuelled through the whole year. Of public baths in Rome during the Republic we find very little in literature and learn nothing from archaeology; we can reasonably infer that they were few, small, and unpretentious. Agrippa's baths in the Campus Martius set a completely new standard and imperial baths became grander and larger as emperors competed to surpass their predecessors. The series was to culminate in the enormous complexes of the baths of Caracalla and of Diocletian, and the maintenance of supplies of wood became an increasingly acute problem in the late Empire.

A more important effect of the increase in population was a revolution in housing. From the boast of Augustus that he had found Rome a city of mud-brick and left it a city of marble it might be assumed that mud-brick was the dominant building material for houses.[46] We know, however, from excavation that concrete walls with a facing of tufa blocks, at first irregular, *opus incertum*, but developing later into regular squares set in a fish-net pattern, *opus reticulatum*, were being increasingly used for private houses as well as for public buildings. Vitruvius realised that it was the density of Rome's population that forced the Romans to build high and he knew that to build high stronger materials had to be used.[47]

For the upper classes, as a passage from Varro indicates, mud-brick was a thing of the past;[48] but in the housing of the common people the transition to the new style of tall house-blocks was by no means complete. Cicero could describe Rome as a city of mud-brick and concrete, and Dio Cassius, in his brief account of a destructive flood in 54 BC, records that the houses, being made of mud-brick, were saturated with the flood waters and collapsed.[49] The houses most affected will have been those nearest the river and these were among the poorest quarters in Rome.

So far as timber was concerned the concrete walls needed no timber framework, but the timber roof-system was unchanged; wood was still needed for the joists supporting upper storeys, for doors, lintels, window-frames, and shutters; and the new tall blocks required strong foundation walls which had to be set in timber casing, which was normally not removed. The new housing was developed to solve the problem of increasing population and was originally designed for the less prosperous sections of society. For the rich the house based on *atrium* and peristyle remained the fashion, but it was extravagant in the use of land and, as the value of land increased, the number of those who could afford the style decreased. By Cicero's time comparatively rich men were not ashamed to take apartments in the new house-blocks.

Our understanding of the new city architecture comes largely from the well-preserved ruins of Ostia, Rome's harbour town at the mouth of the Tiber, and one of the most striking features in the two-thirds of the town that have been uncovered is the apparent absence of slums. There may be meaner housing in the south-east corner of the town, which is still buried, but within the excavated area the building standards are high and there is little shoddy work to be seen. The city we see, however, is primarily a city of the second century AD which had been almost completely rebuilt between the accession of Domitian and the death of Antoninus Pius (81–161), and the standard of housing should not be regarded as reflecting the Rome of Augustus.

It is clear from the passages noted that under Augustus mud-brick houses were not uncommon. How far the decline was speeded by legislation is uncertain, but there is no clear evidence of a legal ban on the material either in the time of Augustus or earlier.[50]* There also survived a much less substantial form of building. Vitruvius makes a sharp attack on wattle walls: 'As for walls of wattle I could wish that they had never been invented.' In the context he may be thinking of the country rather than the city, but walls with timbers framing panels of wattle were certainly to be found in Republican Rome and were probably used for partition walls into the Empire. Vitruvius condemned them, because they were 'like torches ready to start a fire'.[51]

In any consideration of timber consumption in Rome serious account should be taken of wastage from fire. Plutarch records how Crassus took advantage of the recurring fires and collapses that had become an accepted part of Roman life: 'Having built up a force of 500 slaves, architects, and builders, he made a practice of buying up properties that caught fire together with the neighbouring houses whose owners were relieved to be able to sell at any price; and so Crassus came to own more than half of Rome.'[52] There is no doubt a good deal of exaggeration in Plutarch's story, but there is other respectable evidence to confirm that the fire risk in Rome was serious. Strabo, a younger contemporary of Crassus, who visited Rome, emphasises the frequency of fires, collapses, and sales, which often led to the pulling-down of houses for rebuilding.[53] Augustus instituted a fire-fighting force of 6,000 freedmen, distributed in cohorts through the city with a paramilitary organisation; but little more than a generation later Seneca could still regard a house that had no reason to fear fire or collapse as an exception. Oil lamps were particularly dangerous, and when a fire caught hold there was no means of producing a powerful jet of water.

Two main questions now have to be considered. What woods were needed to meet the sharply increased timber requirements of the city, and where was the timber found? Vitruvius who, as a practising architect, should have been familiar with the properties of the various woods, speaks of 'oak (*robur*), elm, poplar, cypress, fir, and the other woods that are useful for building'.[54] Some of these other woods he briefly describes later. They include the *aesculus*-oak which, he says, is an excellent building-wood provided that it is kept dry; it cannot be used for outside work.[55] Ash and elm can be used provided that they are first dried out, and hornbeam (*carpinus*) is another useful hard wood.[56] Pine is mentioned only briefly by Vitruvius, in company with cypress: 'As they have an abundance of moisture they are apt to warp, but they last a long time without decay because the bitterness of their moisture defends them against decay and the small creatures which do so much harm.'[57] Cedar and juniper, he adds, have the same properties. Turkey oak (*cerrus*) and beech he dismisses, because they admit moisture and quickly decay.[58]

No mention of chestnut is made in Vitruvius' section on timber and this is strange because it is now one of the commonest trees on the hills and mountains of Italy and was much used in Rome during and after the Middle Ages, as it was also in England. Theophrastus knew that the tree could grow tall and was used for roof-timbers, and he cites a case at Antandros where chestnut beams in a public bath building gave warning before they broke so that all the people in the building were able to get out before the roof collapsed.[59] He also includes chestnut among woods that are comparatively free from decay.[60] Pliny follows Theophrastus including chestnut among hard close-grained woods that last well.[61] He gives a detailed description of the usefulness of chestnut in producing vine-props and stakes by coppicing, but he nowhere associates it with building. It may be significant that Palladius, a Roman landowner of the fourth century AD, who follows closely an epitome of Vitruvius, adds chestnut to Vitruvius' list of building-timbers. He commends it because it is very strong, and lasts well in the open and in interior work, its only fault being its weight.[62] Perhaps it was not until fir and pine and oak were becoming much scarcer in the Apennines that the Romans turned to chestnut as a good alternative to oak, which could provide long lengths; earlier they may have appreciated the tree most for its fruit and for its value as coppice.

Vitruvius gives little indication of the relative importance of the various woods he describes, but he devotes most space to fir. Its main virtues, he says, are that it is light, not easily bent, and a good weight-bearer; when used for joists supporting an upper floor it does not sag, but it is liable to rot.[63] He closes his section on timber by drawing a distinction between the firs of the two faces of the Apennines. The best-quality fir comes from the western side facing Etruria and Campania, because that side receives more sun, which dries and hardens the trees and so produces timber that will last longer. The slopes on the side of the Adriatic are too shaded and humid; the firs grow very high, but they are full of moisture and when they are cut down they lose their strength.[64] The pre-eminence of fir is brought out more clearly by Vitruvius when he emphasises the need for economy in the choice of building materials: costly materials should not be brought from long distances when adequate alternatives can be found locally: 'You cannot find quarry sand, building-stone, fir, *sappinus*, . . . or marble everywhere . . . The lack of fir will be met by using cypress, poplar, elm, or pine.'[65]

Other literary sources imply that fir and pine were the most widely used woods in Rome. Seneca, looking back to the age of innocence before architects were invented, when beams were rough-hewn rather than sawn to a precise line, adds: 'they did not then bring in pine or fir, with the streets shaking from the long line of carts, simply to supply a support for coffers heavy with gold'.[66] Similarly Juvenal includes in his catalogue of the miseries of life in Rome the danger from the long fir and pine nodding dangerously on their wagons.[67] Apart from its other virtues fir was the tallest of the Italian trees, providing straight lengths up to and sometimes over 100 feet, and when grown in high forest it sheds its lower branches early and is comparatively free from knots: for Virgil it was the fairest of the high mountain trees.[68] The best mountain pines, though not matching the fir, could provide lengths over sixty feet which would have been very difficult to find in other woods. Both fir and pine were also considerably easier to work than the hardwoods.

The need for specially long lengths derives from the Roman

insistence on using single beams to span even the widest spaces. Technically this was not necessary. The standard system of roofing was by tie-beam trusses, and since the cross-beam was in tension two beams firmly jointed together would have served adequately. It seems certain, however, that in their major public buildings the Romans continued to use single beams. The central naves of the great basilicas of Trajan and Constantine had a span of about eighty feet (24.38 m.) and from the earliest engravings of Constantine's fourth-century basilica of St. Peter it is clear that single beams were used.[69] We have seen how one of the beams left over when the roof of the Diribitorium was built was 100 feet long. It is also significant that when Diocletian issued a schedule of maximum prices the first entry in the timber section was for fir timber fifty cubits (75 ft.) long (p. 366).

Among the hardwoods oak was probably the most widely available and the most useful. It was harder to work and heavier than the conifers and it rarely produced straight lengths longer than thirty feet, but it was stronger and lasted longer. There is a good illustration of its use in an inscription from Puteoli which gives the detailed specifications for building a decorative doorway by contract in a boundary wall of a sacred area in 105 BC. The doorposts and lintel, and the corbels carrying the main weight of the roof were to be in oak; fir was to be used for the boards and battens supporting the tiles of the roof of the porch.[70] Elm was the next most useful of the hardwoods. In Greek and Latin sources it was most commonly associated with doorposts and lintels, for which it was well suited because of its strength, but it could also be used for beams, and its common occurrence in the comedies of Plautus shows that in the second century BC it was one of the commonest timbers. Its twisting grain, however, made it harder than other woods to saw. When the increase in population led to large-scale housing developments such as can be seen at Ostia in the second century AD, oak and elm were likely to lose ground to the more easily worked conifers.

Vitruvius includes cypress in his list of building-timbers and, as we have seen, it was widely used in Greek temples; but there is no evidence known to me of its structural use in any building in Rome. We happen to know that it was used for the great door of St. Peter's basilica, where it survived until the papacy of

Eugenius,[71] and we also find cypress-wood used for building warships in the sixth century AD (p. 152), but the Romans of the early Empire seem to associate the cypress primarily with parks and cemeteries, though also finding it useful for marking boundaries and producing poles.[72]

It remains to consider where the massive volume of timber required under the Empire was to be found. Happily for Rome Italy was still well forested when the building programmes of Caesar and Augustus were developed. Dionysius of Halicarnassus, a contemporary, in a glowing description of Italy's agricultural wealth, emphasises the richness in timber: 'Her woodlands on precipitous slopes, in glens, and on unfarmed hills are most impressive; they provide a plentiful supply of fine ship-timber and of timber for other purposes.' Nor was the timber inaccessible: 'the abundance of rivers in all parts of the peninsula makes the transport and exchange of the products of the land easy'.[73]

For the areas from which Rome met her mounting needs our best guide is Strabo, who was writing a description of the known world for Greek and Roman readers during the principate of Augustus. In Rome he was struck above all by the aqueducts and the drainage system, for in practical engineering the Greeks had much to learn from the Romans. The Greeks, he says, in founding their cities were concerned with beauty, security, harbours, and fertile land; the Romans thought first of a good water-supply and an efficient network of drains to carry the city's refuse into the Tiber. Strabo was also impressed by the magnificent new buildings that he saw, especially in the Campus Martius. He asked himself how such a large city, with a continuously increasing population, could be maintained in spite of fires and building collapses. It was possible, he concluded, because of the abundance of accessible stone-quarries and timber and the river system of the Tiber basin: 'First the Anio flowing from Alba, the Latin city next to the territory of the Marsi, through the lower plain till it joins the Tiber; then the Nar and the Tenea which flow through Umbria and also join the Tiber; and the Clanis flowing through Etruria and the territory of Clusium.'[74]

Latium, Umbria, and Etruria were all well wooded. Theophrastus in the late fourth century BC knew the reputation of

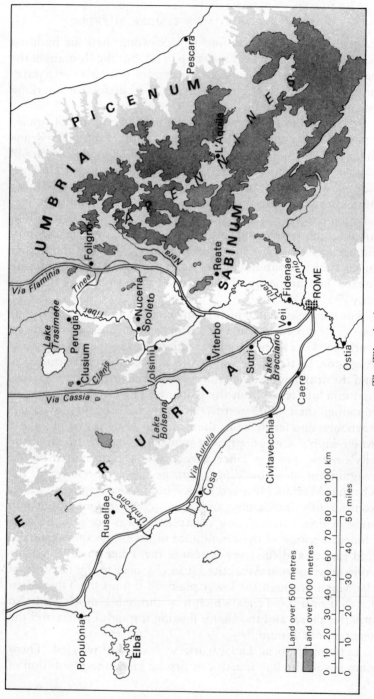

11 The Tiber basin

the trees of Latium: 'The country of the Latins is well supplied with water; the plain has bay, myrtle, and spectacular beech; on the mountains there are pine and fir.'[75] Strabo emphasises the quality of the timber from Etruria: 'most of the straightest and longest beams come from Etruria, and they are brought down from the mountain to the river';[76] and the younger Pliny, describing his estate in Tuscany, says that on the tops of the mountains which form the background of his view there are woods in which the trees are tall and old.[77] In the second Punic War, as we have seen, Perugia, near the Tiber, and Clusium on the Clanis promised firs for the fleet that Scipio was to build to carry the war across to Africa. Volsinii, another Etruscan town near the Tiber, is described by Juvenal as set between wooded hills.[78] And in the excavation of an archaic acropolis at Acquarossa near Viterbo, which was destroyed *c*.500 BC, carbonised traces were found of oak (both *Quercus robur* and *Quercus petraea*), beech, elm, lime, maple, and manna-ash.[79]

In Umbria Strabo distinguishes Nuceria as 'the city which makes the (well-known) wooden vessels', suggesting a well-wooded area.[80] The younger Pliny, describing the attractiveness of the spring of Clitumnus, refers to the venerable cypresses on the hill above the spring and the ashes and poplars on the banks of the stream which flows from the spring and soon becomes a river wide and deep enough for boats.[81] Although this river is not included by Strabo among the tributaries of the Tiber, Pliny's passage suggests that it could have carried timber rafts. Spoleto also must have had access to ample supplies of timber, for in 1455 Pope Callistus III, who wanted to strengthen his small fleet, sent a letter to the governor and priors of Spoleto reminding them sharply that they had not yet sent the carpenters and timber-workers whom he needed to build his ships.[82] South of Umbria was the Sabine country which Strabo describes as particularly suited to olives and vines and producing acorns in plenty, a land of oaks.[83]

Strabo emphasises the importance of water transport, and in the Tiber basin felling will have been mainly concentrated on areas near the Tiber itself, such as Perugia and Volsinii, or on the Tiber's largest tributaries, but the Romans are not likely to have ignored the woodlands on the Alban hills simply because there was no river to carry the timber to Rome. The woods that were identified in Caligula's pleasure-ships recovered from lake Nemi show how wide a range was available in the area.[84] In the larger ship Aleppo pine (*Pinus halepensis*), fir (*Abies*), and the two main oaks corresponding to our *Quercus sessili-flora* and *Quercus pedunculata* were found; the smaller ship had Corsican pine (*Pinus laricio*) and *Quercus sessiliflora*; in the best-preserved section of the palisade round the lake firs and Turkey oaks (*Quercus cerris*) were used. The only surprise is the Turkey oak, which had a poor reputation in Greek and Roman writers.

The network of good roads radiating from Rome made transport by ox-wagon over comparatively short distances reasonably economical. In the fourth century BC Sutrium and Nepete in south Etruria were Roman frontier-towns and beyond them stretched the great Ciminian forest. In 310 BC the Etruscans attempted to regain Sutrium and a Roman army under one of the consuls was sent to relieve the town. The Etruscans were heavily defeated and took refuge in the forest and Livy pauses to dramatise the situation. 'The Ciminian forest in those days was more impenetrable and frightening than until recently were the forests of Germany: up to that time no trader had entered the forest.'[85] The consul's·brother, who spoke fluent Etruscan, disguised as a shepherd and with a single slave to accompany him, reconnoitred the forest area and brought back a detailed report on routes and settlements which enabled the Roman army to advance through the forest and gain a decisive victory over the Etruscans. The Romans were now able to extend their control into central Etruria and a new Roman road, the Via Cassia, helped to open up the forest area. By the end of the Republic much of the woodland had been cut down or burnt to take in more land for agriculture (p. 37). Rome, some twenty-five kilometres distant, would be the most profit-able market for this timber, and it would have travelled by road.

Strabo, in his description of the city, gives the impression that Rome did not go further than the Tiber basin for her timber. This is misleading, for already in the early second century BC there was a timber merchants' portico, *porticus inter lignarios*, in the river-harbour area below the Aventine,[86] and this implies that some of Rome's timber came up rather than down the

Tiber. Strabo himself provides a corrective in his description of Pisa:

> It seems that the city was once prosperous, and it still has a reputation for the fertility of its land, its quarries, and ship-timber. This timber the people of Pisa used in early days to protect themselves by sea: they were tougher fighters than the Etruscans and the Ligurians were bad neighbours. But now most of the timber is used for buildings in Rome and country houses rivalling Persian palaces.[87]

The Ligurians also, according to Strabo, had extensive forests: 'They have very great reserves of ship-timber and large trees, some of which are eight feet in girth; many of these trees are not inferior to finely figured citrus-wood for making tables.'[88] The Ligurians had been conquered the hard way by the Romans in the second century and their timber could have been available to Rome if needed. Strabo says that they took it to Genoa and traded it for Italian oil and wines. There is one other well-forested area of Italy which may have contributed to Rome's timber supplies. Dionysius of Halicarnassus in his *Roman Antiquities* describes the Sila forest in Calabria as 'full of fir as high as heaven and pine, sufficient for the fleets and housing of the whole of Italy'.[89] There is no firm evidence that timber from the Sila forest was used in Rome during our period, but it was a source of beams for the restoration of Rome's basilicas in the early Middle Ages.

While Italy remained rich in forests there was no good reason to go further afield except for such luxury woods as citrus from Africa (p. 286). The mountains behind the head of the Adriatic and its east coast were well forested and were later exploited for Venetian fleets, but we shall need positive evidence before assuming that their timber went to Rome in the early Empire. There may, however, be an exception in Corsica. Theophrastus, while praising the firs and pines of Latium and south Italy, says that both in height and girth they were surpassed by the trees of Corsica.[90] These retained their reputation into modern times. They provided ship-timber for the navies of Genoa, France, and Britain, and Edward Lear, visiting the island shortly before 1870, was particularly impressed by the pines of the Bavello forest: 'The pines are exquisitely beautiful and unlike any I have ever seen: perfectly bare and straight to a great length they seem to rise like giant needles from the deep blue gloom of the abyss below.' There were two main species of pine in the island, *Pinus pinaster* and *Pinus laricio*. The tallest *pinaster* measured was 116 feet high and the tallest *laricio* 150 feet. Lear also writes of timber carts 'each carrying a pine of 100 ft. or more'.[91] It would be strange if Rome did not take advantage of such fine quality so near.

With the firm establishment of the imperial system, distance and other difficulties provided a challenge which was gladly accepted. The Roman emperor was the richest man in the Mediterranean world; for his palaces and his public buildings he wanted the best quality and was able to pay for it. There is no better illustration of this spirit than the introduction of larch to Rome. Vitruvius, writing his treatise on architecture in the principate of Augustus, is the earliest of our sources to call attention to the tree.[92] As a practising architect he had a shrewd understanding of the main properties of Italian woods and, while appreciating the pre-eminence of fir, he had a great respect for Alpine larch. It was first discovered, he tells us, by Caesar when he attacked a native fort in the Alps and was amazed when burning brushwood had no effect on the fort's timber. The reason, he was told, was that the wood was particularly resistant to fire. From the name of the fort, Larignum, the tree was called *larix* and was soon being marketed in north Italy, including Fanum where Vitruvius himself had built a basilica, and down the Adriatic coast as far as Ancona.

Vitruvius regrets that transport to Rome would not be practical, for it could have been very useful round the eaves of buildings in a city where fires were so frequent and so destructive. It was not long before Augustus' successor Tiberius (AD 14–36) had placed a contract for a consignment of larch from the Rhaetian Alps to restore the burnt-out bridge over the Naumachia, the scene of mock naval battles.[93] Had Tiberius read Vitruvius? Was he advised by an architect, or was this a personal choice? Larch was certainly particularly appropriate for the work, because it stands up to the weather, as can be seen from its wide use in Alpine chalets, and, though it does burn, it catches fire more slowly than most woods. It is tempting to think that the decision to use larch was the indirect result of the conquest of Rhaetia in 15 BC when Tiberius had brought an army from the west to join his brother Drusus coming from the east, to break the Alpine tribes that threatened the security of the north Italian plain.

This particular cargo made a great stir in Rome because it included, according to Pliny, 'the largest tree that had ever been seen in Rome, so exceptional that the emperor left it on exhibition on the bridge over the Naumachia. The beam produced from this tree was 120 feet long with a uniform thickness of two feet, which gives some idea of the full height of the tree if one calculates the further length to the top.'[94] Pliny's meaning in the accepted text is not clear, but what he seems to imply is that the tree, and presumably all the other larch trees with it, was transported in the round and, while the remaining trunks may have been shaped into beams or boards, this particular trunk was so enormous that it was kept as an exhibit, in the same spirit as Augustus when he left the great merchantman that brought the larger of his obelisks from Egypt on exhibition in a special dock at Puteoli. When Nero decided to use this famous tree for his wooden amphitheatre it had to be shaped into a beam, but to obtain consistent dimensions the thinner top of the tree had to be cut off. This is a plausible picture. Larches growing in high forest conditions grow very tall and straight, tapering less than most conifers. Many larches of 150 feet and more have been recorded in modern times. There is no difficulty in accepting a larch of up to 150 feet from virgin forest in the Alps.

This giant from the north must have become a talking point in Rome and that is perhaps why the epic poet Lucan, telling the story of Rome's Civil War in rather heavy hexameters, made natives in Africa heap larch logs on the camp-fires.[95] He could not be expected to know that larch is a northern tree, but he was doubly unfortunate in choosing a wood that could not possibly be found in Africa, and whose most endearing quality to the architect was its resistance to fire. Even stranger is Pliny's statement that in Homer's *Odyssey* Circe burnt on her fire larch as well as cedar and *thyon*-wood, but in this passage, as we have seen, Pliny's larch is a mistranslation of the Greek word for pine (*peuke*).[96]

Tiberius' timber from the Rhaetian Alps had to make a very

long journey to reach Rome. Larch was too heavy to be floated[97] and would presumably be rafted on a tributary to the Po and so to Ravenna to be loaded on a ship capable of carrying big timbers. The ship would have to come down the Adriatic, through the Straits of Messina, up the west coast to Ostia, and there be unloaded. In due course the timber would be towed by slaves up the Tiber either in rafts or in special barges such as were built to bring Augustus' obelisks from Ostia to Rome. Vitruvius was not being merely conservative in ruling out the transport of larch to Rome. When fir, pine, and oak were available so much nearer there were good economic reasons for not bringing larch from the Alps. It may be significant that we hear nothing in our sources of larch being used in Rome after Tiberius' spectacular gesture.[98]*

The wooden amphitheatre for which the record larch was used was built in AD 56 in the Campus Martius. If we took Nero seriously it would be nice to imagine that in using larch he was primarily thinking of the fire risk, but he was more probably attracted by the record size of the beam. It is surprising that timber was still used for a building of such large scale, for in AD 27 a timber amphitheatre at Fidenae, only sixteen kilometres from Rome, had collapsed with appalling casualties—50,000 dead or injured according to Tacitus; 20,000 dead according to Suetonius.[99] The amphitheatre had been built with inadequate foundations on ground that was not firm, and the timber seating had not been securely bonded together.

Nero's amphitheatre 'rising to heaven on interlaced beams'[100] had a very short life, for it was destroyed in the disastrous fire that swept through Rome in AD 64. This fire had begun in the valley between the Palatine and Caelian hills and had gathered strength in the Circus Maximus from the two long-stretching tiers of wooden seats. Fires had been not infrequent in the Republic, and, as we have seen, Strabo remarked on their frequency in Augustan Rome, but earlier fires were insignificant when compared with this great conflagration. Tacitus, the only surviving source to give more than a very cursory description, reports that of the fourteen regions of the city four only were unaffected: three were levelled to the ground; in the remaining seven regions only a few buildings were left standing, and they were badly damaged and half burnt.[101]

Tacitus is not likely to have underestimated the damage and the archaeological evidence suggests that he has exaggerated, but it was clearly a traumatic experience for the population and Tacitus' comparison with the Gallic sack is not ridiculous. The mistake made in the uncontrolled rebuilding of the city after that disaster was not repeated now. Tacitus, while always ready to think or at least write the worst of his emperors, admits that Nero took the opportunity to improve building standards in Rome. The rebuilding was controlled by new regulations which limited the height of buildings (Augustus' limit of seventy feet had probably been allowed to lapse), widened streets, provided more open spaces, and added porticoes along streets, whose roofs would form useful platforms for fighting fires. In certain parts of buildings timber beams were to be replaced by the two least inflammable tufas—the grey tufa with fragments of dark lava, *peperino*, found in the Alban district, and the tufa of Gabii, which had the same properties and similar structure but a browner colour.[102]

Tacitus' version of this last regulation is obscure. Literally translated it means that 'the actual buildings in specific parts should be strengthened with Gabine and Alban stone'. It has been suggested that the intention was that *contignationes*, the joists supporting upper floors, should be replaced by vaults; but Roman vaults at this stage would not have been made simply of stone and when concrete was used the type of stone chosen for the fill made little difference to the fire risk. Nor did Nero's reforms mark the end of the use of timber joists. At Ostia in the second century the vault is widely used on the ground floor, but in several Hadrianic buildings the sockets can still be seen into which joists fitted. And even when the rooms of the ground floor were vaulted, it is doubtful whether vaulting would have been used on upper floors. What one would like Nero to have prescribed is that where tufa was used for wall facings it should be the most fire-resistant tufa, and that timber framing should no longer be used, as it had been, for instance, in the *Casa del graticcio* in Herculaneum, whose thin walls are built of rubble within a framework of light vertical and horizontal timbers (pl. 8).[103] This convenient solution, however, cannot be extracted from the text of Tacitus.

The period that followed, from the reforms of Nero to the

death of Antoninus Pius, was again one of great building activity, rivalling the programmes of Caesar and Augustus. Nero took a large area near the centre of the city to set his Golden House within an enormous park. The new palace, however, did not long outlast its creator. Vespasian's answer to Nero's great amphitheatre of wood was a still vaster amphitheatre of stone, built where Nero had excavated an artificial lake. The main building materials of his Colosseum were travertine and tufa, but wood was used for the top gallery with its seating in order to lighten the pressure on the outer wall, and for the floor of the arena.[104] More difficult for the contractor were the 240 massive masts round the building to carry the awning, which could be unfurled over the audience. These masts had to be tall, straight, and strong, and would require specially selected firs. A new set of imperial baths built by Titus occupied part of the site of the Golden House itself, and the rest of the area was rebuilt.

The change that most affected timber in this period was the development of the concrete vault. In the Republic the Romans were very slow to realise the full potential of concrete in roof construction. During the principate of Augustus they had not advanced beyond the simple barrel vault and even this they were reluctant to use to cover large spans such as the warehouses of Agrippa. Although cross-vaulting represents merely the intersection of two barrel vaults, there is little evidence of its use during the Julio-Claudian period. But the architects of Nero's Golden House pointed the way to more adventurous experiments.[105] In most of the rooms the barrel vault was used, but the groined vault made its first known appearance in Roman building. More significant for the future was the concrete vault of an octagonal court.[106] The vault also was eight-sided for some two-thirds of its height, but above this was a hemispherical dome round a central opening at the top. The use of concrete vaulting was extended under the Flavians. In the Colosseum barrel vaulting was used for the principal galleries, entrance corridors, and stairways, but there was cross-vaulting under the landings and the corridors of the upper storeys.

The Flavian palace on the Palatine built by Domitian marked the triumph of the vault. Although the evidence is not decisive, there is a strong case for believing that the three main public rooms, the basilica in which the emperor dispensed justice, the great hall used for public receptions, and the dining-hall were all vaulted.[107] In the basilica, which is 23.50 metres (77 ft.) wide, there was a row of columns along each side of the room, some six feet from the wall. These might have been intended to reduce the central span as in Greek temples, but soon afterwards buttresses were added to the west side, which were surely required to counteract the outward thrust of a vault. The columns were presumably intended to provide an ample seating for the vault. The spans of the other two main public rooms were even larger. The great hall, if roofed with timber, would have needed cross-beams of over 100 feet. It is easier, with Macdonald, to imagine a vault. The crowning triumph of concrete in this period was the immense coffered dome of the Pantheon, which had a diameter of 132 feet (40.23 m.). But though the Pantheon needed no large timbers in its construction, the concrete dome was entirely dependent, like all concrete vaults, on a wooden form, and the composition of the scaffolding to provide the necessary platform must itself have posed a problem to the architect.

It is probable that during the building programmes of Trajan and Hadrian more timber was used for scaffolding than for permanent construction, but scaffolding timber could be reused and when it had lost its strength it could end its life as fuel in public baths, homes, or industries. Not all buildings, however, were vaulted. The basilica still retained its traditional roofing system. When Agrippa's Neptune Basilica was destroyed in the fire of AD 80 it was rebuilt to the same dimensions and in the same style. Even Trajan's basilica which dominated his new Forum used the same system of trusses to support the roof as the Basilica Aemilia, but the span to be covered was about eighty feet (24.38 m.). By contrast, in Trajan's utilitarian market, built on the slope of the Quirinal as part of a grand design with the Forum, the shops on the terraces and the large market-hall on the top of the hill were vaulted.

It might have been thought that the increasing use of vaulting, combined with Nero's building regulations and the dominance of fired bricks in wall faces, would have very considerably reduced the incidence of fire in Rome. There was, however, a devastating fire in 80 which spread from the southern end of the Campus Martius, where several public buildings were burnt, to the Capitol;[108] Juvenal still includes fire as one of the main hazards of life in Rome; and in a fire in the reign of Antoninus Pius no less than 340 houses or house-blocks are said to have been destroyed.[109] This may have been the occasion of a scene recorded by Aulus Gellius: a small company was walking up the Cispian hill when they saw a many-storeyed block engulfed in flames that were spreading to neighbouring properties. One of the company remarked that there was an excellent return on house property in Rome, but the risks were much too great. If there were any way of preventing the constant fires he would have sold his estates in the country and bought city property.[110]

In the early third century Rome suffered from an even more serious fire, and the account in Herodian helps to explain the fire risk. In the rivalry for the succession to the imperial power fighting had broken out between the civilian population and the troops who were quartered in Rome. The troops, being heavily outnumbered, were at first forced to take refuge in their camp, but the mob lacked discipline and patience and the troops were able to break out when the pressure was eased and drive the people off the streets. Afraid of being trapped if they forced their way into the houses, they set fire to the wooden balconies and 'there was so much woodwork exposed in the rows of house-blocks that a large part of the city was quickly destroyed'.[111]*

In the period from the death of Antoninus Pius to the end of the Severan dynasty there are no major changes in building styles. The enlargement of the imperial palace on the Palatine by Septimius Severus and the great baths of Caracalla both illustrate the dominance of concrete in plan and construction. With the full realisation of the virtues of concrete, the curving line in apse, circle, and half-circle become increasingly popular. But with the end of the Severan dynasty came the end of stability. For fifty years few emperors ruled for more than five. Meanwhile the barbarians on the frontiers became stronger and more aggressive. There was considerably less new building in Rome and a general decline in the imperial economy.

There may be signs that the tall firs of the Apennines were becoming more difficult to find during this period. In recording the building of the Diribitorium by Agrippa, Dio Cassius claims that it was the largest building ever constructed with a single roof; and to emphasise the point he adds that in his day (*c.*200) the building was without a roof because it was found impossible to replace it. This is generally taken to mean that the roof was destroyed in the great fire of 80 in which several of Agrippa's buildings in the Campus Martius, including the Diribitorium, were badly burnt. But Dio actually says: 'Now that the whole roof has been taken down the building is open to the sky, because it was impossible to reconstruct it.'[112] The emphasis on the *whole* roof would seem to imply that at some time previously part of the roof had been taken down. This might have happened after the fire of 80, when it may have been possible to restore the roof simply by replacing the timbers that had been destroyed or badly damaged by the fire. It is true that in his brief account of the fire Dio seems to say that the Diribitorium was 'burnt down', but the baths of Agrippa, which were linked in the list of casualties with the Diribitorium, were certainly in use again after the fire.[113] More than a hundred years later the timbers may have been in such a bad state that a completely new roof was needed; but when it was dismantled it may have been decided that it would be impossible to find timbers of such size and in such numbers any longer. There is also a hint in an obsequious poem by Sidonius in honour of Majorian, who was building a fleet with timber from both faces of the Apennines in the middle of the fifth century, that there had for a long time been too much timber taken from them.[114]

But these hints should not be exaggerated. When Diocletian restored a degree of stability to the empire he left his mark on Rome by his buildings. In the magnificent complex of his public baths, whose grandeur can still be appreciated, the huge concrete vaults were the dominant feature of the design; but when he built a new senate house the wide span (58 ft.; 17.68 m.) was covered with a timber roof.[115] In the next generation Maxentius decided otherwise. The original twin temples of Venus and Rome at the east end of the Forum, designed by Hadrian himself, had timber roofs,[116] but when they were burnt down (in 307) Maxentius rebuilt them with coffered barrel vaults, and in his great basilica which was completed by Constantine the central hall was covered by a series of magnificent cross-vaults. This, however, was but a temporary

12 St. Peter's basilica

break in the tradition. The great Christian basilicas of St. Peter and St. Paul in the fourth century reverted to the timber roof. It was not a shortage of building-timber that led to the development of the vault.

There was, however, considerable concern for the supply of fuel. In some areas demand had fallen. By the end of the first century AD inhumation was beginning to take the place of cremation, but the change was not abrupt. Through the second century many family tombs provided both niches for cinerary urns and recesses for coffins or bodies, but by the end of the century inhumation had won the day. The change cannot be attributed to a shortage of wood, but it meant a considerable decrease in demand. It is probable also that the population of Rome had passed its peak and was declining. When the army that had campaigned in the east in the last years of Marcus Aurelius brought back the plague with them the death-toll was alarming, 'so widespread that the bodies were carried out in carts and large wagons'.[117]

These reductions in demand, however, were more than offset by the rising consumption of fuel elsewhere. During the second century, and particularly under Hadrian, there was a tremendous expansion in the production of fired bricks. Nero's building reforms did not lead immediately to an all-brick architecture. Under Domitian and Trajan, and in the early part of Hadrian's rule, private buildings, and to a lesser extent public buildings, tended to combine brick with tufa blocks laid in reticulate fashion. In the second half of Hadrian's rule and for the rest of the century all-brick construction dominated, and more bricks meant more fuel. Meanwhile the consumption of wood in the public baths rose remorselessly with the increase in their number and size.

The increasing popularity of the baths is one of the most striking developments in the social life of Rome during the Empire, and the emperors by their grandiose buildings encouraged it. The baths of Nero were larger and grander than the baths of Agrippa; Trajan's were still larger. All were eclipsed in scale and grandeur by the baths of Caracalla and of Diocletian. Only a very few rich men had sufficient space to include a suite of baths in their town house; the rest of the free population, from senators to casual free labourers, depended on baths open to the public. Martial could expect to find friends in the imperial baths of Agrippa or Titus, in the luxurious baths of Etruscus, famous for the rich variety of their exotic marbles, or in the miserable premises of Stephanus, squeezed into a housing-block. But they all needed brushwood and logs to stoke the furnaces, which provided the hot air that ran through terracotta pipes up the walls of the sweating-rooms, or heated the water of the hot baths. By the time of the regionary catalogues in the middle of the fourth century, there were eleven large sets of imperial baths, *thermae*, and no less than 856 smaller establishments, *balnea*, in the city.[118] It is not surprising that it was becoming difficult to maintain adequate supplies of fuel. The emperor Alexander Severus, who died in 235, is given credit by his biographer for allocating specific woodlands for the supply of Rome's baths;[119] this suggests that it was already difficult to meet the full demand.

A century later the situation had become more serious. In 364 an order was sent by the emperors Valens and Valentinianus to the governor of the province of Africa to allow the African ship operators 'who perform useful service to meet the city's need in bringing logs (for the baths) to retain the privileges that they have long enjoyed'.[120] A little later the same emperors order the urban prefect to safeguard the interests of the contractors operating Rome's salt-beds on the right bank of the Tiber near the coast.[121] Later documents make it clear that these contractors were responsible for supplying logs to the city baths. Some of these supplies were coming from Africa by 364 and in a report to the emperor from Symmachus when he was urban prefect in 384–5 we learn that Terracina on the west coast some ninety kilometres from Rome was required to send regular supplies of lime and logs to Rome.[122] By now the salt-contractors were finding acute difficulties in maintaining regular supplies. They pleaded that the responsibility should be shared by the shipowners, but the shipowners preferred to transfer some of their members. In a further report Symmachus urged the emperor to ensure that the men who had been transferred should be made to stay with the salt-contractors.[123] Some ten years later Symmachus, no longer in office but a man of considerable influence, writes to two men, probably the urban prefect, who controlled the administration of the city, and the prefect of the corn supply, who had special responsibilities in the harbour area, to give what help they can to the salt-contractors, and particularly by enforcing payment from their debtors.[124]

The natural inference from these scraps of evidence is that at some time in the late third or fourth century the emperor assumed responsibility for ensuring adequate supplies of fuel for the baths in Rome. His method was to require various communities in Italy, Tunisia, and perhaps in other provinces to make regular contributions of logs, which the salt-contractors were to deliver to the baths. The employment of the salt-contractors is most easily explained if supplies came by sea to Rome's harbour, for the salt-contractors would have river-boats available, in which they sent their salt to the city. There is no evidence that the supply of fuel for domestic and industrial use was organised in the same way, and it is a reasonable assumption that it was not. Politically a breakdown of the supply of logs for the baths was nearly as dangerous as an interruption of the corn supply. It would have been an astute move for the emperor to have organised new sources of supply for the baths, thus leaving the regular sources in the neighbourhood of Rome to the private market.

Some have inferred from the shipment of African firewood that Italian forests were virtually exhausted in the late Empire. It is important to remember that the evidence for an acute shortage is confined to firewood. It is probable that forests near the Tiber had been seriously depleted, but in the early sixth century, as we have seen (p. 152), Theodoric the Ostrogoth, ruling from Ravenna, was assured that Italy was supplying timber to the province, and he had no difficulty in finding sufficient cypress, pines, and fir to build a fleet of a thousand warships.

9

FARMS, PARKS, AND GARDENS

ALTHOUGH the Greeks wrote more than fifty books on agriculture, the only work that has survived is the first, the *Works and Days* of the Boeotian poet Hesiod who, in the early archaic period (*c.*700 BC), described the hard life of the farmer in hexameters which were to remain scarcely less famous than Homer's epics. Hesiod's father had lived in Cyme on the east side of the Aegean, but poverty forced him to seek a new home with his two sons, Hesiod and Perses. He settled at Ascra under Mt. Helicon in Boeotia, where he seems to have been able to take over land that had not yet been cultivated and leave it when he died to his two sons. While Hesiod worked hard, his brother, according to Hesiod, wasted his time in fighting legal battles and relying on the corruption of the nobles who dispensed justice. Before writing was widespread, poetry was a natural medium of communication to a wider audience and even a hundred years later the Athenian reformer Solon advertised his political views in verse. Hesiod set out to vindicate his own way of life in contrast to his brother's.

Having traced the development of society through the five Ages from the Age of Gold to his own generation, when violence and injustice flourish, but honour and justice still struggle for survival, he appeals to his brother to realise that happiness comes from justice and hard work. He then proceeds to the practical advice that a farmer needs if he is to be successful.[1] General moralising is accompanied by specific advice, and though he is thinking primarily of grain crops and harvest, he assumes a need for timber and timber knowledge: so far as possible the farm must be self-sufficient. Hesiod knew that the best time to cut timber was when the high heat of summer has passed and the leaves fall: 'Then is the time to cut your timber. Cut a mortar three feet wide and a pestle three cubits long, and an axle of seven feet, for so it will fit well: but it you make it eight feet long you can cut a mallet from it too. Cut a felloe three spans across for a wagon of ten palms width.'²

'Cut many curving timbers; and bring back for your plough-tree a holm-oak when you find one, whether on mountain or field; for this is the strongest for oxen to plough with when one of Athena's men has fixed in the share-beam and fastened it into the pole with dowels . . . Poles of laurel or elm are most free from worm; make your share-beam of oak, and plough-tree of holm-oak.' The woodcutter has to watch the calendar carefully. 'On the seventh of the mid-month . . . let the woodcutter cut beams for house building and many ship-timbers, such as are suitable for ships. On the fourth day begin to build narrow ships.'³ The farmer must look ahead and if he needs to build a wagon he must remember that a wagon takes 'a hundred timbers': 'take care to have these ready in time'.⁴

Hesiod's poem is an interesting mixture of moral fervour, shrewd sense, and superstition: 'Happy and blessed is he who knows all these things and works without offence to the immortals, discerning rightly the flight of birds and avoiding transgression.'⁵ Of the many Greek treatises on agriculture written from a more intellectually developed background we have to remain ignorant and there is not much to be gleaned about Greek farms from other branches of literature or from inscriptions. But in agriculture as in so many other things the Romans appreciated the value of Greek experience and Roman writers on agriculture used more Greek than Roman sources.

This, however, was not true of the first Roman writer on agriculture whose book has survived. M. Porcius Cato (234–149 BC) was in fact a strong and stubborn opponent of the growing influence of Greece on Roman character and customs. He fought hard politically to preserve what he regarded as the essential Roman virtues, which were primarily those of an agricultural community. He admits that trade can be more profitable, but there are serious risks involved; money-lending also can be lucrative, but it is dishonourable; agriculture produces the sturdiest soldiers and commands the most respect. Cato had worked hard on his family's Sabine farm when he was growing up and had learnt the basic principles of agriculture by personal experience. His purpose in writing a treatise was not to produce a literary work that would find its way into the libraries, but a practical guide to landowners. He was not thinking primarily of the peasant farmer with a holding of less than ten acres, nor of the very large ranches, but of medium-sized estates with substantial farm buildings and a variety of crops. There is little logical organisation in his work and shrewd practical sense is accompanied by the kind of superstitions that are found in all agricultural societies, and not only among the poorer peasants. Besides advice on crops he discusses the siting of the farm, marketing, and the treatment of the work-force. He gives inventories of equipment required to operate an olive-grove of 140 *iugera* and a vineyard of 100 *iugera*, and detailed instructions for building pressing-rooms for olives.[6]

As a general guide to land-use Cato lists the various crops in order of profitability: 'If the soil produces good wine and plenty of it vines bring the greatest profit; next comes the irrigated garden; third the willow-bed; fourth the olive; fifth the meadow; sixth grain; seventh coppice-wood (*silva caedua*); eighth orchard (*arbustum*); ninth mast-wood (*glandaria silva*).'[7] But while holding that wood brings least profit, he assumes that the farm will grow what timber it needs. 'Plant elms and poplars round the borders of the farm and along the roads to give you leaves for the sheep and cattle and timber when you need it.'[8] If a farmhouse has to be built 'the owner will furnish the timber and materials needed, and also a saw and a plumb-line, but the contractor will fell, square, and cut the timber (into beams and boards)'.[9] Cato gives details for the construction of a pressing-room for the olives and seems to assume that the timber will be provided from the estate, for, in specifying a beam thirty-seven feet (11.28 m.) long, two feet (0.61 m.) broad, and one foot (0.31 m.) thick, he adds: 'If you do not have a single solid beam use two together.'[10] This is the longest timber needed, but the press-beam requires a length of twenty-five feet (7.62 m.).[11] For the anchor-posts and guide-posts oak or pine are specified, for the great disc elm and hazel, because of their strength. Oak is used for dowels, cornel, one of the strongest woods, for nails, and willow for wedges. For the press-beam black hornbeam should be used.[12]

The estate will grow its own trees: Cato discusses the raising from seed of olives, elms, figs, apples, vines, pines, and cypress.[13] In assessing the profitability of crops he ranks the willow-grove higher than coppice-wood, and later writers on agriculture did not find this surprising, for the willow grows fast and served a number of useful purposes. The branches could provide poles and props: the combination of flexibility and strength explains its use for felloes on chariot-wheels in the Bronze Age, and its bark provided ties for vines; willows were also invaluable for basketry and for chair-making.[14] *Silva caedua* is a technical term for coppicing, which involves the encouraging of multiple stems from the base of a tree and cutting them at regular intervals. It was the commonest method of producing props and stakes, firewood, and secondary timbers. *Silva glandaria*, mast-wood, would normally mean oak-woods but could also be applied to beech, whose nuts were valued highly for fattening pigs.[15] Cato puts it last on his list, probably because he is thinking in terms of a mixed farm without much livestock. In Cisalpine Gaul, whose oak forests supplied a large part of the Roman market with pork, *silva glandaria* was a good capital investment.[16]

Cato is anxious that no land should be wasted: 'Where there is a river-bank or wet ground plant poplar cuttings and a reed thicket. Plant Greek willows along the borders of the reed thicket, so that you may have withies for tying up the vines.'[17] But there is to be no planting for the sake of planting: 'The place for planting a willow-grove is on ground that is well watered and remains wet', but 'be sure before you plant that the crop is needed on the estate or that there is a market for it'.[18] Elms and poplars are specially commended because, in addition to providing useful timber, their leaves make good fodder for sheep and cattle; elm leaves are best, followed by poplar, but there are others. 'If you have poplar leaves mix them with the elm to make the latter last longer; and failing elms, feed oak and fig leaves.'[19] Firewood is another by-product that he considers seriously. Normally an orchard has low priority in Cato's mind, but for estates near large towns orchards are highly recommended: 'You can sell logs and faggots (from prunings) and there will also be a supply for the owner.'[20] If there is a surplus of suitable stone a contractor should be employed to provide a lime-kiln and supervise its operations with timber provided by the owner: 'If he has no suitable stone and no market for his surplus logs he should use them to make charcoal.'[21]

Pliny in his *Natural History* paid a nice tribute to Cato by accepting his authority as the final word, nor is this remarkable, because many of the basic principles of agriculture remained unchanged. But there were considerable changes in the pattern of Italian agriculture and the governing class of the Empire would have had little sympathy with Cato's puritanical principles. Conditions had already changed considerably when Varro wrote his book on agriculture. During Cato's lifetime the dramatic series of Roman victories in the east had transformed Rome from an agricultural community that by hard fighting and political generosity had won control over Italy into the greatest power in the Mediterranean. The foundations of a western empire had been laid by the destruction of Carthage, and the Hellenistic kingdoms of the east had been crushed beyond recovery. Those who gained most from these triumphs were the Roman nobles who as generals won the victories and profited most from the booty, and as governors of provinces had unparalleled opportunities to get rich in office. Since land had remained the safest form of investment they had every incentive to enlarge their estates and, at the same time, the long periods of compulsory service in the legions made it tempting to the smallholder to sell his property.

The lack of a firm control over public land also made the accumulation of land easier for the unscrupulous. When the period of almost continuous wars came to an end with the incorporation of Macedon and Greece in the empire in 146 BC, the social dangers of the new developments on the land became increasingly apparent, and some form of land redistribution remained one of the main political issues until the end of the Republic. Tiberius Gracchus set the precedent by a law restricting the amount of public land that a man could hold and distributing public land so recovered among needy citizens (133 BC). Further laws with similar intentions were passed in the following century but no fundamental change was effected. The greater part of Italy was still controlled by the rich and the rich of the late Republic were no longer content with standards that had satisfied Cato. Increasing contact with the culture of Greece and the luxuries of Hellenistic courts encouraged a more relaxed and civilised way of life. Roman noblemen wanted elaborate villas to set off the sculptures which they collected from the Greek world and to entertain their friends in style. The extravagance of Lucullus, Hortensius, and their political associates became a byword and the number of big landowners who took a prudent interest in the proper management of their estates declined.

M. Terentius Varro regretted these changes and in 37 BC, his eightieth year, he settled down to write his own book on agriculture. He was born at Reate in the Sabine country and had followed a senatorial career to the praetorship. He had commanded a naval squadron when Pompey was given a special commission to stamp out piracy in the Mediterranean and, when the rivalry between Pompey and Caesar led to civil war, he again served under Pompey, commanding a squadron on the east side of the Adriatic. But in politics his ambitions were strictly limited. He did not join the competition for the consulship, and during the fifties, while political divisions were sharpening, he chose to devote himself to study and writing. He was the most learned Roman of his day and the range of his interests is amazing: more than fifty of his titles survive and they involve, besides philosophy and history, geography, philology, and medicine. He had already written 490 volumes in 37 BC, when the increasing friction between Octavian, later to become Augustus, and Antony threatened another civil war.

Why did Varro so late in his life and against such a discouraging political background write a book on agriculture? He hoped, he says, that it could be of practical value to his wife when he died, but a much shorter book would have served that purpose very much better. The main reason is probably that after so much writing on academic subjects he was attracted by a subject in which he could add his personal experience to his learning from the library. He had himself built up large herds of sheep and horses in Apulia and at Reate and maintained a lively interest in his estates throughout his political career. While commanding his fleet in the war against the pirates he took the opportunity to discuss breeding with some of the big cattle-ranchers of Epirus,[22] and when he had to lead a military force through Gaul to the Rhine he noticed where the vines and olives, which were such a familiar part of the landscape in the Italy he knew, reached their northern limit.[23]

In form his book was very different from Cato's. Cato had simply provided a practical handbook of recommendations based on experience, set down without any serious consideration of how his material could best be organised. Varro's book was a literary work in dialogue form, designed to interest as well as instruct, and the two men he chose to lead the discussion were well qualified. Gaius Licinius Stolo was descended from one of the two tribunes who in 365 had introduced the law limiting holdings by individuals of public land to 500 *iugera*; Gnaeus Tremellius Scrofa had served on the commission to distribute public land under Caesar's law of 59. Both had considerable experience in managing estates. The book was divided into three sections—agriculture proper, sheep and cattle, birds, and other lesser animals. His material, he tells us, was drawn partly from other authors, partly from consultation with experts, and partly from his own experience.

Varro does not follow Cato in regarding vineyards as the landowner's first choice; he prefers meadows as an investment and concentrates mainly on stock-raising. Like Cato he lays no emphasis on timber but accepts it as an essential element on any large estate. The ideal site for a villa is at the foot of a wooded hill.[24] Trees will be needed to mark the boundary of the estate: 'Some plant pines as does my wife on her Sabine farms, others cypresses as I have done myself near Vesuvius and others in the district of Crustumerium.'[25] He agrees with Cato on the importance of the elm, if the soil and site suit it: it is one of the best nurse-trees for the vine, its leaves are good for cattle and sheep, and the timber is useful for fencing-rails and fuel for fire or furnace.[26] For stakes and props he recommends oak and juniper.[27] The estate will also need a willow-bed and a reed thicket; and different types of land will be needed for coppice.[28] Like Cato he thought that nothing should be bought which could be economically produced on the estate. It would be ridiculous, for instance, to buy such things as baskets, threshing-sledges, fencing, and rakes.[29] There is no suggestion, however, in Varro that a large-scale landowner would expect to provide the timber for building his villa from his own estate. Strabo, writing shortly after the death of Varro, says that the fine timber of Pisa, from which the fleets of Pisa had once been built, were in his day being used for building in Rome or for the luxury palaces of the nobility.[30]

The next of the surviving prose writers on agriculture was, unlike Varro and Cato, a professional specialist; Lucius Junius

Columella, who lived in the first century AD, was born in Spain, held a junior command in the army, but spent most of his life in managing his estates in Italy. He refers in passing to three estates in Latium which he owns or had owned, and one which may be in Etruria.[31] There are no moral undertones or overtones in his writing. His objective is to explain how the landowner can make the most efficient and profitable use of his land. As in all general works on agriculture timber occupies little space, but he is fully aware of its importance. Columella's ideal estate, like Cato's, would be near the sea or a navigable river, in order to provide the most economical transport for the products of the estate that are to be marketed, and for the supply of what the estate needs from outside. It would include different types of land to suit different crops—level land for pasture and arable, willow-groves and reed thickets, but also hills. Some hills should be reserved for grain crops when the slope is not steep, others for olive-groves and vineyards, and the production of stakes for the vines. Hilly country was also required for timber and stone should building be needed, and for grazing.[32]

Columella regards vines as the most profitable investment and discusses the management of the vineyard in great detail.[33] In some parts of Italy it was customary to grow vines on trees and to plant trees specifically for the purpose. In most Latin poetry it is the elm that is most closely associated with the vine. Columella gave first place to the poplar, followed by elm and ash, whose leaves are liked by sheep and goats.[34] But low-growing vines were more widespread and it was an obvious economy to grow the stakes that were needed on the estate itself. These were produced by coppicing and the best woods for the purpose were oak and chestnut. The chestnut grew more quickly and would renew itself after cutting in five years, whereas the oak required seven; it was therefore natural to use chestnut where it already grew or where the soil suited it: 'It likes a dark, loose soil, does not mind a gravelly soil, provided that it is moist, or crumbling tufa; it is at its best on a shady and northward-facing slope',[35] a specification which would be generally accepted today. A detailed description of the planting of the nuts follows and then the cutting: the cut nearest the base should supply four stakes when split, and the second cut two. Every *iugerum* should yield 12,000 stakes.

Pliny closely follows Columella, with minor variations suggesting that he has a second source from which he adds some details that are not in Columella.[36] Only large nuts should be used and they should be planted five together (as an insurance against failures). He also lists other trees that can be coppiced: ash, laurel, peach, hazel, apple, though these grow more slowly. Elder and poplar grow from cuttings. There is a year's difference in Pliny's cycle. According to Columella chestnuts should be cut after five years, oaks two years later. In Pliny chestnut should be cut within the seventh year, oak three years later. This confirmation of a short cycle will reassure those who from current practice in England would expect a much longer cycle of some twenty years. This much longer cycle is comparatively modern, influenced by the sharp decline of the firewood market on the introduction of cheap coal. Practice during the Middle Ages in both Italy and England was very similar to the Roman.[37]

An alternative to producing stakes and props by coppicing from the stump was to use branches from a growing tree. According to Pliny cypress trees were commonly grown for this purpose.[38] Branches after twelve years' growth could be sold for a denarius apiece, making a cypress-grove a profitable investment; which is why they were called a daughter's dowry. It was perhaps just such a grove that was discovered in the territory of Pompeii in the early nineteenth century, when what were at first thought to be the tops of masts of a Pompeian fleet were found to be firmly planted trunks of cypress trees.[39] Poplar branches were also often taken for stakes.[40]

Columella's advice to landowners is to plant vines wherever the soil is suitable, for this was the most profitable investment provided that the vineyards are managed efficiently; but he has to admit that his own view is by no means generally accepted and that there are very many who would prefer to own meadows, mast-woods, or coppice.[41] He defends his preference by quoting figures for the yield of vineyards, 'whereas if meadows, mast-woods, and coppice brought in 100 sesterces for every *iugerum* the owner would seem to be doing very well'. Columella has described coppice only as a means of producing stakes for vines; from his admission that it was a common form of silviculture it follows that there were other markets. Coppice could produce fencing, poles, and firewood as well as stakes and props, and the market was sufficiently large to encourage the peasant as well as the large-scale landowner. When Martial makes the contrast between rich and poor, his rich man, Torquatus, 'has his palatial home by the fourth milestone; at the fourth milestone the poor Otacilius has bought a smallholding. Torquatus has built a splendid set of baths; Otacilius has made a tub for himself. Torquatus has planted a grove of myrtles; Otacilius has sown a hundred chestnuts.'[42] These surely are to be his main source of income. But it is not only the poor who produce for this market. In another epigram Martial addresses a man of property and prays that his woodland at Tivoli (near Rome) 'will hasten when cut down to return again'.[43]

The younger Pliny, consulting a friend when he is considering the purchase of an estate, says that 'the land is fertile and rich and consists of arable fields, vines, and woods producing timber which provides a return that, though modest, can be depended on'.[44] The dependability of the income suggests coppice-wood cut at regular intervals and produced not only for the estate but for sale. Coppicing was the easiest way of producing fuel and all substantial towns would provide a reliable market for land-owners in the neighbourhood. The needs of Rome, however, must have been so large that they could not have been supplied from the immediate neighbourhood; coppicing for the Roman market was probably a common feature on the hillsides of Tuscan and Umbrian estates near the Tiber and its tributaries.

The estate which Pliny was considering was next to an estate which he already owned, and from their common character it is generally assumed that this was his Tuscan estate near Tifernum Tiberinum, the modern Città di Castello in the upper Tiber valley, which he describes in detail:

Picture to yourself an enormous amphitheatre, such as only nature can provide. The broad spreading plain is surrounded by mountains and on the mountain tops are woods of great age, where the trees are tall. These provide hunting in good measure and of great variety. On the slopes below them are coppice-woods; between the woods there are rich fields with plenty of soil (it would be difficult, even if you tried, to find any stones), and they are as productive as the most level fields: the harvest is late but the corn ripens thoroughly and the yield is very good. The slopes further down are covered with vineyards in an unbroken pattern. Where the vineyards end, at the bottom of the slopes, plantations are growing up. Then come meadows and fields which only massive oxen and the strongest of ploughs can break down.[45]

The last surviving Latin treatise on agriculture was written more than three centuries later than Columella. Palladius was a landowner of the late Empire. He knows the works of his predecessors and often follows Columella closely, but he makes new contributions from his own experience. For us his main importance lies in his list of building-timbers, which is based ultimately on Vitruvius but taken by Palladius from Faventius, who wrote an epitome of Vitruvius (c.300).[46] In emphasising the usefulness of larch he is following Faventius:[47] together they imply that larch was more widely marketed, at least in the late Empire, than when Vitruvius wrote. More important, as we have seen (p. 240), Palladius gives us our earliest evidence of the common usage of chestnut for building.

In the Greek and Roman writers on agriculture timber is a minor concern, introduced only because it is a sensible economy for an estate to produce its own timber to maintain the buildings and to supply stakes for the vineyards and fencing, and also firewood. But no advice is given on the economical management of woods other than coppice. We might expect discussions on the age at which the various species of trees should be felled, on the comparative advantages of selling trees standing or felled, and on the most profitable trees to plant for selling outside the estate. The impression that one gains from literature is that woods were appreciated more for pasture and leaf-fodder than for their timber. The poet Catullus, writing maliciously about a man who prides himself on his possessions, seems to regard the 'huge forests' on his estate as a liability.[48] There is ample evidence of olives being planted on a very substantial scale, especially in Africa, but I have found no evidence of the planting of trees to produce timber for the market. There must surely have been some estates in which a significant part of the income came from selling timber, but we hear nothing about them.

We also have to look elsewhere for the growing interest in trees for pleasure in the late Republic. The influences that gave rise to new attitudes to parks and gardens passed to Rome through

Greek channels, particularly in the Hellenistic kingdoms, but they derived ultimately from further east. Assyrian and Babylonian rulers, coming from the comparative treelessness of Mesopotamia, delighted in the great forests of the lands they conquered. Assurnasipal II collected plants and trees 'from all the countries through which he had marched and all the mountains he had crossed' and he lists forty-one species that he claims to have brought to Assyria.[49] Esarhaddon, in his attempt to conciliate the Babylonians after the crushing of their revolt by his father, encourages them to set out plantations and dig irrigation ditches to water them, and by his own palace he laid out a park 'like unto Amanus'.[50] When Alexander came to Babylon after his conquests in the Far East, he found that the cypress had been naturalised by Babylonian rulers.[51]

The Persians inherited this tradition and extended it. A *paradeisos*, or park, was an essential adjunct of a Persian governor's court whether at Ecbatana in Media or in the western satrapies of Phrygia and Lydia, at Dascylium and Sardis. These parks impressed the Greeks, who even adopted the eastern word into their own language. It was the greatest of compliments when Tissaphernes, the Persian governor at Sardis, called his park *The Alcibiades* after the scheming Athenian aristocrat.[52] Xenophon describes the Spartan general Lysander's admiration of the magnificent park at Sardis, for the layout of which the Persian king's younger son Cyrus was himself mainly responsible,[53] and in his account of the expedition of 10,000 Greek mercenaries to place Cyrus on the throne occupied by his brother Xenophon draws attention to the size of the governor of Syria's park full of beauty and every kind of tree.[54] He uses the same language of another park near Sittake on the Tigris which the mercenaries passed on their retreat following the death of Cyrus.[55] It is significant that when the Phoenicians decided to revolt from Persia (361 BC) their first step was to destroy the trees in the Persian governor's park at Tripolis.[56] Theophrastus draws particular attention to the parks in Syria: 'The cedars grow to a marvellous height and girth in the mountains of Syria, but they are even larger and finer in the parks.'[57] Persian appreciation of trees is reflected in a dispatch from the Persian king Darius to one of his governors in the west, probably in Ionia. In the course of his instructions he praises the governor for establishing the fruit-trees of Syria in the precinct of Apollo.[58]

Eastern parks were famous for the size and beauty of their trees; they were also enjoyed as hunting reserves. This aspect is nicely illustrated in Quintus Curtius' description of an episode when Alexander had penetrated into the heart of Asia: 'There is no better indication of the great wealth of the Bazaioi than the herds of noble beasts confined in large forests and open woodland. They choose for the purpose wide spreading forests relieved by abundant springs of running water; the woods are surrounded by walls and there are towers in them for the use of hunters.'[59] One of these parks had not been touched for four generations: Alexander entered it with his army and gave orders for all the beasts to be driven from their cover. They included a magnificent lion which charged at Alexander. Lysimachus was preparing to attack the lion with a hunting-spear, but Alexander rejected the help and dispatched the beast himself with a single thrust.

Alexander had taken with him on his great crusade men who were interested in natural history and the facts of geography. After the expedition there came a flow of literature describing the wonders of the east, including the flora and the fauna. This literature played a considerable part in spreading an interest in and feeling for trees in the Hellenistic world, which found expression not only in the development of aristocratic gardens, but also in the landscape-paintings on the walls of villas. Trees were not only introduced into parks; their value in towns as scenery and shade was also appreciated. Athens had already shown the way when Cimon had plane trees planted in the Agora, and converted the Academy from a dry and treeless place to a well-watered grove laid out with well-shaded walks.[60] It is possible that Cimon conceived the idea when he was reducing the island of Thasos which had revolted from Athens in 465; certainly the magnificent planes with their huge trunks and massive spread of interlacing branches, which are one of the chief delights of the island today, make the suggestion attractive. It is impossible in the present state of the evidence to know whether in bringing trees into their civic centre the Athenians were establishing a precedent or following a practice already introduced elsewhere, for the little evidence that remains comes from a much later period.

A substantial fragment of a description of Greece, dating probably from the second or first century BC, describes Chalcis in Euboea as hilly and well-shaded and the agora of Anthedon on the other side of the Euripus from Chalcis as 'full of trees'.[61] When Pausanias wrote his description of Greece in the second century AD there were planes between the running-tracks in the gymnasium at Elis where Olympic competitors trained, and planes by the racecourse.[62] In Sparta there was an area surrounded by water and accessible only by bridges in which planes grew high and close together. This is where the young Spartans passing from adolescence to manhood did their fighting: it was called *The Planes*.[63] The main development in using trees to improve towns probably came in the Hellenistic period, when architects were particularly interested in the peristyle enclosing a garden of trees and shrubs.

The first reflection of this development in Rome is in the great quadriporticus behind Pompey's theatre, which was dedicated in 55 BC.[64] The large area behind the theatre combined a quadruple colonnade, a garden, and an open-air sculpture gallery. Between four rows of columns there were plane trees and between the plane trees box hedges: within the colonnades was a very mixed collection of sculptures from the Greek world. The backwardness of Rome in planting trees to make life in the city more agreeable is emphasised by comparison with the small town of Pompeii in the Bay of Naples. Greek influences had always been strong in this area, partly from the Greek colonies at Naples and Puteoli on the coast and partly from trade contacts with the Greek world. There were two fine theatres in Pompeii before the first permanent theatre in Rome was built by Pompey. Recent excavations have also shown that when a large open square was built in association with the amphitheatre in the first half of the first century BC two lines of planes were planted round three of the sides. The evidence consists of the moulds that were left in the earth when the trees' roots disintegrated. Concrete has now been poured into the moulds and the very different size of the moulds suggests that during the more than 100 years before the destruction of Pompeii in AD 79 some of the trees had to be replaced.

In Rome Pompey's building operations, as well as those of Caesar, had their influence on Augustan policies. Augustus had his greatest opportunity when he carried out Caesar's plan to extend the monumental area of Rome into the Campus Martius, which during the Republic had been mainly used as an exercise-ground. The aim was to provide a contrast to the crowded streets and fora of the city by a series of temples, porticoes, and other public buildings spaciously planned and relieved by greenery. Agrippa pointed the way with his Basilica of Neptune and his grand set of public baths at the south end of the area, offset by a laurel-grove where he displayed the famous *Fallen Lion* by the Greek sculptor Lysippus, which he had carried off from Lampsacus.[65] At the northern end Strabo particularly admired the great circular mausoleum which Augustus had built for the Julian family early in his rule, with its tumulus encircled by evergreens, presumably cypress trees. Behind the mausoleum a small park was laid out with walks probably flanked by box hedges.[66]

Nero intended an even more spectacular transformation of Rome. When his opportunity came after the great fire of AD 64, which destroyed more than half of the city, he took over a large area of central Rome for a new imperial palace.[67] A rural setting for the palace with lake, meadows, and woodlands brought the country into the city, but this was Nero's Rome in too personal a sense; as soon as Vespasian was firmly established the rebuilding of the area began. The massive Colosseum rose where Nero's lake had been and a new set of imperial baths was built by Titus on part of the site of the 'Golden House'. But the discovery that planted trees improved the crowded city was not forgotten. When Alexander Severus in the middle of the third century built yet another set of public baths he bought up the adjoining properties, pulled them down, and replaced them by a grove of trees.[68]

The taste for decorative trees had affected the nobility before Pompey had provided a precedent in public planning. Lucius Crassus, famous orator and respected elder statesman, had six *lotus* trees (nettle-trees, *Celtis australis*) in the garden of his house on the Palatine.[69] He was said to have been offered a million sesterces for his house and to have accepted the offer, provided that the trees were exempted from the sale. The *lotus* trees, with their spreading branches, survived until the great fire of AD 64. In the last century BC there was a growth in the scale of private gardens in the city. Although the centre of Rome and the river-side districts became more crowded, room was found by the western periphery, especially on and between the Pincian and Esquiline hills, for aristocratic gardens. Some of them were so famous that they retained their names and identity into the late Empire, even when they came into the emperor's possession. Maecenas, the wealthiest patron in Rome, left his garden to Augustus in his will. The garden of Sallustius Crispus, adopted son of the historian, had become imperial property by AD 58.[70] The fate of the garden designed by Lucullus, whose name has remained a byword for extravagance, and further developed by Valerius Asiaticus, twice consul and one of the richest men of his day, was sealed when Messalina, newly wedded to the emperor Claudius, coveted it.[71] It was not difficult to bring charges of treason and to secure the right result. As a special favour Asiaticus was allowed to commit suicide.

Although we know the names and the sites of many of these gardens, no descriptions survive of their designs and we are left to guess what impact they had on public views and what use was made of trees in them. There is, however, a hint in the account given by the historian Tacitus of the death of Asiaticus in the garden of Lucullus. Before he opened his veins he gave instructions for the funeral pyre to be moved 'so that the shade given by the trees should not be diminished by the smoke from the fire'.[72] This surely is a reference to plane trees, which were famous for their shade (p. 277) and the Romans' most fashionable trees for parks and gardens. Trees were more conspicuous in the gardens on the right bank of the Tiber. Propertius is not envious of a river-side garden with a hillside planted with trees as thick as the forest on Caucasus, provided that from his left bank he can see the boats go by.[73] It is probable that Caesar's extensive garden on the right bank, which was left in his will to the people of Rome, was partly woodland, and the grove in memory of Gaius and Lucius, the two grandsons of Augustus who died tragically young, was also on the right bank.[74]

Outside the big towns and in the last generation of the Republic, the magnificent parks and elaborate fish-ponds of Lucullus and other leading senators became notorious. There is a Persian flavour in the large wood that Hortensius stocked with wild animals and enclosed with a wall. He even had a tower built from which his guests could watch the animals responding to the call of a trumpet.[75] Horace in his moralistic mood resents the growth of such luxuries and contrasts the artificialities of an estate near Baiae with its earlier days: 'Few farming acres now remain. A series of lakes stretches from the Lucrine Lake. The plane tree will drive out the elm; beds of violets, myrtles, and scented trees will replace the olive groves.'[76] Seneca asks: 'Why are trees preserved that are going to provide nothing but shade?' and 'Why is my country estate more elaborately designed than my natural requirements demand?'[77] Vitruvius, however, thought otherwise. He considered that those who held office and served their city should have lofty regal vestibules, spacious *atria* with peristyles, and woodland with walks to fit the dignity of their position.[78]

The garden of the younger Pliny's Tuscan villa may be taken as typical. Immediately adjoining the house was a formal garden of box hedges, topiary work, and dwarf shrubs, surrounded by a wall hidden by box rising in tiers. The complex of buildings included a suite of rooms opening off a small court with four plane trees and a fountain. But Pliny prided himself most on his hippodrome, which with its horseshoe shape followed the lines of the Circus Maximus and of the hippodrome attached to the imperial palace on the Palatine. The central area was open so that as you entered you could see the complete design. The riding-ground was flanked by a row of plane trees on each of the two long sides and ivy growing up the trunks linked tree with tree. Between the planes were box trees and on each side there was an outer line of laurels. Round the curving end planes were replaced by cypresses and behind them was another formal garden with an even more extravagant display of topiary, box 'clipped to a thousand shapes—some in the form of letters giving the name of the master of the house and of the designer. Little metal obelisks alternated with fruit-trees and in the middle were two lines of dwarf planes.'[79]

Pliny's choice of plane and box was typical of Roman fashion. The plane was one of the many trees that Rome had adopted from the Greek world. To those who knew the land of Greece or Greek literature the plane was nearly as familiar as the oak. There was the plane near the Ilissus just outside Athens, in whose shade Socrates had discussed the immortality of the soul with Phaedrus,[80] the plane in the Lyceum whose roots stretched some fifty feet,[81] and the plane tree at Aulis where the Achaean heroes sacrificed before leaving for Troy and witnessed a portent that foretold that the war would last ten years.[82] One of the great Ionian craftsmen of the sixth century, Theodorus, had made a plane tree of gold which was presented later to the Persian king Darius,[83] and when Xerxes led his imperial levy against Greece in 480 BC he was so struck by the beauty of a plane tree which he saw on his route from Phrygia to Sardis that he decorated it with gold and made one of the immortals of his guard responsible for preserving it.[84] Dionysius, tyrant of Syracuse in the late fifth and early fourth century BC, had introduced planes to give distinction to his palace at Rhegium,[85] and by the end of the Republic they had found their way all over southern and central Italy.

It is not surprising that they find a place in all or nearly all the gardens of which we have a record. Martial contrasts the well-farmed acres of a friend's villa near Baiae with the unproductive myrtle, plane, and box that are so popular,[86] and in another epigram he refers to myrtle, planes, and pines as a rich man's natural company.[87] He also records a well-grown plane tree that Caesar had planted in Spanish Corduba more than a century ago during the Civil War.[88] The younger Pliny, writing to a friend in Comum, hopes that he is able to enjoy his delightful villa outside the town and is not being always called away on business. Pliny clearly regards his friend's grove of planes as one of the main attractions.[89] His uncle had very different views. For him it was a scandal to bring in a tree from abroad just for the pleasure of its shade; it was worse when the Romans learnt how to produce dwarf planes, 'abortions even in trees',[90] and when a rich freedman introduced an unnatural species from the district of Gortyn in Crete which did not shed it leaves in winter.[91]

In one of his eclogues Virgil chose as the fairest of trees the ash in the woods, the pine in the garden, the poplar by rivers, and the fir on the high mountains.[92] It seems strange at first that the pine, which was one of the commonest building-timbers in Italy, should be regarded as the pride of the garden (hortus), which is a formally-laid-out area of cultivated soil, distinct from park-land. This, together with the inclusion by Martial of pines with box and plane as typical of a rich man's property, suggests that Virgil does not have in mind a pine which is noted for the

umbrella pine

usefulness of its timber. Of the various species of pine the best suited to the context is the umbrella pine, *Pinus pinea*, which was appreciated more for its nuts than its timber, and, as landscape-painters have seen, has a very attractive shape with its tall branchless trunk and broad crown, so very like the mushroom cloud that rises from a violent explosion. The younger Pliny, describing his uncle's death at the time of the great eruption of Vesuvius in AD 79, noticed the resemblance,[93] and the image has become more familiar from its sinister association with the atom bomb.

I O

FURNITURE WOODS

In this survey of trees and timber we have been primarily
concerned with building- and ship-timbers and, to a much lesser
extent, with fuel. Wood was also the main material for furniture,
interior work such as panelling and coffers, and, especially in the
archaic period, for sculpture. In most areas there was a wide
range of woods suitable for making furniture, but some woods
were more useful than others, and some were considerably more
attractive. Native woods in western Europe became less fashionable when mahogany and other exotic hardwoods were introduced; similarly in the ancient world the rich were prepared to
look far afield for special woods for their chairs, couches, and
tables.

The evidence for reconstructing the pattern is very meagre,
except for Egypt where the dry climate and the close sealing
of tombs has left a fine legacy of furniture and sculpture for
the excavator. The royal inscriptions of Egyptian and Mesopotamian kings include furniture in their lists of booty and
several letters to and from the king of Egypt during the half-
century when the court was established at Tel-el-Amarna
record gifts of furniture exchanged between kings. For the Greek
and Roman worlds we have to rely almost exclusively on literary
sources and, not unnaturally, they are more interested in the
luxury trade in fashionable woods than in the woods from which
the ordinary furniture of the average home was made. We could
learn more from archaeology if it became standard practice to
examine microscopically all fragments of carbonised furniture
wood that are found. In Herculaneum at least there should be
no difficulty in identifying the woods used for furniture and
fittings.

In the fourteenth century BC Egyptian power which Tuthmosis III and his vigorous successors had raised to new heights
was in decline. A series of successful campaigns had extended

the Egyptian empire to the Taurus mountains and the Euphrates, but new forces were undermining Egyptian control. The Hittite empire with its capital at Boğaz-Köy had by now become the dominant power in Asia Minor and was penetrating beyond the Taurus into Syria, and at the same time there was growing restlessness among the states of Syria and Phoenicia. The Tel-el-Amarna tablets provide a vivid picture of the increasing helplessness of two very unwarlike Egyptian kings. The governors of cities which remained loyal to Egypt sent pitiful appeals for help.[1] If only the Pharaoh would come forth his enemies would be scattered. Even if he would send his archers a desperate situation might be saved. The governor of Tyre writes: 'The city of Sidon has joined our enemies, we are besieged on all sides. We have no water and no wood. We have nowhere to bury our dead.'[2] The Pharaoh, however, does not come forth and one by one his cities are lost. It is in this desperate crisis that the governor of Byblos is required to send boxwood to the king; his reply is surprisingly restrained: 'Since my lord has written to me for boxwood let him know that it comes from the land of Zali and from the city of Ugarit. I cannot send my ships there for Aziri is hostile and the Hatti people burn the land of Gubla (Byblos).'[3] It was not long before even Byblos had to surrender.

The Egyptian king seems to have been more concerned with his furniture than the fate of his northern cities, and for fine joinery, as for beams and flagstaves of long length, the Egyptians depended mainly on foreign supplies. Box was appreciated by cabinet-makers because it had a close, straight grain, was hard and strong but easily worked, and because it had an attractive pale colour with little difference between heart and sapwood.[4] Box rarely grows to a great height and never produces a thick trunk, but it was a valuable wood for small objects or parts of objects which had to be strong and might need delicate workmanship. It was therefore particularly associated with combs, and musical instruments, especially the flute and lyre.[5] In furniture it could be used for beds, couches, chairs, and small tables, but it was more commonly used in inlays and veneers where its pale colour provided an attractive contrast with darker woods, especially in Egypt with ebony, and with gold, silver, and precious stones. Both Egypt and Mesopotamia probably derived their appreciation of the value of box for furniture from woodworking craftsmen in Syria and Phoenicia from which their supplies came.

The finest box available to Egypt came from Syria where Mt. Amanus is sometimes called the box mountain.[6] Ugarit was the port from which it was shipped, but the traders of Byblos may have acted as middlemen. As we have seen, the governor of Byblos who was required to send boxwood to the Egyptian king explains that he would normally have got his supplies from Ugarit, and Egypt had close ties with Byblos from early in the third millennium (p. 64). Boxwood could also be obtained from Cyprus: this, according to Ezekiel, was a source which supplied Tyre, and when the cities of Cyprus surrendered to the Assyrian Sargon II (721–705 BC) their gifts included objects of boxwood.[7] A century earlier Assurnasipal (881–859 BC) had shown the Assyrian appreciation of boxwood by including in his booty from a campaign in Syria, after he had crossed the Euphrates at Carchemish, 'beds of boxwood, chairs of boxwood, tables of boxwood inlaid with ivory'.[8] It may have been during the period when Assyria dominated the Near East that the lathe was developed for turning wood. There is no clear evidence of turnery in Egyptian furniture of the Bronze Age, but it is very conspicuous in Assyrian reliefs, and the Assyrians may have derived the technique from the Syrians or Phoenicians. It enhanced the value of box which, as Virgil knew, was one of the best woods for turning, *torno rasile buxum*,[9] but it was to have an appalling influence on the design of table-legs.

We have little specific evidence for the use of boxwood by the Greeks, but it can be traced back to the Bronze Age in an inventory from Pylos which includes two tables in which boxwood was combined with the darker yew,[10] a combination which was used with splendid effect on screens found in a royal tomb at Gordium in Phrygia (p. 461). Homer has a mule yoke of boxwood hanging from a peg on a column in Odysseus' megaron.[11] In a neat epigram by the Hellenistic poet Leonidas of Tarentum a young boy dedicates a boxwood rattle with other relics of his childhood.[12] It was used also in Greece for writing exercises[13] and in Rome for drawing exercises[14] as it was in Italy during the Renaissance.[15] In the Erechtheum accounts we find boxwood used for the frames of ceiling coffers.[16] The use of boxwood in the Hellenistic period for such large surfaces as the walls and doors of the library on Hiero's monster merchantman was exceptional, and that presumably was the reason for the choice.[17]

In the Roman period the wood was so closely associated with certain objects that Latin poets used the word *buxum* for comb, flute, and top.[18] A Roman jury law specifies that the ballots shall be of boxwood,[19] and it may be added that balls of box are used in drawing lots for fixtures in the annual English football-cup competition.

For the Greeks and Romans Syria was no longer an important source of supply. The most famous box came from Mt. Cytorus in Paphlagonia and the neighbouring district, and the association of box with the mountain was so close that *cytoreus* was even used as a synonym for *buxeus*,[20] but it is doubtful whether many Greeks or Romans got their boxwood from such a distance. Box grows in the mountains of the Peloponnese and is fairly widely distributed in Greece and Italy, though Theophrastus goes out of his way to emphasise the poor quality of boxwood from Macedonian Mt. Olympus.[21] In the west the box of Corsica had a wide reputation, especially for the thickness of its stem.[22]

In Egyptian documents and in surviving Egyptian furniture box is often linked with ebony. This too was a foreign wood which had to be imported and the only sources available to Egypt in the Bronze Age were in Ethiopia and the south. Queen Hatshepsut in the fifteenth century proudly recorded the tribute in ebony that she brought back from a successful campaign,[23] and in the Bronze Age ebony was the most fashionable furniture wood in Egyptian court circles. After the battle of Megiddo, Tuthmosis III included in his booty six chairs of ivory, ebony, and carob-wood.[24] Among the diplomatic gifts sent by Amenhotep III to the king of Babylon were: 'one bed of ebony, overlaid with ivory and gold, three beds of ebony overlaid with gold, one head-rest of ebony overlaid with gold, one large chair of ebony overlaid with gold, five chairs of ebony overlaid with gold'.[25] His successor sent to the king of Arzawa (possibly in Cilicia) thirteen chairs of ebony and 100 pieces of ebony.[26] Occasionally ebony is used for the main structure, as in an interesting chair which was found in the tomb of the mother of

Senenmut, favourite and chief official of Queen Hatshepsut. This chair, now in the Metropolitan Museum of New York, has a broad, low seat of linen cord and a straight back which is divided into two registers; the lower has three plain panels of boxwood framed by ebony and in the upper register there are cut-out figures, with the god Bes in the centre in boxwood and on either side four hieroglyphs in alternating box and ebony.[27]

This combination of dark ebony with light boxwood is common in Egyptian furniture and a similar effect is achieved more expensively by combining ebony with ivory. Good examples of this combination can be seen among the treasures of Tutankhamun's tomb. These include an impressively simple design in a finely fitted toilet casket. The structural wood has been completely covered by veneers of ebony and ivory; ebony provides the frame on all four sides and the top for large panels of ivory.[28] There is a more elaborate design in a box-like chest standing on four squared legs, which has an ivory-veneered frame and on each of its four sides a large panel of marquetry consisting of small pieces of ivory and ebony inlays set in a herring-bone pattern. In another casket Carter, who discovered the tomb, calculated that 45,000 separate pieces had been glued into place (pl. 5A).[29]

The foot-panel of an ebony bed frames cut-out figures in ivory, ebony, and gold of Bes and Thoueris, gods of the household.[30] Ebony is also used for a richly decorated ceremonial throne with a gracefully curving seat, and here the main effect comes from the interplay of ebony and ivory.[31] On the upper surface of the accompanying footstool the king can stand on his enemies. Within a narrow framing border inlaid with ivory, ebony, faience, glass, and natural stones, there are nine captives: on one side five enemies from the south, on the other, separated by an ivory band with hieroglyphs, four enemies from the north. The head-dresses of all are in ebony, and the dresses in gold, but there is a distinction in the colour of the two groups: for the Asiatics a reddish wood is used, for the Africans a very dark wood. There is a similar theme on a ceremonial walking-stick, in which two figures form the crook, the Asiatic with a face of ivory, the African face in ebony (pl. 5B).[32]

Since in the Bronze Age Mycenaean traders were familiar with the main trading cities of the eastern Mediterranean, it is not unnatural that ebony should find its way into Mycenaean palaces. The Pylos inventories include chairs and tables in which ebony is combined with ivory: 'One ebony chair inlaid with ivory on the back. One ebony chair with ivory back carved with finials and with figures of men. One ebony footstool inlaid with figures of men and lions in ivory.'[33] The tentative translation of another tablet suggests highly decorative tables: 'One *stone* table with *strutting* of *ebony* and ivory, *of encircled* type, a nine-*footer*, carved with a *running spiral*. One ivory table of *projecting* type, decorated with a feather pattern, a six-*footer* carved with a *running spiral*. One *ebony* table with ivory *strutting*, of *encircled* type, a nine-*footer*, decorated with *sea shells*.'[34] The designs of this furniture are very reminiscent of Egyptian pieces such as we have briefly referred to above, and the furniture itself was more probably imported than made by palace craftsmen.

Ebony continued to be in great demand in the Near East in the period of Mesopotamian supremacy which followed the destruction of the Mycenaean palaces and the decline of Egypt. When Assurnasipal, having defeated the Hittites and secured control of Syria, reduced the Phoenician cities of the coast the tribute that he drew from them included, in addition to gold and silver, ebony, boxwood, and ivory.[35] When Sennacherib besieged Jerusalem and Hezekiah was forced to surrender he sent to the Assyrian king among 'all kinds of valuable treasures' ebony and boxwood.[36] Significant quantities of ebony were apparently coming to Palestine and Phoenicia during the period and one would expect the trade to be in the hands of the Phoenicians, because the Egyptians seem to have taken little part themselves in overseas trade; but there may have been competition. The prophet Ezekiel, looking forward to the approaching doom of Tyre, gives a graphic description of the wealth and extravagance of the city. Among her luxury imports he includes ebony and ivory brought by the Rhodians.[37] This was very early in the sixth century, when the Phoenician towns had suffered seriously from invading Assyrian armies and the Greeks were strongly placed in Egypt as a result of help given to the Egyptians when they successfully revolted from Assyria. The Rhodians were in a good position to take advantage of Phoenician weakness.

Ebony was one of the prizes that fell to Persia when, after

having conquered Egypt, she added Ethiopia to her empire and imposed an annual tribute of two hundred ebony logs.[38] But when the Mesopotamian kingdoms and Egypt had become provinces in a vast Persian empire, there were no more royal records of timber-winning campaigns in Syria and Phoenicia and recorded history moves westward. In the great recession that followed the destruction of the Mycenaean palaces the Greeks were in no position to import luxuries, nor were there palaces any longer to encourage demand. But by the eighth century the Dark Age was considerably less dark. The sea-routes to the eastern Mediterranean, which may never have been completely closed, were reopened to Greek traders, and when in addition Egypt had won her independence from Assyria and had reason to be grateful for the help of Greek mercenaries, Egyptian goods probably travelled more widely.

As we shall see later (p. 310), ebony was used, though not on a large scale, by Greek sculptors in the sixth century; Pausanias says that it was also used by Phidias in his very decorative throne of Zeus at Olympia,[39] and it is possible that some use of it was also made in one or more of the temples in the rebuilding of the Athenian acropolis in the fifth century BC (pp. 200, 202). But so far as our evidence goes, it was a wood reserved in Greece for the gods and not used to make fashionable furniture for the rich; had it been so used, we could expect a reference in comedy or the orators. In Egypt, however, it was widely used by kings and nobles for furniture. In the spectacular procession of Ptolemy Philadelphus (286–247 BC) in Alexandria Ethiopian gift-bearers carried 600 ivory tusks and 2,000 ebony logs.[40]

In Roman literature ebony is very elusive. Ovid in his *Metamorphoses* furnished the cave of Sleep with an ebony bed,[41] but this is a reflection of Greek literature rather than Roman habits. It seems that ebony did not become fashionable among the Roman rich even when, by the death of Augustus, trade had been opened up with India and it was known that there were ample supplies of good ebony in the south of that country. Virgil even makes India the sole source of ebony, which suggests that there was little if any ebony to be seen in Rome during the Republic. A hundred years later Pliny knows that Virgil's statement is inconsistent with Herodotus and he has read that ebony was exhibited by Pompey in his triumphal procession to celebrate his victory over Mithridates King of Pontus.[42] He also knows from Theophrastus that ebony is close-grained, heavy, and long-lasting,[43] but he makes no mention of its use in Rome and seems to be more interested in its medical properties. 'They say that its sawdust is a sovereign cure for eye trouble, and that when the wood is ground on the whetstone and mixed with raisin wine it can disperse cataract, while the root if put in water can get rid of white spots in the eyes and clear up a cough provided that an equal quantity of tarragon root and some honey is added.'[44]

Even more significant is the absence of any mention of ebony in the Roman satirists; the silence of Juvenal alone would be almost sufficient to confirm that ebony was not in great demand among the wealthy. Outside Italy it may have had a wider currency: in Egypt, at least, it remained fashionable. Lucan, describing the extravagances of Cleopatra's palace, says that the posts of the great doors, for which you would expect one of the commoner woods to be used, covered perhaps with a veneer, were made of solid ebony.[45]

Apuleius, writing in the middle of the second century AD, introduces the wood in a stranger context. On a journey from his north-African home in Madaura to Alexandria, he had stayed at the coastal city of Oea and had there married a very rich widow. The townspeople, alarmed at the prospect of losing access to one of the biggest local fortunes, accused Apuleius of 'having had a figure of Hermes made secretly from the most precious wood in order to work magic for evil ends'. The figure had a skeletal form and they argued that such a strange shape in such an expensive wood must have a sinister explanation. Apuleius' defence is almost stranger than the charge: he had ordered, he said, a small figure of a god or goddess in wood from a craftsman whom he had seen at work in his shop and he had left him to choose the wood and the god. But while he was out of town his stepson, who had acquired an ebony casket, took it to the shop and asked the man to reuse the ebony for the statuette, hoping to give his stepfather a pleasant surprise.[46]

The furniture wood that most interested the Roman rich and society gossips in the early Empire was called *citrus* by the Romans and *thyon* by the Greeks and to botanists is known as *Callitris quadrivalvis Vent*. We find it first in Homer's *Odyssey* where the wood is burnt on Calypso's fire together with cedar,[47] and the adjective *thyodes* is attached to the clothes given by Calypso to Odysseus when she reluctantly assisted him to leave her, and to Helen's chamber at Sparta.[48] It was clearly an aromatic wood, but it is a little strange to find it in Homer's tree vocabulary because its natural home seems to have been in north Africa. Theophrastus describes the tree briefly: it was like the cypress in its branches, leaves, trunk, and fruit. The wood was proof against decay and the root, which was very compact, was the part which craftsmen chose for the best articles. The tree grew near the oasis of Ammon and in Cyrenaica and, when Theophrastus wrote in the late fourth century BC, it was still common in the neighbourhood of Cyrene itself. But when he says that the people still remember that the roofs of some of the early buildings were made of it, he implies that this was no longer the practice; the natural explanation is that the best trees had been overcut in the area.[49]

Cyrene was brought under Egyptian control in the third century BC and it is natural that a wood which was so much appreciated in Cyrene should be imported by the Ptolemies. It is not surprising, therefore, that Ptolemy Philopator in designing his luxurious river-boat should have chosen citrus-wood for doors.[50] According to Lucan the wood still remained fashionable at the Egyptian court in the last days of independence. Describing the palace in which Cleopatra entertained Caesar, he emphasises that her citrus tables were finer than any that Caesar saw when he captured Juba the Numidian king in his African campaign of 46 BC against the remnants of the republican forces.[51] An earlier prince of Numidia, Masinissa, had sent fifty talents of citrus-wood to Rhodes for making statues after an earthquake in 227 BC.[52] Trade with Africa brought the wood to Sicily, where Hiero II followed Ptolemy Philopator in choosing citrus-wood for the doors of the shrine of Aphrodite on his mammoth merchantman;[53] both kings used ivory to decorate their doors as an effective contrast to the dark wood.

The first known reference in a Roman writer comes from Cato who, in a rousing speech to influence consular elections, denounced the use of the wood as a monstrous extravagance.[54] In the same vein, at the end of the Republic, Varro contrasts simple villas of an earlier generation with a sophisticated villa furnished with *citrus* and gold recently built at Reate,[55] and by then it was also being used as a veneer on sideboards.[56]

Pliny was very surprised that Theophrastus said nothing about tables made from *thyon*, which he rightly identified with *citrus*, because citrus tables had been the talk of the town since the days of Cicero. In his prosecution of Verres for his gross misgovernment of Sicily (78–74 BC), Cicero alleged that Verres unscrupulously confiscated a very large and particularly beautiful citrus table from a man at Lilybaeum who had recently been given Roman citizenship by Sulla.[57] It may have been memories of this table, as well as a determination to keep up with the aristocracy, that made Cicero, who rarely had enough money to keep pace with the villas he insisted on buying, throw caution to the winds and buy a citrus table for half a million sesterces; it could still be seen in Pliny's day after more than a hundred years.[58]

It was probably not until the war against the Numidian Jugurtha in 107–105 BC that the Romans took a keen interest in exploiting the citrus forests for the Roman luxury market, for, though trade sometimes preceded the flag, most traders preferred to wait until the army had paved the way; the elimination of the anti-Roman king would ensure respect for the Roman name. Sensitive Roman imperial consciences should have been pricked by Lucan's lines written when the traders had taken advantage of their opportunities. He is speaking of north-west Africa: 'This was a very fertile area which had never been disturbed in the hunt for metals.' 'The timber of Mauretania was the people's only wealth. They were innocent of its value, it was the leafy shade of the citrus that they enjoyed, and they lived happily. Into the forest hitherto unknown our axes came: we search out tables for our banquets from the end of the earth.'[59]

The reputation of the wood in Rome was enhanced when Caesar made citrus the keynote of the triumph celebrating his conquest of Gaul.[60] This had been long delayed and was the first of four triumphal processions when he returned in 46 BC from Africa. The choice of an African wood for a triumph over Gaul may seem bizarre, but, as Lucan indicates in the lines quoted above, the capture of Juba, who had supported Caesar's enemies in Africa, made available to Rome the citrus trees of

Numidia. With the overcutting of the tree in Cyrenaica, the best citrus trees were now to be found in Numidia and Mauretania. Strabo, writing in the early days of the Empire, emphasises the fertility of Mauretania with its rivers, lakes, and forests. 'This is the land', he says, 'that supplies for the Romans their largest and finest-figured tables from single pieces of wood.'[61] For a hundred years there was fierce competition for size and quality, and when men made fun of women's extravagance in jewellery, Pliny tells us, they countercharged the men with table-mania.[62] Pliny, as a conscientious ascetic, was fascinated by this wild extravagance and went to great trouble to collect prices and sizes and to learn the details of the trade. Seneca had spoken of citrus tables worth a senator's property qualification, which was a million sesterces.[63] Pliny's figures show that he was not exaggerating: the highest price he quotes is 1,300,000 sesterces paid when an antique table, which had belonged to a noted republican family, changed hands. This, as Pliny remarks, would have been enough to buy a large estate. A million sesterces was the price paid for another table by Asinius Gallus, who inherited from his father a strong distaste for the imperial regime and suffered accordingly.

The price depended mainly on the size of the table and the quality of the figure. Pliny, interested as usual in records, gives some examples: the largest citrus table belonged to Ptolemy, king of Mauretania, and was four and a half feet (137 cm.) wide and three inches (7.6 cm.) thick: but the circle was made of two semicircles, though they were so well fitted together that the join was barely visible. The emperor Tiberius had one very nearly as large, but the citrus-wood was only a veneer. It is an interesting sign of the social times that one of the tables in this exalted company was owned by an imperial freedman, Nonius, and his table was in a single piece.[64]

Theophrastus had said that the most valuable part of the citrus tree was the root, which was very compact. Pliny gave more details: 'The table-wood is an excrescence of the root, which is particularly admired when it is completely buried, less so when the burr-wood is found above ground on the trunk and even on the branches. In fact the wood that is bought at such a price is a disease of the trees, the great size of whose roots can be judged by the size of the table-tops.'[65] It would not be difficult to

misunderstand the facts from Pliny's description. The citrus
itself is an unimpressive tree, growing slowly and rarely higher
than thirty feet. But when it is cut down it throws up new growth
immediately and the more often it is cut the wider becomes its
base or stump. It is, however, a very slow process, and a
diameter of four feet would imply a growth of more than two
hundred years. Excrescences, known in the trade as burr-wood,
such as are more commonly seen on horse-chestnut trees, also
grow on the trunk and branches. The wood in these growths
becomes like a hard knot of flesh rolled in a ball, producing a
specially good figure when sawn.

Pliny describes the various patterns that the figure can take:
'The two most fashionable types are the long wavy grain which
is called tiger-wood and the little spiral which is called panther-
wood. Some tables have waves of curly lines which are more
valued if they resemble the eyes in the tail of a peacock; yet
another type is called parsley-wood because it has wavy lines
which look like clusters of grains' (pl. 12).[66] The citrus tree still
survives in Morocco but rarely in large concentrations, and the
stock has sadly degenerated. There is, however, a substantial
forest near Esaouira on the Atlantic coast and cabinet-makers in
the town and in Marrakesh still make boxes and bowls from the
wood; but the days of substantial table-tops are long since gone.

Fashion dictated that the round citrus table should be
supported by an ivory leg. Martial expresses it in terms that
Pliny would have appreciated. 'Your tables support your
Libyan circles on Indian teeth';[67] and those who worked on the
Indian teeth and those who worked on the Libyan circles were
so interdependent that they formed a common guild of citrus-
workers and ivory-workers, *citrarii et eborarii*.[68]

The demand for these tables by the rich remained strong
throughout the first century AD and the philosopher Seneca is
even said by the historian Dio to have had a collection of 500
citrus tables with ivory legs.[69] Occasionally he felt uncomfort-
able and in cross-examining his own conscience in his short
treatise *On the Good Life* he asks himself: 'Why don't you live
according to your principles? Why do you have such elegant
furniture?'[70] Martial composes an elegantly artificial epigram in
the table's honour: 'Accept these blessed woods, the gift of Atlas;
a gift of gold would be a lesser gift.'[71] Statius attending a public

banquet given by Domitian in his new palace on the Palatine would be gazing at 'the Moorish timbers resting on Indian stems', if he wasn't spellbound by the emperor's presence.[72] This is the last we hear of citrus tables in literature, but in the middle Empire there is very little of the kind of literature where we might expect to find references. The silence of the fourth century is more significant.

In the late Republic and early Empire the best-quality citrus-wood was on Mt. Ancorarius in Algeria, but that had been exhausted by Pliny's time and the main supply then came from what is now Morocco.[73] Here too there had probably been no thought of the future in the cutting. The forests had been stripped of their best pieces and only the best could justify the cost of the long journey. While tables provided the strongest demand for citrus-wood, it was also used for interior work in houses.[74] Statius, describing the villa of Manilius Vopiscus at Tivoli, asks: 'where shall my Muse begin, where end? Shall it be the gilded beams and all the Moorish doorposts or the gleaming figured marbles, or the fountains playing in all the bedrooms?'[75] The Moorish doors can only have been made of citrus-wood and the Roman aristocracy in using it for doors were following the example of Hellenistic kings (p. 287). Citrus could also be used for writing-tablets, though, as Martial implies in an epigram entitled *Citrus writing-tablets*, this was rather a humiliation for such an aristocratic wood: 'If our wood were not cut into slender tablets we should be the noble burden of a Libyan tooth.'[76]

When demand for these tables was still strong and the price still high, there was a natural temptation for sharp furniture-dealers. A passage in the *Digest* cites as an example of mis-representation: 'if a man sold tables as if they were citrus tables when they were not'.[77] Maple would best qualify for this role, for like citrus it developed burr-wood, of which, according to Pliny, there were two main types. The finer, known as peacock-maple (corresponding to our bird's-eye maple), had simpler marking and would have been preferred to citrus for tables, but it did not produce the size required, and, apart from writing-tablets and couch veneers, it was seldom used.[78] The other, which was used for ordinary tables, had a darker colour, and was the subject of another neat epigram by Martial. 'I have no wavy grain, nor am I the daughter of a Moorish forest, but my wood too has known fine banquets.'[79] Strabo also probably refers to maple when he says that in the Ligurian forests behind Genoa there were trees which produced wood as finely figured for table-making as the citrus.[80]

Only a small proportion of maple trees produced wood from which expensive tables could be made, but the average maple was a useful tree. It grew in most Mediterranean forests and spread higher up the mountains than most deciduous trees, normally mixed with other species. Its main virtue was its strength, as was appreciated by Aristophanes when he calls the tough Acharnians of his chorus 'hearts of oak, hearts of maple';[81] and that is why it was used for the floor of a chariot in Egypt,[82] and is used for parquet floors in modern houses. It has less character than oak, but its colour is not unattractive and it takes polish well. Theophrastus says that it was used for couches and for the yokes of beasts of burden, and Strabo adds that tables were made from the maples of Sinope.[83] Maple was also used for chairs, and being hard it could be used for writing-tablets. Ovid in his *Amores* pictures the lover waiting for an answer from his mistress; she need only write 'come' and he will dedicate the tablet in the temple of Venus and will write upon it 'Naso dedicates to Venus these servants that have been faithful to her', but 'only a little while ago you were common maple'.[84]

Of the other more fashionable furniture woods the two most important were cedar and cypress, which share many of the same qualities. They are both comparatively unaffected by woodworm and beetle. They both have a fragrant scent, and they both have a very long life. The cedar was considerably less widely distributed than the cypress. It grew abundantly on the coastal mountains of the south of Asia Minor, and behind the coasts of Syria and Phoenicia, it grew well in the Atlas mountains of north-west Africa on the island of Cyprus, and perhaps in Crete (p. 100). Within its own territories it may have been an all-purpose wood as it still seems to be in Marrakesh, but in Egypt, Mesopotamia, and the Greek world it was a precious wood. Homer mentions it only once. In the royal palace at Troy there was a cedar-wood chamber where the aged Priam went for the gifts he was to take as ransom for the body of his dead son Hector.[85] The room was presumably panelled with cedar boards, as were Solomon's temple and Hall of Judgement, 'covering the interior from floor to rafters with wood . . . All was cedar, no stone was left visible'. Similarly, the walls of the Persian royal palace at Persepolis were lined with cedar and cypress and Ptolemy Philopator chose these two woods for the walls of the grand dining-room in his famous pleasure-barge.[86]

The fragrance and durability of cedar-wood made it particularly suitable for storage chests and coffins. A high proportion of Egyptian coffins whose wood has been scientifically identified are of cedar and to them should probably be added the majority of those in the British Museum. Mortuary chests of cedar are also recorded, and in one of his epigrams Theocritus has bees crossing from the meadow to the 'fragrant chest of cedar'.[87] In the Greek world the most famous chest was the chest of Cypselus at Olympia, dedicated in the sixth century BC and still well preserved when Pausanias visited Olympia and described it in detail.[88] The chest itself was made of cedar-wood, and the whole surface was covered with a series of scenes from myth and legend in applied figures made of gold and ivory, and some of cedar-wood, the figures being named in archaic letters decoratively arranged at their side. In the second field on the chest, according to Pausanias, there was a woman carrying a white boy on her right arm and a black boy on the left, representing death and sleep, and in the fourth field Aethra, daughter of Pitheus, was dressed in a black garment.[89] It is attractive to believe that the black in the two scenes was ebony, which in the Bronze Age in the Near East was commonly linked with ivory or boxwood.

Cedar-wood was also the most prized wood for monumental doors in Egypt, and competed on equal terms with cypress in Mesopotamia. In the Greek world it was used for the main door of the temple of Apollo at Delos and for the treasury at Eleusis, but in both Greece and Italy cypress was more often chosen. It is generally thought that cedar-wood was also widely used for fine furniture in Egypt, but until more samples have been tested the extent of its use must remain very uncertain. Samples from boards of the shrines in the tomb of Tutankhamun were found to be cedar-wood, but most of the dowels were of native acacia or sidder.[90]

Cypress-wood, having the same basic qualities as cedar, had the same range. The use of cypress for monumental doors became the established tradition in Greece and Italy, from the

Parthenon at Athens and the temple of Asklepios at Epidaurus to the great Christian basilicas of St. Peter and St. Sabina at Rome in the late Empire. Cypress was also used, like cedar, for chests and boxes and for coffins. The ashes of the Athenians who died in the first year of the Peloponnesian War were placed in cypress coffins,[91] and in most of the best sarcophagi that have been found in the Russian Crimea the basic structure was in cypress (pl. 13).

These sarcophagi are remarkably well preserved because they were found in undisturbed tombs sealed from the atmosphere. They are perhaps the most impressive surviving examples of Greek work in wood and they have been admirably analysed and discussed by N. I. Sokolskii.[92] Most of them were found in the Kerch peninsula. They cover a long period from the fifth century BC to the second century AD and the finest of them come from the second half of the fifth century to the middle of the third. Some of them seem to be by local craftsmen following local traditions, others by local craftsmen following Greek patterns or by resident Greek craftsmen, but the best of them, to judge by their materials and fine craftsmanship, are clearly from Greek workshops and probably from Athens. Many of them were richly decorated with mouldings, inlays, marquetry, or applied carvings (pl. 14). Mouldings included the egg and dart, in one example of which each individual tooth had been separately cut and fixed to the moulding.

The carvings, inlaid and attached, included figures of animals—lion attacking horse, roebuck, or deer; griffins, and panthers; Nereids and sea-monsters; and, in one instance, Greeks fighting barbarians. The subjects of inlays and attachments have no special local reference but are all typically Greek. Three of the sarcophagi had yew boards, but cypress was much commoner; for the decorative elements different woods were chosen, and in some cases ivory. Of the woods used box was the commonest. As we have seen, its closeness of texture is admirably suited to small-scale carving; it is one of the longest-lasting woods, and its pale colour contrasts well with the darker cypress and yew. Microscopic examination of fragments from one sarcophagus suggested a pear or maple type. There are no metal nails in the work; inlays and attachments were fixed by glue and wooden nails.

The woods that we have cursorily reviewed are those which were the most fashionable and therefore most commonly referred to in literature. We hear much less of the ordinary furniture used in ordinary homes. By modern analogy we should expect beech to be one of the most popular furniture woods. As Theophrastus says, the wood has a good colour and a good grain and is also strong;[93] and, because of the straightness of the grain, it is easy to work. Among its uses Theophrastus includes the making of carts, beds, chairs, and tables. Beech is a wood that very rarely occurs in Greek literature apart from Theophrastus, and the natural explanation is that other furniture woods such as oak and maple were much easier to obtain, for beech is a European tree which does not grow in Greece south of Thessaly. It was very different in Italy where beech was one of the commonest trees in the Apennines, and also grew well in the lowlands of Latium, as Theophrastus knew.[94] Martial regarded beech as the poor man's table: 'You hang your circles on Indian teeth; my table is beech, supported by a crock';[95] Pliny says that it was a specially useful wood for boxes and cases and Columella recommends it for chests used for storage.[96]

Oak is another wood that must have been widely used for furniture. If the argument from silence were valid we should conclude that there was very little oak furniture in Greek or Roman society. Theophrastus has plenty to say about the different kinds of oak, their qualities, their usefulness in building, and particularly in underwater work, but he never associates oak with tables, chairs, beds, couches, chests, or boxes. Plutarch, however, regards the Spartans' acceptance of oak benches to sit on for their meals as a good example of Spartan austerity, and Cicero uses it to point the contrast with the Romans of his day.[97] In the archaic period oak was probably the most widespread species in Greece and Italy and it would be very strange if, in the archaic period at least, it was not widely used for tables and chests.

Lime is a very different wood, and was much less common in Greece and Italy. It was too soft to be used in building, but its softness made it very easy to work and particularly suited to turning.[98] It was also a favourite wood for writing-tablets and mummy labels and could be used for chests and boxes. One needs, however, to resist the temptation to believe that

furniture-makers and carpenters always chose the wood that
was by structure or appearance best suited to what they made:
price and availability could also be determining factors. When a
collection of Roman writing-tablets was unexpectedly found at
Vindolanda, a Roman fort near Hadrian's Wall in the north of
England, it was thought that they were made of lime, which
literary sources could have suggested. When fragments of the
tablets were microscopically examined it was found that they
were made from birch and alder.[99] Those who could afford them
might prefer such woods as citrus, cedar, cypress, or even ebony,
but for the common man almost any wood was adequate.

The evidence for the use of nut-wood for furniture is surprisingly scanty, and the value of such evidence as survives is
reduced by the difficulty of distinguishing between chestnut
and walnut in the texts. This confusion will be discussed later
(p. 420); meanwhile we will use the generic term. Juvenal,
recalling the good old days, implies that nut-wood was by no
means fashionable: 'those days saw our tables made at home.
That was what we used the wood for if a storm blew down an
ancient nut-tree.'[100] On the other hand Strabo, referring to
Sinope's reputation for table woods, links mountain nut-trees
with maple.[101] The only other reference known to me comes
from Diocletian's price edict (p. 369), in which maximum prices
are given for three types of bed: for a boxwood bed (or low
couch) 600 denarii, for a nut-wood bed 400 denarii, and for an
inn (or tavern) bed fifty denarii.

Tables, chairs, and couches were not always made from single
woods. Pliny, with his customary contempt for the artificial, had
little sympathy for veneering, 'covering one wood with another,
and giving to a cheaper wood an outer skin of a more expensive
wood. Men have even learnt to cut wood into thin slices to
enable them to keep on selling the same tree.'[102] But veneering
had had a long history by Pliny's day. Examples have been
found in Egypt as early as the first dynasty, and it was
particularly fashionable in the eighteenth dynasty when it was
common practice to cover a native wood with ivory or one of
the finer imported woods, particularly ebony, cedar, cypress,
or box.

Veneering was also practised in Greece, but not apparently
on a large scale. Cratinus, writer of comedies, and one of the

rivals of Aristophanes, mentioned in one of his lost comedies a couch with a veneer of boxwood and this seems to be the only specific reference in Greek literature.[103] In the numerous surviving fragments of the sales of the possessions of men condemned for profaning the Eleusinian Mysteries (413 BC) there is only one example of veneering, a low bed, roughly twice the price of an ordinary bed.[104]

According to Pliny veneering developed late in Rome. It was not until the end of the Republic that sideboards were covered with citrus-wood and maple.[105] During the Empire it must have become much more common, because Pliny gives a long list of the woods best suited to provide veneers. As was to be expected citrus and maple head the list, because their burr-wood provides a particularly attractive figure; alder also formed suitable burr-wood. To these he adds the dark terebinth, box, palm, holly, ilex, the root of the alder, and poplar.[106]

An even more sophisticated treatment of wood was invented in Egypt as early as the third dynasty. In a sarcophagus from a cemetery at Saqqara there was found a small coffin of a young child. The wood was very well preserved and the structure of the coffin could be clearly seen.[107] Throughout there were six layers, roughly four millimetres thick, laid in true cross-grained plywood fashion. A variety of woods were used, including cypress, juniper, cedar, and sidder, and the workmanship was impressive. It has been suggested that the craftsman thought this a good way of using up odd pieces of valuable wood, but there could surely be many simpler ways of doing that. Perhaps the child had been fond of playing with different types of wood. Whatever his motive the pioneer seems to have had no successor until plywood was rediscovered in modern times.

Sometimes, as in sculpture, wood was combined with other materials. From words that have survived in the work of later grammarians we know that ivory and silver were used for the legs of couches,[108] which may explain why the father of Demosthenes, who owned a furniture workshop operated by slaves, had a stock of couch timbers and ivory.[109] The timbers will have been specially selected wood, probably cypress, maple, or box (perhaps prefabricated couch parts); the ivory could have been used either for couch legs, or for carved inlays or attachments.

If furniture is extended to cover kitchen and tableware it is difficult to demarcate the provinces of wood and pottery, which may vary according to date and district. In general, a wide use of wooden vessels was a sign of a simple, unsophisticated society. Strabo regards the use of wooden platters by the mountain peoples of Lusitania in north-west Spain as exceptional.[110] At Rome in the early Republic beech drinking-vessels were fashionable and M! Curius claimed that the only thing he had taken from his battle-won booty was a beech flask for use in sacrifices.[111] By the end of the Republic beech cups were a sign of the old austerity. 'There were no wars in the olden days', says the Augustan poet Tibullus, 'when the cups on our tables at dinner were made of beech-wood.'[112] In the excavation of the area of the Samian Heraeum many dedications in wood have been found, including plates with geometric designs, a perfume vase in the shape of a woman's head, and an oil-flask.[113] Most of them came from the seventh and early sixth centuries BC, but the use of wooden vessels probably lasted longer in Asia Minor and the big offshore islands of Samos, Chios, and Lesbos than in mainland Greece where good clays for potters were common, while in many states wood was scarce.

Even when eating and drinking from wooden vessels had been generally abandoned there remained a limited demand for good craftsmanship in wood. Virgil refers to beech-wood cups decorated by the immortal Alcimedon,[114] and Theophrastus records that the Syrians made cups in the style of the famous potter Thericles from their black terebinth-wood.[115] In a Hellenistic epigram fishermen include in their thanksgiving to Priapus of the Sea-Shore for their catch of tunny fish a mixing bowl of oak.[116]

Wood also continued to be used on a large scale for packing merchandise. Xenophon, writing of the dangers of the north-west coast of the Black Sea, says that it was notorious for its shipwrecks, and the native Thracians collected from the shore large numbers of couches, chests, and books and 'all the many other things that ship captains carry in wooden containers'.[117] Wines and oils were normally in the Mediterranean world carried in large terracotta amphorae, best illustrated by Monte Testaccio in Rome, a considerable hill below the Aventine composed of bases, necks, and other fragments of large amphorae, which had brought oil, wine, and fish-sauce from Spain and Gaul to Rome's river harbour. But reliefs from Neumagen on the Moselle show shiploads of barrels of wine;[118] others can be seen on Trajan's Column. In describing the trade of Aquileia at the head of the Adriatic, Strabo says that local traders carried wine and oil in wooden barrels into the interior to trade for cattle, hides, and slaves.[119] Pliny explains that near the Alps they put wine in wooden barrels because of the low temperatures and even light fires to protect it from the cold.[120]

Wine barrels when emptied were particularly useful for lining wells, and this accounts for the survival of so many of them. They have been found at major settlements along the great northern rivers, the Danube and Rhine, by the Thames in England, and as far north as Scotland.[121] Because of their weight water transport was particularly important for them. One of the barrels found at Silchester in England was six feet four and a half inches high with a diameter of two feet ten inches at the base, tapering to two feet four and a half inches at the end. It could have contained 818 litres, weighing 818 kilograms.[122] The staves ($4\frac{1}{2}$–6 in. at the centre) were made of fir, but the conclusion that the wood came from the Pyrenees and 'without doubt carried Bordeaux wine' is building too much on too little. The firs could have grown in France, Italy, the Balkans, or Spain and a wide choice of wines is available. Fir was also identified in two other barrels, and oak in one.

WOODS FOR SCULPTURE

M OST of the woods that the makers of furniture preferred appealed also to sculptors, who looked for many of the same qualities. They needed woods that would resist decay and insects, and that would not easily split or crack; a pleasant scent was also an advantage. An enquiry into the use of wood in sculpture suffers from the same handicaps as our review of furniture. Egypt, in virtue of its exceptionally dry climate, is the only Mediterranean country in which the study of the sculptor's use of wood can be based on a significant number of surviving statues and reliefs; elsewhere we depend much more on literary sources.

Egyptian sculptures are widely scattered through the museums of the world and a considerable proportion of them are in wood. The earliest date from the early second millennium BC and the series continues into the Roman period. Though there was already sculpture in stone in the pre-dynastic period, it never eclipses wood; whereas in Greece the use of wood in sculpture had been reduced to a very modest role by the end of the archaic period. Nor was wood in Egypt confined to the less prosperous; it was used for the portraits of priests, nobles, and kings. In the rich company of gold and silver in the tomb of Tutankhamun there were no less than seven statues or statuettes of the king in wood. Some eight hundred years later the two portrait statues which King Amasis dedicated to Hera in her great temple at Samos were also carved in wood.

Most of the native woods of Egypt were not well suited to sculpture. Acacia was strong and long-lasting, but it tended to be brittle and its branches were too curving: sycomore fig was more widely used, but it tended to be fibrous; persea-wood was better. Theophrastus says that it was strong, attractive in colour like the nettle-tree, and useful for sculpture and furniture.[1] Although there has been very little microscopic analysis of the wood of Egyptian sculptures and the wide-scale attribution of cedar may not always be justified, it seems that for work of high quality, imported woods were preferred and particularly cedar with cypress from Lebanon or Syria and ebony from the south. But one of the finest heads that have survived, of Queen Tiu, wife of Amenhophet III, is of yew.[2] This is a tree that likes the cold and is not found south of Syria. Fragments of yew have also been identified from Egyptian coffin boards.[3]

For the use of wood by sculptors in the Greek and Roman worlds we have to rely primarily on literary evidence, though during the last fifty years excavations, particularly at the Heraeum on the island of Samos, have recovered sufficient examples of archaic carving in wood to provide useful controls. Of literary sources the most fruitful is the *Description of Greece* written by Pausanias during the reign of Marcus Aurelius (AD 161–80). From his book it is clear that he lived in Asia Minor and he may have been a Lydian, but he had a wide knowledge of Greek history, legend, and myth and he travelled conscientiously through Greece visiting the sites he described and cross-examining local people about their traditions. He shows little interest in the contemporary scene, or even in the Roman government of Greece, though he pays lip-service in passing to Hadrian, who had expressed his affection for Greek culture by practical benefactions as well as words. The primary concerns of Pausanias were antiquarian and religious, and he cared more for sacred groves than natural forests; but his comparative indifference to landscape is more than compensated for by his description of dedications in more than two hundred temples covering more than seven hundred years.

For our purposes his use of words is important. The two words that he most commonly uses for temple sculptures are *agalma* and *xoanon*. *Agalma* literally means something that gives delight, so a gift that pleases the gods, then the statue of a god, and finally a statue without any necessary association with the gods. The derivation and meaning of *xoanon* is more controversial. By some it is taken to refer only to very primitive sculptures. If, however, as many accept, it is derived from the verb *xeein*, which means to give a proper finish to a crude surface with chisel or adze or knife, a *xoanon* should be a figure that has passed beyond the primitive stage to a more realistic form.[4] This controversy mercifully need not detain us, for Pausanias' use of the word is clear and consistent. Two passages show that for him the basic distinction of the *xoanon* is that it is made of wood. In his description of a very old temple of Apollo on the coast of Messenia not far from Corone he says: 'They name the god Crested-lark Apollo and he is represented by a *xoanon*, but the Argive Apollo is an *agalma* in bronze.'[5] Describing the cult of Asklepios at Titane near Corinth, he says that in the stoa by the temple there were figures of Dionysus, Hekate, Aphrodite, Demeter, Tyche: 'These are *xoana*: the Asklepios, Gortynian as he is called, is of stone.'[6] There is a similar contrast in another passage: 'There is a Dionysus Saviour, a seated *xoanon*, and by the sea an *agalma* of Aphrodite in stone.'[7]

In Pausanias a *xoanon* may also be called an *agalma*, but an *agalma* may be of any material. The figure of Dionysus said to have been brought back from Troy is both an *agalma* and a *xoanon*;[8] the statue of Ismenian Apollo in Thebes is made of cedar-wood, but it is called only an *agalma*;[9] the cult statue of Larisian Zeus is an *agalma* made of wood.[10] It is probably significant that the two statues in wood of Olympian victors are not called *xoana*, but *eikones*;[11] *xoanon* was reserved for the gods. In Pausanias the word does not have any chronological significance. Some *xoana* may be described as ancient, but the word can also be used of statues of the late sixth century, and even of fifth-century statues in which wood merely provided the core of the figure as a base for more expensive materials.[12]

Accepting the inference that in Pausanias all *xoana* are made of wood we find more than a hundred wooden statues surviving from a period before 500 BC. What is more surprising is the number of these survivors that Pausanias dates from the Bronze Age, before the collapse of Mycenaean culture. The temple of Wolf-Apollo at Argos was said to have been dedicated together with a *xoanon* by Danaus who, according to tradition, came from Egypt to Argos before the Trojan War; and in the temple were two other *xoana* dedicated not much later, an Aphrodite, a work of Epeios, who built the Trojan horse, and a Hermes dedicated by Hypermnestra, daughter of Danaus.[13] The figure of Dionysus in his temple at Argos had been brought back from Troy after a shipwreck off the island of Euboea.[14] A strange figure of Zeus with two eyes in their normal place and a third in his forehead had once been Priam's Zeus, brought home by Sthenelus from the spoils of Troy.[15] In a double sanctuary on the road from Argos to Mantinea there were *xoana* of Aphrodite and Ares said to have been dedicated by Polynices and the Argives who fought against Thebes in the generation before the Trojan War.[16] On Mt. Taygetus a *xoanon* of Orpheus was attributed to the Pelasgians and at Pyrrhicus *xoana* of Artemis and Apollo were attributed to the Amazons.[17] According to tradition a wooden Hermes in the temple of Athena Polias on the Athenian acropolis was dedicated by Cecrops, first king of Athens, and one of three *xoana* of Ilithya was said to have been brought from Delos by Erysichthon.[18] What value is to be attached to these traditions?

The Greeks of the fifth and later centuries knew very little of their history in the period that followed the destruction of the Mycenaean palaces (*c.*1200 BC); they thought that they knew a very great deal more about the Bronze Age, and about the heroes who fought under Agamemnon in the Trojan War. This knowledge they owed largely to the epics of Homer and his successors and the themes were adopted by their tragedians. The fame of Homer, who had pride of place in all educational systems, ensured that the traditions were kept alive. The prosopography of Homer's characters remained a lively topic among Roman men of learning and the geographer Strabo, who had studied all branches of knowledge, did not question the historicity of Homer's narrative.

A Thucydides, rigorously rational, could question the whole fabric of these traditions, but such bold spirits were rare and Pausanias was not one of them. He finds no difficulty in believing that a plane tree at Caphyae in Arcadia, which was flourishing in his own day, was planted by Menelaus when he was gathering his force to lead against Troy;[19] or that Artemis was called Astrateia at Pyrrhicus, because it was there that the Amazons halted their invasion of Greece;[20] or that ancient *xoana* of Aphrodite in Thebes were made from the figure-heads of the ships of Cadmus who, according to tradition, came from Phoenicia to Thebes before the Trojan War.[21] He can believe that Epidelium on the southern coast of Laconia was called after an image of Apollo at Delos which was thrown into the sea when Delos was sacked by Mithridates' general in 88 BC and washed up on the coast of Laconia.[22] He accepts the tradition that associates Daedalus with the court of Minos King of Cnossus, but he makes sculptors of the seventh and sixth centuries his pupils.[23]

Pausanias can, however, occasionally be sceptical. In the Agora of Elis there was a structure like a temple but without walls, the roof of which was supported by oak columns. The natives maintained that it was a tomb: 'If an old man I asked was right it would be the tomb of Oxylus', a very polite hesitation.[24] When faced with the Athenian tradition that the most sacred image of Athena on the Acropolis fell from heaven, he prefers not to enquire into it.[25] When offered alternatives, he can criticise, but not radically. There was a tradition, made popular by a play of Euripides, that Iphigenia, daughter of Agamemnon, was about to be sacrificed by her father Agamemnon to procure favourable winds to take the Achaean ships to Troy, but was miraculously saved by Artemis, who substituted for her a hind, and made her priestess of the goddess in a temple on the north shore of the Black Sea. There she was found by her brother Orestes and together they fled, bringing with them the figure of the goddess from her temple. It was therefore necessary to trace the history of this famous image, which was claimed by Sparta, Cappadocia, and Lydia.

According to the Athenian tradition it was left by Iphigenia and Orestes at Brauron, the main centre of the cult of Artemis in Attica, taken from Brauron by the Persian invaders in 480 BC, and finally presented by Seleucus to the Syrians of Laodicea 'who still possess it'. Pausanias supports the Spartan claim, based on the tradition that Orestes was once king of their country. Why should Iphigenia have left the image at Brauron and, if she did, why didn't the Athenians take it away when they abandoned Attica?[26] This is a reasonable argument if you accept the traditional story about Iphigenia. But Pausanias did not ask the basic questions and we are too familiar with the attachment of famous names to objects and events with which they can have no connection to have any confidence in local traditions about antique sculptures for which there was no firm evidence.

If, however, we were right in believing that figures were carved in wood by both Minoans and Mycenaeans, we cannot assume that the earliest wooden carved figures that Pausanias saw must necessarily be dated in the eighth century or later. Wood-carving could have been continued on a modest scale through the Dark Ages, and the early temples which were built in the late ninth and eighth centuries will have been intended from the outset to be a home for a community's protecting god or goddess, represented by a wooden image. Two lines of the Alexandrian poet Callimachus have given rise to a very different view of the development of sculptures in wood. Speaking of a figure of Hera in her temple on the island of Samos he says that once it was a crude board, but is now a finely finished figure.[27] From this it has been inferred that in the early archaic period Greek religion was aniconic and that gods were not represented in human form until the seventh century.

This view was developed before any serious consideration had been given to archaic sculpture in wood, but the excavations at the site of the Samian Heraeum have done much to redress the balance. From the considerable number of wooden statuettes (male and female) found in the temple area it is clear that the wood-carvers had made considerable progress by the middle of the seventh century. In particular the small figure of a goddess, probably Hera, with highly decorative costume and towered head-dress shows considerable skill in the craftsman and a good sense of form.[28] Behind such figures there must have been a considerable period of development. It is natural that wood being the softer material should be used before stone could be worked confidently. Stone and bronze began to compete from the middle of the seventh century, but sculptors with international reputations were still working in wood at the end of the sixth century.[29] References to images of wood also continue in the Old Testament during the same period.[30]

In the early archaic period the shape of the material imposed restrictions. If the figure was to be carved in one piece the width was limited by the size of the diameter of the tree-trunk or branch and it was not easy to advance beyond the simple standing figure with legs together and arms straight and close to the side. A rather more difficult alternative was the seated figure, which became the most popular type for a goddess. Pausanias saw a very early seated Hera in the Heraeum at Argos,[31] and the inventories of the temple commissioners of Delos in the Hellenistic period still included the primitive cult image of Leto seated on her throne and they list her wardrobe, for it was customary for seated goddesses to be dressed.[32] It was also a seated Athena in Homer's *Iliad* to whom the Trojans brought a choice robe that Paris had brought from Phoenician Sidon.[33]

Sculpture was more adventurous in the seventh century. In the small statuette of Hera from Samos the goddess holds out her right hand, which was made in a separate piece, and in the sacred marriage of Zeus and Hera, cut in high relief and forming one of the supports of a ceremonial couch, the primitive figures of the early archaic period have been left behind.[34] This relief has been dated in the early seventh century. A more ambitious work from the next generation is included in the record of the dedications in the temple of Athena at Lindos on the island of Rhodes: 'The men of Lindos who with the sons of Panchis joined Battus in founding Cyrene dedicated to Athena and Heracles a figure of Pallas and a lion being strangled by Heracles.'[35]

The sixth century marked the climax of sculpture in wood, stimulated by the growth of wealth reflected in the panhellenic centres of Olympia and Delphi and in the grand new temples of the leading cities. The names of individual sculptors emerge and the growing popularity of the quadrennial Olympic festival led to the building of treasuries by individual cities, encouraging dedications. Pausanias records two dedications in wood from the sixth century of particular interest. For the Epidamnian treasury a Spartan sculptor had carved in wood two of the labours of Hercules—Atlas holding up the firmament, presumably with Heracles standing by to take his place, and Heracles and the apple-tree of the Hesperides with the serpent coiled about the tree.[36] In the Megarian treasury Hercules' struggle with the river Achelous was represented with figures of Zeus, Deianeira, Achelous, Ares, and Athena.[37] The labours of Hercules were to have pride of place in the reliefs of the metopes on the great fifth-century temple of Zeus, but the dedications in the treasuries were not reliefs but compositions of separate figures. When Pausanias saw them the Hesperides had been moved from the Epidamnian treasury to the temple of Hera where they were joined by the figure of Athena from the Megarian treasury.

During the sixth century many states maintained their small

early temples with their primitive cult figures, but most of the richer states built larger temples and, while keeping the ancient images, called on the best sculptors of the day to make new cult statues to match the new temples. There had been more than one early archaic temple of Artemis at Ephesus, but when a new and much grander temple was built in the middle of the sixth century they called on an Athenian sculptor, Endoios.[38] Pausanias saw a seated Athena in marble made by Endoios on the Acropolis, and it has generally been identified with a fine monumental sculpture in the Acropolis museum,[39] but the statue of Artemis in Ephesus was made in wood, as was another large seated Athena which Endoios made for Erythrae.[40] When the Samians rebuilt their temple of Hera on a grander scale they called on the Aeginetan Smilis whose figures of the Seasons seated on thrones Pausanias saw in the temple of Hera at Olympia:[41] there is, however, no evidence that the seated Hera of the Samian Heraeum was made of wood. The famous Apollo of Delos, holding the three Graces in his hand, was the work of Textaeus and Angelion, contemporaries of Smilis and Endoios, and they worked in wood.[42]

No work by any of the sixth-century sculptors in wood whose names were remembered long after their deaths has survived, but attractive examples of the work of local craftsmen have been found in Sicily and near Corinth. Three small figures of goddesses from the first half of the century were discovered in the territory of Acragas near a sulphur spring which had preserved them.[43] The quality of the surface has naturally suffered, but the proportions are good and the craftsman has no difficulty with his tools. It is more difficult to judge the quality of a group of two figures, one standing and one seated, found in a large cave near the village of Pitsa, forty-four kilometres west of Corinth, for the heads have not been preserved and the surface is badly worn.[44] It would be more interesting to see the ox and calf sent to Athena of Lindos from Sybaris by Amphinomos and his sons to commemorate the saving of their ship.[45]

Although almost all our records of sixth-century sculpture in wood are associated with temples, the sculptor's work was no longer strictly confined within a religious context. The first two statues of victors in the games at Olympia were set up soon after the middle of the sixth century and, though sculptors were becoming much more familiar with the working of limestone, marble, and bronze, these two statues were carved from wood.[46] The evidence of Pausanias shows that there was no sharp dividing line between wood and stone and that it was not exceptional for the same sculptor to work in different materials. Canachus who made a statue of Ismenian Apollo in cedar-wood also made a bronze statue of Apollo for the Milesian temple at Branchidae; they were of the same size and the same form.[47] Pausanias also records a wooden cult statue of Hecate on the island of Aegina by Myron,[48] presumably the Athenian sculptor best remembered for his famous statue of the discus-thrower and one of the greatest sculptors in bronze in the generation following the Persian invasion.

The importance of Pausanias for us is not limited to his long catalogue of sculptures and sculptors. He was also interested in the materials that were used and here he is less nervous of using his own judgement. At Pheneus in Arcadia he found the temple of Athena in ruins. Nearby was a bronze statue of Poseidon, named the Horse god, which the local people said was dedicated by Odysseus to commemorate the finding of his lost mares. This is too much even for Pausanias: 'In the rest of their story we can reasonably accept what the people of Pheneus say, but that it was Odysseus who dedicated the bronze statue I cannot believe, for in those days they had not yet learnt how to make bronze statues in a single piece like weaving a garment.' Pausanias thought that bronze-casting was first used by Theodorus and Rhoecus of Samos in the middle of the sixth century.[49] He also likes to differentiate between various woods if he can. When he comes to the ruined temple of Hermes on the top of Mt. Cyllene in Arcadia he is surprised to find that the statue of Hermes, which he guesses to be eight feet high, is made of *thyon*-wood. 'So far as we could learn these are the woods that men of old used to make their *xoana*: ebony, cypress, cedars, oaks, yew, and lotus (nettle-tree); the *agalma* of the Hermes of Cyllene is not made of any of these woods, but of *thyon*-wood.'[50]

This list is not based on his own experience because it omits other woods that he mentions elsewhere; he has found it in a book or by enquiry from another knowledgeable antiquarian. Cedars and oaks are in the plural possibly because the Greek word *kedros* covers some of the junipers as well as cedar, and oaks may include the evergreen oak as well as different species of deciduous oaks. Three of the trees in this list are included in the shorter list that Theophrastus gives of the most suitable woods for sculptors—cedar, cypress, lotus; Theophrastus also adds boxwood and, for smaller figures, the roots of olive.[51] Pausanias gives examples of both: there was a boxwood statue of Apollo in the Sicyonian treasury at Olympia,[52] and he knew of a face of olive-wood that fishermen from Methymna on the island of Lesbos had brought up in their nets. The features were strangely foreign though somehow godlike, so they consulted the Pythian priestess at Delphi to find out what god or hero they had found. When they were told that this was Dionysus they kept the image and honoured it with sacrifices and prayer: 'the image was of wood, the copy that they sent to Delphi was of bronze'.[53]

The ancient, almost shapeless image of Athena on the Acropolis which was said to have fallen from heaven, Athena Polias guardian of the city, was made of olive-wood,[54] as were two other archaic images made famous by Herodotus. His story is that once when the people of Epidaurus were suffering from a crop failure they consulted Delphi and were bidden to set up statues of Damia and Auxesia, goddesses of fertility. The Epidaurians asked whether they should make the statues of bronze or stone and were told to use cultivated olive-wood; so they sent to Athens, whose olive trees they thought to be the most sacred, and asked if they could cut their olive-wood. The Athenians allowed them to take the wood on condition that they sent each year victims to be sacrificed to Athena Polias and to Erechtheus, founder of their city. The statues were set up, Epidaurus flourished, and paid the annual tribute to Athens. At this time the island of Aegina was controlled by Epidaurus, but later the Aeginetans revolted and emphasised their independence by seizing the statues and establishing a festival for them on Aegina. The Athenians now claimed the statues from Aegina on the ground that the wood was theirs; they tried to lift them from their bases with ropes but were interrupted by thunder and earthquake and had to flee. Meanwhile the statues had fallen on their knees and so remained.[55] From Herodotus' charming embroidery it would be unsafe to infer more than that there were on Aegina, from the archaic period, olive-wood statues of two fertility goddesses, Damia and Auxesia, in a kneeling position, the form presumably chosen for their association with birth in nature and in women.

Apart from thyon-wood there are two other woods that are not included in the lists of Pausanias or Theophrastus. When Pausanias came to Argos the cult image in the Heraeum was a gold and ivory statue by the fifth-century Argive sculptor Polyclitus, but near it was an ancient *agalma* of Hera standing on a column. The most ancient image in the temple, however, originally dedicated in Tiryns, and brought to the Heraeum when Argos destroyed Tiryns in the fifth century, was a small seated figure made of wild-pear-wood.[56] This wood is barely noticed in the sources, but the tree is not uncommon in Greece and Asia Minor and, as Theophrastus says, it grows on both mountain and plain.[57] The wood is very hard, suitable for a club[58] and also used by cobblers as a sharpening board for their knives,[59] but it is usually a small tree and could only be useful for small figures. The second wood that Pausanias adds to the list is fig-wood, which was used for the statue at Olympia of a victor in the pankration in 536. Pausanias notes that it was less well preserved than the cypress statue of a victor in the boxing in 534.[60]

All the woods so far mentioned could have been found locally, with the exception of *thyon*-wood, which, according to Pausanias, was used for the larger-than-life-size image of Hermes on Mt. Cyllene.[61] If Pausanias is right the wood, which we have already met as the Roman *citrus* (p. 286), should have come from north Africa and probably from Cyrene, which maintained close relations with the Greek world. The wood is only once associated with sculpture in the Greek and Latin literature that has survived, when Polybius records the gift of *thyon*-wood by the Numidian prince Masinissa to the island of Rhodes after a severe earthquake in 227 BC to make new statues; but traders could have been impressed by the popularity of the wood in Cyrene where it was widely used for roof-timbers.[62] The alternative is to follow Fraser who assumes a confusion of *thyon* with *thuyia*, possibly a form of tall juniper which grew at the top of Mt. Cyllene in Arcadia.[63]

There was, however, one exotic wood at least which must have been imported. Pausanias records four dedications in ebony from the archaic period. There was the cult image of Artemis on the way from Tegea to Laconia[64] and the cult image of Ajax in his ancient temple in the agora of the main town on the island of Salamis.[65] In nearby Megara in the temple of Apollo were three ebony statues of the god represented as the Pythian, the Tithe Gatherer, and the Guide and Leader.[66] These statues had originally stood in a modest temple of mud-brick, but had been transferred to a new marble temple built by Hadrian. The first two, Pausanias says, were very like Egyptian *xoana*, which means that they were stiff and formal; the third was like Aeginetan work, a more relaxed and natural style. In the temple of the Dioscuri at Argos there were figures of Castor and Pollux, with their horses, and of their wives and sons. The figures, which were made by two of the best-known sculptors of the early sixth century, Dipoenus and Scyllis, were all of ebony, apart from a small use of ivory in the horses.[67]

Considerable quantities of ivory were imported by the Greeks in the archaic period and the easiest sources of supply were Syria and Phoenicia; ebony was much rarer and, until trade with India was developed, the only known source was Ethiopia, from which supplies came through Egypt. The ebony used by sculptors during the archaic period might have been brought by Phoenician traders, but it is more likely to have come direct from Egypt and in Aeginetan ships, for Aegina alone of all mainland Greek states was strongly represented at Naucratis, through which all trade to and from Egypt had to pass.[68] But by whichever route the ebony came the cost must have been high. Unfortunately Pausanias gives no indication of the size of the figures; they may have been small, like the little ebony figures that were found in the tomb of Queen Tiu.[69] It is probable that cedar-wood also was imported on a small scale during the archaic period, though the ambiguity of the Greek word *kedros* makes certainty impossible. Pausanias uses the word for the famous chest of Cypselus at Olympia, for representations of two of the labours of Hercules in the Epidamnian treasury at Olympia, and for the statue of Ismenian Apollo.[70] All these dedications would have demanded work of high quality and Greeks trading with the Near East or with Egypt must have known the high reputation of the cedars of Lebanon and their value for sculpture. Pausanias also claims that the figure of Aphrodite Morpho in the temple of Aphrodite at Sparta was made of cedar-wood.[71]

There is some uncertainty concerning the cult statue in the famous temple of Artemis at Ephesus, which ranked with the temples of Hera at Samos and of Apollo at Branchidae near Miletus, the greatest and most famous temples of the Greek world in the archaic period. The original temple was completely rebuilt in the middle of the sixth century and again in the fourth century, but the archaic cult statue of Artemis which was made for the sixth-century temple was preserved into the Roman Empire. Vitruvius said that it was made of cedar,[72] but according to Pliny, who overlooked Vitruvius, in the general tradition the wood was ebony which, as we have seen, could have been appropriate in the archaic period.[73] Mucianus, however, who as governor of Syria in AD 69 urged Vespasian to make his bid for the imperial power, did not agree. In his memoirs he said that it was made from the wood of the vine, which had been chosen by the sculptor Endoios. He added that the statue had survived through several rebuildings of the temple and that nard was injected through a series of holes in order to keep the joins together. Pliny appears to be sceptical; he doubts whether Mucianus could have known the artist's name and is surprised that an archaic statue should have been made in separate pieces. But Mucianus, who in a highly successful career maintained a lively and enquiring interest in nature, may have been right: Pliny himself had earlier said that in olden times the vine was classed among trees because of its size and he had given examples of its use: 'a statue of Jupiter in Etruscan Populonia made from a single vine, and unaffected by decay after all these years; a bowl at Massilia; and at Metapontum (in south Italy) vine-wood columns supporting the temple of Juno'.[74] Nor should Pliny have worried about the joins. In Egypt it was not uncommon even in the Bronze Age to make the limbs, especially arms, separately.

Both Pausanias and Theophrastus included *lotus* in the woods used by sculptors in the archaic period. Theophrastus describes it as, like boxwood, heavy, close-grained, immune to decay, but, unlike boxwood, dark in colour.[75] From this description and the distribution of the tree, it is identified as *Celtis australis*, more generally known from the form of its leaves as the nettle-tree, which requires a warm climate. Pausanias does not mention any example of the wood in the temples he visits, but the figures of

Pallas Athena, and Heracles strangling a lion in the dedication of the Cyrenaean settlers to Athena of Lindos (p. 306) were in lotus-wood. The tree flourished in north Africa, and was also native in Greece, though uncommon. Mulberry-wood is not unlike the wood of the nettle-tree, dark in colour and very hard:[76] Isaiah is familiar with its use in Palestine:

> Or is it mulberry-wood that will not rot which a man chooses,
> seeking out a skilful craftsman for it,
> to mount an image that will not fall?[77]

Of the native woods that could be used for sculpture the Greeks gave pride of place to the cypress, which had many of the qualities of the cedar, but a sweeter scent, and it took a better polish. It was probably used by the Cretans for the cult image of Apollo in his temple at Delphi[78] and at Olympia for the first statue set up to commemorate a victory in the games, when an Aeginetan, Praxidamas, won the boxing-match (544 BC).[79] The wood of two of the three small sixth-century goddess figures found by a sulphur spring in the territory of Acragas was identified as cypress; the third was different and was thought to be probably poplar.[80] This wood is not included by Pausanias or Theophrastus, but Vitruvius notes that, like lime and willow, it is easy to work in sculpture.[81]

From the sixth century we know the name of several sculptors who worked in wood. From the fifth century the only name known to us is Myron. It is significant that when Onatas, a famous Aeginetan sculptor, was commissioned to make a new cult image of Demeter for Phigaleia in Arcadia his copy of the old wooden image was in bronze. If Pausanias' description of the old image is reliable it is the most elaborate archaic sculpture in wood of which there is record. A female figure with a horse's head was seated on a rock. Growing from the head were figures of serpents and other wild creatures and she was dressed in a tunic reaching to her feet. On one hand was a dolphin and on the other a dove. This image was burnt and not replaced, and Demeter's festivals were neglected. Then came a famine and the priestess at Delphi warned the Phigalians to restore her honours to Demeter. Onatas was guided by a painting or by a copy of the original, but he relied mainly, it is said, on directions received in dreams.[82] Perhaps his dreams took him a little further than the original and perhaps memories of the original were influenced by the 'copy'. By now sculptors had mastered the technical difficulties of working in limestone, marble, and bronze; wood ceased to be used for important dedications of public statues except in a more humble role as the junior partner in two new forms of sculpture.

Pausanias claims that at Sparta, on the right side of the temple of Athena of the House of Bronze, he saw the earliest surviving bronze statue. It was a statue of Zeus the All-high and 'it was not made in one piece, but each part was made separately and the parts were fitted together and kept in place by nails'.[83] The natural inference is that the sheets of hammered bronze were fitted over a wooden core as in a group of seventh-century bronze statuettes from Dreros in Crete.[84] The great image of Hyacinthian Apollo at Amyclae represents perhaps an early stage in the technique. Pausanias estimated that the image was thirty cubits high and it was 'ancient and primitive, for apart from face, hands, and feet, the body was like a column of bronze', presumably a wooden core covered with bronze sheeting.[85] The technique of covering wood with hammered bronze may have persisted to the end of the archaic period in Sparta, but when bronze-casting was developed in Ionia, the new technique spread rapidly in Greece. Other techniques combining wood with other materials lasted considerably longer.

In the archaic period it was not uncommon for statues to be in part or whole gilded. The boxwood statue of Apollo in the Sicyonian treasury at Olympia had a gilded head;[86] two figures of Dionysus in the agora at Corinth were gilded with the exception of the faces, which were picked out with red paint.[87] From such experiments there developed a standard form in which the main body was in wood, sometimes gilded, but face, hands, and feet were in a different material, normally limestone or marble, and in exceptional cases ivory. Pausanias describes the figures in the temple of the Graces at Elis as 'xoana, with dress gilded, and face, hands, and feet of marble'.[88] In the statue of Athena in the temple of Zeus at Aegina 'face, hands, and feet are of ivory, but the rest of the xoanon is decorated with gilding and various colours'.[89] The two figures of Demeter in her temple at Onceum in Arcadia are 'agalmata of wood, with

faces, hands, and feet of Parian marble'.[90] It is interesting that
Pausanias uses different words for figures that were basically
of the same form, but the ambiguity is natural. As wood was
the main material, used for all the body except the extremities,
it might be called a wooden statue, but it was a hybrid and not
strictly a *xoanon*. Statues of this form were later called acroliths
and the most famous of them was a great statue made by Phidias
from the spoils of the victory at Marathon for the temple of
Athena Areia, goddess of war, at Plataea. According to
Pausanias it was nearly as tall as the Athena Promachos,
Phidias' colossal bronze statue which stood some forty feet high
on the Athenian acropolis.[91]

The acrolith, which was to have a long life in the Greek
and Roman worlds,[92] was temporarily eclipsed by a more
luxurious form in which ivory was introduced in place of
marble, and sheetgold in place of gilded wood. The earliest
traces of this style in Greece come from Delphi. In 1938 the
French excavators, exploring the area to the south of the temple
of Apollo, found two trenches in which a wide assortment of
objects, most of them in fragments, had been buried. Most of
the objects showed strong traces of fire and those that could
be dated approximately came from the sixth century or the first
half of the fifth. The natural inference is that these were
dedications ruined in a fifth-century fire and carefully buried
near the buildings in which they had been placed originally.
Among the most interesting of the objects were a series of faces,
eyes, toes, and hands in ivory and fragments of a gold alloy.
Amandry's conclusion that these came from figures in which
face, hands, and feet were in ivory and dress in gold is
irresistible.[93] There were no less than eight ivory faces, three
of which were life-size and the rest half-life-size or rather less.
The shape of the head, which is cut straight at the back, shows
that it was fitted on to some other material which was clearly
wood. No wood survives, but there was ample evidence for wood
in the carbonised remains.

Some at least of these faces seem to date from the sixth century and Amandry noted that the style was distinctively Ionic.
We can follow him in believing that the chryselephantine
fashion was adopted from the east by the Ionians of Asia Minor
and further developed on the Greek mainland. We can see a

reflection of the style in Palestine in the sixth-century prophet
Isaiah:

> Is it an image which a craftsman sets up,
> and a goldsmith covers with plate
> and fits with studs of silver as a costly gift?[94]

and in greater detail, in Jeremiah:

> For the carved images of the nations are a sham.
> They are nothing but timber cut from the forest,
> worked with his chisel by a craftsman,
> he adorns it with silver and gold,
> fastening them on with hammer and nails
> so that they do not fall apart.[95]

Of the two earliest statues in gold and ivory known from
literature the first was by Canachus, who also worked in bronze
and wood: it was a seated Aphrodite made for his native
Sicyon.[96] The second was made a little later by two Aetolian
sculptors for Aetolian Calydon, but it had been transferred to
Patrae in the Peloponnese by Augustus.[97] Both of these statues
were probably earlier than the Persian invasion of 480 BC.

It is very doubtful whether any chryselephantine statue
before the middle of the fifth century had exceeded life-size;
Phidias was taking a very bold step when he decided to use the
style for the cult image of the Parthenon, the new temple of
Athena on the Athenian acropolis which was begun in 447/6 BC.
This great statue of Athena was more than thirty feet high, the
wooden core was built round a massive tall post, and the dress
formed a major gold reserve, for the sheets of gold were detach-
able.[98] In the judgement of the ancient world the Parthenos,
much as its splendour was admired, was surpassed by the second
great chryselephantine statue that Phidias made for the temple
of Zeus at Olympia. The Parthenos was a standing figure;
Olympian Zeus was seated on a magnificently decorated
throne, and for once we have evidence for the woods used. Dio
Chrysostom saw the statue at Olympia and reports that the core
was made of cypress and lotus (nettle-wood).[99] These two
woods, both of which could have been found in the Peloponnese,
had the two qualities that were most needed, stability and
endurance.

Polyclitus followed the example of Phidias in a giant seated

Hera for the Argive Heraeum and he in turn was followed by the Parian sculptor Thrasydaeus, who in the early fourth century made the cult statue of ivory and gold for the temple of Asklepios at Epidaurus: 'The god is seated on a throne, grasping a staff in one hand, and holding the other over the head of the serpent, a dog crouching at his side.'[100] On the throne were carved in relief the deeds of Argive heroes. A Megarian sculptor, assisted, it was said, by Phidias, was working on a chryselephantine statue of Zeus for his temple at Megara when the Peloponnesian War broke out. Some of the wood needed for the core of the statue could still be seen by Pausanias.[101] It was in this chryselephantine tradition that the Roman emperor Hadrian, who completed the great temple of Olympian Zeus at Athens, which a Pisistratid tyrant had begun more than six hundred years earlier, had a chryselephantine statue of the god made to match the scale of the temple. 'It is a sight worth seeing', says Pausanias: 'In size, apart from the two colossal statues in Rome and Rhodes, it leaves all others far behind. If the size is considered the work is good.'[102] A little later in the second century a dedication almost as spectacular was made in the temple of Poseidon at the Isthmus by the greatest of Greek private benefactors, Herodes Atticus. We owe the description to Pausanias:

The sculptures inside the temple were dedicated in our day by Herodes the Athenian. There are four horses covered in gold except for the hoofs, which are of ivory; and there are two Tritons by the horses in gold above and ivory below the waist. On the chariot stand Amphiaraus and Poseidon and there is a boy standing on a dolphin, Palaemon. These figures too are in ivory and gold.[103]

In general, from the third century BC the Greeks of the mainland, publicly and privately, were too poor for the chryselephantine style; it may have been more widely used in the wealthier parts of the Hellenistic world. But it does not seem to have appealed to Roman taste: the only evidence in literature or archaeology from Italy is the ivory face and an arm of a life-size female statue, probably Athena.[104] The style is mature classical of the mid-fifth century BC, but though it was found in Sabine country it probably comes from Greece.

Myron is the last well-known sculptor who is recorded to have worked in wood otherwise than in acroliths or chryselephantine statues, but wood was still used for the representations of gods and goddesses in processions. The accounts of the Delian commissioners record the preparations made for the annual processions of Dionysus during his spring festival to the altar where a sacrifice was made.[105] Payments are made for wood for the figure, for the making of the figure, for its painting and decoration. The form of the figure is revealed in a dedication by a certain Karystios commemorating his victory in a choral competition. On the dedicatory altar there is the figure of a cock with wings folded and a phallus in place of head and neck.[106] This was Dionysus, referred to alternately as statue or phallus. Each year a new figure was made and the costs incurred varied from year to year. Some indication of the size is given by the costs. The commonest payment for making the figure is five drachmae, the equivalent of two-and-a-half-days' pay for a skilled man, and the painting of the figure is nearly as expensive, ranging between three and seven drachmae. Several of the annual accounts record the purchase of a 'yard-arm', which in one year cost twenty-four drachmae. The yard-arm, more familiar as a naval timber to carry the mainsail, was needed as the backbone of the figure and since an oak beam twelve feet (3.66 m.) long costs eight drachmae, the yard-arm would probably have been at least twenty feet long. In another account wood for the phallus cost thirty drachmae. That the figure was of substantial size is also shown by the fact that a special carriage was built for it and kept in repair. In some of the later accounts payments are made 'to those who put the lead on the carriage' and 'to those who took the lead away'. This was probably, as has been suggested, designed to prevent the tall figure falling over. A more orthodox procession is recorded in a decree from Magnesia of 196 BC in honour of Artemis, patron goddess of the city. In this procession, which led to the sacrifice of a bull to Zeus Giver of Freedom, the chief magistrate was required to include *xoana* (presumably figures of wood) for all the twelve Olympian gods dressed in fine clothes.[107]

Public processions became a special feature in the competition for prestige and power among the Hellenistic kings who inherited Alexander's conquests. This is a period when the conviction that bigger was better exercised a strong influence on the development of ships and siege equipment; the towering colossus that was 105 feet high and bestrode the harbour of Rhodes was another sign of the times.[108] It was also a period of extravagant display in public festivals, and we are lucky to have detailed descriptions of two great processions which were long remembered. Athenaeus preserves the record of the first, presented by Ptolemy Philadelphus (286–247 BC) in the stadium at Alexandria. This procession included a number of four-wheeler platforms carrying scenes from myth, legend, and religion. Two were in honour of Dionysus. In one, which was pulled by 180 men, there was a statue ten cubits high of the god dressed in a purple tunic extending to the feet, pouring a libation from a gold saucer. The other was more ambitious, illustrating the return of Dionysus from India: the god, twelve cubits high, reclined on the back of an elephant, while a satyr, five cubits high, rode on the animal's neck.

The children in the crowd will have been more excited by a figure which actually moved: Nysa, in a yellow tunic with a gold spangle and wrapped in a Spartan shawl, was made to rise automatically, pour a libation of milk from a gold saucer, and then sit down. There were also figures of the gods, and of the city of Corinth standing beside the Egyptian king. But to inhibited modern societies perhaps the most surprising features in the procession are a Bacchic wand of gold ninety cubits long, and a golden phallus 120 cubits long painted in various colours and bound with fillets of gold.[109] It is reasonable to assume that the gold in the last two curiosities was gilded wood and that although the material is not recorded, the figures of gods and heroes, most of them dressed, were in wood.

The second procession was presented by Antiochus Epiphanes of Syria (175–164 BC) and is described by Polybius. The incentive came from the games given by the Roman general Aemilius Paulus to celebrate his victory over the Macedonian king Perseus, and this accounts for the military character of the procession. The king himself was followed by representative units of the various forces he could call on—infantry, cavalry, chariots, and elephants. The rest of the procession, which was 'almost beyond description', is not recorded in detail by Polybius, but it included 'images of every god, demigod, or hero accepted by man, some gilded and others adorned with gold-embroidered robes; and the myths belonging to each was represented by the most costly symbols. Behind these were carried images of Night and Day, Earth, Heaven, Morning, and Noon.'[110]

Wood also remained a popular material for the making of small-scale sculptures. It was more economical than bronze, stone, or marble and less vulnerable than terracotta. In all major Mediterranean towns there were shops in which crafts-men carved small figures, particularly of gods and goddesses, from wood. Plutarch preserves a scene of Socrates walking with some of his followers in the outskirts of the Agora and passing by the shops of the chest- and box-makers, and of the carvers of Hermes figures to whom Plato also refers in his *Symposium*.[111] Socrates is there compared to the Silenus figures in the shops with flutes or pipes, which when opened are found to have figures of gods inside. Of all the pocket-gods Hermes was by far the most popular, for he was the god who protected travellers and encouraged money-making. Two fables in the collection attributed to Aesop illustrate the point: 'A man made a Hermes of wood and tried to sell it in the market. No one seemed to want to buy it though he insisted that it would bring blessings and profit to the buyer. Why, someone asked, did he not keep it himself?'[112] A less moral story was told of a man who was assured that his wooden Hermes would bring him great good fortune. When his miseries merely increased he took the god by the leg and bashed him against the wall. 'The head was broken and gold fell out.'[113] We have already met Hermes in the sad story of how Apuleius came into possession of an emaciated ebony figure of the god (p. 286). Apuleius claims that he had seen a craftsman working in his shop on small figures and geometric patterns in wood and had asked him to make a small figure in wood of any god or goddess he chose.

Mars was another god in popular demand. Tertullian, anxious to show that the advance of Christianity would not put craftsmen out of work, takes the wood-carver as an example: 'If a man carves a figure of Mars from lime-wood could he not as easily put together a chest?'[114] He has in mind surely a small figure for which lime could be very suitable. Vitruvius knew that it was easy to work and Virgil links it with box as being 'carved and shaped with the sharp iron' (knife).[115] The qualities of lime-wood were no less appreciated in the seventeenth century in England, as John Evelyn records:

It is a shameful negligence that we are no better providers of nurseries for a tree so choice, and universally acceptable. . . . Because of its colour and easie working, and that it is not subject to split, architects make with it models of their designed buildings and small statues. . . . Witness the trophies, festoons, fruitages, encarpia and other ornaments and decorations of admirable invention and performance, to be seen about the choir of St. Paul's and other churches, royal palaces, and noble houses in city and country, all of them the work and invention of our Lysippus, Mr. Gibbons, and for ought appears equal to anything of the ancients.

It is interesting to note that in the Delian records lime-wood is used for architectural mouldings.[116]

The continuing demand for small figures in architectural decorations in wood provided a good livelihood for skilled craftsmen who might be called wood-carvers rather than sculptors. Louis Robert has recently published the funerary inscription of one of them, found in Nicomedia.[117] The inscription is accompanied by outlines of the main tools of his trade, a mallet and a chisel, and the inclusion of a cross proclaims that he was a Christian, probably of the third century.

In passing from the Greek to the Roman world we have no Pausanias to guide us and the evidence, mainly from Pliny, is more fitful. When Virgil's Aeneas visits the Laurentine Picus he sees a long line of the king's ancestors carved in cedar.[118] This is not sound evidence that cedar was imported to Italy in the Bronze Age or later; it is part of Virgil's legacy from Greek writers who knew that cedar was one of the woods used by Greek sculptors in the archaic period. In Italy terracotta was a much more serious competitor than in Greece. The Etruscans were well known for their cult statues in terracotta and the famous Apollo from Veii, now in the Villa Giulia museum in Rome, is a good example of their monumental work. When Rome came into the Etruscan cultural sphere she was naturally influenced by Etruscan practice and when the great temple of Jupiter, Juno, and Minerva was built on the Capitoline hill overlooking the Forum an Etruscan sculptor was employed and he worked in terracotta; but in the seventh century, before Etruscan influence became strong, wood was probably used for most cult images.

The poet Tibullus, following the Augustan fashion of recalling nostalgically the age of innocence, harks back to the time 'when temples were small and their cult images were of wood';[119] and wood remained a common material for public sculpture far longer than in Greece. Pliny is surprised to find in his reading that it did not begin to become obsolete until the Roman conquest of Asia by the defeat of Antiochus in 189 BC when large numbers of Greek craftsmen were brought to Rome.[120] Livy records the dedication of two statues in cypress-wood in the temple of Juno as late as 207 BC,[121] and in 193 BC a cypress-wood statue of the obscure goddess Veiovis was set up on the Capitoline hill; it was still standing there in Pliny's lifetime more than 250 years later, another tribute to the durability of cypress.[122]

In the second century BC the influx of Greek craftsmen and Greek influence hastened the abandonment of wood and terracotta in favour of limestone, tufa, or marble. There is, however, one strange anomaly in the last phase of the Republic. Pliny records that in a temple in Rome there was a cedar-wood statue of Apollo, known as Apollo Sosianus, which had been brought from Seleucia (in Syria).[123] The name comes from C. Sosius who had presumably acquired the statue during his military command in the east under Mark Antony (38–34 BC). It might have had a long history before it came to Seleucia (founded *c*.290 BC) but a Hellenistic date would not be inappropriate. Theocritus (early third century BC) wrote a neat poem about Nicias, a rich Milesian who had a statue of Asklepios made of 'fragrant cedarwood'.[124] It is reasonable to infer that the use of wood for public statues had a longer life in the Greek east than in Greece itself. This is also implied by a statement in Philostratus' *Lives of the sophists*, when in recounting the benefactions of Herodes Atticus, he emphasises that for the roofing of his Odeum at Athens he used cedar 'which is expensive even for sculpture'.[125]

In this brief survey we have concentrated on the mainstreams of Greek and Roman sculpture. If we could look at the countryside and the small towns we should see a much wider use of wood. The younger Pliny had built a shrine for Ceres, goddess of the crops, on his Tuscan estate for the local country people and was anxious to improve it and provide a portico where on days of festival people could take refuge from rain or a too strong sun. He writes to a friend in Rome and asks him to buy four columns

to provide a more dignified frame for the cult figure and says
that he will either have to buy a new statue of Ceres or have one
made, because the old figure which was made of wood is so old
that it has lost some of its parts.[126] Similarly, much earlier when
Xenophon retired to an estate near Olympia he built a little
temple of Artemis and in it placed an Artemis of cypress-
wood.[127] There must have been many such wooden statues in
the Greek and Roman world in small country temples and
wayside shrines. Goddesses of springs particularly attracted
dedications in wood.

In 1963 some 300 wooden figures were uncovered by the
spring at the source of the river Seine which was dedicated to the
goddess Sequana.[128] They had been set up in the open, round
the spring, in the first century AD and had been completely
sealed from the atmosphere by a layer of alluvial soil. Most of the
figures probably represented donors, most of them male. There
were standing figures clothed and nude, heads, and busts, but
there were also arms and legs and other individual limbs, and
one elaborate schematic representation of stomach, heart, and
liver. The dedications were made by men and women invoking
the help of the goddess in maintaining or restoring health, or
paying tribute for health regained. A few of the heads can
compare with contemporary Romano–Gallic sculpture, but the
majority are roughly executed, rustic rather than Celtic,
accepting the restrictions imposed by the shape and size of the
branch from which they were cut, with the features roughly
incised and the main emphasis on the nose. A few wooden
figures in this style had been found in France during the nineteenth century, but had attracted little attention until the Seine
deposit was found. Interest increased when a second deposit of
dedications in wood was found on the site of a mineral spring just
outside Clermont-Ferrand.[129] The number of dedications in this
second deposit was even larger, and the quality of the figures
rather better. The forms of the dedications corresponded closely
with those of the Seine figures, but in addition many of them
took the form of painted wooden plaques, though only the most
meagre traces of paint have survived.

Silvanus, god of the countryside, was also a familiar figure in
the countryside and his images were usually small homely
figures. Those that have been found are of stone or terracotta,

but the majority will probably have been of wood. The only wooden Silvanus that has been found was probably not typical. It came from the harbour at Geneva, was roughly life-size, and seems to have been a well-carved public statue.[130] The most widespread figures in wood, however, were the figures of Priapus, a crude misshapen figure concentrating attention on the phallus, whose function was to protect the garden against trespassers, human and animal. Priapus could not expect fine sculpture. 'Seek not a sculpture wrought by Daedalus, or Polyclitus, or by Phradmon or by Ageladas: let the rough-hewn trunk of an ancient tree be the divine power of Priapus which you honour.'[131] The carving was often very crude: 'a recently carved *xoanon*, with the bark still on, without legs and without ears, but a procreative phallus well capable of doing what the Cyprian goddess wants to be done'.[132] Normally no special attention would be paid to the choice of woods: 'I was till recently useless fig-wood and the craftsman did not know whether to make me a box or a god. So here I am, a god.'[133] So Horace. In the Vergilian Appendix there are rustic figures in poplar and oak.[134] The Priapus figures which Martial celebrates are different; they pride themselves on being made of cypress, 'which has no fear for the passage of a hundred centuries, nor for the wasting sickness of a long-drawn-out old age'.[135]

12

THE TIMBER TRADE

This chapter is concerned with the various processes by which the tree passes into use as timber by acquisition, felling, extraction, transport, conversion, marketing; but there will remain many more questions than answers, for the evidence is miserably exiguous. Of all the major industries the timber industry has been one of the most silent and least recorded. In England there is no lack of books about English woodlands and trees and about the practice and principles of forestry. Good use has been made of timber contracts in the study of medieval and Tudor building, but there has been no serious study of the timber trade, and in most other countries there is a similar gap. It is not surprising, therefore, that so little survives in Greek and Roman writing about the production and marketing of timber as distinct from discussion of the properties of the various woods. There are, however, scattered wisps of evidence and the questions can at least be formulated.

Our first problem concerns the acquisition of timber. There is no difficulty in the case of private estates. The owner is free to sell his trees when and to whom he likes. It is for him to choose whether he will sell the trees standing or already felled and to ensure that the buyer keeps to the terms of the contract. But not all woodlands were privately owned. We have already seen that in Macedon the king controlled the sale of timber. It was King Amyntas who gave authority to the cities of the Chalcidic League to obtain building-timber and ship-timber from Macedonian forests and it was through friendship with Macedonian kings that Athenian politicians and generals were able to acquire timber from Macedon. Similiarly Solomon had to make his bargain with Hiram King of Tyre to procure the cedars and other timber which he needed for his temple and his palace, and Wen Amon, commissioned to get wood for the sacred barge of Amon, pleads his case with the prince of Byblos. A thousand

years later, when Phoenicia had become part of a Roman
province, we find agents of the Roman emperor Hadrian in AD
134 setting up markers over a wide area of the Lebanon range
declaring that all the trees of four species were the property of
the emperor.

In the Greek and Roman republics, and especially in Italy,
the king's place was taken by the state. In her conquest of Italy
Rome had been careful in dictating terms to defeated rivals to
build up a substantial reserve of forest. When the Bruttians, the
southernmost Italian tribe, submitted to Rome, we are told that
they surrendered half their mountain territory.[1] This included
the great Sila forest centred on Cosenza which combined
splendid forests and excellent high pastures. Similar action was
taken by Rome at the end of the long series of wars against the
Samnites in the early second century BC. Varro in his treatise on
agriculture records that the sheep which in the winter pastured
on the plain of Apulia, in the summer were driven up to the
mountains of Samnium and that all sheep had to be registered,
with a penalty for the unregistered.[2] This indicates that the
summer pastures of Samnium were the property of the Roman
people and with them the tracts (*calles*) that led from the plain
into the mountains. Roman landowners had by now realised the
profitability of raising cattle and sheep and this required both
summer and winter pastures. The benefits to the big landowners
is clear and the state could expect a useful annual revenue from
the grazing tax, *scriptura*. Livy's narrative of the early second
century includes references to fines paid by ranchers, presumably for grazing unregistered beasts.[3] One may wonder how
scrupulously this tax was levied later on. In most mountain
systems in Italy forests alternated with open fields, *saltus
silvaeque*. From forests Rome could also expect a steady revenue
from timber and other forest products, particularly charcoal
and pitch. Dionysius of Halicarnassus in his description of the
Sila forest emphasises the importance of the pitch from the pines
'which brought in an annual revenue to the people of Rome'.[4]
In Cicero's *Brutus* we find a company of public contractors, who
had bought a lease from the state, tapping the pines of the Sila
for pitch.[5]

There were also public forests much nearer Rome. Cicero,
allowing himself a liberal measure of rhetorical licence,

describes how Publius Clodius, the notorious tribune of 58 BC, had led down from the Apennines a rabble of foreign slaves working on the land and with them plundered public forests and ravaged Etruria.[6] We have also seen how Scipio cut down firs from public forests, almost certainly in Etruria or Umbria, to build a fleet to take his army to Africa against Carthage (p. 143). It is impossible to draw up a complete list of the public forests of Rome, but the examples given are sufficient to show that by the end of the second century BC Rome had accumulated a very substantial reserve of mountain forests, and it was in the mountains that the best timber for shipwrights and builders were to be found.

The importance attached to the forest reserve by the people is well illustrated by Cicero in his attacks on a bill introduced at the beginning of his consulship in 63 BC by the tribune Servilius Rullus. The professed intention of the bill was to distribute land to the proletariat, and since there was now very little public land suitable for agriculture left, it was essential to buy private land in the open market. To provide the capital needed the bill included a provision for the sale of certain specified public properties. Cicero, not without reason, sensed that there were more powerful political figures behind the tribune and used the formidable force of his rhetoric to convince the common people that a bill which purported to benefit them was in fact primarily designed to give dangerous power to unscrupulous politicians who would threaten the stability of the state. In his first speech, in the senate, he briefly summarised the main sections of the bill, but when he came to the proposal to sell public properties in order to finance the purchase of land he sharpened his attack:

What they need now is ready money, money that cannot be questioned, money that can be counted. I wonder what this watchful and shrewd tribune has in mind? 'The Scantian forest is to be sold', he says. Did you discover the forest in the list of abandoned landholdings, or in the register of pastures controlled by the censors? . . . Would you dare to sell the Scantian forest in my consulship? Would you dare to touch any form of public revenue? Would you rob the Roman people of what gives them strength in war, and in peace a more easy life?[7]

In a later speech, this time to the people, when his attitude has been attacked, Cicero gives the same emphasis to the Scantian forest. He is defending himself against the charge that he is the mouthpiece of the big landowners: 'Now that I have shown you why and in whose interest he has introduced this bill, let him tell us what landowner I am defending when I oppose the agrarian bill.' 'You sell the Scantian forest. It belongs to the Roman people: I oppose.'[8] We know nothing of the *silva Scantia*, neither where it was, nor whether it was large or small, on mountain or plain. If on his return home his brother had suggested that in attaching so much importance to a single forest Cicero was being slightly hysterical, he would have probably agreed. But if Cicero, who was a master at judging the reaction of a mass meeting, laid so much emphasis on a public forest, it is reasonable to infer that the Romans regarded a substantial forest reserve as important.

Forests, however, could be a liability as well as an asset, especially in times of political instability, as we can see from a strange resolution passed by the senate in 60 BC. It was known at the time that Caesar, who had enjoyed a militarily successful year as governor of Spain, was certain to be elected consul for 59 and most of the senate regarded his ambition as dangerous. Their opportunity to prevent him from having an important military command after his consulship came when the consular provinces had to be selected by the senate before the elections were held. They assigned the forests and public tracts, *silvae callesque*.[9] For this strange decision Suetonius the biographer is our only source, but there is no reason to suspect an invention or mistake. In searching for an explanation of such an unprecedented assignment most historians seem to have overlooked the simplest solution. Although the choice may have been politically motivated to check Caesar's ambition, it cannot have seemed at the time completely irrelevant.

In 63 Rome had been seriously shaken by a dangerous conspiracy led by Catiline, a popular noble with a dubious political record, who was advocating revolutionary policies and attracting a considerable body of support. Cicero, who was consul for the year, by clever tactics forced Catiline to battle before he was ready. Catiline was defeated and killed, and his leading followers in Rome were arrested and, after a dramatic debate in the senate, executed. But behind a poorly-planned revolt there was serious social unrest, and the atmosphere remained tense. In such a situation it was not difficult to believe that a slave revolt might be stirred up. Caesar had opposed the death penalty for the conspirators and was strongly suspected of being sympathetic with Catiline's aims. By making him responsible for areas where there were likely to be political refugees who might attempt to enrol slaves, his opponents were putting Caesar in an invidious position.[10]

It is true that Catiline refused to accept the help of slaves in his revolt, since he realised that their aims would be incompatible with his, and to recruit slaves who had run away from their masters would be political suicide. But Sallust, our main authority for the revolt, says that a large number of slaves had approached him as soon as they heard of the conspiracy.[11] These slaves could not have returned to their masters; the only practical alternative was to take refuge in the forest. But though a case could have been made for mopping-up operations in the forests of central Italy, this did not call for men of consular rank. Even Caesar's enemies cannot have been very surprised when a tribune secured a five-year command in Gaul for Caesar.

In maintaining a large reserve of state forests the Romans were also perhaps thinking of the needs of the city of Rome. It was this motive that led colonies and municipalities to have their own public woodlands to provide timber for public buildings and fuel for the public baths.[12] In the charter of the Caesarian colony of Urso in the south of Spain it is specified that the public woods may not be sold or leased for more than five years.[13] This implies the leasing of timber-felling in a wood over a given period, in the same way as the collection of pitch in the Sila forest was leased out to a company of public contractors. It seems that public woods were never operated directly with labour employed by the state and that the same principles were accepted as for public buildings or the collection of taxes.

One would like to know what form such contracts took and how they were controlled. When, for example, the Roman censors placed a contract for the building of a temple and timber for the roof was to be taken from a public forest, how far was the timber merchant allowed to take what he wanted? It is difficult to see how the system could have worked satisfactorily without public employees being responsible for ensuring that the timber merchant did not cut immature trees or more than was specified, and that he cleaned up the area of felling before he left.

This supervision may have been the function of men who are in Latin called *saltuarii*, the *saltus* being an area of woodland and pasture. We find them, for instance, on a large wooded estate on the west coast of Italy south of the Tiber in which the emperor Claudius kept elephants, presumably as a reserve for the arena and for special imperial occasions, as when he himself joined the legions that had invaded Britain. It would have been appropriate for *saltuarii* to keep an eye on felling operations. The number of *saltuarii* looking after this estate was sufficient in number to have a steward (*vilicus*) in charge of them.[14] Legal enactments collected in the Digest throw a little light on the *saltuarius*. His function is 'to look after the crops and keep an eye on the boundaries'. 'An estate that has woodlands and herds of sheep will have shepherds and *saltuarii*.' When an estate is left in a will together with what had been bought or made to cultivate the estate, including the slaves, the *topiarius* and the *saltuarius* are not included, for the function of the *topiarius* is decoration, and the function of the *saltuarius* is the care and protection of the property rather than its cultivation.[15]

To return to our timber merchant. The technique of felling timber changed very little during the long period we are considering. The axe remained the indispensable tool from the Stone Age until the introduction of power-saws in the twentieth century. It was hard to get a really sharp edge to a stone axe-head, but in the Stone Age there was no need to cut large trees. The timbers required to frame huts were very modest in size, and fuel, tool-handles, and simple furniture could come from trees of very modest girth. The introduction of copper made it easier to produce a sharp edge, but copper was too soft to be more effective than stone. The discovery, however, that by mixing copper with a small proportion of tin a metal could be produced which was much stronger but easy to work encouraged men to tackle the much larger trees whose timber was required for palaces and temples. Bronze in turn gave way to iron, which was stronger though much more difficult to produce.

The standard axe of the Minoans was two-headed. Whatever the origin of the type it was an important religious symbol in Minoan society, often associated with the horns of consecration:

but it is also found with working tools and there is no doubt that it was used in the forest; axes with single heads are very rare indeed. There are some advantages in the type. Two blades would have lasted longer than one before needing to be sharpened and the axe may have been better balanced for the swing, but it was more cumbersome and though it was adopted also by the Mycenaeans, it was abandoned by most woodsmen in favour of the single-headed axe in the archaic period. It had a longer life in Greek and Latin poetry, but that was assured by its place in Homer: it was only rarely used by the Romans. The two heads of Minoan axes were of solid cast bronze and usually had a spreading profile above and below the rounded head. Between the two heads was a socket into which the wooden shaft fitted. This socket was at first round, but it was later realised that there was much less likelihood of the head flying off when the socket was given an oval shape. The importance of a tight-fitting shaft was appreciated by Homer: the great bronze axe which Calypso gave to Odysseus had a fine shaft of olive-wood, *well-fitted to the axe*. Felling was not always a straightforward operation. Sometimes it was necessary to guide the fall of the tree; that is why ropes are attached to the falling tree in Seti I's relief at Karnak showing princes of Lebanon felling trees for the Egyptians (pl. 2). In Roman times the Latin poet Ovid writes of 'the tree which, loosened at last by the countless blows of the axe, and drawn down by ropes, crashes to the ground'.[16]

Considerable importance was attached to felling at the proper season, and on the main points there was general agreement. For most purposes trees should be cut when the year's growth has ended, in autumn, and the oak, which sheds its leaves last, should be felled last. But if a tree is to be barked, as for instance when it is to provide a column, then it should be felled when it is coming into leaf because then the bark is most easily stripped.[17] Theophrastus adds a general view that the felling should be done when the moon has set, because the wood is harder then and less likely to rot, but he introduces the point in an unusual way. When he is reporting what others say he usually introduces the point with such phrases as 'the Macedonians (or Arcadians) say', but here he uses a stronger word, 'they demand or insist (*keleuousi*)'.[18] He does not seem to accept the association as a fact of nature, but knows that it is strongly held. Pliny has no such qualms. 'It is of supreme importance to take account of the moon, and people prefer to confine felling to the time between the tenth and thirtieth days of the month; but it is agreed by all that the best time for felling is when the moon is in conjunction with the sun.' Certainly this was the time specified by Tiberius Caesar for felling larches in Raetia for the restoration of the bridge over the Naumachia. 'Some say that the moon should be in conjunction and below the horizon, which is only possible at night.'[19] Such superstitions do not appeal to modern timber merchants or foresters, but they can be paralleled among peasants of all ages, and not only among peasants. Cato, who was accepted as an authority on farming principles and practices long after his death, said that 'timber must not be touched except at new moon or at the end of the second quarter'.[20]

When the tree had been felled it was stripped of its branches with the axe. If long lengths were required the tree-trunk was taken to the timber-yard without cutting, but if the timber merchant was not concerned with special orders and was catering primarily for ordinary housing requirements, the trunk would probably have been cross-cut to make transport easier. For extraction the ancient world relied primarily on oxen and mules. When the prince of Byblos finally consented to give timber to Wen Amon for the sacred barge of Amon at Thebes he sent three hundred men to cut the timber and three hundred cattle to bring it down to the coast (p. 68). When Dionysius of Syracuse (c.400 BC) planned the building of a large fleet 'he collected yokes of oxen to bring the timber down to the coast'.[21] Homer compares Menelaus and Meriones, struggling to drag the dead Patroclus from the battle, to 'mules that throw their great strength into the draught and drag out of the mountain down a rugged track a beam or massive ship-timber, and their hearts are worn within them as they strive with toil and sweat'.[22] Quintus of Smyrna, retelling in epic form the story of the Trojan horse in terms that would not be inappropriate in the fourth century AD when he lived, makes mules and men vie in their toil when they bring down the firs from Mt. Ida.[23]

The same system was still being used in the nineteenth century by the monks of Camaldoli near Arezzo, whose monastery was in large part maintained by the sale of timber, mainly fir, from their well-managed forest. The timber was dragged by oxen to Pioppi on a tributary of the river Arno and there bound into rafts which went down the Arno to Florence and beyond. Payment for the timber was made by the *traino*, the amount that an ox could drag.[24] What may have been a common feature was first observed when a royal burial mound was excavated at Gordium, the Phrygian capital. In this burial the tomb chamber was protected from the very large mound of rubble and clay by an outer casing of round juniper logs averaging about twenty-five feet in length. On some of them it is noted by P. Kuniholm that a notch had been cut at one end with a hole in the middle. Into this hole fitted a peg which was fixed in an axle joining two wheels. The notch kept the log from moving from side to side. In this form the log trailed along the ground, but by adding a second pair of wheels the log could be carried above ground.[25]

Special difficulties must have been met in the extraction of the huge trees needed for the imperial basilicas and for masts for the largest ships. When finally a tree sufficiently tall to provide a mast for Hiero's giant merchantman was found an engineer was required to supervise the transport. The difficulties were similar, though on a smaller scale, to those faced by the woodsmen of Maine and New Hampshire on taking out tall white pines. In the seventeenth and eighteenth centuries the British navy depended on overseas supplies for the masts that she needed for her large gun-ships. The country was well stocked with excellent oak for the main timbers, but English woodland could not produce the tall masts at least 100 feet high that were needed. It was a wonderful stroke of good fortune when Lord Weymouth found that the white pines of the eastern seaboard of America (*Pinus strobus*, often called the Weymouth pine, from the man who discovered it) were exactly what was wanted. These giant trees often grew up to 150 feet, sometimes even to 200 feet, and they were strong, straight, and flexible without a pronounced taper. They were not easily moved. In 1687 Judge Sewell of Boston wrote in his diary: 'Rode out into a swamp to see a mast drawn out of about 26 or 28 inches (diameter), about 30 oxen before and about 4 yokes by the side of the mast between the fore and hinderwheel—a noble sight.'[26] The giant larch that was among the larch logs brought to Rome to restore a bridge over the Naumachia had a diameter nearly as large (24 in., p. 249).

While the Romans, like the Americans, relied mainly on oxen to extract the large trunks from the forest, they probably made more use of human labour than the Americans. On a relief in Gaul from a monument set up by *dendrophori* (literally wood-carriers) four men carry a tree-trunk with the help of a rope from the forest.[27] In the late Empire Ammianus Marcellinus, describing the emperor Julian's efforts to restore the buildings on the Rhine frontier destroyed by the Alemanni, reports that auxiliary troops responded loyally, bringing in fifty-foot timbers on their shoulders. If this seems wild exaggeration a photograph of modern Egyptians moving a sixty-foot board from the sacred boat that was discovered by the pyramid of Cheops will show how it was done.[28]

That manhandling was more common than might be thought is also suggested by an attractive story from the life of St. Columbanus. Coming to Bobbio in the early seventh century, he found St. Peter's basilica in a sorry state and roused the people to restore their church. The fir trees were cut in a nearby forest where the terrain was rocky and precipitous. It was impossible to take them down by cart and there was one timber so enormous that 'thirty or forty men could scarcely carry it on level ground'.[29] That was no problem for the saint. With two or three men to help him he carried it down the steep and difficult mountain path, and all the monks cheerfully followed his example.

There was an alternative to taking the trunk to the timber-yard. Dionysius of Halicarnassus, in his description of the Sila forest in south Italy, says that trees that are felled near sea or river are taken without being further cut to the nearest harbour.[30] Those that are far from sea or river are converted where they are felled into oars, poles, and various household needs. The emphasis on transport by water is sound: transport by land was much more expensive and much slower.[31] Strabo, as we have seen (p. 243), realised the point very clearly; it was the river system of the Tiber basin, as well as the abundance of quarries and forests, that made it possible to supply Rome with the vast quantities of stone and timber needed to sustain so large a population. In England Queen Elizabeth in 1559 imposed a ban on the cutting of oak, beech, and ash trees of timber size —one foot square at the base—to make charcoal for the iron industry, *if the trees were within fourteen miles of a navigable river.* The importance of water transport is no less clearly reflected in an order issued in 1711, the ninth year of the reign of Queen Anne, when the British were concerned at the depletion of the stock of good pines in New England, on which the navy largely relied for masts:

> Whereas there are great numbers of white or other sort of Pine-trees, fit for masts, growing in Her Majestie's Colonies of New Hampshire ... New Jersey, fit for the Masting of Her Majestie's Royal Navy: And whereas the same *growing near the sea, and on Navigable Rivers,* may commodiously be brought into the Kingdom for the Service aforesaid ... (of all pines) of the growth of Twenty four inches diameter upwards cut twelve inches from the Earth ... none are to be cut without Her Majestie's license.[32]

The superiority of water transport is particularly well illustrated by a letter to the Roman emperor Trajan from the younger Pliny, who had been sent out on a special mission to Bithynia by the emperor to correct abuses in the administration of the province and to restore its economic health. Pliny is trying to arouse the emperor's interest and help in a project which could be of great economic benefit to the district of Nicomedia. 'In this territory there is a very large lake. Over this lake marble, fruit, logs, and timbers are carried in boats to the road (leading to the coast). This costs little in money and labour, but it costs a great deal both in labour and money to take these cargoes from the lake to the sea.'[33] Pliny advocates the cutting of a canal from the lake to the sea. He admits that the project would require a lot of labour, but there is no shortage in the district and the project would bring such benefits that all would be happy to join in the work. It would be necessary, however, to ensure that the lake was deep enough not to be drained if the canal was built: he asks the emperor, if he approves the plan, to send a surveyor or architect. Trajan's answer is strikingly different from his standard reply to Pliny's letters, which is little more than a formal acknowledgement.

> This lake of yours is certainly interesting. We would like to link it with the sea, but the project must be investigated thoroughly to ensure that the lake, if linked with the sea, would not be emptied. It is essential to find out the source and volume of the water it receives. You can ask for a surveyor from Calpurnius Macer (governor of the neighbouring

province of Moesia) and I will send you someone from here with experience in this kind of work.[34]

The emperor's enthusiasm, however, did not last. In a second letter Pliny, who is clearly disappointed that Trajan's man has not arrived, suggests various alternative schemes. This time Trajan merely tells Pliny that he is capable of making the right decision himself. 'I think that Calpurnius Macer will provide you with a surveyor, and these provinces of yours have their own surveyors.'[35] It was Pliny's and the province's misfortune that Trajan was becoming too preoccupied with his projected campaign against Parthia.

In water transport rivers were as important as the sea. It is very doubtful if any timber from Pindus Mountains and many other forested regions of Macedon would have gone overseas without the Haliacmon and Axius rivers to carry it to the Aegean and the Achelous to the western coast. It would have been vastly more difficult to exploit the forests of the Apennines for Rome if there had been no Tiber with its tributaries; and it was fortunate that for a large part of their long journey the cedars and other timbers bound for Babylon from Mts. Lebanon and Amanus could be carried down the Euphrates. But not all navigable rivers were navigable throughout the year. The Tiber flowed through the younger Pliny's Tuscan estate and he sent his marketable produce to Rome by river, but only in winter and spring; in summer the upper river-bed was virtually dry.[36] Even in winter it had to flow a long way from its source near Arezzo before it was freely navigable. Pliny says that at first it was a very meagre stream. Like its tributaries the Clanis and the Tinia, its water had to be held back for nine days when rain came, before it was released, and even then it was only negotiable by beams (floated) rather than by rafts.[37] Even in winter it is doubtful whether timber rafts could have begun their journey far from Città di Castello.

The simplest method of sending timber down rivers was to float it. Nebuchadnezzar describes his cedars as floating downstream like reeds,[38] and Vitruvius implies that floating was normal practice on the river Po, when he says that larch was too heavy to float and so had to be carried either in boats or on rafts made of firs.[39] Floating could be effective on wide rivers with a strong current, but in rivers of modest width and winding course logs could easily be stranded. Rafting was common practice on the Tiber in comparatively modern times and though there is no firm evidence it can be assumed that Roman precedent was being followed. When Pliny in his *Natural History* says that the normal price for a raft of timber was 40,000 sesterces, he is probably quoting the standard rate for the Tiber and this implies that there was a standard quantity of timber in the raft.[40] Even on rivers which were suited to floating, rafting was sometimes preferred. Nebuchadnezzar floated his cedars on the Euphrates, but Gudea ruler of Lagash (*c.*2000 BC) made the great timbers that he took from Mt. Amanus into rafts.[41] For most rivers there is no positive evidence, but Roman inscriptions record *ratiarii*, raftsmen, on the upper Rhône and the Isère,[42] and a funerary inscription has been recently published of a rafter (*schedionautes*) from Nicomedia, who will have worked on the river Sangarius, or along the coast of the sea of Marmara.[43]

Rafts could also be used at sea. When Hiram of Tyre undertook to provide the Lebanon timber that Solomon required for his temple and palace in Jerusalem, he said that he would send it in the form of rafts to the place appointed by Solomon, where the rafts would be dismantled.[44] This, however, was a short coastal journey: in high seas rafts were very vulnerable. In the early days of Canadian logging a large timber raft towed by a steamship ran into a fierce storm off San Francisco and came adrift; in the following year it had found its independent way to Japan!

The Romans had learnt their lesson early in their history. Theophrastus records the story to illustrate the exceptional size and quality of the trees in the island of Corsica:

> The Romans once sailed to Corsica with twenty-five ships intending to plant a settlement on the island, and the trees were so enormous that it was difficult to sail into bays and harbours without breaking their masts. The whole island, it was said, was thickly wooded and wild; so they abandoned the idea of a settlement, but some of them landed and cut a great number of trees from a small area, which made a raft so large that it had to use fifty sails. The raft, however, broke up in the open sea.[45]

This is a strange story, so strange indeed that it cannot be rejected as fiction; but while it has been generally agreed that it must be based on fact, however distorted, no satisfactory explanation has yet been found. The view of ancient historians that the idea of a Roman colony outside Italy before the time of Theophrastus is unthinkable has led to the suggestion that the Roman expedition was not intended to settle on the island but to bring back ship-timber. This, however, is even less credible. As Thiel has pointed out, the indefinite mark of time in Theophrastus implies a date substantially earlier than the time when he was writing (c.300 BC).[46] It is true that while Etruria was hostile Rome may not have had access to the Etruscan forests which were so important to her later and Corsican firs and pines certainly provided excellent ship-timbers; but the Romans took no steps to establish a fleet before 311 BC and in an emergency they could have obtained adequate supplies from the firs and pines of Latium, which were praised by Theophrastus.[47] Perhaps an abortive attempt to plant a colony on Corsica is not quite unacceptable. If Meiggs is right in advocating a date in the middle of the fourth century for the establishment of a colony at Ostia, a settlement on Corsica which would embarrass the Etruscans is at least thinkable.[48] Even if the motive of the expedition remains unsolved, we should accept the central point of the story that an attempt to bring big timbers from Corsica in raft form failed.

Dionysius, tyrant of Syracuse (c.400 BC), made no such mistake when he needed timber from south Italy for his ambitious shipbuilding programme. The timber, when brought down from the forest to the shore, was made into rafts and oar-powered boats were sent to tow the rafts swiftly to Syracuse.[49] This again was a comparatively short coastal journey. It is very doubtful whether evidence will be found of rafting for long journeys in the open sea. Once merchantmen had been developed by the fifth century BC to carry heavy cargoes, they will have been quicker and more economical than towed rafts, and by the end of the second century AD at the latest there were ships which specialised in carrying timber, just as there were specially constructed boats for cargoes of marble, which was particularly heavy. Our earliest evidence for timber-carriers comes from the great colonnade behind the theatre at Ostia, where shippers and merchants had small offices to advertise their business. One of these offices was occupied by the timber-shippers, *navicularii lignarii*, and they advertised their business by a mosaic design of the Ostian lighthouse between two merchantmen.[50] There is nothing in the design of these ships to differentiate them from other merchantmen illustrated in the colonnade; the difference probably lay in the organisation of storage capacity. The mosaic dates roughly from near the end of the second century AD, but the lack of earlier evidence is not significant; they are rarely mentioned in the sources and even about the special marble-carriers we find nothing except a single reference in Pliny.

The manifest advantages of water transport have led, not unnaturally, to an exaggerated depreciation of transport by land. In some areas there is no dispute about its use. It is abundantly clear in the sources that asses and mules were widely used as pack-animals. We have seen an Athenian estate-owner keeping six asses to carry wood daily, probably firewood, to Athens (p. 206). No doubt they were often overloaded like the hero of Apuleius' *Metamorphoses*, transformed into an ass and sent to collect firewood on the mountain in the charge of a sadistic boy, who beat him unmercifully and loaded him as if he were an elephant.[51] But though asses were particularly suited to the firewood trade, they could also carry poles, stakes, planks, and boards provided that they were not too long. Varro refers to merchants with trains of asses carrying a mixed range of produce from the country districts to Brundisium.[52]

Mules cost more to buy and maintain, but they could carry a bigger load (300 lb. compared with 200 lb. by asses, according to Diocletian's price edict). They were even more sure-footed than asses in the mountains, and presumably earned a higher fee. In the accounts of the Eleusis commissioners there is an entry of payment to a muleteer for carrying ropes to the sanctuary from the Piraeus,[53] and a passage in Strabo shows that a wood-carrying mule could be profitable. Hybreas of Mylasa in Caria inherited a mule with muleteer from his father. The profit over a short period enabled him to travel to Antioch to sit at the feet of one of the most distinguished teachers of the day and to end his life as the first man in his native Mylasa.[54] The wood that Hybreas' mule carried was more probably building-timber of average lengths than firewood.

It is when we come to heavier loads and larger quantities that the difficulties begin. A. Burford has done a useful service in challenging the view that long-distance travel for heavy goods by road was virtually ruled out in Antiquity.[55] This may have been true in the early days, but we must expect developments in transport on land as well as on sea. It is clear that by the time that the Athenians rebuilt their Acropolis in the fifth century BC they had mastered the business of transporting very heavy blocks of Pentelic marble from the quarry to the building-site, and marble is considerably heavier than timber.

There is a good introduction to the organisation of such heavy transport in one of the annual accounts of the Eleusinian commissioners in the late fourth century BC. It was the year in which the column-drums for a new portico at Eleusis had to be brought from the marble-quarry on Mt. Pentelicus some twenty-five kilometres from Eleusis. These drums were massive and their weight, more than five tons each, required special arrangements. The lines of the account which detail the preparations are very fragmentary. They included repairs to vehicles, the assembling of large quantities of rope, the strengthening of the road, and the buying of troughs from which the oxen could drink. Then follow the accounts for each drum, giving the number of yokes of oxen used, the name of the man who provided them, the time the journey took, in days and half-days, and the sums paid. The most striking feature of the record is the number of yokes of oxen required: the lowest is nineteen, the highest thirty-seven, and the majority near thirty.[56]

We have no evidence for the form of the timber-cart used to transport the marble, but nothing more than a strongly reinforced timber platform on which the column-drum could be securely roped was needed. The weight of the marble, however, was considerably beyond the pulling power of a single yoke of oxen. Xenophon in the fourth century BC gives twenty-five talents for the carrying capacity of a yoke,[57] roughly 1,400 lb. In the fourth century AD the maximum load for heavy transport on the imperial highways was c. 1,050 lb. (1,500 Roman pounds).[58] If all yokes in a team could pull their maximum weight, each column-drum would have needed not more than ten yokes, but in multiple yoking there is a natural loss of efficiency and the greater the number, the greater the loss.[59]

The image of a single block of marble being pulled by a long line of thirty yokes of oxen is to most of us so unexpected that it is important to look for parallels. The best comes from a much later period: Procopius is describing the building of the church of the Virgin Mary in Jerusalem by Justinian in the sixth century AD.[60] The site was difficult, because it was on top of a high hill and special measures had to be taken to bring up the large stones for the walls. Special wagons were built, to carry one block each, and they were each pulled by forty oxen. Some such multiple yoking is also implied by Diodorus in his account of the building of a temple to the Cretan mother goddess at Engyon in Sicily during the archaic period.[61]

These examples of multiple yoking all refer to stone. Timber is considerably lighter but a single fir, for example, of 100 feet might weigh more than three tons and would certainly be far beyond the pulling power of a single yoke.[62] In the ancient sources I can find no evidence of multiple yoking for timber, but we can turn for illustration to the medieval world. In the twelfth century the abbot Faritius needed timber for the rebuilding of his abbey at Abingdon near Oxford:

For all the buildings which the abbot made he caused beams and rafters to come from the district of Wales with great cost and heavy labour. For he had six wains for this purpose, and twelve oxen to each of them. Six or seven weeks was the journey, coming and going, for it was necessary to go as far as Shrewsbury (some 170 km. from Abingdon).[63]

What an abbot could do in the twelfth century a Roman emperor could certainly do in the first or second century AD. Forests that were far from rivers or sea and might seem inaccessible could be exploited if special timber was required. The vast wealth directly controlled by the Roman emperors enabled them to ignore considerations of economy. It did not make economic sense for the emperor Tiberius to order larch from the eastern Alps to restore the bridge over the Naumachia at Rome (p. 248). The history of the marble-quarry near Synnada in Phrygia is a further striking example, as Strabo clearly realised. 'During the Republic', he says, 'only small blocks of marble were quarried, but the present prosperity of the Romans is such that great monolithic columns, with their variegated alabaster-like colours, are taken out of the quarry. And so, in spite of the long carriage of such heavy loads to the sea, columns and blocks of marble are taken to Rome.'[64] The journey to the sea was more than 300 kilometres. For the short

distance from the quarry at Docimium to Synnada there was a
good road, but the next stage of the journey was through difficult country and no river was available. In view of the emphasis
on the expensiveness of land transport, it is widely assumed that
the marble must have travelled as far as possible by river. The
most common view is that the marble was taken by road to
Apamea, an important junction between the interior and the
coast, and from there to the Maeander valley, to complete its
journey by river to Miletus. As an alternative it has been
suggested that the river was the Sangarius, flowing into the
Black Sea, but the Sangarius river implied a very much longer
route to Rome, and the fast current and winding course of the
river is poorly suited for such a cargo. How suitable the
Maeander was is uncertain, but the river was certainly subject
to flooding and it was already silting up badly towards the
mouth. It seems more probable, as Louis Robert suggests, that
the journey was completed by land, possibly to Ephesus.[65]

Strabo had good reason to be impressed by this feat of transport, but it was a very exceptional case. Marble was virtually an
imperial monopoly and emperors who wanted to leave their
mark on Rome would not be deterred by expense. The restrictions on land transport, however, should not be exaggerated.
Strabo explains that the current of the river Rhône was so strong
that it was difficult for merchantmen from Italy to make their
way upstream. As a result some cargoes were carried in covered
wagons to the territory of the Arverni and the river Loire.[66]
Although the river Rhône passed nearby, the land route of
rather more than 100 kilometres was easier. From Narbonne a
river could be used for the first part of a journey to the Garonne,
but there remained not much less than 100 kilometres to be
negotiated by land. Strabo noticed the same point at Aquileia.[67]
Traders carrying goods into the interior used covered wagons
before they reached rivers that would help them.

There is disappointingly little evidence about the wagons
used for the transport of timber. At Pompeii there seem to be
workers who specialise in the carriage of timber and they have
sufficient standing to support a candidate for public office at the
elections: 'The timber-carriers (*lignari plostrari*) support Marcellus for aedile.'[68] Their function presumably was to bring the
timber from the forest to the town, but the name of their wagon,

plaustrum, is no more distinctive than our 'wagon'. At Pompeii the main demand for timber would be for comparatively short lengths, but for the main beams supporting the roofs in the largest *atria* beams of some thirty feet were needed, and one may wonder whether they would have fitted into a standard wagon. The problem becomes much more acute when one considers the massive beams needed for the great Roman basilicas or the cargo of larch trunks ordered by the emperor Tiberius from the Rhaetian Alps. This is more a Roman than a Greek problem, but the biggest timbers of up to thirty-five feet used in the Parthenon had to be carried nine kilometres from the Piraeus to Athens.

The longest carriers recorded to my knowledge are those that were used in the grand procession of Ptolemy Philadelphus in Alexandria. These are called four-wheelers, *tetrakykloi*, and are used as floats carrying groups of statues or scenes from mythology or legend.[69] The greatest length was thirty-seven and a half feet (11.43 m.) and it would seem that the carrier had no sides and was merely a platform on wheels. The principle could be extended by increasing the number of wheels. It was some such carriers that were used in Corsica during the nineteenth century. Edward Lear, who visited the island, has given a vivid account of his experience. He waxed eloquent on the majesty of the pines, but was considerably less enthusiastic about the timber-carts 'loaded each with a single tree trunk 100 ft. or upwards in length and drawn by from 10 to 15 mules . . . from a distance like giant serpents or megalosauri winding down the mountain . . . although guided behind by two men with a sort of helm, dangerously unyielding if encountered unexpectedly at a sharp turn of the road, the mules going down hill being stopped with difficulty'.[70] Unfortunately Lear was so impressed by the pines that he had no time or inclination to sketch the timber-carts. We imagine a timber platform perhaps raised rather high, for the description calls to mind a passage in Juvenal's satire on life in the city in which he includes large timbers among the pedestrian's risks: 'The long fir shakes as the great cart comes along, and another wagon behind it carries a pine: the trees nod on their high platforms and are a threat to the people in the street.'[71] Different names are given to these timber-carriers; the pine is on a *plaustrum*, the normal word for a wagon; the fir is on

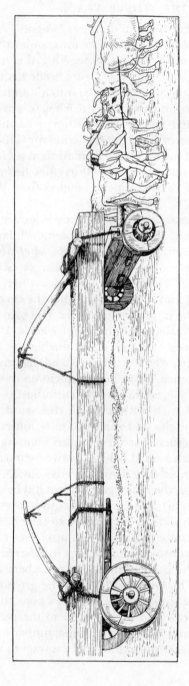

13 Eighteenth-century transport

There is, I think, no evidence that the Romans carried their longest timbers in this way, but it is a natural development from the system used at Gordium where the juniper logs forming the outer protection of the tomb chamber were fastened at one end to an axle, the other end being dragged along the ground (p. 333).

a *serracum*. The difference is not solely for the convenience of the metre; the fir is a considerably taller tree than the pine and *serracum* is a word that is very rarely found and nowhere described, but from the few examples that survive it is clearly a specially large carrier.[72]

The transport of giant firs to Rome from forests that may have been as much as fifty kilometres from the navigable course of the Tiber is an impressive achievement. Even more impressive is the transport of large timbers from the Amanus and Lebanon forests to the kingdoms of Mesopotamia. From Amanus the journey was considerably less difficult. The route from the forest to the Euphrates, though rough, was considerably shorter, and the Euphrates could carry the timber down to Babylon. Gudea claims to have taken cedar logs of sixty cubits and other timbers from Amanus and to have built them into rafts to be carried down by the river.[73] The Assyrians were less fortunate because there was no river to help them. Having crossed the Euphrates they had to go by land, but along the northern end of the Fertile Crescent there was no difficulty in finding water or food. The problems of the Lebanon were more complex, for east of Antilebanon was desert. But if the desert was to be avoided it was necessary to take the timber to a north Syrian port, a distance of more than 100 kilometres, and so to the Euphrates.

It seems certain that Nebuchadnezzar did not do this. In the record that he left in Wadi Brissa on the eastern slope of Lebanon near its northern end he says that he split rocks and made an extraction route for his cedars and made the Arahtu river (the name for the western branch of the middle Euphrates) carry them down to Marduk (the Babylonian god) like reeds.[74] This implies that he did not send the timber down the Orontes, as he might have done, to take the easier route to the Euphrates, but chose the shorter route available, which runs from the coast by the valley of the Al Kabir (Eleutherus) a little north of Tripolis and proceeds through the Homs gap to the Euphrates. The use of this route is also implied in a letter in the Mari archives from the Assyrian king Šamši Adad to his son Iasmah-Adad, whom he had made ruler of Mari.[75] A supply of cypress and other woods had been taken from Quatna to a point on the river near Mari. The timber will have been cut either on

Lebanon or on the coastal hills north of Al Kabir and will have come to the Euphrates by the desert route. At this point it is to be divided into three consignments and while two of the consignments, to Nineveh and Ekallâtum, are to go by land, the timber bound for Subat-Enlil is to go by river (the Habur) for the first stage of the journey.

The desert route seems to be the natural choice for timber cut on either side of the Bekaa valley, whether on the east slopes of Lebanon, on Antilebanon, or on Mt. Hermon. But the best cedar forests were almost certainly on the west slopes of Lebanon, which received considerably more rain. Here too the timber, when brought down to the coast, could have been taken by land to the north end of the Lebanon range and then along the land route to the Euphrates along the valley of the Al Kabir. There is interesting evidence that sometimes at least an alternative route was taken. A large-scale relief from the palace of Sargon II at Khorsabad, now in the Louvre, shows Phoenician vessels transporting timber. Some of the oar-powered ships are carrying large beams, either on deck or towed, while others, empty, are moving in the opposite direction, presumably to reload (pl. 3A). The probable explanation of the relief is that big timbers from the western slopes of Lebanon have been converted into beams in one of the Phoenician cities and are being carried to a Syrian port to take advantage of the shortest land route to the Euphrates.[76]

When timber had completed the journey from the forest to the timber-yard it may sometimes have been left in the round to dry out, but more often it was squared with the axe. In this form it could be sold for export or to local timber merchants, or it could be further processed. The conversion to beams, boards, and battens was normally the work of the saw. Small copper saws had been developed in Egypt and Mesopotamia before the Bronze Age, but it was the Minoans in Crete who were the first to produce saws that could cross-cut large tree-trunks and cut large beams and boards. In the central display-hall of the Heraklion museum it is difficult not to be dazzled by the spontaneity and taste of the pottery and the frescoes, but the large saws are no less impressive.[77] More than twenty of these saws have been found in the palaces and royal villas, and the biggest is five feet seven inches (1.67 m.) long and eight and a half inches (0.21 m.) wide.

The saws are made of bronze sheets hammered into shape, with the top edge usually smooth and straight and the lower cutting edge curving upwards at the end. The pyramidal teeth are regularly cut and average four or five to the inch, sometimes with closer spacing at the narrow end. One of the biggest saws, from the Royal Villa at Hagia Triada, which is five feet six inches long and five inches wide, tapers slightly at the end. There are holes at each end through which wooden handles were riveted. This was a saw for two men, which is probably why the teeth are uniformly spaced for the whole length of the cutting edge. Other large saws have only one handle and there is a more pronounced curve and taper in the blade with teeth closer together at the end.

These saws must often have become choked with sawdust, which was later countered by setting the teeth, as Theophrastus explains: 'Wood which is too green closes when sawn and the sawdust is trapped in the teeth and chokes them; that is why they set the teeth alternate ways to release the sawdust.'[78] It used to be thought that setting was a comparatively late discovery in the archaic period, or even in the classical period, but it has recently been observed that on at least one of these long Minoan saws, though certainly not on all, there is clear evidence of setting, not for the whole length of the saw but at widely spaced intervals, a system that it is not easy to understand.[79] Through most of the archaic period we can assume full setting. These large saws were used to cut panels of gypsum, a soft alabaster-like stone which was widely used, especially at Cnossus and Phaestus, for its decorative quality in pavements, dados, door-jambs, and piers; but the primary motive for their development was their usefulness for cutting round logs, especially for columns, and for sawing the larger timbers into beams and boards.

The extent of sawing in Minoan Crete is uncertain, for cleaving with wedges remained an adequate and simpler process. That was the earlier practice, as Seneca recalls: 'Believe me, blessed were the days before there were architects and plasterers. It was only with the arrival of luxury that timbers were squared and beams cut with the saw straight along the marked line'; and he quotes Virgil to make his point: 'Our early ancestors cleaved wood with wedges.'[80] The fact that one of the thickest beams at Cnossus is nothing more than a length of trunk cut longitudinally down the middle, and that round timbers were sometimes used for ceilings and rounded half-timbers for wall-framing shows that we cannot always expect refinement in

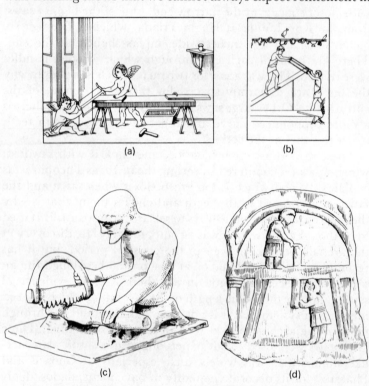

(a)   (b)

(c)   (d)

14 (*a*) and (*b*) Two-men saws in paintings from Herculaneum;
(*c*) Hellenistic bow-saw in terracotta; (*d*) Pit-saw from a tomb relief in Gaul

the preparation of structural timbers. The saws were, however, essential for the production of floor-boards and were probably used for some at least of the main weight-bearing timbers.

In the archaic period iron increasingly replaced bronze in arms and tools and the added strength must have made the sawing of large timbers much easier. A further change was made when it was realised that a blade was more effective when held in tension within a frame. By the Roman period large iron frame-saws operated by two men were the normal tools for cutting large timbers. In modern times the two-handed saw was known in England as a pit-saw, because big logs for sawing were placed across a pit and while one sawyer stood on the log, the other stood in the pit below. There is no trace of this practice in Greek or Latin literature, though Aristophanes in a simile refers to a saw with one man pushing and the other pulling. A crudely carved relief from Gaul, however, shows a large squared timber resting on a high trestle, with one sawyer standing on the beam and the other sawyer below (fig. 14d). A closer parallel may be seen in a long deep trench in a fort where a detachment from a Rhine legion was engaged in sawing timber for camps and forts on the frontier. It has been reasonably interpreted as an elongated saw-pit for the operation of several two-man saws.[81] There is also ample illustration of small frame-saws and bow-saws for single sawyers.

The importance of seasoning some wood before use was appreciated in the ancient world. The timbers that the prince of Byblos gave to Wen Amon were left on the mountain for a season before they were taken down to the coast. Homer's Odysseus knew that dried timber should be used for shipbuilding because of its lightness,[82] and in 205 BC Scipio, having built his ships with green timber, was careful to draw them up for the winter to dry out.[83] But in an emergency there was no option. In the first Punic War the Roman losses were so heavy that there was no time to wait for seasoning;[84] and when the Greeks defeated the Persians at the battle of Salamis in 480 BC many of the Athenian ships must have been built as soon as the timber reached the shipwrights, and launched as soon as they were completed. Special problems were also raised by doors made from wood that was not stable. Theophrastus tells us that doors made of fir-wood were stood up but not finished until the next year, 'for in summer the wood dries and the boards come apart, but in winter they come together again'.[85] The reason, he says, is that the open fleshy texture of the wood of the fir absorbs the moisture in the air.

Various methods of seasoning are referred to in the sources. The simplest, apart from merely leaving the timber in store, was to ring the tree before it was felled, cutting through the sapwood so that the sap, the main source of rot, could drip and the trunk dry out.[86] Vitruvius seems to imply that this was normal practice, but he is saying what should be done rather than what is normally done. Later he refers specifically to ash and elm, which have an excess of moisture and are liable to warp: 'If, however, they dry out either by being stored for a long time or by having the moisture drained from them while still standing, they make good building-timber.'[87] Ringing was probably less popular with the feller than with the architect; a tree is considerably less easy to fell when it is dead than when the timber is green.

Columella recommends that a smoke-room, where newly cut timber could be quickly dried, should be built next to the estate baths, presumably to take advantage of its heating system. Similarly Virgil writes of the smoke of the fire feeling its way through the timbers that have been cut for the plough.[88] Pliny, describing the luxury trade in citrus-wood tables, says that carpenters achieve a surprising reduction in weight by burying the wood in corn for seven days and repeating the process at seven-day intervals. 'It has also been realised', he adds, 'from sea wreckage that timber is dried by the action of salt water.'[89] This is presumably why, according to Palladius, the Sardinians bury their pines in sand by the sea for a year.[90] Cato recommends the putting of wood into a heap of manure or into water to dry it out and harden it, and both Theophrastus and Pliny confirm the practice of smearing manure on vulnerable timbers to prevent them splitting.[91] Both Greeks and Romans also appreciated that wood could be hardened by fire. Odysseus hardened on the fire the olive-wood with which he proposed to gouge out the eye of the Cyclops and then hid it very appropriately in dung.[92] In a different vein Vitruvius recommended the putting of charred olive timbers at close intervals in town walls 'so that the two faces of the wall, tied together by these timbers, should remain strong for ever. For when timber is so treated it cannot be injured by decay, storms, nor age.'[93]

When we come to the marketing of timber the evidence for the Greek world is much fuller than for the Roman. The publication of their annual accounts by commissioners at Eleusis, Epidaurus, Delphi, and Delos provides abundant evidence for the purchase, transport, and use of timber and this is supplemented on a much smaller scale by public decrees and building accounts. The most fruitful of these documents will be examined in more detail in Appendix 4, but the main inference for inter-state trade may be anticipated here. We have seen in the study of Athenian timber supplies that the state of Athens, including Eleusis from which most of our evidence comes, imported timber during the fifth and fourth centuries BC from Macedon, Crete, Samos, Cnidus, Corinth, Thurii, and a single consignment of cedar, presumably from the eastern Mediterranean, for the doors of the sanctuary treasury at Eleusis (p. 437). The most interesting evidence from the accounts of the commissioners who were responsible for supervising an ambitious building programme at Epidaurus comes from the very well-preserved accounts of the temple of Asklepios, which was begun in the first half of the fourth century BC when Epidaurus was becoming an important centre of healing. By comparison with the fifth-century temples on the Athenian acropolis the Epidaurus temple was very modest. It was only 22.5 metres long and 13.20 metres wide and the walls were built with limestone, marble being reserved for the columns and the pediment with its sculpture; but very little of the timber that was required could be found locally.

The fir that was needed for the roof was supplied by a Corinthian, though it was not necessarily grown in Corinthian territory. The cypress for 'the great door' of the temple almost certainly came from Crete whose cypress had the best reputation in the Aegean world. A third contract was for elm, boxwood, and lotus-wood (nettle-tree): the elm was probably to provide doorposts for the temple and for the workshop in which materials were prepared for the main building; the other two woods were decorative and were needed for inlays on the door and probably for the coffers of the ceiling. The elm might have been available locally but for the box and lotus the Epidaurians would have had to go further afield. There should have been box trees on most of the high mountains in the Peloponnese; the lotus was not common in Greece and we have no evidence for its distribution. The fourth and final wood contract was for the supply of beams to the workshop. The wood was not specified and the contract was taken by a local man; it was probably bought locally and pine is the most likely wood.

The temple of Apollo at Delphi was a much grander building. The archaic temple had been burnt down in 548 BC and was handsomely rebuilt, but this temple also was destroyed by fire. Temple commissioners were appointed in the fourth century to supervise the building of a new temple and scattered fragments of their accounts spread over more than twenty years survive. From these fragments it is clear that the main woods used in the building were cypress and fir. Special care was taken in selecting the most important timbers for the temple. The architect went with the commissioners to Sicyon and there they bought from different sellers the best cypress trunks that they could find for the cross-beams that indirectly supported the roof. Two other sources are recorded. A large order for fir timbers, probably from north Arcadia, was divided into two contracts, 571 timbers altogether. Timbers from Macedon are also recorded; they were probably fir or pine.

The evidence for Apollo's birthplace is very much richer than the meagre yield from the seat of his oracle. The accounts of the commissioners of Delos who were responsible for the maintenance of Apollo's temple on the island and the associated temples and other buildings extend over a period of nearly 250 years, and for more than a hundred of those years (c.310–166 BC) there are few years from which no single fragment survives and from some of them more than 300 lines can still be read. Delos had a great quantity of good building-stone but no woodland; all her timber for building, furniture, boat-building, and even fuel had to be imported and the only source specifically recorded is Macedon. Reasonable inferences, however, can be made. Several entries from the first half of the third century BC record cedar, in striking contrast with the rarity of references from the Greek mainland. But it is highly probable that all the cedar references from Delos refer to a single building, the temple of Apollo which had been begun in the fifth century BC but abandoned in the middle of the century and not resumed until Delos was freed from Athenian control towards the end of the fourth century. The cedar could have been found in Lycia, but more probably came from Syria or Phoenicia.

The origin of the many other woods that were imported by the Delian commissioners is considerably more uncertain: oak, ash, elm, beech, lime, cypress, cornel are recorded. All these could have been found in Macedon except perhaps cypress, but the Delians might be expected to buy from nearer sources if adequate supplies were available. For good-quality fir Macedon was probably the nearest as well as the best source, but second-quality fir could have been bought from Euboea. Macedon was also a natural choice for beech, which did not grow south of Thessaly nor in the islands. For the rest of the woods recorded the choice was much wider. Oak, for instance, which was widely used on Delos, grows well on the island of Samos, which at one time was called Dryusa (from *drys*, oak), and it was probably also available in Naxos, Chios, and Lesbos. It is from these islands, together perhaps with Euboea, that the Delians are likely to have acquired most of the large quantities of charcoal and firewood that they needed for their public sacrifices and domestic fuel.

To these detailed illustrations of the wide spread of the Greek timber trade must be added the classification by Theophrastus of timber used by carpenters and joiners in Greece according to quality. Three of his sources are internal—the district of Mt. Oeta near Thermopylae, Euboea, and Parnassus. These are all inferior to imports from outside Greece. The best timber comes from Macedon; the next best from Pontus (the mountain forests behind the south coast of the Black Sea), and the third from the river Rhyndacus (flowing close by thickly forested Mt. Olympus a little south of the sea of Marmara).[94] The implication is that at the end of the fourth century BC when Theophrastus wrote these foreign timbers were widely used in Greece and not only by Athens. It is significant that Syria, Cilicia, Cyprus, and Phoenicia are not included in the list, though Theophrastus was well aware of the timber-richness of their forests.

We know very little indeed of the eastern Mediterranean after the absorption of Cilicia, Syria, and Phoenicia, all of which had a surplus of timber, in the Persian empire. Egypt continued to depend on imported timber for temples, palaces, and fleets and when the Ptolemies ceased to have free access to Syria and Phoenicia they relied largely on Cyprus (p. 135). Rhodes probably needed much more timber than she could produce herself, but from the area she controlled on the mainland she had easy access to the cypress and cedars of Lycia. From Mesopotamia we have no evidence after the Persian conquest, but though Babylon was no longer an imperial power, her domestic resources were still insufficient in her new status as a provincial capital and some of her best timber probably still came from Syria or Phoenicia. As the Greeks could find adequate supplies of good timber in the Aegean it was very uneconomical to import from the eastern Mediterranean. When the very rich Herodes Atticus in the Antonine period bought cedar for the roof of his Odeum in Athens the costliness of the wood was emphasised (p. 216).

For the Roman world the evidence is much less satisfactory. In our study of Roman timber supplies we have examined the sources and attempted to identify the areas of Italy on which the city of Rome was mainly dependent. While the most important area was the Tiber basin, some of her supplies came by sea, from the forests near Pisa and Genoa in the north, and probably from the Sila and Aspromonte forests in the south (p. 462). The citrus-wood for her most fashionable tables came from north-west Africa, and in the late Empire she was importing firewood for the Roman baths from Tunisia (p. 259).

In spite, however, of the great gaps in our evidence, it is clear that timber played a significant part in the sea-borne trade of the Mediterranean and we can identify some of the main timber ports and guess others. Strabo makes it clear that there were substantial exports of timber from Genoa and Pisa on the west coast of Italy.[95] In south Italy the Thurian timbers recorded by the Eleusinian commissioners in their accounts of 408/7 BC[96] will have come down the river Crathis from the Sila forest. The only other river that could bring down timber from the Sila was the Neto, which flows into the sea near enough to Croton to suggest that this was a second port for Sila timber. Further south along the east coast Caulonia was well situated to handle timber from the great fir forest that was later managed by the monks of San Bruno, and in flood time the river Sagra may have carried it down. Thucydides refers to timber stockpiled in the territory of Caulonia, which the Athenians had intended to use during their expedition against Syracuse to repair their ships; but Syracusan raiders burnt the timber.[97] At the southern point of Italy Rhegium's harbour was well sited to send out timber from the large Aspromonte forest above the city. In the north-east Ravenna may have played an important part in the timber trade. She needed considerable quantities of timber herself because her buildings were made of wood and were supported on wooden piles;[98] she could also conveniently provide a wider market for timber from the eastern Alps. Vitruvius in his description of the discovery by Caesar of larch in the Alps says that it was brought down the Po to Ravenna and he adds that the wood could also be bought at Fanum, Pisaurum, Ancona, and the towns in that region.[99] It was probably carried by coastal ships from Ravenna.

There were other important harbours in the Adriatic. In 189 BC the Romans had established a colony at Aquileia as a frontier defence against invasion from the north-east. By the end of the Republic the port was well established and it became considerably more important when the Romans in the early Empire advanced their frontier to the Danube. Strabo describes how the Romans supplied the natives with wine in wooden barrels and oil, while the natives offered slaves, cattle, and hides in exchange.[100] Strabo does not include timber in this trading, but an export trade may well have developed in the Empire, for the district was well wooded. Strabo includes iron workings in the region, which presuppose fuel for the furnaces, and Herodian's account of a third-century attack refers to the dense forests near the city.[101] A survey of the woods in a neighbouring area shows that there were still in the eighteenth century ample stocks of oak, spruce, and fir and lesser quantities of beech, maple, and other hardwoods.[102] An inscription records a dedication to Silvanus by the sawyers of timber at Aquileia, *sectores materiarum*, which suggests that they were of some importance.[103] They may have sawed squared logs for export as well as home consumption.

The mountain chain behind the east coast of the Adriatic and the mountains behind them were rich sources of timber, which later helped to maintain the fleets of Venice. Salona was the best port on this coast.[104] There happens to survive an inscription of a timber merchant, *negotiator materiarius* in the district,[105] and we know that the territory was well wooded.[106] It would be surprising if Salona was not concerned with timber export. Forests continued behind the coast south of Salona into Greece, where Ambracia may be singled out. When the Romans were at war with the Aetolians (190 BC) they were advised to begin their

campaign by attacking Ambracia, which had recently joined
the Aetolian League. The main advantage of Ambracia was
that its territory was a good area to fight in if the Aetolians sent
help to the city. The district could supply abundant timber to
make siege artillery and the river Arachthus flowing under the
walls of the city would be very useful for conveying supplies in
summer and would protect the Roman siege works.[107] The
river was well suited also to bring down timber from the interior,
and as a Corinthian colony Ambracia could have been relied on
to supply timber to Corinth when it was needed.

It is more difficult to determine what were the main harbours
used for the export of Macedonian timber, which was widely
distributed in the Aegean world. The key to the problem should
lie in the two widest rivers in Macedonia, the Haliacmon and
the Axius, by which timber could have been rafted or floated
to the coast from the great Pindus mountain range and other
mountains of the interior. There is no port known to us near
the mouth of the Axius, but some ten kilometres south of the
mouth of the Haliacmon is Methone, a Greek colony which was
a member of the anti-Persian alliance under the leadership
of Athens formed after the defeat of the Persian invaders in
480/479 BC. A series of Athenian decrees from the early years of
the Peloponnesian War has been preserved in which the people
of Methone are rewarded for their loyalty and given various
privileges.[108] Athens undertakes to protect Methone from any
Macedonian encroachment and to send an Athenian embassy to
the Macedonian king to negotiate on Methone's behalf. The
Athenian envoys are to require the king not to harass Methone
and to allow the people of Methone to trade in the interior of
Macedon. This in itself would be a very frail argument for any
connection with timber, but the difficulty of finding any other
suitable port near the Haliacmon makes it an attractive guess.
For timber cut on Mt. Olympus or the Pierian mountains Pydna
would provide a port conveniently near.

East of Macedon the Athenians established the colony of
Amphipolis near the mouth of the river Strymon. It was
intended to promote Athenian economic interests in the area
and when it was captured by the Spartans in the course of the
Peloponnesian War (424 BC) Thucydides emphasises the seri-
ousnesss of the loss to Athens: 'Amphipolis was useful to Athens

for the money revenue it provided and for the ship-timber that it dispatched to Athens.'[109] The timber probably came mainly from Mt. Pangaeus, once well-wooded, but now very bare, and logs may also have come down the Strymon from the interior. East of the Strymon the mountain range behind the coastal plain was also well wooded and there were further mountain forests behind. There were good harbours on the north coast of the Aegean, including Maroneia and Aenos, which were served by rivers that could have brought down timber from the Thracian mountains.

In Asia Minor there were four forested areas which Theophrastus included among the few that provided ship-timber of good quality—Mt. Ida, the river Rhyndacus, Sinope and Amisus, Cilicia.[110] When the Spartan fleet was destroyed at the battle of Cyzicus in 410 BC the Persian governor of the district, who was supporting the Spartans against the Athenians, encouraged the Spartans to build a new fleet from the forests of Mt. Ida,[111] and Strabo calls Aspaneus in the Troad the market for the timber of Mt. Ida, 'for that is where they bring their timber and display it for those who need it'.[112] Some fifty kilometres to the east of Mt. Ida, and some fifteen kilometres south of the sea of Marmara, Mt. Olympus by the river Rhyndacus was a more abundant source of ship-timber and timber for building. Strabo confirms the timber-richness of the mountain,[113] which is also illustrated by the self-styled philosopher Dio Chrysostom, a contemporary of Pliny the younger, who was a citizen of Prusa which lies under the northern slopes of the mountain. In an emotional but laboured appeal for concord he urges his fellow citizens to improve their relations with Apamea, the nearest port: 'They need our timber and many other things and we have no other harbour to use for our imports and exports.'[114] Timber from Mt. Olympus may also have been sent down the river Rhyndacus to Cyzicus, for in Strabo's day Cyzicus had more than 200 ship-sheds, implying a sizeable fleet.[115] Further east Nicomedia in the sea of Marmara had an important harbour with strong seafaring traditions and a well-forested hinterland.[116]

Theophrastus includes Sinope and Amisus among the districts noted for their ship-timber, and of the timber used in Greece for building and general carpentry he placed the timber from the Black Sea next to the Macedonian which was at the head of the list. Ancient and modern sources agree on the impressiveness of the forests that stretch along the south coast of the Black Sea, with their fine fir, beech, pine, oak, maple, and other deciduous trees. Xenophon, returning with the mercenaries who had been forced to make a fighting retreat when Cyrus whom they had hoped to set on the Persian throne was killed in battle, was particularly impressed by the forest between Heraclea and Byzantium. 'There is timber in abundance, including fine ship-timber right on the shore, and dense coastal forest continues for more than twenty stades (c.3 km.) with large timbers of every kind.'[117]

In his description of Cilicia Strabo says that Hamaxia, a little east of Arsinoe (near the western end of the Taurus range), was the place where the ship-timber, which was mostly cedar, was brought down from the mountain.[118] Remnants of a cedar forest can still be seen a little west of Alanya, and most of the long Taurus range was well stocked with cedar and fir. Other ports or anchorages along the coast could also have been used. The forests of western Asia Minor could not be compared with those behind the north and south coasts, and they are not mentioned by Strabo or Theophrastus; but Miletus, Cnidus, and Samos all exported timber to Athens (p. 211). In the last phase of the Peloponnesian War (407 BC) the Spartan commander Lysander organised the building of triremes for the Spartan navy at Ephesus, but Plutarch, who provides our only evidence, may imply that the timber was imported.[119] In the second century AD the city was importing timber on a significant scale, as we learn from a decree by the governor of the Roman province of Asia against abuses in the harbour. Merchants importing marble must not unload it on the quay, because its heavy weight imposed an undue strain on the piers that supported the quay. The importers of timber must not saw their timber on the quay, because the sawdust was threatening to choke the channel of the harbour. A fine was prescribed for these offences and 'since his supreme majesty the emperor has a special concern for the efficiency of harbours', the offenders must also appear before the governor.[120] Timber was not an easy cargo. In Phoenicia Egypt had established close relations with Byblos as early as the third millennium BC and it was from Byblos that she drew her best timber (p. 65). But the other Phoenician cities will have shared in the timber export trade, particularly perhaps Sidon and Tyre.

It remains now to consider the structure and the status of the timber trade and, finally, prices and wages. For the structure of the trade we have to rely mainly on the terms used in inscriptions and literature and on the implications in the accounts of the temple commissioners, to which we have already referred. If we consider the lack of precision in our use in the English language of the words wood, timber, and timber merchant, we shall not be surprised if in Latin and Greek the same words do not mean the same thing to everyone always.

In Latin the words that most concern us are *lignum*, *materia*, *lignarius*, *materiarius*, *negotians materiarius*. The law could make a distinction between *materia* and *lignum*:[121] *materia* was wood used for building; *lignum* was used for fuel. In practice *materia* is the standard word for wood that is used by builders, carpenters, and furniture-makers, but *lignum* is more difficult to restrict. Logs for burning are almost always *ligna* but the *porticus inter lignarios* in the area of the Tiber harbour can hardly have been a firewood market. These *lignarii* are much more likely to have been those who handled imported timber, normally in tree lengths, which came up river from Ostia. There may be a rather different use of the word *lignarius* at Pompeii, where it appears in two graffiti. The *lignari plostrari* are the men who carry wood in wagons, probably from the forest to the town, but possibly also for delivery within the town. But who are the *lignari universi* on another wall?[122] They might be all those who handled wood including fellers, carters, and retailers, or they could mean only the shopkeepers in Pompeii who sold timber. Unlike the Greek language, Latin has no distinctive word for feller and simply uses *lignarius*, which means no more than a man associated with wood. Latin also uses a general word for the timber-seller. In the same Roman district as the *porticus inter lignarios* there was a street of the *materiarii*[123] and a passage in Plautus strongly suggests that these are sellers of timber.[124]

Two surviving inscriptions record a *negotians materiarius*, one from Salona, the other from near Florence,[125] both well-wooded areas. These were probably men who located supplies and negotiated with the landowners or arranged imports from overseas. They may also have supplied the retailer, who did not carry large stocks. Another inscription comes from the tomb of an *abietarius*, who was presumably concerned with firs exclusively and was more probably a trader than a feller. It is therefore particularly interesting that Festus records that *abietaria negotia* was a term once used for 'what we now call *materiaria*',[126] presumably so-called from the trading in fir. This suggests that in the early days, perhaps when the needs of the fleet were paramount, there were men who specialised in firs.

In considering the status of the timber trade we must avoid sweeping conclusions, since the relevant inscriptions are statistically valueless. It may, however, be significant that neither in literature, with one exception, nor in the inscriptions do we find evidence of anyone connected with the timber trade who became politically powerful, or notoriously wealthy. Of the two *negotiantes materiarii*, one had weight-lifting as a hobby, and the other had the tools of his trade cut in relief on his tombstone: his wife was a freedwoman, and his own cognomen Erastus suggests servile ancestry. The three *materiarii* all have short inscriptions on their tombstones; one was a freedman, and the name of one of the others, Tiberius Claudius Probus, shows that he was probably descended from a slave of one of the Julio-Claudian emperors.[127]

There is, however, one man in the record who rose from obscurity. Pertinax, who actually became emperor after Commodus had been murdered, was said to have been a freedman's son who acquired his cognomen from his pertinacity in the timber business.[128] His support in stormy times, however, was inadequate, and he was soon murdered. It is a nice coincidence that when Septimius Severus, who emerged as the victor in the war for the succession, found it politic to pose as the avenger of Pertinax, the guild of the *fabri tignuarii* of Ostia built a temple to Pertinax, now deified.[129] The word *tignuarii* means literally men who worked timbers, but long after wood had ceased to be the main building material the title was still used for builders. It must have had this wider meaning in Ostia because the guild was the largest and wealthiest in the town and had a paramilitary organisation;[130] but it would have included the carpenters who worked the timbers used in building, particularly the roof-timbers.

The Greek terms are no more helpful than the Latin. There is no such distinction in Greek as there is in Latin between *lignum* and *materia*; *xylon* has to do service both for building-timber and for logs for burning, but the word for timber-seller, *xylopolos*, is more explicit than *materiarius*. In the account of the Eleusinian commissioners for 329/8 two purchases are made from *emporoi*; one of these is for three cedar boards for the door of the treasury at Eleusis, and the other for two door-frames. The word *emporos* is used for merchants operating on a substantial scale, often though not always concerned with trade overseas. It is also worth noting that when the contracts for the building of the temple of Asklepius at Epidaurus were made, the Corinthian who contracted for the fir timbers also contracted for the stone for part of the building. Large-scale merchants did not necessarily confine themselves to a single commodity, but the *xylemporos* of an Egyptian papyrus must have been a timber merchant, the equivalent of a *negotians materiarius*.[131] In the retail trade there were some traders who could handle large orders and probably carried large stocks, but perhaps the most striking feature of the accounts is the large number of suppliers used for small-scale orders. Even in the minute island of Delos there seem to have been as many as six different men at the same time selling timber to the commissioners.

The fragmentary nature of our evidence for the timber trade is sharply illustrated by an inscription found near Teos on the coast of Asia Minor towards the end of last century. It records the terms on which a small agricultural community outside the city was absorbed by its larger and more powerful neighbour. The villagers were to have the full citizenship of Teos, and to ease the transition from independence they were to be exempted from the main public liturgies in Teos for ten years, and to receive certain tax concessions. They were not required to pay tax on oxen used for agriculture or timber-carting or on slaves similarly engaged, and they would not have to pay the tax on the sale of timber.[132] This is the only reference known to me of a timber sale tax. If it was a normal feature in most states we should have heard more of it. It may have been introduced at Teos owing to the scarcity of supplies, and one of the reasons why Teos was anxious for the two communities to be united may have been that the village controlled the timber resources of Mt. Kizildağ.

With regard to the status of workers in the timber trade we have very little evidence outside Athens in the Greek world. In the surviving accounts of the Erechtheum no sharp distinction is drawn between citizens and metics (resident aliens): they receive the same wages and undertake the same kind of work. There is also a significant allocation of work to slaves, who receive the same wages as citizens but presumably have to hand over some of their money to their owners.[133] It is, however, dangerous to generalise from the Erechtheum accounts: they cover years of crisis after the great disaster in Sicily, when Athens was fighting desperately to save her empire and most of the free labour force was serving in the fleet or with the army on the east side of the Aegean. At Eleusis nearly a century later the citizens have a larger share of the contracts and the only slaves that are apparently used are the small number who were attached to the sanctuary. As in the Roman world we hear of no fortunes made from timber, nor of any timber merchants who became politically or socially prominent. But this is perhaps to be expected. How many fortunes in England, France, or Germany were based on timber before the nineteenth century?

The important question of prices and wages has deliberately been relegated to the end of this chapter. What readers will hope to find, especially in this age which worships quantification and statistics, is a series of tidy tables showing the rise and fall of prices over the years and the corresponding fluctuations in wages, together with a comparison of these prices and wages with those in other trades. Unfortunately, we can follow the general trend of prices over a substantial period only in two by-products of the timber trade, and in both cases the evidence is confined to Delos. Glotz has analysed the annual purchases of pitch by the Delian commissioners and shown that the fluctuations of prices depend on the relations with the Macedonian king at the time.[134] No such political considerations govern the prices of firewood and charcoal, which are tabulated in Appendix 4.4. But for timber the evidence is fragmented and frustrating. There is indeed no shortage of prices in the accounts from Eleusis, Epidaurus, Delphi, Delos, especially for the fourth and third centuries BC. From Delos in particular we have a large number of prices for timber of various species and of various dimensions, but in no single case can we compare like with like. The main reason for this is the lack of precision which is a characteristic feature of our Greek accounts.

What we should like to know for each purchase is the name of the wood, its dimensions, the use to which it is put, and the supplier. It is very rarely that we are given more than two of these items. We can contrast from Eleusis '3 cedar timbers, 12 ft. × 4 in. × 3 in., from Simmias *emporos* at 210 dr.' (which we know from the next line to have been designed for the door of the treasury) with '12 beams from Phormio resident in Piraeus at 17 dr. each'.[135] There is the same difficulty in comparing prices at different centres. At Delos in the middle of the third century BC oak timbers of twelve feet and fifteen feet were bought for seven drachmae one obol and nine drachmae; at Epidaurus, probably a generation earlier, the prices for timbers of ten feet, fourteen feet, sixteen feet were three drachmae three obols, four drachmae, six drachmae.[136] In comparing the two sets of prices it has to be remembered that the Epidaurian drachma, based on the heavier Aeginetan standard (6.1 g.), had more silver than the Delian based on the Attic standard (4.3 g.). There is, however, no encouragement to make the adjustment, because in both cases the length is the only recorded dimension, and we do not know whether the prices from Epidaurus are for oak, fir, or pine. There does seem to have been a general rise in prices of other materials during the period,[137] but the best that we can say with conviction is that there is nothing in the Delos timber evidence that is inconsistent with the trend.

The evidence for transport costs is no more satisfactory than for timber prices. We have a scatter of interesting figures but they are insufficient to suggest a pattern. Two cases are particularly detailed. In the second half of the fourth century BC the commissioners responsible for supervising the rebuilding of the temple of Apollo at Delphi purchased seventeen cypress logs from Sicyon and the prices, averaging more than 100 drachmae, indicate that they must have been very large, probably up to sixty feet long. They had to be loaded on ship at Sicyon, unloaded at Cirrha, Delphi's port on the other side of the Corinthian Gulf, and taken, presumably by oxen, some seven kilometres up a steep hill to the temple. The timbers had cost 3,047 drachmae; the cost of the transport was probably 500 drachmae, roughly sixteen per cent of the cost of the timber (p. 432). In the second case land and sea transport are again combined. In 339/8 BC a large consignment of elm and ash boards were bought by the commissioners at Eleusis from a Corinthian and the price recorded for transport by land across the Isthmus of Corinth and by sea from Cenchreae to Eleusis was seventy-three drachmae, roughly nineteen per cent of the cost of the timber, 388 drachmae 3 obols (p. 439).

Two more tantalising figures survive. In 306 BC Demetrius son of Antigonus, king of Syria, anxious to win the goodwill of Athens, promised to send her sufficient ship-timber for 100 triremes (p. 145). An Athenian decree authorised the payment of 14,040 drachmae (2 talents, 2,040 dr.) for the transport of the timber.[138] Unfortunately we have no means of calculating the value of the timber sent from Syria. The figure does, however, offer some interesting comparison with the transport of another cargo of timber two generations earlier. The Athenian general Timotheus, having managed to secure a substantial quantity of Macedonian timber as a result of his friendship with the Macedonian king, sent an agent to collect the timber and was charged 1,750 drachmae as the cost of transport.[139] If 14,040 drachmae was the cost of bringing timber for 100 triremes from Syria, 1,750 drachmae should imply sufficient timber for at least ten triremes. In the case brought against Timotheus the prosecutor charged him with having the timber taken to his house in the Piraeus for his own private building.[140] The amount of timber was too large to make the charge plausible: Timotheus had more probably invested in a stock of ship-timber.

The evidence for Roman timber prices and transport costs is even more unsatisfactory. The accounts of expenditure for religious and secular purposes were not publicly displayed as in the Greek world and for most of our period Pliny is our only source. As an imperial procurator concerned with the emperor's finances he had an interest in prices and was also fascinated by records. So he gives us a list of the fantastically high prices paid for citrus tables, and the surprisingly high price (80,000 sesterces) that tall masts could fetch. He gives in detail the total cost of bringing spices and scents to Rome from the east because such extravagance appals him;[141] but he sees no point in recording ordinary market prices for the common timbers used in building. Towards

the end of our period, however, there is a very substantial document that promises to offer considerable compensation for our
frustrations; unfortunately performance does not match promise.
In AD 301 the emperor Diocletian with his three colleagues-in-
power issued an edict which was designed to stabilise prices.[142]
After the close of the Severan dynasty the continuing succession
of ineffective emperors whose reigns were brief, combined with
the decline in the vitality of local government, and the mounting
pressure from the barbarians outside the frontiers, threatened
the disintegration of the empire. Diocletian became emperor in
284 and resolutely attempted to arrest the decay. He was firm at
home and successful in war, but in the long period of instability
prices had soared, and speculators were making big profits.

Diocletian hoped to restore stability by reforming the coinage, but the results were disappointing: 'Who is so insensitive
and so devoid of human feeling that he cannot know, or rather
has not perceived, that in the commerce carried on in the
markets or involved in the daily life of cities immoderate prices
are so widespread that the uncurbed passion for gain is lessened
neither by abundant supplies nor by fruitful years.' Diocletian's
remedy was to determine maximum prices which were to be
binding throughout the empire and no transport or other costs
were to be added, wherever the sale was made. More than one
hundred fragments of the edict have been found, many of them
in the last twenty years, in Asia Minor, Greece, and Egypt, but
none so far in Italy or the west. The preface to the list can now be
completely restored and, although there are still large gaps,
more than half the list has been recovered. Materials are
arranged in sections, beginning with food and drink. Timber is
twelfth on the list and is now virtually complete;[143] section 13 is
entitled 'shuttles' and includes seven items of wood; section 14
contains prices for firewood and for stakes; section 15 gives prices
of wood for vehicles. The sections on wages (7) and transport
charges by land (17) and by sea (35) also concern us.

Before examining these sections it must be admitted that the
list of materials is a very odd compilation. Wine prices (2) are
confined almost exclusively to the wines of Italy and the beers of
Egypt, Pannonia, and the Celts; there is no entry for Spain,
Gaul, or Africa, all of which were large-scale producers, and
many Greek wines travelled. In the second headed 'linen' (26)

the prices for the 139 items, which include second quality and in some cases third quality also, are all related to four production centres only and these are all in the east: Scythopolis, Byblos, Laodicea, Tarsus. In the following section (27), for which the heading has not been recovered, but which includes loincloths and handkerchiefs, the same production centres are the only ones quoted; and in section 28, which also lacks a heading, but includes headbands and bed-linen, the same centres are repeated, but for two of the seventy-seven items other names appear: for bed-ticks and pillow-ticks (28. 46, 47) Tralles, Antinoe, Damascus, and Cyprus are quoted, and prices are given for Gallic towels, first, second, and third qualities (28. 57-9). It is very difficult to explain such selections rationally. How wide would the interest be in the wages of an embroiderer working on a light cloak, made in Laodicea, resembling a cloak from Mutina (20. 4)? One has the impression that the list of prices was compiled by a group of civil servants who put together information collected hurriedly in the east and in Rome. We must therefore approach the timber section with due caution. Under the heading TIMBER the price of various woods is given in terms of length and the girth when the trunk has been squared: normally a squared timber will in fact be a square, so that a girth of four cubits will mean one cubit (one and a half feet) squared. In the table that follows the cubits of the text have been expressed in feet:

	SPECIES	Length (ft.)	Girth when squared (ft.)	Price (den.)
1.	Fir	75	6	50,000
2.	Fir	$67\frac{1}{2}$	6	40,000
3.	Fir	60	6	30,000
4.	Fir	$52\frac{1}{2}$	$6\frac{2}{3}$	12,000
5.	Fir	42	6	10,000
6.	Fir	45	6	8,000
7.	Fir	42	$5\frac{1}{3}$	6,000
8.	Fir	$37\frac{1}{2}$	$5\frac{1}{2}$	5,000
	The same prices are also laid down for pine.			
9.	Oak	21	$5\frac{2}{3}$	250
10.	Ash	21	4	250
11.	Beech	21	3	250
12.	Cypress	18	3	300
13.	*Sappinus*	18	3	250

There are no earlier prices known with which these could be compared, nor could any such comparisons be easy to interpret, since the maximum prices were drafted in a period of very high inflation; nor are comparisons with other materials in the list very fruitful. It means little to know that bartering on the basis of maximum prices one would have had to give a twenty-one-foot squared log of oak for a handkerchief from Scythopolis, or that a massive fir beam seventy-five feet long would only have fetched five hooded Laodicean cloaks in the Nervian style. A slightly better yardstick is the price of wheat at 100 denarii for a *castrensis modius* (20 lb.). The relationship of the prices of different woods may be more revealing. In the following table the prices per cubic foot implied by the figures in the edict have been calculated on the assumption that in each case the squared timber does in fact provide an exact square. This does not necessarily follow, since the figure listed is merely the combined length of the four sides: six feet could represent $1\frac{1}{2} \times 1\frac{1}{2}$ ft. or 2×1 ft., but in most cases the four sides would be equal or very nearly equal. Pliny says that the 100 foot beam which was left over when the Diribitorium was completed had a thickness of one and a half feet (corresponding to the figures in the edict for a 75 ft. fir) and that a 120 foot larch beam had a consistent thickness of two feet.

SPECIES	Length (ft.)	Girth when squared (ft.)	Price per sq. ft. (den.)
Fir/pine	75	6	295
Fir/pine	60	6	222
Fir/pine	45	6	80
Oak	21	$5\frac{2}{3}$	6
Ash	21	4	12
Beech	21	3	21
Cypress	18	3	30
Sappinus	18	3	25

There are several surprises in this table. Since the literary sources concur in regarding fir as the best of timbers for building and shipbuilding, we would expect pine to have a lower price, but it would be dangerous to infer that throughout the Roman period they were regarded as of equal value, especially as this is a list not of fair prices but of maximum prices. The higher cost per cubic foot of longer lengths implies larger differentials than we might expect, but by the fourth century trees that could provide seventy-five feet of straight timber must have been much more difficult to find than in the early Empire. The shorter lengths quoted for hardwoods are to be expected because they do not attain the height of firs and pines. It is a little surprising to find that oak has the cheapest price, but it was probably the commonest of the hardwoods. Beech is more expensive than ash because it had a wider range of uses and was particularly easy to work. The last entry on the list is something of an anomaly. Though the word *sappinus* sometimes seems to be used for a separate species, its main use refers to the part of the fir which is nearest the base and therefore of the best quality because most richly fed from the roots; it was particularly valued for high-quality joinery.[144]

The relationship of the various prices in the list may be unexpected, but they are not sufficiently unexpected to be ignored. Much less easy to explain are the omissions. No fir or pine less than thirty-seven and a half feet is quoted, and though such lengths were required for shipbuilding, basilicas, and temples, the demands for domestic housing, which must surely have been the largest consumer, very rarely included timbers longer than thirty feet. Even the much shorter lengths of hardwoods are longer than most of the purchases of which the lengths are recorded by Greek temple commissioners. It would also be wrong to infer from the list in the edict that no other woods were commonly used. From the literary evidence we should at least expect to find elm, poplar, and maple, and since the edict applies to the whole empire, we should expect it to include cedar, which was one of the dominant species in the Taurus and Lebanon forests and was widely used in the eastern Mediterranean.

After the list of woods, which is now complete, there follow three rates for working with timber, either squaring or, more probably, sawing, and the rates are based on measurement. Oak comes first, with the highest rate (150 den.), because it is the hardest of the more common woods. Next come 'all other woods', for which is prescribed only 'a lower figure' (than oak), a strange anomaly since the objective of the edict was to fix maximum prices. For the third rate specific measurements are given: 'for timbers eight cubits in length and ten fingers wide

(?in section) the rate is 100 denarii'. The first editors take these rates to be for squaring round timbers, but the translation of the Latin is difficult and my preference for sawing needs to be discussed in a note.[145]*

After these rates comes a list of furniture with prices: tables, clothes-presses, chairs, caskets, a set of twenty-four writing-tablets; tent-poles with and without iron ferrule, props with and without iron ferrule: and for both poles and props it is notable that the iron ferrule increases the price very considerably, from 200 to 400 denarii for poles, and from ten to fifty denarii for props. Finally, under a separate heading 'for beds', three types are listed. For a bed of nut-wood (probably walnut, p. 421) the maximum price is 400 denarii, for a boxwood bed 600, and for a hostel bed only fifty.

It is fair to feel sympathy for those who tried to carry out Diocletian's instructions, but it would be perverse to assume that there must be a rational justification for the form and content of this timber section; a reasonable inference concerning wages can, however, be drawn from the relevant section (7), which lists the rates payable in a wide range of employment. The same daily rate of fifty denarii with maintenance is shared by carpenters employed in building, cabinet-makers, wain-wrights, and shipwrights working on river vessels, as distinct from those who work on seagoing vessels who have the higher rate of sixty denarii. The standard rate of fifty denarii is the commonest rate quoted and covers stonemasons, lime-burners, blacksmiths, and plasterers. In Athens (our Greek evidence is confined to Athens) and in Rome wage structures seem to have been simple without elaborate differentials. The accounts of the Erechtheum on the Athenian acropolis provide good examples. Those that have survived come from the last years of the Peloponnesian war, when building was resumed after a long interval. Comparatively little remained to be done and most of the work required a fair degree of skill. The method of organising the work, which was typical of Greek temple building, was to divide it into small units, which were assigned to individual craftsmen who were paid by the piece. Where a daily rate was paid the standard rate was one drachma, and the same rate was paid for working in wood or marble, and no dis-tinction was made between citizens, resident aliens, and slaves.

Different systems were used for the payment of sawyers and they are well illustrated in the Erechtheum accounts. In this final phase of the building Rhaidios, a metic, seems to have been the master sawyer. For himself and his assistant, probably operating a two-man saw, he receives twelve drachmae, the standard rate for two men working for two days, though one may doubt whether Rhaidios divided the money equally. Similarly, for further sawing for twelve days he receives twenty-four drachmae for himself and his assistants, implying that he did not continuously use the same assistant. But for sawing twelve timbers eight feet long he is paid two obols for each cut with six cuts for each timber, while for five cuts in a twenty-four-foot timber he receives one drachma for each cut, implying the same rate per foot as for sawing the eight-foot timbers.[146] At Delphi during the building of the new temple of Apollo in the fourth century a sawyer was paid explicitly by the foot. For sawing squared Macedonian timbers (length unspecified) he receives five coppers ($\frac{5}{16}$ dr.) per foot (p. 433), a rate very slightly higher than that of the Erechtheum sawyer. At the time of the Erechtheum accounts the daily pay of a juror in the people's courts, which was intended to cover subsistence, was three obols. By comparison the timber-worker, who received the same daily pay of one drachma as the oarsmen in the triremes, should have been able to live adequately on his pay.

In the Eleusis accounts from nearly a century later the standard daily rate has been increased to one and a half drachmae, and the same rate was paid to two sawyers (described as a 'yoke') operating a two-men saw for thirty-five days as to labourers carrying mud-bricks and timbers to builders restoring a wall.[147] But sawyers making lintels and door-frames from Macedonian timbers are paid a contract price.[148] The standard wage still seems to compare favourably with the cost of living. Three obols cover the cost of maintenance (excluding clothes etc.) of a slave who worked for the commissioners,[149] and a citizen received one drachma for a day's attendance at the public Assembly. The increase in the rate from the fifth century should have covered the general increase in prices.

13

DEFORESTATION

During the last thirty years more trees have been planted in the world than in all the rest of the world's history. This reflects the public recognition of the long-term effects of cutting down trees without thought for the future, not only on the supply of timber, but also on the total environment including water-supply, wild life, and landscape. Alarm at the progress of deforestation has been expressed by individuals or small groups during the last four hundred years, but the wide-scale realisation that natural resources are not infinite is comparatively modern. Concern is now world-wide and ambitious efforts are being made to halt the devastation and build up reserves by new planting and by the improvement of forest management. This is accompanied by an almost morbid interest in apportioning the guilt for the present sad state of the world's forests. Our concern is to review the part played by the ancient world in the forest history of the Mediterranean.

Most of the forest areas with which we have been concerned in this study present today a very sorry contrast with their past. In the Lebanon range the cedars which in our period were the glory of the forests and the dominant species in a wide band from $c.1,400$ to $c.1,800$ metres over a length of more than 100 kilometres are now reduced to fourteen widely separated stands, none very large, and most of them degraded; and many slopes that were once thickly forested are now bare limestone.[1]

In Italy there remains very little of the fir forests of the Apennines on which Rome primarily relied for her fleet and her major public buildings, especially basilicas. Most of the young firs that one sees are modern planting and their general performance is disappointing. At Spoleto in Umbria, once the centre of a well-forested area, the only native timber in a timber merchant's yard were a few chestnut boards; the rest were Douglas fir from America with pine and spruce from Russia.

Italy, which in our period had a surplus of timber to export, now relies heavily on imports.

The situation in Greece is no more encouraging. There is still plenty of good timber in what in our period was Macedon, but in central and southern Greece most of the woodland is very degraded and the total area of woodland has shrunk seriously even in the last two generations. The forest area that has suffered least in the Mediterranean world is the line of forests behind the south shore of the Black Sea. These forests have never been intensively exploited and their timber is still abundant and of good quality. This cannot be said of the rest of Asia Minor. Even the great forests of the Taurus range, with few exceptions, are thin in density and poor in quality.

At the beginning of our period there was in most Mediterranean areas too much forest rather than too little, and forests were not confined to the hills and mountains. The Neolithic peoples under the pressure of increasing population made substantial inroads into the woodlands of the plain and lower slopes, but it is doubtful whether they had begun to tackle the higher slopes above 1,000 metres. When there were ample resources more easily available to meet their modest needs and when bears as well as boars abounded in the high mountain forests, they may have gone up to hunt, but not to fell trees.

The conversion of forest to agriculture is a natural response to an increase of population and it continued throughout our whole period. As we might expect we meet it early in the history of the Jews:

The sons of Joseph appealed to Joshua and said, 'Why have you given us only one lot and one share as our patrimony? We are a numerous people; so far the Lord has blessed us.' Joshua replied, 'If you are so numerous, go up into the forest in the territory of the Perizzites and the Rephaim and clear it for yourselves. . . . You are a numerous people with great resources. You shall not have one lot only. The hill-country is yours. It is forest land: clear it and it shall be yours to its furthest limits. The Canaanites may be powerful and equipped with chariots of iron, but you will be able to drive them out.'[2]

Where plains were restricted it was natural for agriculture to move into the hills. As Lucretius in his brief outline of the history of agriculture observes: 'Continuously men compelled the forests to withdraw higher up the mountains and to leave the lower slopes to cultivation.'³ But in some areas the deforestation of the plain was a much longer process. Eratosthenes, the most impressive man of learning in the third century BC, described the gradual clearance of forest from the plains of Cyprus.⁴ Even after heavy cutting for the mines and for shipbuilding, further clearance had to be encouraged by offering free possession to anyone who cleared land to bring it under cultivation. The same policy was followed as late as the second century BC by the Romans. In a comprehensive law passed in 111 defining the categories of ownership of public and private land resulting from recent agrarian legislation, a clause was included confirming that anyone who had occupied public land up to thirty *iugera* (20 acres) in extent for the purpose of bringing it under cultivation had a full legal right to the ownership of such land.⁵

Agriculture continued to expand at the expense of forest during the Roman imperial period, but conversion was not always successful. The writers on agriculture were agreed that forest land provided rich soil and good crops, but they also knew that first impressions could be deceptive. The richness came largely from the annual nourishment from the leaves and when there were no more leaves to fall and the roots of the trees had disintegrated, the soil could become considerably less productive unless it was regularly fertilised with manure.⁶ But as governments became more paternal kings and emperors could be interested in winning more land for agriculture. Philip II of Macedon had opened up the great plain of Drama near Philippi to agriculture by cutting down the forest and draining the land.⁷ The Roman emperor Galerius in the third century AD significantly increased the land available for agriculture in Pannonia by cutting down 'immense forests' and draining what was virtually a lake into the Danube.⁸

The most spectacular expansion of agriculture was in the Roman province of Africa, corresponding roughly to Tunisia with eastern Algeria. This area had been controlled by Phoenician Carthage down to 146 BC, when Carthage was destroyed and her territory incorporated as a province in the Roman empire. The Carthaginians had been skilful farmers and an agricultural treatise written by a Carthaginian, Mago, was actually translated into Latin by order of the Roman senate. But though the Carthaginians lived well, there is no reason to believe that they exported grain on any considerable scale: by the end of the first century AD the Roman province of Africa was said to be sending sufficient grain to Rome to maintain a population of nearly a million people for two-thirds of the year. The tremendous increase in production that this implies may have been due in part to more skilful management, but it must also imply a considerable addition of land made suitable for agriculture. It is interesting that inscriptions recording regulations for large imperial estates in Africa offer incentives to workers to take in new land.

Tenants on imperial estates who planted an olive orchard on uncultivated land were entitled to keep for themselves the olive harvest for the first ten years, after which they were required to give annually a third of the oil from the olives to the estate managers. The general policy of the imperial government was clearly stated in the answer to a petition from imperial tenants to plant olive-groves and vineyards in certain lands that were marshy and wooded. The imperial officials give their consent 'since it is our emperor's command, with the unremitting care with which he ceaselessly watches over the interests of his people, that all lands that are suitable for olives and vines as well as for grain crops should be brought into cultivation.'[9] Tertullian, an African priest in the third century, in the course of a eulogy of the Roman empire, emphasises the improvement in communications, in trade, in urbanisation, and in the spread of ordered government. When he comes to agriculture he seems to reflect particularly conditions in the Roman province of Africa: 'Wildernesses have been replaced by most attractive estates, woods have yielded to the plough, the cover of wild beasts has become grazing land, sands are sown, stones are broken up, and marshes are drained.'[10]

The relative importance of another destroyer of the forest is more difficult to assess. The striking evidence of Homer's use of forest fires in his similes has already been emphasised (p. 107). It seems clear that forest fires were part of his own experience, and it would be surprising if they were not. In the dry summers, with occasional thunderstorms, forests, especially of conifers, are very vulnerable. Many of the subsequent references to forest fires in poets may be derived from Homer rather than nature, but a simile used by a Roman historian of the fourth century AD is good evidence that forest fires were still part of the common experience. Ammianus Marcellinus compares the moral disintegration of the emperor Constantius developing from the slightest causes to a fire 'when flying sparks from a dry wood, only lightly fanned by the wind, imperil on their irresistible course the country villagers'.[11] It is not surprising that the myth of a universal flood should be balanced by the myth of a primeval fire which destroyed the forests of Phrygia and the Taurus mountains and then proceeded on its destructive course to India and back by the Lebanon, Egypt, and Libya.[12]

Lucretius, who associated the discovery of metals with forest fires, gives three causes of their origin beside the taking of forest land for agriculture. His first cause is lightning, war his second when armies set fire to forests to intimidate their enemy, and lastly the hunt when animals are driven from their cover by fire. This last cause he qualifies by emphasising that in earlier days men hunted wild animals by digging pits and by fire.[13] In his own day these practices were obsolete; the hunter relied on dogs and his own spear. The other two causes remained continuing dangers. Sargon II describes his ruthless burning of forests in a campaign against Urartu (p. 62).

Lucretius does not include in his list a cause which was commonly given in Greek and Latin literature and which he himself had mentioned earlier. Thucydides, in his description of the siege of Plataea in the Peloponnesian War (430 BC), compares the man-made fire with which the Spartans attempted to burn down the Plataeans' wall to the spontaneous fire which arises when in the mountains 'wood is rubbed against wood by the wind'. Thucydides is the first known to us to have offered this explanation, but he was followed by others, including the architect Vitruvius, down to Quintus of Smyrna in the late Roman Empire, and it is very doubtful whether the authority of Thucydides alone was responsible for the wide acceptance of this explanation.[14] I have tried persistently to save Thucydides' reputation, but have not yet found any forester or timber merchant who is prepared to believe that a forest fire could possibly arise in this way. Presumably it is an early inference from the fact that the normal way of producing fire in Greece was by rubbing two pieces of selected woods together.

A forest fire did not necessarily mean the permanent loss of the forest. In many fires, particularly among deciduous trees rather than conifers, the strongest trees survive and can form the nucleus of a regenerated forest from seeds already in the ground or carried in by birds or the wind. Indeed fire is today deliberately used by some foresters, especially in America, to improve the forest by destroying weak growth. But regeneration is very hazardous. The young growth makes particularly attractive pasture, a godsend to shepherds in charge of sheep or goats and to free-ranging goats a paradise. Unless the burnt area is protected there is very little hope of a forest recovery.

Destruction by flood was less serious than destruction by fire but is not to be ignored in the total reckoning. Vita-Finzi's demonstration that a considerable extent of alluvial soil on Mediterranean plains, which was thought to be from the classical or pre-classical periods, was in fact deposited after the collapse of the Roman empire, has led to a lively controversy about the inference to be drawn from the evidence.[15] This is no place to join the debate except to emphasise what is sometimes forgotten, that, though the clearing of forest from steep slopes will almost inevitably lead to the washing-down of the soil by continuing rain-storms, it does not follow that alluvial deposit always or nearly always implies heavy cutting of timber on the upper course of the river. Pausanias makes this point in wondering why the delta of the river Achelous has not extended to the offshore Echinates islands. The reason, he says, is that the Aetolians had been driven out of their homes near the head-waters of the river, and the land had been neglected; conversely, the Maeander flowing through land in Phrygia and Caria, which was then always under the plough, had continued to make land from the sea between Miletus and Priene.[16] The Romans planted alder trees on the banks of the rivers as barriers against flooding, but they were inadequate to contain rivers in spate.[17] Destruction by flood became a well-worn topos in Greek and Latin literature. It begins with Homer: 'As when a river in spate comes down to the plain, swollen by the rain of Zeus, a winter torrent from the mountain, and carries away with it many a leafless oak and many a pine, and crashes a mass of flotsam into the sea.' It becomes more specific with Virgil, who applies it to the river Po, 'king of rivers', and he is followed by Lucan, who describes the Po as 'shattering forests and sweeping them down to the sea'. In Horace it is the flooding of the Tiber; in Ovid it is the Achelous.[18] Tiber floods were serious long before there was heavy cutting of the Apennine forests.

The losses of forest to flood, fire, and agriculture during our period were serious, but barely significant compared with the cutting-down of trees to satisfy the demand for wood, which increased with the growth of population and the rising standards of public and private building. Although Plato describes the permanent damage to the environment that can be done by deforestation, there is very little evidence elsewhere in Greek or Latin literature of consciences disturbed by an excessive exploitation of forests. The only complaint known to me is a mild protest in the late Roman Empire against overcutting in the Apennine forests (p. 255).

There is certainly no evidence of any general alarm at the depletion of the forests and there is no evidence of any attempts to redress the balance. We hear of massive plantings of olive trees, but never of forest trees. In the agricultural writers there is plenty of information about the propagation of trees from seed, layer, and cutting, but the trees are those which are grown on the estate and for the estate, particularly elm, poplar, and cypress. Coppice-wood is also an integral part of most large estates and detailed accounts are given of how it should be organised; but nothing is said about the proper management of forests designed to produce timber for building, furniture, and joinery.

There were, however, factors in the ancient world that imposed checks on the exploitation of the forests, and of these the most important was the problem of transport. As we have seen, unless use could be made of river or sea, long-distance transport by land, which meant by ox-wagon, was very uneconomical (p. 335). The emperor could ignore the economic factor, but the private trader could not: for practical purposes a substantial proportion of Mediterranean forests were inaccessible until railways were built in the nineteenth century. Theophrastus, expanding the point that trees, if left alone in their natural position and not cut down, grow to a remarkable height and girth, says that the kings of Cyprus used not to cut down their trees. This was partly because they took care of them and wanted to preserve them; but, he adds, 'there was also the difficulty of transport'.[19]

Religion also imposed constraints. Pliny, introducing the section of his natural history devoted to trees, begins by setting them in a religious framework: 'Trees were once the temples of the divine powers and, following traditional ritual, simple country people still dedicate a tree that is particularly grand to a god. Nor do we honour with our worship wooden images gleaming with gold and ivory more than sacred groves and their silence.'[20] Similarly Seneca speaks of a faith in the divine that is inspired by the silence and unbroken shade of a grove of tall trees that shut out the sun.[21] It is not surprising, therefore, that sacred groves should be widely associated with temples or cults.

The rules and rituals of sacred groves could be very strict. Cato records a very elaborate prayer to be recited before thinning a grove.[22] An inscription found near Spoleto enumerates the severe penalties for cutting down trees in a sacred grove.[23] When one of Antony's generals cut timber for ship-building from a grove dedicated to Asklepios on the island of Cos he was later executed by order of Octavian in the grove itself to emphasise his impiety (p. 151). A very special cypress could be cut down in a grove of Apollo on the island of Carpathos, but this was a gift to a goddess, Athena mistress of Athens (p. 201). Enemies, however, were less scrupulous. Sulla had no qualms when he stripped the sacred groves of Attica to build his siege machines for the siege of the Piraeus (p. 171), and when Christianity triumphed the restraint no longer held. The sacred grove was associated with paganism and the trees were cut down with religious fervour. But some groves were converted instead of being cut down. The sacred grove of holm-oaks, Montelucco above Spoleto, still survives, adopted by a Christian community.

It is interesting to note that the Christian religion continued to play a part in the preservation of woodland. The one spectacular cedar-grove which has pride of place in most tourists' visits to Lebanon owes its survival to the protection and care of the Maronite church. In Italy the Camaldoli forest near Arezzo was still in excellent condition when in 1866 it passed with the other papal lands into the possession of the new sovereign state of a united Italy. From the eleventh century the forest had been managed by monks of the Benedictine order, who had evolved good forestry rules and worked to a carefully developed programme of felling and planting. They had enlarged their forest to 1,442 hectares, of which 712 hectares were of fir, and as late as 1832 they were able to provide 380 large fir timbers for the new basilica of St. Paul outside the Walls. Shortly before the forest was taken over by the state, the monastery had been offered 1,000,000 lire for a very large cutting of firs: fortunately they resisted the temptation and what is now a national forest still has the most impressive firs in Italy. The forest of Vallombrosa near Florence, which Milton remembered with affection in his *Paradise Lost*, has a similar history, which can be traced back to a hermit in the twelfth century. It too, as a national forest, remains productive and specially noted for its chestnut and beech.

From the available ancient evidence it is impossible to say how seriously Mediterranean forests were depleted by the end of the Roman Empire. There are indeed a few explicit statements preserved. We learn from Strabo that owing to the exhaustion of fuel on the island, the iron-ore of Elba, the richest source of iron in Italy, had to be taken to Populonia on the Italian coast to be smelted.[24] The ruinous effect of iron production on neighbouring woodlands is amply illustrated in our own history. In the seventeenth century Evelyn, emphasising 'the prodigious waste of these voracious iron and glass works', refers to a forest in Sussex 120 miles long and thirty miles broad—'the ancient Andredswald of old, one entire wood, but of which there remains now little or no sign'.[25] More recently, towards the end of the nineteenth century, the population of a town in eastern Anatolia was reduced from 3,000 to 300 when a lead-mine was closed through lack of wood.[26] How serious was this problem in the ancient world? I know of only two further references.

Eratosthenes said that the first inroad into the forests of the Cyprian plains was for the mines, but he implies that later the demands of shipbuilding and agriculture were more important (p. 397). The production of copper continued to be the main industry in Cyprus, but there still seem to have been ample reserves of timber on the mountains in the late Roman Empire (p. 398). The other passage that is relevant has, I think, been widely misunderstood. Pliny, describing the production of Campanian bronze, says that at Capua the copper is smelted in a wood, not charcoal, fire and the smelting is repeated several times. He adds that bronze of the Campanian style is produced

in many parts of Italy and in the provinces, but there they do the
extra smelting with charcoal because of the shortage of wood.
This is certainly not evidence for a shortage of wood in
Campania, nor is it firm evidence for attributing deforestation
to mining demands, especially when he lays emphasis on Gaul,
'where the metal is smelted between red-hot stones which make
it black and brittle; and they smelt it only once though the
quality is very considerably improved by repeating the smelting'.[27] Most parts of Gaul remained thickly forested during our
period.

A closer examination of the forest history of the main mining
areas in the empire, especially Spain, might reveal a large-scale
depletion of forest, but it is strange that there should not be more
positive evidence. There is perhaps more danger of exaggerating
rather than of underestimating the contribution of metallurgy
to deforestation. A recent very rough estimate of the annual
consumption of fuel for the iron industry in the Roman empire
has been based on estimates of the volume of iron produced, the
volume of iron-ore needed to produce it, and the amount of fuel
needed for the process. An annual deforestation of 5,420
hectares (c.13,392 acres) is a very alarming figure, even though
it is admittedly a very rough estimate.[28] The figure, however, is
based on the annual production of an oak forest of trees
averaging sixty years' growth, and charcoal is not normally
made from whole trees. More often the charcoal-burner obtains
his material as a by-product of felling operations, collecting the
lop and top which is of little value to the timber merchant, who
is interested only in the trunk and the larger branches.
Landowners in mining areas will also probably have realised
that coppice, *silva caedua*, cut at regular intervals, could make
a good profit in supplying the mines with fuel, and without
deforesting the countryside.

Diodorus the Sicilian, in his account of the great shipbuilding
programme of Dionysius (c.400 BC), says that Mt. Etna, from
which Dionysius cut roughly half his timber, was 'still at that
time (some 350 years earlier) full of excellent fir and pine',[29] and,
as we have seen, there is a reference in a fifth-century poem to
the heavy cutting of timber from the Apennines over a long
period (p. 255). There may also have been a deliberate attempt
by Hadrian to conserve the more valuable trees in a large area

of the Lebanon, when he ordered his procurators to set up markers confirming that the trees of four species belonged to the emperor, and must not be cut without authority; but the inference is not certain (p. 86).

Although such evidence is quite inadequate to support any general statement about the damage done to the forest resources of the Mediterranean in our period, we can dismiss some of the more exaggerated claims. It has often been assumed that Plato's account of the deforestation of Attica is valid for the whole country and that even before the Hellenistic period there was very little timber left in Greece. This ignores the difference in rainfall and temperatures between the south with the south-east and the north with the west. Boeotia, Attica, the Argolid, and the southern coast-land of the Peloponnese have poor soils, meagre rainfall, and considerable heat in summer. They can never have produced timber as good as that of the west and the north; but even Attica was by no means treeless. Pausanias says that in his day, the period of the Antonine emperors, there were still bears as well as boars to hunt on Mt. Parnes, which implies a substantial area of forest.[30]

We have seen earlier that Sir Arthur Evans's view that there was an acute shortage of timber on Crete before the end of the Bronze Age is barely consistent with the evidence of Strabo and Pliny (p. 98). Crete was exporting cypresses to Athens in the fifth century BC and Cretan cypresses were being exploited for the Venetian fleet in the Middle Ages and the Renaissance. In the early seventeenth century a Scottish traveller reported that Mt. Ida, the highest mountain in Crete, was 'overclad even to the toppe with Cypre trees, and good store of medicinable hearbes', but little more than a century later Mt. Ida could be described as a barren spot, by one who climbed it.[31] It has also been maintained that the forests of Cyprus were stripped by the demands for ship-timber by the Persians and later by the Hellenistic kings of Syria and Egypt, but in the fourth century AD Ammianus Marcellinus could write that Cyprus was so rich in materials that a ship could be built and fully equipped by the island itself.[32] The forests of Cilicia and Syria, also, were still important in the struggle between Muslims and Byzantium in the early Middle Ages.

In Italy there is less justification for misconceptions, since there is sufficient evidence in local and central archives to reconstruct in broad outline the history of Italian forests, at least from the fourteenth century, and even during our period we are not entirely dependent on guesses. We have seen from Strabo and Dionysius of Halicarnassus, writing shortly after the collapse of the Republic, that Italy was still well forested in their day (p. 243). In a more recent book, concerned with the history of forests, it is claimed that by the end of the Empire the destruction of readily accessible forests in Italy caused the import of wood from north Africa, Spain, and other Mediterranean areas.[33] This is a popular view, but it is not firmly based on evidence and is barely consistent with the situation implied by Cassiodorus in the early sixth century AD (p. 153). Theodoric in 525, ruling Italy from Ravenna, seems to see no difficulty in building at speed a fleet of 1,000 ships with timber supplied from Italy, cypress and pine from the coast-lands and firs from the Po valley. He was assured that Italy at the time was herself sending timber to the provinces.

This evidence does not imply that the forests of Italy in the sixth century were as well stocked as in the period of Augustus, but there is no justification for assuming an acute shortage of wood in Italy as a whole. It is probable that the Apennine fir forests in particular had suffered very heavily and never fully recovered, but Etruria, which had been one of the city of Rome's main suppliers, was still well forested in the fifteenth century; and in the south Pope Gregory the Great ordered long beams for the restoration of the basilicas of St. Peter and St. Paul in Rome from Bruttium (p. 466). The main supply of timber for Orvieto cathedral, begun in 1200, was taken from a local forest [34] and the great rebuilding of Rome by the popes of the fifteenth and sixteenth centuries was carried out with Italian timber, especially fir, chestnut, elm, and beech. A dispatch sent by Pope Nicholas V on 11 July 1451 to a papal secretary at Città di Castello might, with minor changes, have been written by a Roman emperor:

> Seeing that the basilica of the chief of the apostles is showing signs of collapse in the roof and is in such a poor state that there is a danger of the building falling down, we have determined to restore the roof with diligence and care at our expense. And since at other times beams of fir have been brought to Rome from a place in the Alps near Fontanella

[near Arrezo] to restore the roof of the church of St. Paul and since it is known that both the basilica of the chief of the apostles and the church of St. Paul need such restoration, it is our intention to send you to the place referred to above. Be it your earnest endeavour to see that the timbers are cut and then taken from the forest and brought to the Tiber.[35]

The popes during this period were also able to get building-timber from the neighbourhoods of Lake Bracciano, Lake Bolsena, Praeneste, and Narni.

Since the end of the Roman Empire conditions had been favourable for the recovery of forests. The vastly swollen size of the population of Rome during the Empire was dependent on the preservation of power in Rome and a flourishing economy. As Juvenal summed it up, the Roman people had surrendered their political liberties in return for 'bread and the circus': if it had not been metrically inconvenient he would probably have substituted amphitheatre for circus. But to avoid riots on the streets sufficient grain had to be imported from overseas to feed the people, and the emperor had to provide extravagant entertainments. When Rome had been sacked by Goths and Vandals a return to the hard life of the country was preferable to maintaining a precarious existence in an impoverished and vulnerable city. The population of Rome soon dropped sharply. In the early Middle Ages living standards declined, there were no great building programmes in the capital nor in other Italian cities, and the mountain forests were free to regenerate. By the fifteenth century it was even possible to get ship-timber some twelve kilometres from Rome. When Pope Callistus III decided to build a papal fleet he ordered timber from Decima on the Via Laurentina to be carted to the nearest point on the Tiber and taken by river to Rome.[36] The forest from which this timber came may be the descendant of the silva Maesia which, according to Livy, the Romans took from Veii in the reign of Ancus Marcius, under whom Rome advanced her conquests to the sea.[37] The pope, however, had little skilled labour at his disposal and sent to Spoleto requiring the town to send him 100 woodworkers, sufficient evidence that there was plenty of productive woodland in the district.[38]

With the coming of the Renaissance there was a change in the social and economic climate. The growth of trade led to the development of fleets and the fleets of Venice, Genoa, and Pisa made increasing demands on the forests. Changed conditions had led to changes in naval thinking since the days of Athenian naval power. Theophrastus was reflecting Greek practice when he said that the best woods for building the trireme, the standard warship of the fifth and fourth centuries BC, were first the fir and then the pine. The fir was chosen not only because it produced long, straight lengths, was easy to work, and strong, but also because it was a light wood, and when naval tactics depended on speed heavy woods were unsuitable. But the trireme, built for speed and expecting to fight near shore, could not stand up to rough seas.

The Italian fleets of the Renaissance had to protect far-stretching trade routes, especially to Byzantium and the eastern Mediterranean. Strength was vital and oak and larch took the place of fir as the best wood available for the main hull, though fir remained in strong demand for masts and yard-arms, which needed long, straight timbers. In the fifteenth and sixteenth centuries Venice, which had earlier been able to satisfy her needs mainly from the eastern Alps, was having to go further to satisfy her dockyards. She used her control of the east coast of the Adriatic to draw supplies from the forests of the interior, and could look to Crete and other Venetian outposts overseas to make their contributions.[39] Genoa, conveniently served by the Ligurian forests which in Strabo's day were full of good timber, had by the sixteenth century to supplement her supplies from Corsica, though the local forests were by no means exhausted.[40]

The growth of prosperity during the Renaissance was accompanied by an increase of population, especially in the cities, and this led to periodic crises when the supply of grain from home and overseas was inadequate. This in turn put pressure on agriculture and led to the exodus of many people from the cities to the sources of food in the countryside. The natural result was an attempt to bring more land into cultivation and even steep slopes previously neglected were stripped of their trees and terraces were built to safeguard the soil. This was a hard way of earning food and when conditions became easier in the cities such marginal lands tended to be abandoned, with the inevitable result that the walls supporting the terraces disintegrated, the soil was washed away, and the slopes could produce neither trees nor food crops.[41]

In this period, when food was often short and agriculture was trying to expand, the grazing of the goat becomes more important in the history of the forests, so much so that it has often been singled out as the major cause of deforestation. This condemnation has obscured the important part that the goat has played in the agricultural economy of the Mediterranean, ever since it was one of the first animals to be domesticated in the early Neolithic period. The most valuable contribution was the milk of the she-goat, which could also be converted into cheese, not of the best quality, but at its best good enough in Italy to be exported overseas.[42] Its hair could be used for making cheap coats and it was one of the most fertile of animals: twins were common and three kids in a litter not unusual. The male goats were less profitable, but when killed their meat was a welcome supplement and there was a ready market for the hide.[42] The goat also provided a comparatively economical sacrifice. Among the many misconceptions about the goat is the general tendency to associate it only with peasants: but Varro and Columella, whose treatises on agriculture were certainly not directed at peasants, include detailed advice on the feeding and maintenance of goats, and it is clear from Varro that herds of goats could normally be expected on large estates. Opinions differed on the best size of the herd: in the *ager Gallicus* they restricted it to fifty, in the district of Casinum to 100; and the ratio of the male to female differed: 'I keep one buck to ten does, Menas one to fifteen, Murrius one to fifty.'[44]

But the Greeks and Romans were familiar enough with the less attractive habits of the goat. In a comedy by Eupolis, a contemporary of Aristophanes, goats gave their name to the play and formed the chorus, proudly professing their omnivorous grazing habits.[45] Unlike sheep and cattle goats preferred woodland rather than meadow for their grazing and were particularly fond of young growth of whatever texture. That is why, Varro tells us, there was a clause in some colony charters that no goats were to graze on land on which young trees were growing and why some leases had a clause that the tenant was not to graze goats on the land he had leased.[46] Goats could wreck a vineyard and destroy young crops.

To preserve the balance we may turn to Plato: 'Suppose that someone were to commend the keeping of goats or the goat as a valuable property, and someone else, who had seen goats without a goatherd damaging cultivated land by their grazing, were to abuse the wretched animals, can one say that their censure would have any validity?'; and the answer: 'Of course not.'[47] There is little but good to be said about goats as long as they are well controlled; when they are allowed to wander at will there is trouble. They are not, however, a serious danger in well-grown forests, where they will find enough to eat in the undergrowth. But when the forest is cut down wholly or in part the goats will eat all the young growth and prevent regeneration. Italy during the Roman Empire was largely a land of large estates, and the emperor the largest landowner. It is probable that goats were much better controlled than in the sixteenth to nineteenth century.

In the middle of the nineteenth century Giuseppe del Noce published a study of the forest resources of Tuscany and he emphasised the serious decline in forests between 1400 and 1849, caused largely by the taking over of good forest land that was unsuited to agriculture.[48] His statistics showed an average loss of twenty per cent in all the main species. If one had adequate statistics it would almost certainly be seen that the loss of forest between 1849 and 1950 was considerably higher than in the 450 years for which his figures are given.

During the nineteenth century there were great changes in the pattern of demand for wood. From the sixteenth to the nineteenth century the main drain of good-quality timber was for the fleets of Italy, and to a lesser extent France and Britain, but there was some compensation for the forests, since governments were seriously concerned about supplies of naval timbers and Venice in particular made efforts to protect forests and improve their management.[49] But by the middle of the nineteenth century the wooden ships had had their day, and governments became less interested. The demand for wood for fuel from industries had also been considerably reduced by the increasing use of coal. But these reductions in demand for naval timbers and fuel were more than offset by the development of railways. The railways themselves consumed vast quantities of timber for sleepers and for carriages but, more important, they eased the problem of the long-distance transport of heavy loads of timber. Many areas that had been previously inaccessible could now be exploited.

An even more important factor was the spectacular growth of population during the nineteenth century, encouraged by the development of the Industrial Revolution. This naturally led to an intensive increase in public and private building, which involved an increasing demand for timber. And as the forests had become considerably less productive and more timber had to be imported, prices rose and the temptation to take advantage of the situation was difficult to resist. This was very noticeable when the new sovereign Italian state took over the papal lands. As the state finances were desperately weak, many of the estates on these lands were sold and many of the buyers clear-felled the timber on their lands, being more interested in immediate capital than the future prospect of the trees.

The changing pattern is more widely attested in the Sila forest in south Italy. This large area of forested upland had been very little exploited before the nineteenth century. This was partly because of the impoverished state of the south of Italy, but also because the forest area was notoriously inhospitable to strangers and suffered from an almost complete lack of communications. It offered a safe refuge for bandits and outlaws and gave no encouragement to traders interested in timber. This isolation was broken when a railway line was built through Cosenza to the south and high roads were driven through the area. The forests of pine, fir, beech, oak, and chestnut became attractive to timber merchants, and not only from neighbouring coast-lands. In the closing years of the nineteenth and the first thirty years of the twentieth century there was a reckless destruction of forests. Norman Douglas, who spent several years walking in south Italy in 1906 and the following years, published in 1915 a composite but circumstantial account of what he had seen in old Calabria.[50] We should leave him to speak for himself:

It is sad to think that in a few years' time nearly all these forests will have ceased to exist; another generation will hardly recognise the site of them. A society from Morbegno (Valtellina) has acquired rights over the timber, and is hewing down as fast as it can. They import their own workmen from north Italy, and have built at a cost of two million francs (say the newspapers) a special funicular railway, 23 kilometres long, to carry the trunks from the mountain to Francavilla at its foot, where they are sawn up and conveyed to the railway station of Cerchiara, near Sibari. This concession, I am told, extends to twenty-five years—they have now been at work for two, and the results are already apparent in some almost bare slopes once clothed with these huge primeval trees. There are inspectors, some of them conscientious, to see that a due proportion of the timber is left standing; but we all know what the average Italian official is, and must be, considering his salary. One could hardly blame them greatly if, as I have been assured is the case, they often sell the wood which they are paid to protect.

The same fate is about to overtake the extensive hill forests which lie on the watershed between Morano and the Tyrrhenian. These, according to a Castrovillari local paper, have lately been sold to a German firm for exploitation.[51]

Though I passed through some noble groves of chestnut on the way up, the country here was a treeless waste. Yet it must have been forest up to a short time ago, for one could see the beautiful vegetable mould which has not yet had time to be washed down the hill-sides. A driving road passes the Croce Greca; it joins Acri with San Giovanni, the capital of Sila Grande and with Cosenza.[52]

It remains to be seen whether, by the time the lake Ampollina is completed, there will be any water left to flow into it. For the catchment basins are being so conscientiously cleared of their timber that the two rivers cannot but suffer a diminution in volume. By 1896 already, says Marincola San Floro, the destruction of woodlands in the Sila had resulted in a notable lack of moisture. Ever since then the vandalism has been pursued with a zeal worthy of a better cause. One trembles to think what these regions will be like in fifty years; a treeless and waterless tableland—worse than the glaring limestone deserts of the Apennines in so far as they, at least, are diversified in contour.[53]

From whichever side one climbs out of the surrounding lowlands into the Sila plateau, the same succession of trees is encountered. To the warmest zone of olives, lemons and carobs succeeds that of the chestnuts, some of them of gigantic dimensions and yielding a sure though moderate return in fruit, others cut down periodically as coppice for vine-props and scaffoldings. Large tracts of these old chestnut groves are now doomed; a French society in Cosenza, so they tell me, is buying them up for the extraction out of their bark of some chemical or medicine. The vine still flourishes at this height, though dwarfed in size; soon the oaks begin to dominate, and after that we enter into the third and highest region of the pines and beeches. Those accustomed to the stony deserts of nearly all South European mountain districts will find these woodlands intensely refreshing. Their inaccessibility has proved their salvation—up to a short time ago.[54]

By keeping to the left of Circilla, I might have skirted the forest of Gariglione. This tract lies at about four and a half hours' distance from San Giovanni; I found it, some years ago, to be a region of real 'Urwald' or primary jungle; there was nothing like it, to my knowledge, on this side of the Alps themselves; nothing of the kind nearer than Russia. . . . Gariglione was at that time a virgin forest, untouched by the hand of man; a dusky ridge, visible from afar; an impenetrable tangle of forest trees, chiefest among them being the 'garigli' (*Quercus cerris*) whence it derives its name, as well as thousands of pines and bearded firs and all that hoary indigenous vegetation struggling out of the moist soil wherein their progenitors had lain decaying time out of mind. . . .

Well, I am glad my path to-day did not lead me to Gariglione, and so destroy old memories of the place. For the domain, they tell me, has been sold for 350,000 francs to a German company; its primeval silence is now invaded by an army of 260 workmen, who have been cutting down the timber as fast as they can. So vanishes another fair spot from earth! And what is left of the Sila, once these forests are gone?[55]

It was the timber merchants, mainly from outside the area, that were responsible for the most extensive destruction in the forests of Sila during the late nineteenth and early twentieth centuries, but the peasants and the goats made their own contributions:

There followed a pleasant march through pastoral country of streamlets and lush grass, with noble views downwards on our right, over many-folded hills into the distant valley of the Sinno. To the left is the forest region. But the fir trees are generally mutilated—their lower branches lopped off; and the tree resents this treatment and often dies, remaining a melancholy stump among the beeches. They take these branches not for fuel, but as fodder for the cows. A curious kind of fodder, one thinks; but Calabrian cows will eat anything, and their milk tastes accordingly. No wonder the natives prefer even the greasy fluid of their goats to that of cows.

'How' they will ask. 'You Englishmen, with all your money—you drink the milk of cows?'

Goats are over-plentiful here, and the hollies, oaks and thorns along the path have been gnawed by them into quaint patterns like the topiarian work in old-fashioned gardens. If they find nothing to their taste on the ground, they actually climb trees; I have seen them browsing thus, at six feet above the ground. These miserable beasts are the ruin of south Italy, as they are of the whole Mediterranean basin. What malaria and the Barbary pirates have done to the sea-board, the goats have accomplished for the regions further inland; and it is really time that sterner legislation were introduced to limit their grazing-places and incidentally reduce their numbers, as has been done in parts of the Abruzzi, to the great credit of the authorities. But the subject is a well-worn one.[56]

With a single stroke of the pen the municipalities could put an end to the worst form of forest extirpation—that on the hill-sides—by forbidding access to such tracts and placing them under the 'vincolo forestale'. To denude slopes in the moist climate and deep soil of England entails no risk; in this country it is the beginning of the end. And herein lies the ineptitude of the Italian regulations, which entrust the collective wisdom of rapacious farmers with measures of this kind, taking no account of the destructively utilitarian character of the native mind, of that canniness which overlooks a distant profit in its eagerness to grasp the present—that beast avarice which Horace recognised as the root of all evil. As if provisions like this of the 'vincolo forestale' were ever carried out! Peasants naturally prefer to burn the wood in their own chimneys or to sell it; and if a landslide then crashes down, wrecking houses and vineyards—let the government compensate the victims!

An ounce of fact—

In one year alone (1903), and in the sole province of Cosenza wherein San Giovanni lies, there were 156 landslides; they destroyed 1940 hectares of land, and their damage amounted to 432,738 francs. The two other Calabrian provinces—Reggio and Catanzaro—doubtless also had their full quota of these catastrophes, all due to mischievous deforestation. So the bare rock is exposed, and every hope of planting at an end.[57]

When we turn to other forest regions with which we have been concerned, we have to rely on much less satisfactory evidence. For Italy, by examining papal accounts, local records, and descriptions of the country, it would be possible to build up a fairly detailed forest history of most of the regions. In most other Mediterranean countries no such detailed records exist and we have to make what we can of the accounts of travellers from the sixteenth century onwards. We have suggested that in Italy the most critical period in the decline of the forests was the late nineteenth and twentieth centuries. In a very brief and superficial survey of other areas we shall limit our objective to considering how far the emphasis on the nineteenth century in the history of deforestation is applicable elsewhere.

One great difference should first be stressed. As one moves into the eastern Mediterranean, the annual rainfall tends to decrease, and the summer heat becomes more intense and lasts longer. Natural regeneration becomes much more difficult and goats become a more serious menace. In most eastern Mediterranean lands goats have a much more important role in the rural economy, and since the proportion of good agricultural land is very small these peoples have a stronger incentive to convert forest to agriculture or pasture; and they have no coal to relieve the pressure on wood for fuel. As a result of these weaknesses the forests of the east have fared considerably worse than those of the west and while the western Mediterranean countries had established by the end of the nineteenth century more effective forestry services, the gap between east and west has widened.

If we proceed eastward from Italy we find that Yugoslavia has retained more good timber than most Mediterranean countries. There is no evidence that the Adriatic coast and its immediate hinterland were denuded during the Roman period. There may have been a small timber trade between Adriatic ports and the east coast of Italy, but most of the cities on this coast were within easy reach of forests. The records of the Venetian fleet in the sixteenth and seventeenth centuries show that there were still substantial reserves of good naval timber near the Dalmatian coast. The Venetians were also strong enough to exercise a measure of control over the management of the forests, in spite of the opposition of peasants who resisted restrictions on their grazing and cutting. In the interior there was less population pressure than in neighbouring countries and transport problems were a great obstacle to development until the opening-up of the country by railways and new roads in the nineteenth century. But Yugoslavia still has some of the best oak and spruce in Europe.

Greece has had a very different forest history. North Greece, which in our period was Macedon, is closer in climate and soil to Yugoslavia than to central and southern Greece. The rainfall is higher and the summers are cooler and it has suffered less from population pressures. In our period, as we have seen, most of the states of central and southern Greece were not self-supporting in timber. The Athenian fleet was largely dependent on fir and pine from Macedon and Theophrastus lists a wide range of overseas forests from which the Greeks imported timber for building and joinery. But when Greece was overshadowed by Macedon and the patterns of trade changed, she no longer had the resources to afford the quality and quantity of timber that she had drawn from overseas in the fifth and fourth centuries, and economic decline brought with it a decline in population. Appearances could be kept up in some Greek cities by the patronage of Hellenistic kings and, later, Roman emperors, but when, with the collapse of the Roman empire, such props were withdrawn life in Greece became increasingly impoverished. But the decrease in population provided an opportunity for woodlands to recover.

It is a widely held view that the main responsibility for the deterioration of Greek forests rests with the Turks, but the figures suggest that much more has been lost since the establishment of Greek independence. It has been estimated that at the time of independence forty per cent of Greece was under forest: the area has now been reduced to fourteen per cent, and much of this is degraded, with considerably more coppice than high forest.[58] The difference between the Greek forests that Leake saw early in the nineteenth century and their present condition is very revealing.

In Asia Minor the fortunes of the various main forest areas have differed considerably. Strabo found it sufficiently distinctive to draw attention to the fact that Cappadocia was almost entirely treeless,[59] and Livy describing a Roman campaign emphasises the lack of trees in a large area of Phrygia near Pessinus.[60] It is probable that the central plateau, with its extremes of temperature, was never well wooded, but there should have been plenty of woodland on the periphery. It is difficult to reconcile the large area of hypocausts in the Roman baths at Ankara with the bareness of the landscape round the city, but the forest-stripping was not all done by the Romans. In 1402 Tamburlaine was able to conceal his herd of elephants in a wood outside the city. In view of the apparently unrestricted use of wood by the Phrygians in their capital Gordium during the archaic period, there should have been well-stocked forests within easy reach from the city. Today there is little more than a thin scatter of pines and junipers,[61] but we cannot trace the main stages of deforestation.

There is a striking contrast in the forests behind the Black Sea and the sea of Marmara. These forests had a high reputation in the world of Greece and Rome and they have always had a rich range of trees including fir, pine, beech, chestnut, oak, and maple. From Theophrastus we know that their timbers were exported to Greece as well as to other parts of Asia Minor, but we do not know the pattern of the trade. Our evidence suggests that Athens relied on Macedon for her fleet and we know of imports from Samos, Cnidus, and Crete, but there is no hint of a timber trade with Black Sea ports. Megara had established colonies at Byzantium and Heraclea. It would be interesting to know whether she took advantage of the relationship to trade in timber from the Black Sea. Amisus, Sinope, and Heraclea were well known for the quality of their ship-timbers but we do not know which fleets depended on them.

When Byzantium, renamed Constantinople, became the capital of an eastern empire the increasing population of the city will have increased the demand for building-timbers and fuel. But there was no fear of general deforestation. When Cuinet towards the end of the nineteenth century examined the administrative and economic resources of Turkey, he was surprised by the comparative lack of exploitation of these forests. There were still dense forests east of Trebizond. In the district of Sinope, which in the Greek period had been noted for its table woods and ship-timber, Cuinet was greatly impressed by the size of the timbers that were being cut, and they were being exported to Egypt as well as Constantinople. Until recently wooden ships of war had been built in the docks, and merchantmen were still being built there. The forests that Xenophon so much admired to the west of Heraclea were now called the sea of trees, and the hinterland of Nicomedia still had substantial forest reserves.[62] One of the main reasons for the survival of so much forest was

the lack of roads and tracks in mountainous country, where
many of the forests were virtually inaccessible. Nor were local
populations sufficiently large for the maintenance of fuel supplies to impose a serious threat.

Another area that was still well forested in the late nineteenth
century was the south-west of Asia Minor, Lycia and Caria.
Here communications were particularly undeveloped and there
were good reserves, especially of cedar, juniper, and pine, though
cypress, which in our period was one of the commonest trees of
the region, was much less conspicuous. The reports of Philippson and De Planhol provide evidence of the increasing pressure
on the forests in more recent years.[63] Rhodes also was still well
wooded at the end of the nineteenth century with cypress and
pine, but Cuinet found the woods fast disappearing because of
the lack of effective control.[64] Too much timber was being
exported, and trees were being widely burnt to secure grazing.

The Taurus range in the south has suffered much more
seriously over the centuries, but it seems probable that the
greatest damage has been done during the last hundred years.
When Kotschky visited the mountains behind Adana towards
the eastern end of the Taurus in the middle of the nineteenth
century, he found the mountains well-stocked, with oak and
pine on the lower slopes, and on the higher slopes with cedar, fir,
pine, and juniper.[65] He was particularly enthusiastic about the
cedars, considerably more impressive than the firs, and he
implies that there were healthy stands of cedar also all along the
range.[66] On the coastal plain outside Adana there was an
enormous oak forest which seems to have been controlled by
brigands sufficiently formidable to discourage the keenest of
botanists. Less than fifty years later the forest had disappeared.[67]
During the same period at the western end of the Taurus a large
forest that had extended into the coastal plain had now been
heavily overcut and the trees had disappeared from the plain.[68]
Two factors help to explain the very sharp decline of the Taurus
forests. During the nineteenth century there was an increasing
conversion of forest to agriculture and grazing, and there were
still too many goats for the pasture available. At the same time
these forests were called upon to meet the large demands of
Egypt, especially when the Suez Canal was being built.[69]

Meanwhile in north Syria there was no shortage of timber.

Mts. Amanus and Cassius were still well wooded when Cuinet visited them at the end of the nineteenth century. Along the Jebel Ansarieh, running southwards behind the coast from the Orontes to the Nahr Al Kabir just north of the Lebanon range, there had until recently been an abundance of oaks and pines, but Egyptian merchants had nearly stripped the forests.[70] His references to Lebanon are even more gloomy. Cuinet's primary concern was the economic strength of the regions. For him the forests of Lebanon had no economic importance.[71] The days of substantial timber exports from Phoenician cities were long past.

The history of the Lebanon forests is obscure, but it differs sharply from the pattern of the Taurus and Amanus. During the Bronze Age and in the archaic period the pressure on Lebanon was considerably stronger. Egypt relied almost exclusively on Lebanon for the timber which she could not supply from her own resources, and the kingdoms of Mesopotamia, while relying primarily at first on Amanus, tended from the seventh century onward to turn to Lebanon. In the Persian and Hellenistic periods the evidence suggests that the navies of Persia and Syria drew on more timber from Lebanon than from Taurus. Unlike Amanus and Taurus, Lebanon had also to supply the basic needs of large populations in the coastal Phoenician cities, especially Byblos, Beirut, Tyre, and Sidon, and their needs included not only timber for ships and building but also for iron-smelting and glass-making, and in the medieval period for a large silk industry.

There is no clear evidence for the state of the Lebanon forests at the end of the Roman period. Good cedars were still available when the great Christian basilica was built in the fourth century at Tyre (p. 87), and cedar roof-timbers could be found for the church of the Virgin in Jerusalem in the sixth century, though in the account by Procopius they were very difficult to find.[72] Ship-timber was also taken from Lebanon in the struggle between Byzantium and the Moslems, but it seems that the drain on Syria and Cilicia was much heavier.[73] The northern forests of the range were also affected by the migration of the Maronites. This Christian sect had broken away from the Syrian church and had at first settled at Apamea on the Orontes, but under pressure from the Moslems they had taken refuge in Phoenicia and settled with their goats in the mountains. In the records of the Crusades there is strangely little written about the Lebanon forests, but it is interesting to note that in their siege of Beirut in 1110 the Franks could get sufficient timber to make their siege equipment from a pine forest not far from the city. Their siege tower was said to have been fifty cubits high and their rams sixty cubits long.[74]

Towards the end of the seventeenth century Evelyn could write, in reference to western 'cedars':

> I do not speak of those which grow on the mountains of Lebanus or the colder, and northern tracts of Syria. But as I am informed by that curious traveller, Ranwolfius (since also confirmed by that Virtuoso Monsieur Monconys), there remains now not above twenty four of those stately trees, in all the goodly forests, where the mighty prince set four score thousand hewers to work for the materials of one only temple and one palace, 'tis a flagrant example of what time and neglect will bring to ruine, if due and continual care be not taken to propagate timber.[75]

The same impression was given by a French traveller in the early eighteenth century in his account of a visit to Syria and the Lebanon. He described the Bsharre cedar-grove to which Evelyn had referred, and said that none of the natives whom he questioned had ever seen any cedars other than those in this one grove.[76]

More than a hundred years later Hooker in 1862 published a serious study of the famous cedar-grove and wrote emphatically that, in contrast with the flourishing forests on the lower slopes, there were no other cedars in the higher levels, and probably never had been.[77] In the fourth edition of his *Natural history of the Bible* published in 1875 Tristram could write: 'At least nine distinct localities have now been ascertained, some of them containing many thousand trees and with an attendant succession of young saplings springing up round them.'[78] Moreover, there still remain vivid memories of the wholesale felling of cedars and firs before the First World War to feed the railway that was to run from Aleppo to Baghdad, and during the Second World War by the British for a railway from Syria to Palestine. But in spite of these heavy inroads, there are still substantial areas of fir and cedar forests at the northern end of the range and the number of surviving stands of cedar located has been increased to fourteen, spread through the whole length of the range.

It is difficult to explain the aberration of Hooker and his predecessors, but it seems probable that by the end of the seventeenth century, and probably much earlier, the cedars on Lebanon had been reduced to small isolated stands, apart from the Bsharre grove which was protected by the Maronite church, and forests at the north end of the range. So far as Byblos, Beirut, Tyre, and Sidon were concerned the cedars were finished; the northern forests were less accessible. But Hooker found the lower slopes well-forested, and large new forests of the umbrella pine (*Pinus pinea*) were planted in the nineteenth century between Beirut and Sidon. Today they are the most impressive woodlands in the landscape. There is little now to suggest that cypress was once one of the most valued trees on the mountains, but in the middle of the nineteenth century Kotschky seemed to know that there were pure stands of cypress in his day.[79]

In Cyprus we have good evidence for the state of the forests in the late nineteenth century, but the progress of deterioration is as opaque as for Lebanon. Eratosthenes, quoted by Strabo, said that the plains of Cyprus were once covered with woods. The clearing of the land for agriculture began with the provision of fuel (and presumably pit-props) for the production of copper and silver and then of timber for shipbuilders, when the seas could be sailed in safety. But even so, the incentive of free possession of land that had been cleared for agriculture was needed.[80] There is no certain mark of time in this statement. The mining of copper in Cyprus began before the Bronze Age and fleets were being built long before the end of the Bronze Age, but perhaps Eratosthenes had the eighth or seventh century in mind, when at the end of a long recession the sea lanes were again being opened up for trade and colonisation.

While there were plenty of trees on the plains it is unlikely that there was any large-scale cutting in the present two forest areas, the Troodos mountains in the west and the Kyrenia range in the north; nor are the exports of timber likely to have been large before the death of Alexander. During the Hellenistic period it was different. When there was no generally accepted successor to inherit Alexander's newly won empire it was natural that Syria and Egypt should become the bases for rival marshals.

In the continuing long conflict between the Seleucids of Syria and the Ptolemies of Egypt the Ptolemies could very rarely rely on regular supplies of timber from Lebanon. The lines of communication were too long to sustain without a decisive victory. An alternative source of timber supply was essential and Cyprus was the natural choice.

When Demetrius from Syria won possession of the island in 307 he built his famous eleven-oar with Cyprian cedar,[81] and after the Ptolemies had regained control of Cyprus we find Ptolemy Philadelphus building warships in Cyprus.[82] Naval timbers from Cyprus were also used as diplomatic gifts. When Demetrius in 306 promised Athens ship-timbers for a hundred triremes it seems likely that the timber was cut in Cyprus (p. 145), and the pine timbers sent by Ptolemy Euergetes to the city of Rhodes, which had been devastated by a violent earthquake in 227 BC, could not have come from Egypt; they too were probably from Cyprus (p. 145).[83]

When Cyprus became a Roman province and Egypt was also annexed by Rome the strain on the forests of Cyprus should again have been relieved. The timber that was needed for Egypt could again come from Lebanon, Syria, or Cilicia. As late as the fourth century, as we have seen above (p. 381), it could be recorded that in Cyprus a merchantman could be built and fully equipped from keel to topsails from the island's own resources.[84] That the forests were not yet seriously depleted is supported by other frail pieces of evidence. Cyprus was still able to supply ship-timbers in the wars between Byzantium and the Moslems;[85] and, according to Eutychius, fifty 'cedars and firs' were cut in Cyprus for the patriarch of Jerusalem in the early ninth century.[86] It would seem that cedars were then considerably more plentiful than their present state might suggest, but in his description of a journey to Lebanon in 1722 De La Rocque reported that on two journeys to Cyprus he had not found anyone who had seen a cedar tree in the island, 'where it is claimed that there were once large numbers'.

We have to wait until 1872, when Cyprus came under British control, for firm evidence about the general state of the forest. From early reports and from the records of the forestry service established by the British the main stages in the recovery of the forests can be traced. In the early years the goat dominates the story. The forests were being ruined by overgrazing. Mature trees were being burnt to secure more and better grazing, or to produce pitch, which had a good price on the market. Trees large and small were maimed in search of fuel.

How gradual the decline had been must remain uncertain, but a fair case can be made for regarding the nineteenth century as a decisive phase in Cyprus, as in many other forest areas.[87] The governing factor was the rapid growth of population in the island. Villages became towns and much of the common land, which provided grazing, was needed for building and agriculture. At the same time there was an increasing demand for milk and cheese, the main products of the goat. The result was a sharp increase in the number of nomadic shepherds who relied mainly on the forests for their grazing. Forest regulations and forest guards were for a long time powerless to control them effectively.

In north Africa also, in Tunisia, Algeria, and Morocco, the nineteenth century was a critical period, and for Tunisia and Algeria we have a good witness. In 1877 Lieutenant-Colonel R. L. Playfair, Consul-General in Algeria, wrote an account of a tour in the two countries, following in the footsteps of the explorer Bruce, a predecessor in his office who a hundred years earlier had kept a detailed account of what he saw.[88] Playfair was particularly impressed by the striking changes that had been made in the landscape in such a short period. Bruce had frequently alluded to forests through which he passed where there were now no trees to be seen.

Near Sbeitla Bruce had seen a well-stocked wood of pines (called firs by Bruce), from which the inhabitants made pitch; and they were still there, with an admixture of juniper (*Phoenicea*), in 1873 for Desfontaines to see. When Playfair came they had all disappeared: 'At present not a tree or a bush is to be seen on the wide plain as far as the eye can range; its inhabitants have disappeared almost as completely as the pitch they once made.'[89] On his way from Sbeitla to Hydra Bruce had noted that the mountains were covered with pines and cedars, 'the resort of lions'. Playfair, who had not followed Bruce here, was surprised: 'If cedars ever existed in the regency of Tunis they certainly do not at the present day.'[90] From Sbeitla Playfair himself had gone through Sbiba to Mukhter. Near Sbiba he crossed a high plain where Desfontaine had recorded a forest of pines and Phoenician junipers. It was now 'destitute of trees'.[91]

More important light on the nineteenth-century history of the forests comes from the Aures mountains in the south-east of Algeria, a journey, according to Procopius, of thirteen days from Carthage.[92] This vast range runs from south-east to north-west for roughly ninety-five kilometres with a minimum width of about seventy kilometres. The highest mountain in the range is Djebel Chellia (2,286 m.) and several others are higher than 2,000 metres. The Aures mountains were famous for their cedars and when Bruce arrived the forests had been barely touched: 'This mountain (range) is of a very considerable height, but inferior to Atlas, beautifully covered to the top with thick woods of cedar; on the top fine plains and plentiful pasture.'[93] Playfair found great changes. On Djebel Chellia near the summit were woods and clumps of cedars, more dead than living, some of the dead still standing, others torn up by the roots by violent storms. On the other (south) side of the mountain Playfair rode through a dense cedar forest in the valley of Tizoughagkan, with an occasional gnarled yew, but both trees were 'fast disappearing', and the highest timber-level was bare, though whitened stumps showed that it had once been wooded.[94]

But the timber resources of the area were still considerable. Near Lambaesis Playfair found vast oak forests which could supply 'an unlimited quantity of timber' for use at Batna. But the forest 'greatly requires thinning, the mature trees are too crowded'.[95] The finest scenery of the area that Playfair found was near Ain Meimoun, where the vast forest of Belezma of some 14,000 hectares produced a steady supply of timber to two sawing establishments, one military, producing timber for public constructions, the other private, producing timber for the timber trade.[96] But this forest was exceptional. Playfair's general impression was pessimistic. He noted everywhere in Algeria, and especially in the Aures mountains, the absence of young trees, for the sheep and more especially the goats destroyed the young growth as soon as the seeds germinated. But he had some sympathy with the peasants: 'It is difficult to decide whether to protect the young trees by prohibiting the natives from introducing sheep and goats into the forests or to protect the people who, in a country where there is little space for agriculture, can hardly live without their flocks and who have been a pastoral race from the earliest ages.'[97]

But while the goats and sheep were preventing the regeneration of the forests, the demands for fuel and timber for a sharply increasing population encouraged irresponsible cutting: 'Influences which it is difficult to control are causing their (the cedars') gradual disappearance, and there was a time when the reckless extravagance with which timber was consumed threatened to consummate the evil in our own time.' Playfair hoped that new regulations and controls introduced by the French would prove effective. But the coming of French colonists and the changes of land tenure that followed created new problems.[98]

Before the middle of the nineteenth century the populations of Tunisia and Algeria were very small indeed, and were kept small by famine and disease. There was no pressure to grow more food and most of the plains were allowed to remain uncultivated, providing good pasture for increasing flocks of sheep and goats. When the French colonists were settled on the land to bring it into cultivation, most of the natives preferred to move into the hills rather than work on French estates, and in the hills they preferred to live by their flocks rather than take on new land from the forest to cultivate.[99] The natural results were a sharply increased demand for fuel, and overgrazing in the forests. The loss of their grazing in the plains also created a bitterness which found one of its outlets in the systematic burning of forests. Forests were also affected by the increase of population which was partly due to the improvement of public health and communications.[100] However, French forestry services had considerably improved the prospects of the forests when the First World War broke out.

The two World Wars of 1914 and 1939 imposed new pressures on the forests throughout the Mediterranean. With supplies of oil cut off or severely restricted wood again became a major source of energy. It was needed as fuel, for building, for mines, for weapons, and for other less familiar uses. It was even used for fuel on trains in north Africa, as in Phoenicia. Forestry principles were submerged under the demands of war. In the second war some of the Mediterranean countries suffered even more severely than in the first. Occupying armies had little interest in the future of other peoples' forests; Greece and Italy suffered particularly severely.

But the shock of the Second World War sharpened attention on the social and economic effects of deforestation and gave rise to a mood of international concern for the future of the forests. Through the agency of the Food and Agriculture Organisation of the United Nations there was a concerted effort to apply the forestry skills of the more advanced forestry services to the problems of forest reconstruction where they were most needed. Programmes of reafforestation and forest control were drawn up in many countries, including an ambitious attempt to restore the cedar to its pride of place on the Lebanon mountains. The cedar was chosen as the symbol of the independent state of Lebanon and a cedar in the Bsharre grove was reproduced on the national flag and on Lebanese coins. A vigorous attempt has also been made to re-establish it on the mountains, following detailed reports and recommendations by international experts.[101] In 1976 the impressive number of seedlings in the nurseries and young plants on mountain terraces encouraged great hopes for the future, but when the world recession induced by the sudden sharp increase of oil prices in 1973 was followed by civil war and instability, the prospects of the Lebanese forests became very clouded. In the worsening political and economic climate of the eighties, in almost all countries foresters feel considerably less confident than in the fifties and sixties. When national economies come under strain forestry programmes tend to be among the first victims.

Meanwhile great changes have taken place in the position of timber in national economies. In the seventeenth century Evelyn could write:

Since it is certain and demonstrable that all arts and artisans whatsoever, must fail and cease, if there were no timber and wood in a nation (for he that shall take the pen and begin to set down what art, mysteries or trade belonging in any way to human life, could be maintained and exercised without wood, will quickly find that I speak no paradox). I say when this shall be well considered, it will appear that he had better be without gold, than without timber.[102]

Evelyn could not foresee concrete sleepers, steel girders and pit-props, plastic furniture, and the exploitation of oil and gas. Nor could he foresee that in a fast-moving world it would no longer be sound economically to plant oak, beech, and other hardwoods, and that one of the largest demands for wood should come not from the building trade, the mines, nor the railways, but for pulpwood for the production of paper.[103]

APPENDIX 1

Woods from Egypt
in the Ashmolean Museum, Oxford

OLD KINGDOM

| 1914–39 | statuette | fig-wood |

MIDDLE KINGDOM

E 3907	coffin: box and lid	Tamarix sp.
	pegs	Tamarix sp.
	chest	Zizyphus spina-christi
1911. 477	coffin: planks	Ficus sycomorus
	pegs	Tamarix sp.
1895. 153	coffin lid	Ficus sycomorus
1921. 1301	bow	acacia
1912. 600	head-rest	Tamarix sp.

NEW KINGDOM

1885. 375	bow	acacia
1971. 74	figure of Osiris	Tamarix sp. (cf. T. articulata)
	dowel from above figure	Tamarix sp. (cf. T. nilotica)
	chariot-wheel hub:	
	spoke	elm
	flange	Tamarix sp.

UNDATED

1885. 375	arrow	?acacia
1887. 3265[b]	arrow	acacia
1892. 1464	arrow	acacia
1927. 3046	handle of flint engraving-tool	spruce

The woods were identified at the Ashmolean Museum by A. C. Western, who described the construction of the chariot-wheel hub in *JEA* 59 (1973) 91-4.

Egyptian *Ash*-wood

In the main text I have accepted what used to be the popular conception of the cedars of Lebanon. From the splendid language of the Old Testament it was assumed that the cedar was the dominant species at the higher altitudes of the Lebanon range, the glory of the forests. It was an essential element in this picture that the Egyptians relied mainly on these cedars for the long lengths of good-quality timber that they could not supply from their native trees. There was, however, among some botanists considerable scepticism. We have seen that in the middle of the nineteenth century Hooker, one of the outstanding botanists of his day, who made a scientific study of the Bsharre grove of cedars, maintained that this was and probably always had been the only cedar forest on Lebanon. Unknown to Hooker the same claim had been made by De La Rocque more than a hundred years earlier (*Voyage de Syrie et du mont Liban* (1722) 83 ff.); and the local inhabitants whom he questioned maintained that they had never seen any cedars elsewhere. The most extreme form of this scepticism is found in the Loeb edition of the *Enquiry into plants* by Theophrastus. The Greek word *kedros* recurs in several contexts and in all the passages it is taken to mean some species of juniper (Index in vol. 2, p. 455 f.), *oxycedrus*, *excelsa*, or *phoenicea*. In no instance is *kedros*, which admittedly is often used for juniper, made to mean cedar.

Any such extreme view must be rejected. The detailed surveys of the Lebanon range in the period following the Second World War have revealed groups of cedars, most of them degraded, along the whole length of the range. Sufficient samples of ancient wood in Israel and Egypt have been securely identified as cedar to show that there must have been a fair supply of cedar on Lebanon. If all the references to *kedros* in Theophrastus referred to junipers there should be more evidence of juniper-wood used in Egypt. There are admittedly three junipers, *foetidissima* and *excelsa*, and more rarely *drupacea*, that almost certainly grew at the same altitude as the cedar, and were often mixed with cedar. They too could grow high, exceptionally up to eighty feet, but not so high as the cedar and the descriptions of cedars in the Bible do not fit the juniper. But though there are significant differences in the form of the trees, the qualities of the two woods are very similar, and they were probably often cut together.

A more serious attack on the primacy of the cedar has been made by Egyptologists. By far the commonest of the woods that the Egyptians imported was called *ash* (ꜥš), and it was widely assumed that *ash*-wood was cedar. This assumption is now rejected by an increasing number of Egyptologists, who have accepted the main arguments developed by V. Loret in an article published in 1916 (*Annales du service* 16 (1916) 28–51).

Loret rejected the identification with cedar for three main reasons: (1) In Egyptian paintings *ash*-wood was painted yellow or white, whereas cedar, having a reddish-brown heartwood, was painted red. (2) One of the principal uses of the wood was for the flagstaffs erected against the faces of the pylons of temples, which might require lengths of more than eighty feet. Such timbers could not come from cedars, whose main character was their massive girth which limited their height. Moreover most cedars had more than one main stem: a few metres from the ground they split into three or four independent leaders, each with its secondary horizontal branches. (3) *Ash*-wood was important to the Egyptians for its resin in mummification; the cedar has very little resin. Only the fir (*abies*), according to Loret, satisfied the conditions, though the word might be used to cover pine as well. Loret also maintained that the Egyptians represented *ash* as a fir and not a cedar. There are two reliefs in question. Seti I (*c.*1350) commemorated a victorious campaign in Phoenicia and beyond in a series of reliefs on the north wall of the great temple of Amon at Karnak and in one scene princes of Lebanon are felling trees for their Egyptian masters. The trees in this relief (pl. 2) look like straight poles with no branches but nicely balanced leaves (or possibly cones) on short stalks on either side. Very similar trees are depicted on another relief illustrating the capture of a fortress whose site is unknown. These 'trees' are singularly unlike trees of any kind, but perhaps even more unlike cedars than firs. The sculptor, who probably was ignorant of the form of the tree, was more interested in the pattern than realism. It has been suggested that he was familiar with flagstaffs (for which some of these timbers were used) and added leaves to convert them to trees.

Although Loret's arguments have been widely accepted by Egyptologists, no new evidence has been introduced to strengthen them and little attention has been paid to sources other than Egyptian, or to the use of *ash*-wood for other purposes than flagstaffs. It can be admitted that fir would be a more suitable wood for flagstaffs if sufficient good firs were available, but reasons have been given for believing that Lebanon was not well stocked with firs (p. 56) and that cedar was considerably better suited than Loret suggests. Cedars growing close together in high forest will grow up to 100 feet, as they still do in some forests of south Turkey, and Pliny reports that the largest cedar recorded, grown in Cyprus, was 130 feet tall and was cut for a particularly large warship, presumably to make a mast (*NH* 16. 203). Cedars with more than a single stem are exceptional, and usually the result of a goat's browsing when they were young.

The difficulties arise when other uses of *ash*-wood are considered, especially monumental doors, boats, chests, and coffins. If Loret is right fir was used for all monumental doors for which the wood is recorded (*AR* 1. 148; 3. 217, 537, 625; 4. 357, 358, 910, 958M., 970), though cypress and cedar should also have been available. Would the Egyptians choose differently from the Assyrians, Greeks, and Romans? We shall see that the Assyrians almost always used cedar or cypress for the doors of palaces or temples (p. 419). In Greece cypress was much more accessible than cedar and cypress was used for the Parthenon, the temple of Asklepios at Epidaurus, the temple of Artemis at Ephesus, and probably the temple of Apollo at Delphi; cedar was used for the door of Apollo's temple on Delos, and for the treasury at Eleusis. There is no recorded instance in Greece of a temple door of fir. Similarly the Romans used cypress for the doors of the basilicas of St. Peter and St. Sabina, though they had ample supplies of the best-quality firs in the Apennines. The explanation of the preference for cypress and cedar is clear enough: it was the fragrance of the wood, its immunity from rot and insects, and its durability.

Ash-wood was also used for building boats, especially for royal and sacred barges that would carry kings and gods up and down the Nile. Native acacia was used extensively by boat-builders, especially before the second millennium, but for gods and kings *ash*-wood was preferred. Two kings in the seventh and sixth century BC recorded that they found the sacred barge of Osiris built of acacia and built a new barge of *ash*-wood (*AR* 4. 916, 1023). In the summary of the revenues of the gods in the reign of Rameses III (1182–1151 BC) there are twelve ferry-boats and tow-boats of *ash*-wood, seventy-eight tow-boats, canal boats, and boats for the transport of cattle, made of acacia. In the papyrus record from a royal dockyard the main timbers used are *ash*-wood and *meru*-wood, both imported (p. 63 f.); and the same two woods are used by Snefru in the third millennium for boats of 100 cubits (p. 63). In the scene showing Lebanon princes cutting down trees for Seti I some of the timber was to be used for the great barge of the 'Beginning of the river'.

It might be thought that fir was appropriate in these cases because both the Greeks and Romans regarded fir-wood as the best timber for triremes, but here again fragrance and durability were more important: boats for the gods should last, as nearly as possible, for ever. It is also significant that Theophrastus in discussing ship-timbers says that the peoples of Syria and Phoenicia, unlike the Greeks, use *kedros* for their triremes because they have little fir or pine (*HP* 5. 7), and according to Pliny (*NH* 16. 203) who is not here following Vitruvius, the kings of Egypt and Syria are said to have used cedar for their fleets. The introduction of Egypt is derived from a source other than Theophrastus and provides independent confirmation. But perhaps the most telling argument is the boat that was found near the pyramid of Cheops (*c.*2590 BC).

There had been five boat burials by the pyramid. Three had already been robbed, but two had survived, and one has been excavated. This burial was sealed by massive limestone slabs and the boat, which may have been built to carry the king's body to his burial place, was found crushed but in a remarkable state of preservation. All the timbers were delicately raised and the boat, 43.4 metres long, could be put together with its original timbers. The only wood identifications that have been published (M. Z. Nour, M. S. Osman, Z. Iskander, A. Y. Moustafa, *The Cheops boat* (Cairo, 1960) 45) show a surprising variety. Two small pieces of wood from above the limestone blocks were found to be cedar and acacia. A piece from an oar-blade was probably hop-hornbeam of south-east Europe and Asia Minor, another from an oar-shaft was cedar. Pegs from a door were acacia. A piece from a 'board' was juniper, and another, from a 'beam', was probably *Balanites aegyptiacus*. A fragment from a tongue was thought to be *Mangifera indica*, but since it is unlikely that Egypt at that stage was in contact with India, this last identification would need to be confirmed by further sampling. The wide variety in these samples could be misleading, for they omit what we most want to know. They do not include the main timbers and many of these were very large, one at least over sixty feet long (22.72 × 0.52 × 0.10 m.). It is interesting that juniper was used as well as cedar; there is no evidence of fir. The unhesitating impression of the excavators was that the scent of the wood was of cedar or juniper.

Cedar and cypress are also more attractive woods for boxes, chests, particularly chests containing clothes, and coffins. There is a record from the seventh century BC of mortuary chests of *ash*-wood and *meru*-wood (*AR* 4. 966).

In the well-preserved tomb of Rekhmara, chief minister of Tuthmosis III in the later years of his reign, his duties are illustrated in great detail. In his inspection of the work of craftsmen the cabinet-makers are described as 'making chests of ivory, ebony, carob-wood, *meru*-wood, and of cedar of the best of the terraces (*AR* 2. 755; P. E. Newberry, *The life of Rekhmara* (1900) pl. 17). The close association of *ash* and *meru* in these cases, as in the boats of Snefru (p. 63) and the royal dockyard (p. 63 f.), suggests that *meru*-wood was cypress, though this can be little more than a reasonable guess.

For sarcophagi and coffins the superiority of cedar among imported woods is confirmed by identifications already published. In the 1962 edition of Lucas's *Ancient Egyptian materials and industries* there are six coffins and a sarcophagus of cedar, and only one coffin each of cypress, juniper, fir, pine. The next edition should add considerably to cedar identification. Of the thirteen Egyptian coffins in Czechoslovakia that have been examined more recently the majority were made of native woods, especially sycomore; two cedar coffins are the only ones made of imported wood (p. 485 (n. 24)). It will be surprising if the majority of the coffins and sarcophagi in the British Museum are not also found to be made of cedar. But the most important addition to the list will be the coffin of a high official of the Old Kingdom who was 'overseer of the storehouse of *ash*-wood' (H. Junker, *Giza* 8. 91). The wood of his coffin in the Hildesheim museum has now been identified as cedar (Dr Arne Eggebrenlit very kindly gave me this information before its publication). This is not formal proof, but it strengthens the identification of *ash*-wood as cedar.

One final point may be tentatively suggested. Since cedar and the taller junipers grow at the same altitude, and since the properties of their wood are very similar, is it not possible that the same word was used for both species? This might be thought to be ruled out by the inclusion of *wahn*, which is commonly taken to be juniper, with *meru*-wood and *ash*-wood in the timbers cut for Tuthmosis III (p. 66). This difficulty could be met if *wahn*, which is otherwise found only in medical texts, was *Juniperus oxycedrus*, which grows at a lower level, is a much smaller tree, and has very different leaves (sharp-pointed instead of appressed).

APPENDIX 3

Confusion of Species

1. Cedar and Juniper

It is a major embarrassment that in both the Greek and Latin languages the same word is used for cedar and juniper, *kedros* and *cedrus*. The problem is complicated by the fact that both Greek and Latin have a separate word for a tree that is generally regarded as a form of juniper, *arkeuthos* in Greek, *juniperus* in Latin. Vitruvius (2. 9. 13) says that *juniperus* and *cedrus* have the same qualities as the cypress. This confusion has been mentioned in the main text, but unpalatable complications have been evaded. While I cannot offer a comprehensive solution, I need to explain some of the assumptions I have made. A brief discussion of the evidence may save the time of others.

Junipers belong to a large family which have certain properties in common. Their wood is very hard and strong, the colour of their heartwood is reddish-brown, they have an aromatic scent, and their fruit is more like a berry than a cone. They grow extremely slowly. They differ from one another in the form of their leaves and the height to which they will grow. The ones that concern us most are those which grow in the highest zone and produce the most useful timber: *J. excelsa* and *J. foetidissima*, growing exceptionally up to eighty feet, and the much rarer *J. drupacea*, growing up to sixty feet. In the middle zone *J. phoenicea* produces good wood, but does not normally grow higher than thirty feet. In the western Mediterranean *J. thurifera* takes roughly the place of *foetidissima*. The commonest of all junipers in the Mediterranean, *J. oxycedrus*, is more often found as a bush than a tree. It very rarely grows beyond twenty feet but is valued for its berries and oil. The main difference between junipers and cedars lies in their trunks, their leaves, and their fruit. The trunks of junipers are much slimmer and tend to be twisted, their leaves with two exceptions (*oxycedrus* and *drupacea*) are appressed and similar to cypress leaves, whereas the cedar's leaves are needles; whereas the juniper's fruit resembles a berry, the cedar has a cone similar to the other conifers. The trees are easily distinguished in the forest, but their woods are very similar.

It seems reasonable to believe that since *kedros* does not seem to be derived from any of the languages of the Near East, the word was adopted before the Greeks had come into contact with the cedars of the eastern Mediterranean. It may seem strange that when they did become familiar with the ports of Syria and Phoenicia they did not introduce a new word for the new tree; the reason may be that they were influenced by the wood that they saw in the cities, which was so like their own juniper-wood. Some such explanation of the use of words, even if right, does not, however, solve our main practical problem. How do we decide when *kedros* or *cedrus* mean cedar and when they mean juniper? There is no alternative to judging each case according to its context.

There are some passages in which one can be confident that cedar was meant, others where it is probable; some where it is impossible, more where there are inadequate grounds for a decision. The clearest case is Pliny's statement (*NH* 16. 203) that the largest *cedrus* tree recorded grew in Cyprus and was 130 feet tall. There is no other record of cedars in Cyprus in any ancient texts, and early western botanists visiting Cyprus had become convinced that Pliny had made a mistake. It was not until 1879 that S. Baker, a Fellow of the Royal Society, sent a letter to J. D. Hooker, president of the Linnean Society, reporting that he had found unmistakable cedar trees growing in a remote area of the Troodos mountains. He owed the discovery to a monk whose story he did not accept until a branch from one of the trees had been brought to him. We can also be confident that when Strabo (669) says that Antony gave Cleopatra a part of Cilicia which was rich in *kedros* he is referring to cedar, because the coastal town to which the ship-timber was brought, Hamaxia, is a little west of Alanya and there is still a substantial cedar forest in the Taurus range behind the coast at this point.

For our study Syria and Phoenicia are more important. Theophrastus, illustrating the point that the performance of trees depends on how far their situation suits them, says that in the mountains of Syria *kedros* trees are exceptionally tall and massive (*HP* 5. 8. 1); some of them are so large that three men (with outstretched arms) cannot completely encircle them. The emphasis on height and girth should be decisive against juniper, which is less tall than the cedar and considerably smaller in girth. He goes on to say that they are even larger and more beautiful in the parks, and it may be significant that he does not mention height for park cedars: since they were grown more for pleasure than for profit, they would be allowed more room to expand. The mention of parks is more appropriate to Lebanon, where the kings of the richest coastal cities could be expected to have their

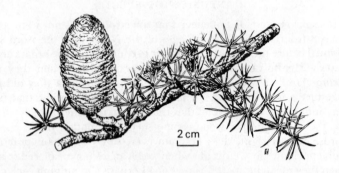

2 cm

(a) *Cedrus libani*

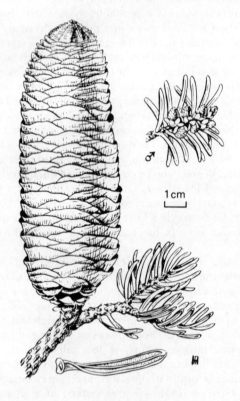

1 cm

♂

(b) *Abies alba*

15 (a) and (b)

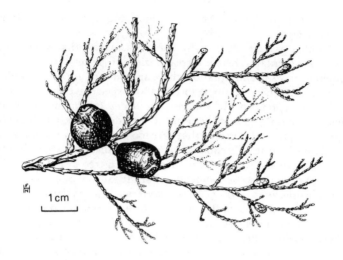

(c) *Juniperus excelsa*

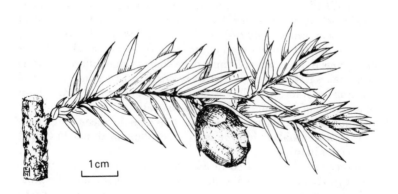

(d) *Juniperus drupacea*

15 (c) and (d)

reserves, than to Syrian Amanus which was more remote from powerful centres.

In another passage (*HP* 3. 2. 6) Theophrastus says that whereas on most great mountains there is a great variety of species of trees, owing to differences of soil and situation, there are some mountains on which the forest is confined to a single species or one species is dominant, and he cites the cypress on Mt. Ida in Crete, *kedros* on the mountains of Cilicia and Syria; and since he seems to include Phoenicia in Syria in the previous passage, I assume that here too he includes Lebanon with Amanus and Taurus. My choice of cedar here is dictated largely by my conviction that the cedar was the more valued tree in Lebanon, for reasons given in the second appendix. For the same reason I infer that when Theophrastus (*HP* 5. 7. 1) says that the Syrians and the Phoenicians used *kedros* for their fleets he means cedar and not juniper.

There is another passage in Theophrastus (*HP* 4. 5. 2) which does not favour cedar. After listing trees and plants that like a cold climate, he says that by contrast fragrant trees grow in hot places and in the south. Warm places, for instance, favour cypress: Crete, Lycia, and Rhodes; but *kedros* grows also in the mountains of Thrace and Phrygia. No cedars have ever been recorded in Thrace, and excavation in the Phrygian capital at Gordium has shown that juniper trees of fine quality and in substantial quantity grew in the neighbourhood (p. 459). It is interesting to note that there was, according to Aristotle (*Hist. An.* 620a 33), a place in Thrace that was once called Kedreipolis. Theophrastus should refer to junipers. There is a strange variant in Pliny (*NH* 16. 137) that is difficult to understand. In a very similar context he says that nature had bestowed *cedrus* on the regions of extreme heat (*aestuosis partibus*), but it grows in Lycia and Phrygia. The intrusion of Lycia in place of Thrace cannot be dismissed as Pliny's carelessness in translation; it must have come from a different source. What makes it interesting is that there is still in Lycia one of the best surviving cedar forests in the eastern Mediterranean, and at Gordium the samples of ancient wood microscopically examined include a small number of cedar-wood (p. 459). This does not mean that Theophrastus was mistaken; but the source that Pliny used may have had *kedros*-cedar in mind.

Juniper may be indicated in an ambiguous passage in Vitruvius (2. 9. 13). He has been saying that *juniperus* and *cedrus* have the same qualities as cypress, being immune from worms and dry rot. 'The tree (*cedrus*) has leaves like the cypress and has a straight grain . . . and it grows best (*nascuntur maxime*) in Crete, Africa, and some parts of Syria.' Pliny follows him closely (*NH* 16. 197). The combination of Africa and parts of Syria might seem to favour cedar, but Crete is placed first and, as we have seen, the grounds for believing that there were once cedars on the island of Crete are controversial (p. 100). Vitruvius' statement that *cedrus* has leaves like the cypress favours juniper, but oddly enough De La Rocque, describing in the early eighteenth century the famous cedars of the Bsharre grove in some detail, thought that they resembled cypress leaves.

In passing from the trees to their woods it is even more difficult to discriminate. I have assumed that the *kedros* beams used for the roof of the Odeum of Herodes Atticus in Athens were cedar-wood (p. 216), because Philostratus emphasises the cost of the wood: it was expensive even for sculptures. This would be natural for cedar-wood imported from the eastern Mediterranean, but much less likely for juniper-wood, which could have been found in Greece. From the use of cedar in this Odeum and the strong preference in Assyria for cedar roofs I have assumed that the *kedros* roof-timbers of the temples of Artemis at Ephesus, of Apollo at Utica, and Apollo on Delos were all cedar-wood. From Philostratus' association of *kedros* with sculpture I have assumed that the *kedros*-wood used by sculptors in the archaic period in Greece (p. 311) and the Apollo Sosianus (*NH* 13. 53; p. 322) were also cedar. But clearly these inferences are not conclusive.

The two words *kedros* and *cedrus* were also associated with an oil or resin which was widely used in Egypt and was well known to the Romans. According to Herodotus (2. 87. 2) it was used by the Egyptians in the process of embalming to destroy the intestines; according to Diodorus (1. 91. 6) it was used to preserve the body. Pliny (*NH* 24. 17) reconciles the apparent contradiction: 'it preserves dead bodies uncorrupted by time and corrupts living bodies'. It is probably what Martial (8. 61. 3–5) calls *oleus cedri* (usually translated as cedar oil), which will preserve for ever the parchment on which he writes. In modern times what is called cedar oil still has the same properties and is sometimes used for medical purposes, but it comes from the tree that the Americans call red cedar, though botanically it is a juniper, *J. virginiana*.

Vitruvius (2. 9. 13) complicates the problem. He says that *cedrus* and *juniperus* have the same virtues and advantages and, as resin comes from cypress and pine, so from *cedrus* comes the oil which is called *cedrium*. When it is put on books and other things they are not harmed by worms or rot. Its leaves are like cypress leaves; the wood has a straight grain. The statue of Diana in the temple at Ephesus and the coffers of the roof are made of it 'because it lasts for ever'. While most of this passage seems to refer to cedar, the comparison of leaves with the cypress suits *J. excelsa* better.

Pliny (*NH* 13. 53, 24. 17) attributes this 'cedar oil' to a tree which he calls *cedrelate*, a name very rarely used: 'Its seed is like that of the cypress. From it is obtained the resin which is so highly valued. Its wood lasts for ever and so they have used it for figures of the gods. The Apollo Sosianus which was brought to Rome from Seleucia is made of it.' This passage is independent of Vitruvius and points more strongly to cedar. The word *cedrelate* suggests a tree that is a cross between a juniper and a fir. This would be an intelligible description of a tree that is like a juniper but taller, and though *cedrelate* is usually taken as *Juniperus excelsa*, Pliny's statement that the seed is like that of the cypress fits the cedar's cone, but not the juniper berry. One other piece of evidence needs to be considered before the cedar is dismissed. What the Akkadian texts call 'the blood of the cedar (*erinu*)' was important enough to be demanded as annual tribute from Syrian princes (p. 74).

It would be convenient if *cedrium* was produced by both cedar and juniper.

2. Cypress and Juniper in Hebrew and Assyrian Texts

The tradition that cedars from Lebanon provided the main building-timbers for Solomon's temple has never been seriously challenged. The identification of the second wood supplied by Hiram has fluctuated considerably. The Hebrew *beroš* has been variously translated as pine, fir, cypress, and juniper. Of these the first two can probably be dismissed: pine certainly, because the climate of Palestine suits Aleppo pine which still grows well there; fir probably, because it is vulnerable to rot and is comparatively short-lived. The choice lies between cypress and juniper which are both well suited because, like the cedar, they remain sound for hundreds of years, have an agreeable aromatic scent, and are virtually immune from decay and insect attack.

Those who have the best command of the languages and of the botany have made a very strong case for juniper and their main arguments are set out by Zohary in the *Hebrew Encyclopaedia of the Bible* (Jerusalem, 1956) 2. 339–41 and by Löw in *Die Flora der Juden* (1926–36) 15. 33–6. These arguments may be briefly summarised: (1) Hebrew *beroš* and Akkadian *burašu* are cognate with the Aramaic *Beruta*, *Berata*, and *Aberata*. (2) The contexts in the Bible (notably Isaiah 14: 8, 37: 24; Zechariah 11: 1–3) suggest that *beroš*, like the cedar, flourishes at high altitudes. The taller junipers, especially *J. excelsa*, are not uncommon in the Lebanon and Taurus forests, and in the forests of Lycia. (3) In Ezekiel 27: 5 *beroš* from Senir is used for the Tyrian ship of State, and while *J. excelsa* is common on Antilebanon, no cypress has been recorded there. (4) Wild cypress still grows in Gilead and Edom; it is reasonable to infer that it was once widespread in Palestine, and would not therefore be needed by Solomon from the Lebanon.

This thesis depends on the identification of *burašu* with juniper, though until recently cypress was preferred, as by Luckenbill in his translation of Babylonian and Assyrian royal documents and by Thureau-Dangin in his translation of Sargon's eighth campaign against Urartu. In this second case juniper suits the context better, because juniper is the dominant high conifer in the Zagros mountains where the campaign was fought. There is also a much stronger case for accepting *šurmenu* as the Akkadian word for cypress (M. B. Rowton, *JNES* 26 (1967) 268; R. Campbell Thompson, *A dictionary of Assyrian botany* 186) related to the Arabic *sarbin* and Syriac *šarwaina*. We can safely follow the *Chicago Assyrian Dictionary* and von Soden's *Wörterbuch* in identifying *burašu* with *J. excelsa*. They also both identify *dapranu*, which occurs frequently in Assyrian texts, as another form of juniper, probably *J. dupracea*, less tall and considerably less common.

The choice of cypress for *beroš* derived from the usage of the Septuagint and Vulgate in which it was translated as *kyparissos* in Greek and *cupressus* in Latin. It could also be added that in modern Hebrew *beroš* is cypress, and that Josephus, who implied that he had access to Phoenician records, also made cypress the second Lebanon wood in the temple, though he says that later Hiram sent cedar and pine to Solomon (*Antiq.* 8. 54, 141). Against these points it can be argued that the translations in the Septuagint and the Vulgate are often unreliable, that in the revival of Hebrew in the nineteenth century many mistakes were made, and that Josephus was living more than a thousand years after the building of Solomon's temple, which was completely rebuilt in the sixth century BC.

The case for cypress becomes stronger when we compare the relative importance of *burašu* and *šurmenu* in Assyrian texts. These suggest to me that of the trees available to the Assyrians cypress was considerably more appreciated than juniper. In the Lipšur litanies (E. Reiner, *JNES* 15 (1956) 129-45) Lebanon is among the cypress mountains (nos. 9-11), while Amanus and Sirara (Hermon) are among the cedar mountains (nos. 5-8). From other sources it is clear that cedar was considered more important, but the description of Lebanon as a cypress mountain shows that cypress was widespread in Lebanon forests. In the same way Amanus which is often called a cedar mountain is sometimes called a box mountain.

More important evidence comes from the imperial inscriptions, which throw light both on the distribution of species and on the uses of the various woods. These uses may be divided into three categories:

(1) Construction, especially for roofing, which is often specified.
(2) Monumental doors, to which special importance was attached.

They were normally not less than twenty feet high and required long straight boards.

(3) Interior work.

The following lists are not complete, especially since I have been unable to use texts that have not yet been translated, but the sample is sufficiently large and representative to be significant. I have assumed that *šurmenu* means cypress and *burašu* means juniper.

Abbreviations: Grayson = A. J. Grayson, *Assyrian royal inscriptions*, vol. 2 (1976); Brown = J. P. Brown, *The Lebanon and Phoenicia* (1969).

(1) *Construction*

1. Gudea prince of Lagash, Amanus: cedar and other timbers insecurely identified, Brown, no. 111, p. 117.
2. King of Mari, ?Amanus (above, p. 73): cedar, box, cypress, *elammaku*, Brown, no. 112, p. 177.
3. Tiglath-Pileser I, Lebanon: cedar, Grayson, 23 (81).
4. Assurnasipal, Amanus: cedar, cypress, *dapranu*, juniper, and from *mehru* land *mehru*, Grayson, 143 (586).
5. Assurnasipal, Lebanon: cedar, cypress, *dapranu*, Grayson, 179 (694).
6. Assurnasipal: cedar for roofs of temple at Ingur-Enlil (Balawat), Grayson, 179 (694).
7. Shalmeneser III, Amanus: in his first, nineteenth, and twenty-first campaigns cedar and juniper (in *ARAB* translated cypress); in his eleventh and seventeenth cedar only. For the text *burašu* see P. Hulin, *Iraq* 25 (1963) 50.
8. Shalmeneser III, from north Syria, but not Amanus, included in indemnities or tribute: cedar and cedar resin, *ARAB* 601.
9. Tiglath-Pileser III, Amanus, Lebanon, Ammanana (?part of Hermon): cedar for roofing, P. Rost, *Die Keilinschrifttexte, Tiglath-Pileser III*, vol. I (1893) 75. 26.
10. Tiglath-Pileser III: pillars (or columns) of cedar, Rost, 61. 13.
11. Sennacherib, Amanus: cedar, D. D. Luckenbill, *The Annals of Sennacherib* (1924) 96. 70.
12. Sennacherib, Amanus and Sirara (Hermon): cedar and cypress, Luckenbill, 106. 23–6.
13. Sennacherib, Amanus: cedar for 'armoury', Luckenbill, 129. 59.
14. Esarhaddon: cedar roof for palace in Nineveh, R. Borger, *Die Inschriften Asarhaddons* (1956) 61, episode 22. 8.
15. Esarhaddon: cedar for temple roof, Borger, 68. 9.
16. Esarhaddon, Amanus: cedar for little palace at Tarbis, Borger, 72. 28.

17. Assurbanipal: cedar from Lebanon, cypress from Sirara (Hermon) for the temple of Sin at Harran, M. Streck, *Assurbanipal und die letzten assyrischen Könige* (1916) 2. 171. 45.
18. Nebuchadnezzar, Lebanon: cedar, Brown, no. 126, p. 196.

(2) *Monumental doors*

19. Gudea: temple doors of cedar, I. M. Price, *The great cylinder inscriptions of Gudea*, Part II (1927) 31. 26.
20. Tiglath-Pileser I: (*ašuhu*) for palace reconstruction at Nineveh, Grayson, 33 (125).
21. Assurnasipal: (*ašuhu*) doors for palace at Nimrud, Grayson, 154 (619).
22. Assurnasipal, Nimrud palace: cedar, cypress, *dapranu*, (mulberry), Grayson, 167 (653).
23. Assurnasipal, for temple at Balawat: cedar, Grayson, 179 (694).
24. Tiglath-Pileser III: cypress and cedar, Rost (no. 9) 77. 28.
25. Sennacherib: cypress, Luckenbill (no. 11) 96. 81.
26. Sennacherib: cedar, cypress, juniper, *sindu*, Luckenbill, 106. 23-6.
27. Sennacherib, for the 'armoury' at Nineveh: *burašu*, Luckenbill, 129. 59-60.
28. Esarhaddon: cypress, Borger (no. 14) 68. 10.
29. Esarhaddon, little palace at Tarbis: cypress, Borger, 72. 28.
30. Assurbanipal: cypress, Streck (no. 17) 2. 173. 50.
31. Nabunidus of Babylon: dilapidated door-leaves replaced in cedar, *ANET* 310.

(3) *Interior work*

In some palace inscriptions longer lists of woods are given, usually introduced by 'a palace of . . .'. The woods always include box, which owing to its colour, texture, and durability was in great demand for furniture and wood-carving. The woods in these lists were used for architectural carving, and other interior work.

32. Assurnasipal, for his Nimrud palace: cedar, cypress, *dapranu*, boxwood, (mulberry), terebinth, tamarisk, Grayson, 166 (653).
33. Assurnasipal, the list repeated in a different order and with one addition: boxwood, (mulberry), cedar, cypress, terebinth, tamarisk, *mehru*, Grayson, 173 (676).
34. Tiglath-Pileser III: doorposts of ivory, *ušu*-wood, boxwood, (mulberry), Rost (no. 9).
35. Sennacherib, Nineveh palace: ivory, (ebony), boxwood, (mulberry), cedar, cypress, juniper, Luckenbill (no. 11) 96. 79.
36. Esarhaddon: ivory, *ušu*, boxwood, (mulberry), cedar, cypress, Borger (no. 14) 61, episode 22. 10.

In these lists the dominance of cedar and cypress is unmistakable and perhaps a little misleading. Campaign records are very compressed. When cedar or cedar and cypress alone are mentioned, it should not be inferred that no other timbers were taken, but it does mean that these were considered the most desirable woods. *Burašu* and *dapranu* are also not uncommon in the texts, but *burašu* is never associated with Lebanon, and Sennacherib is the only Assyrian king in our lists who used it for monumental doors. Its primary use was for roofing where its great strength was invaluable, but it was not chosen for more decorative work. It may be significant that though in the royal Phrygian tomb at Gordium juniper logs were used to protect the burial chamber from the weight of the great mound, pine and a little cedar were used for the boards of the chamber itself (p. 459).

In Solomon's temple the second wood was used for the floor and for the main entrance door. Both cypress and juniper would have been suitable for the floor-boards, and perhaps juniper being stronger might be preferred, but for monumental doors cedar and cypress were the favourite woods in the Near East, as they were later in the world of Greece and Rome. There remain two objections to accepting cypress rather than juniper. Ezekiel (27: 5) in his description of Tyre's ship of State says that *beroš* from Senir was used for the hull. If Senir here means Antilebanon juniper is still the most impressive tree on the range and no cypress has been recorded. But Senir could also mean Mt. Hermon, 'the mountain that the Sidonians called Sirion and the Amorites Senir' (Deut. 3: 10). Cypress could be found in Palestine, but unless it can be shown that there were ample supplies of fine-quality cypress, the Assyrian and Greek texts justify a preference for cypress, but with brackets as a mark of uncertainty.

3. Chestnut and Walnut

It was the belief of the Greeks and Romans that hazel-nuts, almonds, walnuts, and chestnuts came to Europe from the east and, apart from occasional faint doubts about the chestnut, this view is still accepted. It is not surprising that in their passage to the west they should be given different names in different places and that there should be uncertainty in translating from Greek to Latin. In Theophrastus the hazel is the nut of Heraclea (on the south coast of the Black Sea), the walnut is the Persian nut, and the chestnut is the Euboean nut, presumably because it was particularly common in Euboea (*HP* 4. 5. 4). But Theophrastus also calls the chestnut the acorn of Zeus (*HP* 3. 3. 1; 3. 4. 2; 4. 5. 4). Two other names were given to the chestnut by the Greeks. There was a strong tradition that it came to Greece from Lydia, and it was called the Sardis acorn, taking its name from the Lydian capital. It was only later, according to Pliny (*NH* 15. 93), that it was called the acorn of Zeus. Theophrastus even adds a fourth variant, when he calls the chestnut the Castanean nut (*HP* 4. 8. 11). When nut-tree or nut-wood are used without qualification identification is naturally more difficult. In Theophrastus nut alone seems to mean hazel, but Athenaeus quotes an author who said that the Greeks used to call almonds and chestnuts simply nuts, and another author who by nuts meant walnuts (Athen. 52b, 52a).

It is doubtful whether the Romans were familiar with the various nuts when Cato wrote his treatise on agriculture, for he speaks of Greek nuts, bald nuts, and nuts of Abella (in Campania). But by the end of the Republic the Latin names were firmly established, and Pliny's descriptions are unmistakable (*NH* 15. 86–94). The chestnut is *castanea*, the walnut is *iuglans*, meaning the acorn of Jupiter (*Jovis glans*). According to Pliny it was generally agreed that the Greeks sometimes called the walnut *caryon* (κάρυον, nut) from the headache caused by its oppressive scent. We need not be concerned with this fanciful derivation, but if the Greeks called the walnut simply 'the nut', it is reasonable to believe that *nux* the Latin equivalent, like Italian *noce*, might also mean walnut. The nut-tree in Juvenal (11. 119) which in the good old days would have been used, when a storm blew it down, to make a table, will be a walnut and the nut-wood beds of Diocletian's edict will be walnut. On the other hand, the mountain nuts of Sinope (ὀροκάρυα) that, with the maple, are in great demand for tables (Strabo 546) are more probably chestnuts than walnuts because, according to Athenaeus (54d), the name given to Sinope nuts (ἄμωτα) was the name given by one of the authors he quotes to chestnuts, and these have always grown well in the area.

It is not unnatural that there should be some confusion in translation between chestnuts and walnuts, for if *iuglans* is derived from *Jovis glans* it should mean the same as the Greek acorn of Zeus, which is one of the Greek names of the chestnut. This may account for mistakes made by Pliny. Theophrastus, in describing the qualities of the chestnut tree (*HP* 5. 6. 1), says that it grows tall and is used for roofing, and is said to give warning before it breaks. This, he says, happened in the public baths at Antandros, and all the people inside the building rushed out to safety. Pliny repeats the story (*NH* 16. 223) but attaches it to walnut, though in this passage of Theophrastus the chestnut is the Euboean nut. The same mistake is made by Pliny when he says that beech and walnut have a good reputation in water and are among the best woods for use under ground (*NH* 16. 218).

Here again he draws on Theophrastus (*HP* 5. 4. 2 and 5. 7. 6), but Theophrastus' chestnut is again Pliny's walnut.

4. *Picea*

Pliny puts *picea* at the head of his list of resinous conifers, and describes the tree in detail (16. 40, 42, 90). It likes the mountains and the cold. It exudes resin copiously. It begins to branch at the base and the branches are attached to the trunk like arms (in pairs). Its shape is like the fir, and like the fir its leaves are comb-like rather than needles, but unlike the fir, whose wood is highly prized, *picea* serves only for shingles, tubs, and a few other things. This is an admirable description of the spruce, which is valued primarily for its resin, and is mainly used for packaging. *Picea* is not mentioned by Vitruvius, but there are scattered uninformative references in prose and in verse (where *picea* is metrically attractive). But today in Italy, while spruce is widespread in the Alps at high altitudes, south of the Alps native survivals are restricted to a small area in the Tusco-Aemilian Apennines (L. Fenaroli, *Note illustrative della carta della vegetazione reale d'Italia* (1971) 109).

During the last Ice Age spruce spread south from its northern home, but when the warmer weather came it retreated northwards. While it has become very rare in Italy it still grows vigorously in Yugoslavia. It was probably less common in Italy in our period than the sources suggest, because *picea* was sometimes a translation of the Greek *peuke*, the mountain pine (Isidorus, *Etym.* 17. 7. 33). Pliny, for instance, says that Bruttian pitch was made from the resin of *picea* (14. 127) whereas we know from the history of the forests, confirmed by Dionysius of Halicarnassus (*Antiq.* 20. 5), that it came from the pines (*peukai*).

APPENDIX 4

Temple Commissioners' Accounts

1. The Epidaurus Accounts

In 293 BC, after a serious plague, the cult of Asklepios, the god of healing, was introduced to Rome in the form of a sacred serpent from Epidaurus, which had become the recognised centre of the cult in the Graeco-Roman world. The earliest evidence of the cult at Epidaurus comes from the sixth century, when an altar was set up to the god in an area primarily associated with Apollo, some six kilometres from the town. By the early fourth century the reputation of the healing centre at Epidaurus had spread widely beyond her frontiers and it was decided to make more adequate provision for the increasing numbers coming to be healed. There followed a long series of building programmes which included a temple, baths, and other buildings associated with the healing process, and accommodation for the pilgrims. For each new building a separate account was inscribed on stone and publicly displayed.

Some part at least of the accounts of almost all these buildings has been recovered and they are spread over a long period, from the second quarter of the fourth to the early part of the third century BC. Most of the texts are collected in *IG* 4². 1, published in 1927. Further study has led to improvements in some of the texts, and several new fragments have been found. A. Burford reviewed all the texts in *BSA* 61 (1966) 254–323, and suggested a chronological order based on epigraphic factors as well as content: her numbers will be quoted with those of *IG*. In *The Greek temple builders of Epidaurus* (1969) she has analysed the organisation of building operations implied by the documents and provided the foundation for this appendix. For the architecture of the buildings, G. Roux, *L'Architecture de l'Argolide* (1961), is invaluable. The earliest document records the expenditure on the god's temple: it is by far the most important for our purposes and fortunately the best preserved (*IG* 4². 1. 102 = B I).[1]

This temple of Asklepios was small (22.45 × 13.20 m.) by comparison with the great temples of Ionia at Ephesus, Miletus, and Samos, and barely a fifth of the size of the Athenian Parthenon. The style was standard peripteral Doric, with an outer colonnade of six columns at front and back and eleven on each side, and an internal colonnade along three sides. The columns and the walls of the cella were of limestone, but the sculptures of the pediments and the akroteria were in Pentelic marble from Attica. As with all major temple buildings a large workshop was built nearby of less expensive materials: the foundations and lower courses were in stone but the upper part was in mud-brick. The record of expenditure was inscribed on a large stele (1.82 × 0.92 × 0.09 m.) in an unusual form. On both front and back faces (the sides were uninscribed) there are two columns, one considerably wider than the other. The wider column is used for the large contracts for which guarantors were required; the narrower column lists small payments mainly to individual craftsmen for work done, roughly contemporary with the larger payments in the opposite column. The entries in the wider column follow a standard pattern, giving in order the name of the contractor, the work which he undertook, the price for which he undertook it, and his guarantor(s). For our purpose there are four entries of primary importance:

ll. 24–6 Lykios of Corinth took the contract to supply fir; the price was 4,390 drachmae; his guarantor was ——

26 Tychamenes the Cretan took the contract to supply cypress; the price was ——. (No guarantor.)

44–5 Sotairos took the contract to supply elm, nettle-wood, and boxwood for the doors and the workshop for 840 drachmae.

32 Damonoos took the contract to supply beams (*dokoi*) to the workshop, for 299 drachmae five obols; his guarantor was Timodamos.

For the structure of the temple the first of these entries was the most important. Theophrastus emphasises the pre-eminence of firs as building material (*HP* 5. 7. 5). Although cedar, cypress, and juniper were less vulnerable to decay and insect attack and lasted longer, fir was easier to find in Greece in long lengths. Its main use will have been for the roof-timbers, but the span of the temple was broken up by the inner colonnade, and lengths of some twenty-five feet would have been adequate for the cross-beams. The contract was given to a Corinthian and this is not surprising. It is very doubtful whether there were any good firs near Epidaurus and local builders were probably much more familiar with the coastal pine. Corinth, which had been one of the leading trading states of Greece since the archaic period, had probably long been accustomed to supply timber to other states which had no facilities to find their own. Corinthians could expect to find willing sellers in Sicyon, or in Ambracia and other Corinthian colonies on the west coast that had forested hinterlands.

Macedonian fir would have been of better quality, but it is unlikely that Corinth drew on Macedon when she had adequate supplies so much nearer. The price, 4,390 drachmae, is among the higher contract prices and can be compared with the price for quarrying and transporting to the site the limestone blocks for one half of the cella, 6,169 drachmae (ll. 14–16). There is no indication of the form in which the firs were carried, whether in the round, squared with the axe, or cut to the sizes required for the roof. Since there is no trace of any payment for squaring in the accounts we can rule out timber in the round. The same argument makes it unlikely that the firs were squared, for the only significant payment for sawing is for cutting secondary timbers (*stroteres*), usually placed over rafters. A large composite consignment of boards delivered by a Corinthian to Eleusis (p. 434) provides an example of cutting to precise specifications before dispatch.

The second most important timber after fir was cypress, but unfortunately the price has not been preserved and so we have no basis for estimating quantity. It is clear that there must have been sufficient fir for all the major roof-timbers and it is unlikely that a wood as expensive as cypress would have been used for the minor boards and battens over the rafters.[2] Cypress was most appreciated from the Bronze Age onwards, as we have seen, for doors, and Epidaurus would be following such precedents as the temple of Artemis at Ephesus and the Parthenon at Athens. The importance attached to the main door of the temple by the architect is shown by the description of it as 'the great door' and by the costs that it involved for timber.

ll. 45–7   Thrasymedes took the contract to construct the ceiling, the door of the cella, and the decorative panels between the columns; the price was 9,800 drachmae.

64–5   Sotairos took the contract to supply ivory for the door; the price was 3,150 drachmae.

68–70   Kaphisias took the contract to do the inlay work on the door; the price was 2,800 drachmae.

72–3   Damophanes took the contract for hinges with their plates, and bolts for the great door of the cella; the price was ——.

73–5   Damophanes took the contract for the collars for the pivots of the great door; the price was 285 drachmae.

93–4   Damophanes took the contract for (nails), pitch, and (?) for the great door; the price was 230 drachmae.

110   To Damophanes for the lock and key of the great door, 240 drachmae.

50–1   For glue for the doors and ceiling, 802 drachmae two obols.

Thrasymedes was responsible for the general design and actual construction of the door, which would be formed of cypress boards, probably with cross-bands also of cypress over them. He may be identified with Thrasymedes of Paros who, according to Pausanias (2. 27. 1.), made the chryselephantine cult statue for the temple of a seated Asklepios. The ivory was for inlays, small figures, and designs inlaid in the wood, and made by Kaphisias. The fitting of the inlays and the joining together of the cypress boards will have accounted for a considerable part of the high cost of the glue. We have no evidence for the size of the door, but it will have been at least twelve feet high and its height helps to explain the cost of its fittings. Thrasymedes was also responsible for the coffered ceiling, for which cypress boards would have been very appropriate.

The only other references to cypress-wood in the accounts come in the minor expenditures and the sums involved are very small: one drachma three obols was paid for dividing cypress (224–5)[3] and five drachmae 'for carting cypress' (225–6). The main cypress contract was taken by a Cretan, who was apparently not required to provide a guarantor. As has been emphasised above, Crete was noted for her cypress trees, and it was from Crete that Athens imported the cypress that she used in her fifth-century building programmes (p. 200). It is reasonable to infer that Tychamenes was well enough known in Epidaurus not to need a guarantor and was helping the Epidaurians to import good-quality cypress from Crete for their 'great door'.

The three other woods mentioned in the accounts, elm, nettle-wood, and box-wood, were to be delivered to the workshop, but they were not intended for the building of the workshop. Boxwood is too small in its dimensions to be used for building, but its hardness, close grain, and agreeable light colour meant that it was particularly valued for small-scale carvings from the Bronze Age through to the Roman Empire, and we have seen parallels to its use on the great door of the Epidaurus temple in Egyptian furniture, and in sarcophagi found in the Russian Crimea (p. 294). Nettle-wood (*Celtis australis*) is linked by Theophrastus with box as being close-grained and heavy (*HP* 5. 3. 1) and good for carving (*HP* 5. 3. 7). Both these woods would have been used for decoration, particularly perhaps in the coffers of the ceiling, as was box in the ceiling coffers of the Erechtheum (p. 281). Elm was different; it was valued mainly for its strength, liable to twist, but very firm when seasoned. In the literary and epigraphic sources it is particularly associated with doors and its main use was in providing the framework, the pivots, the posts, and sometimes the lintel, but not the door itself. It was probably used for the door-frames in the workshop as well as in the temple.

The contract for these three woods was in the hands of Sotairos, an Epidaurian who would seem to have been of some standing locally because he too was not required to find a guarantor. He might have been able to buy elm locally, but he would probably have had to go further afield to find nettle-wood and boxwood, though not beyond the Peloponnese. He also took the contract for supplying the ivory for the door (64-5), and nails and hinges for the workshop (43-4), and the minor expenditures include a payment to him of twenty-three drachmae four and a half obols for lead (273). He also receives several payments for travel expenses: seven drachmae four obols, six drachmae, four drachmae, ten drachmae. In these four cases all that is recorded is the payment, but in another entry a payment of fourteen drachmae is assigned to a visit to Aegina (256-70). There is no reason to associate any of these journeys with his contracts: perhaps he was visiting neighbouring states to secure subscriptions for a building fund, for Epidaurus was building for others as well as for herself. But to be qualified for his contract to supply special woods it seems probable that he was already experienced in buying timber.

The last of the four timber contracts is the least important and the least expensive. The beams that Damonoos was required to supply were for building the workshop. They would be needed for the roof and possibly also for the framing of the mud-brick that was used for the walls above the stone. This would not have required timber of high quality and local supplies should have been adequate. Today pine grows freely on the site and in the neighbourhood; the name of a small island off the coast nearby, Pityussa, shows that the coastal pine was well established long before the temple of Asklepios was built. This is the only one of the four contracts that specifies the form in which the timber was brought to the site, but *dokos* covers a wide range of sizes; we at least know that it was not just a roughly squared log or timber in the round, and that it was thick enough to carry weight, but the word gives no clue to the length of the beams.

There are several other wood entries among the minor expenditures, but they are mostly concerned with handling timber on the site: fitting beams together (165, 196, 201), repairing doors (275, 297), carting timber (179), none of these costing more than three drachmae. A much more substantial payment (43 dr. 2 ob.) was made to Lachares (215) for beams (*dokoi*). The parcel was not taken from the contractors' timbers and was probably supplied from the local trade. Strangely there is only one payment recorded for sawing, and that is included among the minor expenditures. Euterpidas took a contract to cut secondary timbers (*stroteres*) for forty-eight drachmae (234).[4] If he is the same man as Euterpidas of Corinth who took contracts to quarry and deliver the stone for the walls and also to quarry, deliver, and set in place the stone rubble in the workshop, the combination is at first sight strange; but as he had undertaken the quarrying of so much stone, he must have had men in his labour force who were used to sawing stone and would have regarded sawing wood as light relief.

While the accounts of the temple throw light on the contract system and the use of technical terms, we learn very little of the form and lengths in which timber was bought. But some useful information on these aspects can be gained from two other documents in the Epidaurus series. The more useful of the two, from the early third century, records the expenses of building 'houses of hospitality' on Mt. Kyon (*IG* 4². 1. 109 = B xxi). It is considerably less well preserved than the temple accounts, but it includes a large number of timber entries. Some timbers are brought to the site in the round (*strongula*), others are roughly squared (*tetragona*), but in neither case is the timber further described. When only the length is given—four-footers, ten-footers, etc.—we can infer that we are probably dealing with squared timbers. The commonest lengths in the record are ten feet and four feet. There is one parcel of 150 four-footers (109. II. 84) and another of 157 (II. 86); there is one parcel of 240 ten-footers (I. 126) and in a 'summary of all the timbers' the ten-footers outnumber all other lengths. In this case both lengths and prices are recorded (II. 138–41).

Length (ft.)	Number	Price per piece
24	30	12 dr.
18	400	7 dr.
16	30	6 dr.
14	416	4 dr.
10	450	3 dr. 3 ob.

The numbers suggest a fair degree of standardisation. It is only rarely that both length and price are preserved, but the surviving figures for ten-footers show that the price is not constant. In the parcel of 240 the price is four drachmae (I. 126) as it is in II. 136, but on the next line there are seventeen ten-footers at three drachmae three obols, the price in the 'summary of all the timbers'. A generation earlier twenty ten-footers had been bought at six drachmae (108 = B x. 146). Since we do not know whether all ten-footers were of the same wood and had the same dimensions, we cannot be certain that different suppliers charged different prices for wood of the same species, or that the low price of the largest parcel reflects a reduction for quantity.

Timber could also be bought by the wagon: 'The squared timbers which we bought for the houses of hospitality on Mt. Kyon consist of forty wagons of twenty-two-footers at forty drachmae per wagon' (109. II. 144 = B xxi). In the above table twenty-four-footers are priced at twelve drachmae, eighteen-footers at seven drachmae. It would be reasonable to allow ten drachmae for twenty-two-footers, which would indicate four timbers for a wagon-load. There is, however, an anomaly in the price given for the whole contract. In each of the contract payments in this record ten per cent is deducted for security. With this deduction we should expect the price of forty wagons at forty drachmae to be 1,440 drachmae; the figure on the stone is 1,754 drachmae two obols. The same problem arises in a similar contract in another document, roughly a generation earlier: 'Paid to the contractor Dionysodorus for the squared timbers for the colonnade of Apollo's temple, forty-three wagons at forty-eight drachmae per wagon of twenty-three-footers' (*IG* 4². 1. 108 = B x. 162–3). There is no evidence within this document for the price of any timber over ten feet long, but if a generation later a twenty-two-footer cost ten drachmae, twelve drachmae would be a reasonable price, again indicating four timbers per wagon. The cost of forty-three wagons at forty-eight drachmae should be 2,064 and with ten per cent deducted 1,857 drachmae two obols; the figure on the stone is 1,890 drachmae. In this case the difference is very small and could be accounted for by extra loading, but in the other case no such simple explanation is possible.

If it is a fair inference that there was a standard wagon which could carry four timbers twenty-two or twenty-three feet long we can form a more realistic appreciation of the transport problem. If, with Burford, we assume timbers a foot square in cross-section and ignore the small difference between the Greek foot and our own, and allow thirty-five pounds per cubic foot, a twenty-three-foot timber would weigh 805 pounds. Four timbers at this weight would require at least four yokes of oxen to pull each wagon.

Transport costs also could be priced by the wagon, as well as by the piece: 'Paid to the contractor Demetrius for the carriage of squared timbers bought from Timagathos . . . twenty-five wagons at four drachmae five and a half obols per wagon' (109. II. 158–9). There are similar entries in II. 106–7 and in II. 98–9 (restored), but in these cases the price is five drachmae four obols. On the other hand, Philiades transported fifty-nine round timbers at four and a half obols each (109. II. 156–8; cf. 108).

Most of the records of payments for transport are very lean and do not even mention from which area the timber was brought to Epidaurus. One entry is much more explicit (*IG* 4². 1. 110 = B xviii). Glaukias was paid for transporting thirty round timbers at three and a half obols each. They came from Corinth and it seems that they were bought under the terms of an agreement between Corinth and

Epidaurus.[5] No other reference to such an agreement has survived in the long series of accounts from Epidaurus. Had all timber exports from Corinth been subject to state control there should be further evidence for it in the Eleusinian records of purchases from Corinthian territory.

2. Temple Accounts from Delphi

Delphi was the acknowledged religious centre of the Greeks, and the temple of Apollo at Delphi was their most famous temple. It was there that Apollo delivered his oracles and in the archaic period especially he was consulted by Greek states from east and west as well as the homeland, and by foreign states who wanted to maintain good relations with the Greeks. Apollo's oracles declined in prestige with the growth of rationalism, but the panhellenic significance of Delphi was maintained through the classical period and sacred wars 'to protect the god's interest' could still arouse strong passions in the fourth century. Apollo's temple of the archaic period was destroyed by fire in 548 BC and rebuilt before the end of the century, but in 373 BC this temple also was burnt down. A commission of temple builders, *naopoioi*, was appointed to supervise the work, and fragments of their accounts have been recovered. The texts are published in *Fouilles de Delphes* III. 5 (*FD*). Important revisions have been made by J. Bosquet in *Études delphiques*, *BCH* suppl. 4 (Paris, 1977) 91–105.

These fragments cover a long period because the rebuilding was interrupted by wars, and the fragments which are concerned with timber are among the last, when the time had come to construct the roof. The most informative of these, dated in 335 BC, records the purchase of some very substantial timbers, and a rigorous revision of the text (*FD* 36) by Bosquet (91–5) has brilliantly transformed the interpretation. According to this revision the commission, accompanied by the architect, went to Sicyon and there selected seventeen cypress timbers. Some were bought from single sellers, others from two partners, all Sicyonians. They also made a purchase of cypress-wood from a Corinthian. In the following list the price of each timber, if all the timbers in the transaction had the same price, is added.

   1. From a Sicyonian three timbers for 350 drachmae at 116 drachmae four obols.
   2. From two Sicyonians three timbers for 405 drachmae at 102 drachmae three obols.
   3. From two Sicyonians four timbers for 560 drachmae at 140 drachmae.
   4. From a Sicyonian four timbers for 530 drachmae at 132 drachmae four obols.
   5. From two Sicyonians two timbers for 350 drachmae at 125 drachmae.

6. From a Sicyonian one timber for 140 drachmae at 140 drachmae.

7. From a Corinthian two? for 212 drachmae two and a half obols at 106 drachmae one and a quarter obols.

The total cost of these purchases was 3,047 drachmae, which corresponds very neatly, as Bosquet has pointed out, with the record of a payment by the Delphic treasurers to the temple builders of thirty minae (3,000 dr.) 'for cypress-wood' in May 335 (*FD* 50. 9; Bosquet, 95). This makes it certain that following the precedent of the earlier temple (G. Roux, *REG* 75 (1962) 369–70) cypress was chosen for Apollo. It also justifies the restoration indicating the personal involvement of the templebuilders and their architect in the selection of timbers at Sicyon: ἐν Σικυῶνι μετὰ τοῦ ἀ|ρ] χιτέκτον[ος κυπαρίσσινα ξύλα ἐ|π] ριάμεθα . . . Bosquet's discovery that a letter had been lost at the beginning of each line has also led to some minor modifications, the most important of which is the change from two timbers to one in the sixth transaction, which brings the price into rough conformity with the rest. It is a surprise to find that the second Sicyonian seller in the fifth transaction was a woman: the conclusion is based on Bosquet's observation that the crucial letter is triangular (Σικυωνίας).

The prices of these cypress timbers are exceptionally high. At Epidaurus we know the total cost of the firs bought for the roof of the temple of Asklepios, but we do not know the price of individual timbers. In an account from Epidaurus of the early third century the price for the largest timbers recorded, twenty-four-footers, is only twelve drachmae (p. 428). These, however, were probably oak, fir, or pine; cypress was a more expensive wood. In the Eleusinian accounts of 329/8 BC there is a record of the purchase of four cypress logs for 200 drachmae, an average price of fifty drachmae (p. 434). There is unfortunately no indication of size, but there are no major building operations in the year: they are unlikely to have been more than thirty feet long. The cypresses from Sicyon must surely have been intended for the most important timbers in the temple, the cross-beams that indirectly carried the main weight of the roof. The span to be covered was probably not more than thirty-five feet, but to get the thickness needed they may have had to select timbers of up to sixty feet.

It is interesting that the purchase of seventeen timbers should have involved six separate transactions, but a wide distribution of supplies is characteristic of all timber records. If Sicyon was the main outlet for the timber of northern Arcadia it is understandable that the timber trade could have supported a large number of small businesses. The last transaction in our list is different. The supplier is not a Sicyonian but a Corinthian and what he supplies is different from the rest. The word for timbers, *xyla*, does not fit the space available, which requires a word of seven letters. The word for boards, *sanidas*, would fit the space, but a price of 212 drachmae two and a half obols for two cypress boards would be incredible. Since this last purchase comes immediately before the statement about transport, it is reasonable to infer that it too was made at Sicyon. That it should be a Corinthian is not strange, since Sicyon was probably the main source of Corinth's timber supplies. The timbers were bought at Sicyon but they will have been cut in the mountains to the south. Although poets are notoriously unreliable in the choice of epithets, it may be significant that Ovid describes Mt. Cyllene as *cupressiferus*, cypress-bearing.

The transport of these exceptional timbers was a considerable achievement. If we assume an average length of sixty feet, a diameter of about one foot, and a cypress weight of thirty-five pounds per cubic foot, the weight would be nearly a ton, and those figures are probably a considerable underestimate. To load and unload such timbers was not an easy business, and when they had been unloaded at Cirrha, Delphi's port on the Corinthian gulf, they had to be dragged some six kilometres up a steep hill to Delphi. Each timber would have needed at least two yokes of oxen. The cost of transport, 500 drachmae, was roughly sixteen per cent of the cost of the timber.

Other fragments from the accounts show that the wood used in the temple was not exclusively cypress; very large quantities of fir were also involved. The supply of 481 squared timbers and ninety beams of fir at fifty drachmae per piece was divided into two contracts, one taken by Callicrates, an Arcadian from Cleitor, the other by two partners, an Achaean from Ascheos and a man from Croton in south Italy (*FD* 25. 111B; Bosquet, 96). The total cost of the timber was 28,550 drachmae (4 talents, 4,550 dr.) and the value of each contract 14,275 drachmae. The text does not indicate where the timber was to be cut, but since Callicrates, one of the contractors, was an Arcadian and since Arcadia was the nearest area with ample forest reserves, it is reasonable to believe that these firs, like the cypresses, came from north Arcadia. A little further light is thrown on the contract taken by Callicrates in a payment of 6,423 drachmae by the temple builders for fir timbers, probably for the roof of the peristyle (*FD* 38; Bosquet, 97). It is no coincidence that this payment is precisely half the value of his contract with the usual ten per cent withheld for security. It is the second of two payments to Callicrates and the name is confidently restored by Bosquet: [Καλλικρά]τει in place of [Ἀριστοκρά]τει.

Timber for the temple was also bought from Macedon. Nicodamos, an Argive, sawed 1,729 feet of Macedonian timbers into beams at five coppers per foot and was paid 120 drachmae five coppers (*FD* III. 5. 41, col. III. 7–14). The timbers had presumably been roughly squared before they started on their journey from Macedon and had to be converted into the sizes required, probably for the secondary timbers of the roof. If as is probable these Macedonian timbers were either fir or pine, the combination of roof-timbers may have been similar to the pattern adopted in the Parthenon (p. 202).

One last document (Bosquet, 100), in which Bosquet has combined a new fragment with one already published, records a much humbler assignment. Pancrates provided fifty-four pieces of wood, at seven obols a piece, for sixty-three drachmae. They were to support the tiles of a portico not far from the temple and the very low price suggests that they were timbers laid over the rafters.

3. The Accounts of the Eleusinian Commissioners for 329/8 BC (*IG* 2². 1672)

The cult of Demeter and Persephone at Eleusis, which may originally have been of purely local significance, had by the end of the sixth century extended its influence widely through the Greek world and many states accepted a moral obligation to send each year to the sanctuary the first-fruits from their harvest of grain. The Eleusinian Mysteries continued to exercise a powerful appeal even when Greece had become a mere province of the Roman empire, and as the influence of the cult expanded it was natural that buildings should be enlarged or replaced and new buildings added. The responsibility for maintaining the buildings in good state, supervising new building, and meeting the costs of the cult rested with a board of commissioners who held office for four years and set up the annual record of their income and expenditure on a stone stele which all could see. Fragments from several years have been recovered, but the fullest and for our purposes the most useful is from the year 329/8. In this particular record the expenses were listed by prytany, and the accounts of four of the ten prytanies are fully preserved with parts of two others. In the history of Eleusis it is not a dramatic year. There was no major new building, and almost all the timber entries concern restorations or replacements, but it is the best introduction to the timber trade of Athens.

Our main interest lies in two sets of entries covering respectively the purchase and the use of timber. For purchases the fullest formula gives (a) the name of the wood, (b) the form in which it is bought, (c) the dimensions, (d) the purpose for which it is needed, (e) the person from whom it was bought, (f) the price of the individual piece, (g) the price of the whole parcel: 'seven boards (*sanides*) of elm-wood, twelve feet long, ten fingers wide (7 in.), and three fingers (2 in.) thick, the price of each piece fourteen drachmae, the price of the whole parcel ninety-eight drachmae, from Hagias the Corinthian'. This full formula is found in only two purchases; the wood is rarely named, and more than half the entries do not give measurements. In two cases the name of the seller is not mentioned, though this is more likely to be a careless oversight than a significant silence.

A large number of prices have been preserved but in most cases there is no satisfactory basis for comparison. It soon becomes apparent why, although the inscription was first published in 1883, there has not yet been any comprehensive commentary. Our discussion is strictly limited to questions that concern timber and the evidence that leads to some of the inferences in the main text. It is based on two tables. Table I documents the supply and price of timber. The second lists payments for work done with timber in which the source of supply is not given.

TABLE I

	Line	Description	Dimensions (or weight)	Use	Seller	Price per piece
1.	151	7 elm *sanides*	10 ft. × 7 in. × 2 in.	cross-pieces for doors	Hagias, Corinthian	14 dr.
2.	152	4 elm *sanides*	10 ft. × 6 in. × 3 in.	—	Hagias, Corinthian	13 dr. 3 ob.
3.	153	3 elm *sanides*	16 ft. × 9 in. × 4 in.	—	Hagias, Corinthian	20 dr. 2 ob.
4.	156	2 elm *sanides*	15 ft. × 9 in. × 3 in.	sheaves of the block and pulley	Hagias, Corinthian	23 rd. 4½ ob.
5.	168	8 elm *sanides*	9 ft. × 6 in. × 3 in.	lattice doors	Hagias, Corinthian	9 dr.
6.	155	3 ash *sanides*	—	cross-pieces for doors	Hagias, Corinthian	17 dr.
7.	146	3 cedar timbers	12 ft. × 4 in. × 2 in.	treasury door	Simias, *emporos*	70 dr.
8.	191	4 cypress *kormoi*	—	—	Sophocles, Cnidian	50 dr.
9.	147	16 sawn timbers	12 ft. × 7 in. × 6 in.	doors of posterns and treasury roof	—	32 dr.
10.	145	2 pivots	—	treasury doors	Pamphilos P	25 dr.
11.	150	4 *kanones*	—	—	Phormio P	26 dr.
12.	164	3 *kanones*	—	lintel and porch	Phormio P	25 dr.
13.	62	12 *dokoi*	—	—	Phormio	17 dr.
14.	63	93 *stroteres*	—	—	Agathon, son of Philetairos	1 dr. 4 ob.
15.	64	40 *himantes*	—	—	Archias, Samian	1 dr.
16.	65	400 *epibletes*	—	—	Archias, Samian	1 dr. 3 ob.
17.	9-10	olive-wood	10 talents	for wedges	Heracleides T	1 dr. 2 ob. per talent
18.	124	wood vine prunings	67 talents 60 bundles	for Haloia festival	Kephalaeon P	2 per obol
19.	126	olive-wood vine prunings	4 talents 4 bundles	—	Diodorus, metic, Eleusis	2 per obol
20.	193-4	2 timbers 20 *epibletes*	13 ft.	for the kitchen of the city Eleusinion	Philon	total cost 13 dr.
21.	173	timbers	—	doorposts for the lattice doors	Xanthippus P	30 dr.

	Line	Description	Dimensions (or weight)	Use	Seller	Price per piece
22.	208	*himantes* and beams	—	porch of the sacristan's house etc.	Philon	22 dr. 3 ob.
23.	293–4	timbers	—	doors with door-posts and lintels in the house of priestesses	—	—
24.	70	doorposts	—	for the doors in the religious houses	Syros, *emporos*	28 dr. 3 ob.

P = from the Piraeus, T = from the Theseion.

In the commentary that follows numbers alone refer to numbers in the table. Numbers with 'l.' refer to the text in *IG*.

In the first column the Greek words have been transliterated with two exceptions. *Xyla*, a general term which could be used for round timber, squared timber, or sawn timber, is here translated by timbers; *schista* literally meant cleaved with wedges but comes to mean sawn. *Sanides* covers a wide range of uses: accounts were written on *sanides* before they were inscribed on stone, and artists painted on *sanides*; the word is also appropriate for panels. Board is here perhaps a more appropriate translation than plank. The first meaning of *kanon* in Liddell and Scott's lexicon is 'straight rod, bar' and thence the line used by masons or carpenters, 'a rule or straight edge'. It was normally of wood but could be stone. *Dokoi* is the standard term for substantial weight-carrying beams. *Stroteres, himantes,* and *epibletes* are all shown by their cheap price to be very secondary timbers carrying no weight: *stroter* means a timber placed over a bearing beam; *himas* literally means a strap, and when used for wood usually means a timber placed across a rafter, while *epibles*, literally meaning a coverer, is most often applied to thin battens laid over the *himantes* and immediately under the tiles.

The suppliers are differentiated according to status. For Athenian citizens the name alone is normally given, but occasionally the deme is added and, more rarely, the patronymic. The resident alien, the metic, is described as 'resident' in his deme. For foreigners the name is followed by the ethnic. Two men in our table are called *emporos* (7, 24), which means that their business is on a larger scale than the ordinary trade, and the word is usually associated with trade by sea. There are also two further categories that are differently defined: four of the sellers are described as 'from the Piraeus' (10, 11–13, 18, 21) and one is 'from the Theseion' (17). One might expect that, since the normal metic formula was not used, all these traders were citizens, but the name of Ameinias who is 'from the Theseion' (l. 66) recurs later in the inscription as Ameinias resident in Kydathena (l. 168), and as both entries refer to selling baskets at the same price, the natural inference is that these are the same man, a metic. This, however, is not quite certain. In the record of another year, which is undated but must come close to our year (*IG* 2². 1673; revised, with a new fragment, *Eph. Arch.* 1971, 81–113), the name appears again (l. 45), but this Ameinias is not described as 'from the Theseion', nor is a deme of residence added. He too sells baskets, but at a different price, three and a half obols instead of one drachma. Formally there could be one, two, or three Ameiniases.

That this is not an attempt to create difficulties where none exist is shown by other examples. A large consignment of small timbers (*stroteres*) is bought from Agathon, son of Philetairos (14). The patronymic, for which there is no other example in this record, is presumably added to distinguish him from another Agathon, and this could be the Agathon who sells a substantial quantity of glue (l. 161); but in the same record there are two Agathons who are metics, one resident in Alopeke (l. 18), the other in Scambone (l. 179). There could be one, two, three, or four Agathons. A similar problem arises over the name Pamphilos. Two are distinguished, Pamphilos the stall-holder (ll. 13–15, 171) who sells pitch and ruddle, and Pamphilos Otryneus who makes doors for the city Eleusinion (ll. 165–6) and lattice doors for the temple of Pluto at Eleusis (l. 172), and hires out his block and pulley to the commissioners (l. 235); but there is also a Pamphilos 'from the Piraeus' who sells two pivots for the door of the treasury (10), and an undifferentiated Pamphilos in a poorly preserved context (l. 86). One last example: Syros a merchant (*emporos*) sells two ready-made door posts (24); Syros, a metic resident in the deme Alopeke, is paid for plastering and whitening the altar of Pluto. In the year's record close to ours, referred to above, there is a Syros described as rope-seller, *stuppeiopolos* (*IG* 2². 1673. 41, and probably 15), and Syros a metic from the deme Collytos, who sells cheap tunics (47, ?23).

Until these difficulties are resolved statistics comparing the proportion of metics and Athenian citizens in the building operations recorded in the Erechtheum accounts with the proportion in this Eleusinian record must be suspect. It is doubtful whether there was any significant difference and in both there is no sharp distinction in the type of work undertaken. There is, however, one difference that should be noted. In the Erechtheum accounts payments are made to individual slaves, with the name of their master added. These are presumably slaves who have been trained in various skills and have a limited independence, though presumably most of their earnings go to their masters. There is no sign of the practice at Eleusis: the only slaves mentioned are a team of seventeen attached to the sanctuary and used for work that needs no special skills.

A striking feature of the record is the multiplicity of suppliers from whom the commissioners made their purchases: there is no sign of a timber merchant carrying a large diversified stock. The boards in the first six entries are bought from the same Corinthian seller. We have already met Corinthians supplying timber to Epidaurus (p. 424) and Delphi (p. 431), but it is stranger that Eleusis should go to Corinth rather than the Piraeus for ash and elm. These woods were chosen for their strength, and in the uses specified, for doors and for block and pulley, strength was essential; but the cost of transport from the Piraeus (by sea) should have been considerably cheaper, and almost all the other timbers recorded came from the Piraeus. It would be interesting to know whether it was a question of price, quality, or availability. The three cedar timbers that follow (7) are the most expensive timbers in the record, more than four times the cost of elm boards that are considerably larger. The reason lies in the quality of the wood and the distance it had to come. It was sold by an Athenian merchant and must have come from the south coast of Turkey, Syria, or Lebanon. The special purpose for which it was required is explained in the preceding entry (10), which records the purchase of two pivots 'for the cedar doors of the treasury'. Though the Greek word *kedros* is used for both juniper and cedar, juniper can be ruled out here, because it could have been supplied from much nearer, and would have cost much less.

The nearest in expense to the cedar is the cypress (8), costing fifty drachmae for a log. The word *kormos* is used for a trunk or part of a trunk from which the branches have been cut, the more common word being *strongylos*, round timber. But without knowing the length of the log the relation with other prices cannot be determined. The cypress logs were supplied by a Cnidian and the south-west corner of Asia Minor was well stocked with good cypress. If his origin had not been specified it might have been assumed that the cypresses came from Crete, which was noted for its cypress forests and supplied cypress for Athenian temples (p. 99). Next in price come a large parcel of sawn timbers (9), priced at thirty-two drachmae each and used for doors and for the roof of the treasury; the two most likely woods are fir or cypress: the cost is too high for elm, ash, or pine. The two pivots for the treasury doors (10) would almost certainly be specially selected elm, which was generally recognised as the best wood for the purpose, and they come from the Piraeus which suggests that they were imported. The Phormio of 11 and 12 also did his business in the Piraeus, but the

Phormio from whom the commissioners bought twelve beams is a different man and cannot be placed.

The cost of the *kanones* when compared with the cost of elm and ash boards in our table, shows that they were big pieces of wood; cf. *IG* 7. 3073 (from Lebadeia): 'a *kanon* not less than twenty feet long, six fingers wide, and half a foot thick' (6 m. × 12 cm. × 16 cm.). Of the three purchases of small timbers (14–16) we do not know where Agathon did his business, but Archias came from Samos where the commonest trees, apart from olives, were pine, oak, and cypress; pine would perhaps have been the most suitable for these boards or battens. The wood in the next three purchases (17–19) was sold by weight, not being intended for building or furniture. The olive-wood in 17 was used for wedges because of its strength, but it was also good for burning (19). In the other firewood entry the wood was not specified and was probably a mixed lot. In both cases bundles of vine prunings were added; they made excellent kindling material, and are still commonly so used in Greece. While the olive-wood came from the city of Athens and Eleusis, a much larger consignment of firewood was bought in the Piraeus. This does not necessarily imply that it was imported as firewood, though Euboea probably did supply part of the heavy demand; off-cuts and waste from sawing imported timbers could also have been included.

Costs of transport are set out in detail for the large parcel of elm and ash bought from the Corinthian Hagias (158–9). Seven drachmae had to be paid to hired labour for the first stage of the journey from Corinthian territory; a further ten drachmae went to those who brought the timber across the isthmus to the port of Cenchreae and loaded it on board ship, and the charge of the ferryman for taking it from Cenchreae to Eleusis was fifty-six drachmae. The word used for the first stage, *diakalisasi*, implies the use of rollers or at least something different from taking the timber in a cart: it might mean bringing the timber from rough country where it was stacked to a regular track. For the second stage the timbers might have been put on carts and pulled along the *diolkos*, tram-lines built across the isthmus *c*.600 BC, primarily to enable the Corinthians to pull warships across the isthmus, but also useful for the carriage of cargoes. This second stage to Cenchreae will have been about five kilometres. The third stage cost fifty-six drachmae, which may seem unduly high by comparison with the second stage, but the distance is more than fifty kilometres by sea and not less than forty by land. Judging from the cost of the second stage, Cenchreae to Eleusis by land would have been roughly more than twice as high. This is an excellent example of the desirability of taking timber by water rather than by land, but it also illustrates the high cost of transport. The use of the word *porthmeus*, ferryman, suggests a comparatively small caique. Transport costs 'of all the timbers', making a total of seventy-three drachmae, are added after five of the specifications bought from the Corinthian Hagias. There is a sixth specification recorded later in the accounts of a different prytany, with no transport cost added. If as is more probable this specification is included in the cost of transport, the cost of the timber will be 388 drachmae three obols and the transport cost (73 dr.) will represent nineteen per cent of the cost of the wood. If the isolated specification is excluded the percentage will rise to twenty-three per cent.

Transport costs are recorded in only two other cases. (1) The heavy load of firewood and vine-prunings sold by Kephalaeon in the Piraeus for 105 drachmae three obols (18) also went by sea and seven drachmae three obols was paid to the ferryman, roughly seven per cent of the cost of the wood. The alternative would have been a wagon drawn by a pair of oxen, almost certainly more expensive. (2) A supply of pitch, black pigment, and ruddle bought from Pamphilos the stall-holder (ll. 15–18) was delivered to Eleusis by Diokleides for seven drachmae three obols. The total cost of his load was forty-two drachmae three and a half obols, and transport represents roughly seventeen per cent. Pamphilos' stall was probably in Athens. The addition of the nine kilometres to the Piraeus before the sea passage was sufficient to weight the scale in favour of the land route and we may suspect that he relied on a mule. Admittedly there is no trace of mules in our document, but in the other record to which we have referred two men named in an uncertain context are muleteers (*IG* 2². 1673. 18, 20).

Our second table further illustrates the use of timber at Eleusis and its cost, including the cost of labour:

TABLE II

	Line	Operation	Operator(s)	Price
1.	67	making doors	Dionysius, metic, Eleusis	65 dr.
2.	163	making and fixing the doors to the posterns	Callias, metic, Kydathena	85 dr.
3.	165–6	making the doors and porch of the city Eleusinion	Pamphilos, Otryneus	86 dr.
4.	172	making the lattice doors in the shrine of Pluto	Pamphilos, Otryneus	60 dr.
5.	27	laying bricks by the gateway and the tower, working on the timbers	3 builders	2 dr. 3 ob. per day per man
6.	28	carrying bricks, making mortar, bringing up tiles and timbers	6 labourers	1 dr. 3 ob. per day
7.	60	breaking up and sifting earth to make a coat of clay for the wall and the tower, and preserving them with pitch	labourers	1 dr. 3 ob. per day
8.	180	preserving the roofs with pitch	Leptines, metic, Melite	26 dr.
9.	178	for setting up scaffolding for those who were giving a finish to the colonnade and those who were treating the roofs with pitch	Agathon, metic, Scambone	[50] dr.

[Table continued overleaf]

[*Table II–cont.*]

	Line	Operation	Operator(s)	Price
10.	143-4	making the seating for the festival of the Haloia, providing his own timber	Arimnestos	60 dr.
11.	10	sawing olive-wood into wedges	Ariston, metic, Kollytos	20 dr.
12.	66	sawing 5 Macedonian squared timbers to make lintels, and doors, with their frames	Karion	23 rd.
13.	159-60	sawing timbers	a pair of sawyers	3 dr. per day

The first four entries concern the making of doors, which was one of the most common and important uses of wood. Both in public and private building great emphasis was placed on the door, which explains the use at Eleusis of very expensive cedar for the door of the treasury. The next three entries (5–7) concern the restoration of an old cross-wall built of mud-brick. One of the towers had collapsed (ll. 14–15) and other parts of the wall were in a bad state (l. 23). The rebuilding of the wall requires skilled labour (l. 27) but the auxiliary service of taking the disintegrated bricks and rotted timbers away, bringing up the materials for rebuilding, and making the clay mortar was left to ordinary labourers at the unskilled rate. The inclusion of timbers in the materials to be used is a reminder that mud-brick walls were normally strengthened with timbers.

The next entry (8) is one of several providing for the use of pitch on roof-timbers and doors, and three purchases of pitch are included in the record (ll. 13, 69, 170). The concern to preserve building-timbers with pitch is demonstrated no less strongly in the long series of accounts from Delos. Payments for scaffolding (9) can also be expected in most building accounts. The figure for the payment in this case has not been preserved, but it occupied only one space and fifty drachmae is more likely than either of the other alternatives, ten or 100. In the next entry the meaning of the word (*ikria*) here translated by 'seating' is uncertain. The three last payments are for sawing, of very different kinds. In the first (11) small pieces were being cut from a very rough timber. In the second (12) squared timbers were being cut to specific sizes for specific purposes. In the third case (13) the payment is made to a pair (*zeugos*) of sawyers, presumably using a long two-man cross-saw, who are paid by the day and work for thirty-five days, receiving 105 drachmae, which implies a daily rate of one drachma three obols per day per man, no more than the unskilled rate. This entry comes immediately after the detailed statement of timbers bought from the Corinthian Hagias and the cost of their transport. The natural inference would be that the timbers sawn were the timbers bought from Hagias, but these were bought in specific sizes and should have needed no further sawing. The sawyers were probably converting squared timbers into beams, boards, and battens.

4. The Delian Accounts

The tiny island of Delos, a mere speck on the map, lies in the centre of the Cyclades, surrounded by islands much larger than itself. It owes its place in history to its religious prestige, for in Greek tradition it was the birthplace of Apollo and during the archaic period its annual festival attracted large numbers of Ionians from Asia Minor, the islands, and the Greek mainland. When, after the defeat of the Persian invaders, a grand alliance, mainly of Ionian states, was formed under Athenian leadership to carry on war against Persia it was natural that Delos, as an Ionian religious centre, should be chosen for the meetings of the allies and for their treasury. Athens assumed the role of protector of Apollo's sanctuary and the associated cults and when the treasury was transferred to Athens in 454 BC the meetings of the allies were abandoned.

Athens retained her guardianship of Apollo's interests, which she exercised through a board of Amphiktions. With a brief interruption after the defeat of Athens in the Peloponnesian War (405 BC), Athenian control continued until 314 BC when, after the humiliation of Athens in the Lamian War, Delos was declared independent and managed her own affairs until 166 BC when under Roman direction Athenian control was restored. The inhabitants were driven out, and Athenians were settled in their place. At the same time Delos was made a free port and with this advantage became increasingly attractive to traders at the expense of Rhodes. But after nearly a century of prosperity the island was twice plundered, by one of Mithridates' generals in 88 and by pirates in 67 BC. Delos never recovered.

During this long period annual accounts of income and expenditure continued to be published and fragments large and small from some 300 years have survived. The fullest records come from the period of independence and it is this period only with which we shall be concerned here.[1] The management of the properties of Apollo and the associated cults rested with two Delian commissioners, *epistatai*, holding office for a year, and though there were changes in the organisation of the text, the transactions covered in their reports varied very little during the period of independence: the leasing of properties, normally for ten years; the money loans and the receipt of interest for Apollo acting as a banker; the inventories of the dedications in the various temples and cult centres; the expenditure of the year on new building and the maintenance of old buildings, and on festivals and other religious duties. The year's report opens with a statement of interest inherited over the year and ends with the balance handed over at the end of the year. This is the richest archive for the social and economic history of Greece in the Hellenistic period, but two warnings are needed. The detailed information in 374 inscriptions, some of them more than 300 lines long, is so vast that until a very full index is made it is extremely easy to overlook evidence hidden in obscure contexts. It is also dangerous to generalise from Delos whose conditions were exceptional. A fall in land prices in Delos is poor evidence for the state of agriculture elsewhere, when it can be more easily explained by the improving prospects of trade; and the rise of house prices may reflect nothing more than an increase of immigrants as Delos became increasingly important as a trading centre. In the great scarcity of other evidence the Delian accounts have sometimes been made to carry considerably more weight than they can bear.

Among the states whose timber problems have been briefly reviewed Delos is unique in depending entirely on outside resources. There was admittedly a grove of palms on the island and there is a record of one of the trees being converted into usable timber (144. A. 64), but this was a sacred grove belonging to the gods and not available to the timber merchant. There were also scattered fig trees whose wood was usable, but there was no woodland on the island and even Mt. Kynthos above the town was bare and rugged (Strabo 485). Nor was the soil suited to brick-making, being much too light; bricks as well as timber had to be imported. These weaknesses, however, were made less serious by the abundance and variety of stone that could be easily quarried on the island. It was therefore natural for Delian architects to use stone in places where wood might be expected. There seem to be no wooden thresholds in public or private buildings, stone is more widely used in staircases than elsewhere, and in door- and window-frames. The shortage of wood may also be one of the reasons why flat roofs were preferred in private housing: they dispensed with tiles and were more economical in timber. But there was no alternative to timber for gable roofs, for doors, windows, and shutters, and wooden epistyles were considerably more economical in labour than stone, and could span wider intervals between columns. Had Delos remained prosperous into the Roman imperial period the concrete vault might have been widely used, but there was little new building on Delos after the second century BC, and in the main house-building period architects even in Rome were only feeling their way to the development of concrete construction; upper floors in Delos had to be supported by timber joists. And Delos had to look outside not only for building-timbers, but also for firewood and charcoal, needed not only for the kitchen. Public festivals meant public sacrifices; 'wood for the altars' is perhaps the most regular item of expenditure in the annual records.

The range of woods imported by Delos is surprisingly large. The

TEMPLE COMMISSIONERS' ACCOUNTS

commonest in the records are oak, fir, elm, and cedar, but there is evidence also for ash, beech, box, cornel, cypress, lime, mulberry, olive, palm, and a nut-wood (probably chestnut). Pine is only present in the form of the pine torch associated with firewood for the altars, and this is strange in view of the importance attached to the tree by Theophrastus and its wide distribution in Greek lands. It has to be remembered, however, that in the majority of timber entries the species is not recorded; 'Macedonian timbers' may include pine, oak, or other hardwoods as well as fir. Oak-wood was sometimes bought in large quantities. In 246 BC the commissioners bought forty-eight oak timbers (*ID* 290. 221), in 207 they bought forty-five (*ID* 366. 38). Lengths of eight, ten, and twelve cubits are recorded (*ID* 290. 221, 203. B. 99), and in a few cases prices are added. Oak was used for lintels (*ID* 290. 164, *ID* 440. 88) and for barriers to control entrance to a particular part of a building or latticed panels between columns (*ID* 366. 47).

Fir was regarded by Theophrastus as the best general building-timber (*HP* 5. 7. 4–5) and because, besides being easy to work and strong, it provided longer lengths than any other Mediterranean timber, it was usually the architect's first choice for roofing. Where its use on Delos is specified in the records or can be inferred it is mainly associated with roofs. We read of a squared fir beam in the roof of the temple of Demeter that had broken and been replaced by another, but reused elsewhere (*ID* 290. 173),[2] and of a fir timber bought for the stoa by the sanctuary of Poseidon some twenty years after the stoa was built, presumably as a replacement (*ID* 440. 78). Rafters (*sphekiskoi*) recur often; the wood is normally anonymous, but in one case fir is specified (*ID* 403. 19).

It is also reasonable to believe that the long lengths and high prices recorded in 274 BC (199. A. 57–63) imply fir-wood. The building work of this year was concentrated on the palaestra and the theatre and large quantities of timber were involved. They included the longest lengths in the Delian records (l. 58) thirty-cubit (45 ft.) timbers for the theatre stage. There were also several purchases of eleven-cubit timbers, of which five were bought at sixty-one drachmae, two others at forty-three drachmae and fifty drachmae, and one particular timber 'bought by Menyllos for 133 drachmae' (l. 61). Such high figures are very exceptional at Delos where most of the recorded prices are less than twenty drachmae, but the accounts from Delphi provide points of comparison. The most striking prices at Delphi were for the seventeen special cypress timbers bought by the commissioners at Sicyon, ranging from 102 to 140 drachmae; but contracts were also placed for large numbers of fir timbers at fifty drachmae (p. 432). Cypress timbers occur so very rarely in the Delian records that they can be ruled out here. The only other wood which was commonly used at Delos and for which a comparable price is given is oak. Most of the oak prices recorded are modest. In 246 (*ID* 290. 221) a ten-cubit length of oak cost nine drachmae and an eight-cubit length seven drachmae one obol, but a sixteen-cubit oak timber measuring 16 cu. × 1 ft. × 9 in. cost fifty drachmae. However, it is extremely unlikely that an Aegean oak could produce a length of thirty cubits (45 ft.). Macedonian timbers are also specified in the timber purchases of the year (l. 57). Macedon was noted particularly for its firs.

But fir, though most valued for building, could also be used for joinery. When an extra board was needed for paintings in the theatre it was made from one of the fir timbers in stock (158. A. 68; cf. *HP* 5. 7. 4). Firs occur occasionally in the stock records. In 201 BC twenty-three fir timbers had been handed over by the previous year's commissioners (*ID* 372. A. 162); in another year a single fir timber of eighteen cubits was passed on (203. B. 100). But not all fir timbers were long; a squared timber of fir only eight cubits in length is recorded (*ID* 290. 174), but this was to be sawn into secondary timbers, *himantes*, battens laid across roof-timbers.

There are more references to cedar than in any of the other accounts that we have briefly examined. It does not appear in the accounts from Epidaurus or Delphi, and only once at Eleusis, three cedar boards of twelve feet for the door of the treasury at the high price of seventy drachmae each. But the number of references may be misleading. There were thirty-five cedar timbers in stock in 279 BC (161. D. 92–3) and fourteen in stock in 250 (287. B. 144), eight of which were used in the course of the year (l. 146). But does this represent new buying? The first reference to cedar-wood comes a little earlier than 279 with a record of the handing over of 'the cedar timbers bought for the god' (155. 14). The god must at Delos be Apollo and the reference is to his temple, which had been begun in the second quarter of the fifth century and abandoned, probably when the Athenians transferred the treasury of the Delian League to Athens in 454 BC.

Soon after Delos was made independent of Athens plans were made to complete the building.[3] We find later that cedar was used for both roof-timbers and doors, but the work was still not completed in 250 BC. It is reasonable to ask why cypress was not chosen. It shared the main qualities that made cedar attractive to temple architects: it was comparatively immune from decay and worm or insect attack, and it was thought by many to have a more attractive scent than cedar; there should have been ample supplies available in Asia Minor or Crete, and the price should have been lower.[4] Perhaps the architect's choice may have been influenced by the rulers of Syria or Egypt through whose goodwill and perhaps support cedars from Cyprus, Syria, or Lebanon could have been made available.

The references to elm are not very revealing. There were seven elm timbers in stock in 250 BC (287. B. 144) and there are two fragmentary records of purchases of elm (165. 5, *ID* 403, 29). In one summary elm is associated with doors where its usefulness was widely recognised (161. D. 132), but the only entry that tells us what we should not have guessed otherwise is in 279 BC when elm boarding was used to rest, like an abacus, on the top course of the wall of the temple of Apollo and to provide between the cross-beams the larger frames within which the smaller frames of the coffers were set, as in the Erechtheum, and in the temple of Asklepios at Epidaurus (161. A. 112).

The wood chosen for the smaller frames was cornel, which was appreciated primarily, like elm, for its strength (*HP* 1. 6. 1; 5. 6. 4),[5] and was considered by some to be even better than ash for spears. A payment is recorded for carrying cornel-wood, implying a substantial purchase, but the context is lost (199. A. 32). The only other two references are puzzling (287. A. 77, 161. A. 104); they record the purchase of cornel-wood by weight, a practice which is normally reserved for firewood. But since the two purchases of one talent and one half-talent cost together only six drachmae (for roughly 85 lb.), they probably represent waste from the sawing of bigger timbers. If bought for firewood the price would be more than three times the current price, and one of the purchases was required for the door (287. A. 77). Cornel would, like elm, be suitable for doorposts, or perhaps pivots, but why should it be sold by weight?

Of the remaining woods there is little to be said. Beech is only mentioned twice and in one case there is no clue to size, price, or use (*ID* 290. 226); the other is a purchase of sixty-eight pieces of beech together with forty-five pieces of oak (*ID* 366. A. 36-8). The beech pieces cost only three drachmae each and were required for *gomphoi*, probably dowels to join oak timbers. Cypress is mentioned in only one year, when there were two cypress timbers in stock at the beginning of 250 BC and one of them was cut up in the course of the year, and part of it used for a writing-tablet (287. B. 150). In the same year there were twenty-two pieces (the precise meaning of *phalanges* is uncertain)[6] of boxwood, eleven pieces of which were used for carved decoration (287. B. 146). Lime-wood was also particularly suited to architectural decoration (p. 320 f.), and there are three purchases of lime for that purpose in 280 (165. 4, 32, 45). The references to mulberry (161. A. 43, 199. A. 17) tell us nothing about their size, cost, or use, and of *karya*, a nut-wood, we know only that a beam costing seventeen drachmae was used in building a shed (145. 21) and in 279 there were two boards in stock. As a building-timber it was more probably chestnut than walnut.

For the best correlation between the inscriptions and archaeology we turn to the so-called stoa by the sanctuary of Poseidon. The main work on the building was in 208 and 207 and the accounts of both years are well preserved. Thanks to the ingenuity of French excavators and architects we also have enough evidence to identify and reconstruct, with only a small margin of error, the form of the building. Very little remained to be seen before excavation, but by the patient accumulation of scattered members and surviving fragments of walls and foundations the complete ground-plan was recovered.[7] The stoa was built some 200 metres inland from the main harbour, close to the north-west angle of the sanctuary of Apollo.

The southern façade was emphasised by a fifteen-columned portico, and on the other three sides the stoa had an enclosing wall. Within the walls was a forest of columns, nine columns east to west, five south to north. The outer columns were Doric, the inner columns Ionic, but where the central column should have stood there was no trace of column or foundation. This was a clear indication that there was a central lantern, which would have been needed as an extra source of light. The epistyle over the façade was in marble, over the outer columns in stone, but those over the inner series of columns were in wood. The accounts of 208 cover a series of contracts for stonework. The early stages of building the surrounding wall, the southern façade, and the outer Doric columns had been completed, and work was now concerned with the twenty inner Ionic columns. By 207 the emphasis shifts to the woodwork. The main work is on the epistyles and the roof-timbers and on the lantern.

The year's record includes a list of purchases of timber during the year followed by a summary of the timber in stock at the beginning and at the end of the year (*ID* 366. 37–41).

From Aristophanes sixty-five timbers at three drachmae, a total of 195 drachmae.

From Satyrus one beech timber costing three drachmae and two others costing six drachmae.

From Demeas ten rafters at thirteen drachmae three obols, total 135 drachmae.

From Hierombrotus forty-five oak timbers at seven drachmae three obols, total 337 drachmae three obols.

From the collectors of two-per-cent custom dues twenty-nine rafters at fourteen drachmae, total 406 drachmae.

From the guardians of Aristagoras twenty-nine rafters at fourteen drachmae, total 406 drachmae.

From Soterichus seven rafters at fourteen drachmae four obols, total 102 drachmae four obols, and five ten-cubit lengths at eleven drachmae four obols, total fifty-eight drachmae two obols.

From Callistratus nine rafters, total ninety drachmae, 130 bundles of reeds from Demeas and Dionnus (at 1 dr.), total 130 drachmae.

We also took over, with the architect and the elected committee, all the timber bought from Heraclides and what we bought according to the decree of the people, namely the rafters with the ten-cubit lengths, eighty-seven in all, and the sixty-eight beech timbers and the forty-five oak timbers; also the fifty-nine timbers in stock which we took over from the commissioners Elphinos and Lysandros (our predecessors). Of these timbers we gave, on the instructions of the architect Gorgus who was present, to those who contracted to make the epistyles and set the lantern on the stoa by the sanctuary of Poseidon—Phillis, Callicrates, Pyrracus, Philoxenus, Satyrus—131 timbers from those bought from Heraclides, and the eighty-four rafters and the ten-cubit lengths, and the beech timbers for the dowels, and the oak timbers for the *dryphaktoi*; and the timbers we took over from Elpinos and Lysandros (our predecessors). The remainder of the large timbers bought from Heraclides which are still in the stoa, twenty-two in number, and four rafters and sixty-eight bundles of reeds in the Pythion and 1,000 tiles we handed over to the commissioners Apollodorus and Cleostratus (our successors).

The main contracts for the use of the timber are also well preserved. One contract will be translated in detail, the others summarised:

l. 8   To Phillis who contracted to make the epistyles and upper beams and set them up for 1,310 drachmae we paid the first instalment of 436 drachmae four obols; the second of 436 drachmae four obols; the third of 218 drachmae three obols; and the remainder, when he had completed the work, on the instructions of the architect, 218 drachmae three obols.

10   Callicrates contracted to make and erect thirty-eight beams and set them up for 799 drachmae two obols. He was duly paid on the same principle as Phillis, in instalments.

12   Pyrracus took a similar contract for forty-five beams for 735 drachmae. He is presumably the same man who contracted to put the tiles on the lantern for 298 drachmae (l. 31).

14   Philoxenus contracted for the epistyles for the lantern 'and the other work specified' for 1,200 drachmae. He received three instalments totalling 1,000 drachmae, but 200 drachmae were withheld because the architect complained that he had not completed the work according to the terms of the contract.

16   Satyrus contracted for the beams used in the lantern 'and other work specified' for 997 drachmae three obols. He may be the same Satyrus who sold beech-wood to the commissioners (l. 37).

The contract formula used at the end of the third century BC at Delos differs from the formula used at Epidaurus for the temple of Asklepios in the early fourth century (p. 424). At Epidaurus the guarantors were included in the record, and there is no suggestion that the contract price was paid by instalments or that, when the architect was dissatisfied, the full contract price was not paid. The differences are probably less great than they seem. From the accounts for 208 BC it is clear that the commissioners at Delos safeguarded themselves against defrauding contractors. 'These were the expenses according to the vote of the people and the architect Gorgus specified the tasks to be done and gave the orders according to the contracts and the securities offered, a list of which is in the temple' (*ID* 365. 23). The fact that no payment of instalments is recorded at Epidaurus might be because the record gives only the price of the contract and does not mention payment. The natural inference, however, is that one lump sum was paid.

Timber was required in the stoa for epistyles (from column to column), rafters, and secondary roof-timbers between the rafters and the tiles. If, as seems probable, all the main work in wood was done by the five carpenters whose contracts are listed, the word *dokoi*, which normally means a bearing beam, should be taken to include the secondary roof-timbers, which are not specifically mentioned. Most of the timber that they used came from the 153 'large timbers' bought from Heraclides. These were probably squared timbers (normally called *tetragona*) from which epistyles and roof-timbers could be cut to the required size. The commonest building-timbers on Delos were fir and oak and as oak timbers are separately named it is probable that the 'large timbers' were firs, or perhaps firs and pines. These were supplemented by additional purchases in the course of the year from several suppliers.

Of the eighty-nine rafters bought seventy-four were probably of the same length, for there is only a small variation in the prices, thirteen drachmae three obols, fourteen drachmae, fourteen drachmae four obols, but the length is not given. The remaining fifteen rafters were presumably shorter, five costing one drachma each, and ten costing ten drachmae. The size is also omitted of the forty-five oak timbers included in the other purchases, but the price was seven drachmae three obols, which is close to the price paid for oak timbers of ten cubits in 245, seven drachmae one obol (*ID* 290. 221). These oak timbers were probably used in an internal gallery in the lantern. Some twenty years later thirty-five rafters were used in this stoa (*ID* 440. 75). It is unlikely that it took so long to complete the building: these were probably replacements. In the same year a fir timber was bought for the stoa: it may have been to replace one of the epistyles.

The summary of stock in the accounts of 250 BC (287. B. 144–52) introduces other woods and other procedures:

(At the beginning of our year) there were in stock fourteen cedar timbers, seven elm timbers, twenty pieces of boxwood, two cypress timbers, and three oak off-cuts. The oak-wood was used for the sun-dial. To Ctesias who contracted to make the *koilostathmos* and the doors we gave, with the co-operation of the architect and the official supervisors, eight of the cedar timbers, four of the elm timbers, eleven of the pieces of boxwood, and the two cypress timbers. From the timbers given to Ctesias the following were left over:

There follows a list of what remained at the end of the year from the timbers assigned to Ctesias. The list included five of the boards cut for the doors, ten cubits long; the rest were all off-cuts[8] from the cedar, elm, cypress, and box timbers, and it is noted that one of the cypress off-cuts, three cubits long, was used for a writing-tablet.

The contracts undertaken by Ctesias were for work on the great temple of Apollo, as we learn from an earlier part of the record. He received 1,038 drachmae for the doors of the temple and 767 drachmae for the *koilostathmos* (287. A. 96). A model of the doors had been displayed in the Andrian treasury in 269 (203. B. 96), but it was not until 250 that they were made (287. A. 98). As was normal practice, the two leaves of the door were made up of boards glued together, and since the boards left over were fifteen feet long, that presumably was the height of the main entrance to the temple. The woods given to Ctesias for his work on the doors and *koilostathmos* were cedar, elm, box, cypress. The elm was the natural wood for the pivots, posts, and lintel; cedar or cypress would have been natural choices for the doors, but the relative quantities of the two woods make it certain that the boards of the doors were of cedar, recalling the cedar doors of the treasury at Eleusis (p. 437). Boxwood and cypress will have been used for decoration, the carved inlays or attachments that we have already seen glued on to doors and sarcophagi. As in the temple of Asklepios at Epidaurus ivory too was used for the decoration, but a much smaller quantity, costing only thirty-five drachmae as compared with 1,050 drachmae at Epidaurus, and it was used not on the doors themselves but on the door-frame. Ctesias had two contracts, for the doors and also for the *koilostathmos*. The meaning of this word is very uncertain. The lexicon gives 'coffered ceiling' but the price, 767 drachmae, is far too low. The suggestion made by Courby that it refers to the carved decorations applied to the doorposts is more credible.[9] Other costs are associated with the doors, including 605 drachmae for setting them in place; even the decorative nails for the main doors of the entrance to the cella and the much smaller outer doors of the pronaos, 'the doors exposed to the wind', cost 288 drachmae. The total cost would have been roughly half a talent.

The commissioners were not only responsible for maintaining the buildings associated with the cults of Apollo and the other gods, old and new, who were officially accepted; they also had to see that the buildings were adequately furnished. And so the annual records include contracts for the making and repairing of chairs, couches, and tables. The entries throw a little light on the style of the furniture, but in no surviving entry is the wood named. Another important requirement is more usefully illustrated. Delos, as a religious centre, had many festivals in her calendar and their number increased significantly in the Hellenistic period. When the kings of Macedon, Syria, Egypt, and Pergamum competed for influence in Greece, Delos was a natural magnet for their interested benefactions. Like Athens in the Hellenistic period Delos looked to outside sources for her new buildings; rival kings competed with porticoes, and a natural response was a festival in their honour blurring the line between the human and the divine. One of our documents from the early third century gives a formidable list of such festivals and they include Ptolemaieia, Antigoneia, Philippeia, Attaleia (*ID* 366. A. 53–86).

Festivals involved sacrifices of pigs, goats, sheep, and, in some cases, oxen; all required firewood or charcoal, and the larger animals a very great deal of firewood. And so we find regular entries of 'wood for the altars'. In the early years of independence the purchases for the year were totalled in a single entry, but from 250 BC at the latest each month's total was separately recorded. Firewood does not need to be straight or of any standard size and so it is sold by weight expressed in talents (roughly the equivalent of 56 lb.). Three well-preserved records show the scale of consumption:

TABLE I

Firewood for Festivals

	224 BC (*ID* 338)		
Month	Weight (in talents)	Cost (in drachmae)	Price per talent
Lenaion	—	—	1 dr. 3 ob.
Hieron	20	25	1 dr.
Galaxion	18	—	1 dr.
Artemision	18	18	?1 dr.
Thargelion	18	18	1 dr.
Panemos	16	16	1 dr.
Hekatombaion	18	18	1 dr.
Metageitnion	20	20	1 dr.
Bouphonion	—	—	—
Apaturia	20	21	—
Aresia	15	—	—
Poseidon	—	—	—

Month	200 BC (*ID* 372)		
	Weight (in talents)	Cost (in drachmae)	Price per talent
Lenaion	20	30	1 dr. 3 ob.
Hieron	21	31 dr. 3 ob.	1 dr. 3 ob.
Galaxion	20	33 dr. 2 ob.	1 dr. 4 ob.
Artemision	18	28	1 dr. 3½ ob.
Thargelion	14	28 dr. 2 ob.	2 dr. 1 ob.
Panemos	14	28 dr. 2 ob.	2 dr. 1 ob.
Hekatombaion	13	26 dr. 4 ob.	2 dr. 1½ ob.
Metageitnion	17	28 dr. 2 ob.	2 dr. 4 ob.
Bouphonion	18	30	2 dr. 4 ob.
Apaturia	20	30	1 dr. 3 ob.
Aresia	20	33 dr. 2 ob.	1 dr. 4 ob.
Poseidon	18	30	1 dr. 4 ob.

Month	179 BC (*ID* 442)		
Lenaion	22	27 dr. 3 ob.	—
Hieron	25	37 dr. 3 ob.	—
Galaxion	20	30	1 dr. 3 ob.
Artemision	15	22 dr. 3 ob.	1 dr. 3 ob.
Thargelion	10	15	1 dr. 3 ob.
Panemos	—	—	—
Hekatombäion	15	22 dr. 3 ob.	1 dr. 3 ob.
Metageitnion	10	15	1 dr. 3 ob.
Bouphonion	20	30	1 dr. 3 ob.
Apaturia	15	22 dr. 3 ob.	1 dr. 3 ob.
Aresia	20	30	1 dr. 3 ob.
Poseidon	20	30	1 dr. 3 ob.

Firewood is often accompanied in the accounts by charcoal, an alternative fuel for sacrifices which was measured not by weight but by volume. The standard measure was a basket (*kalathos*), and in one year shortly after 279 BC (203. A. 28) the amount of charcoal bought by the commissioners during the year is recorded as three baskets, a half-basket, and an eighth of a basket (3⅝ baskets) at nine drachmae three obols per basket, making the cost for the year thirty-four drachmae two and a half obols: in the same year the firewood cost sixty drachmae four obols. Later, charcoal purchases were recorded month by month, but only the price is given. In our Table II, when the record for the year is complete, we have marked months with no charcoal payment with a cross: a dash signifies that a payment

was made but the figure has not survived, a blank means that there is
no evidence:

TABLE II

Charcoal Purchases

(in drachmae)

Month	250 BC (ID 287)	224 BC (ID 338)	200 BC (ID 372)	179 BC (ID 442)
Lenaion	7	12	—	12
Hieron	×	12	10	12
Galaxion	4	10	—	15
Artemision	3	—	10	
Thargelion	4 dr. 3 ob.		9	×
Panemos	×	8	9	×
Hekatombaion	3	—	9	9
Metageitnion	3	—	9	14
Bouphonion	3 dr. 4 ob.	8	9	14
Apaturia	4	—	10	12 dr. 3 ob.
Aresia	4 dr. 3 ob.	6	10	18
Poseidon	6	—	10	12

The records give no indication of the principles that governed
the choice between firewood and charcoal; perhaps charcoal was
preferred for the smaller victims and wood for the larger. Both needed
kindling-material, which explains the recurrence of bundles of reeds
(*klematides*) in the accounts.

The figures in our tables, indicating an annual average of *c.*200
talents of firewood (between four and five tons), and charcoal costing
*c.*100 drachmae, do not seem very formidable, but it has to be
remembered that these figures are confined to supplies for public
sacrifices. The population of Delos, increasing during the Hellenistic
period, needed wood and charcoal for cooking and heating and it was
important that supplies should be maintained and should be as cheap
as possible. The concern of the island's government about supplies is
well illustrated by an official regulation, the terms of which have been
preserved on a stone found in 1905 (*ID* 509).

This regulation concerns traders bringing logs, sticks (*rhymoi*), or
charcoal to Delos. The meaning of *rhymoi* is not clear, but the context
here and in similar passages shows that it is material for burning, and it
is generally thought to mean round timber of small size rather than
sawn; 'billet' might perhaps be an appropriate translation. The document lays down that traders bringing firewood or charcoal to Delos
must have it weighed on proper timber-scales and must sell it in the
market at the price registered with the collectors of the two-per-cent

import duty, which they must declare in advance to the market officials. To charge more or less will be an offence liable to prosecution and anyone may bring a charge against an offender before the market officials, who are to take the case to the court of the thirty-one before the end of the month. If any such trader has been exempted officially from customs dues he must declare his price before he sells and may not change it. No trader from outside may sell any firewood or charcoal that he has himself bought on the island.[10] This is a gallant attempt to protect the consumer.

One other forest product recurs regularly in the Delian accounts. Pitch was an important preservative used on ships and buildings, particularly on altars, doors, and roof-timbers. The purchases of pitch, unlike firewood and charcoal, are nearly always concentrated in a single payment rather than spread over the year and occur normally in summer, in the month Pamenos or Hekatombaion. The standard measure is at first called an *amphora*, later a *metretes*. In Table III we give the changing price of the measure during our period and, where the evidence is available, the number of measures bought for the year:

TABLE III

Purchases of Pitch

Date BC	Price per measure (in drachmae)	No. of measures
c.310	15–19	
305–303	22	
302	17	
296	18	
282	24	
279	40	
276	28	
275	27	
274	20	
269	25	9
268	23	
250	14	11
246	15	
231	18	15
c.223	16	
218	15	
200	15	9
179	9	11
169	16	8

It is difficult to reconstruct the pattern of the timber trade implied by the annual accounts of the Delian commissioners. The ultimate source of the timber is only once mentioned, in 274 BC. Menon supplied 'Macedonian timbers' (199. A. 57) and 'Macedonian timbers' are also recorded in the accounts from Eleusis and from Delphi. The quality of Macedonian timber was well known throughout the Aegean world and especially Macedonian fir, which had been the mainstay of the Athenian fleet in the fifth and fourth centuries. Macedon would be the natural source for the large quantities of fir needed for roofing in Delos, and was also probably the source of the beech-wood used in the island. Beech needs a colder and wetter climate than most of the Aegean coast-lands provide: it did not grow on the islands and on the mainland it did not extend south of Thessaly. It would also be natural to look to Macedon for elm, boxwood, and lime.

But Macedon could not have supplied the cedar for Apollo's temple, which must have come from the eastern Mediterranean; and better cypress could have been bought much nearer in Crete, Samos, or Miletus. Oak, the price of which seems to be substantially lower than elm, could probably have been bought from Naxos, Andros, or Samos. We should also look to these and other islands close to Delos for the supplies of firewood, for which there was an all-the-year-round demand. There were many other small islands in the Aegean which, as Plato emphasised (p. 188), were virtually treeless even before the Hellenistic period. Island-hopping traders from Euboea and Samos, and other large islands that were still well wooded, could have done good business. Timber from Mt. Ida may also have found its way into the Aegean, especially when the Attalids of Pergamum were anxious to foster good relations with Greece.

On Delos itself, as at Eleusis, one of the most striking features is the number of timber sellers and the small scale of so many of the purchases. In 189 BC eight elm timbers were bought and the order was spread over three sellers at three different prices, six drachmae four and a half obols, seven drachmae, six drachmae three obols (*ID* 403. 29). When roof-timbers and epistyles were needed for the stoa by the sanctuary of Poseidon supplies were bought from seven different sellers (*ID* 366, p. 446). But large orders were also placed. A year's account of the early third century (155. C. 4) includes 'cedar timbers bought for the god'. This was a major consignment for Apollo's temple and, as we have noted, there were still thirty-five cedar timbers left in stock in 279 (161. D. 92-3). When the stoa by the sanctuary of Poseidon was being built towards the end of the third century, Heraclides was able to supply 153 'large timbers' (p. 447). Similarly, in 274, when there was much building activity on a palaestra and the theatre a certain Menon had a stock of Macedonian timbers (199. A. 57) and it may be significant that he also sold pitch to the commissioners (199. A. 38), for Macedon was the source of the most valued pitch in the Aegean. Menon probably had regular trade links with Macedonian exporters.

But even in these years when substantial orders are implied we have a wide distribution of smaller purchases. During the building of the stoa by the sanctuary of Poseidon, in addition to the 'large timbers' supplied by Heraclides, rafters were bought in small numbers, ten, seven, five, and nine, from other suppliers (p. 446); and in 274, in addition to Menon, there were six others who sold timber to the commissioners during the year. In a much later year (*ID* 440) when there was apparently no important new building work-timber was bought from five suppliers.

The Delian accounts provide an important source for the movement of prices during the Hellenistic period. One of the results of the opening-up of the east that followed Alexander's conquest was to move the centre of gravity of trade eastward, and away from the Aegean. Athens was no longer the busiest harbour of the Mediterranean; the island of Rhodes was much better placed to seize the new opportunities of eastward trading, and became the most prosperous trading community in the Greek world. The recession in the Aegean is reflected in a general fall of prices in the first half of the third century while the new kingdoms carved from Alexander's empire were settling down. But by the middle of the third century a new stability was emerging and prices in the second half of the century were generally higher.

Timber records contribute very little to this general picture, because it is only very rarely that the wood, its dimensions, and prices are given. Although rafters are often mentioned in the records, those that give the price rarely give the length and those that give the length rarely give the price; very few indeed specify the wood. Boards (*sanides*) also are occasionally mentioned, but never with both dimensions and wood. The commonest term is simply *xylon*, timber, which can mean either round log or squared timber, but gives no indication of size. It is in fact very difficult to find points of comparison. Some, however, have found a glimmer of hope in oak prices. In 246 BC oak timbers of ten cubits were bought for nine drachmae and of eight cubits for seven drachmae one obol (*ID* 290. 221); in 207 oak timbers were bought at a price of seven drachmae three obols, and in 189 two purchases were made at ten drachmae two obols and nine drachmae four and a half obols (*ID* 403. 24). If the seven drachmae three obols of 207 refers to the same size as the seven drachmae one obol of 246 and the two prices of 189 refer to the same sizes as the nine drachmae and seven drachmae one obol of 246, the figures would show increases at the right time, but this would be a very frail foundation for a general rise in prices. If the price of eight-cubit timbers had risen by two drachmae three and a half obols it is incredible that the price of ten-cubit timber should have risen by only one drachma two obols. We meet the same kind of frustration if we try to compare prices at Delos with prices at Epidaurus. While fifteen-foot oak timbers cost nine drachmae at Delos, at Epidaurus at roughly the same time sixteen-foot timbers cost only six drachmae (p. 428), but we know neither the species nor the width and thickness.

A study of firewood and charcoal prices is more rewarding. In 279 BC (161) the cost per talent of firewood was one drachma two obols; in 268 it was one drachma; in 250 it varied from one drachma one obol to one drachma two obols and by 224, as can be seen from our Table I, there was no appreciable change. In 200 (*ID* 372) the prices were considerably higher and there was a much wider variation within the year, no less than six different prices between one drachma three obols and two drachmae four obols. This did not, however, set the pattern for the future; in 179 BC the price was constant throughout the year at one drachma three obols. Some special explanation must be found for the fluctuations in price during 200. From the general movement of prices in the Aegean during the second half of the century the increase in the price of firewood is what we should expect, and the same pattern can be seen in the price of charcoal.

Since in the period covered by our Table II only the price of charcoal is recorded, we cannot tell how much of the increase in cost is due to an increase in consumption and how much to an increase in price. The figures suggest a sharp increase between 250 and 224, a modest increase between 224 and 200. The marked fluctuation in firewood prices in 200 is not reflected in the prices of charcoal, which seem to drop precisely when the firewood prices rise. This makes it more difficult but not impossible to see an explanation of the firewood prices in the tensions generated by the prospect of a Roman war to punish Philip of Macedon for his alliance with Hannibal.

While the prices of firewood and charcoal correspond with what seems to be the general movement of prices in the third and second centuries, the price of pitch, the general importance of which will be discussed in a later appendix, does not follow the same pattern. Purchases of pitch are recorded in every annual account and for nineteen years the price is preserved, though the quantity purchased during the year is known for only six years. In our Table III it can be seen that, while the prices of firewood and charcoal rise in the second half of the third century, and again in the first half of the second

century, pitch prices fall, and in two years the figure is in sharp
contrast with its neighbours: in 279 forty drachmae between twenty-
four and twenty-eight drachmae, and in 179 only nine drachmae
between fifteen and sixteen. These anomalies have been convincingly
explained by Glotz, who shows that the decisive factor in determining
the price is the situation in Macedon, and particularly the relations of
the Macedonian king with Delos.

Although pitch was widely produced in the Greek world, Macedonian pitch was accepted as the best pitch in the Aegean and
Macedonian pitch, like Macedonian timber, was a royal monopoly.
The year 179 saw the destructive invasion of the Gauls, when
production could have been seriously interrupted with a consequent
shortage of supplies and rise in prices. The specially low price of 179
can most easily be explained, as Glotz shows, by the anxiety of the
Macedonian king to win as much support as possible in the Aegean in
view of an expected war with Rome. Similarly the high prices from 282
to 268 may reflect the stronger influence of the Ptolemies on Delos.

A Royal Tomb at Gordium

In the excavation of large burial mounds there have been many frustrations. It is not unknown for the burial chamber to be missed altogether: more often it is found to have been already robbed of its contents. Few can have expected the dramatic success of the American excavation of the largest of the burial mounds outside the Phrygian capital, the so-called Midas Mound, which is no less than 250 metres in diameter and roughly fifty metres high. Rodney Young, directing the excavation, first drilled into the mound to locate the stone pile that could be expected over the burial chamber. He then dug an open trench from the south-west angle for seventy metres, which showed that the outer coating of the mound was formed by material washed down from above: the original mound of rubble and clay had a considerably smaller diameter, but was significantly higher.

From the end of the trench a tunnel was opened in the direction indicated by the drilling and after a further seventy metres the workmen came to a rough wall of soft limestone blocks about three metres high. When a hole was made in this wall rubble poured in. When the rubble had been cleared away it was seen that there was another wall, made of round logs, some with traces of bark still on them. The branches had been cut off but they were otherwise unworked, and they were piled one on another and kept in place by rubble packing on either side. The logs averaged eight metres in length and their diameters ranged between thirty and sixty centimetres. Beyond this wall, at a distance of only thirty-five centimetres, was a very different type of wall, made with squared beams closely fitted together. This proved to be the south wall of the burial chamber.

When an entrance had been cut through this wall the chamber was found to be remarkably well preserved. The length (N.-S.) was 5.15 metres, and the width (E.-W.) 6.25 metres, and the height of the walls 3.25 metres. The beams were thirty-eight centimetres thick and their width averaged thirty-five centimetres. The timbers of the short sides were socketed into grooves at the ends of the long sides. The workmanship of the tomb chamber was very impressive (pl. 7A): the beams were so close-fitting that the joins were inconspicuous; knots and other imperfections had been cut out and replaced by small pieces of wood glued in. There were clear signs that after the beams had been squared they were smoothed with the adze and then sanded. The floor rested on a rubble base and was composed of fourteen beams, thirty-three centimetres thick and with widths varying from twenty to fifty-three centimetres. There were no doors to the chamber, which implies that the corpse was lowered into the chamber from above. The roof that was then added was double-sloping with three triangular gables at the north and south ends and in the centre. Special strength was given to the ridge-beam by using three thick timbers, one on top of the other.

The reason why this chamber was found in such excellent condition was that it had been protected from the pressure of the mountain of rubble and clay of the mound by an outer defence of round logs on all four sides and also over the roof. The total consumption of wood was therefore very considerable, ninety squared beams for the chamber and 105 round logs. The microscopic examination of the structure of the wood in samples from the timbers and the study of annual growth rings tells us a great deal more. When the excavators came to the outer wall of round logs they were struck by the cedar-like scent of the wood; of twelve samples from round logs one was found to be yew, all the others were juniper, the majority probably *J. excelsa*. No juniper, however, was found in the burial chamber. Five samples from the walls were all pine. From the ceiling two samples were yew and one cedar; two samples from cross-beams and one from the floor were pine. A somewhat similar pattern was found in the wood indentifications from excavation within the city. Of some seventy samples only one was identified as cedar, and a split-log sarcophagus of cedar was found in a burial mound outside the city. The great majority of samples were pine, both *P. silvestris* and *P. nigra*. Juniper was probably chosen for the outer defences of the burial chamber in the great mound because it was one of the strongest of woods as well as long-lasting; pine was preferred for the finer work of the chamber.

Today one would have to go either to the Taurus range in the south, or the Black Sea mountains in the north to find timber on the scale required for the great burial mound. It seems extremely unlikely that the timber was brought to Gordium from such long distances, especially as there is no sign of economy in the use of wood in the city. It is reasonable to infer that in the neighbourhood of Gordium, which is now almost treeless, there were in the archaic period still substantial supplies of pine and juniper and a sprinkling of cedars.

The study by P. Kuniholm of the annual growth rings in the round logs and beams of the great burial mound adds interesting information and raises a difficult problem. His study shows that there was great variety in the age of the trees that were felled for the tomb. The oldest was a little over 800 years and there were very few less than 200 years old. As might be expected the slow-growing junipers were much older than the pines; there were eight junipers more than 400 years old, no pines older than 300 years. A comparison of the tree-rings in the beams of the tomb chamber with those in the round logs of the outer wall has disturbing implications. There is apparently a difference of 184 years between the last preserved tree-ring of the chamber beams and those of the round logs and there seem to be only two logical explanations of this anomaly. Either the trees used for the beams had been felled 184 years before the tomb was built and kept in stock (the reuse of old timber for a royal tomb can be ruled out) or the outer casings were added 184 years after the tomb chamber was built. The difficulty might be removed if we could believe that 184 year-rings had been lost in the squaring of the beams for the chamber; but Kuniholm, well aware of the anomaly, feels bound to reject this solution.

The excavation of the Midas tomb has also added to our appreciation of furniture in wood during the archaic period. Among the objects which accompanied the dead king to his burial chamber were the royal bed, tables, stools, and screens (pl. 7B). These were found in varying stages of disintegration but sufficient remained to make clear their form and structure.

The bed, a four-poster with headboard and footboard, was a large bed for a small person (estimated height less than five feet). The simple frame was supported by four substantial blocks of wood at the corners and the long planks of the bed rested on iron bars. The king's skeleton lay on the central plank sixty centimetres wide with narrower planks on either side, and traces of the side-rails showed that they were made of strips of light and dark wood joined together. Most of the tables, all three-legged, were in a poor state, but eight of the nine were of a standard type, familiar from literature and partially illustrated by substantial fragments found near the Samian Heraeum. These tables were low, adapted to reclining rather than sitting, with tops averaging $c.80 \times 65$ centimetres. The table-top was normally made from a single piece of wood, the rim was slightly raised, and the corners rounded. There was a triangle of rectangular or square holes into which the three legs fitted. The legs were turned on the lathe and had outward-curving feet, bent by steam or long soaking in water. Long tenons from the legs fitted into the holes in the table-top and to improve stability at the joints a cushion or collar of wood was added round the tenon and the top of the leg. The ninth table provides a striking contrast to the simple elegance of the others. The craftsman who made it revelled in his ingenuity and anticipated the decorative excesses of Victorian enthusiasm.

But the most impressive of the wooden objects are two screens which now add distinction to the museum in Ankara (pl. 7B). These screens (195 × 80 cm.) were made from different pieces of wood held together by tenons fitting into sockets. They were badly crushed when heavy bronze vessels, which had been hung on iron nails in the wall, fell on them, but sufficient pieces were recognisable to explain the structure, and the faces of the screens, which are a fine example of geometric decoration, were particularly well preserved. The basis of the design is a series of squares enclosing a swastika-type pattern, arranged in rows, eight rows of fourteen rectangles in the upper half, and seven rows of ten rectangles in the lower half, where the centre is taken by the curving legs of the screen ending in scroll feet. The areas between the rectangles are filled with minute inlays of triangles and lozenges in neat rows. At first sight the rectangles seem all to repeat the same design; I was surprised to be convinced by my grandson that there are at least seven variations on the theme. The total effect owes much to the choice of woods, the dark yew of the inlays providing an effective contrast with the white boxwood into which they were fitted. The fine workmanship of these screens is as striking a tribute to the craftsmanship of the Phrygians as the intricate decoration in stone of some of the faces of their rock tombs.

Sources: Preliminary excavation reports, *AJA* 1955–68 (for the royal burial mound, *AJA* 62 (1968) 149–54); the final report has been prepared for publication. R. S. Young, 'Phrygian furniture from Gordion', *Expedition* 16 (1974) 2–13; P. I. Kuniholm, *Dendrochronology at Gordion and on the high plateau of Anatolia*, see Bibliography, p. 532.

The Forests of south Italy

(see fig. 16, p. 480)

For the Greeks and Romans Italy south of Lucania was the land of the Bruttians (Brettians in Greek), but on the two coasts there was a fringe of Greek colonies, more important on the east than on the west. The interior was very mountainous and most of the coastal plains, particularly on the west coast, were restricted. The Romans regarded the mountains as a continuation of the Apennine range, but they were different and older. The Apennines were limestone, the mountains of south Italy were formed from granite. Unlike the Apennines these southern mountains had once been rich in minerals. The area is divided into two halves by the isthmus of Tiriolo. Here Italy has its narrowest waist. From the Gulf of Squillace to the Gulf of Euphemia are only thirty-one kilometres and on each side the mountains descend to 250 metres, sharpening the division. This isthmus was once sea and the land to the south is geologically closer to Sicily than to Italy.

North of the isthmus the name Sila is now given to the mountain forests that rise over the plain of Sybaris (later Thurii) and continue to the isthmus. Tradition has divided the area into three, though the divisions are not sharp: in the north Sila Greca (so-called from Greek-speaking settlers from Sicily); in the centre Sila Grande centred on Cosenza, the old native capital of the Bruttians; and to the south Sila Piccola with Cantanzaro its main settlement. The mountains are more accessible from the east than from the west where the coastal plain is extremely narrow and the mountain face particularly steep and uninviting. The high upland plains provide excellent pasture and the mountains that rise from them are attractively rounded in form. Mountain streams are abundant, but there are few rivers which could carry timber to the coast. In the west the river Savuto provides the only easy extraction route. The east is well served by the Crathis in the north reaching the sea near Thurii, and the Neto whose mouth is in the territory of Croton. In the spring floods some of the smaller streams on the east side may have carried timber down.

There is sufficient rain to suit both conifers and hardwoods and there is a rich variety of trees. On the lower slopes there are varieties of oak, including the Turkey oak (*cerrus*), ash, maple, and other hardwoods. Above them come chestnuts, widely spread, and on the higher levels pine, fir, and beech which is often coppiced. The pride of the Sila forest is a distinctive variety of the Corsican pine which grows fast and can grow over 100 feet. It is valuable for construction, but also has a special reputation for the richness of its pitch. Today the fir is not remarkable for quantity or quality but this might be partly explained by overcutting for the navy.

Below the isthmus the character of the scenery changes. There are no individual mountains but a high ridge of varying width running south for nearly 100 kilometres and leading to the wide spreading Aspromonte forest, which stretches westward to reach its highest point on Monte Alto (1,947 m.) above Rhegium. In both these areas the firs have a better reputation than the Sila firs and are preferred to pines by the timber trade, but the pines here too are noted for their pitch.

When we now turn to our ancient sources interpretation becomes unexpectedly difficult. For the Greeks Italy was only Italy south of a line between the river Laos on the west coast and Metapontum on the east coast.[1] Theophrastus can compare the fir and pine of Latium with those of Italy and when he includes Italy in his short list of forests that provide good ship-timber he means south Italy.[2] Similarly when Thucydides makes Alcibiades refer to the timber-richness of Italy he is thinking only of the south.[3] Very occasionally the area from which the timber is taken is more closely defined. The Thurian squared timbers included in their accounts by the Eleusinian commissioners of 408/7 BC were probably cut from trees that had been carried down the river Crathis from the Sila Greca.[4] The naval timber that was stockpiled at Caulonia for the Athenians during their siege of Syracuse may have been cut from firs in the famous forest later controlled by the monks of San Bruno.[5] When Dionysius tyrant of Syracuse, in his preparations for building a large fleet in 399 BC, sent woodcutters to Italy, the trees would have been cut either in the Aspromonte forest or on the mountain ridge north of the Heraclean promontory. As Rhegium at the time was probably hostile and Locri friendly, Dionysius will have probably chosen the latter.

The name Sila does not survive in our sources until the Roman period, and for its siting we have to turn to the geographers reflected in Pliny and Strabo. Pliny, after tracing the west coast of Italy from north to south, comes to Rhegium 'where the Apennine Sila forest begins'.[6] He makes no further mention of the forest but frequently refers to Bruttian pitch. Strabo is much more specific.[7] He traces the coastline from Rhegium to the promontory of Leucopetra, past the promontory of Heracles, and so to Locri which, he says, is 600 stades from Rhegium. At this point there is a diversion. 'Above these cities (from Rhegium to Locri) the Brettians inhabit the interior and there is a forest which produces the Brettian pitch, finest of all pitches. Sila is the name of the forest. It has fine trees and a good water-supply, and is 700 stades (*c*.130 km.) long.'[8] He then proceeds along the coast to the river Sagra, Caulonia, and Scylletium. From the combined evidence of Pliny and Strabo the natural conclusion is that the Sila forest stretched from Rhegium to the isthmus and not beyond. It is impossible to include the modern Sila in Strabo's definition.

Nor is his brief description of the forest inappropriate. The mountains in this area were well forested and there was an abundance of mountain streams. The reference to Bruttian pitch is justified, for the pitch from the territory of Locri had a wide reputation. Virgil can set together the groves of Narycian (Locrian) pitch and the famous box trees of Cytorus as spectacles that delighted the eye.[9] It is a nice coincidence that the inventory on a bronze tablet of the income of a Locrian temple includes a large quantity of pitch.[10]

There is one other important description of the forest to be considered. Dionysius of Halicarnassus, a slightly older contemporary of Strabo, describes the Sila forest in more detail: 'When the Brettians came under Roman control they freely surrendered half of their mountain country, Sila by name. It is full of timber well-suited for building houses and ships and all manner of other things. For there is much fir, heaven-high, in the forest, much alder, and much rich mountain pine (*peuke*), beech, and coastal pine (*pitys*), spreading oak, and ash.'[11] Does this description refer to the forests south of the isthmus? Is the land that was surrendered to Rome, becoming Roman *ager publicus*, the southern half of Bruttium?

If we did not have the evidence of Strabo and Pliny there would be a strong case for making the modern Sila forest the area which was surrendered to Rome. This annexation has usually been associated with the initial subjugation of the Bruttians in the context of the war against Pyrrhus. When Pyrrhus brought over an army from Epirus to champion the Greeks against Rome he met with considerable successes at first and the Bruttian tribesmen gave him assistance. Between 278 and 272 BC the Romans celebrated six triumphs over the Lucanians and Bruttians. The Roman victories over Pyrrhus and his Italian friends could have been followed by a substantial confiscation of territory. There is, however, another possible context. In the closing years of the second Punic War Hannibal, having failed to win over the Italians of central Italy and Campania, made Bruttium his base, where the mountains and the hostility of a majority of the tribesmen to Rome offered him security and the opportunity of raids into enemy country. When Hannibal had withdrawn his forces to Africa and

Rome had won her final victory in the war, the Bruttians could not expect to go unpunished.

Livy is virtually silent on what happened in Bruttium in the years following the war. He does, however, refer to a Roman praetor assigned to the province of Bruttium who had sent a dispatch to the senate about a theft of money from a sanctuary at Locri:[12] he was presumably in charge of the whole of Bruttium both north and south of the isthmus. It was, however, the area north of the isthmus that had proved the greater danger to Rome, both in the time of Pyrrhus and of Hannibal. The importance attached to the area is seen in the establishment of colonies. In 194 BC citizen colonies were sent to Croton and Tempsa.[13] Croton provided the easiest access to the modern Sila and was one of the main outlets for its timber; Tempsa near the river Savuto offered the only easy route into the interior from the west. In the same year two Latin colonies were sent out, one to Thurii near the mouth of the Crathis, which was important for the timber that passed through it as well as for its rich agriculture; of the other Livy merely says that it was sent to Bruttian territory.[14] In 192 a colony was sent to Hipponium at the west end of the isthmus, which the Romans renamed Vibo Valentia (and where, according to Velleius, a Roman colony had been sent in 237),[15] and later Augustus distributed land in the territory of Cosenza, which may have been envisaged as an area for settlement at the time of the agrarian law of Gaius Gracchus.[16]

It is tempting therefore to believe that the modern Sila derives its name from the Roman period and that the name which originally applied only to the forests south of the isthmus was extended to the forests to the north after the second Punic War. This view may receive some support from the wording of Dionysius. When he says that the Bruttians handed over half their mountainous territory which is called Sila he could possibly mean that the half which was handed over was called Sila, but the more natural meaning of the Greek is that the whole mountainous territory was called Sila.

The Latin references, apart from Pliny, do not resolve the problem. The most familiar is Virgil's picture of two bulls with locked horns battling for the favours of an attractive heifer 'in the huge Sila forest'.[17] We could not expect a poet to provide a map reference, but we could hope for more precision in Cicero. He refers in his *Brutus* to the notorious killing of well-known men in the Sila forest. Suspicion fell on the slaves of a company of public contractors who had bought a lease for taking pitch from the pines, and even free men were thought to be involved. The scandal created such a stir that the senate instructed the two consuls to hold an enquiry.[18] We are left to wonder who killed how many, why, and when. The earliest of the references is the most tantalising.

A line is preserved from Sallust's *Histories* where, referring to slaves in revolt, he said that 'they were in the Sila forest'.[19] This is a reference to the great slave revolt led by Spartacus (74-71 BC). The main force of the rebels, after indecisive successes in Campania, moved south through Lucania into Bruttium making for the Straits of Messina. They had reason to believe that the pirates, who at the time were a formidable force, would provide ships to take them to Sicily. But the pirates did not co-operate. Meanwhile Crassus, who in 71 commanded the Roman forces, took his army to the Tiriolo isthmus and fortified the line between Scolacium and Vibo Valentia.[20] He hoped to cut off their return northward and bring them to battle in the south. But on a stormy night the rebels broke through the defences. Sallust's passage might refer to this episode, meaning by Sila the forest to the south of the isthmus. There is, however, another incident which could provide a suitable context. Cicero, in his attack on Verres, who was governor of Sicily during the slave revolt, refers to a disaster at Tempsa, on the west coast a little north of the isthmus (*incommodum Tempsanum*); presumably the slaves had sacked or raided the town on their way south. Leading men from the colony of Vibo, a Roman colony at the west end of the isthmus, appealed to Verres for help, but he took no action.[21] Sallust may have been giving the background to the attack on Tempsa before the slaves had crossed the isthmus.

These references in Virgil, Cicero, and Sallust mention the Sila forest but make no mention of timber-cuttings. For that we have to wait until the post-classical period. Towards the end of the sixth century Pope Gregory the Great, needing specially long timbers to restore the roofs of the great basilicas of St. Peter and St. Paul in Rome, instructed a subdeacon to cut the timber 'in the land of the Bruttians'. Further dispatches were sent to other officials in the region to assist in the organization of transport for the tree-trunks from the forest to the sea.[22] There is, however, nothing in the correspondence to determine whether the timber was cut in the modern Sila or south of the isthmus.

The main questions that arise concerning the forests of south Italy cannot be answered. What we would most like to know is how extensively timber was cut in the three main forest areas that can be distinguished, how widely it was distributed, and what was the pattern of the trade. Perhaps our main hope of learning more lies in the dicovery of funerary inscriptions of timber merchants from the coastal towns.

Modern sources: H. Nissen, *Italische Landeskunde* 1. 244-7, 2. 924-67; G. Rogliano, *La Sila* (2 vols. 1963-5, Cosenza) (useful for physical features); G. V. Zurlo, *Storia della Sila* (1862).

Pitch

Plutarch's table-talk includes a discussion in Corinth at the time of the Isthmian festival on the reasons why the *pitys*-pine, which was used for the victor's wreath at the festival, was sacred to both Poseidon and Dionysus. After various ingenious derivations had been rejected, it was agreed that the special association with Poseidon was due to the value of *pitys* for building ships. *Pitys* (coastal pine) and kindred trees, *peuke* (mountain pine) and *strobilos* (umbrella pine), produce the most suitable woods for ships, and also pitch and resin without which no ships are seaworthy. *Pitys* was dedicated to Dionysus because pitch is used to seal wine-vessels, and so preserve the wine, and some people mix it with wine, because they think that it improves the quality.[1]

From this passage alone the importance of pitch in Greek and Roman life can be appreciated. The need of pitch for naval and merchant shipping is amply illustrated in the sources. When the Macedonian king in the early fourth century BC authorised the cities of Chalcidice to take timber from Macedonian forests, he included pitch in the concessions and in the treaty pitch precedes the timber.[2] When Hellenistic kings sent relief to Rhodes after the disastrous earthquake of 227 BC, Antigonus of Macedon and Seleucus of Syria both added substantial quantities of pitch to their generous gifts of timber.[3] The pitch was regarded as essential to seal the joins of ships' boards, and was sometimes also used to cover the entire hull. Warships were vulnerable to fire-arrows because 'their timbers were coated with pitch and resin'.[4] When Procopius saw the ships in the Red Sea he was amazed that they made no use of pitch or iron nails, but relied entirely on cords to hold the boards together.[5]

There is less emphasis in the sources on the use of pitch for building-timbers but it is clear from the accounts of temple commissioners that for important buildings, at least, it was regarded as indispensable. In the Eleusis account for 329/8 BC three purchases of pitch are recorded, totalling ten measures (c.258 litres).[6] The uses include the pitching of the roof and doors of the Eleusinium in Athens and a wall with its towers at Eleusis.[7] At Epidaurus the accounts of the temple of Asklepios include payments for pitching the workshop (4½ dr. representing roughly three days' work) and doors.[8] In Delos, as we have seen, purchases of pitch appear in all the annual accounts and it is used not only for roofs and doors but also for altars, particularly the great horned altar.[9] One entry specifies that the pitch is to be used for the altars and porches 'and for whatever else is normally treated with pitch'.[10] Presumably this would include the roof-timbers that were structurally the most important, and timbers exposed to the weather. In a comedy by Plautus it is said of doorposts that are looking the worse for wear: 'They are good enough if only they can get a coat of pitch.'[11] From Delphi we find the block and tackle used at the port of Cirrha being pitched.[12]

Pitch also played an important part in the production and distribution of wine. The recovery of ancient shipwrecks in recent years has reminded us of the importance of the wine trade in Mediterranean economies. Shiploads of amphorae are a more vivid reflection of the export of Italian wine to Gaul than passing references in literature. It was taken for granted that the containers in which wine was stored, and particularly if it was to travel, must be thoroughly coated with pitch to make them waterproof. When preparations were made for the vine-harvest it was essential to see that all containers had been pitched.[13] Columella describes the process in detail. If the vessel, normally a terracotta amphora, was to remain above ground or to travel, it was first raised from the ground mouth downwards and a fire lit underneath it until the sides of the vessel were too hot to touch; then the amphora was put on its side, hot pitch poured in, and spread evenly over the whole surface with a wooden ladle.[14]

Pitch in a more liquid form was also used to flavour wine, being mixed with it in the first stage of fermentation.[15] It was thought to give the wine a more attractive fragrance and to add body to it. In the passage from which we started Plutarch says that the practice of resinating wine was common in Euboea in Greece and in Cisalpine Gaul in Italy, implying that it was by no means universal. He adds that resinated wine from the south of Gaul was also popular among Romans.[16]

There were other miscellaneous uses for pitch and resin. Pitch is included by Pliny in a wide range of medical recipes, including cures for gout, consumption, skin irritation, and ulcers.[17] It was even used as a male depilatory, much to Pliny's disgust.[18] It was also used by perfumers,[19] and black paint could be made from the soot produced by burning resin or pitch.[20] *Peuke*-pines, particularly rich in resin, were used as torches.[21]

Pitch and resin came almost exclusively from conifers. Pliny gives a fairly complete list.[22] Theophrastus is particularly useful for his detailed description of the production processes, and Dioscorides, who is mainly interested in their medical properties, adds a little independent information. According to Pliny the most prolific provider of pitch was *picea*,[23] which from his description can be confidently identified with *Picea excelsa*, the Norway spruce, more familiar in Great Britain as a Christmas tree. But spruce, needing colder temperatures and a higher rainfall, was not suited to the Mediterranean climate, and though it had retreated southwards in the last Ice Age, it moved northwards when the climate became warmer and in our period was probably of little importance except in and near the Alps and in the forests behind the south coast of the Black Sea. Most of the Mediterranean world relied primarily on the pines for pitch.

Of the various pines the umbrella pine (*Pinus pinea*) was regarded as the least productive.[24] The maritime pine (*Pinus pinaster*) is now considered the richest in resin, but it is a western Mediterranean tree. In the areas that most concern us the commonest pines are the coastal pine (*halepensis*, or *brutis*) and the mountain pine (*Pinus laricio* or *nigra*). Theophrastus, describing the pines of Mt. Ida, says that the mountain pine was more resinous than the coastal pine,[25] and in south Italy it was the mountain pines that were famous for their pitch.[26] Dioscorides, however, links the *peuke*-pine with the umbrella pine, as less productive.[27] The quantity and quality of the pitch probably depended on the locality as well as the species. But whatever the species, pitch-producing trees need plenty of sun.

The fir (*abies*), unlike the pines, has no resin ducts, but it is distinctive in exuding 'tears' of resin from its bark, though not in large quantities.[28] Larch also is distinctive. It is rich in resin of a reddish colour and penetrating scent, but unlike the resin of the other conifers it remains liquid when heated.[29] Dioscorides includes cypress in his list, but only as a modest provider.[30] In the east two species of *Pistacia* provided a resinous substance which was particularly prized. The quality of *Pistacia terebinthus*, the turpentine tree, which was particularly common in north-east Syria, but also grew freely in Cyprus, was considered the best by Theophrastus;[31] *Pistacia lentiscus* produced a very gummy liquid, commonly called mastic, which was particularly associated with Chios.[32]

There were two principle methods of producing pitch, by tapping, and by burning. By the first a section of wood was cut out from near the bottom of the trunk. Into this cavity the sap from the resinous ducts percolated.[33] The process could then be repeated in a different place in the same tree and as long as the tree was given time to recover it was not seriously crippled. If, however, the process was repeated too frequently the tree was seriously weakened and of no further use for timber or pitch. It was then cut down and the heartwood burnt to extract pitch. The liquid that was collected in the cavity was oleo-resin, a combination of resin and essential oils, which could be removed by heating, and the oils that were given off by the heat could be collected and used for medical and other purposes. The residue was pitch, liquid at first (*pix liquida*), but becoming gradually thicker until it formed a hard substance (*pix dura*).

The second method of producing pitch was similar to the production of charcoal. Straight pieces of wood were closely stacked in a large circle which, according to Theophrastus, could be as much as 180 cubits in circumference and up to fifty cubits high.[34] A chimney was left in the middle of the pile and when the pile was completed it was covered with turfs or earth to ensure slow burning. Lighted wood was put into the chimney, which was then closed and the fire was kept alive by judicious prodding with sharpened poles. A channel had been cut from the pile to a recess into which the liquid released from the burning wood percolated. The first flow was very liquid and it was this that was used to flavour the wine. As the fire progressed the liquid became stiffer. When the fire was completely burnt out the accumulated residue could be heated again to reach the required stiffness and finally become solid.

Wherever there were pines there could be pitch, but certain forests acquired special reputations. Macedon, which had the best ship-timber in the Aegean, would be expected to produce good pitch. It seems to have been the source of most of the pitch used on Delos (p. 457), and Macedonian pitch was probably widely distributed in Greece. Theophrastus draws attention to the pitch of the pines of Mt. Ida.[35] Strabo emphasises the 'amazing' pitch production of Cisalpine Gaul and reports that south-west Spain, which had good supplies of ship-timbers, also exported pitch.[36] Hiero of Syracuse sent to the Rhône valley for the pitch for his monster merchantman.[37] Columella recommended pitch from the well-forested mountains of Liguria,[38] but the most famous pitch, in Italy at least, was the Bruttian pitch from the Sila forest in the south.[39] Dionysius of Halicarnassus notes the contribution to the Roman treasury of its *peuke*-pine and in Cicero's *Brutus* we find public contractors who have taken a lease to produce pitch from the forest (p. 326).[40] Bruttian pitch was recommended in particular for pitching the large amphorae in which wine was stored.

But it was generally agreed that for many other purposes the resinous yield from the *Pistacia* trees was superior, and this was recognised in the prices established in Diocletian's maximum-price edict. The common hard pitch (*pix dura*) is priced at twelve denarii for a pound, terebinth at forty denarii.[41] There is a separate price for resin from Colophon, which had a considerable reputation, but the figure has not survived. Chian mastic also had its own special price. This section of the edict includes *kedria* (in Greek; in Latin *cedrium* or *cedria*). As we have seen, it is uncertain whether the resinous liquid which can destroy living tissue but preserve dead bodies and parchment comes from cedar, juniper, or both (p. 415).

In the economy of the Roman empire the expensive resins of the *Pistacia* trees played a very small part, but the pitch of the pines was one of the commonest articles of trade. In Egyptian papyri pitch figures prominently in the customs account of a village,[42] and in what seems to be an inventory of naval stores,[43] but the commonest context is in accounts of sales and purchases. Most of the quantities are small[44] but there is a record of twelve talents of pitch, costing 3,400 drachmae per talent, bought for a local authority.[45] We cannot expect such varied evidence from other provinces but archaeology should increase our knowledge of the major centres of production, and the varying ways in which pitch was used.[46]

For a good account of the Greek and Latin terminology for pitch and resin, see J. André, 'La résine et la poix dans l'antiquité, technique et terminologie', *Ant. Class.* 33 (1964) 86-97.

Tall Trees and Long Timbers

This appendix is intended to assemble the evidence for trees and timbers of exceptional size, most of which have been mentioned in the text, and to offer some parallels.

Tree heights

Pine (*peuke*), 230 ft. Described in detail by Attalus I, first king of Pergamum (269-197 BC), Strabo 603. Circumference 24 ft. Straight for 67 ft., then dividing into three stems, but uniting in a single crown. *c.*25 km. north of Adramyttium (in or near the forest of Mt. Ida). For such a height we should now have to look to the redwoods or Douglas firs of America, or the metasequoias of China. No other height near it has been recorded from the Mediterranean world, but to be described so carefully by a king it must have been a very exceptional tree.

Cedar (*cedrus*) from Cyprus, 130 ft., *NH* 16. 263. Used, probably as a mast, for the eleven-oar built by Demetrius (*c.*300 BC).

Larch from Rhaetian Alps, 130+ ft., *NH* 16. 203. Intended for the restoration of a bridge, but retained for exhibition because of its size. Converted to a beam of 130 ft. for Nero's wooden amphitheatre. As the beam had no taper (*crassitudine aequalis*), I assume that the top of the log had been cut off, implying a height for the tree of 140-50 ft.

Trees in north-west India, seventy cubits (105 ft.), Diod. 17. 90. 5.

Tree girth

Sometimes the girth of trees is recorded.

Pine of Attalus, 24 ft.

Ilex near Tusculum, 34 ft., *NH* 16. 242.

Cedars (*kedros*) on 'Syrian' mountains (probably including Phoenicia); three men with outstretched arms could not encircle them (*c.*18+ ft.), *HP* 5. 8. 1.

Cedar from Cyprus (above), three men needed to encircle it (*c.*18+ ft.), *NH* 16. 203.

Fir (*abies*) used for mast of obelisk ship, built for the emperor (Caligula), four men needed to encircle it (*c*.24 ft.), *NH* 16. 202.

Trees in north-west India, four men could barely encircle them (*c*.24 + ft.), Diod. 17. 90. 4.

Round timbers

Cedar, sixty and fifty cubits, cut for Gudea of Lagash from Amanus, *ANET* 269a.

Cedar, sixty cubits, cut for Tuthmosis III from Lebanon, *ANET* 243.

Masts

Recorded heights for cedar masts are confined to Egypt where several heights over 45 ft. are recorded, the highest being forty-two cubits (63 ft.), *ZÄ* 68 (1931) 20, n. 48. The masts of the largest seagoing ships will have been much higher. Pliny refers to the 130 ft. cedar in Cyprus, which was presumably used for a mast, and the fir mast of Caligula's obelisk ship which took four men to encircle its girth will have been *c*.100 ft. high (*NH* 16. 202). The main mast of Hiero's famous merchantman must have been in the same class, because a professional engineer was required to supervise its transport to the coast (Athen. 208).

Squared beams

Larch, 130 ft. long, 2 ft. thick, from the Rhaetian Alps, *NH* 16. 200.

Fir, 100 ft. long, 1½ ft. thick, for the roof of Agrippa's Diribitorium, *NH* 16. 201. Larch had not yet been introduced in Rome. Pine is just possible.

Fir and Pine, 75 ft., Diocletian's edict, 12. 1.

Cherry-wood, 60 ft. long, 3 ft. thick, *NH* 16. 125.

From Gaul 40 ft. beams in Gallic walls, Caesar *BG* 7. 23.

From Rhineland timbers (*materias*) 50 ft. long and longer, carried by auxiliary troops.

Rams

80 ft., cut for Antony's Parthian campaign, Plut. *Antony* 38. 2. If cut in the mountains of Armenia, probably juniper or cypress; if cut in Syria, cedar and fir would have been available.

104 ft., cut for Hagetor of Byzantium's 'tortoise', 15 in. wide and 1 ft. thick at the base, tapering to 1 ft. in width and 9 in. thick (Vitr. 10. 15. 2).

The difficulty of transporting a ram is well illustrated by an incident recorded by Ammianus Marcellinus (20. 11. 11-18). In the middle of the fourth century the Romans under Constantius, advancing against the Persians, came across a huge ram (*molem arietis magnam*) which the Persians had used to break down the wall of Antioch. When they withdrew they had cut down the ram to make transport easier, but even so had abandoned it at Carrhae, where the Romans found it and used it with considerable success at the siege of Bezabde. But while the sizes recorded for the rams of Antony and Hagetor are credible, we cannot accept a length of 120 cubits given by Diodorus (20. 95. 1) for a ram used by Demetrius in the siege of Rhodes.

We are also justified in assuming that beams more than seventy feet long were used for Agrippa's Odeum in Athens (p. 216), probably of Macedonian fir, and in Rome for Trajan's basilica, and the great fourth-century basilicas of St. Peter and St. Paul-outside-the-walls, all three probably of fir from the Apennines. These large spans in Rome are matched by the fourth-century basilica in Trier. We are fortunate in having later records which give a more realistic impression of the size of these beams. R. Lanciani (*Pagan and Christian Rome* (1895) 138) quotes from a description of St. Peter's by Philippo Bonani. In a visit on 21 February 1601 he measured the horizontal beam of the first truss from the façade which Carlo Maderno had just lowered to the floor; it was seventy-seven feet long and three feet thick. It is doubtful whether an original fir beam could have lasted so long (nearly 1,300 years), but Lanciani adds an extract from the fourteenth-century diary of Rutilio Alberini: 'I have seen one (beam in St. Peter's) marked with the name of the builder of the church (Constantine); it was so huge that all kinds of animals had bored their holes and nests in it. The holes looked like small caverns, many yards long, and gave shelter to thousands of rats.'

It becomes easier to appreciate the scale of operations in roofing the great basilicas by comparison with the building of the roof of Westminster Hall in 1394-5. This hall is comparable in size to the central hall of Trajan's basilica—240 ft. long and 67 ft. 6 in. wide, compared with *c.*390 × 80 ft. for Trajan's hall. The original King's Hall had been built by William II at the end of the eleventh century with two internal rows of columns or piers, in the Greek manner, to break the width of the span. English architecture was largely governed by the timbers available and there were no tall conifers in England to provide the long timbers that made the tie-beam truss the natural solution in Italy. Oak remained the dominant building-timber until trade with the Baltic was more widely developed, and oaks could not provide timbers to bridge a sixty-seven-foot span. But by the time of Richard II the poor condition of the walls, doubts about the roof, and the inconvenience of the internal supports, combined with the excitement of the introduction of the Gothic style, led to a decision to rebuild the walls and design a completely new roof which could leave the whole floor of the hall unencumbered.

The organisation of the work was divided between a master mason and a master carpenter, Hugh Herland, who had won a reputation for his work on timber roofs. His magnificently original design was based on trusses consisting of hammer-beam, supported by curving brace, hammer-post, and collar-beam. The timbers, almost entirely of oak, were taken from forests in Hampshire, Surrey, and Hertfordshire, and it was decided to build the roof at Farnham in Surrey, away from the Westminster site. There the round timbers were sawn to the required sizes and the timbers for the curving braces bent. By the end of 1395 the construction of the roof had been completed. The multiple components had been fitted together and the timbers duly numbered were dismantled for transport. Instructions were sent to the sheriffs of Berkshire, Hampshire, and Surrey to 'go to a place called the Frame by Farnham for the carriage of the timbers there wrought for the King's Great Hall at Westminster'. They were each to provide thirty 'strong wains' which were to make five journeys each during the four weeks after Trinity. We read later of two carts with sixteen horses making fifty-two journeys of sixteen leagues (c.58 km.) to Hamme on the Thames to be taken by river to Westminster.

There are of course sharp differences between the English and Roman operations. The roof of Westminster Hall was revolutionary, complex, and highly decorative; Trajan's basilica roof was traditional, simple, and austere. The range of specifications for timbers in Herland's design, including curving timbers, was considerably larger than for Trajan's building. For Trajan's basilica there would be standard sizes for cross-beams, rafters, and secondary timbers over the rafters, and none curved. For the cross-beams of their largest basilicas the Romans required timbers 75–80 feet long; the longest timber used by Herland was not more than thirty-two feet. The greatest thicknesses in Westminster Hall were 25 in. for the hammer-posts, and $22\frac{1}{2}$ in. for the hammer-beams. In the giant beams used by the Romans there seems to have been a wide diversity in the thickness. The record larch beam of 130 feet recorded by Pliny (*NH* 16. 200) was two feet thick, the 100-feet beam from the roof of the Diribitorium was $1\frac{1}{2}$ ft. thick (ibid. 201); but the seventy-seven-feet beam from St. Peter's is said to have been three feet thick. In both operations timbers of special quality had to be selected, but during the early Empire, at least, it was easier to find high-quality firs in Italy than it was to find oak of the standard required in fourteenth-century England. Even so it would probably have been necessary to go to more than one forest for the cross-beams.

The roof of Westminster Hall was built a long way from Westminster. The building-site would have been too restricted for the large working force and as the design had no precedents to follow and it might be necessary to modify it while work was in progress, there was a great advantage in being away from the distractions of the capital. Should we imagine the Romans adopting the same practice? Was the roof of Trajan's basilica constructed outside the walls? On this point we have no evidence direct or indirect. By the time the roof was needed the main work on the walls would have been completed. There should have been room on the site for sawyers to convert squared timbers into rafters and secondary roof-timbers, but the preparation of the massive cross-beams might have been an embarrassment. If, as is likely, the tree-trunks had merely been stripped of their branches in the forest, they had to be cross-cut to the required length (c.80 ft.) with the saw and then squared with the axe. These must have been familiar operations in importers' timber-yards and were better done there.

For another Roman operation with long timbers we can find a closer parallel. One of the results of the battle of Actium was the annexation of Cleopatra's Egypt, which was later celebrated by the bringing to Rome of two Egyptian obelisks. The erection of the first obelisk in the Circus Maximus must have been one of the most exciting spectacles that the people of Rome, by no means starved of lavish entertainments, had ever seen, but it has left strangely little mark in the surviving literature. The scene can be partially recovered from the account by the fourth-century historian Ammianus Marcellinus of the entry into Rome and the erection in the reign of Constantius II (357) of the largest obelisk ever to be seen there. Unlike the earlier obelisks which had been transferred to special barges at Ostia, this obelisk remained in the ship that had brought it from Alexandria, and 300 oarsmen rowed the great ship up the narrow Tiber. It was unloaded some four kilometres outside the walls to avoid the crowded river harbour under the Aventine and, placed on a timber cradle, it was pulled carefully through the Porta Ostiensis to the Circus Maximus. A literal translation that is technically credible eludes me, and it is doubtful whether the historian had a clear understanding of the operation, but he knew that there was a forest of long sturdy timbers, quantities of long stout rope (web-like in pattern), and 'thousands of men' working machines, like men turning round the upper grindstone of a mill.

It is easier to appreciate the Roman achievement by reading the detailed account, magnificently illustrated, by Domenico Fontana, the architect appointed by Pope Sixtus V to move the obelisk from Caligula's Circus to the square in front of St. Peter's. His preparations included sending a work-force to bring in a massive quantity of the largest and tallest oak beams from Campo Morto near the Porto di Nettuno, not far from Anzio, forty-five kilometres from Rome. They were carried on carts with two huge wheels, each cart drawn by seven pairs of buffaloes. A great quantity of elm timbers were also brought from Terracina to provide a casing round the obelisk, and ilex (because of its great strength) was used for the vital parts of the capstans. The oak timbers were used to build a great timber tower to provide a framework for the lifting of the obelisk by means of a series of capstans worked by horses and men. No less than 800 men and 140 horses were employed on forty capstans.

Very few specific figures are given for the timbers but most of them, to judge by the illustrations and the general description, were more than twenty feet long and some must have been more than forty feet. Of the four long levers that were also used one was seventy feet long. Our respect for the Roman engineers is increased when we realise that the obelisk of Constantius, now standing in front of the Lateran, is thirty feet taller than the Vatican obelisk.

Sources: Westminster Hall: H. M. Colvin, *A history of the King's works* 1 (1963) 527–33; *Restoration of Westminster Hall* (typescript, Bodleian Library, April 1922); G. L. Ware, 'Farnham and the King's work', *Journ. Farnham Museum Soc.* 1 (1971) 3–9.
Obelisks: Amm. Marc. 17. 4. 13–16; Domenico Fontana, *Trasportazione del obelisco Vaticano* (1950); C. d'Onofrio, *Gli obelischi di Roma*² (1967); E. Iversen, *The obelisks of Rome* (1968).

APPENDIX 9

Measures, Coins, Weights

Measures

Greek and Roman measurements are derived from parts of the body—finger (length), palm (breadth), foot (length), cubit (from elbow to end of hand), fathom (the span between outstretched arms). There is a wide variation in the length of the foot used by Greek architects. Scholars disagree about the number of standards and their precise measurements, and there are also differences in the names given to them. It is, however, generally agreed that there are at least three recognisable standards, measuring approximately 35 cm., 33 cm., 29.5 cm., and that the largest of these is the least common. Since both the more common standards are used in buildings at Athens, and also, if a recent interpretation of a difficult inscription is correct (*BCH* 104 (1980) 158), at Delos, it is perhaps less invidious if the three feet are called large, medium, and small.

What is certain, from rulers that have been found as well as from buildings, is that the Roman foot is 29.6 cm., less than half a centimetre longer than the short Greek foot, and both are close to the British foot of 30.48 cm. There is a difference that is not negligible between the British foot and the larger Greek foot. In the arsenal at the Piraeus, for example, the length, including the walls, is 405 ft. in the inscription. Converted to the British foot this gives a length of 433 ft. 10 in. In many inscriptions, however, it is uncertain which foot is implied. More could be lost than gained if I attempted to make the minor adjustments that are theoretically desirable. There are also different forms of the cubit: the measurement is sometimes taken from the elbow to the beginning of the fingers and sometimes to the knuckles of a closed fist. Such differences are only very rarely recorded in the texts. For convenience we have assumed that all cubits mentioned without qualification are the standard cubit from elbow to the end of the middle finger:

$$1 \text{ palm} = 4 \text{ fingers} = 3 \text{ in.}$$
$$1 \text{ foot} = 4 \text{ palms}$$
$$1 \text{ cubit} = 6 \text{ palms} = 1\tfrac{1}{2} \text{ ft.}$$
$$1 \text{ fathom} = 6 \text{ feet}$$

Distances are measured by feet:

$$Bema = \quad 1\tfrac{1}{2} \text{ ft.}$$
$$Plethron = 100 \text{ ft.}$$
$$Stadion = 600 \text{ ft.}$$

The Romans usually follow the Greek division of the foot into sixteen fingers, but sometimes they divide it into twelve inches. For distances their basic measure is the *passus* of five feet, the mile consisting of 1,000 paces, about ninety-five yards less than the English mile.

From feet to metres			
ft.	m.	ft.	m.
1	0.305	40	12.19
5	1.52	50	15.24
10	3.05	60	18.29
12	3.66	65	19.81
14	4.27	70	21.34
16	4.88	75	22.86
20	6.10	80	24.38
22	6.71	85	25.91
24	7.32	90	27.43
30	9.14	100	30.48

Liquid measure: The amphora mentioned in connection with wine and pitch represents the volume of a cubic Roman foot, 25.79 litres.

Area: 1 *iugerum* = $\frac{5}{8}$ acre = $\frac{1}{4}$ hectare.

Weights

In Greece and Rome timber was sold by measure (though not by cubic feet) and firewood, in Greece at least, was sold by weight. Only talents and half-talents are recorded and we have no evidence for the weight of the talent. If at Athens the timber talent was based on the coinage standard, the talent would weigh 25.58 kg. (*c.*56 lb.), but references to an Alexandria timber talent and an Antioch timber talent suggest that there may have been special weights for wood. This might help to explain apparent inconsistencies in the evidence for the carrying capacity of a yoke of oxen. Xenophon (*Cyr.* 6. 52) gives the normal expectation as twenty-five talents. If this is the Athenian coinage talent it would be *c.*1,400 lb. But in the Theodosian Code the maximum load permitted is 1,050 lb. (1,500 Roman pounds), and in Diocletian's edict

(14.8) a wagon-load of timbers is 860 lb. (1,200 Roman pounds). The figures derived from the coinage talent seem too high.

1 Roman pound = 11½ ounces = 321 grams.

Coins

Greece
6 obols	= 1 drachma
60 drachmae	= 1 mina
60 minae	= 1 talent

There were two main standards in the Greek world, the Attic-Euboic adopted by Athens, Corinth, Euboea, and the majority of the islands, and the Aeginetan which was the dominant standard in the Peloponnese. In the Aeginetan standard the drachma weighed 6.1 grams, in the Attic-Euboic 4.3 grams.

Rome
16 asses	= 1 sesterce (bronze)
4 sesterces	= 1 denarius (silver)
25 denarii	= 1 aureus (gold)

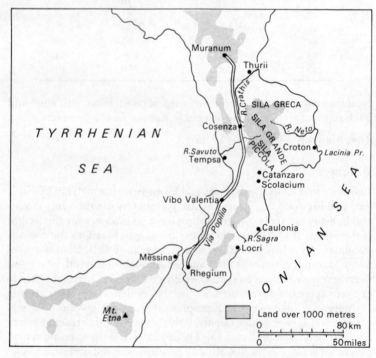

16 The forests of south Italy

NOTES

Chapter 1

1. A. Burford, *The Greek temple builders of Epidaurus* (1969).
2. *IG* 1². 1084.
3. *ILS* 7725.
4. 7540.
5. E. Espérandieu, *Recueil général des bas-reliefs* . . . *de la Gaule romaine* (1907–66) 2. 1096.
6. Text and translation by Sir Andrew Hort in the Loeb series (1916). It should be noted that botanists now draw a sharper distinction between fir and pine; *peuke* should be translated by pine rather than fir. The treatment of *kedros* in the text and in the useful index of plants by Thiselton Dyer also needs reconsideration (see p. 405). For a general survey of the life and work of Theophrastus, see O. Regenbogen, *RE Suppl.* 7 (1940) 1435–79.
7. Diogenes Laertius 5. 55.
8. *HP* 3. 8. 1.
9. 3. 10. 4.
10. 3. 9. 6.
11. 3. 9. 3.
12. *NH* 16. 141.
13. Text and translation in ten volumes of the Loeb series. His main contribution to our study is in vol. 4 (books 12–16) by H. Rackham. There are valuable commentaries on these books by J. André in the Guillaume Budé series. For a detailed survey, see W. Kroll, *RE* 21 (1951) 270–439 (for books 12–17, see 319–32).
14. Pliny, *Ep.* 3. 5.
15. *NH* 16. 9: Pliny, discussing the civic crown, says that originally it was given only to a god; that is why Homer uses the word 'crown' only for heaven and for a whole battlefield; 16. 19: Homer has a special word for the acorn of a holm-oak; 16. 110: the willow loses its seed early; that is why Homer calls it 'fruit-losing'. These look like the burrowings in Homer of Hellenistic grammarians.
16. *NH* 16. 144: *HP* 4. 4. 1. Pliny says that ivy is now said to grow in Asia, whereas Theophrastus had said that it did not. What Theophrastus did say was that in Asia ivy did not grow in those parts of Syria that were five days from the sea.
17. *HP* 4. 5. 6; *NH* 12. 8.
18. *HP* 3. 10. 2; *NH* 16. 62.
19. *HP* 3. 9. 1; *NH* 16. 48.
20. *HP* 3. 9. 5; *NH* 16. 46.
21. Homer, *Od.* 5. 60; *NH* 13. 100.
22. Verg. *Aen.* 7. 13. Virgil's Circe is a poet's conflation of Calypso and Circe.

23. I am grateful to Professor Gordon Williams for introducing me to Detlefsen, who suggests, for κέδρου τ᾽ εὐκεάτοιο θύου τ᾽, κέδρου τε πεύκης τε θύου τ᾽. Since the scholiasts comment on εὐκεάτοιο it seems that Pliny or his source used an unorthodox text.

24. *HP* 5. 6. 1: *NH* 16. 223; *HP* 5. 44: *NH* 16. 218.

25. *HP* 3. 8. 2: *NH* 16. 16.

26. *HP* 1. 9. 5: *NH* 16. 81.

27. *NH* 12. 11.

28. *HP* 5. 2. 1: *NH* 16. 197.

29. *NH* 16. 218.

30. *HP* 5. 44; Vitr. 2. 9. 9.

31. *HP* 5. 8. 3.

32. *NH* 16. 139-42, 215: 14. 122.

33. 16. 80.

34. *HP* 5. 3. 7.

35. *NH* 13. 102.

36. 12. 9.

37. 5. 14.

38. 16. 64. There is no other reference, ancient or modern, to ash leaves being poisonous, but Pliny insists that this was a personal experience, and we should not doubt him. A little earlier (16. 62) he confuses the Greek words for ash and yew; he is probably making the same mistake here. Perhaps his company was Greek-speaking! Cf. *Sylva* 43: 'I am astonished at the universal confidence of the botanists . . . ; this is an old imposture of Pliny who either took it on trust or was mistaken in the tree.'

39. *NH* 16. 5.

40. 5. 25; 18. 163.

41. 14. 147.

42. 16. 194.

43. For the relation of Vitruvius to the architecture of his age, see A. Boethius in *Dragma* (studies presented to P. Nilsson, 1939) 116-34; P. Gros, *Aurea templa* (1976) 54-6.

44. Vitr. 2. 9.

45. For a fuller review of Strabo's life and work, see E. Honigmann, *RE* 4. A. 76-155.

46. Polyb. 2. 15-16.

47. Conceived by Philostratus (*Imagines* 2. 17), son-in-law of the more famous Philostratus who wrote lives of the sophists in the second century AD. He pictures woodcutters at work: 'One of them is drawing his axe out, another has set his axe in, and a third is sharpening his axe which has lost its edge. Another inspects the fir assessing its suitability for a mast. Separate from them woodsmen are cutting trees that are young and straight for oars.'

48. Archilochus fr. 18 (Diehl).

49. Plato, *Phaedrus* 230 d.

50. Suet. *Vita Verg.* 1.

51. Verg. *Aen.* 2. 16, 112, 258.

52. 5. 663; 10. 230.

53. 6. 179-82.

54. Ennius 6, fr. 10 (Vahlen). Later catalogues: Ovid, *Met.* 10. 90-104; Seneca, *Oedipus* 566-75; Lucan 3. 640-3; Statius, *Theb.* 6. 98-106; Claudian, *De raptu Proserpinae* 2. 107-11.
55. Theocr. *Id.* 12. 8.
56. Verg. *Georg.* 3. 172; Homer, *Il.* 5. 838.
57. Verg. *Georg.* 1. 173. Maple and hornbeam were commonly used: *HP* 5. 7. 6; Vitr. 2. 9. 12.
58. Seneca, *Ep.* 86. 15.
59. Verg. *Georg.* 2. 440-3.
60. Horace, *Odes* 1. 14. 11.
61. Homer, *Il.* 2. 829; Strabo 588.
62. Paus. 2. 34. 8.
63. Strabo 167; Diod. 5. 16. 1.
64. *NH* 5. 135.
65. Strabo 589; for Chios see also *NH* 5. 136.
66. Hdt. 1. 56. 3; 8. 31; Strabo 434.
67. Hdt. 7. 218. 1.
68. Hdt. 1. 146; 8. 43, 46.
69. Paus. 10. 33. 12.
70. Strabo 445.
71. Hdt. 9. 39. 1
72. *NH* 5. 135.
73. Thuc. 8. 31. 3.
74. Strabo 433; Homer, *Il.* 2. 697; Strabo 349; 329 fr. 6.
75. Thuc. 8. 24. 2, 31. 3.
76. Paus. 4. 36. 7, referring also to a sanctuary of Athena Cyparissia; Homer, *Il.* 2. 553.
77. M. Ventris and J. Chadwick, *Documents in Mycenaean Greek*[2] (1973) no. 284, p. 273.
78. Homer, *Il.* 2. 519; Paus. 10. 37. 5.
79. *HP* 4. 54.
80. *NH* 4. 35; Ptolemy 3. 13. 36.
81. *NH* 5. 9.
82. J. R. A. Greig and J. Turner, 'Some pollen diagrams for Greece and their archaeological significance', *Journ. Arch. Sci.* 1 (1976) 177-94; Theophr. *Caus. Plant.* 5. 14. 5. Discussed by J. L. Bintliff, *Natural environment and human settlement in prehistoric Greece, BAR* Suppl. series 28, 1 (1977) 77 f.
83. E. Corona, 'Dendrocronologia radiocarbonio e palinologia al Colosseo', *Italia Forestale e Montana* 29 (1974) 117-18.

Chapter 2

1. My main sources for this chapter have been: M. Rikli, *Das Pflanzenkleid der Mittelmeerlanden* (3 vols. 1943-8); P. Boudy, *Économie forestière nord-africaine* (4 vols. 1948-55); W. Dallimore and A. B. Jackson, *A handbook of conifers* (1966).
2. [Xen.] *Ath. Pol.* 2. 12.

3. *HP* 5. 2. 1.
4. W. B. Critchfield and E. L. Little, *Geographic distribution of the pines of the world*, U.S. Dept. of Agriculture Misc. Publications 991 (1966).
5. A. Camus, *Les Chênes* (2 vols. 1936–54).
6. *HP* 3. 8. 2–7.
7. *NH* 16. 19.
8. *ILS* 5317.
9. *SIG* 969; described p. 213.
10. *HP* 4. 5. 2.
11. App. 3. 1.
12. Vitr. 2. 9. 14–16; discussed p. 248.
13. *NH* 15. 102.
14. *NH* 12. 6–7.
15. *NH* 16. 139.

Chapter 3

1. J. B. Pritchard (ed.), *Ancient Near-Eastern texts relating to the Old Testament*[3] (1969) 82 (tablet 5).
2. J. Hansman, 'Gilgamesh, Humbaba and the land of the *erinu* trees', *Iraq* 38 (176) 25–35. The argument depends on evidence that I am not competent to assess.
3. Ezekiel 31: 3–7.
4. P. Mouterde, *La Végétation arborescente des pays du Levant* (1947) 15.
5. Song of Songs 4: 8.
6. Deuteronomy 3: 10, 4: 48.
7. *ANET* 280. Professor Rowton (in a letter) suggests an attractive explanation: 'The answer may be that Mt. Hermon was viewed as a southern outcrop of the Antilebanon. Viewed that way, the mountain range as a whole has two dominant 'peaks', one Mt. Hermon, the other, somewhat less conspicuous, the Jebel Sherqi, to the north of Hermon. Either of the two could have given its name to the whole range. Hermon was the higher of the two but Sherqi was almost at the centre of the range. The latter prevailed and gave its ancient name, Senir, to the range as a whole. The result is that the name Senir is ambiguous; it denotes both the Jebel Sherqi and Antilebanon plus Hermon.'
8. See Bibliography, The Near East.
9. J. D. Hooker, 'The cedars of Lebanon', *Nat. Hist. Rev.* 2 (1862) 11–17.
10. V. Loret, 'Quelques notes sur l'arbre âch', *Annales du service* 16 (1916) 33–51.
11. *NH* 16. 213. Vitruvius (2. 9. 13) refers only to cedar coffers.
12. *NH* 16. 203.
13. *HP* 3. 2. 5–6.
14. 5. 7. 1.
15. Diod. 19. 58. 3.
16. M. B. Rowton, 'The woodlands of ancient western Asia', *JNES* 26 (1967) 269.

17. Discussions of Egypt's timber problems: A. Lucas, *Ancient Egyptian materials and industries*[4], ed. J. R. Harris (1962) 429–56; D. M. Dixon, 'Timber in ancient Egypt', *Commonwealth For. Rev.* 53 (1974) 205–9; R. K. Winters, *The forest and man* (1974) 36–83; D. W. Beekman, *Hout in alle tijden* (1949) I. 401–578.

18. *HP* 4. 2; *NH* 13. 56–67.

19. Lucas (n. 17), foreign timbers 429–31; native 439–48.

20. Hdt. 2. 96.

21. *HP* 4. 2. 8.

22. *AR* 4. 1023; cf. 4. 916.

23. Exodus 36: 20–38.

24. *HP* 4. 2. 1–2. The popularity of sycomore coffins is confirmed by further identifications since 1962. Of 23 Egyptian coffins in Czechoslovakia 16 were found to be made of sycomore (D. Březinová and B. Hurda, 'Xylotomic examination of timber from ancient Egyptian coffins', *ZA* 103 (1976) 139–41). Two more can be added from the Ashmolean Museum (App. 1).

25. *HP* 4. 2. 5.

26. 4. 2. 6.

27. 4. 2. 7.

28. 4. 2. 4; Strabo 822.

29. *NH* 13. 92.

30. Lucas (n. 17) 440.

31. Hdt. 2. 148. 7.

32. A. J. Spencer, *The brick architecture of ancient Egypt* (1980) 263–76.

33. F. Petrie, *The royal tombs of the first dynasty* (1900–1) 8–11 (beams of over 20 ft.); G. A. Reisner, *The development of the Egyptian tomb down to the accession of Cheops* (1936).

34. M. Zohary, *Flora Palestina* (1966) 1. 17–19.

35. Strabo 739.

36. *ARAB* 2. 142, 161. But *burašu*, here translated cypress, is more probably juniper (see p. 417).

37. L. Waterman, *Royal correspondence of the Assyrian empire* (1930–6) 1. 424; cf. 705.

38. M. B. Rowton, 'The woodlands of ancient western Asia', *JNES* 26 (1967) 261, 277. Trajan in AD 116 was able to build a large number of ships from the forests near Nisibis: Dio 68. 26. 1.

39. *ANET* 227.

40. *BM* 10056. S. R. K. Glanville, 'Records of a royal dockyard of the time of Tuthmosis III', *ZA* 66 (1931) 105–21 (text and translation); 68 (1932) 7–41 (commentary).

41. *Meru*-wood, Glanville, text, 113–15; *ash*-wood 115–21. Set of seven *meru*-wood timbers (in cubits) 113, col. 10, 9–15: [2]8, [2]6, (?20½), 22, 21, 19, 13.

42. Mast, Glanville, text, 115, col. 14. 11. Other *ash*-wood masts, Glanville, commentary (1932) n. 48. In his preface to the commentary (8 f.) Glanville accepts Loret's identification of *ash*-wood as fir or fir and pine, but suggests that a more general term might be appropriate and uses deal,

meaning cut timber. But in that case would *meru*-wood and sycomore have separate names? For the identification of *ash*-wood with cedar, App. 2, pp. 405-9.

43. *AR* 3. 217.

44. *AR* 4. 357, 358.

45. N. Jidejian, *Byblos through the ages* (1968).

46. P. Montet, 'Le pays de Negau', *Syria* 4 (1923) 181-92.

47. A. H. Gardiner, *The admonitions of an Egyptian sage* (1909) 32.

48. *ANET* 240; J. P. Brown, *The Lebanon and Phoenicia* (1969) no. 113, p. 178.

49. *AR* 2. 321; cf. 2. 492.

50. *ANET* 243. As early as the fourth dynasty (*c.*2500 BC) the title of 'leader of an expedition to bring back cedar-wood' is found on the coffin of a high official: H. Junker, *Giza* 7 (1944) 151 with pl. 29c.

51. S. A. B. Mercer, *The Tel-el-Amarna tablets* (1939) 1. 102-2. 138.

52. Ibid. 2. 147-55.

53. Ibid. 1. 35. 27-9.

54. *ANET* 254b; J. P. Brown (n. 48) no. 114, p. 178.

55. *ANET* 25-9.

56. 1 Kings 5-7; 2 Chronicles 2-4; cf. Josephus, *Antiq.* 8. 50-60, 141-3. Translation of these main sources with notes, Brown (n. 48) no. 119, p. 181.

57. Reasons for preferring cypress are set out in Appendix 3. 2 (pp. 416-20).

58. 1 Kings 10: 27; cf. Isaiah 9: 10: 'The bricks are fallen, but we will build in hewn stone: the sycomores are hacked down, but we will use cedars instead.' Excavation at Beer-Sheba: Y. Aharoni (ed.) *Beer-Sheba* 1 (1973) including wood indentifications by N. Lipschitz and Y. Waisel, pp. 97-105.

59.* The Red Sea fleet: 1 Kings 9: 26-8; 2 Chron. 8: 17-18. *Almug* (*algum*) associated with Ophir: 1 Kings 10: 11; 2 Chron. 9: 10. *Algum* requested from Hiram: 2 Chron. 2: 8. Until recently it was commonly thought that the wood (whether *almug* or *algum*) was sandalwood from India. It has now been shown that the Sanskrit word which encouraged the indentification was of later origin (J. G. Greenfield and M. Mayrhofer, The 'algummim/almuggim problem re-examined', Suppl. to *Vetus Test.* 6 (1967) 83-9) and it is extremely doubtful whether at this early time there was any trade between Egypt or Arabia and India. This has given rise to the suggestion (based on 2 Chron. 2: 8) that *almug* may in fact be a Lebanon wood, and support for this view was found in a text from Ugarit (C. H. Gordon, *Ugaritic textbook* (1965) text 120, p. 191, which includes *lmg* together with (?cypress wood) in an inventory. It is a short, philologically respectable step to identify *lmg* with *elammaku*, which was one of the woods cut by the king of Mari (p. 73) and which is not uncommon in Akkadian texts (s.v. *elammaku, CAD*)). This attractive hypothesis, however, does not explain the association with Ophir. In both accounts the natural implication is that the wood came by the Red Sea to Eloth, and only after the main buildings were completed. Two uses are given for the wood. In both accounts it is used for harps and lutes; for the second use two different words are used and the meaning of neither is certain. One should look for a precious hardwood used for furnishings rather than a building-timber. The rarity of the wood is emphasised in both accounts, which fits an exotic from the south much better than a wood that seems to have been fairly common in Syria, and therefore perhaps in Lebanon also.

60. *ANET* 268.
61. *ANET* 269, 3b; Brown (n. 48) no. 111, p. 176.
62. Brown (n. 48) no. 112, p. 177; A. Malamat, 'The campaigns to the Mediterranean by Iahdumlin and other early Mesopotamian rulers', *Assyr. Stud.* 16 (1965) 365-73.
63. Brown (n. 48) no. 116, p. 179.
64. *ANET* 276; Brown (n. 48) no. 120, p. 189.
65. *ARAB* 1. 575.
66. 1. 583.
67. 1. 601.
68. 1. 804.
69. 2. 19-22, 139-78.
70. W. F. Saggs, 'The Nimrud letters', *Iraq* 17 (1955) 127-31, letter 12. The text is taken from a revised translation by J. N. Postgate, *Taxation and conscription in the Assyrian empire* (Rome, 1974) 390-1.
71. *ARAB* 2. 319.
72. 2 Kings 19: 35.
73. Hdt. 2. 141. 6.
74. Isaiah 37: 24.
75. *ARAB* 2. 411.
76. 2. 653.
77. 2. 697, 698.
78. Nahum 3: 19.
79. *ARAB* 2. 804.
80. 2. 914.
81. A. H. Layard, *Nineveh and Babylon* (1853) 357.
82. M. E. L. Mallowan, *Nimrud and its remains* (1966) 270, 377 f.
83. A. H. Layard, *Nineveh and its remains* (1849) 258.
84. Mallowan (n. 82) 443.
85. Waterman (n. 37) 1. 92, 705.
86. A. K. Grayson, *Assyrian royal inscriptions* (1972) 1. 166 (653): discussed by D. J. Wiseman, *Iraq* 14 (1952) 28.
87. Mallowan (n. 82) 152-6.
88. *ANET* 307; Brown (n. 48) no. 48, p. 196.
89. Isaiah 14: 7-8.
90. Brown (n. 48) no. 128, p. 201.
91. Nehemiah 2: 8.
92. R. G. Kent, *Old Persian, grammar, texts, lexicon*[2] (1953) 142-6; Brown (n. 48) no. 127, p. 199.
93. Curtius Rufus 5. 7. 5.
94. Polyb. 10. 27. 10.
95. Cleopatra had persuaded Antony to give her Phoenicia and Palestine: Josephus, *Antiq.* 15. 1.
96. Ibid. 12. 141.

97. Josephus, *BJ* 5. 37.
98. *NH* 5. 78 with R. Mouterde, *Regards sur Beyrouth* (1966).
99. Strabo 756.
100. In one inscription the legion that became VIII Augusta after Octavian had become Augustus in 27 BC was named VIII Gallica, reflecting its service under Caesar in his conquest of Gaul.
101. J. P. Rey Coquais, 'Syrie romaine de Pompé a Diocletien', *JRS* 68 (1978) 52.
102. The earliest evidence is a rough inscription of AD 60 on the top drum of one of the columns, *IGLS* 6. 2733. Rey Coquais suggests that building may have begun under Augustus, *The Princeton encyclopaedia of classical sites* (1976) 380.
103. E. Renan, *Mission de Phénicie* (2 vols., Paris, 1864-74) 1. 257-74; distribution map E. Honigmann, *RE* 13 (1927) 6.
104. Vegetius 4. 34.
105. *HP* 5. 3. 1.
106. Eusebius, *Eccles. Hist.* 10. 4. 42-3; Brown (n. 48) 136.

Chapter 4

1. A. Parrot, *Mission archéologique de Mari, Le Palais*, vol. 2: *Architecture* (1958).
2. Vitr. 2. 8. 16.
3. Parrot (n. 1) 113-15.
4. *PM* 2. 408; J. W. Graham, *The palaces of Crete* (1962) 159. I have taken Graham's slightly revised measurements. The trunk was more probably split than sawn.
5. *PM* 2. 406.
6. *PM* 4. 968-70; Graham (n. 4) 159.
7. Graham (n. 4) figs. 46, 48.
8. *PM* 1. 337-41.
9. L. Banti, *Il palazzo minoico di Festo* (1935) 69, 320, 457; cf. Cnossus: *PM* 2. 688; Graham (n. 4) 194.
10. *PM* 2. 521; 1. 344; 3. 323.
11. *PM* 3. 321; 1. 342; Graham (n. 4) 193.
12. *PM* 1. 443, fig. 19; 2. 601, fig. 373d.
13. *PM* 3. 318-48; 1. 349-51; Graham (n. 4) 86 f.
14. *PM* 3. 333-9.
15. S. Marinatos, *Excavations at Thera* (Athens, 1974) 6.
16. D. M. Ohly, 'Holz', *AM* 68 (1953) 79 ff.; G. Kopcke, 'Neue Holzfunde aus der Heraion von Samos', *AM* 82 (1967) 115 ff.
17. *PM* 3. 522 with fig. 365. I am grateful to Mr Sinclair Hood for drawing my attention to other bronze curls in *PM* 3. 429-32. These are flat and Evans thought that they came from a lion's mane; Mr Hood suggests that they resemble the locks of human figures as represented in frescos. He further suggests that the finding of heads in stone, plaster, and ivory without any associated body parts in Mycenae and in Crete may be

because the wood has perished. This is attractive and could become persuasive if more such isolated heads are found.

18. J. C. Caskey, *Hesp.* 35 (1966) 369-71.
19. *PM* 2. 565, 518-19.
20. Banti (n. 9) 420.
21. Strabo 475.
22. Hermippus, quoted in Athen. 27de.
23. *HP* 4. 5. 2.
24. 3. 1. 6; 3. 2. 6; 4. 1. 3.
25. *NH* 16. 141-2.
26. F. Thiriet, *La Romanie vénitienne au Moyen Âge* (1959) 322, 416.
27. *PM* 1. 344.
28. *PM* 3. 21.
29. J. W. Shaw, *Minoan architecture: materials and technique, Ann. della scuola arch. di Atene* 49 (1971) 135 f; Marinatos, *Ann. Arch. Arch.* 7 (1974) 95.
30. *AA* 1934, 251-4; 1935, 248-51.
31. Vitr. 2. 9. 13 followed by Pliny (*NH* 16. 197).
32. P. Warren, 'British travellers in Crete', *Κρητ. Χρον.* 24 (1972) 70.
33. Identified by Netolitzsky (n. 30), who also identified *Picea orientalis*, but the spruce, which is common in the forests south of the Black Sea, would seem to be much too far south in Crete.
34. P. Warren, *Myrtos* (1972) 299-30 (appendix by O. Rackham).
35. M. Ventris and J. Chadwick, *Documents in Mycenaean Greek*² (1973) nos. 278-82 f.; *NH* 16. 110.
36. Ventris and Chadwick (n. 35) p. 141.
37. The history of the excavation and the description of the site: Carl W. Blegen and Marion Rawson, *The palace of Nestor at Pylos in western Messenia,* vol. 1 (1966).
38. Ibid. 76-92.
39. W. G. Loy, *The land of Nestor* (1966); W. A. McDonald and G. R. Rapp, Jr., *The Minnesota Messenian expedition* (1972), especially ch. 12.
40. Ventris and Chadwick (n. 35) no. 284, p. 273.
41. no. 240. 241, pp. 341 f.
42. no. 242; *HP* 3. 4. 6.
43. Homer, *Od.* 19. 428-54.
44. *Il.* 13. 198-200.
45. *Il.* 5. 560.
46. 13. 178.
47. 13. 389-91 (repeated 16. 482-4).
48. 14. 413-16.
49. 4. 482-7.
50. 12. 132-4.
51. 16. 765-9.
52. 13. 633.
53. 14. 396-7.
54. 20. 490-4.
55. 11. 493-5
56. 11. 86-90

57. 23. 110–26.
58. *Od.* 5. 64.
59. 5. 239.
60. n. 47.
61. *Od.* 17. 208.
62. 5. 239.
63. *Od.* 7. 105–6.
64. *Il.* 5. 692.
65. 2. 307.
66. Schol. *Il.* 11. 86.
67. *Od.* 21. 43.
68. 14. 12.
69. 12. 357.
70. 14. 328.
71. *Il.* 18. 558.
72. *Od.* 9. 125–6.
73. *Il.* 16. 143.
74. *Od.* 17. 339.
75. *Il.* 21. 242.
76. 6. 419.
77. *Od.* 5. 64.
78. 17. 340.
79. 6. 292.
80. 17. 208.
81. *Od.* 7. 105–6; *Il.* 4. 482–7.
82. *Od.* 5. 236.
83. 13. 612.
84. 9. 322–3.
85. *Il.* 16. 767.
86. *Od.* 10. 242.
87. *HP* 5. 7. 1 and 4–5.
88. 5. 1. 7.
89. *Od.* 2. 424.
90. *Il.* 7. 5.
91. *Od.* 19. 38.
92. *Il.* 24. 448–54.
93. n. 47.
94. *Od.* 9. 186.
95. *Il.* 11. 494; 23. 328.
96. *Il.* 24. 269.
97. 24. 192.
98. *Od.* 5. 60.
99. *HP* 5. 3. 7.
100. *Od.* 5. 234–45.
101. 5. 246–8.
102. *Od.* 17. 384.
103. *Il.* 23. 315.
104. J. Levy, *Isis* 52 (1961) 78–86.

105. *Il.* 11. 494; 23. 328.
106. *Od.* 9. 186.
107. *HP* 3. 8. 2.
108. *Il.* 5. 693.
109. 5. 838.
110. *Od.* 5. 60. The adjective *thyōdes* is also used in *Od.* 4. 121 (of Helen's chamber) and 5. 264 (of clothes given by Calypso to Odysseus).
111. Ventris and Chadwick (n. 35) no. 252.
112. *Od.* 9. 391-5.

Chapter 5

1. For a useful introduction see A. C. Johnson, 'Ancient forests and navies', TAPA 58 (1927) 199-209.
2. Thuc. 8. 1. 3.
3. Strabo 669.
4. *BG* 3. 13. 3.
5. *HP* 5. 7. 1-3.
6. Plato, *Laws* 705c.
7. Diod. 17. 89. 4.
8. Verg. *Aen.* 5. 663; 8. 91.
9. Tod, *GHI* 2. 111. 10-15.
10. For a description of firs, see W. Dallimore and A. B. Jackson, *A handbook of conifers and ginkgoaceae* (1966): *Alba* 34 f.; *Cephalonica* 44; *Cilicica* 46; *Nordmanniana* 70.
11. *HP* 5. 1. 5.
12. *IG* 1³. 89. 31.
13. *HP* 5. 1. 7. In an inscription from Cos the oar-makers, a specialist trade, are called oar-shavers (*kopoxystae*): *SIG* 1000. 18.
14. *IG* 2². 1604. 34, 35, 53-4.
15. Ar. *Knights* 1307-10.
16. Strabo 741; Arrian 7. 19. 4; Antigonus used cedar and cypress for his fleet in 315 BC (Diod. 19. 58. 3).
17. Vegetius 43. 4; Plut. *Symp.* 1. 2. 5 (618b) regards the pine of the Isthmus and the cypress of Crete as the best ship-timbers (not thinking primarily of warships).
18. Thuc. 1. 8. 1.
19. Hdt. 7. 139. 1-4.
20. Thuc. 1. 14. 3.
21. Hdt. 7. 1. 144; Arist. *Ath. Pol.* 22. 7.
22. Diod. 14. 41. 3.
23. *HP* 4. 5. 5.
24. Hdt. 5. 94. 1; Arist. *Ath. Pol.* 15. 2.
25. Hdt. 8. 136. 1.
26. M. B. Wallace, 'Early Greek *proxenoi*', *Phoenix* 24 (1970) 199.
27. Hdt. 5. 23. 2.
28. Thuc. 6. 90. 3.
29. *IG* 1³. 386. 100-1.

30. Hdt. 8. 62. 2.
31. Plut. *Them.* 24. 1; Thuc. 1. 136. 1.
32. *NH* 16. 192; cf. Strabo 833 (the Carthaginians built 120 ships in two months).
33. *BC* 1. 58. 3.
34. Livy 29. 1. 14.
35. Vegetius 4. 36.
36. Xen. *Hell.* 6. 1. 11.
37. Meiggs, in *The Athenian Empire* (1972) 428-30, preferred a date in the mid-thirties. This provides a very suitable context, but, as Lewis in *IG* 1³. 141. 89 emphasises, the length of line and the fullness of the text favour a much later date.
38. Andoc. 2. 11.
39. The Athenians had established a settlement at Eion at the mouth of the river Strymon in 476/5 BC.
40. Thuc. 1. 100. 2-3.
41. 1. 105-6.
42. 4. 108. 1.
43. 1. 57. 2-3.
44. 4. 132. 1
45. 8. 1. 3.
46. 7. 25. 2.
47. Meiggs and Lewis, *GHI* 91.
48. Xen. *Hell.* 1. 6. 31.
49. Thuc. 2. 91. 3.
50.* A very different pattern is advocated by R. P. Legon in 'The Megarian decree and the balance of Greek naval power', *Class. Phil.* 68 (1973) 161-71. One of the most striking achievements in the events that led up to the Peloponnesian War is the dramatic increase in the Corinthian fleet from thirty triremes at the battle of Leukimme when they were defeated by Corcyra (Thuc. 1. 27. 2) to ninety at the battle of Sybota less than two years later (1. 46. 1). Legon assumes that there were no adequate supplies of timber in the Peloponnese and that after the defeat of Leukimme Corinth could have been cut off from her normal supplies in the north-west. She will therefore have needed to turn to the forests of the north Aegean. Since she had abandoned the Aegean as a result of the dominance of Athens, she will have relied on Megara to bring her supplies. This, Legon thinks, produces a more convincing explanation of the decree in which Athens banned the Megarians from all the harbours of her empire.

The silence of Thucydides, who makes no mention of the Corinthians in connection with the decree, is serious but not fatal, because there are other strange omissions in Thucydides. The basic assumptions, however, are invalid. There is ample evidence in the fourth-century accounts of the temple commissioners at Delphi that there were considerable supplies of fir and cypress in Arcadia (p. 432), and during this period Corinth was not cut off from all her western colonies. Although the immediate result of the defeat at Leukimme was that the Corcyraeans controlled the local seas and could even raid Leucas and Elis, the Corinthians then established a base at Actium 'to protect Leucas and their other friends' (l. 30. 3). Ambracia which had a particularly well-forested hinterland (p. 356) supplied eight ships at Leukimme, twenty-seven at Sybota. Her timber would also have been available to Corinth. Nor should the island of Cephalonia be ignored. It has given its name to the commonest fir in Greece and had provided four ships at Leukimme.

51. Xen. *Hell.* 1. 1. 23.
52. 1. 1. 25.
53. Diod. 14. 42. 4.
54. *IG* 2². 1611.
55. [Dem.] 17. 28.
56. Arrian 2. 13. 7.
57. Diod. 17. 89. 4; Strabo 698.
58. Strabo 741; Arrian 7. 19. 3-4.
59. Diod. 19. 58. 2-5.
60. 20. 47-52.
61. *NH* 16. 203, *HP* 5. 8. 1. Cedars discovered, S. W. Baker, *Cyprus as I saw it* (London, 1879) 489; described in detail, *For Treasures* 6 (1949) 14-19. For the wider distribution of cedars, *HP* 5. 8. 1. Dr Michaelides, Director of the Department of Forests in Cyprus, has kindly sent me the following notes:
    (*a*) At Skouriotissa Mines pit-props of cedars, pines, cypresses and alders used by the Romans were found.
    (*b*) It is certain that cedars formerly covered a wider area of the southern-range mountains. The reasons for believing this are the following:
        (i) There are a few cedars in private lands (Tsakistra and Pedhoulas) far from their present sites in the forest.
        (ii) Cedars planted in forest areas away from their present site grow exceedingly well.
A fragment of a pit-prop sent to me from Skouriotissa unfortunately was too mineralised to be precisely indentified.
62. *OGIS* 39.
63. Diod. 14. 41. 3; 16. 44. 6. *IG* 2². 1627. 275-8; 1629. 808-42.
64. L. Casson, *Ships and seamanship in the ancient world* (1971) 97-125.
65. *IG* 2². 1628.
66. Diod. 20. 49. 2, 50. 2-3.
67. Plut. *Demetrius* 43.
68. *HP* 5. 8. 1.
69. *NH* 16. 203.
70. Athen. 203e-204d. The platform used to launch the vessel was said to have been built from the timber of fifty quinqueremes.
71. Casson (n. 64) 110-16.
72. Plut. *Antonius* 64. 1; Dio. 50. 23. 2.
73. Athen. 206d-209b.
74. *NH* 16. 192.
75. Polyb. 1. 22; F. W. Walbank, *A historical commentary on Polybius* 2 (1967) 77-9; Casson (n. 64) 121.

76. Polyb. 1. 63. 5.
77. P. Boudy, *Économie forestière nord-africaine* 4 (1955) 417–59; Admiralty Handbook, *Tunisia* (1945) 91–5. The ancient sources: S. Gsell, *Histoire ancienne de l'Afrique du nord* 1 (1920) 137–58.
78. Appian, *Lib.* 97. Plentiful timber supplies near Tunis, 'because of the multitude of trees': *BC* 2. 37. 4.
79. A full report by Honor Frost of the wreck will shortly be published. The woods and plants are analysed in an appendix by Nigel Hepper of the Kew Herbarium which he has kindly allowed me to read.
80. Livy 28. 45. 18.
81. Appian, *Hannibal* 59.
82. Livy 33. 30. 5.
83. A. McDonald and F. W. Walbank, *JRS* 59 (1969) 30–9.
84. Polyb. 5. 89 with Walbank (n. 75) 1. 619 f.; Holleaux, *REG* (1923) 480–7.
85. *HP* 5. 7. 1.
86. *NH* 16. 203.
87. *IG* 2². 1492. 120 f.: εἰς τὴν τ[ῶ]ν [ξύ|λω]ν κομίδ[η]ν τῶν π[ε]υ[κῶν τῶν πα]ρὰ [βασιλ]έων [εἰ]ς τὰς ναῦς. I am grateful to Mrs Karapa-Molisani for examining the stone and sending me a squeeze. In the critical word πευκῶν she read a stroke of upsilon, but in the fourth rather than third letter-space: her reading was confirmed by David Lewis from the squeeze. Unless there was a flaw in the stone at this point π[ε]υ[κῶν must be ruled out. π[ιτ]ύ[ων, however, would fit in and this is the word used by Theophrastus for Cyprian pine (*HP* 5. 7. 1). Even so, the proportion of restoration is high and the restored text as a whole is not completely convincing.
88. *HP* 5. 8. 1.
89. Polyb. 25. 4.
90. Livy 45. 29. 14.
91. The Ligurian coast offered similar facilities, but was more securely controlled by Rome.
92. Thuc. 2. 69. 1.
93. Cic. *De imperio Cn. Pompeii* 33.
94. Appian, *Mith.* 96.
95. *BC* 2. 33. 3.
96. *BC* 3. 3.
97. Dio 48. 49–50.
98. Strabo 244.
99. Dio 51. 8. 3; Val. Max. 1. 49 adds that he was executed in the grove itself.
100. *Pineta*: Jordanes, *Getica* 57. 293; Strabo 213. The guild of builders had at least twenty-eight sections (*CIL* 11. 132) and may have included builders of ships. The tombstone of a shipwright from Ravenna has a relief showing him at work (*CIL* 11. 139).
101. Strabo 243. Juvenal (3. 306–7) calls it a pinewood which attracted the lawless.
102. Vitr. 2. 10. 1.
103. Sidonius 5. 441–5.
104. Cassiodorus, *Var.* 5. 16–18, 20.

Chapter 6

1. *BC* 3. 15. 2.
2. *BG* 5. 39. 2. For the construction see K. Saatman *et al.*, *Bonn. Jahrb.* 143 (1938) 83-208.
3. *BG* 5. 40. 2.
4. 4. 17.
5. 8. 14. 4.
6. G. Matherat, 'Les ponts-de-fascines de Jules César à Breuil', *Rev. Arch.* 7 (1936) 53-94; 9 (1937) 38-67.
7. *BG* 5. 11. 1-8.
8. 2. 30-1.
9. 3. 29.
10. Thuc. 2. 75-7.
11. Cf. Ezekiel 4: 1: 'Man, take a tile and set it before you. Draw a city on it, the city of Jerusalem: lay siege to it, erect watch-towers against it, raise a siege-ramp, put mantelets in position, and bring battering-rams against it all round.'
12. For evidence of attempts to undermine the mound, and the discovery within it of heads of arrows, spears, and javelins, see F. G. Maier, *Report of the Department of Antiquities, Cyprus* (1967) 31 and 39.
13. Diod. 14. 51-3.
14. 16. 74. 2-6.
15. Vitr. 10. 13. 3.
16. Arrian, *Anabasis* 2. 15. 6-24. 6; Diod. 17. 40-6.
17. Diod. 17. 42. 6.
18. 20. 47-52; Plut. *Demetrius* 15-16.
19. 20. 81-8; 91-9; Plut. *Demetrius* 21.
20. Diod. 20. 91.
21. 20. 95. 1-2.
22. E. W. Marsden, *Greek and Roman artillery. Technical treatises* (1971) 70-1.
23. Firs could have been cut on the Taurus range in Cilicia, as well as cedars, junipers, and pines.
24. Vitr. 10. 13. 6.
25. 10. 15.
26. *BG* 2. 4; Vitr. 10. 14.
27. *BC* 1. 36.
28. 2. 15. 1.
29. Lucan 3. 394 ff.
30. Plut. *Sulla* 12.
31. Plut. *Antony* 38. 2.
32. Vegetius 2. 10, 11.
33. 2. 25.
34. *BG* 5. 12. 5.
35. H. Godwin, *The history of the British flora*[2] (1973) 273-6. It seems improbable that Caesar should, as Godwin suggests, have confused beech, which was very common in Italy, with chestnut.
36. *BG* 5. 15. 19; Tac. *Ann.* 14. 34. 3; Tac. *Agricola* 20. 2; 25. 1; 26. 1; 37. 4; Herodian 3. 14. 10.

37. Tac. *Agricola* 25-39 with commentary (R. M. Ogilvie and I. A. Richmond, 1967) 239-87; see also J. K. S. St. Joseph, 'The camp of Durno and Mons Graupius', *Britannia* 9 (1978) 271-87.

38. Tac. *Hist.* 1. 2.

39. Annual reports in *JRS* 43-56 (1953-66): a useful summary by K. A. Steer in *The Princeton encyclopaedia of classical sites* (1976) 409. For Roman military timber-building see I. A. Richmond in W. E. M. Jope, *Studies in building history* (1961) 15-26.

40. I. A. Richmond, *Hod Hill* 2 (1968) 84 f.; cf. B. Cunliffe, *Fishbourne* (1971) 27-30.

41. J. P. Bushe-Fox, *Richborough report* 4 (1969) 26.

42. In a detailed study of Roman military timber granaries W. A. Manning, in *Saalburg Jahrb.* 32 (1975) 105-29, emphasises that there is no firm evidence for the use of a timber sill, but only for the trench, and he argues that it would have no purpose. But the sill would provide a better defence than a trench alone against uneven sinking of the posts, and it would protect the open ends of the posts from direct contact with the earth.

43. In the headquarters building (*principia*) and in the officers' houses the framing timbers were more substantial (1 ft. square in the *principia*), but none of the lengths approached thirty feet.

44. I. A. Richmond and J. McIntyre, *Proc. Soc. Antiq. Scot.* 73 (1938-9) 110-54.

45. Ibid. 154.

46. Richmond (n. 39) 25.

47. W. S. Hanson, 'The organisation of Roman military timber supply', *Britannia* 9 (1978) 293-305.

48. Seasoning discussed, p. 349 f.

49. Pollen: S. E. Durno, 'Pollen analysis of peat deposits in Scotland', *Scottish Geog. Mag.* 72 (1956) 177-87; 73 (1957) 176-84. Ecology: H. M. Steven and A. Carlisle, *The native pine-woods of Scotland* (1959) 49; D. N. McVean in J. H. Burnett (ed.) *The vegetation of Scotland* (1964) 144 f., 568-72. The Visitor of Balliol College has kindly introduced me to a not irrelevant contribution from an unexpected source. In Queen Victoria's *More leaves from the journal of a life in the Highlands* there is a description of an excursion on 12 September 1873. Her Majesty was staying at Inverlochy just north of Fort William and made an expedition to Achnacarry. When they got to Loch Arkaig they 'embarked on board a very small but nice screw steamer which belongs to Cameron of Lochiel . . . We went about halfway up the Loch . . . Both sides are beautifully wooded all along the lower part of the fine hills which rise on either side, and the trees are all oaks, which Cameron of Lochiel said were "the weed of the country", and all natural—none were planted.'

50. M. L. Anderson, *A history of Scottish forestry* (1967) 67-71.

51. Tac. *Agricola* 25: *Silvarum et montium profunda.*

52. Dio 77. 13; Herodian 3. 14. 10.

53. S. S. Frere and J. K. S. St. Joseph, *Britannia* 5 (1974) 1-129.

54. D. J. Breeze, *Britannia* 8 (1977) 130-61.

55. F. H. Thompson, *Roman Chester* (1965) 42.

56. Tac. *Ann.* 2. 63. 5.
57. M. L. Anderson (n. 50) 66-86; cf. from Belgium, J. Bastin, 'La via Mansuerisca', *Antiq. class.* 3 (1934) 363-83.
58. Vegetius 3. 7.
59. D. A. Jackson and T. M. Ambrose, 'Timber bridge at Aldwinkle', *Britannia* 7 (1976) 39-72.
60. D. P. Dymond, 'Roman bridges on Dere Street' (with appendix on the evidence for Roman bridges in Britain), *Journ. Arch.* 118 (1961) 136-64. For a more general survey of Roman bridges in the western provinces, see H. Cüpper, *Die Trierer Römerbrücken* (1969) 173.
61. Dymond (n. 60) 146. This bridge would have needed beams of a little more than thirty feet to provide a foundation for the road.
62. Tac. *Agricola* 21. 1.
63. S. S. Frere, *Verulamium excavations* 1 (1972) 5-23, 49 f. There is evidence of mud-brick at Colchester: B. R. K. Dunnett (*Journ. Arch.* 123 (1966) 31.
64. D. S. Neale, 'The Roman villa at Boxmoor', *Britannia* 1 (1970) 156-62.
65. H. Cleere, 'Ironmaking in a Roman furnace', *Britannia* 2 (1971) 206. A heap of slag found at Beaufort Park, Battle, is estimated to have contained *c.*50,000 tons before it was quarried for road metalling in the nineteenth century.
66. *BG* 6. 25; *NH* 16. 6.
67. *NH* 16. 5; Tac. *Ann.* 1. 51. 6-8, 56. 5, 64. 7; 2. 11. 3, 16. 3, 17. 2.
68. For a general review of the Rhine frontier, see H. Schönberger, 'The Roman frontier in Germany', *JRS* 59 (1969) 146-97.
69. *CIL* 13. 6618, 6623.
70. H. Bingemer, *Saalburg Jahrb.* 10 (1951) 29-33.
71. C. Cichorius, *Die Reliefs der Traianssäule* (2 vols. text and 2 vols. photographs, 1896-1900). For the form of the monument, and detailed descriptions of selected scenes, see I. A. Richmond, 'Trajan's army on Trajan's Column', *PBSR* 13 (1935) 1-40.

Chapter 7

1. Plato, *Critias* 111c.
2. W. M. Leake, *Travels in northern Greece* (1835) 2. 420.
3. Hdt. 9. 39. 1.
4. Thuc. 2. 75-8.
5. Leake (n. 2) 2. 372 f.
6. Euripides, *Bacchae* 1051-1104.
7. A. T. Hodge, *The woodwork of Greek roofs* (1960) 7.
8. Woods for sculpture in the archaic period are discussed in ch. 11, pp. 300-24.
9. J. Travlos, *Pictorial dictionary of Athens* (1971) 402-11. The total area dedicated to Zeus was 205.80 × 63.68 metres. Within this area the double peripteral temple measured 110.55 × 43.63 metres.
10. Thuc. 1. 14. 3.
11. Thuc. 1. 89. 3.

12. Plut. *Cimon* 13. 7.
13. Ibid. 4. 6; Paus. 1. 15. 1.
14. Synesius, *Ep.* 54. 135.
15. I can find no positive evidence.
16. H. A. Thompson and R. E. Wycherley, *The Agora of Athens* (1972) 41-6; Travlos (n. 9) 583.
17. Travlos (n. 9) 140-9.
18. *IG* 1³. 472. 155-60.
19. Meiggs, *Athenian Empire* (1972) 185 f.
20. In his admirable study of Greek roofs A. T. Hodge (n. 7, 38-42) inferred from the exceptional size of the spans covered in Sicilian temples (see table, Hodge, 39) that the western Greeks must have discovered the principle of the tie-beam truss in the late archaic period and since it was unknown to the Greeks of the mainland it must have been learnt from the Phoenicians. The only alternative was to believe that the western Greeks had access to timber of special size and strength; this he thought to be very unlikely. It is, however, much more difficult to believe that such a dramatic step forward should have been ignored by the mainland Greeks for more than a hundred years. The western Greeks had access in Mt. Etna and the forests of south Italy to some of the best timber in the Mediterranean (App. 6, p. 462).
21. *Hesp.* 55 (1958) 251 n.
22. Hodge (n. 7) 246.
23. I. T. Tallon, *The ancient city of Athens* (1953) 153.
24. G. P. Stevens, *Hesp.* 24 (1955) 244-6.
25. Plut. *Pericles* 13. 9-10.
26. Vitr. 5. 9. 1.
27. Travlos (n. 9) 387-91.
28. Appian, *Mith.* 38.
29. Plut. *Pericles* 12-13.
30. For a detailed discrediting of the debate, see A. Andrewes, 'The opposition to Pericles', *JHS* 98 (1978) 1-8. Against the great majority I am not convinced that Pericles was uninterested in the employment of the poor; cf. Isocrates 7. 42.
31. The fragment is published in *IG* 1². 388. For the identification see *IG* 1³. 461.
32. *HP* 5. 6. 4.
33. App. 4. 1, p. 424 f.
34. Pindar, *Pyth.* 5. 44-5 with G. Roux, 'Pindare, le prétendu trésor des Crétois et l'ancienne statue d'Apollon à Delphes', *REG* 75 (1962) 366-80.
35. Hermippus, quoted in Athen. 27d-e.
36. Tod, *GHI* 2. 110. David Lewis agrees that the letter-forms demand a fifth-century date and would prefer the third quarter.
37. A. Wilhelm, *Sitzb. -Wien.* 220 (5) 85 f.
38. J. M. Paton, *The Erechtheum* (1927) 239, xiii, col. 1. 3-4.
39. An *empolion* from the bottom of the capital of the south-east corner of the eastern portico of the Erechtheum was scientifically identified as cypress: Paton (n. 38) 226. Previously (196) the *empolia* of the north portico had been described as cedar, but presumably without microscopic examination.

40. E. G. Mariolopoulos, *Geofisica pura e applicata* 51 (1962) 243–50.
41. *NH* 16. 141–2.
42. Paton (n. 38) 338 f.
43. Ibid. 239.
44. Paus. 5. 11. 2.
45. *IG* 1³. 439. 107.
46. The evidence is discussed in A. W. Gomme, *The population of Athens in the fifth and fourth centuries* (1933).
47. A. N. Balci, *Timber trends and prospects in Turkish forestry* (1968).
48. Sophocles, *Ajax* 1220.
49. Dem. 21. 167.
50. The building of furnaces nearer to the coast may be a reflection of this trade.
51. *IG* 1³. 435. 17, 39, 75, 110; 472. 151.
52. Fuel for metallurgy: J. Healy, *Mining and metallurgy in the Greek and Roman world* (1978) 148–52.
53. Thuc. 2. 38. 1.
54. [Xen.] *Ath. Pol.* 2. 9–10; 3. 2.
55. App. 4. 4.
56. G. E. M. de Ste. Croix, *Ehrenberg studies* (*Ancient society and institutions*) (1966) 109–14.
57. Dem. 42. 10.
58. App. 4. 1, p. 424.
59. *Hesp.* 22 (1953) 288.
60. *SIG* 987; A. Wilhelm 'Die Pachturkunden der Klytiden', *Jahreshefte* 28 (1933) 197–210.
61. Dicaearchus 1. 21 (*Geographical minores*, p. 103).
62. Xen. *Mem.* 3. 1. 7.
63. Thuc. 2. 75. 5.
64. D. M. Robinson and G. W. Graham, *Olynthus* 8 (1930).
65. *The Agora of Athens* (n. 16) 173–85.
66. Thuc. 2. 4. 1.
67. Hdt. 1. 17. 2.
68. *Hesp.* 25 (1956) 233–40. Doors could also be taken as securities by the authorities: Dem. 24. 197.
69. *Hellenica Oxyrhyncia* (Bartoletti, 1954) 17. 4.
70. Dem. 49. 25–36.
71. Theophr. *Characters* 6. 14; cf. Dem. 19. 265: a corrupt politician of Olynthus bribed by Philip with Macedonian roof-timbers.
72. *IG* 1³. 386. 134.
73. Thuc. 7. 28. 1.
74. Thuc. 8. 96. 2.
75. Dem. 3. 26.
76. L. E. Jones, A. J. Graham, and L. H. Sackett, 'The Dema house in Attica', *BSA* 57 (1962), 75–114; 'An Attic country house below the cave of Pan at Vari', *BSA* 68 (1973) 355–452.
77. Thuc. 2. 65. 2.
78. *Hell. Ox.* (n. 69) 17. 4.

79. App. 4. 3, p. 433.
80. *HP* 5. 2. 1.
81. *The Agora of Athens* (n. 16) 74; Travlos (n. 9) 534.
82. W. B. Dinsmoor, *The architecture of ancient Greece*[3] (1950) 241.
83. Travlos (n. 9) 522-7; J. J. Coulton, *The architectural development of the Greek stoa* (1976) 69.
84. Travlos (n. 9) 505-20; Coulton (n. 83) 69.
85. Paus. 1. 8. 6; *Hesp.* 19 (1950) 31-161; Travlos (n. 9) 505-20.
86. Paus. 7. 20. 6; Travlos (n. 9) 522-7.
87. Philostr. *Vit. soph.* 2. 1. 8.

Chapter 8

1. Ovid, *Fasti* 5. 93-4.
2. Propertius 4. 1. 1-2; cf. Tibullus 2. 5. 25-31.
3. Verg. *Aen.* 8. 313-65.
4. *NH* 16. 237.
5. 16. 38, 139.
6. Tac. *Ann.* 4. 15. 1.
7. Dion. Hal. *Antiq.* 1. 79. 11; Dio 54. 29. 8.
8. *Mon. Ant.* 41 (1951) 1-146.
9. *HP* 5. 8. 3.
10. M. E. Hirst, *PBSR* 1 (1938) 137-51; *NH* 36. 100.
11. Livy 40. 51. 4.
12. D. Marchetti, *Bull. comm. arch. Rom.* 19 (1891) 45-60.
13. E. G. Gjerstad, *Early Rome* (1953-73) 4. 1. 399.
14. Ibid. 3. 108-90; 4. 1. 168-207. For the need for wooden architraves, see Vitr. 3. 3. 5.
15. Vitr. 2. 1. 3-7.
16. Gjerstad (n. 13) 4. 1. 403-17.
17. Livy 5. 41. 7.
18. F. Prayon, *Frühetruskische Grab- und Hausarchitektur* (Heidelberg, 1978); A. Boethius and J. B. Ward-Perkins, *Etruscan and Roman architecture* (1970) 63-76 with pls. 35-46.
19. Livy 5. 55. 3.
20. *NH* 16. 36.
21. Cicero, *De oratore* 1. 62.
22. Livy 35. 10. 12.
23. Livy 35. 41. 10; 40. 51. 6.
24. For the form of the basilica see Boethius and Ward-Perkins (n. 18) 127-31; Ward-Perkins, *Roman architecture* (1977) 20, 22.
25. Platner and Ashby, *Topographical dictionary of ancient Rome* (1929) 72; F. Coarelli, *Guida archeologica di Roma* (1975) 60.
26. Livy 1. 35. 7-9.
27. Livy 8. 20. 2.
28. Platner and Ashby (n. 25) 114.
29. Plut. *Gaius Gracchus* 12.
30. Livy, *Epit.* 48.

31. *NH* 36. 114-15.
32. *NH* 116.
33. Tac. *Ann.* 14. 20.
34. Vitr. 5. 5. 7.
35. Plut. *Caes.* 29. 3.
36. Cic. *Ad Atticum* 4. 11. 8.
37. Cic. *De lege agraria* 2. 59.
38. Suet. *Caes.* 30. 2.
39. Cic. *Ad Atticum* 13. 33.
40. Augustus, *Res gestae* 20.
41. F. W. Shipley, 'Chronology of the building operations in Rome from the death of Caesar to the death of Augustus', *Mem. Am. Acad. Rome* 9 (1930) 7-60.
42. *NH* 16. 191.
43. Dio 55. 8. 4.
44. *NH* 16. 201. Pliny includes this roof among the wonders of Rome (36. 102).
45. A detailed discussion of the evidence: P. A. Brunt, *Italian manpower* (1971) 376-88.
46. Suet. *Augustus* 28. 3.
47. Vitr. 2. 8. 17: 'pilis lapideis, *structuris testaceis*, parietibus caementiciis'. Vitruvius has exaggerated the importance of burnt brick in the new architecture. Archaeology has shown that under Augustus tufa blocks remained the standard facing of walls. Burnt bricks are still very rare and only gradually supersede tufa. All-brick facings are not the norm until the late years of Hadrian.
48. Varro, *Sat. Menipp. reliquiae* (ed. A. Riese) 225. xv.
49. Cic. *De divin.* 2. 99; Dio 39. 61. 2.
50.* Vitruvius (2. 8. 17) seems to regard legislation as relevant when, at the end of a description of mud-brick walls, he explains why they should not be used in Rome. 'Public statutes do not allow walls *loco communi* to be built thicker than one and a half feet; moreover, the other walls are built to the same thickness in order that room-space should not be reduced. But, if walls are not two or three bricks thick, they cannot with a thickness of one foot and a half support more than one storey.' That walls *loco communi*, meaning literally on ground that is shared, refers to party-walls is clear from Pliny (*NH* 35. 73): 'A wall of one and a half feet cannot support more than one storey, *cautumque est ne communis crassior fiat.*' From the muddled explanation of Vitruvius all that can safely be inferred is that at some time the thickness of party-walls was restricted to one and a half feet and since he refers to statutes and not a single statute, it can be inferred that in a succession of public laws such a clause was included. Rutilius Rufus, for instance, who was consul in 105 BC, delivered a speech 'On building regulations' which Augustus read out in the senate (Suet. *Aug.* 88. 2.) The original purpose of the law may have been to economise in the use of land.
51. Vitr. 2. 8. 20; 7. 8. 11. For the timber framing, see Vitr. 7. 3. 11. There is a good example of wattle walling in Republican Rome in Orosius (5. 12). When Gaius Gracchus and his followers were being hunted (121 BC) the

ex-consul Flaccus and his son fled through the temple of the moon goddess into a private house. They bolted the door, but their pursuers broke through the wattle wall and cut them down.

52. Plut. *Crassus* 2. 3.
53. Strabo 235.
54. Vitr. 2. 9. 5.
55. 2. 9. 9.
56. 2. 9. 11–12.
57. 2. 9. 12.
58. 2. 9. 9.
59. *HP* 5. 6. 1.
60. 5. 4. 2.
61. *NH* 16. 206, 212.
62. Palladius 12. 15. 2; H. Plommer, *Vitruvius and later Roman building manuals* (1979) 7; *Sylva* 45: 'The chestnut is (next the oak) one of the most sought-after by the carpenter and joiner.'
63. Vitr. 2. 9. 6.
64. 2. 9. 10.
65. 1. 2. 8.
66. Seneca, *Ep.* 90. 9.
67. Juv. 3. 254–6; discussed p. 343.
68. Verg. *Ecl.* 7. 66.
69. W. Sackur, *Vitruv und die Poliorketiker* (1925) 133–9.
70. *ILS* 53 17.
71. Evelyn, *Sylva* 123.
72. *NH* 16. 140, 141; Varro, *RR* 1. 15 (boundaries).
73. Dion. Hal. *Antiq.* 1. 37. 4; cf. Strabo 286; Brunt (*Italian manpower* 128 f.) regards these descriptions of Italy as grossly exaggerated. Admittedly the praise of Italy was a literary topos, but the evidence of Strabo and Roman historians confirms that Italy was very well forested and her navigable rivers, Po, Tiber, Arno, Crathis, compared favourably with those of Greece and several other Mediterranean lands.
74. Strabo 235.
75. *HP* 5. 8. 3. Lucan (2. 431) refers to the pine-clad rocks of the Apennines.
76. Strabo 222; cf. Varro 1. 9. 6.
77. Pliny, *Ep.* 5. 16. 7.
78. Juv. 3. 191.
79. C. E. Österberg, *Case Etrusche di Acquarossa* (1975) 4.
80. Strabo 227.
81. Pliny, *Ep.* 8. 8. 3 and 6.
82. P. A. Guglielmotti, *Storia della marina pontificale nel medio evo* (1886–93) 2. 209–15.
83. Strabo 228.
84. G. Ucelli, *Le navi di Nemi* (1956) 138, 147.
85. Livy 9. 36. 1; Florus 1. 12. 3.
86. Livy 35. 41. 10.
87. Strabo 223.
88. 202. Ligurian forests: Livy 39. 20; Diod. 5. 39. 2.

89. Dion. Hal. *Antiq.* 20. 15.
90. *HP* 5. 8. 1; cf. *NH* 16. 71.
91. Edward Lear, *Journal of a landscape painter in Corsica* (1870) 90, 137.
92. Vitr. 2. 9. 15–16.
93. *NH* 16. 190.
94. *NH* 16. 200.
95. Lucan 9. 920.
96. *NH* 100: Homer, *Od.* 5. 60.
97. Vitr. 2. 9. 14.
98.* Faventius (*c.*300), writing an epitome of Vitruvius, includes larch in his list of building-timbers, but he merely paraphrases Vitruvius. Palladius (12. 15. 1) follows him but adds nothing significant. Neither provides evidence that the use of larch had extended to central Italy and Rome. It has, however, been identified in two boats found within the Claudian harbour at Ostia, a large barge in which it was combined with oak, and a small fishing-boat (O. Testaguzza, *Porto* (1970) 132). It is very surprising that larch, which had come all the way by sea from the Alps, should be used rather than pine or oak for a small fishing-boat. But if it was so used at Ostia, it should have been not uncommon in Rome.
99. Tac. *Ann* 4. 12. 1–2; Suet. *Tiberius* 40.
100. Calpurnius Siculus 7. 23. Tacitus refers to the lavish praise by contemporary writers of the foundations and beams of the amphitheatre (*Ann.* 13. 31. 8).
101. Tac. *Ann.* 15. 38–41.
102. 15. 43. 4.
103. A. Maiuri, *Ercolano* (1958) 407–19.
104. *ILS* 5049; wooden floor: G. Cozzo, *The Colosseum* (1971) 56–7.
105. A. Boethius, *Nero's Golden House* (1960).
106. W. L. Macdonald, *The architecture of the Roman Empire* (1965) pls. 25–34; J. B. Ward-Perkins, *Roman architecture* (1977) 103–5.
107. Macdonald (n. 106) 56–73. Boethius and Ward-Perkins (n. 18) 232 questioning the vault over the main hall.
108. Dio 66. 24. 2.
109. Juv. 3. 7; SHA, *Antoninus Pius* 9.
110. Aulus Gellius 15. 1. 2–3.
111.* Herodian 7. 12. 5–6. The Greek is ambiguous. The Loeb edition translates: 'The buildings adjoined one another very closely and a great number of them were made of wood.' It is unlikely that buildings made entirely or mainly of wood were tolerated in Rome after the great fire of Nero's reign. The passage follows immediately after the firing of balconies, and may refer to the widespread use of wooden balconies in the great house-blocks.
112. Dio 55. 8. 4. The Loeb edition is misleading in translating καθαιρεθείσης by 'destroyed'. In Dio the verb consistently means 'to take down' or remove by human agency.
113. Martial 3. 20. 15 shows the baths of Agrippa in use after the fire of 80.
114. Sidonius 5. 441–5.
115. Coarelli (n. 25) 66.

117. SHA, *Marcus Aurelius* 13.
118. L. Homo, *Rome impériale* (1925) 352-5.
119. SHA, *Alexander Severus* 24. 5. A shortage of fuel may have been a contributory factor in the increasing use of stone and reused brick in the third century before brick production was revitalised by Diocletian.
120. *Cod. Theod.* 13. 5. 10.
121. 14. 5. 1.
122. Symmachus (Seeck) 10. 40.
123. 10. 44.
124. 9. 103, 104.

Chapter 9

1. The composition is more complex than this simple outline suggests: see M. L. West, *Hesiod Works and Days* (text and commentary, 1978).
2. Hesiod, *Works and Days* 427-36.
3. 805-9.
4. 456-7.
5. 826-8.
6. Cato, *De agricultura* 10. 11.
7. 1. 7.
8. 6. 3. For the importance of leaves as fodder, Columella, *Res rusticae* 11. 2. 99.
9. 14. 3.
10. 18. 5.
11. 18. 2.
12. 31. 1.
13. 28. 1.
14. 33. 5, 31. 1.
15. *NH* 16. 25.
16. Strabo 218.
17. Cato 6. 4.
18. 9.
19. 5. 8, 6. 1, 6. 3.
20. 7. 1.
21. 38. 4.
22. Varro, *RR*, Book 2, Introduction, 6.
23. 1. 7. 8.
24. 1. 12. 1.
25. 1. 15.
26. Ibid.
27. 1. 8. 4.
28. 1. 23. 5.
29. 1. 22. 1.
30. Strabo 223.
31. Col. 3. 9. 2; 3. 3. 3.
32. 1. 2. 3-4.

33. Book 3.
34. Col. *De arboribus* 16. 1.
35. 4. 33.
36. *NH* 17. 147-9.
37. O. Rackham, *Trees and woodlands in the British landscape* (1976) 72-3. In England the seventeenth century was a transitional period, when both short and long cycles are found: *Sylva* 146-50.
38. *NH* 16. 141.
39. Edith Clay, *Sir William Gell in Italy* (London, 1976) 92, 94, 102, 110, 125.
40. *NH* 16. 206.
41. Col. 3. 3. 1-3.
42. Mart. 10. 79.
43. 7. 28. 1-2.
44. Pliny, *Ep.* 3. 19.
45. 5. 6.
46. H. Plommer, *Vitruvius and later Roman building manuals* (1979).
47. Faventius 12: Palladius 12. 15. 1.
48. Catullus 114, 115.
49. D. J. Wiseman, *Iraq* 14 (1952) 30, ll. 36-52.
50. *ARAB* 2. 698.
51. Strabo 741.
52. Plut. *Alc.* 24. 7.
53. Xen. *Oeconomica* 4. 20.
54. Xen. *Anab.* 1. 4. 10.
55. 2. 4. 14.
56. Diod. 16. 41. 5 with J. P. Brown, *The Lebanon and Phoenicia* (1969) p. 204, no. 130.
57. *HP* 5. 8. 1.
58. Meiggs and Lewis, *GHI* 12, p. 20.
59. Quintus Curtius 8. 1. 11.
60. Plut. *Cimon* 13. 7. 1.
61. Dicaearchus 1. 26, 27 (*Geog. graeci minores* 1. 105).
62. Paus. 6. 23. 1; 5. 27. 11.
63. Paus. 3. 14. 8.
64. Propertius 2. 32. 11-16.
65. Strabo 596.
66. 236.
67. Tac. *Ann.* 15. 42. 1; Suet. *Nero* 31.
68. SHA, *Alexander Severus* 25. 4.
69. *NH* 17. 2-5.
70. Tac. *Ann.* 13. 47. 3.
71. 11. 3. 1.
72. 11. 3. 2.
73. Propertius 1. 14. 1-8.
74. Augustus, *Res gestae* 23.
75. Varro, *RR* 3. 13. 2.
76. Horace, *Odes* 2. 15.
77. Seneca, *De vita beata* 17. 2; *NH* 12. 6.

78. Vitr. 6. 5. 2.
79. Pliny, *Ep.* 5. 6. 4–40.
80. Plato, *Phaedrus* 229b.
81. *HP* 1. 7. 1.
82. Homer, *Il.* 2. 307.
83. Hdt. 7. 27. 2.
84. 7. 31.
85. *NH* 12. 7; cf. *Sylva* 118: 'I am persuaded, that with very ordinary industry, they (plane trees), might be propagated to the incredible ornament of the walks and avenues of great-men's houses. The introduction of the true plane among us is due to the honourable gentleman, Sir Geo. Cook of Oxfordshire from whose bounty I received a hopeful plant now growing in my villa.'
86. Mart. 3. 58.
87. 12. 50.
88. 9. 61.
89. Pliny, *Ep.* 1. 2. 1.
90. *NH* 12. 13.
91. 12. 12.
92. Verg. *Ecl.* 7. 65.
93. Pliny, *Ep.* 6. 16. 5–6.

Chapter 10

1. S. A. B. Mercer, *The Tel-el-Amarna tablets* (1939) 1. 103–55.
2. Ibid. 149. 51–3.
3. Ibid. 126. 4–6.
4. *HP* 1. 5. 4–5; 1. 6. 2; 5. 3. 1; *NH* 16. 70.
5. Philostratus, *Imag.* 2. 10; Calpurnius Siculus 4. 72; Ovid, *Tristia* 6. 697; *Ex Ponto* 1. 45; *NH* 16. 172.
6. *ANET* 282.
7. Ezekiel 27: 6, but the text is uncertain; *ANET* 284.
8. *ANET* 275. From a second campaign, in a neighbouring area, he extracted as tribute from another prince 'chairs of boxwood with insets (and) mountings, beds of boxwood, beds with insets, tables with ivory inlay (on boxwood)'.
9. Verg. *Georg.* 2. 449.
10. M. Ventris and J. Chadwick, *Documents in Mycenaean Greek*[2] (1973) no. 240, p. 342.
11. Homer, *Il.* 24. 269.
12. *Anth. Pal.* 6. 309.
13. Pollux 10. 59.
14. *NH* 35. 77.
15. Cennino d'Andrea Cennini (trans. D. V. Thompson), *The craftsman's handbook* (New York, 1960).
16. J. M. Paton, *Erechtheum*, p. 339, XI. col. 2. 31.
17. Athen. 207e.

18. Mart. 14. 25; Ovid, *Met.* 14. 537; Verg. *Aen.* 7. 352.

19. E. G. Hardy, *Roman laws and charters* (1912), p. 25 (*Lex Acilia repetundarum*, 37).

20. *HP* 3. 15. 5; Strabo 545; Verg. *Georg.* 2. 437. 'Box to Cytorus' was equivalent to Britain's 'coals to Newcastle'.

21. *HP* 5. 7. 7.

22. *NH* 16. 71; cf. Diod. 5. 14. 3.

23. E. Naville, *The temple of Deir el Bahari* 2 (1896) 1-3.

24. *ANET* 237.

25. Mercer (n. 1) 1. 5. 20-5.

26. Ibid. 31. 36-8.

27. Hollis S. Baker, *Furniture in the ancient world* (1966) 131, fig. 182.

28. Ibid. 147, fig. 227.

29. H. Carter, *The tomb of Tutankhamen* 3. 66. with pls. 15A and B.

30. H. S. Baker (n. 27) 104, fig. 135.

31. Ibid. 81, 91-4.

32. P. Fox, *Tutankhamun's treasure* (1951) pl. 14A.

33. Ventris and Chadwick (n. 10) no. 242, p. 342.

34. Ibid. no. 240, p. 341.

35. *ANET* 276.

36. Ibid. 288.

37. Ezekiel 27: 15, but the text is not quite certain.

38. Hdt. 3. 97. 3.

39. Paus. 5. 11. 2.

40. Athen. 201a.

41. Ovid, *Met.* 11. 610.

42. Verg. *Georg.* 2. 116; *NH* 12. 17-20.

43. *HP* 1. 5. 5; 5. 4. 2.

44. *NH* 24. 89.

45. Lucan 10. 117-19.

46. Apuleius, *Apol.* 61.

47. Homer, *Od.* 5. 60.

48. 5. 264; 4. 121.

49. *HP* 5. 3. 7.

50. Athen. 205b.

51. Lucan 10. 144-6.

52. *Suda* s.v. θύον.

53. Athen. 207e.

54. Festus (Lindsay) 292.

55. Varro, *RR* 3. 2. 4.

56. *NH* 33. 146.

57. Cic. *Verr.* 4. 37.

58. *NH* 13. 92.

59. Lucan 9. 426-30.

60. Velleius Paterculus 2. 56. 2. The suggestion that Caesar chose citrus-wood for his Gallic triumph because there were large workshops using citrus-wood in Gaul (Blümner) is much less probable.

61. Strabo 826.

62. *NH* 13. 91.
63. Seneca, *De beneficiis* 7. 9. 2.
64. *NH* 13. 94.
65. *NH* 13. 95; cf. Petronius, *Satyricon* 119. 27-31: 'The table of citrus dug out of the soil of Africa'.
66. *NH* 13. 96-7; cf. Seneca, *De ira* 3. 35. 5.
67. Mart. 2. 43. 9; cf. Juv. 11. 122-7.
68. *CIL* 6. 9258.
69. Dio 61. 10. 3.
70. Seneca, *De vita beata* 17. 2.
71. Mart. 14. 89; cf. 9. 59. 7; 10. 80: citrus tables among the luxuries displayed in fashionable shops in the Saepta.
72. Statius, *Silvae* 4. 2. 38-40.
73. *NH* 13. 95.
74. Horace, *Odes* 4. 1. 20, reading *sub trabe citrea*; Apuleius, *Met.* 5. 1: citrus ceiling coffers in a dream palace.
75. Statius, *Silvae* 1. 3. 35.
76. Mart. 14. 3.
77. *Dig.* 19. 21. 3.
78. *NH* 16. 68.
79. Mart. 14. 90. A rich man's maple table: Horace, *Odes* 2. 8. 10; a poor man's: Ovid *Met.* 12. 254.
80. Strabo 202. G. M. A. Richter, *The furniture of the Greeks, Etruscans, and Romans* (1966) 123 assumes that they were juniper trees.
81. Ar. *Acharnians* 180.
82. A. Lucas, *Ancient Egyptian materials and industries*[4] (ed. J. R. Harris, 1962) 429.
83. *HP* 5. 7. 6; Strabo 546.
84. Verg. *Aen.* 8. 178; Ovid, *Amores* 1. 11. 27-8.
85. Homer, *Il.* 24. 192.
86. 1 Kings 6; Polyb. 6. 10. 27.
87. *AR* 4. 966; Theocr. *Ep.* 8. 56.
88. Paus. 5. 17-19 with J. G. Frazer, *Pausanias* 2. 600 ff.; E. Simon, *Encycl. It. arte class. orient.* 4 (1961) 427-32.
89. Paus. 5. 18. 1, 19. 3.
90. Lucas (n. 82) 431; R. K. Winters, *The forest and man* (1974) 68 f.
91. Thuc. 2. 34. 3.
92. N. I. Sokolskii, *Sarcophagi from the northern shore of the Black Sea* (1969). I was able to enjoy the book by the kindness of W. L. Goodman who had made his own translation.
93. *HP* 3. 10. 1.
94. 5. 8. 3.
95. Mart. 2. 43. 10.
96. *NH* 16. 229.
97. Cic. *Pro Murena* 74.
98. *HP* 5. 6. 2, 7. 5; *NH* 16. 65.
99. A. K. Bowman and J. D. Thomas, 'The Vindolanda writing tablets and their significance', *Hist.* 24 (1975) 463-78.

100. Juv. 11. 117-19.
101. Strabo 546.
102. *NH* 16. 232.
103. Pollux 10. 34.
104. W. K. Pritchett, 'The Attic stelae', *Hesp.* 25 (1956) 321.
105. *NH* 33. 146.
106. 16. 231.
107. A. Lucas, *Annales du Service* 26 (1931) 1-4.
108. Athen. 255e.
109. Dem. 27. 10.
110. Strabo 155.
111. *NH* 16. 185.
112. Tib. 1. 10. 6.
113. J. Kopcke, 'Neue Holzfunde aus der Heraion von Samos', *AM* 82 (1967) 115 ff; D. M. Ohly, 'Holz', *AM* 68 (1953) 89 ff.
114. Verg. *Ecl.* 3. 36-7.
115. *HP* 5. 3. 2, misunderstood by Pliny, *NH* 16. 205.
116. Anth. Pal. 6. 33.
117. Xen. *Anab.* 7. 5. 14.
118. E. Espérandieu, *Recueil général des bas-reliefs* . . . *de la Gaule romaine* (1907-66) 6. 5184, 5193, 5198; A. Grenier, *Manuel d'arch. Gall-Rom.* 2. 2 (1934) 601-13.
119. Strabo 214.
120. *NH* 14. 132.
121. G. Ulbert, 'Römische Holzfässer aus Regensburg', *Bayerische Vorgeschichtsblätter* 24 (1959) 6-29.
122. Ibid. 26.

Chapter 11

1. *HP* 4. 2. 5; Pliny *NH* 13. 60.
2. L. Borchardt, *Der Porträtkopf der Königin Teje* (1911) 10.
3. A. Lucas, *Ancient Egyptian materials and industries*⁴ (ed. J. R. Harris, 1962) 430.
4. Studies of the word *xoanon*: F. M. Bennett, *AJA* 21 (1917) 8-21; W. H. Gross, *RE* 9. A2 (1969) 2140-9. More general discussions of the importance of wood in archaic sculpture: H.-V. Herrmann, *Zum Problem der Entstehung der griechischen Großplastik*, in *Wandlungen* (Festschrift Hermann-Wedeking, 1975); S. S. Ridgway, *The archaic style in Greek sculpture* (1977).
5. Paus. 4. 34. 7.
6. 2. 11. 8.
7. 2. 37. 2.
8. 2. 23. 1.
9. 9. 10. 2.
10. 2. 24. 3.
11. 6. 18. 5.

12. 9. 4. 1.
13. 2. 19. 3-6.
14. 2. 23. 1.
15. 2. 24. 3.
16. 2. 25. 1.
17. 3. 25. 3.
18. 1. 27. 1, 18. 5.
19. 8. 23. 4.
20. 3. 25. 3.
21. 9. 16. 3.
22. 3. 23. 3.
23. 7. 4. 5; 2. 15. 1; 3. 17. 6.
24. 6. 24. 9.
25. 1. 26. 6.
26. 3. 16. 7-10.
27. Callimachus (Pfeiffer) I. 144, *Aetia* 4, fr. 100.
28. D. M. Ohly, *AM* 82 (1967) 88-99.
29. Paus. 9. 10. 2; 2. 30. 2.
30. Isaiah 37: 19; 2 Kings 19: 18.
31. Paus. 2. 17. 5.
32. *ID* 1417, col. 1. 100; E. Willemsen, *Frühe griechische Kultbilder* (1939).
33. Homer, *Il.* 6. 286-304; Strabo 601.
34. D. M. Ohly, 'Holz', *AM* 68 (1953) 77-83 with pls. 13-15, 18-19.
35. *FGH* 531. 17.
36. Paus. 6. 19. 8.
37. 6. 19. 12.
38. *NH* 16. 214.
39. Paus. 1. 26. 4; G. M. A. Richter, *The sculpture and sculptors of the Greeks* (1966) p. 60, fig. 64.
40. Paus. 7. 5. 9.
41. 5. 17. 1.
42. 9. 35. 3; 2. 32. 5.
43. *Mon Ant.* 37 (1938) 630.
44. E. Blegen, *AJA* 39 (1935) 134.
45. *FGH* 531. 26.
46. Paus. 6. 18. 7.
47. 9. 10. 2.
48. 2. 30. 2.
49. 8. 14. 5-8.
50. 8. 17. 2.
51. *HP* 5. 3. 9.
52. Paus. 6. 19. 6.
53. 10. 19. 3.
54. 1. 26. 6; schol. Dem. 22. 13.
55. Paus. 2. 30. 4; Hdt. 5. 82. 3.
56. 2. 17. 4-5.
57. *HP* 3. 3. 1.
58. Alciphron 38. 2.

59. *HP* 5. 5. 1.
60. Paus. 6. 18. 7.
61. 8. 17. 2.
62. *HP* 5. 3. 7.
63. J. G. Frazer, *Pausanias* 4. 452.
64. Paus. 8. 53. 11.
65. 1. 35. 3.
66. 1. 42. 5.
67. 2. 22. 5.
68. Hdt. 2. 178. 3.
69. L. Borchardt (n. 2) 14: statuettes of Amenhophet III (6 cm. high), and Queen Tiu (6.4 cm.).
70. Paus. 5. 17. 5; 6. 19. 8 and 12; 9. 10. 2.
71. 3. 15. 11.
72. Vitr. 2. 19. 3.
73. *NH* 16. 213.
74. 14. 9.
75. *HP* 1. 6. 1; 5. 3. 1; 5. 4. 2; *NH* 13. 104–6.
76. *HP* 5. 4. 2; 5. 6. 2.
77. Isaiah 40: 20.
78. G. Roux, 'Pindare, le prétendu trésor des Crétois et l'ancienne statue d'Apollon à Delphes', *REG* 75 (1962) 379.
79. Paus. 6. 18. 7.
80. See n. 43.
81. Vitr. 2. 9. 9; *NH* 16. 209.
82. Paus. 8. 42. 4–7.
83. 3. 17. 6.
84. *AA* 1936, 217.
85. Paus. 3. 19. 2.
86. 6. 19. 6.
87. 2. 2. 6.
88. 6. 24. 6.
89. 7. 26. 4.
90. 8. 25. 6.
91. 9. 4. 1.
92. Mau, *RE* 1. 1198.
93. P. Amandry, *BCH* 63 (1939) 86–119.
94. Isaiah 40: 19.
95. Jeremiah 10: 3–4.
96. *NH* 36. 47.
97. Paus. 7. 18. 10.
98. Thuc. 2. 13. 5.
99. Dio. Chrys. 12. 49.
100. Paus. 2. 27. 2.
101. 1. 40. 4.
102. 1. 18. 6.
103. 2. 1. 7–8.

104. C. Albizzati, 'Two ivory fragments of a statue of Athena', *JHS* 35 (1916) 373-402.
105. P. Bruneau, *Recherches sur les cultes de Délos à l'époque hellénistique et à l'époque impériale* (1976) 312-16.
106. R. Vallois, *BCH* 46 (1922) 94-113.
107. *SIG* 589. 22-68.
108. Strabo 652; *NH* 34. 41.
109. Athen. 197a-203b.
110. Polyb. 31. 3.
111. *Plut. De Soc. genio* 580e; Plato, *Symp.* 215b.
112. Aesop 2.
113. Ibid. 66.
114. Tertullian, *De idol.* 8. 3.
115. Vitr. 2. 9. 9; Verg. *Georg.* 2. 449.
116. *Sylva* 65; *IG* 11(2). 165. 32, 45.
117. L. Robert, 'Documents d'Asie Mineure', *BCH* 102 (1978) 413.
118. Verg. *Aen.* 7. 178.
119. Tib. 1. 10. 5.
120. *NH* 34. 34.
121. Livy 27. 37. 12.
122. *NH* 16. 216.
123. *NH* 13. 53.
124. Theocr. *Epigr.* 8. The assumption by P. Gros in *Aurea templa* (1976) 163 that Apollo Sosianus was a primitive figure, valued for its antiquity, seems to me less probable.
125. Philostr. *Vit. soph.* 2. 1.
126. Pliny, *Ep.* 9. 39. 4.
127. Xen. *Anab.* 5. 3. 11-13.
128. R. Martin, *Antiquity* 39 (1965) 247-52.
129. C. Vatin, *Antiquity* 46 (1972) 39-42.
130. A. Grenier, *Arch. Gallo-Rom.* 2. 2 (1934) 568.
131. Col. 10. 29-34.
132. Theocr. *Epigr.* 4.
133. Horace, *Sat.* 1. 8. 1.
134. Appendix Verg., *Priapea* 2. 2; 3. 3.
135. Mart. 6. 49. 73.

Chapter 12

1. Dion. Hal. *Antiq.* 20. 15, discussed p. 464.
2. Varro, *RR* 3. 16.
3. Livy 33. 42. 10; 35. 10. 18.
4. Dion. Hal. 20. 15. 2; Strabo 261.
5. Cic. *Brutus* 85.
6. Cic. *Pro Milone* 26.
7. Cic. *De lege agraria* 1. 3.
8. Ibid. 3. 15.

9. Suet. *Caesar* 19. 2.
10. This explanation has been anticipated in part by P. A. Brunt (*Italian manpower* 291) who believes that the declared objective of the assignment was the crushing of brigands, but he might not accept my interpretation of the special relevance to Caesar.
11. Sallust, *Cat.* 56. 5.
12. K. Lachmann, *Die Schriften der römischen Feldmesser* (1848) 114. 3 (Hyginus): 'There are woods reserved for the supply of timber for the repairs to public buildings'; 55. 4 (Frontinus): 'There are woods from which firewood is cut for the public baths.' Private woods could be assigned to the state for such purposes; a magistrate of Misenum promised 400 loads of hardwood annually for the public baths, and assigned the woodland from which it was to come (*ILS* 5689).
13. E. G. Hardy, *Roman laws and charters* (1912) p. 36, clause 82.
14. Meiggs, *Roman Ostia*² (1973) 343.
15. Dig. 33. 12. 4; 33. 7; 32. 60. 3.
16. Ovid, *Met.* 8. 775.
17. *NH* 16. 188; Vitr. 2. 9. 1; Vegetius 4. 35.
18. *HP* 5. 1. 3.
19. *NH* 16. 190.
20. Cato 37. 3.
21. Diod. 14. 42. 4-5.
22. Homer, *Il.* 12. 123; repeated in 17. 702.
23. Quintus Smyrnaeus 12. 126.
24. D. G. M. Cacciamani, *L'antica foresta di Camaldoli* (ed. Camaldoli, 1965; out of print).
25. P. I. Kuniholm, *Dendrochronology at Gordion* (see Bibliography under Timber).
26. Quoted by R. E. Pike, *Tall trees, tough men* (1969) 40, an excellent description of the white-pine trade. For the subsequent supply of white pines from Canada, see M. C. More, *Canadian Geogr.* 99 (1980) 66.
27. Espérandieu, *Recueil* 2. 1096.
28. Amm. Mar. 18. 2. 5; M. Z. Nour, *The Cheops boat* (1960) pl. 60.
29. *Ionae vitae sanctorum* (Krusch, 1925) 221-2.
30. Dion. Hal. 20. 15. 2.
31. A. H. M. Jones, *The later Roman Empire* (3 vols. Oxford, 1964).
32. *Statutes of the realm*, vol. 4, part 1, p. 377 (1559); 9, p. 480 (1710).
33. Pliny, *Ep.* 10. 41.
34. 10. 42.
35. 61, 62.
36. 5. 6. 12.
37. *NH* 3. 53.
38. *ANET* 307.
39. Vitr. 2. 9. 14.
40. *NH* 16. 202.
41. *ANET* 268 (3a).
42. *CIL* 13. 2035, 2331; 12. 2597.
43. L. Robert, *BCH* 102 (1978) 426.

44. 1 Kings 5: 9.
45. *HP* 5. 8. 2.
46. J. H. Thiel, *A history of Roman sea-power before the second Punic War* (1954) 19 f.
47. *HP* 5. 8. 3.
48. Meiggs (n. 14) 22.
49. Diod. 14. 42. 4.
50. Meiggs (n. 14) 286.
51. Apuleius, *Met.* 7. 17-24.
52. Varro, *RR* 2. 6. 5.
53. *IG* 2². 1675. 26; a second muleteer, l. 20.
54. Strabo 659.
55. A. Burford, 'Heavy transport in the ancient world', *Eng. Hist. Rev.* 13 (1960) 1-18.
56. *IG* 2². 1673 with G. Glotz, *REG* 36 (1923) 26-45.
57. Xen. *Cyr.* 6. 52. The weight of the talent is uncertain, discussed on p. 479.
58. *Cod. Theod.* 8. 5. 30.
59. Xenophon (n. 57) says that when eight yokes pulled a siege tower the share of the load for each yoke was only fifteen talents. A Kenya farmer tells me that he used eighteen oxen to pull 6,800 lb. of wheat on a full-sized wooden wagon.
60. *De aedificiis* 5. 6.
61. Diod. 4. 80. 4-5.
62. For the rough estimate I assume: length 100 ft.; section 1½ × 1½ ft. (*NH* 12. 201); 30 lb. per cu. ft. (F. H. Titmus, *Commercial timbers of the world*³ (1965) 124).
63. Quoted by L. F. Salzman, *Building in England down to 1540* (1952) 245.
64. Strabo 577.
65. D. Pensabene, *Journ. internat. naut. arch.* 7 (1978) 317-18; L. Robert, *Journal des savants* 1962, 26.
66. Strabo 189.
67. 207: 'not much more than 400 stades' (*c.*30 km.).
68. *ILS* 6417b.
69. Athen. 198c-200b.
70. E. Lear, *Journal of a landscape painter in Corsica* (1870) 90.
71. Juv. 3. 255.
72. Quintilian 8. 3. 21; SHA, *M. Aurelius* 13; Amm. Mar. 31. 2. 18.
73. *ANET* 268 (3a).
74. *ANET* 307; J. P. Brown, *The Lebanon and Phoenicia* (1969) 196.
75. G. Dossin, *Archives royales de Mari*, I. *Correspondence de Šamši-Adad* (1950) n. 7, p. 35.
76. The relief (pl. 3A) is discussed on p. 524 f.
77. J. W. Shaw, *Minoan architecture: materials and technique*, *Ann. della scuola arch. di Atene* 33 (1971) 55-8.
78. *HP* 5. 6. 3; Pliny, *NH* 16. 227.
79. First noted by R. K. Winters, *The forest and man* (1974) 163; discussed and illustrated, *Expedition* 10 (1974) 2-8.
80. Seneca, *Ep.* 90. 9; Verg. *Georg.* 1. 144. There was a practical advantage in

NOTES TO PAGES 348-57 515

cleaving rather than sawing, as Evelyn (*Sylva* 201) notes: 'The grain of timber ought to be observed, since the more you work according to it, especially in cleaving, and the less you saw, the stronger will be your work.'

81. Fig. 14d; H. Bingemer, 'Die Ohrenbacher Schanze', *Saalburg Jahrb.* 10 (1951) 29-37.
82. Homer, *Od.* 5. 240.
83. Livy 29. 1. 14.
84. *NH* 16. 192.
85. *HP* 5. 3. 5.
86. Vitr. 2. 9. 3; *NH* 16. 192, 219; Palladius 12. 5. 3.
87. Vitr. 2. 9. 11.
88. Col. 1. 6. 19: 'fumarium quoque, quo materia, si non sit iam pridem caesa, festinato siccetur.' W. S. Hanson, 'The organisation of Roman military timber supply', *Britannia* 9 (1978) 297 assumes that this must be firewood. The normal word for firewood is *ligna*, as in Col. 12. 20. 8. The distinction is brought out clearly in a Roman arbitration between two Ligurian tribes. The Roman ruling is that in a disputed area both tribes shall have the right to pasture animals and to take firewood and timber, *ligna et materiam* (*ILS* 5946). For a similar drying of timber, see Verg. *Georg.* 1. 175.
89. *NH* 13. 99.
90. Palladius 12. 5. 3.
91. Cato 31; *HP* 5. 5. 6; *NH* 16. 222.
92. Homer, *Od.* 9. 328-9.
93. Vitr. 1. 5. 3.
94. *HP* 5. 2 1. I take πρὸς τὴν τεκτονικὴν χρείαν to mean both joinery and building.
95. Strabo 202.
96. *IG* 1³. 387. 101.
97. Thuc. 7. 25. 2.
98. Strabo 213.
99. Vitr. 2. 9. 16.
100. Strabo 214.
101. Herodian 8. 1. 6; cf. Amm. Mar. 21. 12. 8-9.
102. P. Piussi, *Un inventario forestale del xviii secolo per i boschi costieri dell'Alto Adriatico* (Collana Verde 41, 1970).
103. *CIL* 5. 908.
104. Strabo 315.
105. *CIL* 3. 12924.
106. Dio 56. 14. 7.
107. Polyb. 21. 26.
108. Meiggs and Lewis, GHI 75.
109. Thuc. 4. 108. 1.
110. *HP* 4. 5. 5.
111. Xen. *Hell.* 1. 1. 25.
112. Strabo 606.
113. Strabo 574, 572.
114. Dio. Chrys. 30. 40.

115. Strabo 575.
116. L. Robert, *BCH* 102 (1978) 419-26.
117. Xen. *Anab.* 6. 4. 5.
118. Strabo 669.
119. Plut. *Lys.* 3.
120. J. Keil, *Jahreshefte* 44 (1959) 242-6.
121. *Dig.* 32. 55.
122. *ILS* 6417b, 6419d; *lignarii*: *CIL* 4. 951.
123. *CIL* 6. 975, col. 3. 36.
124. Plautus, *Miles gloriosus* 915-21: 'The keel is laid, the architect and shipwrights are ready, if the *materiarius* does not hold us up.'
125. *CIL* 35. 1294; 11. 1620.
126. *CIL* 6. 9104; Festus (Lindsay) 25.
127. *CIL* 4. 6212; 6. 9561; 10. 3965.
128. SHA, *Pertinax* 1. 1.
129. Meiggs (n. 14) 328 with 595.
130. Ibid. 319.
131. *Ox. Pap.* 2981.
132. *SEG* 2. 579. This well-preserved inscription had been strangely neglected until Louis and Jean Robert, in a typically definitive analysis, interpreted its clauses and explained its significance. The text is reprinted and discussed by them in the *Journ. des savants*, 1976, 175-89 in the course of a study of a new document giving the terms of a union between Teos and Kyrbissos (pp. 153-235).
133. R. H. Randall, 'The Erechtheum workers', *AJA* 57 (1953) 199-210.
134. G. Glotz, 'L'histoire de Délos d'après les prix d'une denrée', *REG* 29 (1916) 281-325.
135. *IG* 2². 1672. 146: 62.
136. *IG* 11(2). 290. 221; for Epidaurus, see Appendix 4.1 (p. 424).
137. F. M. Heichelheim, *An ancient economic history* (1958-70) 3. 24-38; G. Glotz, *Ancient Greece at work* (1926) 330 f.; *Journ. des savants*, 1913, 16-29.
138. *IG* 2². 1492. B 121-2; the text discussed, p. 494 n. 87.
139. [Dem.] 49. 29.
140. Ibid. 36.
141. *NH* 16. 202.
142. S. Lauffer, *Diokletians Preisedikt: Texte und Kommentar* (1971).
143. K. T. Erim and J. Reynolds, *JRS* 60 (1970) 120-41; a later addition to the timber section: M. Crawford and J. Reynolds, *Zeitschr. für Pap. und Epigr.* 26 (1977) 134-5 with 143-6.
144. *Sappinus* can mean either a species similar to a fir (Vitr. 1. 2. 8; Varro, *RR* 1. 6. 4) or the lower part of the trunk of a fir, specially suitable for interior work (Vitr. 2. 9. 7; *NH* 16. 191).
145.* The main difficulty lies in translating 12. 15: *sectori materiarum robore [a]r[um] in pede per pede(m)* (in the latest fragment the text is *in pedae per pedae*). The editors, puzzled by the precise meaning of *in pede per pede(m)*, the more reliable text, have assumed that the operation must be squaring, which preceded the further conversion of the timber. Columella, reviewing winter work on the farm, includes squaring

timbers, and gives the amount that could be expected from a day's work. Oak comes first as in the edict and twenty feet is the standard for a day's work; for pine it is twenty-five feet, for elm and ash thirty feet, for cypress forty feet, sixty feet for fir and poplar. But the word for squaring used by Columella is *dolari*. We should expect *sectori* to mean a sawyer and the third rate (100 den.) suggests that this is the right solution: *materiarum cubitoru[m] in longum* [vac.] *latitudinis in quadru[m] digitorum*. This formulation corresponds closely with the definition of measurements in the list of prices of the various woods, as in the first entry: [*Ma*]*teria abiegna* [*cu*]*bitorum L* [*la*]*titudinis in quadrum cubitorum iiii*. In these entries *latitudo* means the girth of the timber when squared, four cubits implying four sides of approximately one and half feet. But in 12. 17 the *latitudo* measurement is only ten fingers ($\frac{5}{8}$ ft.), which must surely refer to one side only. The rate prescribed for a timber twelve feet long and about seven and a half inches wide is 100 denarii, and since the maximum daily rate for a timber-worker in the edict is fifty denarii, 100 denarii should imply roughly two days' work. Taking two days to square twelve feet, in the light of Columella's figures, is far too long even in the late Empire.

Greek records suggest that the figures might make sense if related to sawing. In the Erechtheum accounts a sawyer is paid for sawing fourteen timbers eight feet long. In each timber there had to be six cuts, and for each cut he was paid two obols, or a quarter of an obol per foot (J. M. Paton, *The Erechtheum* (1927) 331, col. 9. 14-17). Since at this time the daily wage was one drachma, in two days he should have sawn roughly forty-eight feet, which in this case would represent one large squared timber cut into six boards. At Delphi, nearly a century later, a sawyer was paid five coppers (equivalent to five-sixteenths of a drachma) per foot, a very slightly higher rate (*FD* 3. 5. 41). The twelve-foot timber of the edict was barely big enough (*c*.7$\frac{1}{2}$ in. wide, and presumably roughly the same thickness) for six cuts, but four would be acceptable. This would give about forty-eight feet (4×12) for two days' work. The coincidence of the two totals is not significant, and they can both be only approximate figures, but they make it easier to give *sectori* its more likely meaning of sawyer.

146. Paton, *Erechtheum* 331, col. 9.
147. *IG* 2². 1672. 160, 79.
148. Ibid. 66.
149. Ibid. 117.

Chapter 13

1. M. W. Mikesell, 'The deforestation of Mt. Lebanon', *Geog. Rev.* 59 (1969) 1-28.
2. Joshua 17: 14-18.
3. Lucretius 5. 1370 f.
4. Strabo 684.
5. E. G. Hardy, *Roman laws and charters* 59, clause 13.

6. Col. 2. 1. 5–6; Verg. *Georg.* 2. 207–13.

7. Theophrastus, *CP* 5. 14. 6.

8. Aurelius Victor, *Caes.* 40. 9.

9. *CIL* 8. 25903, 25943.

10. Tertullian, *De anima* 30. 3.

11. Amm. Mar. 21. 16. 11.

12. Diod. 3. 70. 3–6.

13. Lucr. 5. 1241 ff.

14. Thuc. 2. 77. 4; followed by Lucretius 5. 1091–5; Vitr. 2. 1. 1; Q. Smyrn. 13. 488 ff. A letter to the *Quarterly Journal of Forestry* (1972) refers to an article in *An Claidheamh Soluis* (10, 1908) by Seán Longáen pointing out that the old people of Glenealy, Co. Tyrone, accounted for the blackened tree-stumps found in local bogs by saying, 'There came three years of wind from the southwest and with the dint of the trees rubbing against one another they caught fire on the tops of the hills.'

15. C. Vita-Finzi, *Mediterranean valleys* (1969).

16. Paus. 8. 24. 11.

17. *NH* 16. 173.

18. Homer, *Il.* 11. 492–5; Verg. *Georg.* 1. 481–3; cf. *Aen.* 2. 305–7; Luc. 2. 408; Horace, *Odes* 3. 29. 33–6; Ov. *Met.* 8. 552–5.

19. *HP* 5. 8. 1.

20. *NH* 12. 3.

21. Sen. *Ep.* 44. 3.

22. Cato 139.

23. *CIL* 11. 4766; cf. records of the Arval Brothers, *ILS* 5042, 5045–7, and decrees governing the sacred grove of Daphnae in Syria, *Cod. Just.* 11. 78. 1–2.

24. Strabo 223; Diod. 5. 13. 1–2.

25. *Sylva* 238.

26. V. Cuinet, *La Turquie d'Asie* (1891–1900) 2. 232–5.

27. *NH* 34. 95–6.

28. J. Healy, *Mining and metallurgy in the Greek and Roman world* (1978) 151.

29. Diod. 14. 42. 4. But the loss of trees may be primarily the result of a volcanic eruption: Strabo 274–5.

30. Paus. 1. 32. 1.

31. P. Warren, 'British travellers in Crete', Κρητ. Χρον. 24 (1972) 70, 73, 83.

32. Amm. Mar. 14. 8. 14.

33. R. K. Winters, *The forest and man* (1974) 185.

34. L. Funi, *Il duomo di Orvieto* (1891).

35. *Bullarium Vaticanum* 2. 138. A somewhat similar missive authorising the payment of fifty golden florins to Master Bartholomew carpenter of Florence for the purchase and transport of round and sawn timbers from the district of Borgo San Sepolcro for work on the basilica of St. Mark in Rome: A. S. Roma, Camerale I. Mandato Camerali, Reg. 839. c. 80 v.

36. P. A. Guglielmotti, *Storia della marina pontificale nel medio evo* (1886–93) 2. 209.

37. Livy 1. 33. 9.

38. Guglielmotti (n. 36) 213.

39. F. C. Lane, *Navires et construction à Venise pendant la Renaissance* (1965) 204–16.

40. M. Quaini, *Riv. geog. ital.* 78 (1968) 508-37.
41. Well illustrated in Umbria by H. Desplanques, *Campagnes Ombriennes* (1969) 235-56.
42. Col. 7. 8. 6.
43. Verg. *Georg.* 3. 305, 317; Exodus 26: 7 (goat-hair hangings).
44. Varro, *RR* 2. 3. 11.
45. J. M. Edmonds, *The fragments of Attic Comedy* 1. 317-33.
46. Varro, *RR* 1. 2. 14-16.
47. Plato, *Laws* 639a.
48. Giuseppe del Noce, *Trattato istorico scientifico ed economico delle macchie e foreste del grande ducato Toscano* (1849).
49. F. C. Lane (n. 39).
50. Norman Douglas, *In old Calabria* (London, 1915). References are to the Modern Library (New York) edition.
51. 197.
52. 264.
53. 294-5.
54. 298.
55. 301.
56. 198-9.
57. 295-6.
58. G. Tsoumis, *The forests of Greece and Cyprus* (1976); A. Prentice, 'Reafforestation in Greece', *Scot. Geog. Mag.* 72 (1956) 25-31.
59. Strabo 538.
60. Livy 38. 18. 4.
61. C. H. E. Haspels, *The highlands of Phrygia* (1971) 101, 112.
62. V. Cuinet, *La Turquie d'Asie* (4 vols. 1891-1900). In vol. 4 there are brief descriptions of these forests: Sinope, p. 567; Heraclea, p. 499; hinterland of Nicomedia, pp. 315-18 with L. Robert, *BCH* 102 (1978) 413-28. See also Cuinet, pp. 24, 97.
63. A. Philippson, *PGM* 65 (1919) 168-73; X. De Planhol, *Rev. géog. alpine* 42 (1954) 665-73; 47 (1959) 373-85.
64. Cuinet (n. 62) 374-5.
65. T. Kotschy, *Reise in den cilicischen Taurus über Tarsus* (1858).
66. Ibid. 57 ff.
67. Ibid. 282; F. Schaffer, 'Cilicicia', *PMG* Ergänz. 1903 (141) 39.
68. De Planhol, *La Plaine Pamphylienne*; Cuinet (n. 62) 1. 812.
69. *Vnasylva* 6 (1952) 119 f.
70. V. Cuinet, *Liban et Palestine* (1896) 153.
71. Ibid. 217.
72. Procopius, *De aedificiis* 5. 6.
73. M. Lombard, 'Le bois dans la Méditerranie Musulmane, vii-ix siècles', *Annales: écon. soc. civ.* 14 (1959) 239.
74. William of Tyre, *Historia rerum transmarinarum*, book 12, ch. 13. More detail from Ibn al Galanasi, *The Damascus Chronicle of the Crusades* (trans. H. A. R. Gibb, 1932), who gives the measurements of tower and rams.
75. *Sylva* 119.
76. De La Rocque, *Voyage de Syrie et du mont Liban* (1722) 85.

77. J. D. Hooker, *Nat. Hist. Rev.* 2 (1862) 11-17.

78. H. B. Tristram, *The natural history of the Bible*[4] (1875) 341.

79. Kotschy (n. 65) 300.

80. Strabo 684.

81. *NH* 16. 203, *HP* 5. 8. 1, with p. 136.

82. *OGIS* 39.

83. *IG* 2². 1492. 201; Polyb. 5. 89. 1, with p. 145.

84. Amm. Mar. 14. 8. 14.

85. M. Lombard (n. 73) 240.

86. Eutychius, Migne, *PG* 111, 423B.

87. A. H. Unwin, *Goat-grazing and forestry in Cyprus* (1928).

88. Lt.-Col. R. L. Playfair, *Travel in the footsteps of Bruce in Algeria and Tunisia* (1877).

89. Ibid. 179.

90. 188.

91. 191.

92. Procopius, *Bell. Vand.* 8. 5.

93. Playfair (n. 88) 62.

94. Ibid. 93-5.

95. 172-3.

96. 96.

97. 73. For the late deforestation of the Aures forests, see also P. Boudy, *Économie forestière nord-africaine* 4. 188-91.

98. Playfair (n. 88) 96 f.

99. J. Battandier and L. Trabert, *L'Algérie* (1898) 25; M. Benchetrit, *Rev. géog. alpine* 43 (1955) 628-9.

100. From 2,307,000 in 1858 to 4,071,000 by the end of the century.

101. W. R. Chaney and M. Basbous, 'The cedars of Lebanon', *Econ. Bot.* 32 (1978) 118-23. For reports see Bibliography, The Near East.

102. *Sylva* 197.

103. From the *Yearbook of Forest Products 1967-78* (FAO, Rome, 1980), 1978 production, in cubic metres:

all categories	2,600,000,000
fuel and charcoal	1,218,000,000
sawlogs and veneers	862,000,000
pulpwood	314,000,000.

Appendix 4.1

1. In the *Corpus* text it is assumed that there are two missing lines before the first line that can be read on the stone. Burford found no traces of inscribed or painted letters and concluded that the first surviving line, a contract for supplying stone, was in fact the first line of the document. The omission of an explicit reference to the building concerned would be extremely unusual, and since all references will still be to the *Corpus* text, the numbering of the lines in that text will be

followed here. The complete account is translated by Burford, 212-30 and by Roux, 424-32.

2. It seems probable that both in the Parthenon (p. 200) and in the fourth-century temple of Apollo at Delphi (p. 431), cypress was used for the cross-beams. The reason for preferring fir at Epidaurus is that the cost of the fir would seem too high if the cross-beams, the most expensive timbers in the building, were not included.

3. The word διαίρεσις has been translated by 'squaring' or 'cutting', but cf. ll. 165-6: ξύλων συνθέσιος καὶ διαιρέσιος, which should mean fitting and taking apart timbers.

4. The payment of 48 dr. represents roughly a month's work by a sawyer (at 1 dr. 3 ob. per day). This should have been sufficient to produce all the secondary timbers over the principal rafters.

5. Burford's interpretation (p. 179) of κὰτ τὰν ἐξαίρεσιν τᾶν πόλεων is followed uneasily for, as she admits, ἐξαίρεσις does not mean agreement. It should mean taking away, extraction.

Appendix 4.4

1. The records of the Delian commissioners during the period of independence, from 314 to 166 BC, are published in *IG* 11(2). 135-289, and the series is continued in *Inscriptions de Délos* 290-510. Numbers alone refer to *IG*; *ID* is added for the second series.

2. *IG* 11 (2). For a similar economy cf. 154. 7, the payment of 1 dr. 2 ob. to a sawyer to saw a beam in order to reuse the part that was still sound, *ID* 408.

3. For the history of the various temples of Apollo on Delos, see F. Courby, *Les Temples d'Apollon*, *Délos* 12 (1931). For the temple completed in the third century, see pp. 218-20, with the text of most of the relevant inscriptions, 225-30.

4. The Eleusis commissioners bought cypress logs from Cnidus (p. 434); Philopator used Milesian cypress for panelling on his giant pleasure-barge, Athen. 205b.

5. *Sylva* 118: 'cornel, though not mentioned by Pliny for its timber, is exceedingly commended for its durableness, and use in wheel work, pinns, and wedges, in which it lasts like the hardest iron'.

6. The Greek word φάλαγξ, here translated as 'piece', is used also by Herodotus (3. 97) for the ebony tribute imposed on the Ethiopians by the Persians. Hesychius describes φάλαγγες as ξύλα στρογγύλα καί σύμμετρα, round timbers of standard length.

7. J. Leroux, *La Salle hypostyle* (1909); R. Vallois and G. Poulsen, *Nouvelles recherches sur la salle hypostyle* (1914), *Délos* 2. 1 and 2.

8. The Greek words translated as 'off-cuts' are ἀπότομα and παράτομα. Presumably the timbers given to Ctesias were large squared timbers, which he had to cut down to the sizes he required. Cutting could reduce either the thickness or the length. ἀπότομα are the pieces left when the length is reduced, παράτομα when the thickness is reduced.

9. Courby (n. 3) 329; cf. Theocr. *Id.* 24. 15: σταθμὰ κοῖλα θυράων with A. S. F. Gow, *Theocritus* 2. 419; *Flinders Petrie Pap.* III (Mahaffy, Smyly) no. 48, p. 141 θυρίδας κοιλοστάθμους.

10. *SIG* 975. Detailed commentary, E. Schulten and P. Huvelin, *BCH* 31 (1907) 46-93. Text and translation, Larsen, *ESAR* 4. 352. Text and bibliography, H. W. Pleket, *Epigraphica* 1 (1964) *Texts in the economic history of the Greek world* no. 10.

Appendix 6

1. Strabo 254.
2. *HP* 5. 8. 1; 4. 5. 5.
3. Thuc. 6. 90. 3.
4. *IG* 1³. 387. 100-1.
5. Thuc. 7. 25. 2.
6. *NH* 3. 74.
7. Strabo 259-65.
8. 261.
9. Verg. *Georg.* 2. 438.
10. A. de Franciscis, *Stato e società in Locri Epizefiri* (1972) Tablet 15, p. 29.
11. Dion. Hal. 20. 15.
12. Livy 31. 12. 1.
13. 34. 45. 4.
14. 34. 53.
15. 35. 40. 5; Vell. Pat. 1. 14. 8.
16. K. Lachmann, *Die Schriften der römischen Feldmesser* (1848) 1. 209: 'Ager Consentinus ab imp. Augusto est adsignatus limitibus Graccanis'; cf. Cic. *De leg. agraria* 2. 66.
17. Verg. *Aen.* 12. 715.
18. Cic. *Brutus* 85.
19. Sall. *Hist.* 4. 32 (Maurenbrecher).
20. Plut. *Crassus* 10.
21. Cic. *Verr.* 5. 39-41.
22. Greg. *Ep.* 9. 124-7.

Appendix 7

1. Plut. *Mor.* 676a.
2. Tod, *GHI* 2. 111. 10.
3. Polyb. 5. 89. 3, 6.
4. Vegetius 4. 44. The inflammability of pitch is further illustrated by the sad story in a Hellenistic epigram (*Anth. Pal.* 11. 248): 'The ship's hull was completed, right up to the benches. They were anointing the timbers with the rich juice of the pine, when the pitch boiled over and destroyed the ship.'
5. Procopius, *Bell. Pers.* 1. 19. 23.

6. *IG* 2². 1672. 13, 69, 170.
7. Ibid. 170. 60, 69.
8. *IG* 4². 1. 102. 245, 277.
9. *ID* 372. 84; 442. A.188.
10. Ibid. 372. A.84-5.
11. Plaut. *Most.* 827 ff.
12. *FD* 5 (3) 19. 55.
13. Cato 23; *NH* 14. 134.
14. Col. 12. 18. 3-6.
15. *NH* 14. 124.
16. Plut. *Mor.* 676c; *NH* 14. 120, 124.
17. *NH* 28. 137, 138, 139, 243.
18. *NH* 14. 123.
19. 16. 40.
20. 35. 41.
21. Sophocles, *OT* 215.
22. *NH* 16. 38-49.
23. 16. 40.
24. 16. 38. Pliny distinguishes only two pines, *Pinus* and *Pinaster*. *Pinus* can be identified with *Pinus pinea* (the umbrella pine) because it branches from the top.
25. *HP* 9. 2. 35.
26. Dion. Hal. 20. 15. 2.
27. Diosc. 71. 3.
28. *NH* 16. 42.
29. 16. 63.
30. Diosc. 71. 3.
31. *HP* 9. 2. 2; *NH* 14. 122.
32. Diosc. 70.
33. *HP* 9. 2. 1-8; *NH* 16. 57-60.
34. *HP* 9. 3. 1-3; *NH* 16. 52-5.
35. *HP* 9. 2. 5.
36. Strabo 218, 144.
37. Athen. 206 f.
38. Col. 12. 232.
39. Dion. Hal. 20. 15. 2.
40. Cic. *Brutus* 85.
41. *Zeitschr. Pap. Epigr.* 34 (1979) 179.
42. *BM* 3. 929. There is also evidence in a Greek inscription of customs duty on the import and export of pitch at Caunus in Lycia: G. E. Bean, 'Notes and inscriptions from Caunus', *JHS* 74 (1954) 97-105.
43. Preisigke, *Sammelbuch* 1.
44. e.g. *BM* 3. 1191; *Ox. Pap.* 14. 1721, 1751.
45. *Ox. Pap.* 12. 1497.
46. An interesting account of a cargo of resin sunk off the south coast of Gaul, L. Balsan 'L'industrie de la résine dans les Causses et son extension dans l'empire romain', *Gallia* 9 (1952-3) 53.

NOTES ON THE PLATES

1A   Close-growing cedars in a Lycian forest.

1B   The two tallest juniper species, *excelsa* and *foetidissima*, are not uncommonly found in cedar forests in south Turkey and in the Lebanon range.

1C   These larches, with occasional pines (*Pinus silvestris*), are from the Musfair valley , Grison, Switzerland, which is in the region where the impressive larches were cut for the restoration of the Naumachia in Rome by the emperor Tiberius.

2   This relief is from the illustrated record of the victorious campaign of Seti I (1318–1304 BC) on the north wall of the great temple of Amun at Karnak. Its place in the series can be seen in J. B. Pritchard's *The ancient Near-East in pictures relating to the Old Testament* (1954) fig. 327, p. 108. Lebanon princes make obeisance to an Egyptian high official while trees are being cut for the Egyptians. The fall of the trees is being guided with ropes.

    These trees are very schematic and very similar trees are depicted on another relief illustrating the siege of a city which has not been identified (M. Burchardt, 'Die Einnahme von Satuna', *ZÄ* 51–2 (1914–15) 106–9). Loret, *Annales du service* 16 (1916) 43–5, maintained that they were much more like firs than cedars, and it has been suggested that the 'leaves' may be intended to represent cones, for the long cone is especially characteristic of the fir. The accompanying inscription refers to the trees as *ash*. If in fact they were firs the identification of *ash* with cedar would have to be abandoned. I prefer to believe that the sculptor was more concerned with pattern than with nature. Positive reasons for accepting the traditional identification are given in Appendix 2, p. 405.

3A   E. Pottier, Musée du Louvre: *Catalogue des antiquités assyriennes* 86–8; M. P. E. Botta, *Le Monument de Ninève* 1 (1849) pl. 34 with 5 (1850) 99–102; G. Contenau, *Journ. Asiatique* 9 (1917) 181–9.

    This is one of a series of five reliefs cut on orthostats in the palace of Sargon II (721–705) at Khorsabad. Of four ships carrying long timbers of standard length, some on board, others towed, three are already unloading, the fourth is approaching. Two ships are being rowed empty in the opposite direction. Three of the other reliefs are much less well preserved. Drawings were made by Flandin at the time of discovery and published by Botta in 1849, but they are difficult to interpret. In three of the reliefs ships are taking timbers to a place that cannot be identified and returning empty, presumably to reload. The form of the ships with high raised bow and stern is typically Phoenician. What may be the first of the series of reliefs shows a rocky mountain with four lines of men carrying with the help of ropes what seem to be long round timbers. Botta, followed by Pottier, suggested that the timber was required for an attack on a fortress; it is surely more probable that the timber is required for building the palace, cut on the western slopes of Lebanon, converted to beams by Phoenicians, and carried on Phoenician ships to a port in northern Syria to shorten the land route to the Euphrates.

3B   A bull colossus, carved in the quarry, has been placed on a sledge to be taken to Sennacherib's palace, where it will be one of a pair flanking the main entrance. The sledge is being pulled by four long lines of men straining on very stout ropes (R. D. Barnett, *Assyrian palace reliefs in the British Museum* (1971) pls. 7 and 8). The exceptionally long lever (?considerably more than 30 ft.) is to ease the sledge over rollers. In the background can be seen carts with two very large wheels, loaded with substantial timbers. They seem to anticipate the carts used in the sixteenth century to transport big oak timbers from near Anzio to Rome for moving an obelisk from Caligula's Circus to the Vatican (p. 477). In the right bottom corner men are carrying a long round timber.

5A   This casket or chest has an ivory veneer with panels of ivory and ebony inlays. Howard Carter (*The tomb of Tutankhamun* 3. 66, pl. 15B) calculated that there were more than 45,000 pieces in the panels on sides and top.

6   The photographs were taken from *PM* 1, 328, fig. 239, and 3. 436, fig. 211.

7A   Gordium royal tomb chamber showing central cross-beam and gable, south face from south-west.

7B   Bronze and wood found in the tomb: a screen, the main parts of a highly decorative table, and bronze vessels. See p. 460 f.

8   For the *Casa del graticcio* see A. Maiuri, *Ercolano* (1958) 407–20. Most of the walls are thin, built with rubble framed in light vertical and horizontal timbers. A wall in the first floor upstairs has the imprint of reeds which were often used to line walls of wattle in order to provide a better bed for the plaster (Vitr. 7. 3. 11).

9   Maiuri (n. 8) 252–5. Above, a domestic shrine with pronaos framed by Corinthian columns. Below, a cupboard containing vessels in terracotta and glass and a bronze statuette of Heracles.

10A   Dedication from the Samian Heraeum. D. M. Ohly, *AM* 68 (1953) 88–91 with pls. 22–7. Side of a footstool balanced by a similar piece on the other side, joined by boards with a geometric design. ?Early archaic period. Remains of similar footstools found later, H. Kyrieilis, *AM* 95 (1980) 107, showing by an incised wheel that the stools represented the chariot of the goddess.

11A   Pine (*Pinus laricio*) from the Sila forest, *c.*400 years old, over-mature with crown broken. Length 80 ft., diam. 4 ft.

11B   Douglas fir from the state of Washington. The tree was felled by the

English Logging Company in Skagit county. The beam was hand-hewn and not sawn and was exhibited at the Alaska-Yukon Exhibition on the University of Washington campus in 1909.

12   Box and bowl from the collection of Dr Pauline Gregg, bought in Marrakesh and Agadir. Citrus-wood discussed on pp. 286–91. In describing the various figures that the wood assumes Pliny says: 'One form has the curving line of waves and is more highly valued when it resembles the eyes of a peacock. In another figure which is appreciated, though not so highly, there are clusters of what look like grains. They call the wood parsley wood because it is so like parsley' (*NH* 13. 96–7). Pliny also notes that the wood is very liable to surface cracks. Such hair-checks can be seen in both photographs.

15A   Richmond, *PBSR* 13 (1935) 5–8. Legionaries and praetorian troops cross the Danube at the beginning of Trajan's first campaign against the Dacians, on two parallel boat bridges. This was one of the commonest military methods of crossing rivers and the legions carried with them log boats carved from single timbers, chosen for lightness and strength (Vegetius 3. 7). In the centre of each boat is a support formed of close-packed vertical timbers on which the planks of the roadway rested. The legionaries are on the nearer bridge, the praetorians on the other. Both carry their different standards. In front of the line of legionaries is an officer and next to him two legionaries carrying eagles, the reward for distinguished service.

15B   Richmond (n. 15A) 32–4. The historian Dio Cassius (68. 13) describes Trajan's bridge over the Danube as the greatest of his building achievements. It had, he said, twenty piers of squared stone, one hundred and fifty feet high and sixty feet wide, seventy feet apart, and connected by arches. 'The fact that the river is here contracted from a great flood to such a narrow channel, after which it again expands into a wider flood, makes it all the more violent and deep and this factor must be considered in judging the difficulty of building the bridge.' The superstructure, including the segmented arches on which the roadway rests, is all of wood and the road is flanked by typical wooden criss-cross railings. At each end of the bridge is a fort. The two long tiled buildings of the fort on the Roman side of the river may represent granaries. The plain arch in front marks the entrance to the bridge.

A sacrifice is being prepared for victory in the first Dacian campaign. In the centre the emperor pours a libation on to a wreath-covered altar; in front of him a small boy (*camillus*) holds an open incense box. On the other side of the altar stands the executioner holding the ox about to be sacrificed. To the left of the picture are legionaries holding javelins (in metal which has disappeared); two of them hold legionary standards and the figure at their head is probably a legionary commander. The figures with the emperor are his personal following (*comites*).

16A   Cichorius, *Die Reliefs der Traiansäule* 2. 73–6. On the right Trajan approaches a fortified camp built on a rocky hill overlooking a stream.

In the foreground three legionaries cross a light bridge, with typical criss-cross railings, while another draws water from the stream. On the right troops fell oak trees and two are carrying away on their shoulders a trunk stripped of its branches with a second attached to it by a sling. The oak is the dominant tree on the column, as it still is in the areas fought over in Trajan's Dacian campaigns. The quality of the trees suggests that the work on camp buildings was considerably rougher than the sculptor has made it.

16B Richmond (n. 15A) 23-5. This scene immediately follows A. On the left in the foreground the emperor, who is with three of his personal followers, has turned to speak to one of his men at work. In the background a fort is being built. On the left a man is using a straight edge. Two others are working with hammer (on the right) and an adze (on the left). On the right one man, kneeling, is driving in the last stake in a palisade and two others are crossing a light bridge. Behind the palisade are two pyramidal straw beacons to be used for signalling. In the background a man is carrying a long timber to be used in the fort. This longer timber may have come from a conifer, two of which are shown. These trees are very different from the oaks; they may be pines. The walls in the background represent a temporary camp for the building party. The walls are probably made of turfs, and one can see the round ends of logs that supported a rampart walk.

ADDENDA

P. 62. The general statement on Mesopotamia is largely based on G. M. Lees and N. L. Falcon, 'The geographical history of the Mesopotamian plains', *Geog. Journ.* 118 (1952) 26–39. Even if in the period 2000–900 BC trees were much more common, they would have been inferior for building to the mountain conifers in the west.

P. 142. At the time of writing I had not seen Honor Frost's final report on the Punic ship sunk off the north-western coast of Sicily: *Lilybaeum*, in *Notizie degli scavi* 30 Suppl. (1976). Various dating criteria converge on a date *c.*235 BC (± 65 yrs.), which makes the suggested association with the final battle of the first Punic war highly probable. It is surprising that the datable artefacts seem to come from central Italy and that some of the ballast stones are of a type which can only be found in the neighbourhoods of Naples and Rome. This has led (p. 116) to the interesting inference that the ship might have been built in one of the Etruscan coastal cities. These had all been subdued by Rome, but they had had close ties in trade with the Carthaginians and there may still have been resentment of Rome's domination.

In the woods sampled from the superstructure (pp. 98–100, by Nigel Hepper) the most puzzling is a sample of cedar, the nearest known source of which is north Africa. Today the nearest cedars to Carthage and Utica are in the Aures mountains in the south and the Djurdjuria and Babor mountains near the coast, but both areas are much too remote from Carthage to be a normal source of supply. If we accept the tradition that the temple of Apollo at Utica was built with cedar roof-timbers, a nearer source is needed. Lieutenant-Colonel R. L. Playfair, in his *Travels in the footsteps of Bruce in Algeria and Tunisia* (1877) 188, records that in his journey from Sbeitla to Hydra he saw 'mountains covered with cedars and fir [?pine] very thick, the resort of lions'. This was roughly five kilometres from Roman Sicca, and Sicca was very near the Mejerda river, which could have carried timber to the coast near Utica.

P. 178. W. S. Hanson's 'Military timber buildings: construction, re-construction', in *Woodworking techniques before AD 1500*, ed. S. McGrail (National Maritime Museum, Greenwich, Archaeological Series 7; *BAR* International Series 129) 169–86, is a useful supplement to his earlier article (p. 180 above) and includes a good discussion of the use of timber sills.

Pp. 257-8. 'Allevamenti ed economia delle silve' by A. Giardina, in *L'Italia: insediamenti e forme economiche* (Rome, 1981), is a refreshingly original discussion of the relations between agriculture and forestry. He agrees that the early deforestation of Italy has been grossly exaggerated, but rejects the view that there was a fuel crisis in the city of Rome during the late Empire. The question depends on the meaning of the emperors' direction to the governor of the Roman province of Africa to respect 'the long-established privileges of the African ship-masters, who convey *ligna* suited to our dispositions and needs'. I accepted the general assumption that the reference was to logs for the Roman baths. *Ligna* is the normal word for firewood but Rome is not mentioned. Giardina draws attention to a Greek papyrus from Egypt of the second century BC mentioning Italian logs for burning (*ligna causima Italica*, ξύλα καύσιμα), and suggests that the African ship-masters might be carrying logs for the baths in Egypt. The papyrus reflects the growing interest of Italian merchants in trade with the east. Wood was plentiful in Campania and the forests of south Italy and was badly needed during the Empire in Egypt. If the Roman emperors were concerned for the supply of fuel to Egyptian baths the easiest solution was to send wood back in the large merchantmen that brought Egyptian corn to Rome. They could have picked up supplies at Puteoli on the return journey. The main duty of the African shipmasters was to bring corn to Rome; they could add firewood to their cargo.

Pp. 341-2. J. B. Ward-Perkins, 'Nicomedia in the marble trade', *PBSR* 48 (1980) 23-68, discusses in more detail the transport of marble from Docimium to Rome (p. 30). In view of the decisive advantages of transport by water, he thinks that the marble would have been taken to the river Sangarius but unloaded before the river reached the Black Sea. From Pliny *Ep.* 10. 41 he infers that a short cut would have been taken from the river across the narrow isthmus to Nicomedia. Pliny in his letter to Trajan explains that marble, crops, firewood, and timber from the interior cross lake Sophon and then have to complete the journey by road. He strongly recommends the digging of a canal to replace the road. There are two main difficulties. It has to be assumed that the early course of the river, which is now barely navigable above Gordium, was larger in the early Empire. The considerable amount of extra loading and unloading would also be a serious disadvantage. The distribution map of sarcophagi of Docimium marble (p. 29) shows that these heavy loads could be carried for more than 150 kilometres without the help of any river.

P. 450. In one of the fine mosaics from Sousse (Hadrumetum) that are now in the Bardo museum at Tunis there is an unloading scene which is not easy to explain. According to the latest comprehensive survey of the African mosaics the scene shows 'three men carrying bars of lead: two inspectors weighing them' (K. M. D. Dunbabin, *The mosaics of Roman north Africa* (Oxford, 1978) pl. 48. 121, p. 270 no. 21). Lead would seem to be much too heavy to be carried on the shoulders and this would not explain the slight projections that look like the stubs of branches that have been cut off from the main stem. Though timbers were sold by measure, firewood seems always to have been weighed. Sousse is olive country not likely to have been favourable to other trees. Ample supplies of firewood would be available from the Tunis area.

Ch. 13 (pp. 371–403). J. V. Thirgood, *Man and the Mediterranean forest* (Academic Press, 1981) is an excellent analysis of deforestation by a geographer.

P. 503 n. 98. Dr Valnea Scrinari, superintendent of excavations at Ostia, has now published a detailed account of the six boats that were found embedded in the mud of the Claudian harbour at Ostia: *Le navi del porto di Claudio* (Rome, 1979). Ilex is the only wood cited even for the small fishing-boat. This is unexpected because, though growing locally, ilex is a very hard wood normally used only where strength is the primary requirement. The earlier attribution of larch is almost equally strange, since it would have had to come from the Alps. Further samples from the boats should resolve the problem.

BIBLIOGRAPHY

The Near East

Y. Aharoni (ed.) *Beer-Sheba* 1. (Tel-Aviv, 1973)

*A. Baltaxe, *On mapping the forests of Lebanon 1 : 50,000* (Beirut, 1966)

*M. Basbous and W. R. Chaney, 'The cedars of Lebanon the witnesses of history', *Econ. Botany* 33 (1978) 118-25

*E. W. Beals, 'The remnant cedar forests of Lebanon', *Journ. Ecol.* 53 (1955) 669-94

D. W. Beekman, *Hout in alle tijden* (2 vols., Deventer, 1949)

R. Borger, *Die Inschriften Asarhaddons Königs von Assyrien* (Graz, 1956)

D. Brezinova and B. Hurda, 'Xylotomic examination of timber from ancient Egyptian coffins', *ZA* 103 (1971) 139-41

J. P. Brown, *The Lebanon and Phoenicia* (Beirut, 1969)

G. G. Cameron, 'The annals of Shalmeneser III', *Sumer* 6 (1959) 1-20

Chicago Assyrian Dictionary (1964-)

G. Contenau, 'Un bas-relief assyrien du musée du Louvre', *Journ. asiatique* 9 (1917) 181-9

D. M. Dixon, 'Timber in ancient Egypt', *Commonwealth For. Rev.* 53 (1974) 205-9

FAO, 'Forestry in the Middle East', *Unasylva* 6 (1957) 104-23

P. Fox, *Treasures of Tutankhamun* (London, 1951)

A. H. Gardiner, *The admonitions of an Egyptian sage* (Leipzig, 1909)

—— *Egypt of the Pharaohs* (Oxford, 1961)

*E. Giordano, 'The Mediterranean', in *A world survey of forest resources* (ed. S. Haden Guest, New York, 1966) 317-52

—— 'Montagne e foreste del Lebano', *Monti e boschi* 13 (1967) 105-21

S. R. K. Glanville, 'Records of a royal dockyard of the time of Tuthmosis III', *ZA* 66 (1931) 105-21 (text and translation); 68 (1932) 7-41 (commentary)

A. K. Grayson, *Assyrian royal inscriptions* (2 vols., Wiesbaden, 1976)

J. C. Greenfield and M. Mayrhofer, 'The algummim/almuggim problem re-examined', Suppl. to *Vetus Testamentum* 6 (1967) 83-9

W. Helck, *Die Beziehungen Ägyptens zu Vorderasien im 3. und 2. Jarhtausend²* (Wiesbaden, 1971)

P. K. Hitti, *The history of Syria²* (London, 1957)

—— *Lebanon in history³* (London, 1967)

E. Honigmann, *Libanos*, *RE* 13 (1927) 1-11

*J. D. Hooker, 'The cedars of Lebanon', *Nat. Hist. Rev.* 2 (1862) 11-17

N. Jidejian, *Byblos through the ages* (Beirut, 1968)

J. Killen, *Ancient Egyptian furniture* (Warminster, 1980)

H. Klenger, 'Die Libanon und seine Zedern in der Geschichte des alten Vorder-Orient', *Das Altertum* 13 (1967) 67-76

J. Landström, *Ships of the Pharaohs* (London, 1970)

T. LAUFFROY, 'Les bois d'œuvre d'origine Libanaise', *Mélanges St Joseph* 46 (1970–1) 153–63

A. H. LAYARD, *Nineveh and its remains* (London, 1849)

—— *Nineveh and Babylon* (London, 1853)

*V. LORET, 'Quelques notes sur l'arbre *âch*', *Annales du service* 16 (1916) 33–51

A. LUCAS, *Ancient Egyptian materials and industries*[4], ed. J. R. Harris (London, 1962)

D. D. LUCKENBILL, *The Annals of Sennacherib* (Chicago, 1924)

—— *Ancient records of Assyria and Babylonia* (2 vols., Chicago, 1926–7)

A. MALAMAT, 'The campaigns to the Mediterranean by Iahdumlim and other early Mesopotamian rulers', *Assyr. Stud.* 16 (1965) 365–73

M. E. L. MALLOWAN, *Nimrud and its remains* (London, 1966)

*R. D. MEICKLE, *Flora of Cyprus* (Kew, 1977)

S. A. B. MERCER, *The Tel-el-Amarna tablets* (2 vols., Toronto, 1939)

M. W. MIKESELL, 'The deforestation of mount Lebanon', *Geog. Rev.* 59 (1969) 1–28

P. MONTET, 'Le pays de Negau', *Syria* 4 (1923) 181–92

*P. MOUTERDE, *La Végétation arborescente des pays du Levant* (Beirut, 1947)

—— *Regards sur Beyrouth phénicienne, hellénistique et romaine* (Beirut, 1966)

*H. PABOT, *La Végétation sylvo-pastorale du Liban et son écologie* (FAO, Rome, 1959)

F. PETRIE, *The royal tombs of the first dynasty* (London, 1900–1)

*G. E. POST, *Flora of Syria, Palestine, and Sinai*[2] (2 vols., Beirut, 1932–3)

J. B. PRITCHARD, *The ancient Near-East in pictures relating to the Old Testament* (Princeton, 1954)

—— (ed.) *Ancient Near-Eastern texts relating to the Old Testament*[3] (Princeton, 1969)

P. RAPHAEL, *Le cèdre du Liban dans l'histoire* (Beirut, 1924)

E. REINER, 'The Lipšur litanies', *JNES* 15 (1956) 129–45

G. A. REISNER, *The development of the Egyptian tomb down to the accession of Cheops* (Cambridge, Mass., 1936)

*M. B. ROWTON, 'A topographical factor in the Ḫapiru problem', *Assyr. Stud.* 16 (1965) 375–87

*—— 'The woodlands of ancient western Asia', *JNES* 26 (1967) 261–77

W. F. SAGGS, 'The Nimrud letters', *Iraq* 17 (1955) 127–31

W. VON SODEN, *Akkadisches Handwörterbuch* (Wiesbaden, 1959–)

A. J. SPENCER, *The brick architecture of ancient Egypt* (Warminster, 1980)

M. STRECK, *Assurbanipal und die letzten assyrischen Könige* (Leipzig, 1916)

R. CAMPBELL THOMPSON, *A dictionary of Assyrian botany* (Oxford, 1949)

*H. B. TRISTRAM, *The natural history of the Bible*[4] (London, 1875)

E. DE VAUMAS, *Le Liban, étude de géographie physique* (3 vols., Paris, 1954)

L. WATERMAN, *Royal correspondence of the Assyrian empire* (4 vols., Ann Arbor, 1930–6)

Trees

M. L. ANDERSON, *A history of Scottish forestry* (Edinburgh, 1967)

J. ANDRÉ, *Lexique des termes de botanique en latin* (Paris, 1956)

M. Benchetrit, 'Le problème de l'érosion de sol de montagne et le cas du tell algérien', *Rev. géog. alpine* 43 (1955) 605-40

J. L. Bintliff, *Natural environment and human settlement in prehistoric Greece, BAR* Suppl. series 28, 1 and 2 (Oxford, 1977)

B. Bonacelli, 'La natura e gli Etruschi', *Stud. Etrusc.* 2 (1928) 427-569

P. Boudy, *Économie forestière nord-africaine* (4 vols., Paris, 1948-55)

D. G. M. Cacciamani, *L'antica foresta di Camaldoli* (ed. Camaldoli, 1965; out of print)

A. Camus, *Les Chênes* (2 vols. 1936-54)

W. B. Critchfield and E. Little, *Geographic distribution of the pines of the world*, U.S. Dept. of Agriculture Misc. Publications, 991 (1966)

W. Dallimore and A. B. Jackson, *A handbook of conifers and ginkgoaceae* (ed. S. G. Harrison, London, 1966)

E. J. Davis, *Anatolia (Caria, Phrygia, Lycia, Pisidia)* (London, 1876)

P. H. Davis, *The flora of Turkey and the East Aegean islands* (vol. 1, Edinburgh, 1965)

H. Desplanques, *Campagnes ombriennes* (Paris, 1969)

S. E. Durno, 'Pollen analysis of peat deposits in Scotland', *Scottish Geog. Mag.* 72 (1956) 166-87

—— 'Certain aspects of vegetational history in north-east Scotland', *Scottish Geog. Mag.* 73 (1957) 176-84

L. Fenaroli, *Note illustrative della carta della vegetazione reale d'Italia* (Collana Verde 28, 1971)

T. Garfield, 'Atlas cedars', *Quarterly Journ. Forestry* 52 (1966) 54-9

H. Godwin, *The history of the British flora*[2] (1973)

J. R. A. Greig and J. Turner, 'Some pollen diagrams for Greece and their archaeological significance', *Journ. Arch. Sci.* (1976) 177-94

P. Grimal, *Les Jardins romains* (Paris, 1969)

S. Gsell, *Histoire ancienne de l'Afrique du nord* (vol. 1, Paris, 1920)

J. M. Houston, *The western Mediterranean world* (London, 1964)

F. Jeshemeni, *The gardens of Pompeii, Herculaneum and the villas destroyed by Vesuvius* (New York, 1979)

T. Kotschy, *Reise in den cilicischen Taurus über Tarsus* (Gotha, 1858)

W. M. Leake, *Travels in northern Greece* (4 vols., London, 1835)

E. Lear, *Journal of a landscape painter in Corsica* (London, 1870)

W. G. Loy, *The land of Nestor* (Washington, 1966)

W. A. McDonald and G. R. Rapp, Jr., *The Minnesota Messenian expedition* (Minneapolis, 1972)

P. C. Magaldi, *Lucania Romana* (Rome, 1947)

K. I. Makres, *Preliminary study of the natural forests in Greece from the point of view of timber production* (Thessaloniki, 1973)

R. D. Meikle, *Flora of Cyprus* 1 (Oxford, 1980)

M. W. Mikesell, 'The deforestation of north Africa', *Science* 132 (1960) 441-9

H. Nissen, *Italische Landeskunde* (2 vols., Berlin, 1883-1902)

G. del Noce, *Trattato istorico scientifico ed economico delle macchie e foreste del grande ducato Toscano* (Florence, 1849)

G. Passerini, 'Residui di una abetina originaria a Monte Amiata', *Stud. Etrusc.* 17 (1943) 389-418

A. DE PHILIPPIS, 'Problemi e tecnica del rimboschimento nel territorio italiano a clima mediterraneo', *Italia forestale e montana* 17 (1962) 1-12

R. E. PIKE, *Tall trees, tough men* (New York, 1969)

P. PIUSSI, *Un inventario forestale del xviii. secolo per i boschi costieri dell'Alto Adriatico* (Collana Verde 41, 1970)

M. QUAINI, 'I boschi della Ligura e la loro utilizzazione per i cantieri navali', *Riv. geog. It.* 78 (1969) 508-37

M. RIKLI, *Das Pflanzenkleid der Mittelmeerlanden* (3 vols., Bern, 1943-8)

A. SEIDENSTICKER, *Waldegeschichte des Altertums* (2 vols., 1886)

F. TRIFORE, *Storia del diritto forestale in Italia* (Rome, 1959)

G. TSOUMIS, *The forests of Greece and Cyprus* (Thessaloniki, 1976)

—— *A forest botanical garden at the Aristotelian University of Thessaloniki* (Thessaloniki, 1976)

P. WARREN, 'British travellers in Crete', Κρητ. Χρον. 24 (1972)

M. ZOHARY, *Plant life of Palestine, Israel and Jordan* (1962)

—— *Flora Palestina* (1966)

Timber

L. BANTI, *Il palazzo minoico di Festo* (1935)

J. BASTIN, 'La via Mansuerisca', *Antiq. class.* 3 (1934) 363-83

H. BINGEMER, 'Die Ohrenbacher Schanze', *Saalburg Jahrb.* 10 (1951) 29-37

C. W. BLEGEN and M. RAWSON, *The palace of Nestor at Pylos in western Messenia* 1 (Princeton, 1966)

—— 'Architectural notes from Pylos', *Orlandos Festschrift* (4 vols., Athens, 1965-8) 1. 117-25

H. BLÜMNER, *Technologie und Terminologie der Gewerbe und Künste bei Griechen und Römern* (Berlin, 1875-87; 2nd edn., vol. 1, 1912)

A. BOETHIUS, 'Vitruvius and the Roman architecture of his age', *Dragma* (studies presented to P. Nilsson, Lund, 1939) 114-43

—— and J. B. WARD-PERKINS, *Etruscan and Roman architecture* (Harmondsworth, 1970)

A. K. BOWMAN and J. D. THOMAS, 'The Vindolanda writing tablets and their significance', *Historia* 24 (1975) 463-78

D. T. BREEZE, 'The Roman fortlet at Bamburgh Mill, Dumfriesshire', *Britannia* (1974) 130-61

A. BURFORD, 'Heavy transport in the ancient world' *Eng. Hist. Rev.* 13 (1960) 1-18

—— 'Notes on the Epidaurian inscriptions', *BSA* 61 (1966) 254-334

—— *The Greek temple builders of Epidaurus* (Liverpool, 1969)

J. P. BUSHE-FOX, *Richborough report* 4 (1969)

L. D. CASKEY, 'The roofed gallery of the walls of Athens', *AJA* 14 (1910) 298-309

L. CASSON, *Ships and seamanship in the ancient world* (Princeton, 1971)

C. CICHORIUS, *Die Reliefs der Traiansäule* (2 vols. plates, commentary, Berlin, 1896-1900)

H. CLEERE, 'Ironmaking in a Roman furnace', *Britannia* 2 (1971) 203-17

P. Coarelli, *Guida archeologica di Roma* (Rome, 1975)

J. J. Coulton, *The architectural development of the Greek stoa* (Oxford, 1976)

—— *Greek architects at work* (London, 1977)

G. Cozzo, *Ingegneria romana* (Rome, 1928)

—— *The Colosseum* (Rome, 1971)

D. P. Dymond, 'Roman bridges on Dere Street', *Journ. Arch.* 118 (1961) 136–64

H. van Effenterre, *Le Palais de Mallia* (2 vols., Paris, 1980)

A. Evans, *The palace of Minos* (4 vols., London, 1921–36)

Domenico Fontana, *Della trasportazione dell'obelischo Vaticano* (Rome, 1590)

S. S. Frere, *Verulamium excavations* i (Oxford, 1972).

—— and J. K. S. St. Joseph, 'The Roman fortress at Longthorpe', *Britannia* 5 (1974) 1–129

L. Funi, *Il duomo di Orvieto e suoi restauri* (1891)

E. G. Gjerstad, *Early Rome* (6 vols., Lund, 1953–73)

J. W. Graham, *The palaces of Crete* (Princeton, 1962)

P. A. Guglielmotti, *Storia della marina pontificale nel medio evo* (10 vols., Rome, 1886–93)

W. S. Hanson, 'The organisation of Roman military timber supply', *Britannia* 9 (1978) 293–308

J. Healy, *Mining and metallurgy in the Greek and Roman world* (London, 1978)

A. T. Hodge, *The woodwork of Greek roofs* (Cambridge, 1960)

L. P. Holland and P. Davis, 'The porch ceiling of the temple of Apollo on Delos', *AJA* 38 (1934) 71–80

A. C. Johnson, 'Ancient forests and navies', *TAPA* 58 (1927) 199–209

L. E. Jones, A. J. Graham, and L. H. Sackett, 'The Dema house in Attica', *BSA* 57 (1962) 75–114

—— 'An Attic country house below the cave of Pan at Vari', *BSA* 68 (1973) 355–452

J. Keil, *Jahreshefte* 44 (1959) 242–7

P. I. Kuniholm, *Dendrochronology at Gordion and on the high plateau of Anatolia* (Univ. of Penn. thesis, order no. 78-06607, obtainable from University Microfilms Ltd., High Wycombe, Surrey)

F. C. Lane, *Navires et construction à Venise pendant la Renaissance* (1965)

S. Lauffer, *Diokletians Preisedikt: Texte und Kommentar* (Berlin, 1971)

R. P. Legon, 'The Megarian decree and the balance of Greek naval power', *Class. Phil.* 68 (1973) 161–71

A. R. Lewis, *Naval power and trade in the Mediterranean, A.D. 500–1100* (Princeton, 1951)

M. Lombard, 'Le bois dans la Méditerranée musulmane, viie–ixe siècles', *Annales: économies, sociétés, civilisations* 14 (1959) 234–54

W. L. Macdonald, *The architecture of the Roman Empire* (New Haven, 1965)

W. H. Manning, 'Roman military timber granaries', *Saalburg Jahrb.* 32 (1975) 105–29

E. G. Mariolopoulos, 'Fluctuation of rainfall in Attica during the years of erection of the Parthenon', *Geofisica pura e applicata* 51 (1962) 243–53

E. W. Marsden, *Greek and Roman artillery. Technical treatises* (Oxford, 1971)

R. Martin, *Manuel d'architecture grecque* (vol. 1, Paris, 1965)

536   BIBLIOGRAPHY

G. MATHERAT, 'Les ponts-de-fascines de Jules César à Breuil', *Rev. Arch.* 7 (1936) 53-94; 9 (1937) 38-67

D. S. NEALE, 'The Roman villa at Boxmoor', *Britannia* 1 (1970) 156-62

A. K. ORLANDOS, *Les Matériaux de construction et la technique architecturale des anciens Grecs* 1 (Athens, 1955) trans. V. Hadjimichalis (Paris, 1966)

—— *The architecture of the Parthenon* (2 vols., 1977-8)

C. ÖSTERBERG, *Case etrusche d'Acquarossa* (Rome, 1975)

J. M. PATON, *The Erechtheum* (Cambridge, Mass., 1927)

R. E. PIKE, *Tall trees, tough men* (New York, 1967)

H. PLOMMER, *Vitruvius and later Roman building manuals* (Cambridge, 1979)

W. K. PRITCHETT, 'The Attic stelai', *Hesp.* 25 (1956) 178-328 (commentary); *Hesp.* 22 (1953) 225-311 (texts)

J. REYNOLDS and M. CRAWFORD, 'The Aezani copy of the Price Edict', *Zeitschr. Pap. Epigr.* 26 (1977) 125-41

—— and K. ERIM, 'The copy of Diocletian's Edict on Maximum Prices from Aphrodisias', *JRS* 60 (1970) 120-41

I. A. RICHMOND, 'Trajan's army on Trajan's Column', *PBSR* 13 (1935) 1-40

—— 'Roman timber building', in W. E. M. Jope, *Studies in building history* (London, 1961) 15-26

—— *Hod Hill* 2 (London, 1968)

—— 'Roman military engineering', in *Roman archaeology and art*, ed. P. Salway (London, 1969) 194-8

L. ROBERT, 'Documents d'Asie Mineure', *BCH* 102 (1978) 395-543

—— and J. ROBERT, 'Une inscription grecque de Téos en Ionie: L'Union de Téos et de Kyrbissos', *Journ. des savants* (1976), 153-235

D. M. ROBINSON and G. W. GRAHAM, *Olynthus* 8 (Baltimore, 1930)

G. ROUX, *L'architecture de L'Argolide aux iv. et iii. siècles* (Paris, 1961)

—— 'Pindare, le prétendu trésor des Crétois et l'ancienne statue d'Apollon à Delphes', *REG* 75 (1962) 366-81

W. SACKUR, *Vitruv und die Poliorketiker* (Berlin, 1925)

H. SCHÖNBERGER, 'The Roman frontier in Germany: an archaeological survey', *JRS* 59 (1969) 146-97

F. THIRIET, *La Romanie vénitienne au Moyen Âge* (Paris, 1959)

F. H. THOMPSON, *Roman Chester* (Chester, 1965)

H. A. THOMPSON and R. E. WYCHERLEY, *The Agora of Athens (The Athenian Agora* 14, 1972)

J. TRAVLOS, *Pictorial dictionary of Athens* (London, 1971)

G. UCELLI, *Le navi di Nemi* (Rome, 1956)

M. B. WALLACE, 'Early Greek proxenoi', *Phoenix* 24 (1970) 189-208

J. B. WARD-PERKINS, *Roman architecture* (New York, 1977)

T. WIEGAND, *Die Puteolanischer Bauinschrift*, Suppl. 21 *Jahrb. Class. Phil.* (1894)

A. WILHELM, 'Die Pachturkunden der Klytiden', *Jahreshefte* 28 (1933) 197-221

Furniture and Sculpture

C. ALBIZZATI, 'Two ivory fragments of a statue of Athena', *JHS* 35 (1916) 373-402

P. Amandry, 'Rapports préliminaires sur les statues chryséléphantines de Delphes', *BCH* 63 (1939) 86-119.

H. S. Baker, *Furniture in the ancient world* (London, 1966)

F. M. Bennett, 'A study of the word *xoanon*', *AJA* 21 (1917) 8-21

P. Bruneau, *Recherches sur les cultes de Délos à l'époque hellénistique et à l'époque impériale* (Paris, 1976)

E. Espérandieu, *Recueil général des bas-reliefs, statues, et bustes de la Gaule romaine* (1907-66)

H.-V. Herrmann, 'Zum Problem der Entstehung der griechischen Großplastik', *Wandlungen* (Festschrift Homann Wedeking, Waldsessen, 1975)

J. Killen, *Ancient Egyptian furniture* (Warmington, 1980)

J. Kopcke, 'Neue Holzfunde aus der Heraion von Samos', *AM* 82 (1967) 100-48

A. Maiuri, *Ercolano* (Rome, 1958)

R. Martin, 'Wooden figures from the source of the Seine', *Antiquity* 39 (1965) 247-52

D. M. Ohly, 'Holz' (Samos), *AM* 68 (1953) 77-176

—— 'Der Herastatuette' (Samos), *AM* 82 (1967) 89-99

G. M. A. Richter, *The furniture of the Greeks, Etruscans, and Romans* (London, 1966)

S. S. Ridgway, *The archaic style in Greek sculpture* (Princeton, 1977)

N. I. Sokolskii, *Sarcophagi from the northern shore of the Black Sea* (Moscow, 1969)

R. Vallois, 'L'*agalma* des Dionysies de Délos', *BCH* 46 (1922) 94-113

A. Wasowicz, *Le Travail du bois en Grèce antique* (Polish text with summary in French)

Miscellaneous

A. Andrewes, 'The opposition to Pericles', *JHS* 98 (1978) 1-8

L. Balsan, 'L'industrie de la résine dans les Causses et son extension dans l'empire romain', *Gallia* 9 (1952-3) 53-5

A. di Bérenger, *Studi di archeologia forestale* (1859-65; reprinted Florence, 1965)

F. Braudel, *The Mediterranean and the Mediterranean world in the age of Philip II* (2 vols., London, 1972-3)

P. A. Brunt, *Italian manpower* (Oxford, 1971)

V. Cuinet, *La Turquie d'Asie* (4 vols., Paris, 1891-1900)

—— *Liban et Palestine* (Paris, 1896)

J. Evelyn, *Sylva*[3]. *A discourse on forest trees and the propagation of timber* (London, 1679)

R. J. Forbes, *Studies in ancient technology*, 1-9 (Leiden, 1956-71), *Heating, cooking, lighting* XI (1964)

A. de Franciscis, *Stato e società in Locri Epizefiri* (1972)

T. Frank, *An economic survey of ancient Rome* (5 vols., Baltimore, 1933-40)

J. Le Gall, *Le Tibre* (Paris, 1958)

C. T. Glacken, *Traces on the Rhodian shore* (Berkeley, 1967)

G. Glotz, 'Le prix des denrées à Delos', *Journal des savants* (1913), 16-29

G. GLOTZ, 'L'histoire de Délos d'après les prix d'une denrée', *REG* 29 (1916) 281-325

—— *Ancient Greece at work* (London, 1926)

W. L. GOODMAN, *The history of woodworking tools* (London, 1964)

P. GROS, *Aurea templa* (Paris, 1976)

N. G. L. HAMMOND, *A history of Macedon* (Oxford, 1976)

E. G. HARDY, *Roman laws and charters* (Oxford, 1912)

F. M. HEICHELHEIM, *An ancient economic history* (3 vols., Leiden, 1958-70)

E. HONIGMANN, 'Strabo', *RE* 4. A. 76-155

F. JESHEMSKI, *The gardens of Pompeii and the villas destroyed by Vesuvius* (New York, 1979)

W. KROLL, *The elder Pliny, RE* 21 (1951) 271-439

K. LACHMANN, *Die Schriften der römischen Feldmesser* (Berlin, 1848)

W. LAIDLAW, *A history of Delos* (Oxford, 1932)

P. LAWSON, *Renaissance Italy* (1967)

A. MAGIE, *Roman rule in Asia Minor* (Princeton, 1930) .

O. MAKONNEN, *Ancient forestry, Acta Forestalia Fennica* (Helsinki) 82 (1967), 95 (1969)

R. MARCILLE, 'La poix antique', *Rev. Tunisienne* (1941) 216-19

—— La résine et la poix dans Pline', *Rev. Tunisienne* (1941) 220-3

R. MEIGGS, *The Athenian Empire* (Oxford, 1972)

—— *Roman Ostia*² (Oxford, 1973)

R. M. OGILVIE and I. A. RICHMOND, *Tacitus, Agricola*, text and commentary (Oxford, 1967)

C. D'ONOFRIO, *Gli obelischi di Roma*² (Roma, 1967)

The Princeton Encyclopaedia of classical sites (1976)

R. H. RANDALL, 'The Erechtheum workers', *AJA* 57 (1953) 199-210

O. REGENBOGEN, *Theophrastus, RE* Suppl. 7 (1940) 1354-1512

E. SCHULHOF and P. HUVELIN, 'Loi réglant la vente du bois et du charbon à Délos', *BCH* 31 (1907) 46-93

E. C. SEMPLE, *The geography of the Mediterranean region: its relation to ancient history* (London, 1932)

M. VENTRIS and J. CHADWICK, *Documents in Mycenaean Greek*² (Cambridge, 1973)

J. B. WARD-PERKINS, 'Landscape and history in central Etruria' (Myres Memorial Lecture, 1964)

R. K. WINTERS, *The forest and man* (New York, 1974)

INDEX OF TREES AND
THEIR WOODS

Since the particular species within the genus can only very rarely be distinguished in the
sources, the botanic name is only added when the English name is unfamiliar.

Acacia (ἄκανθα, *acacia*) 59, 300, 404, 408
Alder (κλήθρα, *alnus*) 42, 109, 296
Algum 72, 486 n. 59*
Ash, (μελία, *fraxinus*) 407, 438; leaves as
fodder 267, but *see also* 28; spears 110

Beech (ὀξύη, *fagus*): in Apennines 47,
Latium 219, Sila forest 464, Britain 174;
in Greece 454; uses 295, 298, 445
Birch (*betula*) 296
Box (πύξος, *buxus*): on Amanus 73, in
Cyprus 281, near Ugarit 280; special
quality in Corsica and on Mt. Cytorus,
poor quality on Mt. Olympus (Macedon) 282; properties of the wood 280;
uses 281 f., 426, 449; with ebony 282,
with yew 461

Carob (κερατωνία, *ceratonia*) 41; 60, 408
Cedar (κέδρος, *cedrus*): on Lebanon 49 f.,
53, 405-9, Amanus 73, 74, in Cyprus
47, 55, 135 f., 398, Lycia 394, on Taurus 395,? in Crete 99 f.; for doors 293,
407, 419; roof-timbers 78, 415, 418;
Solomon's temple and palace 69-71,
Darius' palace 82 f.; furniture 292 f.;
ship-timbers 118, 134, 136, 408; sculpture 308 f., 311 f.
Cherry (κερασός, *cerasus*) 47, 473
Chestnut (καρύα ἡ Εὐβοϊκή, *castanea*): for
building 240; coppice 267 f.; confused
with walnut 420-3; in modern Sila 463;
place name 36
Citrus (θύον, *Callitris quadrivalvis*) 286-91;
in Homer 112
Cornel (κράνεια, *cornus*) 110, 111, 443
Cypress (κυπάρισσος, *cupressus*) 46; on
Lebanon 416-20; for doors 78, 293,
419; roof-timbers, 78, 200, 430; furniture 293 f.; grown to produce poles 268;
for shipbuilding 86, ?134, 120, 152;

sculpture 308, 313, 322; modest supply
of pitch 469

Ebony (ἔβενος, *ebenus*): for furniture 282,
with boxwood 283, with ivory 284; used
by Phidias at Olympia 285, ?and on
Athenian acropolis 202; for sculpture
65, 286, 310 f.; as tribute to Persia 284 f.,
carried in Alexandrian procession 285,
exhibited in Pompey's triumph 285
Elm (πτελέα, *ulmus*): useful to plant for
timber, leaves as fodder 263; nurse for
vines 266; uses 445, 426, 433

Fig (ἐρίνεος, *ficus*): wood used for sculpture
310, 324; 442
Fir (ἐλάτη, *abies*) 119, 444; distribution of
species 43; on Lebanon 56, in Crete
99; best timber for triremes 118; good
building-timber, particularly important in Rome 241; transport of 343;
resin 469; 424, 432, 448

Ilex (ἀρία) 45; in Crete 100, Italy 218

Juniper (ἄρκευθος, *juniperus*) 43, 47, 54; at
Gordium 459, in Lycia 394, on Taurus
394; confusion with cedar 410-16

Larch (*larix*): discovered by Romans 248,
brought to Rome for Tiberius 248 f.;
used for shipbuilding 86; special form of
pitch 469; confused by Pliny with pine
24; place name 36
Laurel (δάφνη, *laurus*) 276
Lime (φιλύρα, *tilia*): for furniture 295;
carving 320

Maple (σφένδαμνος, *acer*) 54, 143, 291 f.,
297
Mulberry (συκάμινος, *morus*) 313, 445

SELECT INDEX OF REFERENCES
TO CLASSICAL AUTHORS

A note-number in parenthesis after a page-number indicates that the reference is to be found near the cue to that note.

INDEX OF PASSAGES FROM
THE BIBLE

A note-number in parenthesis after a page-number indicates that the reference is to be found near the cue to that note.

INDEX OF INSCRIPTIONS

A note-number in parenthesis after a page-number indicates that the reference is to be found near the cue to that note.

GENERAL INDEX

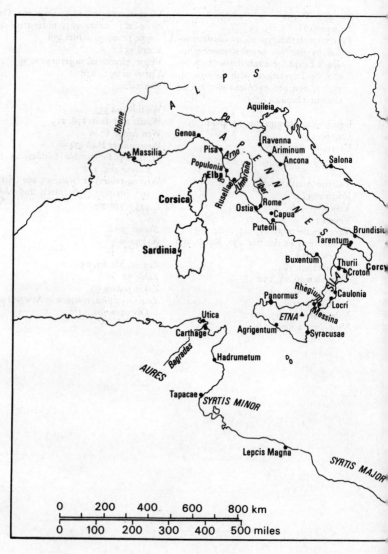

17 Central and eas

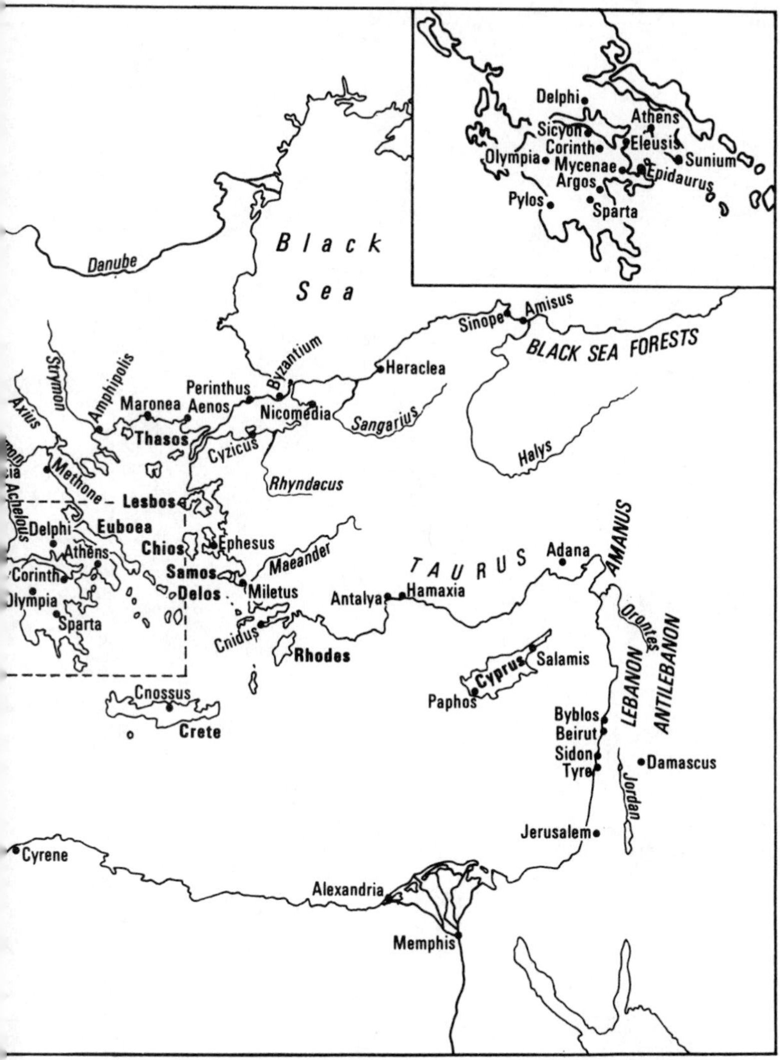
Delphi
Athens
Sicyon
Eleusis
Corinth
Olympia
Mycenae
Sunium
Argos
Epidaurus
Pylos
Sparta
Black Sea
Danube
Amisus
Sinope
BLACK SEA FORESTS
Byzantium
Heraclea
Strymon
Amphipolis
Perinthus
Maronea
Aenos
Nicomedia
Sangarius
Axius
Thasos
Cyzicus
Halys
Methone
Rhyndacus
Lesbos
AMANUS
Achelous
Delphi
Euboea
Ephesus
Adana
Chios
Maeander
Athens
TAURUS
Corinth
Samos
Miletus
Antalya
Hamaxia
Olympia
Delos
Orontes
Sparta
Cnidus
Salamis
Rhodes
LEBANON
ANTILEBANON
Cyprus
Paphos
Cnossus
Byblos
Crete
Beirut
Sidon
Damascus
Tyre
Jordan
Jerusalem
Cyrene
Alexandria
Memphis

iterranean

PLATES

1B *Cedrus libani with Juniperus foetidissima*

1A *Cedrus libani*

1C *Larix decidua with Pinus silvestris*

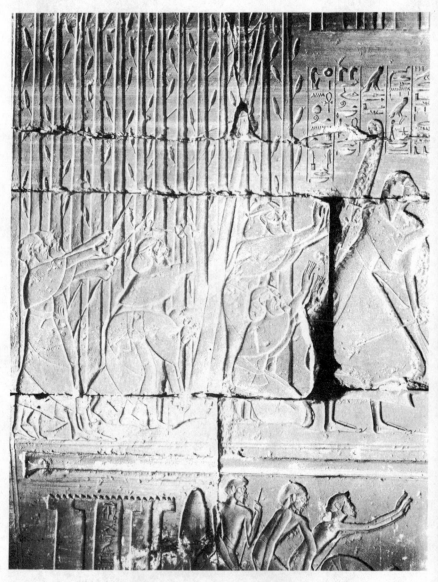

2 Cutting Lebanon trees for the Egyptians

3A Phoenician transport of Lebanon timber for the Assyrians

3B Assyrian transport of bull colossus

4 Team of oxen pulling logs, near Fort Bragg, California, *c.*1900

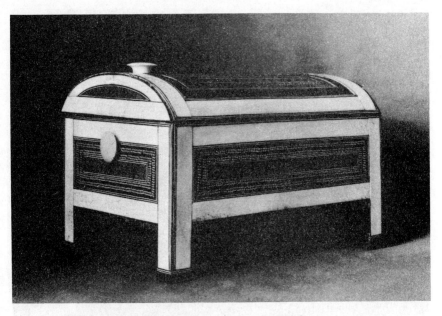

5A Casket with ivory and ebony inlays

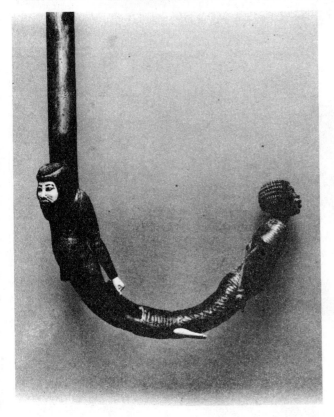

5B Walking-stick
with African and
Asiatic figures

6A The Hall of the Double Axes, south wall

6B The wall restored

7 Gordium tomb chamber

8 The *Casa del graticcio* in Herculaneum

9 Lararium in Herculaneum

10A Footstool from Samian Heraeum

10B Bowl or cup from Samian Heraeum

11A Pine from Sila forest

11B From an American Douglas fir

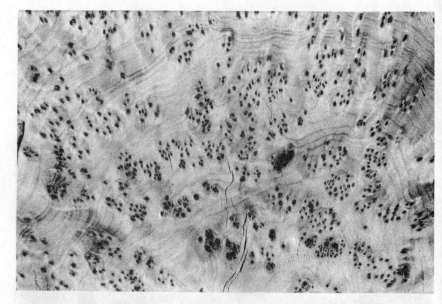

12A Citrus-wood box

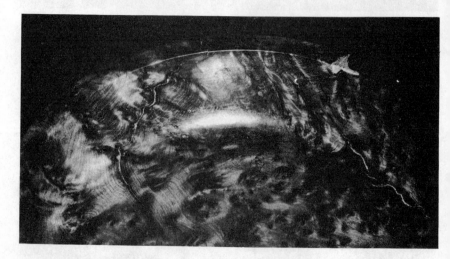

12B Citrus-wood bowl

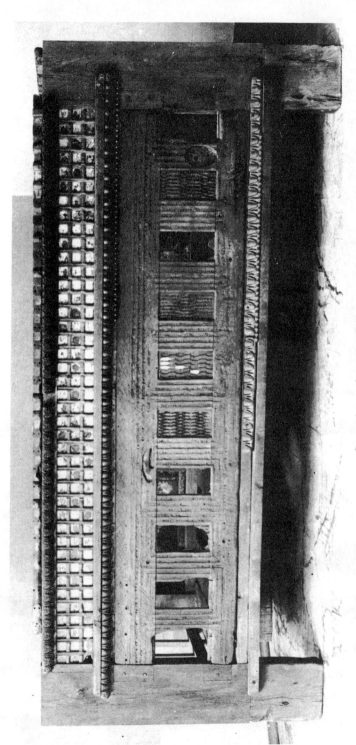

13 Sarcophagus from the Crimea

14 Decorations from Crimean sarcophagi

15A Crossing the Danube by bridge of boats

15B Trajan's Danube bridge

16A Trajan's Column: timber-felling operations

16B Trajan's Column: building a fort

OTHER TITLES IN THIS HARDBACK REPRINT PROGRAMME FROM SANDPIPER BOOKS LTD (LONDON) AND POWELLS BOOKS (CHICAGO)

ISBN 0–19–	Author	Title
8143567	ALFÖLDI A.	The Conversion of Constantine and Pagan Rome
6286409	ANDERSON George K.	The Literature of the Anglo-Saxons
8228813	BARTLETT & MacKAY	Medieval Frontier Societies
8114222	BROOKS Kenneth R.	Andreas and the Fates of the Apostles
8148348	CAMPBELL J.B.	The Emperor and the Roman Army 31 BC to 235 AD
826643X	CHADWICK Henry	Priscillian of Avila
826447X	CHADWICK Henry	Boethius
8219393	COWDREY H.E.J.	The Age of Abbot Desiderius
8148992	DAVIES M.	Sophocles: Trachiniae
825301X	DOWNER L.	Leges Henrici Primi
8143109	FRAENKEL Edward	Horace
8201540	GOLDBERG P.J.P.	Women, Work and Life Cycle in a Medieval Economy
8140215	GOTTSCHALK H.B.	Heraclides of Pontus
8266162	HANSON R.P.C.	Saint Patrick
8224354	HARRISS G.L.	King, Parliament and Public Finance in Medieval England to 1369
8581114	HEATH Sir Thomas	Aristarchus of Samos
8140444	HOLLIS A.S.	Callimachus: Hecale
8212968	HOLLISTER C. Warren	Anglo-Saxon Military Institutions
8223129	HURNARD Naomi	The King's Pardon for Homicide – before AD 1307
8140401	HUTCHINSON G.O.	Hellenistic Poetry
8142560	JONES A.H.M.	The Greek City
8218354	JONES Michael	Ducal Brittany 1364–1399
8271484	KNOX & PELCZYNSKI	Hegel's Political Writings
8225253	LE PATOUREL John	The Norman Empire
8212720	LENNARD Reginald	Rural England 1086–1135
8212321	LEVISON W.	England and the Continent in the 8th century
8148224	LIEBESCHUETZ J.H.W.G.	Continuity and Change in Roman Religion
8141378	LOBEL Edgar & PAGE Sir Denys	Poetarum Lesbiorum Fragmenta
8152442	MAAS P. & TRYPANIS C.A .	Sancti Romani Melodi Cantica
8148178	MATTHEWS John	Western Aristocracies and Imperial Court AD 364–425
8223447	McFARLANE K.B.	Lancastrian Kings and Lollard Knights
8226578	McFARLANE K.B.	The Nobility of Later Medieval England
8148100	MEIGGS Russell	Roman Ostia
8148402	MEIGGS Russell	Trees and Timber in the Ancient Mediterranean World
8142641	MILLER J. Innes	The Spice Trade of the Roman Empire
8147813	MOORHEAD John	Theoderic in Italy
8264259	MOORMAN John	A History of the Franciscan Order
8116020	OWEN A.L.	The Famous Druids
8143427	PFEIFFER R.	History of Classical Scholarship (vol 1)
8111649	PHEIFER J.D.	Old English Glosses in the Epinal-Erfurt Glossary
8142277	PICKARD–CAMBRIDGE A.W.	Dithyramb Tragedy and Comedy
8269765	PLATER & WHITE	Grammar of the Vulgate
8213891	PLUMMER Charles	Lives of Irish Saints (2 vols)
820695X	POWICKE Michael	Military Obligation in Medieval England
8269684	POWICKE Sir Maurice	Stephen Langton
821460X	POWICKE Sir Maurice	The Christian Life in the Middle Ages
8225369	PRAWER Joshua	Crusader Institutions
8225571	PRAWER Joshua	The History of The Jews in the Latin Kingdom of Jerusalem
8143249	RABY F.J.E.	A History of Christian Latin Poetry
8143257	RABY F.J.E.	A History of Secular Latin Poetry in the Middle Ages (2 vols)
8214316	RASHDALL & POWICKE	The Universities of Europe in the Middle Ages (3 vols)
8148380	RICKMAN Geoffrey	The Corn Supply of Ancient Rome
8141076	ROSS Sir David	Aristotle: Metaphysics (2 vols)
8141092	ROSS Sir David	Aristotle: Physics
8264178	RUNCIMAN Sir Steven	The Eastern Schism
814833X	SALMON J.B.	Wealthy Corinth
8171587	SALZMAN L.F.	Building in England Down to 1540
8218362	SAYERS Jane E.	Papal Judges Delegate in the Province of Canterbury 1198–1254
8221657	SCHEIN Sylvia	Fideles Crucis
8148135	SHERWIN WHITE A.N.	The Roman Citizenship
8642040	SOUTER Alexander	A Glossary of Later Latin to 600 AD
8222254	SOUTHERN R.W.	Eadmer: Life of St. Anselm
8251408	SQUIBB G.	The High Court of Chivalry
8212011	STEVENSON & WHITELOCK	Asser's Life of King Alfred
8212011	SWEET Henry	A Second Anglo-Saxon Reader—Archaic and Dialectical
8148259	SYME Sir Ronald	History in Ovid